Yearbook of the Maimonides Centre for Advanced Studies 2018

Yearbook of the Maimonides Centre for Advanced Studies

Edited by
Giuseppe Veltri

Yearbook of the Maimonides Centre for Advanced Studies 2018

Volume Editor
Bill Rebiger

DE GRUYTER

The Yearbook is published on behalf of the Maimonides Centre
for Advanced Studies

ISBN 978-3-11-057560-6
e-ISBN (PDF) 978-3-11-057768-6
e-ISBN (EPUB) 978-3-11-057624-5

This work is licensed under the Creative Commons Attribution-NonCommercial-NoDerivs
4.0 License. For details go to http://creativecommons.org/licenses/by-nc-nd/4.0/.

Bibliographic information published by the Deutsche Nationalbibliothek
The Deutsche Nationalbibliothek lists this publication in the Deutsche Nationalbibliografie;
detailed bibliographic data are available in the Internet at http://dnb.dnb.de.

© 2018 Walter de Gruyter GmbH, Berlin/Boston
Cover: Staats- und Universitätsbibliothek Hamburg, Ms Cod. Levy 115, fol. 158r:
Maimonides, More Nevukhim, Beginn von Teil III.
Printing and binding: CPI books GmbH, Leck

www.degruyter.com

Contents

Editorial —— VII

Part I: Articles

Dirk Westerkamp
Quaestio sceptica disputata de philosophia judaeorum: Is there a Jewish Philosophy? —— 3

Hanna Liss
Scepticism, Critique, and the Art of Writing: Preliminary Considerations on the Question of Textual Authority in Medieval *Peshaṭ* Exegesis —— 15

Bill Rebiger
Sceptical Elements in a Dogmatic Stance: Isaac Polqar against Kabbalah —— 47

Giuseppe Veltri
Apologetic, Empiricism, and Sceptical Strategies in Simone Luzzatto —— 67

Oded Schechter
Spinoza's Miracles: Scepticism, Dogmatism, and Critical Hermeneutics —— 89

Diego Lucci
Political Scepticism, Moral Scepticism, and the Scope and Limits of Toleration in John Locke —— 109

Guido Bartolucci
Jewish Scepticism in Christian Eyes: Jacob F. Reimmann and the Transformation of Jewish Philosophy —— 145

Lukas Lang
Reidian Common Sense: An Antidote to Scepticism? —— 165

Ze'ev Strauss
The Ground Floor of Judaism: Scepticism and Certainty in Moses Mendelssohn's *Jerusalem* —— 179

Andreas Brämer
Abraham Geiger—skeptischer Pionier einer Glaubenslehre des Reformjudentums? —— 207

Asher Salah
Are Karaites Sceptics? The Jewish Perception of Karaism in Nineteenth Century Italy —— 231

Libera Pisano
Anarchic Scepticism: Language, Mysticism and Revolution in Gustav Landauer —— 251

Part II Reports

Activities and Events —— 275

Yoav Meyrav
Report on the International Conference on Abraham Abulafia and the Early Maimonideans: Trends, Approaches, and Sceptical Strategies (March 12–15, 2018) —— 307

Silke Schaeper
Report on the Library of Jewish Scepticism —— 319

Editorial

The *Yearbook of the Maimonides Centre for Advanced Studies 2018* is already the third volume containing articles resulting from the research done by fellows and research associates in the first section as well as reports on the events which took place at the Maimonides Centre in the second section.

In the first section, articles dealing with a variety of topics related to scepticism are chronologically structured from the Middle Ages to the early twentieth century. All articles have been subject to a double-blind peer review. In a programmatic way, Dirk Westerkamp's article opens this section, posing the question, 'Is there a Jewish philosophy.' As his contribution was first presented in a Dialectical Evening at the Maimonides Centre, the form of his article discussing the pros and cons is reminiscent of a mediaeval scholastic *quaestio*.

In her article on textual authority in medieval *peshaṭ* exegesis, Hanna Liss examines exegetical glosses in Ms Vienna, Österreichische Nationalbibliothek, cod. hebr. 220. She focusses on the question whether, and in what manner, the gloss's comments convey negative criticism of Rashi's Torah commentary, and how and in which way they challenge the authority of this sage. With regard to her topic, Liss concludes that an extension of the term 'scepticism' beyond its epistemological meaning, actually causes more problems than it solves.

Bill Rebiger analyses a passage attacking the Kabbalah from *'Ezer ha-Dat* ('In Support of the Religion') written by the Jewish Averroist Isaac Polqar in the first half of the fourteenth century. Rebiger provides the reader with the first translation of the entire passage into English and a commentary exposing the sceptical elements detected therein.

Giuseppe Veltri presents some subtle sceptical strategies implemented by the Venetian Rabbi Simone Luzzatto in his *Discorso* to substantiate the right of existence of the Jews despite and because of their differences in the face of the Venetian society and government. In the same way, Veltri studies Luzzatto's *Socrate* which is the first existing treatise on scepticism written by a Jew.

The starting point of Oded Schechter's article is the riddle first formulated by Leo Strauss: Is Spinoza's interpretation of miracles consistent with his literal-sense hermeneutics? In contrast to Strauss' view, Schechter suggests that closer reading of Spinoza's critique of both sceptic and dogmatic hermeneutics clears the path for solving the Straussian riddle.

Diego Lucci reconsiders the impact of John Locke's moral and soteriological concerns on his approach to religious toleration and, thus, on the scope and limits of Locke's views on toleration in their development from his *A Letter concerning Toleration* to *The Reasonableness of Christianity*. As a result, he focusses on the sceptical dimension of Locke's thought.

Guido Bartolucci's article deals with the Lutheran scholar Jacob F. Reimmann who published a short essay in 1704 under the provocative title "An Salomon fuerit scepticus?" ("Was Solomon Sceptic?") arguing that the essence of Jewish philosophy is scepticism. Actually, Reimmann's claim is the first evidence for this interpretation and Bartolucci studies its historical background.

Remaining in the eighteenth century, Lukas Lang discusses Thomas Reid's common-sense-based version of the well-known *apraxia* objection, as it appears to be immune to Sextus Empiricus' reply countering it and so still has a chance to succeed.

The following three articles are devoted to the Jewish Enlightenment in Germany and Italy. Ze'ev Strauss explores Moses Mendelssohn's equivocal application of doubt in *Jerusalem oder über religiöse Macht und Judentum* (*Jerusalem or on Religious Power and Judaism*), and demonstrates that he, despite his rather unfavourable view of scepticism as a 'disease of the soul,' nonetheless draws heavily on it.

In his article on Abraham Geiger, one of the most influential rabbis in German Reform Judaism, Andreas Brämer considers him to be a sceptical pioneer of a theology of the new Jewish trend. While Geiger was interested in contemporary outcomes of Protestant theology as a role model on the one hand and a contrasting concept on the other, at the end he hesitated in writing a matching theology suitable for Jewish Reform concepts. Due to the many unpublished German sources provided by the author this article was not translated into English.

Asher Salah surveys the Jewish perception of Karaism as ambivalent objects of attraction and repulsion in debates between traditionalists and reformers of nineteenth century Italy. The selected texts the author discusses pose the leading question 'Are Karaites Sceptics?'

In the last article of this section, Libera Pisano introduces the anarchic sceptic Gustav Landauer and analyses his unique concepts concerning language, mysticism, and revolution. Pisano focusses on Landauer's place within the German discourse of *Sprachkrise* at the turn of the nineteenth into the twentieth century.

The second section of the *Yearbook* consists of three reports. The first presents all activities and events taking place at the Maimonides Centre between August 2017 and August 2018. Yoav Meyrav summarises the papers delivered at the international conference on Abraham Abulafia and the early Maimonideans hosted at the Centre in March 12–15, 2018. Finally, the Centre's librarian Silke Schaeper reports on the new acquisitions of the Library of Jewish Scepticism.

We would like to thank James Rumball who worked on the language editing of this volume. First and foremost, we owe many thanks to the *Deutsche Forschungsgemeinschaft* for the generous funding that maintains the Centre, to the Board of Trustees for their supervisory role, the advisory board for their engagement in selecting the fellows, and the President of the Universität Hamburg, Dieter Lenzen, the Chancellor, Martin Hecht, the Dean of the faculty, Oliver Huck, and the head of the Philosophy department, Benjamin Schnieder, for all their efforts that have made the Maimonides Centre a unique venue in the scholarly world.

Hamburg, August 2018
                                            Giuseppe Veltri (Chief Editor)
                                               Bill Rebiger (Volume Editor)

Part I: **Articles**

Dirk Westerkamp
Quaestio sceptica disputata de philosophia judaeorum: Is there a Jewish Philosophy?

> *Listen to the truth whoever speaks it.*
> (Maimonides, Eight Chapters)

Quaestio

The question reads: Is there a Jewish Philosophy (JP) or Can there be a JP? This question evidently entails the question: What is JP?

Videtur quod

It seems that there is a JP. JP is taught at departments of philosophy and Jewish thought around the world. JP looks back on a long history and rich tradition. Sometimes JP is put to use in public debates.[1] We speak of Philo, Maimonides, Mendelssohn and Lévinas as Jewish thinkers. JP is a philosophical *tradition* and we should not underestimate that traditions are important for (the history of) philosophy.[2] They are constituents of philosophical discourse and the simple fact that they emerge, change or come out of fashion over time does not imply that they don't exist or do not *matter*. So, yes, arguably there is such thing as JP.

1. However, since ontological, epistemological and methodological matters do not seem to be determinable as specifically 'Jewish', Tirosh-Samuelson/Hughes argue that JP is not primarily a theoretical enterprise but a practical philosophy 'heavily invested in matters of Jewish peoplehood and in articulating its aims and

---

Paper given at the Dialectical Evening at the Maimonides Centre for Advanced Studies, Universität Hamburg, August 22, 2017. Many thanks to all its participants for the helpful comments and the lively discussion. In order to encourage a debate this paper was presented in the form of a scholastic *quaestio*. It should be noted, however, that this is a kind of sketch. Neither do I want to pretend that it is a *bona fide* Quaestio in the formal scholastic sense; nor do I think that this stylised form of a Quaestio is the best and only way to discuss this matter. I trust that the irony of its presentation does not distract from the seriousness of the arguments.

1 Cf., e.g., Eliezer Schweid, *New Gordonian Essays: Globalization, Post-Modernism, Post-Humanism and the Jewish People* [in Hebrew] (Tel Aviv: Hakibbutz Hameuchad, 2005).
2 Josef Stern, "What is Jewish Philosophy? A view from the Middle Ages," in *Yearbook of the Maimonides Centre for Advanced Studies 2017*, ed. Bill Rebiger (Berlin and Boston: De Gruyter, 2017): 199.

objectives.'³ To this aim, it constantly and always had to apply ideas of 'non-Jewish' origins 'to Jewish ideas and values.'⁴ Thus, JP is 'in tune with certain principles of rationalism.'⁵

2. JP aims at harmonising philosophy and the Jewish tradition;⁶ JP agrees with the 'Jewish religious tradition.' JP 'explain[s] and rationalize[s]' the 'essential core of Judaism.'⁷ Complementary to this *essentialist account*, the *formalist account* of JP maintains that
- JP is 'any philosophy produced by a Jewish person, whatever the definition given for "Jewish"'⁸ (= *necessary condition*);
- JP has to address Jewish issues to define a philosophy as Jewish (= *sufficient condition*): 'While essentialism focusses on the Jewish content, moderate formalism rather takes into account the Jewish context.'⁹

3. It seems that there is JP as long as JP matches the standards of philosophical discourse: analysis, argument, distinction, critical evaluation, problem-solving.¹⁰ Likewise, Melamed argues that the reality

> [...] for modern Jewish philosophy was that most of its participants were either good philosophers (Spinoza and Cohen) or well informed in Jewish texts (Mendelssohn, Krochmal, Soloveitchik), though unfortunately in many cases they were neither Jewishly informed nor good philosophers.¹¹

Thus, there can be JP if it meets the—given—standards of state of the art philosophy (that seems to be one of the differences between JP and Jewish Thought, JT) *plus* the standards of erudite scholarship in Jewish studies. As for Modern JP, then, it seems that the 'real question is not "Is there a Jewish Philosophy?"' but: 'Is Jewish philosophy (still) *philosophy?*'¹² On this view, there can also be an Analytic Jewish Philos-

---

3 Hava Tirosh-Samuelson and Aaron W. Hughes, "Editors' Introduction to Series," in *Eliezer Schweid: The Responsibility of Jewish Philosophy*, Library of Contemporary Jewish Philosophers, vol. 1, eds. Hava Tirosh-Samuelson and Aaron W. Hughes (Leiden and Boston: Brill, 2013): xi.
4 *Ibidem*.
5 *Ibidem*, xii.
6 Raphael Jospe, *Jewish Philosophy: Foundations and Extensions*, vol. 2: *On Philosophers and Their Thought* (Lanham: University Press of America, 2008), 20.
7 Stefan Goltzberg, "Three Moments in Jewish Philosophy," *Bulletin du Centre de recherche français à Jérusalem* 22 (2011): 1.
8 Raphael Jospe, "Teaching Judah Ha-Levi: Defining and Shattering Myths in Jewish Philosophy," in *Paradigms in Jewish Philosophy*, ed. Raphael Jospe (London: Associated University Press, 1997): 113.
9 Goltzberg, "Three Moments in Jewish Philosophy," 2.
10 See Stern, "What is Jewish Philosophy? A view from the Middle Ages," 189.
11 Yitzhak Melamed, "Salomon Maimon et l'échec de la philosophie juive modern," *Revue germanique internationale* 9 (2009): 186–187.
12 Josef Stern, "Was jüdische Philosophie sein könnte (wenn es sie gäbe). Ein mediävistischer Blick," *Zeitschrift für Kulturphilosophie* 11 (2017): 296.

ophy applying the tools of logical and conceptual analysis for example to talmudic reasoning[13] or to Wittgensteinian accounts of lifeforms.[14]

4. In this sense, we may speak of JP if it is (i) philosophy (in the above mentioned sense) and (ii) concerned with Jewish religious and cultural practices. Melamed seems to adhere to the essentialist rather than to the formalist account of JP:

> Unlike many others, I do not take a Jewish philosopher to be someone who is (a) Jewish and (b) a philosopher, but rather suggest that Jewish philosophy is the attempt to provide a well-argued and informed account of Jewish religious and cultural beliefs and practices.[15]

Being Jewish, then, would neither be a necessary nor a sufficient condition for doing JP whereas providing an 'account of Jewish religious and cultural beliefs and practices' would be the necessary condition.

5. JP is the philosophy of Judaism; it is 'invested in matters of Jewish peoplehood,' 'in tune with certain principles of rationalism,' and providing an 'account of Jewish religious and cultural beliefs and practices.' It is contested, however, as to whether this *essentialist account* of JP has to be *critical* as well—meaning that it should critically reflect JP's own *historicity*: 'The critical approach takes into account the history of the texts, their modification over time, their successive editions. This critical approach is philosophically and historically receivable.' From the *non-critical essentialist's* point of view, 'a text of Jewish philosophy does not have to meet the criteria of the critical approach.'[16]

6. According to the *critical essentialist view*, JP and JT form a 'dynamic space of thought' (*dynamischer Denkraum*),[17] consisting of three 'spatial' elements: philosophy, mysticism, and theology. This space, however, is systematically nuanced, thematically inclusive (there can be more, for example the *musar*-movement etc.), and interculturally open. This essentialist view of JP is critical insofar as it holds that the essence of JP (and Judaism) is not *static* and *stable* but in constant transition, antithesis, and dynamic.

7. Furthermore, the *critical essentialist account* of JP can be divided into two camps: (i) Either JP fully (though not without self-criticism) endorses, promotes and defends Jewish beliefs, practices and convictions; or (ii) JP aims at being rather a 'philosophy of Judaism,' implying that JP seeks to 'achieve a critical understanding

---

13 Cf., e.g., Eli Hirsch, "Identity in the Talmud," *Midwest Studies in Philosophy* 23 (1999): 166–180.
14 Cf. Hilary Putnam, *Jewish Philosophy as a Guide to Life: Rosenzweig, Buber, Levinas, Wittgenstein* (Bloomington: Indiana University Press, 2008).
15 Melamed, "Salomon Maimon et l'échec de la philosophie juive modern," 176.
16 Goltzberg, "Three Moments in Jewish Philosophy," 4.
17 Frederek Musall, "Jüdisches Denken denken," in *Jewish Lifeworlds and Jewish Thought* (FS Grözinger), ed. Nathanael Riemer (Wiesbaden: Harrassowitz, 2012): 141–149.

of the foundational beliefs, logical structure, and presuppositions articulated in its data, *not to promote them*.'[18]

8. Some currents of the second strand of *critical essentialist account* of JP can be interpreted as *negativistic*. On this view, we better not define the critical essence of JP in *positive* terms (since its *Denkraum* is systematically and historically open and shifting). Rather, it can be determined through *negative* distinctions. According to the negativistic critical essentialist account, JP is
- *not* a school (for example Kalam; Aristotelians, Neo-Platonists),
- *not* a style (analytic philosophy, phenomenology, hermeneutics),
- *not* philosophy done by Jews (not an ethnic category),
- *not* philosophy written in Hebrew.[19]

Some positive attributes, however, can be formulated. Medieval JP, for instance, was a network of a 'continuous dialogue' of Jewish authors 'embedded' in the 'tradition of Islamic philosophy and its Greek sources' and, later, encountering Christian scholastic philosophy.[20] Within this discourse-network, the question of the relation *between Philosophy and Torah* is debated. JP is 'a causally-intraconnected discourse, or conversation, what I called a "tradition"'[21] following the agenda of discussing the relation between philosophy and Torah set by Maimonides' *Guide*.

Sed contra

On the other hand, the existence of a JP is heavily contested, abrogated, and denied. To highlight this, let me report a somewhat funny, yet illuminating personal conversation I had with one of my academic advisors, Yossef Schwartz, while returning to the Hebrew University of Jerusalem as a Visiting Research Fellow (in 2000):

> Schwartz: 'What do you want to study with me while you are a Visiting Research Fellow at the Hebrew University?'
> Westerkamp: 'Medieval Jewish Philosophy.'
> Schwartz: '*Ein davar*—there is no such thing as Medieval Jewish Philosophy. Study with someone else or study something else.'

1. It can be argued against the *formalist account* of JP (see *Videtur quod*, 2.) that since there is no Jewish physics, no Jewish biology and no Jewish sociology (being radically different from social studies on Judaism), there can be no JP. This is drastically canvassed by Jospe, saying that some Jews playing football doesn't make their playing

---

[18] Stern, "Was jüdische Philosophie sein könnte (wenn es sie gäbe). Ein mediävistischer Blick," 278 (emphasis added).
[19] Cf. Stern, "What is Jewish Philosophy? A view from the Middle Ages," 186–190.
[20] *Ibidem*, 198.
[21] *Ibidem*, 201.

football a Jewish football game. The formalist account of JP can be formalistically challenged also by the following example: Suppose that a philosopher discovers at the end of her career that she was Jewish. Would this 'retroactively turn' her work 'into a contribution to Jewish philosophy'?[22] Taking the example of the late Hilary Putnam who towards the end of his life cared more and more about his 'Jewishness', does not mean that his earlier work becomes JP retrospectively.

2. According to the *critical historiographical account* of JP (JP_{CHA}), JP was simply 'the creation of the academic discipline, the "History of Jewish Philosophy," an artefact *made* by an academic discipline as much as the discipline *studies* it.'[23] Within the camp of JP_{CHA}, however, there is an ongoing controversial debate on the origins of this 'artefact'. Whereas Leora Batnizky claims that JP is a 'modern academic construct,'[24] Daniel Frank traces the idea of its tradition back to nineteenth century German-Jewish *Wissenschaft des Judentums*. The *Wissenschaft des Judentums* sought to legitimate Jewish philosophical texts as a respected academic subject.[25] I have shown that the idea of a *philosophia judaeorum perennis* is even older, stemming from seventeenth century French-German discourse on 'historiographical holism'[26] and German Enlightenment historiography of Jewish Thought.[27] Even prior to that, so Giuseppe Veltri argues, the 'first sketch of a Jewish [...] history of philosophy was formulated by the Venetian Rabbi Simone Luzzatto (1583–1663),'[28] consequently dating the 'artefact' of JP back into sixteenth century humanism.

3. In addition, JP_{CHA} demonstrates that JP was not only a historiographical invention but also a highly *polemical* one.[29] Within seventeenth and eighteenth century 'historiographical holism,' JP was introduced as an allegedly continuous tradition (from the prophets [= *philosophia haebraeorum*] up until Moses Mendelssohn) only in the end to be expelled from the kingdom of 'serious' philosophy. More bluntly: JP was invented for no other purpose than to be excluded as a mere *philosophia extra-graecanica* or *philosophia orientali*.

As a consequence, any essentialist account of JP has to question itself as to whether it wants—however unconsciously—to continue this polemical tradition of

---

22 Goltzberg, "Three Moments in Jewish Philosophy," 3.
23 Stern, "What is Jewish Philosophy? A view from the Middle Ages," 186.
24 Leora Batnizky, "The Nature and History of Jewish Philosophy," in *Jewish Philosophy Past and Present*, eds. Daniel H. Frank and Aaron Segal (New York and London: Routledge, 2016): 72.
25 Daniel Frank, "What is Jewish philosophy?," in *History of Jewish Philosophy*, eds. Daniel H. Frank and Oliver Leaman (London: Routledge, 2004).
26 Dirk Westerkamp, *Die philonische Unterscheidung. Aufklärung, Orientalismus und Konstruktion der Philosophie* (München: Fink, 2009); cf. also idem, "The Philonic Distinction. German Enlightenment Historiography of Jewish Thought," *History and Theory* 47 (2008): 533–559.
27 Westerkamp, *Die philonische Unterscheidung*, 15–90.
28 Giuseppe Veltri,"Die arabische Philosophie und der Islam im modernen jüdischen Denken," in *Jewish Lifeworlds and Jewish Thought* (FS Grözinger), ed. Nathanael Riemer (Wiesbaden: Harassowitz, 2012): 100.
29 Westerkamp, *Die philonische Unterscheidung*, 71–74.

tradition-construction or not. If not, this would mean either to write a different history of the tradition of *philosophia judaeorum perennis* or to give up its very idea altogether. In sum: according to JP$_{CHA}$, there is no such category as JP prior to Early Modernity and, as a consequence, Philo or Maimonides never were (and never have or could have considered themselves to be) Jewish philosophers.

4. According to the *anti-essentialist account* of JP (JP$_{AEA}$), JP is philosophically unoriginal; its philosophical issues, methods and solutions are second hand news. The 'philosophy' in JP is borrowed from philosophically genuine *non*-Jewish backgrounds: Greek thought, Islamic philosophy, scholastic thinking, and later (with regard to Moses Mendelssohn and Hermann Cohen) from Leibnizian or Kantian philosophy etc. In this sense, Veltri and others (Stern, Samuelson, Leaman etc.) argue that JP can not be conceived of independently from Arabic Muslim philosophy etc.; it can only be determined in 'interaction' (*Wechselwirkung*) with other philosophical cultures. Hence, JP can be studied only by taking into account the multifaceted and underlying processes of 'cultural transfer.'[30] This position could be termed the *culturalist anti-essentialist account* of JP (JP$_{CAEA}$).

5. Even more radical, some interpreters claim the principal irreconcilability of Judaism and philosophy, the latter concerned with pure reason, the former stemming from religious experience. Alexander Altmann's JP$_{AEA}$ maintains the irreconcilability of reason and revelation (this is, according to Altmann, philosophy's central project in the *mediaevum* as well as in eighteenth century Enlightenment). Accordingly, it is

> [...] futile to attempt a presentation of Judaism as a philosophical system. [...] Judaism is a religion, and the truths it teaches are religious truths. They spring from the source of religious experience, not from pure reason.[31]

Altmann's position can be labelled the *irreconcilabilist anti-essentialist account* of JP (JP$_{IAEA}$).

6. JP$_{IAEA}$ leads to yet another prominent *anti-essentialist account* of JP, the *anti-universalist account* of JP (JP$_{AUA}$). According to this view, doing JP is 'insular', 'parochial' – in all a 'particularistic' enterprise. Restricted to Jewish matters, JP has to give up the very 'universal concerns'[32] which construct the core of any *serious* thinking that may deservedly be called 'philosophy'. Thus, there can be no JP, or at least JP is *not* philosophy for it does not exhibit a 'universal curiosity and a universal questioning'[33] into the foundations of existence. Likewise, Veltri argues that the epithet 'Jewish' restricts philosophy to particularistic (historical and cultural contingent) in-

---

30 Veltri, "Die arabische Philosophie und der Islam im modernen jüdischen Denken."
31 Alexander Altmann, "Judaism and World Philosophy," in *The Jews: Their History, Culture, and Religion*, ed. L. Finkelstein (Philadelphia: Jewish Publication Society of America, 1949): 954.
32 Tirosh-Samuelson/Hughes, "Editors' Introduction to Series," x.
33 Leon Roth, "Is there a Jewish philosophy?," in *Jewish Philosophy and Philosophers*, ed. R. Goldwater (London: Hillel Foundation, 1962): 8.

terests, whereas philosophy (*en sens large*) has to 'go beyond the contingent.'³⁴ JP$_{AUA}$ leads to the separation of general philosophy and Judaism. According to Leon Roth, there can be no such thing as JP may be a 'philosophy of Judaism' whereas conceivable: as 'the thinking and rethinking of the fundamental ideas involved in Judaism and the attempt to see them fundamentally, that is, in coherent relation one with another so that they form one intelligible whole.'³⁵

7. JP$_{AUA}$ has led to yet another position: the *paradoxical* or *self-contradictory conception* of JP (JP$_{PARA}$): JP somehow *is* and *is not*. According to Tirosh-Samuelson/Hughes, Jewish philosophy is 'rooted in a paradox'—if not contradiction: 'As philosophy, this activity makes claims of universal validity.' Insofar as this activity is interpreted as a Jewish activity, philosophising becomes 'an activity by a well-defined group of people' and, therefore, 'it is inherently particularistic.' Hence, JP is ruled by a contradiction as the 'collision of particularistic demands and universal concerns.'³⁶ JP, then, would be a philosophical tradition (or stance) which heroically accepts the impossible task of trying to reconcile the irreconcilable: particularist faith and universalist reason, philosophical truths and religious practice. JP would accordingly be the heroic but (im)possible endeavour to at least try to bring the impossible into the form of philosophical discourse.

8. JP$_{CHA}$, JP$_{AEA}$, JP$_{CAEA}$, JP$_{IAEA}$, and JP$_{AUA}$ amount to the conclusion that (i) either there is no JP (as an essential or even formal entity) or (ii) that JP is an academic artefact or (iii) that JP is not possible (in terms of 'consistently conceivable')—or that JP is possible only as the philosophical possibility of facing and formulating the philosophically impossible (JP$_{PARA}$).

Responsio / Dicendum quod

For the sake of the argument, I seek to take a dogmatist stance in the *corpus articuli*. Thus, I will—*contre cœur* (see *Sed contra*, 3.)—argue for an *essentialist* answer to the *quaestio sceptica disputata*. To do so, I will not only refute the *Sed contra*-theses but develop further decisive arguments which amount to a definition (or better: explication) of what JP was and is. Among these arguments are:
1. an *argumentum ad verecundiam* or argument from authority;
2. an empirico-transcendental argument against performative self-contradiction (which can be read as an *argumentum ad hominem* as well);
3. a pragmatic conceptual argument;
4. a methodological argument with regard to the distinction of scientific subject and object (implicitly rejecting the *Sed-contra*-arguments of JP$_{CHA}$ 2.–4.);

---

34 Veltri, "Die arabische Philosophie und der Islam im modernen jüdischen Denken," 99.
35 Roth, "Is there a Jewish philosophy?," 8.
36 Tirosh-Samuelson/Hughes, "Editors' Introduction to Series," ix-x.

5. an anti-dogmatic *tertium datur*-argument with regard to the relation between reason and revelation (implicitly rejecting the *Sed-contra*-argument of JP$_{IAEA}$ 5.);
6. an anti-particularistic *reductio ad-absurdum*-argument (implicitly refuting the *Sed contra*-argument of JP$_{AUA}$ 6.);
7. an anti-positivist argument in favour of a methodologically sound distinction between scientific subjects and literary categories (implicitly refuting the account of JP$_{AUA}$, namely *Sed contra*-arguments 1. and 7.);
8. a counterfactual classification-argument;
9. an argument from autonomy; and, finally, a
10. definition with the *genus proximum* 'philosophy' and three restrictive *differentiae specificae*.

It has to be said that (*dicendum quod*) there is a JP. This conclusion becomes evident (*ex ergo patet*) from the following arguments that serve as premises to the overall conclusion:

1. Eminent scholars work on medieval Jewish philosophy; other prominent scholars in the field have edited book series such as the "Library of Contemporary Jewish Philosophers" (Tirosh-Samuelson/Hughes). If we agree that these authorities are not 'bluffers' but actually know what they are doing, we must suppose that there is something that may be termed JP or JT[37] or at least that there are indeed 'contemporary Jewish philosophers.'

2. There are chairs of Jewish Thought and Jewish Philosophy (Israel, US, Europe).[38] In Germany, there are, to the best of my knowledge, at least four chairs of JP or JT.[39] Denying that there is such a thing as JP would be a performative contradiction for those occupying the chairs.

3. The existential copula 'is' in the question 'Is there a Jewish Philosophy?' does not refer to a quantificational-ontological question on 'what there is' (as Popperian

---

[37] The difference between Jewish Philosophy (JP) and Jewish Thought (JT) may recall Heidegger's distinction between 'philosophy' and 'thinking' (*Denken*). Whereas 'philosophy' became a watered-down form of philosophy such as *Betrieb* or professionalised business, Heidegger favours 'thinking' (as 'real' philosophy) over philosophy; for him, 'thinking' stands in proximity/neighbourhood (*Nachbarschaft*) to poetry (*Dichten*). I trust that the difference between JP and JT does not imply the Heideggerian motive.

[38] Just some random name-dropping: Paul Franks is Professor of Philosophy, Jewish Philosophy, and Religious Studies at Yale University; Benjamin Pollock is Sol Rosenbloom Chair in Jewish Philosophy and Associate Professor of Jewish Thought at the Hebrew University of Jerusalem; Haim Kreisel is Professor of Medieval Jewish Philosophy in the Department of Jewish Thought at Ben-Gurion University of the Negev; Noam Zohar is Associate Professor of Jewish Philosophy and Chair (General Philosophy) at Bar-Ilan University.

[39] Jewish Philosophy and Religion: Giuseppe Veltri (Universität Hamburg); Religious Studies and Jewish Thought: Sina Rauschenbach (Universität Potsdam); Modern Jewish Philosophy: Walter Homolka (Universität Potsdam); Jüd. Philosophie und Geistesgeschichte: Frederek Musall (Hochschule für Jüdische Studien, Heidelberg).

world 1-objects, for instance). Instead it refers to something that *matters* for us. It refers, moreover, to a *category* (a world 3-object/ideal object). These objects are not eternal but come into being through our scientific practices. JP is such a category. That it was 'invented' or is an 'artefact'[40] does not mean that it does not matter for us now. The fact that Maimonides didn't regard himself *as* a Jewish philosopher (but as an Aristotelian philosopher and a pious Jew) because he didn't know of the artificial category 'JP' does not imply that he was not a Jewish philosopher.

4. There is a difference between doing JP (i.e. constituting/establishing the category itself) and doing research in the history of JP (i.e. always already using the category). Even if it may be that the *history* of JP was in fact an invention of the sixteenth- (Veltri), seventeenth/eighteenth- (Westerkamp), nineteenth- (Frank) or twentieth-century (Batnizky) scholarship and historiography, JP (as the subject of this scholarship) is not. This would mean that science and scholarship can sometimes produce their scientific objects. It is, however, a sign of good scientific practice to clearly distinguish the subject and object of science (the historian of nationalism need not to be a nationalist).

With the help of arguments 3./4., one can reject the *Sed-contra*-arguments of JP_{CHA} (2.–4.).

Ad 2. Even historiographical artefacts and categories exist (in the sense that they matter, that they can be useful scientific objects) since the subject of these artefacts are series or bundles of existing texts by real authors. Traditions may be 'invented' but can nevertheless have a hold on us. JP is such a tradition.

Ad 3. Against the polemical classification of JP as non-philosophy (and the argument of JP_{CHA}), Jewish philosophers may invoke the 'counter-memory' (Jan Assmann) of their own tradition.

Ad 4. Against JP_{AEA}'s argument of the 'non-originality' of JP ('borrowed' methods, rationalism etc.) one can show that in the history of *philosophia perennis* everyone borrows something from someone (so to speak). The scholastics thought highly of the Islamic and Jewish philosophical pioneer-work in metaphysics. Surely, cultural transfer is never a one-way street. Philosophical transfer always was a *non-asymmetrical* or a *transitive* relation. There has been an immense 'backflow' from JP to philosophy (especially to scholastic thinking).

5. JP_{AEA} (see *Sed contra*, 5.) intends to develop an anti-dogmatist argument. Yet it is in itself highly dogmatic. The position according to which philosophy and Judaism or reason and revelation are irreconcilable, rests on a dogmatic *a priori* assumption. It follows the problematic logic of *tertium non datur*. And it shows a deep misunderstanding of JP. Contrary to that, Jewish philosophers like Maimonides tried to show that revelation is in itself rational. To say that religion is only irrational is in itself dogmatic, at best arrogant. In this vein, Horkheimer/Adorno argued that myths already have some inner rationality whereas pure and abstract reason can itself depra-

---

[40] Stern, "What is Jewish Philosophy? A view from the Middle Ages," 186.

vate into a myth and become a quasi-religious idol. So it seems that JP$_{AEA}$'s view is not only dogmatic but extremely ahistorical and privileges a restricted modern view on historical matters.

6. Doing *Jewish* philosophy does not necessarily imply that it is 'insular', 'particularistic' or 'parochial', since being Jewish does not rule out (a) that this philosophy can at the same time be heavily influenced by Hellenistic, Islamic, Christian, hermeneutical, analytical, phenomenological or any other strand of thought. Denying that would ignore that, e. g., the medieval Jewish-philosophical enterprises were clearly intercultural and interreligious enterprises.[41] And it does not rule out (b) that JP makes universal claims pertaining to every living creature. That is to say that philosophy can be particularistically Jewish without giving up its 'universal concerns' (Tirosh-Samuelson/Hughes).

If specifying epithets cause problems of particularism then this would also cast doubt on the possibility of any analytic, phenomenological or sceptical philosophy at all. Again, the sharp alternative between particularistic *or* universal philosophical claims rests on a problematic presupposition, on a binary opposition ruling out any third possibility. If any restriction of philosophy endangers its philosophical substance, then only ontology (as first philosophy) could be (absurdly) called philosophy.

With this argument, we may also refute *Sed contra*, 6. (JP$_{AUA}$): Every philosophy, every philosophical text (even Hegel's majestic, allegedly all-encompassing system) is somewhat particularistic. Any *anti-universalist account* of JP would have the burden of proof to show what instead could be a full-fledged universalistic account of philosophy. What is philosophically 'universal' at all? Hence, the argument against 'insularism' collapses into itself.

7. Universalism and particularism do not necessarily contradict. Something can universalistically be philosophy but particularistically be done in a Jewish garb; thus the analogy—if there a 22 Jews playing football it does not mean that what they do is Jewish football—does not hold; the same is true with 'Jewish physics' and the like. The analogy is bad since it contaminates two incomparable subjects. Philosophy is concerned with thoughts and arguments (expressed in speech and text) not primarily with natural objects. Since there can be a specific Jewish literature and a specific Jewish temple but no specific Jewish stone or planet, there can also be philosophical Jewish texts. Not to distinguish subjects and to convey the same passe-partout-method on them is positivism or logical empiricism. Both are bad philosophy.

JP thus is a *textual category*. Edmund Husserl never produced a text which falls under this category but both the phenomenologist Emmanuel Lévinas and the analytic philosopher Hilary Putnam did.

---

[41] Stern, "What is Jewish Philosophy? A view from the Middle Ages," 198.

With this in mind, JP$_{AUA}$—namely *Sed contra*, 1. and 7.—can be rejected: *Ad* 7. The view that Jewish philosophy is 'rooted in a paradox' is no *Alleinstellungsmerkmal* of JP but holds true also with regard to Islamic Philosophy (IP) and Christian Philosophy (CP) (e. g. Neo-Thomism).

Ad 1. The formalist view is wrong since it is not the Jew which makes philosophy Jewish but that is a certain sort (and tradition) of texts that makes a philosophical text belong to JP.

8. Let us consider some simple yes/no-cases. Was Salomon a Jewish philosopher? Not in a technical sense. Was Philo of Alexandria a Jewish philosopher? Definitely! Maimonides? He too! Was Spinoza a Jewish philosopher? Not so much the author of the *Ethica* but rather the author of the *Tractatus Theologico-Politicus*. Husserl was not a Jewish philosopher, Lévinas was. Scholem was not, being a Jew but not a philosopher (calling himself a 'historian of religion'). Were Benjamin and Derrida Jewish philosophers? Difficult to say, at least not according to the definition with which this paper concludes. So here comes the eighth argument: What would we do if the historiographical category 'JP' were missing (or similar categories such as 'Islamic philosophy' or 'Christian philosophy')? How would we classify thinkers such as Maimonides, Crescas, Luzzatto? Thus, JP—if well-defined—seems to be a useful category.

9. As already seen, it is not a necessary condition for JP that an author interprets him- or herself as a Jewish philosopher in order to be one. This does not imply, however, that the self-attribution or self-understanding of authors is generally irrelevant. If some colleague came up to me and said, 'I am a Jewish philosopher'—who am I to disagree or tell he/she is not or he/she is a victim of a 'scientific self-misunderstanding' (Habermas). To a great extent, simply out of sheer respect, we would have to accept the autonomous philosophical self-interpretation of the other. If there were a group of philosophers calling themselves Jewish philosophers with good reasons to back this up, then they actually *are* Jewish philosophers that form the category 'JP'.

10. Without debating what 'philosophy' or 'philosophising' exactly means and reminding Nietzsche's insight that: we can only define that which has no history, the following definition (or less technically: explication) of the term JP can be given: JP is a philosophy of a specific historical tradition which philosophises out of the sources of Judaism, involves an account of the relation between reason and revelation and accepts (or in a weaker sense – reflects) the truth claims of the Jewish tradition as developed in the sources mentioned. Schematically:

JP is   philosophy (or philosophising)   (*genus proximum*; *genos*)
- in a specific historical tradition ('-ish')   (*species*; *eidos*)
- 'out of the sources of Judaism' (H. Cohen) (i.e. Torah, Midrash, Talmud plus their commentaries)   (1st *differentia specifica*)
- giving an account of the relation between reason and revelation   (2nd *differentia specifica*)

- accepting (or at least: reflecting) the truth claims of Jewish tradition developed in the mentioned sources (truth claims: One God, importance of prophecy, liability of the Halakhah etc.) (3rd *differentia specifica*)

Some explanations of the *differentiae specificae* or sufficient conditions/restrictions may be useful. *Ad* 1st *differentia specifica:* The 'sources' of Judaism (however that category is defined) may in themselves already contain 'philosophemata' or 'theologoumena' or any elements prone to philosophical thinking. *Ad* 2nd *differentia specifica:* Whatever 'reconciliation' means—it has to work with an 'update' of a certain philosophical terminology developed in former (Late-Antiquity, Mediaeval, or Enlightenment period) discourses on the topic. *Ad* 3rd *differentia specifica:* A crucial, yet extremely difficult question is whether one has to fully accept the truth claims of the Jewish texts or may one adopt a neutral stance towards them when doing JP. My understanding is that one has to fully subscribe to these truth claims in order to write a JP. However, one could further distinguish between the attempt to ground the truth claims and to show how and why they are *possible* (i.e. moderate foundationalist position) and the attempt to show that they are not only grounded but that they are *necessary* and therefore have to be affirmed *in toto* (i.e. fundamentalist position).

From all this we may draw the *conclusion:* If it can be proved that there are authors and texts satisfying the conditions of this (internally open) definition, then there is JP.

Hanna Liss
Scepticism, Critique, and the Art of Writing: Preliminary Considerations on the Question of Textual Authority in Medieval *Peshaṭ* Exegesis

The glossed book's lay-out, difficult to set up and copy, was reserved for works that were among the most fully institutionalized [...] the works of certain classical authors.
(Mary Carruthers)

Glosses not only use a variety of strategies to preserve and create authority, but also to undermine and, occasionally, to usurp it.
(Suzanne Reynolds)

1 Introduction

'Scepticism' among the tosafists? Glosses as a means for a sceptical discourse? The two opening quotations[1] will define the edges of a research field whose outline may be delineated by the question regarding 'scepticism' in Northern French *peshaṭ* exegesis revealing 'doubts about the claims of authorities'[2] on the one hand, and the '"authorizing" of a text'[3] on the other.[4]

---

[1] 'The glossed book's lay-out [...]' stems from Mary Carruthers, *The Book of Memory: A Study of Memory in Medieval Culture* (Cambridge: Cambridge University Press, 2008), 265; 'Glosses not only use a variety of strategies [...]' is quoted from Suzanne Reynolds, *Medieval Reading: Grammar, Rhetoric, and the Classical Text* (Cambridge: Cambridge University Press, 1996), 7.
[2] Cf. the definition from the Maimonides Centre's mission statement: 'One of the most important research objectives is to examine whether the method of enquiry implied in the term 'scepticism' could be regarded an anthropological constant [...] across both Eastern and Western philosophy and culture. The assumption would be that people in every culture express doubts about the claims of authorities to truth, the reliability of texts, and their social or mystical relevance, doubts about the power and presence of divinities, or about the power of reason and the controlling power of social structures and their respective consequences [...].' (https://www.maimonides-centre.uni-hamburg.de; accessed March 2018).
[3] A term introduced by Carruthers, *Book of Memory*, 243.
[4] This paper is based on my article '"Daneben steht immer ein kluger Kopf": Die Glossenformationen im Codex Wien hebr. 220," in *Diligens scrutator sacri eloquii. Beiträge zur Exegese- und Theologiegeschichte des Mittelalters. Festgabe für Rainer Berndt SJ*, eds. Hanns Peter Neuheuser, Ralf M. W. Stammberger, and Matthias M. Tischler (Münster: Aschendorff, 2016): 53–85, and was reworked under the respective topic during my stay as Senior Fellow at the Maimonides Centre for Advanced Studies—Jewish Scepticism, Universität Hamburg (October 2017–March 2018). My thanks to Jonas Leipziger who arranged, in particular, the edition of the gloss material in this paper, Bettina Burghardt who translated parts of this paper from German into English. Thanks also to all the staff mem-

OpenAccess. © 2018 Hanna Liss, published by De Gruyter. This work is licensed under the Creative Commons Attribution-NonCommercial-NoDerivatives 4.0 License.
https://doi.org/10.1515/978-3-11-057768-6-003

In its specific philosophical sense, sourced in Ancient Greek philosophy, scepticism and/or the sceptical approach seek to refrain from any of its own judgements regarding religious beliefs or philosophical views. In that sense, the question is easily declined: There is no philosophical scepticism among the tosafists, for the tosafists were neither philosophers, nor did their critical glosses on the Bible and the Talmud (more precisely: their critical notes and questions on Rashi's commentaries on the Bible and the Talmud) intend reaching a state of mind beyond any affirmation or denial of religious knowledge or beliefs. However, even if we take 'scepticism' in an extended sense, comprised of sceptical and critical strategies, concepts, and attitudes against elements of tradition,[5] we would hardly label the tosafists' exegetical discourses as 'scepticism' or sceptical thought, although they challenge traditional rabbinic exegesis, and in some cases utter harsh criticism of the *Rishonim* as their exegetical forerunners. For instance, in Ms Oxford, Bodleian Library, Opp. 34 (Neubauer 186), fol. 116v,[6] we find various exegetical *dicta* attributed to Rashbam[7] describing the new exegetical approach 'according to the ways of the world', thus criticising the former exegetical explanations for being 'neither in accordance with the way of the world, [based on] common knowledge, nor in line with the [meaning of] the verse.'[8] Moreover, in the same context, we find harsh criticism of his grandfather Rashi whose explanation of Deuteronomy 20:19 is rejected, almost scoffed at, as 'foolishness.'[9] However, when dealing with medieval Jewish literature, one always has to wrestle with the question of *textual* authority, and so we may accede the *dictum* conveys an undermining of the exegetical authority. But I would like to propose the question: Is textual authority identical with exegetical authority?[10] And if so, must it be labelled a sceptical mode or strategy, even in a very broad sense? Are these exegetical comments a means for conveying sceptical thought? Is a critical attitude towards rabbinic understanding tantamount to a sceptical approach? And

---

bers of the Centre for their kind and attentive support, and my colleagues Bill Rebiger and Friedhelm Hartenstein for many discussions about the issue at hand.
5 See Bill Rebiger, "Sceptical Strategies in Simone Luzzatto's Presentation of the Kabbalists in his *Discorso*," in *Yearbook of the Maimonides Centre for Advanced Studies 2017*, ed. Bill Rebiger (Berlin and Boston: De Gruyter, 2017): 53.
6 The manuscript is fully digitised online (accessed March 2018).
7 This text was written in a second (later) hand on fol. 116v, after the poem at the end of *Parashat Zot ha-Berakha*. It is signed with the words מיסוד רב׳ שמואל in line 26, and זצ״ל מאיר בר שמואל ר׳ בפתרי (first letter hardly readable due to page-cut). This text is not laid out as a gloss to the Rashi commentary, but is a collection of biblical explanations attributed to Rashbam (starting with Deuteronomy 34:1 in line 1); for the details see Moshe Sokolow, "כ״י - לרשב״ם מפירוש התורה חדשים קטעים :המתחדשים הפשטות," *Ale Sefer* 11 (1984): 74–76.
8 אם יראו הרואים פירושי׳ קדומים שנוטים לצד אחר פשט אחר בעניינים אחרים יתנו לב כי אינם דרך ארץ לפי חכמת דברי בני אדם, או כפי׳ הפסוק (line 8–10).
9 הלא תראה מה פירש זקיני זצ״ל [...] הלא זה הדבר הבל (line 12–14).
10 See above note 2.

last, but not least: in which way have 'sceptical' strategies, concepts, and attitudes to be qualified in relation to the literary genre in which they appear?

In the following study on the exegetical glosses in Ms Vienna, Österreichische Nationalbibliothek, cod. hebr. 220, I will present an edition of selected glosses[11] and examine, if, and in what manner, these gloss comments convey negative criticism of Rashi's Torah commentary, and how and in which way they challenge the authority of the great sage. As some of these glosses have already been attributed to Rashbam, my study will compare them to the printed editions of Rashbam's Torah commentary (henceforth RTC).[12]

2 The Manuscript Tradition of Rashi and his School

2.1 Textual Witnesses of Rashi's Torah Commentary

The so-called *peshaṭ* exegesis by Northern French Jews of the eleventh and twelfth centuries, and the question of how exactly it is to be understood, has engaged scholars of Jewish Studies almost continuously for the last 150 years. The main focal point has been—and remains—the commentary by R. Shelomo Yiṣḥaqi (acronym Rashi; ca. 1040–1105), for even to this day, it is considered the fundamental text of Jewish Bible exegesis.[13] His commentary is present in each and every traditional Bible edition. Regarding manuscript tradition and contemporary print editions, Jewish Medieval studies are in a much less comfortable position than their Christian counterparts.[14] This has became even more so in recent years, when the relationship between the literary

---

11 An edition of the entire gloss corpus is currently being prepared. All the glosses will be diplomatically edited, and presented as an annotated digital edition according to their *mise-en-forme* and arrangement on the manuscript's folio. I am deeply indebted to Clemens Liedtke, M.A., Center for Jewish Studies Heidelberg (Project Corpus Masoreticum; accessed March 2018) for providing me with the electronic tools for the digital edition.
12 See below section 2.3.
13 Among others see for instance Gilbert Dahan, Gérard Nahon, and Elie Nicolas, eds., *Rashi et la Culture Juive en France du Nord au Moyen Âge* (Paris: E. Peeters, 1997); Avraham Grossman, *The Early Sages of France: Their Lives, Leadership and Works* [in Hebrew] (Jerusalem: Magnes Press, ²1996); Avraham Grossman, *Rashi* [in Hebrew] (Jerusalem: The Zalman Shazar Center for Jewish History, 2006); English edition: (Oxford and Portland, OR: The Littman Library of Jewish Civilization, 2012); Jason Kalman, "Medieval Jewish Biblical Commentaries and the State of Parshanut Studies," *Religion Compass* 2.5 (2008): 819–843; Robert Salters, "The Exegesis of Rashi and Rashbam on Qoheleth," in *Rashi et la Culture Juive en France du Nord au Moyen Âge*, eds. Gilbert Dahan, Gérard Nahon, and Elie Nicolas (Paris: E. Peeters, 1997): 151–161; Barry Dov Walfish, "An Annotated Bibliography of Medieval Jewish Commentaries on the Song of Songs," in *The Bible in the Light of Its Interpreters: Sarah Kamin Memorial Volume*, ed. Sara Japhet (Jerusalem: Magnes Press, 1994): 518–571.
14 Cf. Matthias M. Tischler, *Die Bibel in Saint-Victor zu Paris: das Buch der Bücher als Gradmesser für wissenschaftliche, soziale und ordensgeschichtliche Umbrüche im europäischen Hoch- und Spätmittelalter* (Münster: Aschendorff, 2014).

heritage of Rashi and the documentary evidence of his pupils came under closer scrutiny. It was revealed that *the* Rashi commentary never really existed,[15] at least not before it made its way into the typographic world. The first printing of Rashi's commentary on the Torah also marks the beginning of Hebrew book printing *per se* (Reggio di Calabria, 1475).[16]

Even the handwritten text-witnesses existing today originate from a noticeably later period and are everything but uniform: the oldest manuscript, Ms Munich, Bayerische Staatsbibliothek, cod. hebr. 5 (commentary only) was copied in 1233 in Würzburg and also constitutes the oldest dated, illuminated Ashkenazi manuscript. The second important Rashi manuscript, Ms Leipzig, Universitätsbibliothek, hebr. 1 (B.H. fol. 1) originates from the thirteenth century (undated) and contains, aside from the Masoretic biblical text (with eclectic annotated Masoretic glosses), the Targum and a commentary attributed to Rashi and is also accompanied by a number of glosses by Rashi's most eminent pupil, Shemaʿya, and the scribe Makhir.[17] The third manuscript, considered to be one of the most important objects for research into Rashi, Ms Vienna, hebr. 220 (Schwarz 23) is also undated, but originates from a considerably later period (thirteenth/fourteenth century). Strictly speaking, the printed editions are unusable for academic purposes: aside from the traditional Bible, editions in the so-called Rabbinic Bibles (*Miqra'ot Gedolot*) are severely flawed. Today one resorts to either Rashi's Torah commentary in the Abraham Berliner[18] edition or the one contained in *Miqra'ot Gedolot Haketer*.[19] There is as yet, no *critical* edition available, and of the existing Rashi commentaries, the deviations are occasionally overly extreme. Such findings resulted in numerous discussions among scholars on whether to describe the Rashi corpus as 'author commentary' or 'compilatory commentary'. The discussions, however, were largely too narrowly focussed (providing basically no result).[20] Scholarly results emanating from Modern Languages and

---

15 See in particular the forthcoming book by Kay Joe Petzold, *Masora und Exegese. Untersuchungen zur Masora und Bibeltextüberlieferung im Kommentar des R. Schlomo ben Yitzchaq (Raschi)* (Berlin and Boston: De Gruyter, 2018).
16 See, e.g., Joseph Hacker and Adam Shear, eds., *The Hebrew Book in Early Modern Italy* (Philadelphia: University of Pennsylvania Press, 2011); Moshe Rosenfeld, *Hebrew Printing from its Beginning until 1948: A Gazetteer of Printing, the First Books and their Dates with Photographed Title-Pages and Bibliographical Notes* [in Hebrew] (Jerusalem: M. Rosenfeld, 1992).
17 On the significance of Ms Leipzig, hebr. 1, cf. Grossman, *The Early Sages of France*, 187–193.
18 Abraham Berliner, *Der Kommentar des Salomo B. Isak über den Pentateuch: nach Handschriften, seltenen Ausgaben u. dem Talmud* (Berlin 1866; Frankfurt am Main: Kauffmann, ²1905) drew on a wealth of manuscripts but compiled an eclectic text.
19 Menachem Cohen, ed., *Miqra'ot Gedolot 'Haketer': A Revised and Augmented Scientific Edition of Miqra'ot Gedolot* (Jerusalem and Ramat Gan: Bar-Ilan University Press, 1996); online: Miqra'ot Gedolot 'Haketer' (accessed March 2018).
20 See in particular the discussion between Sara Japhet, "The Nature and Distribution of Medieval Compilatory Commentaries in the Light of Rabbi Joseph Kara's Commentary on the Book of Job," in *The Midrashic Imagination: Jewish Exegesis, Thought, and History*, ed. Michael Fishbane (Albany: State

Medieval Latin[21] studies already dealing in detail with literary theory in medieval literature, gloss hermeneutics, and medieval reading theories were insufficiently integrated into studies of Hebrew material. However, a number of important published studies conclude that neither the romantic notion of the 'author' as found in the nineteenth century nor the battle cry of the 'death of the author' based on a one-sided, exaggerated reception of Foucault's theories are the only alternatives.[22] I have demonstrated elsewhere that Rashi's commentaries are better considered the first 'Jewish Glossa Ordinaria', and in terms of their ambition, bear comparison with Gilbert of Poitiers' (ca. 1080–1154) *Media Glossatura* or the *Magna Glossatura* compiled by Petrus Lombardus (ca. 1100–1160).[23] Rashi collects the most fitting Midrashim to highlight the *peshaṭ* of a verse or word, while simultaneously introducing new exegetical and grammatical approaches and insights by intertwining them with classical material well known from the rabbinic texts.

2.2 Tosafist, Copyist, Writer, or Author

The problem of a fluctuating tradition, and the question of whether one single 'author' (if so, which one?) may have been the guiding spirit of the Northern French exegetic tradition is not confined only to the Rashi tradition, but also includes his school, i.e. the Bible commentators and tosafists he himself trained and bore connection to his *Beit Midrash*. Aside from his acolyte and chronicler R. Shemaʻya (ca. 1060–1130),[24] this school include his grandsons R. Yaʻaqov ben Meïr (Rabbenu Tam; ca. 1100–1171) and R. Shemuʼel ben Meïr (acronym Rashbam; ca. 1088–after

---

University of New York Press, 1993): 98–130, and Martin I. Lockshin, "'Rashbam' on Job: A Reconsideration," *Jewish Studies Quarterly* 8.1 (2001): 80–104.
21 See, e.g., Carruthers, *Book of Memory*; Michael T. Clanchy, *From Memory to Written Record: England 1066–1307* (Oxford: Blackwell, ²1993), esp. 224–252; 270–272; Alastair J. Minnis, "Discussions of 'Authorial Role' and 'Literary Form' in Late Medieval Scriptural Exegesis," *Beiträge zur Geschichte der deutschen Sprache und Literatur* 99 (1977): 37–65; idem, *Medieval Theory of Authorship: Scholastic Literary Attitudes in the Later Middle Ages* (Aldershot: Scolar Press, 1988); Reynolds, *Medieval Reading*; Richard H. Rouse and Mary A. Rouse, "Ordinatio and Compilatio Revisited," in *Ad litteram: Authoritative Texts and Their Medieval Readers*, ed. Mark D. Jordan (Kent Emery: Notre Dame, 1992): 113–134.
22 Michel Foucault, *Schriften zur Literatur* (Frankfurt am Main: Fischer, 1991).
23 Cf. Hanna Liss, *Creating Fictional Worlds: Peshat Exegesis and Narrativity in Rashbam's Commentary on the Torah* (Leiden and Boston: Brill, 2011), 35–44.
24 Reconstructing R. Shemaʻya's biography is beyond our ability, but he is known as the one who first disseminated Rashi's literary legacy. Rashi mentions him by name in his commentaries on Genesis 35:16 and Ezekiel 42:11 (source: *Miqra'ot Gedolot Haketer*). It is unclear if and to what degree they were related, by blood or by marriage. According to Grossman, he probably was some sort of 'assistant' to Rashi: he edited his commentaries, augmented them with his own glosses (Ms Leipzig, hebr. 1 alone contains more than 250 of Shemaʻya's glosses) and probably also influenced Rashi to no small degree on halakhic matters; cf. Grossman, *Early Sages*, esp. 43–45; 132–133.

1158),²⁵ and R. Yosef ben Shim'on (ca. 1050–1125)²⁶ in particular. The latter had probably already received his epithet 'Qara' (Hebrew קרא) at Rashi's *Beit Midrash* for his efforts as a Bible teacher and reader.

Abraham Geiger had already referred to R. Yosef Qara as a glossator.²⁷ According to Geiger, R. Yosef commented less on the biblical text itself than on Rashi's commentary. Geiger relied on handwritten text-witnesses referring to R. Yosef Qara as מעתיק ('copyist') or כותב ('scribe').²⁸ Difficulties in the debate arise due to many of the Hebrew manuscripts not labelling the various tosafists consistently, thus far no criteria have been established enabling accurate attribution of text authorship and precisely its authorial intention. Terminological distinctions between *scriptor*, *compilator*, *commentator* and *auctor*, as known from Latin medieval contexts,²⁹ cannot simply be transferred to Hebrew settings, and the relevant manuscripts are at least 130 years more recent than the tosafists mentioned.

Attribution of exegetic commentaries to specific tosafists is also problematic as existing text-witnesses specify the glosses differently to one another. There exist glosses labelled with the originator's name ('R. Yosef'; 'R. Shemu'el'), and those without attribution and glosses that are similar to others yet bear differing names. With such the written evidence hasty attributions are ill-advised. The online resource *AlhaTorah* cites a comment on Genesis 41:7 in Ms Vienna, hebr. 220 attributed to R. Yosef Qara's Torah commentary³⁰ and cross-references it to commentaries by Rashbam, Ḥizzequni, and Rashi (Ms Leipzig, hebr. 1), and they are, indeed, very similar to one another and very close to R. Yosef Bekhor Shor's comment (twelfth century; Orléans).

Before an exegetic attribution to one specific exegete is attempted and his approach towards former (rabbinic) commentaries outlined, the gloss-inventory should be assessed and evaluated for each individual manuscript. The debates over attribu-

---

25 On the discussion about Rashbam's biographical data, cf. most recently Liss, *Creating Fictional Worlds*, 57–61.
26 On R. Yosef ben Shim'on Qara, cf. Ingeborg Lederer-Brüchner, *Kommentare zum Buch Rut von Josef Kara. Editionen, Übersetzungen, Interpretationen: Kontextualisierung mittelalterlicher Auslegungsliteratur* (Frankfurt am Main: Peter Lang, 2017), 23–60; Qara's biographical dates are contested, cf. Mayer I. Gruber, ed., *Rashi's Commentary on Psalms* (Leiden and Boston: Brill, 2004), 64, arguing for the dates 1060–1130, contra Grossman, *Early Sages*, 258, who assumes the period 1050/1055–1120/1130.
27 Abraham Geiger, *Parschandata. Die nordfranzösische Exegetenschule. Ein Beitrag zur Geschichte der Bibel-Exegese und der jüdischen Literatur* (Leipzig: Leopold Schnauss, 1855), 20 [German part], 22 [Hebrew part]. According to Geiger, R. Yosef Qara added only glosses to Rashi's commentary, because he was not capable of composing his own commentary.
28 Cf. Abraham Berliner, "Eine wiederaufgefundene Handschrift," *Monatsschrift für Geschichte und Wissenschaft des Judentums* 6 (1864): 218, who distinguishes between an 'unknown copyist' (מעתיק) and the author (of a commentary); see also the entry on Qara in *AlhaTorah*; online: Introduction to Qara's commentary on the Torah (accessed March 2018).
29 See Minnis, "Discussions of 'Authorial Role';" idem, *Medieval Theory of Authorship*, esp. 94–95.
30 *AlhaTorah*; online (accessed March 2018).

tion that used to focus on a single commentator and/or his school can now be extended to incorporate information on the geo-cultural background of a specific manuscript and its scribal tradition. In addition, one can prevent the premature attribution of a gloss on one single Bible verse. Not all exegetic glosses relate the comment unambiguously, via a prefixed lemma or other paratextual elements (e.g. circles or ornaments), to one, and only one, Bible verse. The reason for this may be that some glosses do refer directly to the biblical text, while others relate to the already existing commentary as their hypotext. According to Suzanne Reynolds, it is the teacher, the *grammaticus*, who 'reads' for the others, the pupils. In that, the glosses turn into 'written traces of a much fuller reading practice.'[31]

2.3 Rashbam's Torah Commentary: A Gloss Commentary?

In his introduction to the edition of Rashbam's Torah commentary, David Rosin held the view that Rashbam had probably written his commentary as a gloss commentary:

> Rashbam wrote his commentary in the margins of his Bible editions [בפאת ספרי הקדש], and the first copyist [הסופר הראשון], who introduces himself as 'the young (man)' and who was a pupil of R. Eliʻezer of Beaugency,[32] added the beginnings of the biblical verses on which Rashbam commented [as *lemmata*] when he copied his commentary into a separate book, in order to render Rashbam's gloss explanations [פתרוני רשב״ם] easier to understand.[33]

Rosin understood Rashbam's commentary on the Torah to be a gloss commentary, as it was a way but not the only way of commenting on the Bible and other (pagan) classical texts in the Middle Ages. Nonetheless, Rosin's evaluation is remarkable, since the (compound) manuscript he used for his edition[34] was not a glossed Bible, but a Rashi commentary arranged according to the weekly Torah portions which, in most cases, were appended by Rashbam's comments. Hence the manuscript did not contain Rashbam's commentary as a separate book but as a compilation (drawn from a different source), re-arranged according to the Rashi commentary as its hypotext. Un-

---

31 Reynolds, *Medieval Reading*, 29.
32 Cf. the addenda in RTC to Deuteronomy 1:2; more in David Rosin, *Der Pentateuch-Commentar des Samuel ben Meir nach Handschriften und Druckwerken berichtigt und mit kritischen, erklärenden, vergleichenden und den Nachweis der Stellen enthaltenden Anmerkungen* (Breslau: S. Schottlaender, 1881), 199 incl. n. 20.
33 Rosin, *Pentateuch-Commentar*, XXXVI [Hebrew; my translation]; similarly, also David Rosin, "R. Samuel b. Meïr (רשב״ם) als Schrifterklärer," *Jahresbericht des Jüdisch-Theologischen Seminars Fraenckel'scher Stiftung* (1880): 91.
34 Described in detail in Rosin, *Pentateuch-Commentar*, XXXII–XLIII; on this manuscript, see also Rainer Wenzel, *Moses Mendelssohn, Einleitungen, Anmerkungen und Register zu den Pentateuchkommentaren in deutscher Übersetzung* [Moses Mendelssohn, *Gesammelte Schriften*, JUB vol. 9,4: *Schriften zum Judentum*, vol. III,4, ed. Daniel Krochmalnik] (Stuttgart-Bad Cannstatt: Frommann-Holzboog, 2016), 41.

fortunately, the manuscript of Rashbam's Torah commentary is the only manuscript in existence. It found its way into the Breslau Seminary by way of the Mendelssohn and Fraenckel families and vanished as a result of the Nazi persecutions. The Rosin edition was re-edited and annotated in 2009 by Martin Lockshin.[35]

In 1985, Sara Japhet and Robert Salters discussed the literary form of Rashbam's commentary, and concluded with a qualitative distinction between 'glossary' and 'well-structured, premeditated composition'[36] In their introduction to the Qohelet commentary, Japhet/Salters took up a position contrary to Rosin's assumption, arguing that Rashbam's commentary was 'by no means a glossary,' but a 'well-structured, premeditated composition, the writing of which is guided by a literary insight into the book of Qoheleth.'[37] In distinguishing between a gloss and 'a continuous and fluent presentation, comprising complete sentences and written in a brief and concise idiom,'[38] Japhet/Salters (at least implicitly) characterised the 'act of glossing' as inferior to the 'act of writing/composing.'

Japhet/Salters also attempted the same claim for Rashbam's Torah commentary but had to acknowledge the dearth of available manuscripts—a dearth far worse today than that of Rosin's period, as the very manuscript he used to prepare his edition no longer exists. Similarly, Elazar Touitou rejects Rosin's opinion with the argument that it is hardly conceivable that the space between the lines or in the margins would allow for a commentary of such proportions.[39] He added that one would also expect a commentary noted in the margins to have been intended for private perusal and not publication.

The debate appears to have gone down a blind alley. As a result, this study proposes accessing the glosses differently and focussing on external parameters. To determine the function of a gloss text it seems reasonable to not only compare the glosses in a manuscript to other texts in terms of their semantic content, but also to make the most thorough going investigations possible of their placement on the page, their shape and form and as a result, make their communicative function become apparent. Accessing the exegetic glosses via the manuscript's layout, *mise-en-page*, *mise-en-texte*, and the direction of the writing can also focus attention to details, hitherto unnoticed, concerning the relationship between the gloss and the hypotext.

---

35 Martin I. Lockshin, ed., פירוש התורה לרבינו שמואל בן מאיר. עם שינויי נוסחאות, ציוני מקורות, הערות ומפתחות, 2 vols. [Hebrew] (Jerusalem: Chorev, 2009) [henceforth quoted as: Lockshin, *Perush ha-Tora*].
36 See Sara Japhet and Robert B. Salters, eds., *The Commentary of R. Samuel ben Meir Rashbam on Qohelet*. Edited and translated (Jerusalem: Magnes Press; Leiden and Boston: Brill, 1985), esp. 42. Cf. also Eran Viezel, "'The Anxiety of Influence': Raschbam's Approach to Rashi's Commentary on the Torah," *AJS Review* 40.2 (2016): 290 incl. n. 47, who, in a very similar way, takes Rashbam as an 'author' and, thus, regrets the idea of gloss commentary.
37 Japhet/Salters, *Commentary on Qohelet*, 42.
38 Ibidem, 38.
39 Cf. Elazar Touitou, *Exegesis in Perpetual Motion: Studies in the Pentateuchal Commentary of Rabbi Samuel Ben Meir* [in Hebrew] (Ramat Gan: Bar-Ilan University Press, ²2005), 81.

2.4 The Glosses in Ms Vienna, ÖNB, Cod. Hebr. 220

Ms Vienna, Österreichische Nationalbibliothek, cod. hebr. 220 (Schwarz no. 23;[40] vellum; undated; thirteenth/fourteenth century) comprises 276 folios and contains a recension of Rashi's commentary on the Torah, the Prophets (*Nevi'im*) and almost all Hagiographa (*Ketuvim*). Schwarz distinguishes two scribes who identify themselves as Menaḥem (מנחם) fol. 16v (he penned 1v–22v) and Avraham (אברהם, אברם) fol. 25rv, 26v.[41] The Rashi commentary is arranged in three columns[42] of continuous text, almost without any further formation and formal arrangement.[43] At first glance, there appears to be no distinction between biblical lemma and commentary.

The manuscript is heavily glossed by several hands, especially on the first 25 folios (i.e. in the Book of Genesis/*Bereshit*; the Book of Exodus/*Shemot* begins on fol. 26r). At least two groups of glosses, written in two hands, can be recognised: the first group GL¹, which, according to Schwarz, originates, from the first scribe (upon which we will focus subsequently) and a second, GL², which continues beyond fol. 22v and glosses intensely beginning on fol. 25. GL² in particular, originates from a distinctly later period; written in Italian cursive script indicates the late fifteenth and sixteenth century. The hypotext commented on is thus not the biblical text itself, but the recension of Rashi's commentary. As a result, from the outset, the glosses can have several functions: They may re-explain the biblical text, largely independently of Rashi, or perhaps expand upon, modify, or disprove Rashi's commentary.

GL¹ was written with a different pen, but the same ink as the main text, allowing one to assume that the manuscript's scribe (Menaḥem) is also responsible for the glosses. The script indicates the time of the manuscript's copying, and in a marginal gloss on fol. 152v, the scribe ponders the fact that, in his *Vorlage* the tribe of Gad was missing in the listing of tribes: ואני הכותב תמהתי שלא מצאתי שבט גד מצוייר. The glosses from GL¹ can be attributed to different (groups of) authors:[44]

---

[40] See Arthur Zacharias Schwarz, *Die hebräischen Handschriften der Nationalbibliothek in Wien* (Wien, Prague and Leipzig: Strache, 1925); online: Manuscripta Mediaevalia, 28–29 (accessed March 2018).
[41] Cf. Schwarz, *Die hebräischen Handschriften*, 28. The Catalogue of the *Institute of Microfilmed Hebrew Manuscripts* (accessed March 2018) names one Avraham ben Menaḥem (אברהם אבן מנחם) as scribe, but leaves open whether other scribes contributed. However, different hands (in particular, Avraham over-elongates the Hebrew letters *Quf* and *Nun*) as well as a change in ink are easily observed (cf. the transit from fol. 22v to 23r). In addition, beginning with fol. 30rv, fantastical animal-creatures, depicted in the same ink used for the main text, start showing up. Finally, the peculiar distribution of the glosses (cf. the following table) points to a change of scribe.
[42] With the exception of the transitional pages, fol. 20v, 21r, which are arranged in one or two columns, resp.
[43] Only the beginning of the weekly Torah portions is highlighted.
[44] Unfortunately, some pages are cut off at the bottom, making it impossible to discern ascriptions.

a. ר׳ יוסף R. Yosef⁴⁵
b. תוספת, mostly abbreviated as תו or ת *tosefet*⁴⁶ (pl. *tosafot*); '(supplementary or explanatory) addendum;'⁴⁷ anonymous glosses, by the so-called tosafists, to the comments by Rashi that are, depending on the manuscript, occasionally integrated directly into Rashi's commentary
c. ר׳ שמואל בר יצחק R. Shemu'el bar Yiṣḥaq⁴⁸
d. ר׳ שמואל / ר׳ שמ R. Shemu'el⁴⁹
e. ר׳ שמשון R. Shimshon⁵⁰
f. ר׳ ון? בר׳ יצחק מלוצײנא R.[?] bar Yiṣḥaq from Lucena (?) or Luziza (?).⁵¹

Furthermore, an entire array of gloss information in group GL¹ does not provide an ascription (we will see, however, that at least some imply an ascription!). Moreover, one further group was prevented from giving us an ascription because the last and crucial line at the bottom or lateral margin has been cut off.⁵² The Torah segment, beginning on fol. 23r, shows only faint traces of the later glossator's ink (GL²).

---

45 Torah: Fol. 1v; 2r; 2v; 3v; 4r; 6v; 7r; 8v; 9r; 12r; 13r; 13v; 14v; 15r; 16r; 17v; 18r; 19r; 19v; 20v as ת׳ ר׳ יוסף; '*tosefet R. Yosef*'; 21r; *haftarot* and commentaries to the prophets: 95r; 101v; 103r; 103v; 107v.
46 Explicitly on fol. 2r.
47 Torah: Fol. 1v; 2r; 3r; 4v; 5r; 6r; 6v; 7r; 8r; 8v; 10v; 11r; 11v; 12r; 12v; 13r; 13v; 14r; 14v; 15r; 16r; 17v; 19v; 21r; 21v; 22r; *haftarot* and commentaries to the prophets: 149r; 149v. Tosafot are (anonymous) meta-commentaries by the tosafists (*Baʻale ha-Tosafot*), whether on Rashi's commentaries on the Bible or on the talmudic tractates.
48 Fol. 19r; cf. Efraim Elimelek Urbach, *The Tosaphists: Their History, Writings and Methods* [in Hebrew] (Jerusalem: Bialik Institute, ⁴1986), 630 incl. n. 43, 643 incl. n. 18. Urbach's discussion shows a similar tangle of ascriptions in the Talmud commentaries); Simcha Emanuel, *Fragments of the Tablets: Lost Books of the Tosaphists* [in Hebrew] (Jerusalem: Magnes Press, 2006), 358, only names R. Shemu'el bar Yiṣḥaq ha-Levi of Worms, who is probably not identical with the R. Shemu'el discussed here.
49 Torah: Fol. 8v; 9v; 11r; 15v; 16v.—On the question of whether R. Shemu'el is indeed identical with Rashbam, Rashi's grandson, cf. in particular the discussion in section 3.4.3.
50 Fol. 18r; the identity of R. Shimshon, is impossible to determine from this gloss alone. Any attempt to resolve this issue, is dependent on the tosafists' glosses being comprehensively documented and comparing the results with their parallels in the Bible and Talmud commentaries
51 This last attribution is rather interesting, fol. 2v; Schwarz, *Die hebräischen Handschriften*, 28, transcribes יודן בר׳ יצחק מלוצײנא, but without solving the problems of identity and location (Lucena?; Córdoba province). Heinrich Gross, *Gallia Judaica: Dictionnaire géographique de la France d'après les sources rabbiniques* (Paris: Publications de la Société des Etudes Juives, 1897), 291, identifies the toponym as לוציצא Lisieux/Lizieux, a town in Basse-Normandie, which would be fitting, since all of the names identified so far, point to tosafists from Northern France. Regarding a commentary on Job, Leopold Zunz, *Zur Geschichte und Literatur*, vol. 1 (Berlin: Veit und Comp., 1845), 79, mentions Shemu'el, the grammarian, and a certain R. Meir of לוציצא in addition to Rashi and Qara (again without solving the problem of the toponym).
52 Torah: Fol. 1v; 2r; 2v; 3r; 4r; 4v; 5r; 6v; 7r; 8r; 9r; 9v; 10v; 11r; 11v; 12r; 13v; 14r; 16r; 16v; 17r; 18r; 18v; 19r; 19v; 20r; 20v; 21v; *haftarot* and commentaries to the prophets: 95r; 102v; 103r; 107v; 108v; 149r; 149v; 150v; 151r.

Elazar Touitou and myself have already edited some of the glosses attributed to one 'R. Shemu'el' (this is all we have with which to identify him) and analysed their relationship to Rashbam's commentary on the Torah.[53] While Touitou acknowledges an attribution to Rashbam as secure, I feel this leaves some serious questions unanswered raising fresh problems. They pertain, in particular, to the relationship between these glosses and the RTC.[54] It is important to state that the glosses have only been evaluated thus far in terms of their exegetic statements and not in light of their placement in the manuscript or outward appearance. Such an extension of the questions concerning the glosses, (bearing in mind that the commentaries could well have been used in a scholastic context), may provide important results, which, in turn, could assist in solving problems of the glosses' authorship or, more generally, how *peshaṭ* comments were actually implemented in the Middle Ages.

Indeed, it is notable that each gloss possesses a specific *mise-en-forme*, even if it is not quite consistently applied. This finding has so far not been taken into account. It is possible that it is nothing more than an arbitrary way of embellishing the manuscript: The scribe did not wishing to write the glosses in the margins in a 'boring' manner. But the shape of the glosses may be a clue to the utilisation of the manuscript. The glosses are certainly eye-catching, since only the smallest part appears as rectangles or simply unarranged. Some texts go around corners and are arranged at right angles;[55] 'balls' or 'heads', i.e. circles with or without directly attached texts;[56] sharply pointed triangles (mostly, but not always when the gloss is closed with 'ת *tosefet/tosafot*);[57] and combinations of circles and triangles.[58] The glosses specifically attributed to R. Shemu'el are mostly in the shape of a 'head' (with or without 'shoulders'). Perhaps the glossator let the abbreviation ר' שמואל evolve via ר"ש into ראש ('head').[59] However, some glosses explicitly attributed to R. Shemu'el do not display a head's form, whereas some of the heads explicitly bear other signatures (e.g. R. Yosef).[60] A page cut prevents some glosses to connect to a name, others remain anonymous.

---

53 Cf. Touitou, *Exegesis in Perpetual Motion*, 189–195 (however, Touitou missed some connections between the glosses, having ascribed no significance to the glosses' shape); Liss, *Creating Fictional Worlds*, 45–55; eadem, "Glossenformationen," 24–26.

54 See above section 2.3.

55 Fol. 2rv; 4r and on other folios.

56 Fol. 6v; 7r and on other folios.

57 Fol. 1v; 4rv and on other folios.

58 Fol. 4v; 5r.

59 Thanks to Dr. Kay Joe Petzold (Project Corpus Masoreticum; accessed March 2018) for sharing this idea with me.

60 See for instance fol. 6v that displays two heads, of which the left one is signed with ר' יוסף"; the head on fol. 7r is signed with ת", the heads on the bottom of fol. 8v, 9v are, again, signed with ר' יוסף"; see above note 44.

The subject of book 'forms' (including *mise-en-texte* and *mise-en-page*) has come in for renewed academic scrutiny recently. Implementing text-anthropological means here requires more than simply identifying the commentaries' *Sitz im Leben* but to consider the history of their materiality. By using materiality in its broadest sense, we have also to regard the people who dealt with the artefacts/manuscripts as the original 'locus of the text'.[61] The goal is not so much to write a history of the manuscript as to write the story of the people involved in it, by extrapolating the narrative contained in the materiality of the document. So far, this aspect has barely been considered in Judaic Medieval studies, in spite of its potential to bear fruitful results. The following sample descriptions of several glosses in Ms Vienna, hebr. 220, are to be understood as the first step towards a better understanding of the exegetical glosses of the Northern French exegetic school and their disputes with elder exegetical traditions. In order to relate an 'author' to these glosses, I will focus on some of the glosses explicitly attributed to R. Shemu'el, and present a description of the gloss, edition/translation, and a short comment.

3 Edition, Translation, and Explanation of the Glosses

3.1 Fol. 8v

3.1.1 Description

The first gloss explicitly attributed to R. Shemu'el is found on fol. 8v, where the main text containing Rashi's commentary on Genesis 20:16 begins. This gloss, written in the top margin above the middle column, is attributed in its first section to R. Shemu'el (ר' שמו). Furthermore, the gloss contains a French translation of the biblical lemma מי מלל (*who [would have] said*) from Genesis 21:7. As this translation is located after the name ascription, it is not entirely clear whether it was part of the original comment. The gloss was centred above the second column, apparently consciously arranged into a circular form, a 'head' of sorts; this is clear from the abbreviation of the name שמו' (row 7) and the inclusion of a space filler ר" (row 8). Judging from the biblical lemma, it belongs to the Rashi text which begins in the middle column in row 11 with מי מלל (lemma Genesis 21:7). The Bible text says (Genesis 21:7): *And she said: 'Who said unto Abraham, that Sarah should give children suck? For I have borne him a son in his old age.'* The Rashi commentary reads:[62] מי מלל לאב'

---

61 In this respect, this effort is committed to answering the basic questions put forward by Heidelberg's *Collaborative Research Centre 933 Material Text Cultures*. One objective is to try and apply the notion of 'text anthropology' to various artefacts (including those from manuscript cultures); see in particular Markus Hilgert, "'Text-Anthropologie': Die Erforschung von Materialität und Präsenz des Geschriebenen als hermeneutische Strategie," in *Altorientalistik im 21. Jahrhundert: Selbstverständnis, Herausforderungen, Ziele*, ed. Markus Hilgert (Berlin: Deutsche Orientgesellschaft, 2010): 85–124.
62 Ms Vienna, hebr. 220, fol. 8v, middle column, row 11.

'Who said
unto Abraham*—This is an expression of praise and importance (in the sense of): לאברהם לשון שבח וחשיבות ראו מי הוא ומה הוא גדול ושומר אבטחה מבטיח ועושה
"See, Who it is, and how great He is. He keeps (his) promise, he promises and performs!"' However, the two comments—the gloss and Rashi—are not connected with paratextual elements. This could be seen as a clue that this comment was intended not so much as a super-commentary on Rashi, but as an alternative comment on the biblical text. Another clue pointing to this is the gloss being placed on top of the French translation of the biblical lemma מי מלל as a concluding, almost categorically final, comment.

3.1.2 Edition and Translation

מי מלל
לאברהם. מוסב
לכל השומע יצחק
לי. כשמללו אברהם
יולד לך בן זכר שמח
שמחהו שילדתי בן
לזקוניו״. ר׳ שמו׳
מי מלל קי רי
ריישייט
כל השומע היה מצחק״

Who said to Abraham: This refers to [the previous verse] *Everyone who hears will laugh with me* (Genesis 21:6): *Who brought my father the news and said, A boy is born to you, and gave him such joy* (Jeremiah 20:15), *Yet I have borne a son in his old age* (Genesis 21:7). [An explanation by] R. Shemu'el. [The Hebrew expression] מי מלל [means in Old French] קי ריישייט 'qui riseit/risoit,'[63] '[Everybody] laughed [about it].' *Everybody who heard* (Genesis 21:6) [such a thing] laughed [about it].

---

[63] The form קי ריישייט *qy ryysyyṭ* [riseit/risoit] is a verbal form of the Old French *ris* (→ *riser*) 'laughter/ laugh'; see the references in MousketR (online: Dictionnaire Étymologique de l'Ancien Français), 29377: *et cil risent* (date: 1243), or ChevCygnePrNaissT (online: Dictionnaire Étymologique de l'Ancien Français), 100,4: *s'en risent moult boinement* (date: end of thirteenth century).—I thank Dr. Marc Kiwitt (former member of the team) and Dr. Stephen Dörr from the project Dictionnaire Étymologique de l'Ancien Français for explaining and contextualising the Old French gloss. The reading קי מושייט *qui musait* [Old French] = 'qui imaginait' as proposed by Touitou, *Exegesis in Perpetual Motion*, 189–195, is unlikely.

3.1.3 Explanation

The gloss (G_8v/1) takes up the same lemma from Genesis 21:7 as in the Rashi commentary. It begins, using intertextual exegesis, by explaining the Hebrew expression מי מלל לאברהם as directly connected with the preceding text (Genesis 21:6b), according to which Sarah interprets the laughter in the sense of 'being laughed at.' This understanding is also paraphrased in the last sentence of the gloss: Anyone who heard about the two old people's bliss would make fun of such news. By doing so, the gloss stands in direct opposition to Rashi's commentary in the main text body. Rashi justifies the usage of the uncommon verb מלל with the importance of the divine promise and Sarah's appropriate reaction to this great deed of God. RTC argues similarly.[64] Therefore, both Rashi and RTC understand the subject of the lemma מי מלל to be divine,[65] while our R. Shemu'el to whom the gloss is attributed assumes a human subject who is unable to comprehend such a miracle and therefore jokes about it: Divine greatness (in the indicative mode) is in contrast with the expression of human doubt (in the subjunctive mode). In its first part (lines 1–7) the gloss insists on a decidedly different understanding as in the Rashi commentary (and in the printed RTC) without explicitly refuting Rashi's explanation.

In order to leave no doubt about the intended exegetic message of the Hebrew expression, the gloss concludes with an Old French translation (*pitron*[66]) that segues into another Hebrew summary. The fact that the Old French translation appears after the name ascription to R. Shemu'el leads one to conclude that only the actual *peshaṭ* exegesis belongs to Shemu'el's commentary, and that the French gloss was added by the scribe. Interestingly, there is another Old French rendering for מלל in this context in the so-called *Glossaire de Leipzig*:[67] Drawing on Job 8:2 (עד אן תמלל), מלל in this *Glossaire* it is translated as פַּרְלָא (*parla*; in Modern French: 'affirma/déclara').[68] Irrespective of our scribe knowing this translation or not, and from wherever he obtained this translation, it certainly intends to support the *peshaṭ* at hand. The explanatory gloss (*pitron*) is the result of French cultural contacts,[69] indicating this

---

64 ותאמר מי מלל לאברהם כלומר ידעו ויבינו כל השומעים מי הוא האלהים שמלל לאברהם להיות לו בן משרה [...] כי אין גדול כאלהים 'She said: Who said to Abraham?, that means: Let all those who hear know and understand who is the God who said to Abraham that he would have a son from Sarah [...]. Indeed, there is none as great as God!' (ed. Lockshin, *Perush ha-Tora*, vol. 1, 33 [Hebrew quotation unvocalised].
65 This understanding was taken up by Benno Jacob, *Das erste Buch der Tora: Genesis* (Berlin: Schocken, 1934), 479.
66 *Pitron* ('explanation') is an exegetical gloss that often, though not always, arises out of a translation into the vernacular.
67 Menahem Banitt, ed., *Le glossaire de Leipzig, Corpus glossariorum biblicorum Hebraico-Gallicorum medii aevi*, vol. 1 (Jerusalem: Acad. National des Sciences et des Lettres d'Israël, 1995), 45, #599.
68 Cf. the different reading in the gloss on Job 8:2 (פרלוש) in Menahem Banitt, ed., *Le glossaire de Leipzig, Corpus glossariorum biblicorum Hebraico-Gallicorum medii aevi*, vol. 3 (Jerusalem: Acad. National des Sciences et des Lettres d'Israël, 1995), 1305, #17095.
69 Cf. Kirsten A. Fudeman, *Vernacular Voices: Language and Identity in Medieval French Jewish Communities* (Philadelphia: University of Pennsylvania Press, 2010); Marc Kiwitt, "The Problem of Judeo-

manuscript was still used in a French-speaking *and* French-reading environment and auditorium. The French gloss does not simply support the *peshaṭ* exegesis, at the same time it demonstrates that here, the *peshaṭ* is guided by the protagonists' logic insinuated in the narrative. As the gloss contrasts so vividly with Rashi's and RTC's explanations, one may consider either the glossator (as an independently thinking 'head') placed the explanation in its specific shape as a sign indicating he favours R. Shemu'el's explanation (not merely for ease of access), or that he wished, for the first time, to place R. Shemu'el 'ahead' of his fellow scholars.

To sum up: by presenting a comment on the same lemma as in the Rashi commentary yet not in the margins of a Bible codex, but in the margins of a Rashi commentary as its hypotext, the gloss not only adds a second, alternative reading, but by means of the French *pitron* exposes Rashi's understanding of the verse as erroneous, and, thereby, undermines his exegetical authority.

3.2 Fol. 9v

3.2.1 Description

On fol. 9v, three glosses are marked with the signature ר' שמואל. The first one (G_9v/1; 4 lines) is written upside down in the top margin. This one, too, displays a very specific form; its first two lines run precisely above the middle and left columns, but its third and fourth only above the left and, in accordance with the reading direction, last column on this folio. The gloss is signed with the full name of R. Shemu'el. The biblical lemma quoted at the outset contains the beginnings of the sentences of Genesis 23:17–18. It is, therefore, related to the Rashi commentary that starts in the left column in row 30. As in our latest example, there are no additional paratextual signs that connect the gloss to Rashi's commentary. The commentary closes with a summarising remark that encapsulates the whole explanation in one short sentence.

G_9v/4 (starting with שים נא) and G_9v/5 (starting with הוא ישלח; directly underneath G_9v/4) are located in the bottom margin, below the left column, and display several peculiarities. Firstly, they are clearly linked together. At the end of each line, G_9v/4 is shaped into a left- and up-turning peak; they are joined by a line from G_9v/5, moving upwards and curving in the direction of the circle/head. Judging by the form, one would expect this to be a single gloss. However, the two *lemmata* are obviously distinct, having been taken from different verses and are introductions to two different commentaries, each of which is expressly ascribed to ר' שמואל. At any

---

French: Between Language and Cultural Dynamics," *International Journal of the Sociology of Language* 226 (2014): 25–56; idem, "Les glossaires hébreu-français du XIIIe siècle et la culture juive en France du nord," in *Cultures et Lexicographie. Actes des Troisièmes Journées allemandes des dictionnaires en l'honneur d'Alain Rey*, eds. Michaela Heinz and Alain Rey (Berlin: Frank & Timme, 2010): 113–125; see Liss, *Creating Fictional Worlds*, 229–249, 257–268.

rate, row 6 of G_9v/4 features a paratextual symbol, a circle, pointing to Rashi's commentary (left column, row 39), thereby identifying the gloss more as an engagement with Rashi's commentary than with the biblical lemma itself.

G_9v/5 comments on the biblical lemma from Genesis 24:7, one that neither Rashi nor RTC discuss.[70] RTC, however, does comment on the very similarly structured passage in Genesis 24:40.

3.2.2 Edition and Translation

So Ephron's field arose [...] etc. *to Abraham as his possession* (Genesis 23:17): The silver was paid in the presence of the Hittites, so that they witnessed the proceedings, and only after he [Abraham] had buried her [Sarah], the text says: *Thus the field* [...] *passed from the Hittites to Abraham, as a burial site* (Genesis 23:20). [Even] after the land passed from Ephron (to Abraham) as his possession in the presence of the Hittites, it did not yet have the character of a burial site. [This was only the case] after he had buried Sarah, with the permission of the sons of the city. Only then [the piece of land] [...] *passed from the Hittites to Abraham, as a burial site* (Genesis 23:20). No one re-designates [a piece of] land as a burial site without permission by the neighbouring [landowners]. [An explanation by] R. Shemu'el.

---

70 On fol. 9v and 10r, Rashi's commentary discusses placing the hand under the thigh as the expression of a covenant.

G_9v/4: *Place your hand under my thigh* (Genesis 24:2; 47:29): There are [different] ways to seal a covenant in the Torah: *The calf they cut in two* (Jeremiah 34:18), [or rather] passing between its halves—that is a [way of] sealing of a covenant. *The palm of Zebah and Zalmunna in your hand* (Judges 8:6.15). *If you have stood surety for your fellow, given your hand for another* (Proverbs 6:1) —this is also a [way of] sealing of a covenant. We see this placing of the hand under the thigh [both] with the son—Josef—[and] with the servant—Eli'ezer—when he makes an oath to the father or master, and the honouring by son and servant are comparable, as it is written: *A son should honour his father, and a slave his master* (Malachi 1:6). And they had this custom in these days. [An explanation by] R. Shemu'el.

G_9v/5: *He will send His angel before you* (Genesis 24:7): This is prophetic speech [by Abraham]: 'I know that he [i.e. the servant] will succeed [in his mission].' Likewise, [this refers to] the whole section: Just as he took me out of my father's house, he promised me that he would make me successful. Therefore, I am sure that you will succeed in [fulfilling your mission]. *And she said: drink* (Genesis 24:14) [...] and I know that she [i.e., Rebecca] will say: 'Drink!' and will not rebuff me, *which proves* that [God] granted [him] some of the indications and omens [he had asked for]. *[We cannot say anything to you], either bad or good* (Genesis 24:50). They were not [?] and they could not delay [the matter], since *the matter proceeded from YHWH* (Genesis 24:50). *We will call the girl* (Genesis 24:57). You said that your master was quite sure that you would accomplish [your mission]. 'If she will go with that man, we will know that *it is from YHWH* (Genesis 24:50) and that all your words were right.' [An explanation by] R. Shemu'el.

3.2.3 Explanation

G_9v/1 discusses a biblical turn of phrase that, at first glance, seems redundant: according to Genesis 23:17, a piece of land passed to Abraham '*as his possession*' (in the presence of the Hittites), while Genesis 23:20 states that it passed to him '*as a burial site.*' The gloss explains that initially, the piece of land is bought by Abraham and passes into his possession (witnessed by the Hittites), but that it took another act '*from the Hittites,*' i.e. their permission, to convert it into a burial ground. This is also emphasised by the last sentence: only with the permission of surrounding real-estate owners can a piece of land be re-zoned as a cemetery. As a result, R. Shemu'el's explanation agrees neither with Rashi's[71] nor with RTC's comment.[72] Rashi's commentary is not at issue in this gloss at all, as its primary concern, on the basis of *Bereshit Rabbah* 58:8, is the use of the root קום from Genesis 23:17 to signify the 'elevation'[73] of a piece of land's status when it passes into a king's hands by way of sale by a private citizen (הדיוט). Rashi focusses on the changeover of the owner, and in addition exposes Genesis 23:17 to be an incomplete sentence that has to be supplemented by Genesis 23:18. RTC claims, following the Babylonian Talmud, *Qiddushin* 27a, that Abraham's transaction was only brought to a final and irrevocable end after he put the piece of land to use by burying his wife. But this aspect is not at issue in the handwritten gloss, as indicated by the last sentence, which does not concern itself with the act of purchase but with the social context in which it occurred. G_9v/1 presents a *peshaṭ* explanation that harmonises the social conventions of the biblical narrative with contemporary regulations, i.e. an exegesis compliant with the *sensus historicus*, or rather, what the exegete believed it to be. The question still remains as to why the gloss was written upside down. Possibly, the writer wanted to make it obvious, even at first glance, that in this instance, a *peshaṭ* commentary is forwarded that runs contrary to the usual aggadic and halakhic explanation as given by Rashi and RTC. The argument is exposed rather indirectly and with the help of graphic means (*mise-en-forme; mise-en-page*). We may therefore characterise the glossator's 'challenge of tradition' a fight with closed visor.

---

[71] ויקם שדה עפרון. תקומה היתה לו שיצא מיד הדיוט ליד מלך ופשוטו של מקרא ויקם השדה והמערה וכל העץ לאברהם למקנה וגו' (Ms Vienna, hebr. 220, fol. 9v, left column, row 30): '*So Ephron's field arose*: It was a raising [as regards the importance of its owner], since it passed from the possession of an ordinary person into the possession of a king (cf. BerR 58:8). However, the plain meaning of the verse is: *The field and the cave and all the trees were made sure* (Genesis 23:17) *to Abraham as a possession* (Genesis 23:18) etc.'

[72] לאברהם למקנה קם לאחר נתינת הכסף, כדכתיב: ונתן הכסף וקם לו, אבל לאחזת קבר מאת בני חת לא קם והחזק לאברהם עד שקבר שרה אשתו אז ויקם [וגו'] לאחזת קבר מאת בני חת (ed. Lockshin, *Perush ha-Tora*, vol. 1, 42 [Hebrew quotation unvocalised]): '*To Abraham as his purchase*: when the money was given—as it is written '*he shall give the money and it will become his.*' However, it passed [to Abraham] *as a burial site from the children of Heth* (Genesis 23:18), and was secured to Abraham [as his purchase] only after he had buried Sarah, his wife. Only then *it passed as a burial site from the children of Heth* (Genesis 23:20).'

[73] ויקם is the 3rd pers. sg. of the consecutive imperfect of קום 'rise.'

Contrary to Rashi's explanation,⁷⁴ where he argues that a person entering into a covenant has to take a holy object into his hand, e.g., a Torah scroll or Tefillin, G_9v/4 insists that 'placing under the thigh' has nothing to do with the body part, but, rather, with the manner and degree of submission (son to father; servant to master). In addition, the gloss explains that biblical tradition knows of different ways to seal a covenant, and that even a handshake between parties was recognised. This line of argument fully agrees with the *sensus historicus*.

G_9v/5 expounds a lemma that is ignored by Rashi's commentary. The relation to RTC is of particular interest in this instance, as G_9v/5 seems to elaborate on a commentary that RTC offers as an explanation to Genesis 24:40–50,⁷⁵ according to which Abraham already knew that they would succeed in their endeavour. G_9v/5 uses this literary context to ascribe prophetic qualities to Abraham, then extends this reasoning to the whole paragraph, Genesis 24:7–57 (with the result that all its protagonists are considered to have prophetic ability!). Notably, this means G_9v/5 tells us that even the servant was endowed by God with prophetic powers, as he established a sign that he already knew Rebecca would enact. Furthermore, contrary to RTC's explanation, stating the family agreed to the terms rather hesitantly, here they are portrayed taking a much more positive stance for Abraham's (prophetic) confidence helps to guarantee the servant's success. The 'art of narration' displayed in G_9v/5 is similar to RTC in as much as direct speech is interwoven with the commentary, turning it into more of a retelling than an exegesis, which is characteristic of the *peshaṭ* exegesis of the second generation after Rashi.⁷⁶ This gloss simply ignores its hypotext (Rashi) and refers directly to the biblical narrative.

---

74 Ms Vienna, hebr. 220, fol. 9v, left column, row 37—fol. 10r, right column, row 2: תחת ירכי. שהנשבע צריך ליטול בידו חפץ של מצוה״ כגון ספר תורה או ת׳ תפילין, והמילה היתה מצוה ראשונה לו באה לו על ידי צער והיתה חביבה עליו '*Under my thigh:* Whoever takes an oath must take some sacred object in his hand, such as a Torah scroll or Tefillin (cf. bShev 38b). As circumcision was the first command given to Abraham, and it was very special to him because he suffered great pains while complying, he chose this (bodily) 'object' (cf. BerR 59:8).' see also Rashi on Genesis 47:29.

75 Ed. Lockshin, *Perush ha-Tora*, vol. 1, 47–49 [Hebrew quotation unvocalised]): ישלח מלאכו. יודע אני שיתנו לך. ואמר ה׳ אלהי אדני אברהם וגו׳. כל אריכות דברים, להודיעם שמאת הקדוש ברוך הוא יצא הדבר. [...] לא נוכל דבר אליך רע או טוב. לא הסתירה ולא הבנין תלוי ברצוננו, כי בעל כרחנו, רוצים ולא רוצים, כי הקדוש ברוך הוא עשה, שהיכולת בידו [...] נקרא לנער [וגו׳]. אם תרצה להתעכב ימים או עשור כדברינו, או מיד לילך כדבריך '*He will send his angel. I know that they will allow you* [to take her]. *And I said: 'Oh, YHWH, the God of my master Abraham,'* etc. The reason for the extended speech is to let them know [for sure] *that the matter proceeded from YHWH* (Genesis 24:50). [...] *We cannot say anything to you, either bad or good*. Neither destroying nor establishing [the matter at hand] depends on us, since [it will happen] willy-nilly, whether we like it or not, for YHWH, who is all-powerful has arranged for it. [...] *We will call the girl* [in order to see] whether she would like to wait *a full year or ten months* (Genesis 24:55) as we suggested, or to go immediately, as you suggested.' On this paragraph, see in detail also Liss, *Creating Fictional Worlds*, 61–63.

76 See Liss, *Creating Fictional Worlds*, esp. 120–135.

3.3 Fol. 11r

3.3.1 Description

Fol. 11r is a textbook example of how, and with what purpose in mind, the writer integrated exegetic commentaries as glosses into his work. It also illustrates why it is important to pay proper attention to the glosses' *mise-en-forme*.

On fol. 11r, there are three glosses sitting side-by-side (G_11r/1–3, from right to left), two of which are (discernibly) un-signed. Only the left one bears the signature of שמואל ר׳ (hereinafter: G_11r/3). The gloss in the centre is signed with the letter ת׳ *tosafot*—the signature appears in the middle of the gloss. All three glosses were deliberately shaped, with the use of abbreviations and/or space fillers, into R. Shemu'el's characteristic layout of a head or circle form, and each was placed under one column of Rashi's commentary. The first anonymous gloss (hereinafter G_11r/1) begins with the lemma to Genesis 25:21, לנכח אשתו, and is found below the right column, whose first row contains Rashi's commentary to Genesis 25:16.[77] The second gloss (hereinafter G_11r/2), signed with a ת׳ in the third row and therefore identifiable as a gloss by an anonymous tosafist, is located below the second column whose first row contains Rashi's commentary to Genesis 25:20. The biblical lemma to G_11r/2, however, does not begin there, but in the last row of G_11r/1[78] (with את בכורתי לקח from Genesis 27:36) and is therefore linked to this commentary. The third gloss (G_11r/3) was placed below the leftmost column, which contains Rashi's commentary to Genesis 25:22 (starting already in row 31 of the middle column) and whose last row contains the commentary to Genesis 25:27, concluding on fol. 11v/row 10. A paratextual link to Rashi's commentary is absent in all three glosses.

3.3.2 Edition and Translation

אל תרד	לקח ולא	לנכח אשתו
מצרימה כמו ש׳	ראה את הנולד…	בשביל אשתו. למה
שעשה אביך שתת	ת״	זה אנכי. היתה יריאה
שתתברך בארץ הזאת	מלבד הרעב הראשון	למות על עצבונה והנבי׳
וכן מצא ויזרע יצחק	וג׳. בא להגיד שכשם	השיבה אל תיראי כי לא
וגום׳ ויברכהו יי… ר׳	שירד אברהם למצרים	תמות אך מנהג יולדת
ר	בימי הרעב כמו כן רצה	תומים הוא זה שהרי
שמואל	יצחק לירד למצרים	שני גוים בבטנך. ה׳
	דרך פלשתים שזה	הולך למות. לסוף
	דרך קרוב	ימי כמ׳
	לבא מארץ כנען למצרים. כדכת׳ ולא	הנה אנכי הולך בדרך כל הארץ. ויבז
	נחם אלקים דרך וג׳. וזהו שאמ׳ הק׳ לו	לבסוף נתחרט כדכת׳ את בכורתי ל׳

G_11r/1: [...] *on behalf of his wife* (Genesis 25:21): for his wife. *If so, why do I exist?* (Genesis 25:22): She feared dying of her affliction, but the prophet answered her: Don't be afraid! You will not

---

[77] This commentary already begins on fol. 10v, column 3, last row.
[78] It concludes with the space filler ל׳, from the word לקח.

die. It is just the way of women who are pregnant with twins, because *two nations are in your womb* (Genesis 25:23). Behold, often enough *I am at the point of death* (Genesis 25:32), that is to say, close to the end of my days, like: *He will bring my term to an end* (Job 23:14). *Thus did Esau spurn* (Genesis 25:34): In the end he would regret it (after all), since it is written (there): *he [took away] (from me) my birthright* (Genesis 27:36).

G_11r/2: *He took away (from me)* (Genesis 27:36), but (at that time) he had not yet seen the future. ת [=] (an anonymous, explanatory) addendum. *Aside from the previous famine* etc. (Genesis 26:1): This (verse) is meant to convey that, just as Abraham moved to Egypt in the days of the (first) famine, Isaac intended to move to Egypt, (that is) through the Philistines' land, because this was the shortest way from Canaan to Egypt. (But,) as it is written: *God did not lead them by way of the (land of the) Philistines* etc. (Exodus 13:17), (so) it is also (meant) here, because the Holy One said:

G_11r/3: *Do not go down to Egypt* (Genesis 26:2), as your father (once) did, since you are blessed in this land, and so one (thereafter) finds *Isaac sowed* etc. and *YHWH blessed him* (Genesis 26:12). (An explanation by) R. Shemu'el.

3.3.3 Explanation

G_11r/1–3 are glosses on the biblical text of Genesis 25:21–26:2. First of all, the exegesis to Genesis 25:22f., which both the Midrash and Rashi's commentary conduct in a strongly anti-Christian tone,[79] is here reduced to its *peshaṭ*: Rebecca's worries were unfounded, as the prophet informs her, because her condition is the result of being pregnant with twins. This exegesis closely parallels the commentary in RTC, though they are not verbatim copies.[80] The other comments, too, show close kinship

---

79 Ms Vienna, hebr. 220, fol. 11r, middle column, row 31–37: יתרוצצו. על כורחך המקרא אומר לך דורשיני שסתם מה היא רציצה זו וכתב אם כן למה זה אנכי. רבותי׳ דרשוהו לשו׳ ריצה עוברת על פתחי תורה של שם ועבר. ויעקב רץ ומפ׳ ומפרכס לצאת עוברת על פתחי ע״ז ועשו מפרכס לצאת *'And [the children] struggled*: You must admit that this verse says "Expound me!" because it leaves unexplained what this struggling was about, and it writes [that she said]: "If it be so, wherefore do I live." Our masters interpreted [this word] as an expression of running: Whenever she passed by the doors of the Torah [i.e. the School] of Shem and Eber) Jacob would run and jerked to go out, whenever she passed by the doors of [a place of] idol worship, Esau jerked to go out.'

80 לנכח בשביל [...] לדרוש את ה׳. אל הנביאים שבאותן הימים, כדכתיב לדרוש את ה׳ מאתו, וכתיב כי יבא אלי העם לדרש אלהים. ויאמר ה׳ לה. על ידי נביא. שני גוים. אל תיראי, כי צער העיבור שלך בשביל ששני תאומים יש בבטנך, שמרובה צער העבור של שנים מעיבור אחד [...] הנה אנכי הולך למות. בכל יום אני הולך לצוד חיות ביערים המצויים שם דובים ואריות וחיות רעות, ואני מסוכן למות למה זה [לי] להמתין חלק בכרה לאחר מיתת אבינו? כך פירש אבי הרב רבי מאיר מנוחתו כבוד. [זהו] ויבז עשו את הבכורה [...] ויבז עשו. לפי שלסוף נתחרט על כך כדכתיב את בכרתי לקח, לכן הקדים כאן להודיע שטותו. עתה, בשעת אכילה, בזה את הבכורה, אבל לבסוף היה מתחרט (ed. Lockshin, *Perush ha-Tora*, vol. 1, 53–58 [excerpts; Hebrew quotation unvocalised]: 'For [his wife]: for the sake of [...] to inquire of YHWH. From the prophets of those days, as in *[one man] through whom we may inquire of YHWH* (1 Kings 22:8), and in *it is because the people come to me to inquire of YHWH* (Exodus 18:15).1 (23) YHWH said to her through a prophet. Two nations. Do not be afraid! The discomfort of your pregnancy is because you are carrying twins in your womb, and the discomfort of a pregnancy with two [fetuses] is greater than of a pregnancy with [only] one [child] [...] "Behold, I am about to die:" Every day I go to hunt animals in the forest, where one can find bears and lions and other fenot with Rashi's comments but with RTC, which is in part due to the fact that they also concern themselves with the narrative's literary arc—as the cross-reference between Genesis 25:34 and Genesis 27:36 demonstrates.

G_11r/1 deserves special attention; firstly, it appears to be an unsigned gloss and only when closely scrutinised does it reveal itself to be closely tied to G_11r/2. Secondly, it compresses a major biblical literary arc (Genesis 25:21–34) into a form whose exegetical content parallels that of RTC. In G_11r/2, however, this is labelled as a tosafist's addendum. At this point, it should be clear that the circular form of R. Shemu'el's commentaries is not chosen arbitrarily. There are two possible explanations for this:

1. The explanation to Genesis 25:34 (including the reference to Genesis 27:36) was available to the glossator as an anonymous tosafist's addendum. He felt that it went well with other literary-theoretical *peshaṭ* explanations of R. Shemu'el, and therefore integrated it into the triple configuration of glosses signed with R. Shemu'el. This being the case, he would have bestowed an 'author' upon an anonymous explanation, but also left a hint for future scholars by adding the attribution ת', enabling us to reconstruct how medieval gloss collections turned into 'author's collections', like RTC, that provide commentary without any hypotext. Alternatively,

2. the commentary on Genesis 25:34 (including the reference to Genesis 27:36) was available to the glossator bot as an anonymous tosafist's addendum *and* as an explanation by R. Shemu'el. In this instance, he would have wished to credit both originators (by using signature and head shape).

G_11r/2 and G_11r/3 explain why going to Egypt would not have been in Isaac's best interest, while pointedly disagreeing with Rashi's commentary on Genesis 26:2.[81] In particular, drawing on the Midrash, Rashi explains that Isaac is comparable to a burnt offering (*'olah*) which one is not allowed to present on the wrong side of the curtain, for it would be rendered void. G_11r/3, however, insists (indirectly) on the *peshaṭ* that follows from the immediate literary context. There is no need for the Midrash.

---

rocious animals. I am [always] in danger of dying. What use is there for me to await the share of the first-born after our father's death?—Thus elucidated my father, R. Meir, may he rest in honour. [And this is the reason why the text continues]: *Thus Esau spurned his birthright* (Genesis 25:34) [...] *And Esau spurned [his birthright]*. Since [according to the plot of the story] in the end he would regret this [arrangement]—as it is written [later on]: *[First] he took away my birthright* (Genesis 27:36)—the biblical [author] anticipates this verse in order to make known his foolishness: "Now," [i.e., at this point of the narrative] when he was eating, he spurned his birthright. However, later on he had regrets.' On RTC's literary-theoretical implications, cf. Liss, *Creating Fictional Worlds*, 135–141.

81 Ms Vienna, hebr. 220, fol. 11v, middle column, row 2: שירד כמ׳ מצרים לרדת דעתו שהיה .מצרימה תרד אל '*Do not go down to Egypt*: Since he thought of going down to Egypt as his father had gone down in times of famine. *Do not go down to Egypt* for you are a burnt-offering without blemish, and [residence] outside the Holy Land is not worthy of you.' Cf. BerR 64:3 and TanB, Toldot 6.

Strictly speaking, G_11r/3 is already part of fol. 11v, because Rashi's commentary ad loc. begins there (second column, second row ff.). That it was nevertheless placed on fol. 11r can be explained by the desire to combine G_11r/3 with G_11r/1 and G_11r/2, thereby identifying the three heads as a connected commentary by R. Shemu'el. It is apparent that the glossator focussed much more on the biblical text as his hypotext than on Rashi's: the triple-form appears on the page on which, with *Parashat Toldot* (Genesis 25:19–28:9), the specific narrative arc, to which these commentaries pertain, arises.

3.4 Fol. 15v

3.4.1 Description

There is only one gloss (G_15v/1) on fol. 15v that was written by the first scribe (Menaḥem).[82] It is attributed to R. Shemu'el, and it, too, is instantly recognisable as a Shemu'el 'head', as it was given this form by filling in blank space where necessary. This gloss was placed below the first (right) column, in which the last row of Rashi's commentary on Genesis 32:25 begins. The lemma ויאבק ('*and [...] wrestled*') comes with a paratextual reference (circle), which, however, is not repeated in the gloss itself, and is probably meant to refer explicitly to the biblical lemma to link the gloss to the biblical hypotext and not to Rashi's commentary.

3.4.2 Edition and Translation

ויאבק א̇
איש וגו'. הק̇ הב̇ט̇
הבטיחו הטב אי̇טיב
עמך ולא האמין לו ויירא
יעקב מאד ויצר לו. ולפיכך
ניזק. וכן מצינו במשה ש̇
שאמ' לו הק̇ לך שוב מצר̇
מצרימה וְאהיה עמך
והשיב לו שלח נא
ביד תשלח
וניזק ויפגשהו י֝י ויבקש המיתו, וכן מצינו
בבלעם ויחר אף אלקים כי הולך הוא וניזק.
כן לכל המעבירין על דעת קונם ניזיקין∵
ר שמואל"

And there wrestled a man with him (Genesis 32:25). The Holy One, Blessed be He, promised him *I will surely do you good* (Genesis 32:13), but he did not believe him, and Jacob was greatly afraid

---

[82] There is, however, an additional gloss on fol. 15v, introduced with ד"ך and written in the later hand (below the left column).

and distressed, and therefore, he was struck. Likewise, we find in the [story of the call of] Moses that the Holy One, Blessed be He, said to him: *Go back to Egypt, and I will be with you*, but he answered him: '*Send someone else, whomever you want!*' (Exodus 4:13), and [immediately] he was struck. YHWH met him and sought to kill him (Exodus 4:24). Similarly, in [the story of] Balaam, *God's anger blazed up, because he was going* (Numbers 22:22), and [immediately] he was struck. Likewise, this happens to all those who disobey a vow that they will get struck. [An explanation by] R. Shemu'el.

3.4.3 Explanation

The commentary begins with the wrestling match, which it interprets as a punishment for Jacob's lack of trust. It attempts to establish a cause-and-effect chain between Jacob's fear (Genesis 32:8) and the wrestling match at the Jabbok (Genesis 32:25ff.): Jacob did not react properly to God's promise and was punished for it. In contrast to Rashi[83] who not only focusses on the morphology of the verbal form ויאבק, but also devotes significant attention to the 'man' (איש) whom he labels Esau's guardian angel (שרו של עשו), the gloss tries to trace the greater narrative arc, and additionally cites other examples from the Torah (Moses and Balaam) to prove how God punishes those who show reluctance in trusting in the divine word. It is clear the gloss is not dealing with Rashi's comments on the immediate verse, but addressing the biblical text directly.

There is an analogous argument in RTC, in which the examples of Moses' and Balaam's divine punishment are also present (though their inclusion feels rather forced).[84] However, the commentary in RTC is clearly accentuated differently, since

---

83 Ms Vienna, hebr. 220, fol. 15v, right column, last row: ויאבק איש. מנחם פירש ויתעפר איש עמו לשו' אבק שהיו מעלין עפר ברגליהן על ידי ניענועם ולי נרא' שהוא לשון ויתקשר. ולשון ארמי הוא בתלמוד בתר דאביקו בה. ואביק להו מיבק לשון עניבה. שכן דרך שנים המתע' המתעצמים להפיל איש את רעהו. שחובקן ואובקן בזרועותיו. ופירשו רבותי שהוא שרו של עשו.. '*And there wrestled a man with him*: Menaḥem [ibn Saruq] explained it as "a man covered himself with dust," as an expression [belonging to the semantic field of] "dust," since they were raising the dust with their feet through their movements. However, it appears to me that it means "*he became bound up*" (2 Kings 9:14) and this is an Aramaic expression, as in "after they became bound up [with it]" (cf. bSan 63b) and "and he would bound the [four threads unto the loop to form] a slipknot" (cf. bMen 42a)—an expression of entanglement, for such is the way of two people who are struggling to throw each other—that one hugs and twines himself round [the other] with his arms. Our Masters of blessed memory explained that he was Esau's ministering angel (cf. BerR 77:3).' **84** ויאבק. מלאך עמו, שלא יוכל לברח, ויראה קיום [הבטחתו] של הקדוש ברוך הוא, שלא יזיקהו עשו. כי לא יכל לו. המלאך. ורצה לעבר ולברח בעל כרחו [...] ומה שלקה יעקב ונצלע, לפי שהקדוש ברוך הוא הבטיחו, והוא היה בורח. וכן מצינו בכל ההולכים בדרך שלא ברצון הקדוש ברוך הוא או ממאנים ללכת, שנענשו. במשה כתיב שלח נא ביד תשלח, ויחר אף ה' במשה [...] אך לפי הפשט, לפי שהיה מתעצל ללכת כתוב ויהי בדרך במלון ויפגשהו [ה'] ויבקש המיתו. וכן ביונה שנבלע במעי הדגה. וכן בבלעם ויחר אף אלהים כי הולך הוא, ונעשה חיגר, כדכתיב ותלחץ [את] רגל בלעם, ויל"ד שפי', חיגר כמו ושפו עצמתיו (ed. Lockshin, *Perush ha-Tora*, vol. 1, 88–90 [excerpts; Hebrew quotation unvocalised]: '*But an angel wrestled with him*, so as to not allow him to flee in order that he might see the fulfilment of God's promise that Esau would not harm him. *When he saw that he could not prevail*, i.e., the angel saw, and that [Jacob] was trying to cross and flee against the angel's will [...] But the reason that Jacob was punished and lamed was because the Holy One, Blessed be He, promised him, but he still [repeatedly] attempted to flee. Similarly, we find that anyone who attempts

its 'retelling', which deals with the motif of Jacob's flight on an almost epic scale, reflects another developmental stage of *peshaṭ* exegesis, both with respect to literary technique and the psychological characterisation of the biblical protagonist.[85] If the gloss at hand in Ms Vienna, hebr. 220, did indeed originate with Rashbam, it would be compelling evidence that the commentary in RTC should be attributed to a (later) scholar: *mi-de-ve-Rashbam* (Ps.-Rashbam) rather than Rashbam himself.[86]

4 Conclusion

Already this initial glimpse on the case studies presented here shows that these tosafists' glosses do not comment on their hypotext, Rashi, but expound the biblical text by focussing on the plot of the biblical narrative and its story line, the psychology of the biblical characters, or on contemporary profane lore and knowledge. However, with regard to their literary shape, it is important to underline that they do not constitute a continuous and fluent presentation, but a gloss commentary that along with its external *mise-en-texte* represents the *consensus patrum*, in this case: the *consensus magistri*, i.e. Rashi. By adding explanations on the *biblical text* into (a recension of) the *Rashi commentary*, the tosafists not only show that in the Christian environment the Bible had become an important tool for their intellectual discourse at

---

a journey or refuses a journey against God's will, is punished: In the [story of the call of] Moses it is written [first]: *"Send someone else, whomever you want!"* (Exodus 4:13), [and then the text goes on]: *And YHWH's anger blazed up against Moses* [...] However, according to the *peshaṭ* [there is a more explicit perceivable effect]: Since Moses was reluctant to go, *it came to pass on the way at the lodging-place, YHWH met him and sought to kill him* (Exodus 4:24). Likewise, in [the case of] Jonah, who was swallowed up into the belly of the fish [as a result of his refusal to go] (cf. Jonah 2:1). Similarly, in [the case of] Balaam, *God's anger blazed up, because he was going* (Numbers 22:22), and [as a result] he became lame, as it is written: *And [the ass] squeezed Balaam's foot* [...] (Numbers 22:25) and he went off lame [שפי] (Numbers 23:3) [which means] "lame," [as in] *"And his bones were dislocated"* (Job 33:21).'

85 I have demonstrated elsewhere that RTC displays a quite fascinating psychological sensitivity. Jacob's fear of Esau is the main reason for his attempt to flee. However, RTC does not refer to this emotional state of mind explicitly, but rather indirectly through the motif of Jacob's attempt to flee, i.e., the depiction of his preparations for escape and the events occurring to him. I compared this literary technique, in which a character's activities are indicators of his internal state of mind, to literary features in the romances of Chrétien de Troyes (c. 1140–c. 1190) which often make use of this specific literary practice. On the whole subject, cf., in detail, Liss, *Creating Fictional Worlds*, 66–67, 154–161; eadem, "Kommentieren als Erzählen: Narrativität und Literarizität im Tora-Kommentar des Rashbam," *Frankfurter Judaistische Beiträge* 34–35 (2009): esp. 103–110 and 118–121.

86 This would also solve some of the problems that occur when comparing the RTC with the romances of Chrétien de Troyes and their literary features, since Chrétien wrote his major poems and romances (Erec and Enide; Cligès; Yvain, the Knight of the Lion; Lancelot, the Knight of the Cart, and Perceval, the Story of the Grail) in the last third of the twelfth century, not earlier than 1170, a date in time that Rashbam did not experience any more, as he died probably no later than 1158. I will address this question in more detail in the edition of the entire gloss material to follow.

eye-level with the (Babylonian) Talmud, but also elevate (a recension of) the Rashi commentary to the status of a 'canonical' text: Instead of glossing the Bible (any Bible manuscript) and thereby labelling it as the basic authority, they chose a Rashi commentary to adhere the glosses to. In that, these glosses constitute Rashi as an *auctor* (comparable to the biblical '*auctor*'), an authority that from now on will become a further authoritative *source-text* for all later generations. This means that, although their comments, in most cases, pointedly disagree with their *teacher* Rashi (i.e. Rashi, the man), and thereby seem to undermine his exegetical authority, they create Rashi for the first time, i.e. the Rashi commentary *in toto* as a *textual* authority:[87] the second *torah* alongside the Torah. In so doing, the tosafists' writings from Northern France match perfectly with the formal Latin scribal culture: 'This textual format [...] is thus an applied mnemonic containing numerous visual helps to memory in its features, and also laying out graphically the relationship of the auctor and all its progeny, including their disagreements.'[88] Furthermore, by means of a gloss commentary the glossator does not intend to create a sharp demarcation line between his own literary creation and the hypotext to which he appends his glosses. Due to the fact that the glossator appends exegetical remarks on the Bible to a Rashi text, the claim of authorities is hidden by means of a literary form that supports the Rashi as a textual authority while at the same time refuting his exegetical results. In other words: The glosses transform an *individual* person—Rashi—as the exegetical teacher and author of a Bible commentary into a *textual authority*.

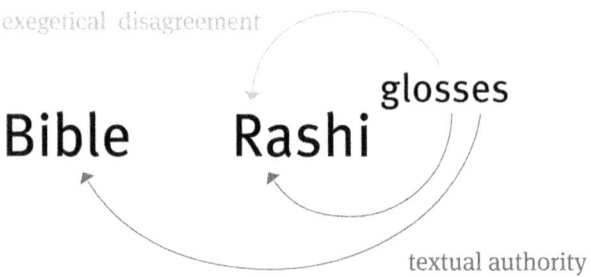

Quite a different picture emerges in comparing medieval gloss commentaries to Judeo-Arabic authored works of which we find its earliest exponents, not by chance, in the works of savants living in the Islamic cultural context and active in the fields of either philosophy or grammar in the tenth and eleventh centuries (R. Saadiah Gaon, R. Shelomo ibn Gabirol, R. Judah Halevi, Menaḥem ibn Saruq or Dunash ibn Labrat and, later, R. Abraham ibn Ezra). The figures here reveal themselves as authors by constantly exhibiting a clear-cut hermeneutical starting point and a dis-

---

87 Cf. the introductory quote by Reynolds, *Medieval Reading* (see note 1).
88 Carruthers, *Book of Memory*, 268.

tinctive grammatical, exegetical, or philosophical approach in their attempt to demarcate themselves from other authors. In philosophical as well as in most of the grammatical and exegetical treatises one finds an introduction (*haqdama*), in which the author's method as well as his critique is explicitly stated, or, as in philosophical as well as (later) kabbalistic exegesis, forward the claim that any exegetical endeavour should lead to the discovery of some deeper meaning 'behind' the literal surface.[89] A 'doubting author' sets up a counter authority about a subject, a belief, in medieval philosophical terms: a *res*. By constrast, a gloss does not necessarily aim to explicitly doubt anything, but to explain the issue at hand or append new ideas on a *text*: a *verbum*.[90] Scepticism/sceptical thought always expresses doubts about a *res*. We might, therefore, conclude at this point that the investigation of glosses in a medieval manuscript as a form of test case could prove that when dealing with medieval Jewish tosafist literature an extension of the term scepticism/sceptical thought beyond its epistemological meaning actually causes more problems than it solves. In addition, future studies on the question of the different patterns of critical thought in tosafist literature should be carried out far more in relation to the literary form in which it is expressed than has been done up to the present.

---

89 See Bill Rebiger, "The Early Opponents of the Kabbalah and the Role of Sceptical Argumentations: An Outline," in *Yearbook of the Maimonides Centre for Advanced Studies 2016*, eds. Giuseppe Veltri and Bill Rebiger (Berlin and Boston: De Gruyter, 2016): 51.
90 On the distinction between *res* and *verbum*, see also Carruthers, *Book of Memory*, esp. 234–237.

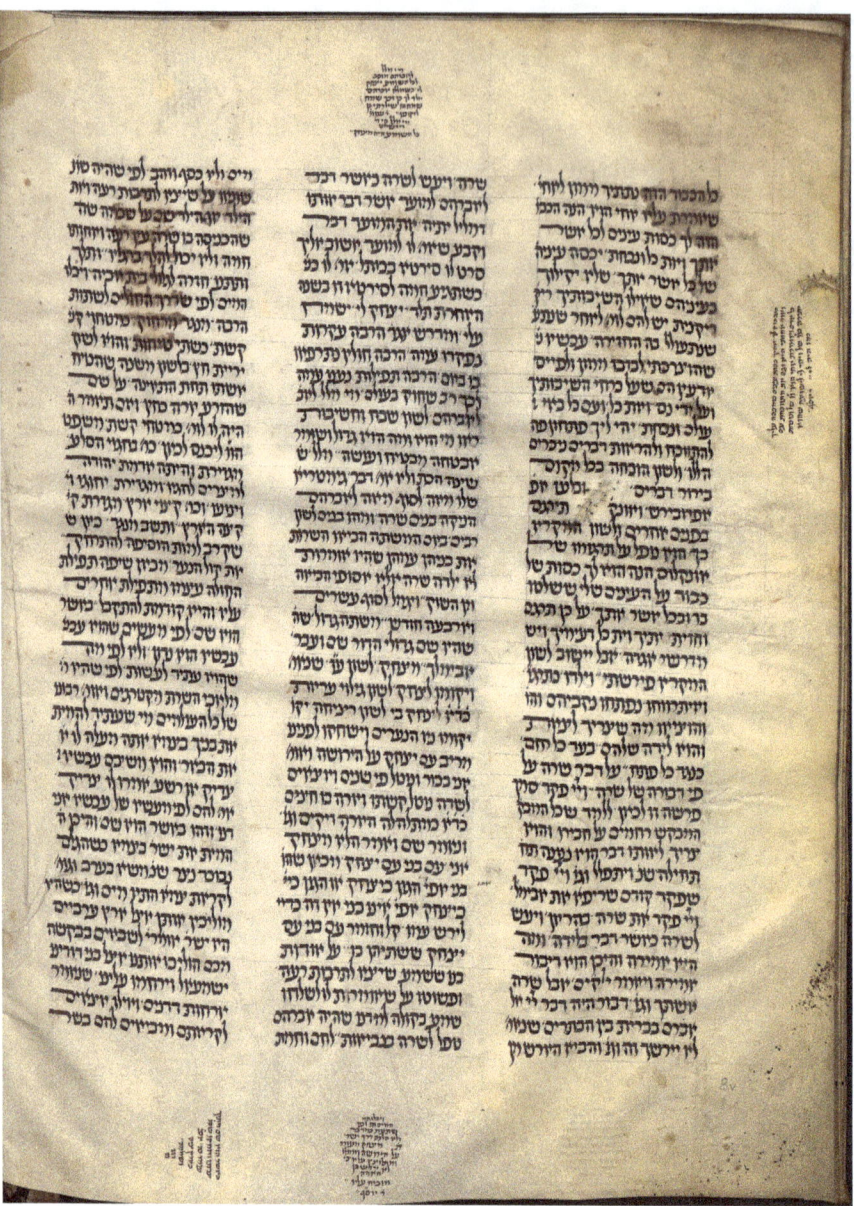

Illustration I: Ms Vienna, hebr. 220, fol. 8v. © Österreichische Nationalbibliothek

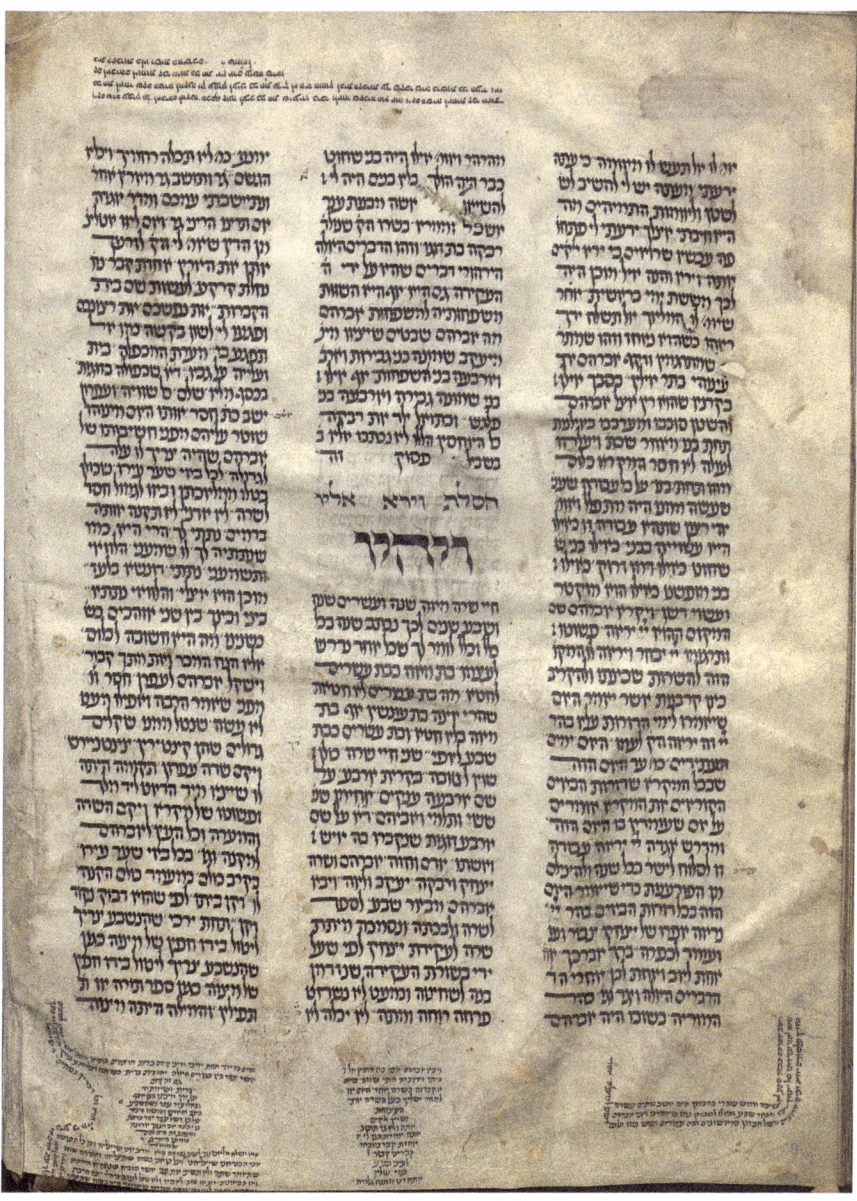

Illustration II: Ms Vienna, hebr. 220, fol. 9v. © Österreichische Nationalbibliothek

Illustration III: Ms Vienna, hebr. 220, fol. 11r. © Österreichische Nationalbibliothek

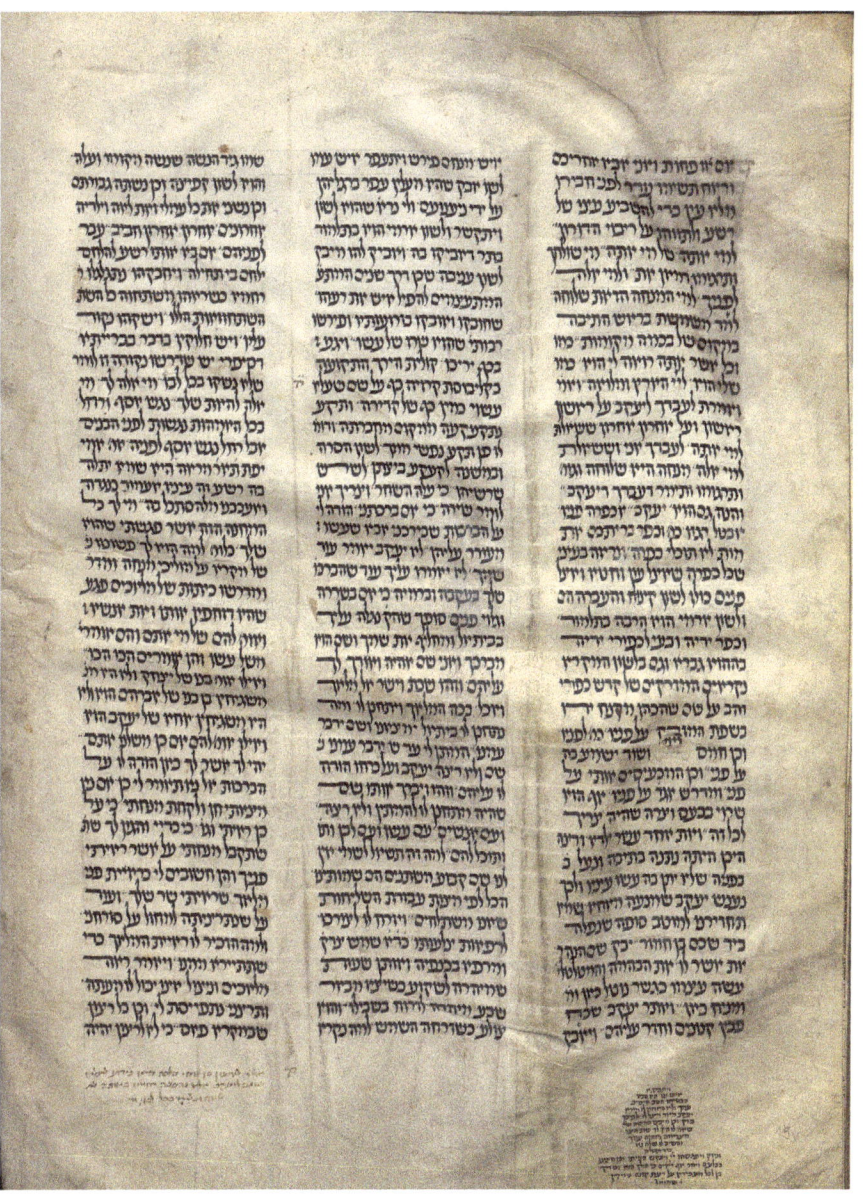

Illustration IV: Ms Vienna, hebr. 220, fol. 15v. © Österreichische Nationalbibliothek

Bill Rebiger
Sceptical Elements in a Dogmatic Stance: Isaac Polqar against Kabbalah

Introduction

As already announced elsewhere, I am going to publish a series of articles on the early opponents of Kabbalah focussing on sceptical elements and strategies.[1] Jewish philosophers—especially those who were indebted, to one degree or another, to the philosophy of Aristotle as interpreted in the Middle Ages—presented a major field of opposition to Kabbalah. The fundamental arguments of any philosophical criticism of Kabbalah had already been provided by Maimonides, although it appears he barely knew anything of its esoteric lore. Menachem Kellner's monograph *Maimonides' Confrontation with Mysticism* is a very useful starting point for understanding why Maimonides is so vital to many opponents of Kabbalah.[2] According to Kellner, Maimonides' philosophy can provide the blueprint for any philosophical criticism of mystical and kabbalistic claims. Kellner's 'proto-kabbalistic' examples of Maimonides' criticism encompass Heikhalot literature and the *Sefer Yeṣirah* ('Book of Creation') as well as the Jewish magical tradition.[3] It is well known that Maimonides' philosophy is deeply engaged with Aristotle as the latter was transmitted and revised in the Arabic tradition. The commentaries of Averroes, who was also known as Ibn Rushd (1126–1198), on various works of Aristotle are especially important for the later Jewish reception of Aristotelian philosophy within the tradition of Maimonidean philosophers.[4]

This article is a result of a long-term research project carried out at the Maimonides Centre for Advanced Studies at the University of Hamburg. I am indebted to my colleagues there and to our visiting fellows for presenting and discussing different aspects of Isaac Polqar at several Reading and Dialectical Evenings as well as for personal conversations I have had with them. I am especially grateful to Racheli Haliva, Lawrence Kaplan, Yuval Harari, and Elisa Carandina.

1 Bill Rebiger, "The Early Opponents of the Kabbalah and the Role of Sceptical Argumentations: An Outline," in *Yearbook of the Maimonides Centre for Advanced Studies 2016*, eds. Giuseppe Veltri and Bill Rebiger (Berlin and Boston: De Gruyter, 2016): 39–57.
2 Menachem Kellner, *Maimonides' Confrontation with Mysticism* (Oxford and Portland, OR: The Littman Library of Jewish Civilization, 2006).
3 Ibidem, 18–25.
4 Cf., e.g., Alfred Ivry, "Remnants of Jewish Averroism in the Renaissance," in *Jewish Thought in the Sixteenth Century*, ed. Bernard D. Cooperman (Cambridge: Cambridge University Press, 1983): 243–265; Steven Harvey, "Arabic into Hebrew: The Hebrew Translation Movement and the Influence of Averroes upon Medieval Jewish Thought," in *The Cambridge Companion to Medieval Jewish Philosophy*, eds. Daniel H. Frank and Oliver Leaman (Cambridge: Cambridge University Press, 2003): 268–272.

OpenAccess. © 2018 Bill Rebiger, published by De Gruyter. This work is licensed under the Creative Commons Attribution-NonCommercial-NoDerivatives 4.0 License.
https://doi.org/10.1515/978-3-11-057768-6-004

Regarding these preliminary considerations, it is not surprising that opposition to Kabbalah was to a large extent formed by philosophers who belong to the Aristotelian–Maimonidean tradition. In particular, several Jewish Averroists, among whom I would like to mention Jacob Anatoli, Isaac Albalag, Isaac Polqar, Moses Narboni, and Elijah Delmedigo, contributed polemics against Kabbalah in their works. In fact, the designation of 'Jewish Averroists' gathers together various distinctive philosophers who first and foremost share an interest in Averroes' works, particularly his commentaries on Aristotle. As a rule, this interest does not imply that every Averroist entirely agreed with Averroes and vice versa.[5] Another distinguishing feature of Jewish Averroists is clearly outlined in their efforts to somehow combine Averroes' thought with that of Maimonides. The Averroistic precondition that a human being —provided he or she is a philosopher—may explain not only everything that exists, but also the underlying principle(s), leads to a general mistrust or even criticism of mystical and—in the Jewish context—kabbalistic interpretations. The knowledge for which the philosopher strives even includes knowledge of God or—at least from the Averroistic point of view—of the active intellect. This is indeed a dogmatic statement and apparently quite distant from any sceptical position regarding epistemology. However, despite the observation that many Jewish Averroists were non-sceptics, at least in their epistemological concepts, nonetheless certain sceptical elements or strategies can be detected in their works. It is the aim of my intended case studies to discuss certain sceptical elements and strategies implemented by the aforementioned Jewish Averroists.

The *a priori* of any polemic is the assumption that the adversary's knowledge is necessarily wrong and that his claims are to be refuted and disproved. Thus, the front line a polemic evokes must appear extremely clear-cut. In this regard, any statement intended for the purposes of polemics appears in no way akin to the sceptical approach. In contrast to sceptical enquiry, discussion, or open-ended dispute— which, to be more specific, may even be without any intention or purpose, following the tradition of Sextus Empiricus—the intention of polemics is at the very outset to affirm only the truth of one side, i.e. that of the polemicist. In this sense, criticism of Kabbalah, especially in the camp of Jewish Averroists, is very often non-sceptical or dogmatic insofar as the final truth of their philosophical claims of knowledge is obviously not in question.

What the rationalist philosophers actually criticise is Kabbalah's all-too-frequent absence of argumentation by reasoning according to philosophical principles. Or, to put it another way, the kabbalistic discourse was considered to be completely different to the philosophical one. Sceptical elements or strategies are especially fruitful when the participants of a debate do not share the same discourse or logic of argumentation and proofs, as is expressed in the Latin maxim *contra principia negantem*

---

[5] Cf., e.g., Oliver Leaman, "Is Averroes an Averroist?," in *Averroismus im Mittelalter und in der Renaissance*, eds. Friedrich Niewöhner and Loris Sturlese (Zürich: Spur Verlag, 1994): 9–22.

non est disputandum. Thus, the argumentation against certain content-related claims is less important than the attempt to undermine the certainty, authority, or legitimacy of a text, person, or institution as a source of knowledge. Therefore, the sceptical element found in many anti-kabbalistic texts is often expressed as doubt about authority and tradition as sources of knowledge, as will be discussed below. These sceptical elements could eventually be elaborated into sceptical strategies by later authors, such as, for instance, the Venetian Rabbi Simone Luzzatto (?1583–1663).[6] When the rather simplistic doubting of authority and tradition termed here as only a 'sceptical element' is transformed into a subversive method for systematically undermining the reliability of sources of knowledge which are accepted only by authority or tradition, I would then like to call this a 'sceptical strategy.'

In the following, my aim is to present a case study devoted to the philosopher and polemicist Isaac Polqar (second half of the thirteenth century–c. 1330). The present article provides the reader with the first translation of a passage dealing with his attack on kabbalists into a modern language and a commentary on it through a close reading focussing on the sceptical elements to be detected therein.

1 Isaac Polqar

Isaac ben Joseph ibn Polqar[7] lived in Christian Spain, or more precisely, in the Kingdom of Castile. Not much of his biography is known to us. Polqar was clearly a philosopher in the tradition of Maimonides, Averroes, and Isaac Albalag.[8] According to a poem dedicated to him by Samuel ibn Sasson, Polqar was an expert in the study of

---

[6] On my definition of sceptical strategies such as relativisation, objectification, historicisation, indictment of heresy, and delegitimation, see Bill Rebiger, "Sceptical Strategies in Simone Luzzatto's Presentation of the Kabbalists in his *Discorso*," in *Yearbook of the Maimonides Centre for Advanced Studies 2017*, ed. Bill Rebiger (Berlin and Boston: De Gruyter, 2017): 53–64.

[7] Variants of the correct spelling of Polqar, such as Policar, Pollegar, Polgar, or Pulgar, can be found elsewhere.

[8] On Polqar, cf., e.g., Racheli Halevi, *Isaac Polqar—A Jewish Philosopher or a Philosopher and a Jew? A Study of the Relationship between Philosophy and Religion in Isaac Polqar's 'Ezer ha-Dat [In Support of the Religion] and Teshuvat Apikoros [A Response to the Heretic]* (typescript, PhD McGill Montreal, 2015; Berlin and Boston: De Gruyter, forthcoming); Shalom Sadik, "La différence entre judaïsme et christianisme selon deux averroïstes juifs espagnols," *Viator* 47 (2016): 191–204; idem, "Negation of Political Success in the Thought of Rabbi Isaac Pulgar," *AJS Review* 39 (2015): 1–13 (Hebrew section); Shlomo Pines, "Spinoza's *Tractatus Theologico-Politicus* and the Jewish Philosophical Tradition," in *Jewish Thought in the Seventeenth Century*, eds. Isadore Twersky and Bernard Septimus (Cambridge, MA: Harvard University Press, 1987): 499–521; idem, "Some Topics on Polqar's Treatise *'Ezer ha-Dat* and their Parallels in Spinoza's View," in *Studies in Jewish Mysticism, Philosophy and Ethical Literature, Presented to Isaiah Tishby on his Seventy-Five Birthday*, eds. Joseph Dan and Joseph Hacker [in Hebrew] (Jerusalem: Magnes Press, 1986): 395–457; Colette Sirat, *A History of Jewish Philosophy in the Middle Ages* (Cambridge: Cambridge University Press, 1985): 315–322; Isidore Loeb, "Polémistes Chrétiens et Juifs en France et en Espagne," *Revue des études juives* 18 (1889): 63–70.

the Hebrew Bible and the Mishnah. He was also known as a poet and physician and was an acknowledged authority in his congregation.[9] However, Polqar is first and foremost known as the student of the Jewish scholar Abner of Burgos, whom he admired as his beloved master. Abner lived between 1265 and 1347 and eventually converted to Christianity between 1320 and 1322. After his conversion, he adopted the Christian name Alfonso of Valladolid and began writing anti-Jewish polemics in Hebrew.[10] Abner's conversion was an essential event for Polqar and one that caused him to question his Jewish self-confidence. As a result, he began to compose his own polemics against Christianity in general and against Abner in particular.

Most of Polqar's books have not survived. Among his lost works, he reportedly wrote commentaries on the biblical books of Genesis, Ecclesiastes, and the Psalms. Nevertheless, only two of Polqar's works exist today. The first is a letter addressed to Abner known by the title *Teshuvat Apikoros* ('A Response to the Heretic').[11] Unfortunately, this is the only surviving text of a far larger correspondence between Polqar and Abner. The second of Polqar's works to have survived is his magnum opus *'Ezer ha-Dat* ('In Support of the Religion'). I will proceed by presenting the chapter of this book that contains Polqar's attack on the kabbalists and discussing it at length. In addition, one of his lost writings, a book entitled *Musar ha-Banim* ('Instruction of the Sons'), is mentioned in the passage translated below.

In his writings, Polqar attempted to defend the Jewish faith not only against Christians by birth, but also against Jewish converts, particularly those well trained in biblical and talmudic sources. Polqar was a fiery adept of Aristotelian philosophy and Averroes' commentaries on Aristotle's works. In Polqar's view, Judaism is a true religion because its beliefs are possible according to their philosophical principles.[12] Therefore, Judaism is superior to Christianity and its theological concepts of the Trinity and the Incarnation are beliefs which Polqar deems and dismisses as logically impossible.[13] Another target of his polemics takes on other philosophical schools as

---

[9] Cf. Yitzhak Baer, "Fragments from Castilian Poets in the Fourteenth Century," in *Minḥah le-David: Collected Studies on Jewish Wisdom Presented to David Yellin for his Seventieth Birthday* [in Hebrew], ed. Jubilee Committee (Jerusalem: Ruben Mass, 1935): 200.

[10] On Abner, see Jonathan L. Hecht, *The Polemical Exchange between Isaac Pollegar and Abner of Burgos/Alfonso of Valladolid according to Parma MS 2440* (PhD Diss., New York University, 1993); Ryan Szpiech, *From Testimonia to Testimony: Thirteenth-Century Anti-Jewish Polemic and the Mostrador de justicia of Abner of Burgos/Alfonso de Valladolid* (PhD Diss., Yale University, New Haven, CT, 2006); Shalom Sadik, "Abner de Burgos and the Transfer of Philosophical Knowledge between Judaism and Christianity," *Medieval Encounters* 22 (2016): 95–112.

[11] The only manuscript evidence is Ms Parma, Pal. 2440, where no title for this letter is given; see Hecht, *Polemical Exchange*. However, the title *Teshuvat Apikoros* is referred to by Isaac Polgar, *Ezer HaDat. A Defense of Judaism* [in Hebrew], ed. Jacob S. Levinger (Tel Aviv: The Chaim Rosenberg School of Jewish Studies, 1984), 30 and 76.

[12] Cf. Polgar, *Ezer HaDat*, ed. Levinger, 34–40.

[13] On the distinction between possible and impossible religious beliefs according to Maimonides, cf. Daniel J. Lasker, *Jewish Philosophical Polemics Against Christianity in the Middle Ages* (Oxford and Portland, Oregon: The Littman Library of Jewish Civilization, 2007), 28–43.

well as astrologers and kabbalists. Polqar attacked the latter as they argued against the philosophical interpretation of the Jewish religion, particularly in its Aristotelian–Averroistic form. A further reason to attack Kabbalah lay in the probability that Abner had implemented kabbalistic ideas to support himself in his conversion.[14]

2 Polqar against the Kabbalists in his *'Ezer ha-Dat* ('In Support of the Religion')

In literary terms, *'Ezer ha-Dat* is made up of dialogues and essays. The first and fourth chapters are written as essays, while the second, third, and fifth chapters are composed in dialogue form. I would like to emphasise that already in the last dialogue of the second chapter between the old traditionalist and the young philosopher about the limits of human knowledge and the exalted rank of the prophets, the traditionalist mentions various secrets including, among others, divine names, the kabbalistic concept of the ten Sefirot, and the *Sefer Yeṣirah*.[15] According to the traditionalist, who evidently became a kabbalist during his life, the prophets transmitted these secrets to him via the chain of tradition.

However, the polemic against the kabbalists presented below can be found in the fourth chapter in which he attacks four different groups, accusing all of them of being Judaism's greatest enemies. Among these are the self-proclaimed true believers who reject science, the kabbalists, the philosophers who hold radical naturalistic views, and lastly adepts of magic and superstition. According to Polqar, the kabbalists are dangerous because they assert that they have knowledge that does not follow Aristotle's philosophical methods and logical rules.[16] In contrast, the knowledge that the kabbalists claim to have is provided by an esoteric tradition reaching back to the time of the prophets, as they claim.

The Hebrew word 'Kabbalah' literally means 'tradition.' Both philosophy and Kabbalah express truth claims with regard to the interpretation of texts. They both agree that truth is mostly hidden and not obvious in the texts, or that truth is nothing but the deeper meaning behind the surface of the literal sense. Thus, kabbalists frequently qualify their interpretations of the Torah, for instance, as being found 'by the

---

14 Cf. Yitzhak Baer, "The Use of Kabbalah in the Christological Thought of Abner of Burgos," *Tarbiz* 16 (1909): 280–289; Shoshana Gershenzon, *A Study of Teshuvot La-Meḥaref by Abner of Burgos* (PhD Diss., Jewish Theological Seminary of America, 1984); but see the critique by Shalom Sadik, *Trinity and Determinism in the Thought of Abner of Burgos* (PhD Diss., Ben-Gurion University of the Negev, 2011).
15 See Polgar, *Ezer HaDat*, ed. Levinger, 84–87; however, the term 'Kabbalah' is not explicitly mentioned here.
16 Cf. the short summary in Carlos del Valle, "La critique de la Qabbale chez Isaac ibn Polgar," in *Expérience et écriture mystique dans les religions du livre*, eds. Paul B. Fenton and Roland Goetschel (Leiden: Brill, 2000): 131–141.

way of truth' ('*al derekh ha-'emet* in Hebrew). Among many Jewish scholars of Polqar's time, Kabbalah was firstly a 'generally accepted opinion' and secondly acknowledged as a tradition received by trustworthy persons. According to Maimonides' *Treatise on the Art of Logic*,[17] these two sources of kabbalistic knowledge—more precisely, generally accepted opinions and traditions—are not self-evident because they depend solely on the social environment and testimony. Therefore, Kabbalah cannot be accepted as a source of knowledge whose conclusions are already certain from the outset. However, the majority of kabbalists would not accept this kind of epistemological argument simply by dint of the fact that they do not agree with Aristotelian standards of philosophy and logic. Furthermore, content-related attempts to falsify kabbalistic ideas would not be accepted because of the pluralistic hermeneutics concerning truth claims shared by most kabbalists. Therefore, another, more subversive way to undermine the meta-level or frame of the kabbalistic self-image appears to be more effective. Thus, the assertion that Kabbalah is indeed an ancient tradition, as the literal meaning of the term suggests, was something that Polqar particularly doubted, and a sceptical element can be seen in Polqar's attempt to undermine the acceptance of his contemporaries' kabbalistic opinions when he claims Kabbalah is neither an ancient tradition nor a real one. In this way, he attempts to undermine the reliability of kabbalistic genealogy and authorities. Polqar's main sceptical element is to assert doubts concerning the textual accuracy of kabbalistic sources. He deconstructs Kabbalah's presentation of itself as a reliable tradition continuously transmitted since antiquity. However, Polqar's dogmatic stance concerning Kabbalah is evident throughout this passage. In general, he has no doubt that Kabbalah cannot be accepted because of its non-philosophical means of arguing. On several occasions, he goes so far as to explicitly debunk Kabbalah as 'foolishness' and castigates kabbalists as 'ignorants.'

What follows is a complete English translation of the passage from '*Ezer ha-Dat* in which Polqar attacks the kabbalists. The translation is based on the Jacob S. Levinger edition of the original Hebrew text.[18] The passage has been divided into smaller portions to enable me to comment on them directly in the close reading. The Hebrew original of the quoted passages is given in the footnotes according to Levinger's edition.

---

[17] Cf. Hannah Kasher, "Maimonides: Halakhic Philosopher or Philosophical Halakhist? On Skeptical Epistemology and Its Implications," in *Moses Maimonides (1138–1204): His Religious, Scientific, and Philosophical Wirkungsgeschichte in Different Cultural Contexts*, eds. Görge K. Hasselhoff and Otfried Fraisse (Würzburg: Ergon 2004): 51–63.
[18] Polgar, *Ezer HaDat*, ed. Levinger, 156–158.

3 Translation and Commentary

After his attack on Jews defining themselves as true believers while actually rejecting science, Polqar commences his polemic against the second group, the kabbalists, with the following lines:

> And the second objection is the objection of the group of people who are called 'kabbalists' [*mequbbalim*] in this generation. And these are those who say that since man's intellect is unable to apprehend anything hidden through his contemplation, that is to say, by seeking a conclusion from known premises, the only way is that of a Kabbalah ['tradition'] that was taken from a prophet. And (they furthermore say) that they know and recognise in truth that the Kabbalah that today is in their possession is the one which was heard from the mouths of the prophets.[19]

The second group Polqar attacks consists of 'people who are called "kabbalists" in this generation.' In the beginning, Polqar already emphasises that they are merely called 'kabbalists,' that is, 'receivers of a tradition,' but they are not even such receivers in his view. In this passage, Polqar tries to argue precisely both that the kabbalists are not reliable receivers of the tradition and that the kabbalistic tradition itself is not reliable. However, the kabbalists were obviously a distinctive group in the first half of the fourteenth century. Christian Spain, where Polqar resided, was one of the most important sites of kabbalistic writing in Polqar's period, as it had been in the previous century. Major works of the kabbalistic tradition, such as the *Sefer ha-Bahir*, most of the texts later compiled in the *Sefer ha-Zohar*, and kabbalistic commentaries on the Hebrew Bible or the *Sefer Yeṣirah*, had already been written and disseminated. Crucial authors of various kabbalistic trends such as Isaac the Blind (c. 1160–1235), Azriel of Gerona (c. 1160—c. 1238), Moses Naḥmanides (1194–1270), Menaḥem Recanati (1223–1290), Moses de Leon (c. 1240–1305), Abraham Abulafia (1240—after 1291), Joseph Gikatilla (1248—after 1305), or Isaac of Acre (thirteenth to fourteenth century) had been active long before Polqar arrived on the scene. Nevertheless, Kabbalah was still a set of various lores studied first and foremost by the Jewish elite.[20] However, magical practices were much more popular among less educated people, and in this period they begin to intermingle with kabbalistic ideas.[21] The results of

---

[19] *Ibidem*, 156, lines 3–8: והטענה השנית היא טענת כת האנשים הנקראים בדור זה מקובלים, והם האומרים כי אין שום יכולת בשכל האדם להשיג שום נעלם בהתבוננותו, ר"ל בבקשו תולדה מהקדמות ידועות, כי אם בדרך קבלה לקוחה מנביא, וכי הם יודעים ומכירים באמת, כי הקבלה אשר היא היום בידם היא הנשמעת מפי הנביאים.

[20] For surveys on the early history of Kabbalah, cf., e.g., Gershom Scholem, *Origins of the Kabbalah*, trans. Allan Arkush (Philadelphia: Jewish Publication Society and Princeton University Press, 1990); Joseph Dan, *The Early Kabbalah* (New York: Paulist Press, 1986); Hava Tirosh-Samuelson, "Philosophy and Kabbalah: 1200–1600," in *The Cambridge Companion to Medieval Jewish Philosophy*, eds. Daniel H. Frank and Oliver Leaman (Cambridge: Cambridge University Press, 2003): 218–257; Jonathan Dauber, *Knowledge of God and the Development of Early Kabbalah* (Leiden and Boston: Brill, 2012).

[21] On mediaeval Jewish magic, cf. Joshua Trachtenberg, *Jewish Magic and Superstition. A Study in Folk Religion* (New York: Behrman's Jewish Book House, 1939; reprinted Philadelphia: University of

this process were eventually dubbed 'practical Kabbalah' and, as we will see later, they became of some relevance for Polqar.²²

Polqar introduces the kabbalists in a very significant way: surprisingly, he does not focus on kabbalistic ideas, but rather on the epistemological difference between kabbalistic and philosophical approaches for obtaining true and certain knowledge. In Polqar's philosophy, men gain truth with the assistance of the rational speculation of the intellectual faculty. Using the intellectual faculty, the philosopher is also able to apprehend hidden things by means of Aristotelian reasoning and to draw a conclusion from known premises. By contrast, the kabbalist denies this ability of the philosopher in particular and human beings in general by means of a virtually sceptical approach. Instead, the kabbalist prefers to rely on a tradition that goes back to the prophets when it comes to hidden truths. Therefore, in an anonymous text entitled 'Chapter on the *kawwanah*, by the ancient kabbalists,' for instance, which according to Gershom Scholem was probably written by the early kabbalist Azriel of Gerona, the following identification with prophecy is included at the end of a passage dealing with the kabbalistic concept of *kawwanah* or the required intention or devotion while praying or fulfilling the commandments:

> And this [i.e. *kawwanah*] is the path among the paths of prophecy, upon which he who makes himself familiar with it will be capable of rising to the rank of prophecy.²³

However, the most important example of a prophetic interpretation of Kabbalah is provided by Abraham Abulafia, who claimed to be a prophet, a mystic, and the messiah all at once.²⁴ In Polqar's view, prophecy has nothing to do with true knowledge, since it is nothing but imagination.²⁵ Maimonides argues that every prophet is nec-

---

Pennsylvania Press, 2004); Yuval Harari, *Jewish Magic before the Rise of Kabbalah* (Detroit: Wayne State University Press, 2017).

22 On practical Kabbalah, cf. Gershom Scholem, *Kabbalah* (Jerusalem: Keter, 1988): 182–189; Moshe Idel, "Defining Kabbalah: The Kabbalah of the Divine Names," in *Mystics of the Book: Themes, Topics, and Typologies*, ed. Robert A. Herrera (New York: Peter Lang, 1993): 97–122; idem, "On the Theologization of Kabbalah in Modern Scholarship," in *Religious Apologetics—Philosophical Argumentation*, eds. Yossef Schwartz and Volkhard Krech (Tübingen: Mohr Siebeck, 2004): 142–145.

23 See Scholem, *Origins of the Kabbalah*, 419. On the view of another late thirteenth-century kabbalist, Rabbi Joseph ben Shalom Ashkenazi, concerning the visualisation of letters and colours as a technique for achieving the prophetic state, cf. Moshe Idel, *Kabbalah: New Perspectives* (New Haven and London: Yale University Press, 1988), 105–106.

24 On Abraham Abulafia, cf. the many books and articles written by Moshe Idel, e.g., idem, *The Mystical Experience in Abraham Abulafia* (Albany: SUNY Press, 1987); idem, *Studies in Ecstatic Kabbalah* (Albany: SUNY Press, 1988); idem, *Language, Torah, and Hermeneutics in Abraham Abulafia* (Albany: SUNY Press, 1989).

25 On Polqar's inventive view of prophecy and the prophet's knowledge being differentiated from the philosopher's knowledge, see also Polgar, *Ezer HaDat*, ed. Levinger, 88–89 and 116–118; cf. Pines, "Some Topics on Polqar's Treatise '*Ezer ha-Dat* and their Parallels in Spinoza's View," 420–432; idem, "Spinoza's *Tractatus Theologico-Politicus* and the Jewish Philosophical Tradition," 501–503;

essarily a philosopher and that a prophet is provided with both a perfect imaginative faculty and a perfect rational one.[26] In contrast, Polqar clearly differentiates between the prophet and the philosopher. He maintains that although only Moses was both a perfect philosopher and a perfect prophet, all the other prophets are not philosophers because they use only imagination and intuition. In line with this, Polqar acknowledges the kabbalists insofar as they are similar to traditionalist Jews, for both maintain that the only source of true knowledge is tradition that goes back to the prophets. Both reject the philosophers by dint of the alleged limitations of man's intellectual faculty.[27] In this epistemological regard, both the kabbalist and the traditionalist are sceptics. However, Polqar too is a sceptic insofar as he continues to question the kabbalists on the certainty of their own claims regarding the sources of knowledge that they use:

> But if one will say to them [i.e. the kabbalists]: 'Whence do you know this?' or 'How is it that you do not take note and raise doubts (about your claim) and admit that it would be possible that these views (of the kabbalists) are not those that were heard from the mouths of the prophets? For (the views of the prophets) were forgotten and lost in the course of time in the crisis of changes, and in the troubles of sufferings which happened to our congregation due to our sins.'[28]

One major characteristic of the philosophical approach in general and the sceptical approach in particular is to question one's own claims and enquire into their certainty. Obviously, this approach differs from the kabbalistic one, which accepts claims simply by following the tradition provided by the chain of genealogy and filiation from master to student without any opportunity to doubt. The problem, Polqar states, is the fact that prophecy already came to an end in biblical times. The historical explanation for the end of prophecy he gives is also intriguing. Israel's sins are the reason for the end of prophecy and the loss of the prophets' knowledge. The long period between the end of prophecy and the Kabbalah of his contemporaries is what Polqar's mistrust is founded upon. How can one rely with certainty on a tradition claiming to be that ancient? According to Polqar, the kabbalists would equate this situation with the reliability of the Torah and the writings of the prophets:

> They [i.e. the kabbalists] will reply and say: 'Far be it from us that we should cast any doubt on those of our beliefs which were received [ha-mequbbalot] by us from the mouths of the people

---

Dov Schwartz, "Prophecy according to Isaac Polqar, Rabbi Shlomo Al-Konstantin, and Spinoza" [in Hebrew], *Asufot* 4 (1990): 60–61; Shalom Sadik, *Trinity and Determinism in the Thought of Abner of Burgos*, 93–98; Haliva, *Isaac Polqar*, 251–268.
26 See Maimonides, *Guide of the Perplexed*, II:35–38 and II:45.
27 Polqar already ascribes this view to the traditionalist in the last dialogue of the second chapter, but without mentioning the kabbalist; see Polgar, *Ezer HaDat*, ed. Levinger, 84–87.
28 Polgar, *Ezer HaDat*, ed. Levinger, 156, lines 8–12: וכשיאמר אליהם אדם מאין תדעו זאת, ואיך לא תשימו לבכם להסתפק ולומר כי איפשר שלא היו דעות אלה הם הנשמעים מפי הנביאים, כי היו נשכחים ונעדרים באורך הזמנים, ובחלופי השניים ובטרדת התלאות אשר קרו בעונותינו לעדתינו?

> who are approved in our eyes, just as we do not doubt either the book of our Torah or the writings of our prophets, peace be upon them.' And they are so brazen as to compare and equate the stories of their foolishness to the Holy Scriptures.[29]

Regarding the kabbalists' equation of Kabbalah with Torah, any general doubt regarding the reliability of all these ancient texts would be inappropriate. This evokes a subtle dilemma for Polqar as he must avoid any conflict concerning the acceptance of the Torah as a source of knowledge while trying to argue against Kabbalah. At first, Polqar clearly states, in a very dogmatic way, that the equation of Kabbalah with Torah is brazen because the kabbalistic stories are to be considered nothing but foolishness. In mentioning 'stories,' Polqar is most likely alluding to kabbalistic Midrashim to be found, for instance, in the *Sefer ha-Zohar*.[30] However, Polqar has to differentiate between the characteristics of Kabbalah and Torah. Thus, he presents two rather odd examples for the purpose of degrading Kabbalah as an allegedly ancient tradition. The first reads as follows:

> And they (obviously) do not know that from the day of the death of Moses, our master, all the people of our nation made constant efforts, were diligent and occupied themselves with preserving the traditional text of their writings, so that no (single) letter of them would be missed or others would be added. And all of them stated their intention to bequeath their children firm and wise[31] books copied and checked from one another until today. But despite all their diligence and their efforts in (preserving) their traditional text, today there are to be found variants in the Holy Scriptures in several places. And this is known to anyone who examines the book of the Torah, which is well known among us as being in the handwriting of Ezra the priest, for there are to be found in it words that differ from similar (words) in the other checked books which are in our possession.[32]

In his first example, Polqar compares the transmission of the Holy Scriptures and kabbalistic sources. The argument *ad antiquitatem* (appeal to antiquity or tradition) provides the general background: a source is deemed correct on the basis that it is correlated with some past or present tradition. The widely accepted idea is that the antiquity of the source guarantees the truth of its text. In this case, Polqar adopts

---

29 *Ibidem*, 156, lines 12–16: ישיבו ויאמרו חלילה לנו מלשום שום ספק באמונ[ו]תינו אלה המקובלות אצלנו מפי האנשים המוחזקים בעינינו, כאשר לא נסתפק בספר תורתינו ובכתבי נביאינו ע״ה, ויעיזו פניהם להשוות ולדמות ספורי הבליהם לספרי הקדש.

30 Cf. Oded Yisraeli, *Temple Portals: Studies in Aggadah and Midrash in the Zohar* (Berlin and Boston: De Gruyter, 2016).

31 The Hebrew *nevonim* edited here by Levinger should probably be corrected to *nekhonim*, 'correct.'

32 Polgar, *Ezer HaDat*, ed. Levinger, 156, lines 16–25: ולא ידעו כי מיום מות משה אדונינו השתדלו והחריצו והתעסקו תמיד כל אנשי אומתינו בשמור את מסורת כתביהם כדי שלא תחסר מהם אות או תעדיף אחרת וכולם שמו כונתם להוריש את בניהם ספרים ישרים ונבונים מועתקים ומוגהים זה מזה עד היום, ועם כל חריצותם והשתדלותם במסורתם נמצא היום שנויים בכתבי הקודש במקצת מקומות. וזה ידוע אצל המעיין בספר התורה אשר הוא מפורסם אצלנו שהוא כתיבת יד עזרא הכהן, כי ימצאו בו מלות שונות לדומיהן בשאר הספרים המוגהים אשר בידינו.

the traditional view that the Torah was revealed to Moses and put into writing by Ezra the priest, who was also called the scribe.[33]

However, Polqar's implicit premise states the fundamental difference between both literary traditions concerning the quality and accuracy of the textual transmission. Beginning already in rabbinic literature, evidence of textual variants and emendations in the circulating copies of the Hebrew Bible was discussed and guidelines for accurate copying were introduced.[34] In the history of textual criticism, Christian authors such as Origen of Alexandria (c. 184–c. 253) and Jerome (347–420) or Jewish authors such as Abraham ibn Ezra (1089–c. 1167) and David Kimhi (1160–1235) were early forerunners who were aware of textual variants and related problems in the transmission of the Bible.

Polqar seems to accept, at least for a moment, that Kabbalah could indeed rely on ancient sources, only for the purpose of his argumentation. Hence, he aims to imply a so-called *qal wa-ḥomer* conclusion or an *argumentum a fortiori:* if there are variants in even the Holy Scriptures despite the efforts made in copying and checking them, then the kabbalistic sources must be all the more deficient and therefore full of (scribal) errors and simply unreliable. But the implicit opposite case would probably be even more subversive: should there be no textual variants in a specific kabbalistic source of purported old age, such an absence of variants would prove that the source was not an ancient one.

Polqar's implicit sceptical argument of doubting the textual accuracy of kabbalistic sources concerning their transmission since antiquity deconstructs Kabbalah's presentation of itself as an ancient tradition. Later, in the seventeenth century, this argument was elaborated into the philological method of textual criticism (e.g. Jean Morin and Richard Simon) and eventually into a general scepticism concerning ancient sources and the Holy Scriptures. However, in my view, Polqar did not intend this kind of general sceptical strategy regarding textual reliability. In addition, I would like to emphasise that in Polqar's view, Kabbalah is understood first and foremost as a written text based on ancient written sources. This may apply for kabbalistic works as the *Sefer ha-Bahir* attributed to Rabbi Neḥuniah ben ha-Qanah or the *Sefer ha-Zohar* attributed to Rabbi Shim'on bar Yoḥai. However, he does not consider either the possibility of an oral transmission of kabbalistic lores via filiation from master to student from ancient times or the recent or contemporary production of kabbalistic texts in his time.

In the following, Polqar describes the peculiarities of kabbalistic writings:

> And when a man reads the books found among these kabbalists, he will find their words in two ways:

---

[33] Cf. Ezra 7:6; 2 Esdras 14:44–46; Babylonian Talmud, Sanhedrin 21b.
[34] Cf. Saul Lieberman, *Hellenism in Jewish Palestine* (New York: The Jewish Theological Seminary of America, 1994), 20–37; Emanuel Tov, *Textual Criticism of the Hebrew Bible* (Minneapolis: Fortress Press, 2001).

The first is strange words (which) frighten the listener (but) without signifying any matter of internal logic, and they are only babbling of the lips. And (the) wickedness of their hearts and (the) strength of their stupidity cause them to justify and believe in a matter before its perception, something which it is forbidden (to do) according to the art of logic. *For they know not, neither will they understand; they walk on in darkness* [Psalm 82:5].
And the second is that the majority of things (they write) which are possible for man to contemplate on any matter by internal logic will be found to be the opposite of what the intellect and the judgment[35] would approve. And others of them are complete heresy due to the contradiction of the unity of God, blessed be He, and a denial of His real attributes.[36]

As in the previous example, Polqar does not refer to the essentials of the (theosophical) Kabbalah such as the concept of the Sefirot or the theurgical interpretation of the commandments. Instead, he focusses on the meaning of logic and intellectual approaches from a philosophical or epistemological perspective. First, the aforementioned 'strange words' are a literal translation of the Latin technical term *nomina barbara*, known as the divine, angelic, or demonic magical names used in adjurations. These names—usually without a semantic meaning in the language of the magical text and its users—are nevertheless acknowledged by magicians and clients as the agents of magical efficacy.[37] As these names are often used in maleficent magic, they are frightening for the reader. A broader interpretation of those 'strange words' emphasises the lack of internal logic and argument. Therefore, they are nothing but nonsense or 'babbling of the lips.' Again, Polqar dogmatically adjudges the kabbalists as wicked and stupid.

Secondly, according to Polqar, kabbalistic texts contradict logical principles in most cases. Incidentally, the Hebrew phrase for 'judgment' that Polqar uses is *shiqqul ha-da'at* or 'balancing of the mind.' Perhaps this phrase somehow recalls the sceptical ability to balance out the persuasive force of arguments for and against any disputed claim (*equipollence*). Furthermore, Polqar asserts Kabbalah to be not only non-logical, but also heretical. Indictment of heresy is often used in polemics.[38] At the end of the quoted passage, Polqar is very probably alluding to the kabbalistic concept of the ten Sefirot when he writes: 'Others of them are complete heresy due to

---

35 Literally 'the balancing of the mind' or 'common sense.'
36 Polgar, *Ezer HaDat*, ed. Levinger, 156, line 25 to 157, line 6: וכשיקרא האדם בספרים הנמצאים מהמקובלים האלה ימצא דבריהם בשני פנים: האחת מלות זרות מבהילות אל השומע בלתי מורות על שום ענין בהגיון הפנימי ואינם כי אם מוצא שפתים בלבד, וזדון לבם ותוקף סכלותם יביאם להצדיק ולהאמין בדבר טרם ציורו, מה שהוא נאסר במלאכת ההגיון, כי לא ידעו ולא יבינו בחשכה יתהלכו. והשני כי רוב הדברים אשר אפשר להתבונן בהם האדם שום ענין בהגיון הפנימי (!) ימצאו בהפך מה שיחייב השכל ושקול הדעת ומקצתם כפירה גמורה מסתירת יחוד האל ב״ה והכחשת תאריו האמתיים.
37 On *nomina barbara* and the use of magical names in Jewish magic, cf. Trachtenberg, *Jewish Magic and Superstition*, 78–103; Idel, *Language, Torah, and Hermeneutics in Abraham Abulafia*, 82–124; Daniel Abrams, "From Germany to Spain: Numerology as a Mystical Technique," *Journal of Jewish Studies* 47 (1996): 43–63.
38 On indictment of heresy as a sceptical strategy, cf. Rebiger, "Sceptical Strategies in Simone Luzzatto's Presentation of the Kabbalists in his *Discorso*," 63–64.

the contradiction of the unity of God, blessed be He, and a denial of His real attributes.' The concept of the ten Sefirot contradicting the unity of God and, in doing so, the core concept of a monotheistic religion, is one of the major arguments levelled by the Jewish opponents of Kabbalah. Thus, it is no coincidence that many anti-kabbalistic criticisms are embedded in the context of anti-Christian polemics against the concept of the Trinity. Accordingly, circa 1230–1235, Meir ben Simon ha-Me'ili of Narbonne, most probably the first known opponent of Kabbalah, wrote about the kabbalists in his anti-Christian polemical work *Milḥemet Miṣwah* ('War by Commandment') in a passage comparing the concept of the Trinity with that of the Sefirot: 'Do there exist in our time, even among the religions of the gentiles, deniers[39] of the unity of God, blessed be He, more (worthless) than these [i.e. kabbalists]?'[40] Some decades later, circa 1280, the ecstatic kabbalist Abraham Abulafia further elaborated this line of argument in an epistle to his disciple entitled *Ve-Zot le-Yehudah*. In his letter, Abulafia sharply criticised the even worse case of the concept of the ten Sefirot in the theosophic Kabbalah.[41]

The next lines of Polqar's attack on the second group deal with the opposition between kabbalists and philosophers:

> And those kabbalists to whom I speak are so brazen as to raise their voices to mock and despise those who make efforts to read the books of philosophy. And they say to them [i.e. the philosophers]: 'Why do you waste your days in studying these books of foolishness, since man's intellect is unable to attain hidden (matters), to perform miracles, and to change their nature?' And they [i.e. the kabbalists] are so presumptuous in themselves as (to claim that) they attain these matters without any effort and labour, but only by copying those books which are venerated in

---

39 Here I follow the conjecture of ספרים ('books') to כופרים suggested by Alon Goshen-Gottstein; cf. idem, "The Triune and the Decaune God: Christianity and Kabbalah as Objects of Jewish Polemics with Special Reference to Meir ben Simeon of Narbonne's *Milhemet Mitzva*," in *Religious Polemics in Context*, eds. Theo L. Hettema and Arie van der Kooij (Assen: Royal Van Gorcum, 2004): 190 n. 76.
40 The Hebrew text is found in the only manuscript attesting *Milḥemet Miṣwah*—that is, the Sephardic manuscript written around 1300, MS Parma 2749 (De Rossi 155), fol. 231b—and was published in a slightly abridged form by Gershom Scholem, "Te'udah ḥadašah le-rešit ha-qabbalah" [Hebrew], in *Sefer Bialik*, ed. Ya'akov Fikhman (Tel Aviv: Hoṣa'at va'ad ha-yovel uve-hishtatfut hoṣa'at omanut, 1934): 146–149, reprinted in Gershom Scholem, *Studies in Kabbalah*, ed. Yosef ben Shelomo, vol. 1 (Tel Aviv: 'Am 'Oved, 1998), 7–38; cf. the English translation of the whole passage in idem, *Origins of the Kabbalah*, 398–400; cf. furthermore Heinrich Gross, "Meïr b. Simon und seine Schrift Milchemeth Mizwa," *Monatsschrift für Geschichte und Wissenschaft des Judentums* 30 (1881): 295–305, 444–452 and 554–569; Adolf Neubauer, "The Bahir and the Zohar," *Jewish Quarterly Review* 4 (1892): 357–360.
41 Abraham Abulafia, *Sefer Razei Ḥayyei 'Olam ha-Ba* (Jerusalem: Amnon Gross, 1999), 22ff.; cf. Moshe Idel, *Kabbalah: New Perspectives*, xii; idem, *Studies in Ecstatic Kabbalah*, 139; Elliot R. Wolfson, "The Doctrine of Sefirot in the Prophetic Kabbalah of Abraham Abulafia," *Jewish Studies Quarterly* 2.4 (1995): 341–343.

their eyes (and) which were concealed and hidden in the houses of the glorious sages until God delivered their being copied into their hands.⁴²

In this passage, Polqar reflects the frontline between kabbalists and philosophers mockingly calling one another as foolish and non-effective. When the kabbalist claims that the philosopher is not able to attain hidden matters, to perform miracles, or to change nature, according to Polqar he implicitly states that he himself is able to do so. All three abilities define the specific features of a biblical prophet. In contrast, a philosopher such as Polqar cannot understand how one could claim such an ability without any intellectual effort but relying only on transmitted texts. Here, the textual criticism concerning the accuracy and reliability of the transmission of kabbalistic texts already implicitly presented in the previous section leads to the final subversive goal of his argument, which is specifically the complete neglect of that which is essential to Kabbalah according to its abovementioned literal meaning, i.e. its claim of being a reliable tradition.

The sentence about the books 'which were concealed and hidden in the houses of the glorious sages' probably alludes to the pseudepigraphical attribution of the *Sefer ha-Zohar* to Rabbi Shimʻon bar Yoḥai, who lived in the second century, and to the thirteenth-century kabbalists' explanation as to why this and similar texts had only appeared now after centuries of being hidden. So, for example, Moses de Leon, who was, at least to a certain degree, engaged in the production of zoharic literature, writes in his *Sefer Mishkan ha-ʻEdut*:

> Concerning this matter, there are hidden mysteries and secret things which are unknown to men. You will now see that I am revealing deep and secret mysteries which the holy sages regarded as sacred and hidden, profound matters which properly speaking are not fit for revelation so that they may not become a target for the wit of every idle person. [...] And they [the sages] have closed and locked the door behind their words and hidden all their mystical books, because they saw that the time had not come to reveal and publish them.⁴³

In his second example, Polqar presents Kabbalah as first and foremost being practical Kabbalah, although in this case it is actually non-kabbalistic magic. In Polqar's

---

42 Polgar, *Ezer HaDat*, ed. Levinger, 157, lines 6–14: והמקובלים האלה אשר אני מדבר עמהם יעיזו פניהם וירימו קולם להלעיג ולבזות את המשתדלים לקרוא בספרי הפילוסופיא ואומרים אליהם, למה זה תבלו ימיכם בהגות ספרי ההבלים אלה אחר אשר אין כח לשכל האדם להשיג הנעלמות ולעשות הנפלאות ולשנות הטבע, ומתנשאים בעצמם כי הם ישיגו דברים אלה מבלי שום יגיעה ועמל רק בהעתקת ספרים הנכבדים בעיניהם, אשר היו גנוזים ונסתרים בבתי החכמים המפוארים, עד אשר אנה האלהים לידם העתקתם.

43 Moses de Leon, *Sefer Mishkan ha-ʻEdut*, ed. Avishai Bar Asher (Los Angeles: Cherub Press, 2013), 118–119; English translation by Gershom Scholem, *Major Trends in Jewish Mysticism* (New York: Schocken Books, 1961), 201–202; cf. Boaz Huss, *The Zohar: Reception and Impact* (Oxford and Portland, OR: The Littman Library of Jewish Civilization, 2016), 42.

view, magicians—as well as astrologers—believe only in a concept of causality that is entirely erroneous.⁴⁴ In continuing the passage quoted, he tells the following story:

> And a man who is acknowledged among our masses for (his) knowledge of Kabbalah and (his) performance of miracles, whose name is Maestre Marcus, told me that in his youth his only activity was seeking for wisdom. And he heard people saying that in a land far away from the islands of Ashkenaz (there lived) a very wise man, and he sought him out. And he went and travelled until he reached him in his land. And he dwelt with him for many days, he worked in his house and served him. When this man saw his diligence and the swiftness of his service, his work was highly esteemed in his eyes, he greatly honoured him and provided him with hospitality. He only avoided teaching him anything, lest he learn (it) and escape from him and return to his land. *When he had been there a long time* [Genesis 26:8], he was concerned that he was (overly) delayed and detained there, and he was sorry for him.⁴⁵

Polqar claims that a certain man called Maestre Marcus told him how he had received esoteric or magical knowledge in his youth. The peculiar name 'Marcus' is also mentioned in other sources in the context of magical techniques and practices, as well as their transmissions. Thus, in the collection of magical recipes in Ms Bibliothèque de Genève, Comites Latentes 145, Rabbi Elijah Menaḥem ben Moses of London (c. 1220–1284) is connected to a certain Marcus.⁴⁶ But if this Marcus is the same in both accounts, then the 'very wise man' could probably be identified as Rabbi Elijah of London. Rabbi Elijah is indeed known for his use of divine names for protective purposes and for transmitting magical adjurations.⁴⁷ In line with Rabbi Elijah and his relation to Marcus, the obscure 'islands of Ashkenaz' mentioned in Polqar's text quoted above may quite probably be identified as England. Already in the third chapter of his *'Ezer ha-Dat*, Polqar mentions Ashkenaz—together with France—as places where magic dealing with the names of angels and demons is quite popular among the Jews.⁴⁸ However, it is not entirely clear whether Polqar's Marcus is a fictitious or historical character and whether Polqar's account describes a real personal encounter with him.⁴⁹ Obviously, it is not quite plausible that Marcus had in fact told the story of his acquisition of esoteric knowledge to Polqar in such a self-effacing

---

44 Cf. the fourth chapter in *ibidem*, 159–161.
45 *Ibidem*, 157, lines 14–23: והגיד לי איש מוחזק בהמונינו בידיעת הקבלה ובמעשה נפלאות, שמו מאישטרי מרקוש, כי בנערותו לא היתה מלאכתו כי אם בבקשת החחמה, ושמע אומרים, כי בארץ רחוקה מאי אשכנז איש חכם מאד, ושם מגמתו אליו. וילך הלוך ונסוע עד הגיעו לארצו, וישב עמו ימים רבים ויעבוד בביתו וישמשהו. וכראות האיש חריצותו וקלות שמושו יקרה מאד בעיניו עבודתו וירב כבודו ומשאת ארוחתו, רק חדל מלמדו דבר פן ילמד ויברח ממנו וישוב אל ארצו. ויהי כי ארכו לו שם הימים וידאג על בוששו והתמהמהו שם ויצר לו.
46 Ms Bibliothèque de Genève, Comites Latentes 145 (formerly Ms Sassoon 290), pp. 379–381.
47 Cf. Ephraim Kanarfogel, *"Peering through the Lattices": Mystical, Magical, and Pietistic Dimensions in the Tosafist Period* (Detroit: Wayne State University Press, 2000), 232–233.
48 See Polgar, *Ezer HaDat*, ed. Levinger, 115.
49 On Marcus and Rabbi Elijah of London, including Polqar's account, cf. Amos Goldreich, *Automatic Writing in Zoharic Literature and Modernism* [in Hebrew] (Los Angeles: Cherub Press, 2010), 289–298.

way. Moreover, the Latin name Marcus sounds more Christian than Jewish. It is most likely that Polqar wished to indicate some Christian influence on this Jew or that he was a former Jew who had converted to Christianity, which is quite fitting regarding his adversary Abner, who called himself Alfonso of Valladolid.

A crucial point mentioned above is that the wise man 'avoided teaching him anything.' Thus from the outset, Maestre Marcus was obviously not a dignified student deserving of at least some of his master's knowledge. His not being worthy of this acquisition will become clear as the story continues:

> And he said to himself, 'Since the man is not interested in teaching me, *I will therefore turn aside* [Exodus 3:3] if I can take a look in his book and see it, then I will cast my eye on it and copy it.' And night fell, and he peered into the innermost part of his chamber and, behold, the man was reclining on his bed, reading in a respected and fine[50] book. And when fatigue weighed heavily upon him and sleep overtook him, he placed the book under his head and fell asleep. And when he [i.e. Maestre Marcus] saw that he was deeply asleep, he came into the chamber and stealthily placed his hand under his head and stole the book, and then he hastened to the ink and parchment to write it out. And when the sun rose, behold, he had finished copying it, and then he returned it to the place where it was taken from.[51]

It is explicit here that Maestre Marcus planned to steal the book for a short period and to copy it while its owner was asleep. This was obviously the only way for him to obtain the secrets that his master had chosen to withhold from him. The placing of a secret book under the head of someone who is asleep probably alludes to the magical practice of a dream request (*she'elat ḥalom* in Hebrew).[52] Therefore, in one magical fragment from the Cairo Genizah destined for this purpose, the following instruction is preserved: 'Write the entire issue and place it under your head.'[53] Here, it is clear from the context that 'entire issue' means divine names. And in fact, the secret book under the head contains divine names, as mentioned in the continuation of

---

50 The Hebrew *na'eh* should probably be corrected to *nora*, 'awesome.'
51 Polgar, *Ezer HaDat*, ed. Levinger, 157, line 23 to 158, line 3: ויאמר בלבו אחר אשר אין חפץ האיש ללמדני אסורה נא אם אוכל לחזות בספרו ואראהו, אשימה עיני עליו ואעתיקהו. ויהי בלילה והשגיח בחדרי חדרו והנה האיש מוסב על מטתו, קורא בספר נכבד ונאה. וכאשר כבדה עליו העייפות ואנסתהו השינה, שם הספר תחת מראשותיו ויישן, וכאשר ראה תוקף שנתו בא תוך החדר ויבא ידו מראשותיו בלט, ויגנוב הספר וימהר אל הדיו ואל הקלף ויכתבהו. ויהי כעלות השחר והנה כלה מהעתיקו, וישיבהו אל המקום אשר לקחו משם.
52 On dream requests in medieval Jewish magic, cf., e.g., Trachtenberg, *Jewish Magic and Superstition*, 241–243; Moshe Idel, "On Še'elat Ḥalom in Ḥasidei Aškenaz: Sources and Influences," *Materia Giudaica* 10 (2005): 99–109.
53 See the Cairo Genizah fragment, Pennsylvania University H457, fol. 1a/10 (unpublished, my translation). The same magical practice can be found in another Genizah fragment concerning the recovery of lost property, cf. CUL T.-S. K 1.96, fol. 2a/12–13, in *Magische Texte aus der Kairoer Geniza*, vol. 3, eds. Peter Schäfer and Shaul Shaked (Tübingen: Mohr Siebeck, 1999): 369 (No. 84). On this fragment and the placing of the adjuration text under one's head, see Yuval Harari, "Metatron and the Treasure of Gold: Notes on a Dream Inquiry Text from the Cairo Genizah," in *Continuity and Innovation in the Magical Tradition*, eds. Gideon Bohak, Yuval Harari, and Shaul Shaked (Leiden and Boston: Brill, 2011): 307–308.

Polqar's story. It is striking that in one of the magical adjurations transmitted by Rabbi Elijah of London, a dream request is also intended.⁵⁴ However, the placing of the book under the head can also simply serve to protect it from thieves, even though—as we learn from Polqar's story—this precaution against theft was somewhat unsuccessful. The concluding part of the story of Maestre Marcus reads as follows:

> And when he saw that God had caused his way to succeed, and that he had achieved his desire and yearning, he set out for his land, which was a distance of four months away. But the distance was shortened for him by the power of the adjuration of one of the (divine) names which were written in this book. And he came to his home before a third of the day (was over). Beliefs in such stories of foolishness and all types of nonsense are, on account of our sins, very prevalent among many of the people from the dignities of our nation.⁵⁵

Here, a well-known magical technique is mentioned, the so-called 'shortening of the path' or 'path jumping' (*qefiṣat ha-derekh* in Hebrew). The goal of this technique is a miraculous journey between two distant places in a short time.⁵⁶ Polqar describes Maestre Marcus' return to his homeland using the technical terminology established in Jewish magic. The use of magical names in an adjuration for this purpose is well attested in medieval Jewish magic.⁵⁷ The details in the story of Maestre Marcus that Polqar presents clearly show his familiarity with Jewish magical traditions, their features, and their technical language. In any case, it is decisive that Polqar does not provide the reader either with a description of the magical practice itself, including an adjuration, or with any mention of the effective name(s) of God.⁵⁸ Thus, the continuous dissemination of the content and essence of magic is not supported, at least by Polqar. Instead, he chooses another way of dealing with the challenge of magical beliefs and practices performed by Jews. In fact, those who execute magical practices

---

54 Cf. Kanarfogel, *Peering through the Lattices*, 232.
55 Polgar, *Ezer HaDat*, ed. Levinger, 158, lines 3–9: ובראותו כי הצליח האל את דרכו, והשיג תאותו וחשקו, וישם לבו אל ארצו אשר היתה רחוקה מהלך ארבעה חדשים, ותקפוץ לו הארץ בכח אזכרת שם מן השמות הכתובים בספר ההוא, ויבא אל ביתו טרם שלישית היום. ואמונות סיפורי הבלים כאלה ומיני ההתולים רבים מאד בעונותינו בהרבה אנשים מנכבדי אומתינו.
56 Cf. Mark Verman and Shulamit H. Adler, "Path Jumping in the Jewish Magical Tradition," *Jewish Studies Quarterly* 1 (1993/94): 131–148; Gedalyah Nigal, *Magic, Mysticism and Hasidism: The Supernatural in Jewish Thought* (Northvale, NJ: Jason Aronson, 1994), 33–49.
57 Cf., e.g., the magical fragments stemming from the Cairo Genizah JTSL ENA 2871, fol. 7b/7, in *Magische Texte aus der Kairoer Geniza*, vol. 2, eds. Peter Schäfer and Shaul Shaked (Tübingen: Mohr Siebeck, 1997): 127 (No. 28); CUL T.-S. K 1.115, fol. 1b/9–12, in *ibidem*, 155 (No. 31); CUL T.-S. AS 143.171, fol. 2b/1–2, in *Magische Texte aus der Kairoer Geniza*, vol. 3, eds. Peter Schäfer and Shaul Shaked (Tübingen: Mohr Siebeck, 1999): 137 (No. 68).
58 In the last dialogue of the second chapter, the traditionalist mentions the divine names of forty-two and seventy-two letters among the secrets he has acquired; see Polgar, *Ezer HaDat*, ed. Levinger, 86. On these names, see Trachtenberg, *Jewish Magic and Superstition*, 94–97. In the section on magicians also included in the fourth chapter, Polqar actually describes two examples of magic—a love spell and a spell for winning games of dice. However, in both cases, neither an incantation nor any magical name is mentioned; see Polgar, *Ezer HaDat*, ed. Levinger, 160–161.

do not necessarily claim to have theoretical knowledge (*scientia*) concerning the reasons for the efficacy of magic, but usually the practitioner only has practical skills (*ars*) for performing a magical act. As epistemological scepticism would be directed against a knowledge claim but not against practical skills, Polqar chose another sceptical element in his polemic. Usually, the well-known *topos* of 'stolen wisdom' or 'theft of wisdom' deals with knowledge transfer between different nations, such as the Jews and the Greeks.[59] Here, Polqar uses this *topos* in a slightly different way to deconstruct the self-conception and self-image of Jewish kabbalists. For the purpose of his argument, Polqar does not doubt the quality of wisdom with regard to kabbalistic claims, but rather the legitimation of their ownership of this wisdom. Therefore, his purpose is to delegitimise his opponents' authority and reliability by using stories and experiences acknowledged by the kabbalists.[60] The crucial point of his method is to avoid answering the question regarding the kabbalists' claims that Kabbalah is knowledge or indeed even wisdom.

At the end of this passage, Polqar once again presents his epistemological premises on the possibility of knowledge. At the same moment, he aims to define 'true tradition' as opposed to the self-image of Kabbalah:

> And these ignorants[61] do not know, nor do they understand, that we possess no faculty more honoured and more elevated than the rational faculty, through which we can attain the hidden (matters). And the only way to attain this faculty is through seeking out the middle term and the construction of a demonstration. To be sure, the apprehension of the prophet is not (attained) through combining the premises and seeking out the demonstration, but through a way more honoured and elevated than them. However, the apprehension of the hearers of his words and (what) they receive [*meqabbelim*] from him cannot be compared to it [i.e. the prophet's apprehension] in any way. And the topic of the true tradition [*qabbalah*] and the measure of the apprehension of those who receive [*meqabbelim*] it from the mouth of the prophet or from one who receives [*meqabbel*] (it) from another who received [*mequbbal*] it is written in the book *Musar ha-Banim* ['The Instruction of the Sons'] (written) by me.[62]

For a philosopher such as Polqar, men are able to attain hidden things with the help of the rational faculty, which is only possible by following the principles of Aristotelian syllogisms. The prophet's way of attaining hidden matters is not only different to this philosophical approach, but also 'more honoured and elevated.' Nevertheless,

---

59 Cf. Abraham Melamed, *The Myth of the Jewish Origins of Science and Philosophy* [in Hebrew] (Jerusalem: Magnes Press, 2010), 178–219 and now Giuseppe Veltri, *Alienated Wisdom: Enquiry into Jewish Philosophy and Scepticism* (Berlin and Boston: De Gruyter, 2018), 21–42.
60 On delegitimation as a sceptical strategy, cf. Rebiger, "Sceptical Strategies in Simone Luzzatto's Presentation of the Kabbalists in his *Discorso*," 64–66.
61 Literally 'those who are lacking understanding,' here meaning the kabbalists.
62 Polgar, *Ezer HaDat*, ed. Levinger, 158, lines 9–17: וחסרי דעת אלה לא ידעו ולא יתבוננו כי אין בנו כח אחר נכבד ומעולה מן ההוגה אשר בו ניכל להשיג הנעלמות, והשגת הכח הזה אינה כי אם בבקשת גבול אמצעי ובנין מופת. אף אמנם השגת הנביא איננה בהרכבת הקדמות ובקשת מופת, כי אם בדרך נכבד ומעולה ממנו, רק חשגת שומעי דבריו ומקבלים ממנו דומה אליה בשום ענין. ועסק הקבלה האמתית ושיעור השגת המקבלים אותה מפי הנביא או ממי שמקבל ממקובל אחר, הלא הוא כתוב בספר "מוסר הבנים" אשר לי.

neither the receiver of the prophetic tradition nor the tradition itself share the same quality of apprehension. The assumption that the prophet and the receivers of his tradition are epistemologically equal is considered the kabbalists' main mistake. Unfortunately, the elaboration of the true Kabbalah in Polqar's *Musar ha-Banim* (mentioned above) is unknown as the book did not survive.

Conclusion

The Hebrew word 'Kabbalah' literally means 'tradition.' Polqar's goal in his attack on the kabbalists is to undermine the acceptance of kabbalistic opinions among his contemporaries by implementing a sceptical element which argues that Kabbalah is not a real tradition. In doing so, he attempts to undermine the reliability of the claim that the Kabbalah possesses a tradition that dates back to the time of the ancient prophets. Polqar's main sceptical elements are the focus on doubts about the textual accuracy of kabbalistic sources and the question of whether the kabbalists acquired their knowledge honestly. Thus, Polqar deconstructs Kabbalah's self-presentation as an ancient tradition continuously transmitted since antiquity on the one hand and the legitimacy of kabbalistic authorities on the other. In both examples, Polqar does not deal with the specific content of kabbalistic claims, but with the general framework of tradition and its reception of them, thus emphasising the literal meaning of Kabbalah. The *qal wa-ḥomer* conclusion or *argumentum a fortiori* used in the first example concerning the deficiency of kabbalistic texts is not convincing when kabbalists claim that they copied and checked kabbalistic texts in the same way as the Holy Scriptures. The weakness of Polqar's argument in his second example implementing the story of Maestre Marcus is found in the inductive reasoning: even if one accepts the veracity of Polqar's personal story of Maestre Marcus, it nonetheless provides only one example of the *topos* of stolen wisdom but cannot as such guarantee its general validity for all kabbalistic texts. Therefore, I would not call Polqar's approach a fully-fledged sceptical strategy, but rather one which only contains elements of scepticism which, in turn, are embedded in a dogmatic stance.

Giuseppe Veltri
Apologetic, Empiricism, and Sceptical Strategies in Simone Luzzatto

Introduction

Simone Luzzatto (?1583–1663)[1] is the first Jew of the early modern period who, imbued with political philosophical ideas and a sceptical attitude, presented a new empirical concept of Judaism as an integral part of society while also remaining a sceptic intellectual who critically engaged modern sciences and philosophy. He is philosophically in step with the work of the rabbi, preacher, and philosopher Judah Moscato (c. 1533–1590), who asserted the near perfection of mathematics against the weakness of the (new) sciences.[2]

For the first time in the history of Jewish philosophy, a scholar proclaimed himself a sceptic following the New Academy. Already in his first rather apologetic-political work, the *Discorso circa il stato degli Hebrei* (1638), Luzzatto qualifies himself as new academician:

> Political matters are full of alterations and contingencies, and in this Discorso I promised I would follow the probable and the verisimilar,[3] just as a new academician would, and in so doing [the academician] differs from the mathematicians that are used to following the absolutely verifiable and undeniable.[4]

This article is a chapter I published in my recent book *Alienated Wisdom. Enquiry into Jewish Philosophy and Scepticism* (Boston and Berlin: De Gruyter, 2018), 213–232, here reprinted for the Yearbook.

1 For a bibliography of and on Luzzatto, see Simone Luzzatto, *Scritti politici e filosofici di un ebreo scettico nella Venezia del Seicento*, eds. Giuseppe Veltri in cooperation with Anna Lissa and Paola Ferruta (Milan: Bompiani, 2013), 465–499. In this volume the *Discorso* as well as the *Socrate* are edited; all quotations of the original text are from this edition.
2 This was also a topic of the Italian academies, in which the study of science and mathematics together with the liberal arts was both common and appreciated; see Michele Battagia, *Delle accademie Veneziane dissertazione storica* (Venice: Orlandelli, 1826), 35.
3 For a discussion on the term πιθανός as 'verisimilar', see Pierre Gassendi in *Sintagma* (1658) I, De logicae fine, 5, *Opera* 1, 79b; cf. Robert Pasnau, *After Certainty: A History of Our Epistemic Ideals and Illusions* (Oxford: Oxford University Press, 2017); on the second volume of the *Exercitationes paradoxicae adversus Aristoteleos* II, VI,6 (1659), cf. Delphine Bellis, "Nos in Diem Vivimus: Gassendi's Probabilism and Academic Philosophy from Day to Day," in *Academic Scepticism in the Development of Early Modern Philosophy*, eds. Plinio Junqueira Smith and Sébastien Charles (New York: Springer, 2016): 125–152; on probable and verisimilar, see *ibidem*, 130–131.
4 Luzzatto, *Discorso*, 30r.

Being a mathematician, as we can infer at least from some parts of his *Socrate* (1651),[5] Luzzatto was acquainted with axiomatic systems, demonstrably consistent because of their absence of contradiction *per definitionem*. He was, however, of the opinion that axiomatic logic does not work in the consideration of human affairs and political matters, and that the philosopher cannot reach a judgment on them with the sole help of probable and verisimilar argumentations because contradiction is here more often the rule than the exception. The adoption of the categories of plausibility and verisimilitude occurred first in the *Discorso*, the first field of his sceptical training, while in *Socrate* he presents very detailed strategies against dogmatic thought in almost every branch of human science and wisdom. To my knowledge, *Socrate* is the first extant treatise on scepticism written by a Jew.

The main emphasis here will be, therefore, to evince some subtle sceptical strategies Luzzatto used to substantiate the (right of) existence of the Jews despite and because of their differences in the face of the Venetian society and government; he weakened the arguments against Judaism and the Jews that were generated by their detractors and enemies.

Although the *Discorso* and *Socrate* do have very different literary structures and therefore belong to different genres and address two different types of audience, it is my conviction that both of them follow the same sceptic logic: to counter dogmatic ideas and preconceptions with the intent to create at least an equipollence of arguments and culminate politically with the pragmatic issue of how to integrate the Jews into Venetian society. In the *Discorso*, Luzzatto defends the *integral* role of the Jews in the Venetian society against the alleged reason of political and religious *incompatibilities* between them and Christianity. In his philosophical work *Socrate*, he is in favour of the suspension of judgment for Socrates because of the impossibility of an impartial process and correspondent plausible judgment. In the first case, we have empiricism against dogmatism, in the second we observe the necessity of the *epoché*; all of them are sceptical strategies. In this essay, I will deal primarily with the *Discorso*.

1 Apology and Apologetic

According to some scholars, Luzzatto's *Discorso* falls into the category of the apology or 'modern' apologetics of Judaism in Venice.[6] Because of my special research interest focussed on sceptical strategies, it is worthwhile to explain some concepts surrounding the field of apology/apologia in modern (English) language.

---

[5] Cf. Luzzatto, *Socrate*, 68.
[6] Cf. Francesca Trivellato, "Jews and Early Modern Economy," in *The Cambridge History of Judaism*, vol. 7: *The Early Modern World, 1500–1815*, eds. Jonathan Karp and Adam Sutcliffe (Cambridge: Cambridge University Press, 2018): 161.

The terms apology, apologia, and apologetics seem to philologically include the same concept, but philology does not play the decisive role here. Today the English word apology means 'the act of declaring one's regret, remorse, or sorrow for having insulted, failed, injured, harmed or wronged another.'[7] Yet, apologia derives from the same Latin word *apologia* and means what the Greek coinage ἀπολογία in substance addresses: 'verbal defence, speech in defence.' The first literary and philosophical occurrence known to me is the *Apologia of Socrates*.

By contrast, apologetics is systematic argumentative discourse in defence of a doctrine/ religion, as every dictionary confirms.[8] The method of the defence of apologetics may be similar to apologia but the goal is very different. Apologetics may and could have a missionary objective to convert people to the 'true' religion, the 'right' doctrine, while an apologia is primarily a defence designed to convince the judge of one's innocence in opposition to a prosecutor's arguments. The goal is to reach at least an equipollence of arguments. At any rate, an apologia is by no means an apology; it is not a remorseful speech or a term acknowledging wrongful or offensive action and it must also be properly located in the realm of jurisprudence and in philosophical/rhetoric dialectic discussions.

Further, it is well-known that in an accusatorial process the task of the defendant is to try to abate every charge of the accusation by using an arsenal of rhetorical tools, adducing evidence, (accurate) testimony, and (alleged or consistent) proof: all strategies in order to undermine the claim and argument of the (state) prosecutor. I will come back to this point later in my discussion of rhetorical logic and the results of a rabbinic discussion. At this point, I would like to confine myself only to written apologias by emphasising that *writings* in defence of individual or (political, religious, ethnic) groups against the charges of the majority or the ruling powers, are called 'apologia' because they are defending their own point of view, behaviour, or identity which are different from that of the majority. The strategies involved in apologia and apologetics are similar: to produce evidence to counter the adversary, to reduce an accusation to a self-contradiction, and to disavow the charges, removing all legitimacy and plausibility from the construction of the prosecutor's indictment.

Luzzatto adopts this strategy for dismantling the accusation that the Jews are unsuitable to Christian society due to their identity as a different ethnic group and religion. He does not repeat ancient and traditional arguments of antiquity and (messianic) legitimacy in favour of the Jews, but he refers to the experiential, empirical argument of the socially cohesive nature and economic usefulness of the Jews of Venice. It is of course well known that empiricism and scepticism are not the same philosophical movement; however, they use very similar strategies and base their arguments on pragmatic facts based on experience.

---

7 Quoted from Mihaela Mihai, "Apology," in *Internet Encyclopedia of Philosophy*, http://www.iep.utm.edu/apology/ (accessed 3 May, 2018).
8 See, for example, https://www.britannica.com/topic/apologetics (accessed 3 May, 2018).

A few words and notations should be addressed towards the topic of experience as a *philosophoumenon* both of the empiricism and scepticism.⁹ The question of similarity between the two Greek schools is very old and goes back to Sextus Empiricus. Nevertheless, there is more. The discussion of whether Sextus, author of the main fonts of ancient scepticism, was an empiricist or not, as some ancient sources suggest,¹⁰ does not obscure the fact that ancient empiricism did not admit a dogmatic vision of healing in its methods. Sextus recognises some validity to their strategies, when he affirms:

> Some say that the Sceptical philosophy is the same as the Empiric school in medicine. But you must realize that if this form of Empiricism makes affirmations about the inapprehensibility of unclear matters, then it is not the same as Scepticism, nor would it be appropriate for Sceptics to take up with that school.¹¹

Although he seems to counter medical empiricism, he does seem to accept the medical method:

> They might rather adopt, as it seems to me, what is called the Method; for this alone of the medical schools seems to practise no rashness in unclear matters and [the empiricist school] does not presume to say whether they are apprehensible or inapprehensible, but it follows what is apparent, taking thence, in line with Sceptical practice, what seems to be expedient.¹²

Independent from the question of the goals and of the approach to medicine, Sextus cannot negate the fact that empiricism and scepticism adopt very similar tactics.¹³ Both of them back their strategies with experience (ἐμπειρία), a medical attitude of general significance, as an example of linguistic scepticism. To abate the grammarian's dogmatic vision of the 'natural significance' of words, he bases his criticism on the experience with the 'Barbarians' and comments:

> If nouns exist 'by nature' and are not significant in each instance by reason of convention, then all men ought to understand the speech of all, Greeks that of barbarians and barbarians that of

---

9 Cf. Emidio Spinelli, "L'esperienza scettica: Sesto Empirico fra metodologia scientifica e scelte etiche," *Quaestio* 4 (2004): 25–43.
10 Cf. Alan Bailey, *Sextus Empiricus and Pyrrhonean Scepticism* (Oxford: Oxford University Press, 2002), 93–99; cf. Roderick M. Chisholm, "Sextus Empiricus and Modern Empiricism," *Philosophy of Science* 8.3 (1941): 371–384.
11 Sextus Empiricus, *Outlines of Pyrrhonism* I:236; all English translations are taken from Sextus Empiricus, *Outlines of Scepticism*, eds. Julia Annas and Jonathan Barnes (Cambridge: Cambridge University Press, 2000).
12 Sextus Empiricus, *Outlines of Pyrrhonism* I:236–237.
13 It is not my intent here to deal with every aspect this topic involves. I refer the reader to the detailed study of Emidio Spinelli, "Sextus Empiricus," in *Dictionnaire des philosophes antiques*, ed. Richard Goulet (Paris: CNRS éditions, 2016): 265–300; on empiricism, see *ibidem*, 279–282.

Greeks and barbarians that of (other) barbarians. But this is not the case; therefore, nouns are not 'naturally' significant.[14]

The argument used here is from experience (that of the Barbarians and the Greeks), not from the realm of logic or metaphysics. Also well-known is his argument about the moral(s) of society: every people have different moral standards, ergo there is not a common morality 'by nature.' Furthermore, the argumentation 'by nature' can be but treacherous for the dogmatic because of the experience of good and bad, or according to his words:

> For those who hold the opinion that things are good or bad by nature are perpetually troubled. When they lack what they believe to be good, they take themselves to be persecuted by natural evils [...].[15]

Empiricism as a school and as a medical practice is not confined to ancient philosophy and medicine, it has a long history in the Middle Ages, Renaissance, and early modern period. Beginning with the schools of Roger Bacon and William of Ockham in Middle Ages, its apex occurred in the late Renaissance with Machiavelli and Guicciardini. Yet, from the *De rerum natura iuxta propria principia* (*On the Nature of Things According to their Own Principles*) by Bernardino Telesio in 1586 and Michel de Montaigne's "On Experience"[16] to Francis Bacon onwards, empiricism experienced new modes of transmission and discussion. Luzzatto's acquaintance with it may derive from his study of Pierre Gassendi, a very probable source of his writing and perhaps a favourite reading.[17] Additionally, Francis Bacon was one of the sources of Luzzatto's attitude towards the sciences, mostly plausibly his first address for the doctrine of the induction. Francis Bacon is often indirectly quoted in the *Discorso*, as I have demonstrated elsewhere.[18]

---

14 Sextus Empiricus, *Against the Professors*, I:VII, §144–145 (Loeb, 1949, 86–87).
15 Sextus Empiricus, *Outlines of Pyrrhonism* I:27; see also I:30. Cf. Michael Frede, "The Sceptic's Beliefs," in *The Original Sceptics: A Controversy*, eds. Myles Burnyeat and Michael Frede (Indianapolis: Hackett, 1997): 22.
16 Michel de Montaigne, "Of Experience," ed. Patrick Madden, trans. Charles Cotton (1588; 13 September, 2006). http://essays.quotidiana.org/montaigne/experience/ (accessed 3 May, 2018).
17 Cf. Giuseppe Veltri, "Opere e pensiero di Simone Luzzatto," in Luzzatto, *Scritti politici e filosofici:* LXXX.
18 Giuseppe Veltri, "Economic and Social Arguments and the Doctrine of the Antiperistasis in Simone Luzzatto's Political Thought: Venetian Reverberations of Francis Bacon's Philosophy," *Frühneuzeit-Info* 23 (2011): 23–32.

2 Luzzatto's Strategies and the *Tropoi* of Sextus

Concerning the strategies of Luzzatto it is valuable to foreground some observations before we handle them in detail. In the *Discorso*, the rabbi uses some strategies to abate dogmatic principle (read: main, current, and influential opinions). The reader may be sceptical about my approach in this book on Luzzatto's language of scepticism and relative strategies. While it is true that the *tropoi* are indirect, they are the basic elements of the *Socrate*, as Michela Torbidoni has demonstrated,[19] and, in the *Discorso*, the Rabbi twice directly quotes Sextus Empiricus, on both occasions from the *tropoi*, which I would call strategies of scepticism.

In the first quotation, he speaks of moral scepticism, attacking Tacitus's calumny 'to defame the Jewish Nation,' painting it as dissolute in its carnal impulses: 'and although as a race, they are prone to lust, they abstain from intercourse with foreign women; yet among themselves nothing is unlawful.'[20] He adds:[21]

> But if this refers to the customs of the Jews, it could not be further from the truth, since there has never been a nation more restricted regarding carnal relationships than the Jews. The Egyptians, who were by no means barbarians, but in fact passed on many doctrines to the Greeks, took their sisters for wives, and the Ptolemaic kings set an example [of this habit] to the common people. The Persians, who enjoyed dominion over Asia and the subjugation of Greece, passed to a higher level of turpitude, permitting sons to wed their own mothers. Chrysippus, the propagator of Stoic philosophy, claimed that he was responsible for the reform of the human race. And yet he remained indifferent in the face of such a detestable practice; on the contrary, by means of some of his reasoning he sought toss describe it as almost honest, as one can read in the books of Sextus Empiricus.[22]

The argumentation is here highly imperative: Luzzatto's defence of Jewish custom neither takes into consideration the (im)morality of an act commanded by the God of the Jews (to refrain from intercourse with foreign women), thereby avoiding a return to the argument of a heteronomous moral act, nor does he found it on morality based on 'nature.' He infers the immorality from the discrepancy with the high esteem in which other peoples in the world community (Egyptian and Greeks) were held despite their incestuous and lascivious customs. With reference to the above listed sexual practices, Luzzatto states that the moral code of the Jews is more restrictive than that of Egyptian and Greeks, although they are judged as 'barbarians' despite their probity. This is not a dogmatic argument, but a strategy taken from experience grounded in moral scepticism and relativism. The Sextian argument against natural

---

19 Michela Torbidoni, "Il metodo del dubbio nel Socrate," in *Filosofo e Rabbino nella Venezia del Seicento. Studi su Simone Luzzatto (ca.1583–1663). Con un'appendice di documenti inediti dall'Archivio di Stato*, ed. Giuseppe Veltri (Rome: Aracne, 2015): 183–245.
20 Tacitus, *Historiae* V:5.
21 Luzzatto, *Discorso*, 59v–60r.
22 Sextus Empiricus, *Outlines of Pyrrhonism* I:152 and 160.

morality was very similar: he quoted several examples of different customs in decisive moral acts like sexuality, which differed among Romans, Greek, Indians etc., an argument rooted in a multifaceted approach to law and custom.[23] Luzzatto emphasises a particular element: the high esteem in which some cultures were held despite their even more radical difference in morality, e.g. the Egyptians enjoy our elevated cultural esteem despite their flagrant, according to our standards, immorality.

The second direct quotation is more complicated because he, speaking of the phenomenon of the Kabbalah, associates the 10 principles (the Sefirot) and their flux to some ideas of the Platonic system of object and motion. It is not my intention here to analyse the strategies of the anti-kabbalistic essay of Luzzatto, already examined by Bill Rebiger in the *Yearbook* of 2017,[24] but only his *ars relationis* of the Sefirot, their relation and Plato's world of the ideas. Luzzatto writes:

> Plato, however, adhering in part to the said opinion, yet in a calmer manner, was not satisfied with entirely denying the existence and permanence of the being of whatever thing. For he conjectured that beyond the apprehension of our senses there were some firm and fixed substances. [According to his view,] these substances need neither a confrontation nor a relation to others, and thus could have a stable and firm existence in themselves. Furthermore, these [substances] were the origins of those apprehensions that we perceive and could be called shadows and unsubstantial appearances. This is the doctrine he affirms in his Letters,[25] which involves a great application of mind and a great force of intellect to apprehend a thing as pure, genuine, and bared of the commingling of relation and motion. For every object is burdened and wrapped up in these. This is what Sextus Empiricus demonstrated, i.e. that every phenomenon and object is mixed and involved in five kinds of relations. Proceeding in his examination, he even demonstrated that it is almost impossible to grasp anything about objects other than their relation. This thing [the relation] would be so feeble and slight that the Stoics, and after them the Nominalists, negated its existence, [by saying that] it was chimerical and imaginary, or even better, verbal.[26]

The reference to Sextus in confirming a Platonic view of the system of the ideas and their relationship is tricky because Sextus does negate the existence of all fixed and firm substances. It is enough to refer here to *Outlines of Pyrrhonism* III:3:

> Now, since some of the Dogmatists say that god is a body, others that he is incorporeal, some that he is anthropomorphic, others not, some in space, others not—and of those who say that he is in space, some say that he is within the universe, others that he is outside it—how shall we be able to acquire a conception of god if we possess neither an agreed substance for him nor a form nor a place in which he is?

---

[23] Sextus Empiricus, *Outlines of Pyrrhonism*, I:152: 'We oppose custom to the others—for example, to law, when we say that in Persia homosexual acts are customary, while in Rome they are forbidden by law.'
[24] Bill Rebiger, "Sceptical Strategies in Simone Luzzatto's Presentation of the Kabbalists in his *Discorso*," in *Yearbook of the Maimonides Centre for Advanced Studies* 2017, ed. Bill Rebiger (Berlin and Boston: De Gruyter, 2017): 51–69.
[25] Luzzatto probably refers to the 7th Epistle of Plato.
[26] Luzzatto, *Discorso*, 81v-82r.

But that is only one side of the question because Luzzatto connects the theory of the Sefirot to Plato's world of substances. Besides the tradition of this theory, already examined by Moshe Idel,[27] Luzzatto's strategic aspect cannot be concealed: fixed substances have a firm existence in themselves and therefore cannot be apprehended if not in their shadowy and unsubstantial appearances. According to Luzzatto's rendition of Sextus 'every phenomenon and object is mixed and involved in five kinds of relations.' He concludes 'that it is almost impossible to grasp anything about objects other than their relation.' As Emidio Spinelli wrote to me in an epistolary communication, Luzzatto may be referring here to the sceptic Agrippa. Sextus reported Agrippas' *tropoi*,[28] among them that of relativity, in his *Outlines of Pyrrhonism*.[29] The confusion has probably resulted, I imagine, because Agrippas' five modes are quoted by Sextus, as mentioned before.

Yet, as Spinelli comments, Sextus also speaks of the relativity in *Outlines of Pyrrhonism* I:38–39 as a hierarchical submission of all *tropoi* to it. Expressly in *Outlines of Pyrrhonism* I:140, he affirms:

> So, since we have established in this way that everything is relative, it is clear that we shall not be able to say what each existing object is like in its own nature and purely, but only what it appears to be like relative to something. It follows that we must suspend judgement about the nature of objects.

Ancient authors convey that Pyrrhonians were also relativists,[30] but an assimilation of their thoughts is not without problems, as Annas and Barnes sustain.[31] The *pros ti* of relations/relativity is also a topic of Stoic philosophy, as Luzzatto notes, which introduces or sustains the insubstantiality of relation in the cases of verbal definition, as 'father' is father so long as he has a child, as Simplicius, in his *Commentary* on Aristotle's *Categories* comments.[32]

---

27 That is, Isaac Abravanel; cf. Moshe Idel, "Jewish Kabbalah and Platonism," in *Neoplatonism and Jewish Thought*, ed. Lenn E. Goodman (Albany: State University of New York Press, 1992): 332–333. He speaks of the Sefirot as Platonic ideas and 'separate universal forms.' Yoḥanan Alemanno also speaks of the Sefirot as the primordial ideas of Plato.
28 Sextus Empiricus, *Outlines of Pyrrhonism* I:164–177: "The Five Modes."
29 See Emidio Spinelli, *Questioni scettiche. Letture introduttive al pirronismo antico* (Rome: Lithos, 2005), 32–33.
30 Cf. Julia Annas and Jonathan Barnes, *The Modes of Scepticism: Ancient Texts and Modern Interpretations* (Cambridge: Cambridge University Press, 1997), 97.
31 Ibidem, 98.
32 Cf. ibidem, 134–135: 'But when it is observed not in virtue of an internal difference but solely in virtue of its relation to something else, it will be a thing somehow in relation to something. Sons and people on the right require certain external things for their subsistence. That is why, even if no change takes place in themselves, a man may cease to be a father when his son dies and someone may cease to be on the right when what was next to him has changed position.' The interpretation of Annas and Barnes does not take into account the oral element of stoic discourse.

Luzzatto likes to demonstrate that a precise analysis of relations results in the conclusion that we cannot grasp the object of anything. The goal of his sentence is the negation of the dogmatic assertion of the existence of Plato's substances and, in this way, the Sefirot. From given relations we cannot infer a given substance.

It is important here to realise that sceptical strategies are at work in the *Discorso*, especially because Luzzatto considers himself in step with Sextus' scepticism, although he defines himself a New Academician and, therefore, not a Pyrrhonian. In the following section I will present some sceptical strategies present in Luzzatto's work, all of which are based on experience and achieved in history and society. Nevertheless, I suppose that Luzzatto is also using the *tropoi*, or strategy, of Sextus and Agrippa, using it as a political tool for describing, defending, and apologising for the Jews of Venice. I will select the political strategies of relation/relativity, recess, and necessity, and end with the argument concerning the 'nude truth.'

3 The Strategy of Relation/Relativity

Sextus Empiricus and Agrippa[33] agree—as I discuss above—that things are together by virtue of their relation and not due their nature. We will return to this idea with reference to usury. Here I would like to stress that the 'relationship' between the elements of society is the backbone of its political structure, as well as the commitment of Luzzatto to the apologia. The presence of the Jews in Venice is due to their integration into every part of its fabric and life. Integration is not the deprivation of their factuality as Jews (i.e. conversion) but the recognition of their very clear position in society. This participation is not substantial but relative to the 'state of the Jews in Venice.' But first something on the *Discorso*.

Luzzatto's political thesis in the first part of the *Discorso* is simple and, at the same time, temerarious: Venice can put an end to its political decline, he argues, by offering to the Jews a monopoly on overseas commercial activity. This proposal recommends itself because the Jews are 'well suited for trade,' far more so than others (such as 'foreigners'). The Rabbi opens his argument by recalling that trade and usury are the only occupations permitted to Jews. Within the confines of their historical situation, the Venetian Jews became particularly adept at trade with partners from the Orient. This talent could be put to the use by the Venetian government for maintaining—or, more accurately—recovering its political importance as an intermediary between the East and the West. Luzzatto was the first to define the role of the Jews on the basis of their economic and social functions, disregarding the classic categorisation of Judaism's (privileged?) religious status in world history.

---

[33] A Pyrrhonian philosopher probably of the first century BCE and author of five *tropoi*, reported by Sextus, *Outlines of Pyrrhonism* I:164–169.

Luzzatto prefaces his treatise with an "Introduction,"[34] ostensibly intended to provide a theoretical outline of the political and economic aspects of his subject, a reflection also of his vision of the customs and ways of life followed by the Jews of the Diaspora. In this introduction to the 'whole' tractate, he deals, in fact, with only *one* issue: the status of the Jews of Venice and their economic situation, which is, in turn, the topic to which the entire first part of the *Discorso* is devoted. Luzzatto clearly states his central thesis right from the outset: the ancient people of the Jews, present today in the illustrious city of Venice, are, in their constitution and way of life, a 'fragment' of the God's original creation.[35] Nobody, he claims, can contest the proposition that Venetian Jews are a 'reward' (*emolumento*) to the city of Venice and that they constitute an integral part of the common populace.[36]

The Rabbi of the Ghetto of Venice avails himself of the fragment metaphor: the Jewish community of Venice is as a Democritian atom in the Milky Way of the Venetian *res publica*.[37] Although the Rabbi has serious doubts as to the cosmological value of Democritus' philosophy, he seems to accept its usefulness as a source of metaphor:

> And if this opinion was rightly condemned, what occurred to those men was more a result of the casual coupling of small bodies, which those philosophers proposed, rather than a result of the absurdity of the construction.[38]

The purpose of his treatise is not primarily to celebrate the antiquity of the Jews but rather to present some of the advantages they bring to the State. He considers the Jewish people as an integral part of city of Venice or, better, of the entire world. The function of the Jews, he claims, is similar to that of the atoms of Democritus that populate the 'Lower World,' which, in turn, feeds with its vapour the sun, the moon, and the other stars: a stoic idea. In this sense, every kingdom on the earth is comparable to the galaxy.[39]

The metaphors he uses to describe the composition of society serve to draw attention to two specific points: that every element of society, and in particular that of

---

34 Luzzatto, *Discorso*, 7r–8r.
35 *Ibidem*, 6v: 'because the common consensus among men agrees that there was a time when this People took their form of government and social institutions from the Highest Artist.'
36 *Ibidem*, 7v.
37 *Ibidem*, 7r.
38 *Ibidem*. Luzzatto seems here to refer to a criticism of atomistic theory, which was introduced into European intellectual circles by Gassendi. Luzzatto himself was a follower of sceptical theory. On Gassendi and scepticism, see Richard H. Popkin, *The History of Scepticism from Erasmus to Spinoza* (Berkeley: University of California Press, 1979).
39 Cf. Francis Bacon, *Essays XIX: Of Empire:* 'Princes are like to heavenly bodies, which cause good or evil times; and which have much veneration, but no rest. All precepts concerning kings, are in effect comprehended in those two remembrances: memento quod es homo; and memento quod es Deus, or vice Dei; the one bridleth their power, and the other their will.' On the classical origin of the idea, see A. I. Ellis, "Some Notes," *The Classical Review* 23 (1909): 246–247.

Venice, should be fully integrated as a prerequisite to their contribution to the welfare of the whole. That is also the logic of the human body as Luzzatto expressly indicates, citing indirectly the fable of Menenius Agrippa:[40]

> [...] So too when our stomach suffers from lack of food, it lives on suitable humours with great pain and distress of other limbs.[41] But when the opposite occurs, and there is an abundance of nourishment, there is respite from the plundering, and this relief spreads to other parts of the body. Similarly, the preponderance of duties and passage taxes not only frees the populace from the burden of taxes and contributions—which they would be obliged to pay in emergencies and for the needs of the Prince—but also itself profits of this abundance of public money with not little advantage.[42]

In sixteenth century, the metaphor of the stomach becomes more specific: in 1612 Francis Bacon writes in his *Of Empire* 11:

> For their merchants, they are vena porta; and if they flourish not, a kingdom may have good limbs, but will have empty veins, and nourish little. Taxes and imposts upon them, do seldom good to the king's revenue; for that that wins in the hundred, he leeseth in the shire; the particular rates being increased, but the total bulk of trading, rather decreased.[43]

Luzzatto substantially agrees with Bacon. Taxes on imports and exports are lethal for an economy because they lead to a decrease in trade volume. In the end, the state treasury will end up with little more than usual. In addition, there is a moral aspect that should be also taken into consideration: the state should avoid imitating the ancient Romans who 'ultimately imposed taxes on human excrement [...] and even disgraceful and obscene operations such as these helped enrich the treasury.'[44] In contrast to this depravity on the part of the ruling power, the Republic of Venice 'has the custom of imposing taxes only on the industry of men, and not on their lives; to punish their vices, and not to profit from them.'[45] We have here, then, the principal ingredients of Luzzatto's political theory: 1) the Jews of Venice are an integral part of the Republic; 2) their function in commerce is vital and can be of true benefit only if the taxes imposed remain limited, since the taxes on imports and exports have a lethal effect on the general economy; 3) the Republic of Venice was founded on pragmatic ideas.

---

40 Livius, *Ad urbe condita*, II 32.
41 Galen thought that blood was produced in the liver from the food the stomach transported there via the portal vein. On the state of medicine at this time, based largely Galen, see Rudolph E. Siegel, *Galen's System of Physiology and Medicine: An Analysis of his Doctrines and Observations on Bloodflow, Respiration, Humors and Internal Diseases* (Urbana: University of Illinois Press, 1993).
42 Luzzatto, *Discorso*, 7v.
43 *The Works of Francis Bacon*, vol. 6, eds. James Spedding *et alii* (London: Longman and co., 1857–1874; reprint 2011), 422.
44 Luzzatto, *Discorso*, 8r.
45 *Ibidem*.

We can add that Luzzatto—if using the sceptic *topos* of relativity—argues that the relation of the Jews to the *Serenissima* is a profitable one and that changes to this relation (i.e. their expulsion from Venice) would also change the 'state' of the Jews in Venice, and perhaps also Venice itself.

Another application of the political strategy of relation/relativity can be found in chapter 12 of the *Discorso* in which Luzzatto addresses the criticism of the Jewish presence as voiced by three different groups: religious zealots, politicians and statesmen, and the common people. The religious zealots claim that toleration of a religion that differs from the official faith is contemptuous; politicians argue that there is no utility to tolerating a diversity of religions in the same city, both because of the possibility of sacrilege and because of bad example that one group may provide to the remainder of the population; and the common people simply believe and repeat any calumny and false slander invented out of hatred for the Jewish nation.

In response to the religious zealots, Luzzatto notes that the Pope himself admitted Jews into the city of his own residence, and that they have been living there for over 800 years. To the politicians he offers a very detailed response, stressing the physical separation between Jews and Christians, which is reinforced by Jewish law, according to which ritual contact and sexual relations with non-Jews are prohibited, as is proselytism. As for the crime of usury practiced by the Jews—he adds that it is only tolerated by their laws rather than expressly permitted, referring indirectly to Francis Bacon.

As for the denunciations of the common people, Luzzatto responds:

> Truth alone is harsh, and not very pleasing, whereas falsity is admired and delightful. The former is subjected to the occurrence of events; the latter free and wandering. The former is produced by the action of the object that impressed it in our mind, while the latter depends upon human judgments, and like our offspring, one brings them loving affection.[46]

He then deals more specifically with the calumny of the Jews having been unfaithful, and with their purported friendship with pirates. Contrary to what his opponents maintain, Luzzatto describes the Jews as a harmonious part of society, living in reciprocal sympathy with their neighbours in keeping with the will of God, who 'decreed that all humanity should conform together in unanimous amity, each man considering himself a citizen of one commonwealth.'[47] Religious differences, as he points out in chapter 14 and as we have analysed in the second part of my book *Alienated Wisdom*, are by no means a good reason for war.[48]

The perspicacious reader recognises here a typical strategy of referring to the successful integration of Jews into the Venetian city and their utility under the sky

---

46 *Ibidem*, 44r.
47 *Ibidem*.
48 *Ibidem*, 51v. Cf. Isaac Abravanel, *Perush al nevi'im aaronim* (Tel Aviv, n.d.): 9; and Johann Maier, *Kriegsrecht und Friedensordnung in jüdischer Tradition* (Stuttgart: Kohlhammer, 2000), 403.

of the *Serenissima*. The reason given is not a dogmatic reference to the Revelation on Sinai, but rather the activity of the Jews, originating in historical necessity. Their success is dependent on the conservation of their status as Jews as well as their utility for Venice;[49] that is, the key for the Jews' integration into Venetian society is to fill and to continue to fulfil the social position they already hold, a kind of political *recess ad infinitum*.

4 Strategy of Necessity, or, How to Explain *recess ad infinitum* Politically

Luzzatto uses a typical political-economic category, 'necessity'. *Necessitas* as a category must not be confused with the Aristotelian logical concept of *necessitas*,[50] and it also occurs in sceptical philosophy: necessity is the reason, according to the sceptical philosophy of Sextus, to suspend every judgment.[51] The context of Sextus' use is totally different, but Luzzatto's logical use of necessity is very similar: to search for the major cause of necessity would regress to an analysis of animals, which do not possess reason. Luzzatto indirectly refers to regress to the causes of the situation of the Jews, because necessity *is* the situation into which humans are born and to which man can positively react, or, according to Luzzatto's wording:

> The majority of men claim that nature has thrust upon them and vexed them with obligations and necessities in greater abundance than other animals which are deprived of reason. But these men [the majority] complain of duty, because poverty and need are the true stimuli and incentives that result in the inventions and discoveries of the most worthy and excellent arts, which so ennoble the human race.[52]

The proverb *mater artium necessitas*, 'necessity is the mother of invention,' has a long tradition. In the Middle Ages, it was an operative concept of the political tradition, used in conjunction with other political terms such as *virtus* and *fortuna*.[53] There is of course a common use of the proverb which probably first appeared in print in 1519 in the *Vulgaria* of William Horman, 'a book of aphorisms for the boys

---

49 On both categories during the Renaissance, see Paul-Erik Korvela, *The Machiavellian Reformation: An Essay in Political Theory* (PhD dissertation, University of Jyvaskyla, 2016), 119–120.
50 Lambert Marie de Rijk, *Aristotle: Semantics and Ontology. Philosophia Antiqua*, vol. 91, no. 1 (Leiden: Brill, 2002), 569; Nathanael Stein, "Causal Necessity in Aristotle," *British Journal for the History of Philosophy* 20 (2012): 855–879.
51 For *Outlines of Pyrrhonism* I:175–176, see Casey Perin, *The Demands of Reason: An Essay on Pyrrhonian Scepticism* (Oxford: Oxford University Press, 2010).
52 Luzzatto, *Discorso*, 18r.
53 On the triad, cf. Felix Gilbert's chapter "Fortune, Necessity, and Virtù" in idem, *Machiavelli and Guicciardini: Politics and History in Sixteenth-Century Florence* (Princeton: Princeton University Press, 1965): 191–200.

of the schools to learn by heart.'⁵⁴ Yet numerous individuals and intellectuals were acquainted with this proverb and its inherent political-philosophical meaning. One such person was Leonardo da Vinci.⁵⁵ The category of necessity, however, did not become a political category with clear-cut criteria until Machiavelli's opus,⁵⁶ to which Luzzatto most likely refers.

According to the Rabbi of Venice and in agreement with the generally accepted history of the Jews since the Middle Ages, trade and money-lending were the only occupations permitted to the Jews. This historical necessity engendered in the Venetian Jews a highly developed capacity for these occupations. Consequently, they were considered by Luzzatto potentially capable of assisting the Venetian government in maintaining, or, to be historically more accurate, *recovering*, a position of political equilibrium between the East and the West. To put this briefly with respect to a very intriguing aspect of the political life of the Jews in Venice: the *Discorso* was published in 1638 in a period in which the political power of Venice was beginning to wane. His philosophical work *Socrate*, published in 1651, expressly refers to the Turkish threat against Crete and to the war in which Venice was involved. Hence, Luzzatto tried to offer the Governor of the *Serenissima* a political-economic prescription to restore the vital trade of Venice by offering the Jews more economic and social freedom.

Bacon's conviction was that 'It is against nature for money to beget money,'⁵⁷ echoing an Aristotelian-Thomistic conviction.⁵⁸ However, that is only a superficial read of Bacon's analysis, vision, and inferences.

---

54 It is very difficult to locate the origin of the proverb. Recent works refer it to Curtius Rufus's *Historia Alexandri Magni*, 4,3,24: 'Efficacior omni arte imminens necessitas;' see Hubertus Kudla, ed., *Lexikon der lateinischen Zitate. 3500 Originale mit Übersetzungen und Belegstellen*, 3rd edition (Munich: Beck, 2007), n. 1439. I think that there is no precise Latin quote, but for a Latin sapiential tradition of it, see all the proverbs on 'necessity' quoted by the *Hoyt's New Cyclopedia of Practical Quotations* (New York: Funk & Wagnalls, 1922), 559; see also the collection of examples of this phrase at http://www.phrases.org.uk./meanings/necessity-is-the-mother-of-invention.html (accessed 3 May, 2018).
55 Cf. *Scritti letterari di Leonardo da Vinci*, ed. Augusto Marinoni (Milan: Rizzoli, 1974), 7: 'La necessità è tema e inventrice della natura, e freno e regola eterna.' See the very interesting philosophical evaluation of the maxim in Herr von Prantl, "Leonardo da Vinci in philosophischer Beziehung," *Sitzungsberichte der königlichen bayerischen Akademie der Wissenschaften zu München. Philosophisch-philologische Classe*. Jahrgang 1885 (Munich: Akademische Buchdruckerei, 1886), 17.
56 On the use of '*necessitas*' in Machiavelli, see *Machiavellism: The Doctrine of Raison D'Aetat and Its Place in Modern History*, trans. Douglas Scott (New Haven: Yale University Press, 1957).
57 Francis Bacon, "Of Usury," in idem, *Essays* (1625); see William Shakespeare, *The Merchant of Venice*, I, 3: 'Antonio. Or is your gold and silver Eues and Rams? Shylock. I cannot tell, I make it breede as fast.' See Francis Bacon, *The Essays or Counsels, Civil and Moral*, ed. Brian Vickers (Oxford: Oxford University Press, 1999), 94.
58 Thomas Aquinas, *Summa Theologica*, trans. Fathers of the English Dominican Province (London: R. T. Washburne, Ltd., 1918), 330–340, reprinted in Roy C. Cave and Herbert H. Coulson, *A Source Book for Medieval Economic History* (Milwaukee: The Bruce Publishing Co., 1936; reprinted, New

An in-depth study of Bacon's conception of usury reveals a more complex attitude which, as we shall see, is similar to that of the Rabbi of Venice. Bacon is adamant in his opposition to usury, and it should be borne in mind that this activity as perceived by Luzzatto and Bacon was not only the act or practice of lending money at an exorbitant rate of interest, but rather simply the practice of lending money at any rate of interest at all.[59] However, the Lord of Verulam was well aware of the advantages of such activities. In his "Essay on Usury," he enumerated the advantages and disadvantages of usury, including the danger of capitalisation:

> The fourth [disadvantage of usury is], that it bringeth the treasure of a realm, or state, into a few hands. For the usurer being at certainties, and others at uncertainties, at the end of the game, most of the money will be in the box; and ever a state flourisheth, when wealth is more equally spread.[60]

Luzzatto also refers to an ideal situation of greater equality, always desired but never attained. He states:

> [T]he aspiration to a rigorous reduction of one's possessions to a moderate size has been considered a desirable undertaking to this day, but it is hardly ever practiced, especially with regard to the equal distribution of moveable assets and cash. Whenever this was attempted with real estate, the result was for the most part unsuccessful.[61]

Bacon's position is in fact very pragmatic: whoever thinks that one can lend money without profit belongs *ipso dicto* to the realm of utopian dreamers:

> It is a vanity to conceive, that there would be ordinary borrowing without profit; and it is impossible to conceive, the number of inconveniences that will ensue, if borrowing be cramped. Therefore, to speak of the abolishing of usury is idle. All states have ever had it, in one kind or rate, or other. So as that opinion must be sent to Utopia.[62]

York: Biblo & Tannen, 1965), 182. Walter S. H. Lim, "Surety and Spiritual Commercialism in *The Merchant of Venice*," *Studies in English Literature* 50.2 (2010): 371.

59 Cf. Benjamin Ravid, "Money Lending in Seventeenth-Century Jewish Vernacular Apologetica," in *Jewish Thought in the Seventeenth Century*, eds. Isadore Twersky and Bernard Septimus (Cambridge: Harvard University Press, 1987): 262.

60 See above n. 58 for the reference.

61 Luzzatto, *Discorso*, 25v: 'Ma il volere con rigore ridure li haveri a segno di moderata proporzione, fu impresa sin ora desiderata, ma non giamai praticata, e massime l'uguaglianza de beni mobili, e danari contanti, e se fu alcuna volta attentata nelli beni stabili riuscì sempre con infelice successo' (English translation by Ariella Lang).

62 Bacon, *The Works*, vol. 14, 416. Cf. *The English Renaissance: An Anthology of Sources and Documents*, ed. Kate Aughterson (London: Routledge, 1998), 548; Robert Appelbaum, *Literature and Utopian Politics in Seventeenth-Century England* (Cambridge: Cambridge University Press, 2002), 4.

Luzzatto also refers to Thomas More's *Utopia* as concretisation of the 'machinate repubbliche' ('ingenious republics') of Socrates and Plato, where the distribution of goods was the chief element of their political thought.[63] Bacon sums up his opinion on the re-integration of usury, stating that it should be reserved for a small group under government control: For 'it is better to mitigate usury, by declaration, than to suffer it to rage, by connivance.'[64] In his response to some criticisms of money lending, made both by philosophers and statesmen, Luzzatto uses the same argument as advanced by Bacon, focussing on the stimulus generated by the moneylenders:

> [...] usury is a sin constantly condemned, but in every time and place practiced. For two stimuli of our fragility, contribute to it: the necessity of those who need the money and therefore give the interest, and the avidity of the moneylender. When such a transgression was not committed by a Jew, there was perhaps no lack of others, who with greater extortion of the poor and needy would practice such a contemptible profession, reducing the number of usurers. And I do not say this to defend such actions, but merely to demonstrate that such enormity, like some others, is not an essential property of the Jews, as many presume to assert; rather it is an accidental result that comes from the strictness of the life and conditions of the time.[65]

The reader acquainted with sceptical strategies will have already recognised here the argument against an *essential* property of the Jews (that is, 'is not an essential property of the Jews;' also see Sextus' usage of 'by nature') and the recurrence of the strategy of infinite regress as factual relation used in political discourse: If agent A^1 does not do a practise P, there will be an A^2 which will do P. The argumentation does not presuppose a direct causality between A^1 viz. A^n and P, but it implies the experienced fact P which requited a non-essential but accidental relation to P. The only experienced fact is P, the agent A which/who produces P is only accidental and therefore theoretically infinite. The relation from P to A is not essential, therefore it leads to A^n.

---

63 Luzzatto, *Discorso*, 22r–v: 'La massa degli huomini mentre non fosse stata dalla prudente diligenza di legislatori, e formatori di governi civili, distinta in varii ordini, e differenti classi rassembrarebbe maggior diformità che l'antico, e decantato cahos all'imaginatione de poeti giamai rappresentasse. Socrate, e Platone, nelle loro machinate republiche posero tal distribuitione, come principale elemento delle loro politie, e l'istesso osservò il moderno inventore della Utopia, et il simile ancora eseguirono tutti li praticanti, come parimente Aristotile nel primo della Politica, ch'impiegò ogni suo spi|rito in riordinare, e correggere le divisioni fatte da quelli doi gran maestri dell'umanità.'
64 Bacon, *On Usury*, XLI.
65 Luzzatto, *Discorso*, 42r–v: '[...] usura, peccato continuamente dannato, ma in ogni tempo e loco essercitato, concorrendovi due stimoli maggiori, ch'habbia la nostra fragilità, la necessità del mutuario che contribuisce l'usura, e l'avidità insaziabile del mutuante, che la riceve, e quando non fusse commessa dall'hebreo tal transgressione, non vi mancarebbeno forsi altri, che con maggior estorsione dell'indigente, e bisogno, essercitassero tal prava professione, riducendosi a minor numero gl'usurarii' (English translation by Ariella Lang).

5 Moral Scepticism, or, Stoic Teaching in Sceptical Dress: The *Charakteres*

Chapter 11 of the *Discorso* marks the beginning of its second part. Luzzatto begins by observing, with Socrates, that the human being is nothing but 'a multiplicity of different animals, wrapped and entangled within themselves.'[66] Luzzatto refers to letter CXIII by Seneca *ad Lucilium* in which he purposely mentions the stoic doctrine of the multiple or animal soul in human beings, because virtues can only be animal in nature: *virtutes esse animalia*.[67] The statement *virtutes esse animalia* goes back, according to the Stoic fragments, probably to Chrysippus.[68] Luzzatto wishes to find a philosophical connection to affirm that the human soul is a mixture. He indirectly cites the theory of *omomerie* (ὁμοιομέρειαι) by Anaxagoras, that is to say of the principles or roots of cosmological anthropological compositions forming a mixture in the body:

> And if Anaxagoras, who denied that natural things are generated and because of this he introduced a certain confused mass composed of all things, and who judged that in all things there is another one annexed and attached, an opinion considered as absurd, had a similar thing proposed about human soul, may be his opinion would have been received with more applause by the learned, because if one considered attentively the movements of the soul, it would appear as a universal mixture of infinite things.[69]

Luzzatto's main objective is not so much contemplation about the composition of human personality, but rather discussion of the theme of virtue and vice in human beings. What follows is in fact a long passage on virtues and their obverse as individual characteristics in different moments and different locations:

---

66 *Ibidem*, 35v: '[Socrate] pronunziò non sapere se egli fosse un solo animale, overo una moltiplicità di diversi in se stessi anodati, ed invilupati, talmente trovava in se medesimo confuse le virtù, e li vizii, li eccessi, e le moderazioni.'

67 Seneca, *ad Luciulium espistolae morales*, liber XIX, CXIII,3: [2] 'Animum constat animal esse, cum ipse efficiat ut simus animalia, cum ab illo animalia nomen hoc traxerint; virtus autem nihil aliud est quam animus quodam modo se habens; ergo animal est. Deinde virtus agit aliquid; agi autem nihil sine impetu potest; si impetum habet, qui nulli est nisi animali, animal est. [3] "Si animal est" inquit "virtus, habet ipsa virtutem." Quidni habeat se ipsam? quomodo sapiens omnia per virtutem gerit, sic virtus per se. "Ergo" inquit "et omnes artes animalia sunt et omnia quae cogitamus quaeque mente conplectimur. Sequitur ut multa millia animalium habitent in his angustiis pectoris, et singuli multa simus animalia aut multa habeamus animalia." Quaeris quid adversus istud respondeatur? Unaquaeque ex istis res animal erit: multa animalia non erunt. Quare? dicam, si mihi accommodaveris subtilitatem et intentionem tuam. [4] Singula animalia singulas habere debent substantias; ista omnia unum animum habent; itaque singula esse possunt, multa esse non possunt.'

68 *Stoicorum veterum fragmenta*, vol. 3, ed. Hans F. von Arnim (Stuttgart: Teubner, 1964), 75; Stobaeus Ecl. 64,18 and 65,1; see also Thomas G. Rosenmeyer, *Senecan Drama and Stoic Cosmology* (Berkeley: University of California Press, 1989), 96.

69 Luzzatto, *Discorso*, 36r.

The courage of living an adventurous life often derives from the fear one has of vulgar whispers and gossips, as on the contrary Fabius, cowardly in attacking Hannibal but intrepid scorner of the tongue of the plebeians, the greediness of prolonging life and enjoying its pleasures putting the weak but durable avidities before the vehement and short ones, makes us tempered and moderate: whereas Socrates following Plato who discovered in his Phaedo this great arcane called morality that the moderates, 'intemperantia quadam temperantes sint, e cosi timiditate forte sint,' and Solomon in Ecclesiastes c. 4 said, 'et contemplatus sum omnem laborem, et omnem rectitudinem operum, et ecce ipsa esse invidia hominis de socio suo,' as in Hebrew; that is to say that the vulgar virtues are envy, competition and emulation keeping men close to one another, confusing in the way virtues and vices.

[36v] Pleasure, the principal and most attractive object of our soul, is always mixed together with pain, its contrary, as Plato demonstrates in Philebus, hunger and thirst are the major condiments for out taste, tragic representations move us and produce in us indignation against tyrants, nevertheless we feel a certain hidden pleasurable itch and irritation, which amuses and captures us; the Jews express pleasure with the word תענוג which derives from the verb ענה which also means affliction and therefore confirms the above mentioned mixture.

The impulsive agitation of rage was commended by Homer as full of pleasantness and sweetness, in the same way in the fervour of love jealousy gets generated and therefore hate, as Tacitus said about Mount Lebanon mirum dictu tantos inter ardores opacum fidumque niuibus. Alexander, famous for his victories not less than for the virtues of his soul, so compassionate toward Darius and his women, was afterwards so inhuman against Parmenion and Clitus, who had put the dominion of the world in his hands, and also so cruel with Callisthenes, his master. Julius Caesar, ferocious and inhuman in Pharsalia but clement with Marcellus and indulgent with Brutus, his assassin. Nero, a monster for all times, sometimes was displeased by the fact that he was able to write, especially when he had to sentence criminals to death, even though he did not hesitate in applying it against his own mother [37r] and against Seneca, his master; he was a friend of virtue and doctrine but he hated those characters in others, and for that the most humorous of the poets who ever existed, Lucan, lost his life. At the time of the cruel proscription ordered by the triumvirate, where faith, charity and gratitude were exiled from the most eminent and well composed spirits of the republic, because these virtues could not be found in fathers, children and sibling, they took refuge among the abjections of the serfs and the obscenity of the harlots; among many, one of them suffered the last torments in order not to reveal the names of her dishonest friends. Socrates in the height of his wisdom found ignorance, and was therefore judged by the very wise oracle. Little irritated meekness becomes untamed haughtiness, and this, with masterful dexterity, converts itself in meek and flexible pleasantness.[70]

The careful reader has probably recognised part of the catalogue of the second book of Aristotle's *Rhetoric:* pleasure-pain, rage-meekness, friendship-hate, fear-courage, shame-shamelessness, compassion-disdain, envy-emulation. This list has a particular purpose: to demonstrate the multifaceted dimensions of the human soul. In the words of our character:

> The internal image of our soul is composed of a mosaic which apparently forms a single idea, but once it approaches, it shows how it is accompanied by various fragments and vile little and precious stones connected and committed together. In the same way, our soul is mostly com-

---

70 *Ibidem*, 36r-37r.

posed by different and divergent pieces; in various occasions each one of them shows itself with a different appearance. Therefore, describing the nature and condition of a single man is very hard and difficult, and even more so is the will to refer his actions and ideas to a single norm. This explains why so many authors can be found [37v] who have written on the nature of horses, dogs and falcons, and who have devised with such an exactitude their customs and conditions, while very few have wanted to deal with men, and even so only in passing. The one who talked about them better was Theophrastus, Aristotle's disciple, who reserved the enterprise for the last years of his life as he was already eighty years old, and compiled a historical treatise about it with observations on the characters of the human soul; a fragment of his work made it all the way down to us, the rest was destroyed by the inclemency of times.[71]

Luzzatto refers here to Theophrastus of Eresos, author of *Charakteres*, a series of characterisations of the human soul. Angelo Ambrogini, nicknamed Poliziano, translated the first fifteen characters into Latin. These characters were published in Basel in 1532 by Andreas Cratander and did not feature Poliziano as the translator.[72] They were published again, this time with Poliziano's name, in Paris in 1583 by Frédéric Morel. Already in 1552 an edition of these works by Aldo Manuzio, with eight more characters added, had appeared thanks to the efforts of Giovanni Battista Camozza. In 1599, a second edition, titled *Caratteri*, was published in Leiden, including five more characters (21–28). This edition was discovered by Isaac Casaubon and copied once more by Marquard Freher. In 1620, Ansaldo Cebà[73] published an Italian version of the first fifteen characters, probably without taking into consideration Manuzio's edition, possibly because, as Romizi believes, he was too young to know of it. In any case, he does not utilise the 1552 edition. Cebà's book was, however, present in Venice, as the ancient catalogue of the Marciana Library reveals. This publication most likely circulated even in the Venetian Ghetto because at that time Cebà, a priest, had an epistolary love affair with a famous poet of Jewish origins, Sara Copio Sullam, who we have previously discussed.[74]

The Venetian Rabbi's objective is now evident: referring not only to Aristotelian rhetoric or to Theophrastus' composition, he underlines a very popular rhetorical device of that time: the use of typical characters of seventeenth-century theatre.[75] This representation of the affects of the human soul, and of its different characters, was a sign of distinction in a century of comedies and tragedies performed and sung on the stage. It will be exactly the above mentioned Cebà who publishes a detailed commentary to accompany Theophrastus' text. Something which does not escape the attentive reader is that emphasising the theatrical character of human soul also means

---

71 *Ibidem*, 37r-v.
72 I refer the reader to my source for this paragraph, Andreas Cratander, *I caratteri Morali di Teofrasto*, ed. Augusto Romiti (Florence: Sansoni, 1899), which is the critical edition of the Greeek text with Italian translation and notes.
73 Ansaldo Cebà, *I Charatteri morali di Teofrasto interpretati per Ansaldo Cebà*, ed. Cardinale Federigo Borromeo (Genoa: Pavoni, 1620).
74 Cf. Giuseppe Veltri, *Renaissance*, 226–247.
75 Cf. Silvia Carandini, *Teatro e spettacolo nel Seicento* (Rome: Laterza, 1990).

negating objective responsibility: everyone is an actor on the *theatrum mundi* stage, always playing at a passion/affection or its reverse.

Conclusion: Reluctant and Nude Truth

At the end of this section of which the intent was to illustrate only some aspects of the *Discorso*, I would like to conclude with a central concept of Luzzatto's apologia of Jewish life in Venice: the 'reluctant and nude truth.'

Just at the beginning of the small treatise, the Rabbi ventures to present an image of Judaism that goes beyond prejudices and atavistic hatred. It is specifically addressed to the 'cultori dell'invita verità.' Exactly what is meant by this expression, which was used in the dedication, is not clear at first sight. Earlier translators have preferred to consider it as a misprint and to amend the text to 'invicta verità' ('unconquerable truth'). There is, however, no need to change the wording of the text, which in translation sounds.

> I dare to bring this work, neglected and stripped of ornate diction, to your noble attention, while indeed being aware that lovers of reluctant Truth appreciate simplicity. For [this reluctant truth] takes the greatest delight in [its] very nakedness. I do not claim [3v] undeserved favour, nor extorted applause from you, as I recognize how unworthy and unmerited it would be; but I plead for the most candid and honest judgment of the issues discussed.[76]

The concept of 'reluctant truth' fits very well into the system of Luzzatto's political. Lovers of the 'reluctant/unwilling' truth accept it, regardless of the form in which it may be propagated. In Luzzatto's own words:

> Therefore, with a minimum of talent that divine majesty granted me, I proposed to compose a concise but truthful account of this nation's principal rites and most commonly shared opinions, which are not dissonant or discrepant from the universal ones. In writing this text, I tried with all of my powers (even though I am from the same nation) to abstain from any emotionality or passion that could make me deviate from the truth. Thus I hope to meet discreet readers, who, void of any anticipation or troubled judgment, are not about to follow the vulgar custom of only approving and favouring happy and adventurous individuals, and always damning those who are disheartened and afflicted. Rather, with upright judgment they will balance their opinions on the subject, which my imperfection dictated to me, and in saying this I will omit an extended reflection on the antiquity of this race, on its unmixed blood, which has existed for such a long period of time, on the tenacity of this nation's rites and belief, and on its inflexibility during times of oppressions. I will only add to my aforementioned proposal a discussion of some of the profits that the Jewish nation that lives in Venice brings to this illustrious city. With this, I do not intend to offer any ambitious apparatus of profits and gains; rather I only wish to demonstrate that this nation is anything but a useless member of the general population of this city.[77]

---

[76] Luzzatto, *Discorso*, 3r-v. A similar parallel appears in Francis Bacon, *The New Organon*, 14: 'For a naked mind is the companion of innocence and simplicity, as once upon a time the naked body was.'
[77] Luzzatto, *Discorso*, 5r–v.

The author's commitment to his truth should not hide the fact that Luzzatto is not speaking of the Aristotelian principle of non-contradiction, but of the political perception of that condition. His intention is to provide as neutral a portrait of the Jews as possible, describing their presence in Venice and the (economic) advantages they bring. Although himself a member of the Jewish 'nation', a *pars in causa*, he will nevertheless maintain his impartiality. In return for his unbiased presentation of the argument, he expects his readers to form their opinion on the subject without prejudice.

The expression 'nudity of the truth' is very intriguing. The reader of Luzzatto was acquainted with the concept of *nuda veritas* since Horace,[78] but also of its contradictory nature. For the nudity was, obviously, tantamount to purity and simplicity but also implied a lack of defences. The Florentine painter Sergio Botticelli recreated the *Calumny of Apelles*, a lost painting of the Greek painter Apelles, the story of which has been reported or perhaps invented by Lucian.[79] A slander, a rival of Apelles, accused the painter of revolt in front of King Midas:

> On the right sits a man with long ears almost of the Midas pattern, stretching out a hand to Slander, who is still some way off, but coming. About him are two females whom I take for Ignorance and Assumption. Slander, approaching from the left, is an extraordinarily beautiful woman, but with a heated, excitable air that suggests delusion and impulsiveness; in her left hand is a lighted torch, and with her right she is holding a youth by the hair; he holds up hands to heaven and calls the Gods to witness his innocence. Showing Slander the way is a man with piercing eyes, but pale, deformed, and shrunken as from long illness; one may easily guess him to be Envy. Two female attendants encourage Slander, acting as tire-women, and adding touches to her beauty; according to the cicerone, one of these is Malice, and the other Deceit. Following behind in mourning guise, black-robed and with torn hair, comes (I think he named her) Repentance. She looks tearfully behind her, awaiting shame-faced the approach of Truth. That was how Apelles translated his peril into paint.[80]

In the depiction of Botticelli, the Truth is naked, a nakedness which can have three possible meanings: 1) purity and simplicity, which causes or it is caused by innocence; 2) lack of defence; and 3) extreme difficulty in catching an adversary (e.g. in the Olympic games). While the first and the second possibilities are expressions of weakness and literary 'imbecility' (incapability of fighting and defending oneself),

---

[78] Horace, *Odes and Epodes*, eds. Paul Shorey and Gordon J. Laing (Chicago: Benj. H. Sanborn & Company, 1919), 1.24:
  cui Pudor et Iustitiae soror
  incorrupta Fides nudaque Veritas
  quando ullum inveniet parem?
[79] Cf. Rudolph Altrocchi, "The Calumny of Apelles in the Literature of the Quattrocento," *Modern Language Association* 36.3 (1921): 454–491.
[80] *The Works of Lucian of Samosata*, vol. 4, eds. Henri W. Fowler and Francis G. Fowler (Oxford: The Clarendon Press, 1905), 2–3.

the third one is almost the reverse, revealing the 'sceptic' attitude of a bodily description.

Back to the picture: a very similar 'translation' of a process of judgment into a piece of theatre has been presented by Luzzatto in his *Socrate*, where the theatrical figures of Defamation, Suspicion, Ignorance, Fame, and Custom (as ministers of Authority/Slander) appear.[81] In another passage of the *Socrate*, he comes back to the comparison between truth and nudity.[82] Here he is dealing with the consequences of his attitude to his enquiry 'concerning the cognition of the truth, convinced to suspend and withhold [my] assent.' His hesitation and perplexity lead him 'to consider whether it was a profitable decision to publicly discredit our alleged knowledge.' Disclosing the truth, he maintains, does not always fulfil our interest, like the nudity of our body, although 'the members were masterly constructed by the supreme Nature it often turns out to be indecent that the truth should appear to vulgar men without any ornament.'

The truth of cognition is like nudity, appreciated by lovers but also likely considered indecent by common people. The indirect reference is obviously to Genesis 3 and the creation of the feeling of shame in seeing nudity after the primordial sin. For Luzzatto, this indecency is a feeling of vulgar men, provoked by the nudity of the truth. This indecency can also prompt scepticism concerning the effectiveness of the decision to 'publicly discredit our alleged knowledge.' That is an extreme aspect of sceptical attitude: to be sceptical about one's own scepticism.

---

81 Luzzatto, *Socrate*, 6–7: 'Yet, as soon as the traitor [i.e. Authority] had achieved so noble a rank and become impudent through the simple obedience and easy credulity of the stupid folk, it began conspiring against me. Felony went so far that it chased me out of my royal seat and brought and relegated me to a dark and lonely prison. Hence, as I have indeed lost my freedom, it was forbidden to have intercourse with my favourites and thus I became infertile and sterile [...] Indeed, it came so far only by means of sumptuous cloths, authoritative bearings, frowning, intimidating glances, furrowing its brows, concise and ambiguous words, brief and reluctant conversations, contemptuous and delusory manners, obstinate and Custom, both of them promoters of its acclaims and commendations.' Also *ibidem*, 65: 'retinenza di giuditio, tanto da miei adversarii calunniata, et al Vostro spettabile tribunale acramente hora accusata;' cf. *ibidem* 74, 77, and 299 (of the Italian original).
82 *Ibidem*, 256 (of the Italian original).

Oded Schechter
Spinoza's Miracles: Scepticism, Dogmatism, and Critical Hermeneutics

Introduction

An old riddle, which was first formulated by Leo Strauss,[1] has resurfaced in the last decade, capturing the imagination of several prominent scholars:[2] is Spinoza's interpretation of miracles consistent with his literal sense hermeneutics? A review of the rhetoric used by several scholars when depicting this problem provides sufficient evidence in order to indicate the fundamentality of the philosophical beliefs that this puzzlement undermines. Thus, Warren Zev Harvey speaks about it in terms of 'enigmatic statements,'[3] stating that 'Spinoza is *playing a game*—but what?'[4] Steven Nadler speaks about 'the *perplexity* generated by these *anomalous passages*,'[5] concluding his paper discussing the question in terms of mystery:

> It is still a *mystery* why Spinoza believes, as he argues in chapter six, that as a matter of fact Scripture itself—or, rather, its prophetic authors—when properly interpreted does in fact ascribe natural causes to all events, even those it presents as miracles.[6]

Critical hermeneutics requires the reader to look for the *meaning* of prophecy and biblical teaching within only the biblical text. How can one derive the *meaning* of the biblical prophecy from the Bible itself? The first stage, according to Spinoza, is ach-

---

I am greatly thankful to the anonymous reader, Racheli Haliva, Zev Harvey, Ilil Hoz, Yitzhak Melamed, Amanda Parris, and Stephan Schmid, for their helpful comments.

1 Cf. Steven Nadler, "Scripture and Truth: A Problem in Spinoza's *Tractatus Theologico-Politicus*," *Journal of the History of Ideas* 74.4 (2013): 639, n. 40: 'For a long time, and as far as I could tell, only Leo Strauss took the incongruity of these passages with Spinoza's "whole principle of interpretation, that objective truth may not be used as the key for interpreting Scripture" seriously. But Strauss only concluded that all this shows is "how little Spinoza finds himself at ease in [his] critique of miracles."'
2 Nadler, "Scripture and Truth: A Problem in Spinoza's *Tractatus Theologico-Politicus*," 623–642; Carlos Fraenkel, "Spinoza on Miracles and the Truth of the Bible," *Journal of the History of Ideas* 74.4 (2013): 643–658; Michah Gottlieb, "Spinoza's Method(s) of Biblical Interpretation Reconsidered," *Jewish Studies Quarterly* 14 (2007): 286–317; Warren Zev Harvey, "Spinoza on Biblical Miracles," *Journal of the History of Ideas* 74.4 (2013): 659–675.
3 Harvey, "Spinoza on Biblical Miracles," 659, 673 and 675.
4 Ibidem, 667 (my italics).
5 Nadler, "Scripture and Truth: A Problem in Spinoza's *Tractatus Theologico-Politicus*," 623 (my italics).
6 Ibidem, 641–642 (my italics).

ieved by using his *literal sense* method, i.e. deciphering the *meaning* of biblical prophecy requires us to study the prophetic statement taking its linguistic use as a starting point. If we know how a particular language was used at the specific time of the prophecy, we can reconstruct the its meaning. Spinoza posits his critical hermeneutics in stark contrast to dogmatic hermeneutics, which he defines as any interpretation which deciphers meaning according to the interpreter's own already established philosophical opinions rather than deriving it from the biblical text itself.[7]

Spinoza's hermeneutics is compatible with his *separation thesis;* theology and philosophy are two distinct domains that should not be conflated. Thus, a prophet's claim should not be explicated by means of a philosophical claim, and a philosophical claim should not be addressed in a theological manner. According to the *separation thesis*, regardless of whatever philosophical thesis the prophet holds (even an entirely false one), it does not imply that his *prophecy* contradicts or conflicts with the true philosophical view; the prophet's opinion is as little a part of the theological aspect of his prophecy as, for instance, the length of his hair; the only prophetic teaching is theological, and theological teaching has nothing to do with philosophical teaching.

Now, here is the question that puzzles scholars: when analysed philosophically, Spinoza argues, miracles are absurd and impossible; we would not have expected him to formulate it any differently. However, strangely enough, Spinoza claims that *because* miracles are impossible, we have to interpret the biblical miracles in such a way that the biblical text does not imply anything which is not in accordance with reason. Moreover, Spinoza claims that miracles are, in fact, a philosophical issue, and hence that we should explain the meaning of a prophetic statement in a way which would not result in a contradiction between the philosophical view of miracles and the prophet's view of miracles.

Hence, the riddle that Spinoza's reader is faced with is this: what reason could Spinoza have that would explain his deviation from critical hermeneutics, namely what reason could he have for applying dogmatic hermeneutics to the biblical miracles? Although the riddle focusses on miracles, Harvey claims, in a Straussian spirit, that Spinoza deliberately presented this contradiction in order to teach the reader how the *TTP* should be read as a whole. Harvey compares Spinoza's manner of composing a contradictory text to that of Maimonides in his *Guide*. Other scholars have offered other resolutions,[8] but they all agree that 1) Spinoza's analysis of miracles is

---

[7] I skip the important discussion concerning Spinoza's hermeneutics, as it is not essential for the purpose of this paper. For the sake of the main argument in this paper, I distinguish between *literal sense method* and *critical hermeneutics* as follows: *literal sense method* concerns the *meaning* of specific phrase or passage, whereas *critical hermeneutics* ascertains the prophetic/philosophic nature of the biblical expression or passage.

[8] For an interesting discussion of the different approaches, see Harvey, "Spinoza on Biblical Miracles," 672ff.; Harvey names three types of resolution: the biographical (Strauss and Fraenkel), the harmonizing (Nadler), and the dialectical one (Harvey).

dogmatic to some extent, and 2) the dogmatic interpretation of miracles stands in contrast to his critical hermeneutics, which requires us to study the prophet's view in light of the literal sense rule.

In contrast to this widely shared agreement, I would like to suggest an alternative interpretation which consists of the following theses:
1. Spinoza's analysis of miracles is, in fact, an expression of his *anti-dogmatic* commitments.
2. Spinoza's claim that the prophets were, in fact, committed to the same Spinozian view of miracles is the result of his critical hermeneutics.
3. Spinoza's analysis of miracles can contribute to an understanding of the biblical conception of miracles.

This alternative interpretation will help in resolving the puzzle. The order of presentation I will take in this paper will be:
1. The puzzle: Spinoza's analysis of miracles as a violation of his critical hermeneutics.
2. Miracles as a problem for Spinoza's hermeneutics.
3. Showing Spinoza's way out—Spinoza's hermeneutics actually informs our understanding of biblical miracles.
4. Claiming that Spinoza's analysis of miracles is, in fact, a clear expression of his commitment to anti-dogmatic hermeneutics.

The Puzzle: Spinoza's Analysis of Miracles as a Violation of his Critical Hermeneutics

For the sake of clarity, I will briefly present the link between Spinoza's *separation thesis* and his *literal sense method*. Then, I will present the puzzling deviation of Spinoza's analysis of miracles from his critical hermeneutics.

Critical hermeneutics and the *separation thesis*

Spinoza's critical hermeneutics can be crudely explained as consisting of two parts:
1. Application of the *separation thesis*—theology and philosophy are two distinct domains, distinguished in the following way:
    I) Each has its own source of knowledge: the source of theological knowledge is prophetic revelation, whereas the source of philosophical knowledge is the natural light of reason.
    II) Theology's medium for thinking the world is imagination, whereas philosophy's is reason.
    III) The aim of philosophy is truth, whereas the aim of theology is obedience and piety.

According to the *separation thesis*, the prophetic aspect of the Bible should consist of teachings in which the medium of thinking is imagination. The kind of teaching or knowledge that prophecy conveys has to do with piety and obedience.[9]

2. Literal sense method—the literal sense method enables the reader to separate the theological content of the prophet's expression from its philosophical content. Thus, the critical reader is not bothered by the truth or falsity of the prophet's expressions; the philosophical value of the prophet's opinion does not affect the theological value of prophetic expression, e.g., the prophet's view of God may be invalid philosophically, but entirely valid theologically.

Miracles: a Deviation from Critical Hermeneutics

I will now focus on two central discussions: the first is Nadler's discussion of Spinoza's deviation and the second is Harvey's discussion of Spinoza's *apology*. Let me just briefly elaborate on them.

Nadler's Question: Spinoza's Dogmatic Deviation

Nadler's discussion brings the reader directly to the heart of the problem. Summarising it, he says:

> The issue is why Spinoza believes that Scripture's authentically prophetic authors cannot possibly assert anything about miracles that is 'contrary to reason.'[10]

Let us now examine Spinoza's dogmatic thesis, the argument he provides to support it, and Nadler's question. Concerning the biblical view of miracles, Spinoza says:

> If anything should be found [in scripture] which can be conclusively demonstrated to be contrary to the laws of nature, or to have been unable to follow from them, *we must believe without reservation that it has been added to the Sacred Texts by sacrilegious men. For whatever is contrary to nature is contrary to reason; and what is contrary to reason is absurd, and therefore to be rejected.* (*TTP*, 6 [51]; my italics)

Spinoza's conclusion here is that any passage found in the Bible which conveys the opinion that something happens which is 'contrary to the laws of nature' must be

---

[9] I will skip the discussion as to how the mind's possession of revealed knowledge and the person's disposition to obey this knowledge are actually one and the same according to Spinoza. Spinoza does have an argument in store in favour of this equation, but it is beyond the scope of this paper.
[10] Nadler, "Scripture and Truth: A Problem in Spinoza's *Tractatus Theologico-Politicus*," 639.

considered a corrupt passage. He supports this claim by arguing that 'whatever is contrary to nature is contrary to reason; and what is contrary to reason is absurd.'

Now, does the argument support the thesis? It seems that according to Spinoza's own objection to dogmatic interpretation, his argument does not support his conclusion, since the fact that from the perspective of reason nothing can be contrary to nature does not necessarily entail that the prophet cannot believe that this is exactly the case. Nadler puts this question very convincingly, saying:

> Given everything that Spinoza has said about the nature of prophecy, the content of the prophetic writings, and the interpretation of Scripture, it is very surprising to see him say what he does in passage C.[11] In fact, it would seem to be precisely what he should not say, since it is inconsistent with his overall account of the interpretation of Scripture. His remarks in this passage are something that we might expect from Maimonides or Meijer, but not from Spinoza. According to Spinoza's considered account of Scripture, it is perfectly reasonable to expect the Bible's untutored authors to regard events as having supernatural causes and thus sincerely to narrate them in such a way that they 'contravene the laws of Nature,' or to possess an understanding of things that is 'contrary to reason' and, from reason's perspective, 'absurd'. But the prophets were not intellectually gifted individuals, much less Spinozist philosophers who identify God with Nature. Thus, there is no reason to expect, as a matter of principle, that the prophets believed that every event has a natural cause or can be explained through the laws of nature. Why, then, should it not at least be possible to find 'something in Scripture contrary to the light of Nature' without suspecting the piety of its author? As Spinoza himself says, in his objections to Maimonides's view that 'there is nothing in Scripture which contradicts reason,' 'I insist that Scripture expressly affirms and teaches that God is jealous [. . .] this is contrary to reason.'[12]

Spinoza's thesis here is apparently a dogmatic one; however, his argument does not seem to support his thesis. Moreover, the reason for his deviation is quite puzzling: what could have been his reason for introducing such a dogmatic thesis that explicitly contradicts his own critical hermeneutics and possibly jeopardizes the aim of the *TTP*, namely the *separation thesis*?

Harvey's Questioning of Spinoza's **Apology**

In a passage that Harvey describes as Spinoza's *apology*, Spinoza explicitly addresses our question. Yet Harvey claims that instead of offering an answer, Spinoza's *apology* only expands the question. According to Harvey, Spinoza's *apology* is so puzzling that we must assume that Spinoza was playing a game which needs to be explained in a different way. Let us follow Spinoza's *apology* and Harvey's question. Spinoza's *apology* reads:

---

11 Referring to the passage I have just quoted above.
12 Nadler, "Scripture and Truth: A Problem in Spinoza's *Tractatus Theologico-Politicus*," 637.

> Before I end this chapter, there's something else I want to note. I've proceeded regarding miracles according to a method completely different from the one I followed regarding Prophecy. Concerning Prophecy I affirmed nothing but what I could infer from foundations revealed in the Sacred Texts. But here I've elicited the main points only from principles known to the natural light. I did this deliberately. For since Prophecy surpasses man's power of understanding, and is a purely Theological question, I could affirm nothing about it, nor even know in what it chiefly consisted, except from the foundations which have been revealed. I was compelled to put together a history of Prophecy, and to formulate certain doctrines from it, which would teach me the nature and properties of Prophecy, as far as this can be done. [66] But concerning miracles what we are asking is completely philosophical: can we grant that something happens in nature contrary to its laws, or something which couldn't follow from them? So I didn't need anything like that. (*TTP*, 6 [65–6])

Spinoza is thus completely aware that in his analysis of miracles, he deviates from the critical hermeneutics which he used for the analysis of prophecy. Harvey boldly questions Spinoza's distinction between miracles and prophecy, saying:

> The apologia begins with Spinoza's admission that he has treated the subject of biblical miracles completely differently from that of biblical prophecy. He explains that in discussing prophecy in chapter one he had based himself on 'foundations revealed in Sacred Writ,' for prophecy is a 'purely theological' subject, but in discussing miracles he has based himself on 'foundations known by means of the *lumen naturale*,' for the subject of miracles is 'plainly philosophical.' The *petitio principii* here is so flagrant that it must be supposed to be intentional.
> Spinoza is playing a game—but what? One would have thought that the subjects of prophecy and miracles are for Spinoza very similar. Prophecy may be understood as being rational and natural (e.g., the natural knowledge of the intelligent individual) or imaginary and supernatural (e.g., the visions of the biblical prophets which are said to be 'beyond the limits' of natural knowledge and inexplicable by 'the laws of human nature'); and so too miracles may be understood as being rational and natural (e.g., the extra light at Gibeon was caused by the hail) or imaginary and supernatural (e.g., the light was caused by the sun's standing still in the heavens). Spinoza claims that the subject of prophecy is 'theological' because it 'surpasses human knowledge' (*captum humanum superat*), whereas that of miracles is 'philosophical' because it involves the philosophical question of 'whether we can concede that something may happen in Nature that contravenes its Laws.' However, he might just as easily have said: the subject of prophecy is 'philosophical,' for it involves the philosophical question of whether there can be suprarational knowledge, whereas that of miracles is 'theological,'[13]

Harvey's puzzlement assumes that Spinoza's critical hermeneutics provides no reason to explicate miracles and prophecy differently; if what is at stake is the difference between natural light and supernatural light (reason or imagination), then both prophecy and miracles can be addressed either philosophically or theologically. Spinoza's claim that miracles are the object of philosophy whereas prophecy is the object of theology is as arbitrary as it gets.

I think we are now in a position to summarise the different aspects of the main problem, which is Spinoza's inconsistency: despite his strong commitment to his own

---

13 Harvey, "Spinoza on Biblical Miracles," 666–667.

critical hermeneutics, his analysis of miracles is committed to dogmatic hermeneutics. More specifically, there are two issues:
1. That the prophet's understanding of miracles is compatible with the philosophical one. Thus, in cases where we cannot explain a biblical paragraph concerning miracles in a philosophical way, we have to censor this paragraph.
2. Spinoza's distinction between miracles and prophecy on the basis of reason and the prophetic kind of cognition does not make any sense.

Miracles as a Problem for Spinoza's Hermeneutics

In this part, I will suggest the following thesis: a miracle—when interpreted according to Spinoza's literal sense method—is apparently a significant problem for Spinoza's critical hermeneutics, if we suppose that the latter assumes that the literal sense method and the *separation thesis* are compatible.

In his *apology*, Spinoza states: 'I affirmed nothing but what I could infer from foundations revealed in the Sacred Texts' (*TTP*, 6 [65]). It might be helpful to review the last paragraph of chapter 2, in which Spinoza summarises the thesis he infers from his analysis of prophecy:

> Although only the things we have said about the Prophets and Prophecy pertain particularly to my purpose of separating Philosophy from Theology, nevertheless, because I have treated Prophecy generally, I want to ask now whether the gift of Prophecy was peculiar to the Hebrews or whether it was common to all nations. We also need to ask what we must maintain about the calling of the Hebrews. That's the object of the following chapter. (*TTP*, 2 [58])

Spinoza's claim is quite explicit: the literal sense analysis of prophecy is intended to support the *separation thesis*. Now, how does it achieve this? Spinoza briefly explains the *separation thesis* in the preface:

> Having shown the fundamentals of faith [in chapter 14], I conclude finally that revealed knowledge has no object but obedience, and indeed that it is *entirely distinct from natural knowledge, both in its object and in its foundation and means. Revealed knowledge has nothing in common with natural knowledge*, but each is in charge of its own domain, without any conflict with the other. [In chapter 15 I show that] neither ought to be the handmaid of the other. (*TTP*, preface [27]; my italics)

The *separation thesis*, then, stipulates that the distinction between revealed knowledge and natural knowledge (theology and philosophy) is clear-cut: these are two completely distinct domains of knowledge which have 'nothing in common' with each other and cannot conflict. The first two chapters on prophecy and the prophet are rich in content. However, according to Spinoza's claim, all of the discussions concerning prophecy were designed to support his *separation thesis*. How do they support it? Skipping a detailed analysis, I will point out two kinds of discussions which do so:

1. The analysis of prophecy shows that the foundations of revealed knowledge are different from the foundations of natural knowledge. Thus, since revealed knowledge is knowledge of the imagination, one should not take the prophet's philosophical opinions to have any theological validity. For instance, regarding the revelation to Cain, Spinoza says:

> For example, *the revelation to Cain* [Genesis 4:6–7] *teaches us only* that God warned him to lead a true life, for that was the only intent and substance of the revelation, not teach the freedom of the will or Philosophic matters. So even though the freedom of the will is contained very clearly in the words and reasonings of that warning, we are permitted to think the will is not free, since those words and reasonings were only accommodated to Cain's power of understanding. (*TTP*, 2 [53]; my italics)

2. Critical hermeneutics can disclose the meaning in which revealed knowledge is a domain in and of itself. Thus, for instance, by disclosing the manner in which a revelation is validated, we see that revealed knowledge does not appeal to reason.

One of Spinoza's main discussions revolves around the source of certainty. Literal sense hermeneutics, he argues, helps us to decipher the inner criteria for certainty with regards to revealed knowledge. Spinoza concludes the first chapter with the following telling passage:

> As a result, we're now forced to ask how the Prophets could have come to be certain of things they perceived only through the imagination, and not from certain principles of the mind. But whatever we can say about this, we must seek from Scripture. As we have already said, we do not have true 'knowledge of this matter, or we cannot explain it through its first causes. What Scripture teaches concerning the certainty of the Prophets, I shall show in the following chapter, where I have decided to treat of the Prophets. (*TTP*, 1 [48])

Certainty, according to Spinoza, accompanies any piece of knowledge which is deduced by reason. [See *TTP*, 2 [4–6]] There is no need for any further act of the mind in order to become certain of the truth of any piece of knowledge which is derived by reason. In contrast, knowledge achieved by imagination requires an additional element in order to be endowed with certainty.

It is important to note here that Spinoza's comment—'we're now forced to ask how the Prophets could have come to be certain of things they perceived only through the imagination, and not from certain principles of the mind' (*TTP*, 1 [48]) —turns out to be very telling. Why are we forced to ask this when the certainty is coming from the imagination, but not when it comes from the principles of the mind? If we were to derive this certainty from our principles of reason, then the *separation thesis* could not be as strong as Spinoza claimed it was, namely we could not claim that 'revealed knowledge has nothing in common with natural knowledge, but each is in charge of its own domain, without any conflict with the other' (*TTP*, preface [27]). Thus, being committed to the strong version of the *separation thesis*, Spinoza has to reject the premise that prophecy obtains its certainty from certain principles of the mind. To summarize: Spinoza's strong *separation thesis* is intimately linked with his view that the certainty of prophecy cannot originate in reason.

Yet to come to our point now: Spinoza claims that in order to determine the source of certainty when it comes to revealed knowledge, we must read the Bible using his method.

Certainty and Revealed Knowledge

In the last section, we showed the significance of Spinoza's hermeneutics to his *separation thesis*. Moreover, we have seen that Spinoza is committed to the strong version of the *separation thesis*, namely that revealed knowledge should not be supported by means of reason. According to Spinoza, it is part of the task of chapter 2 to show that the certainty which accompanies revealed knowledge is not being informed through reason. If we fail to make this distinction, we will not be able to abide by the strong version of the *separation thesis*.

So, what is it indeed that endows revealed knowledge with certainty?

> But first I must treat the certainty of the Prophets, both because it concerns the theme of this chapter, but also because it will help in some measure to get to the conclusion we intend to demonstrate. [4] Unlike a clear and distinct idea, a simple imagination does not, by its nature, involve certainty. So to be able to be certain of things we imagine, we must add something to the imagination—viz., reasoning. It follows that, by itself, Prophecy cannot involve certainty. As we've shown, it depended only on the imagination. So the Prophets were not certain about God's revelation by the revelation itself, but by some sign. (*TTP*, 2 [3–4])

The certainty which accompanies revealed knowledge is not revelation, but a sign. After giving different examples from the Bible, Spinoza concludes:

> This shows that the Prophets always had some sign by which they became certain of the things they imagined Prophetically. That's why Moses warns [the Jews] to seek a sign from [anyone claiming to be] a Prophet, viz. the outcome of some future event (Deuteronomy 18:22). [6] In this respect, then, Prophecy is inferior to natural knowledge, which needs no sign, but of its own nature involves certainty. (*TTP*, 2 [5–6])

Indeed, the certainty which accompanies revealed knowledge is inferior to the certainty which accompanies natural knowledge. Yet Spinoza has successfully shown that this certainty does not come from reason. The certainty to which the prophet aspires is achieved through a sign which is as imaginary as prophecy itself.

To summarise: according to our explication, the only way we can account for the certainty of revealed knowledge without violating the strong version of the *separation thesis* is by pointing our the exact role of the sign plays in endowing certainty to prophetic knowledge; we can understand the role of the sign only by closely critically studying the biblical text.

Signs and Miracles

But what is the kind of sign that endow prophetic revelations with certainty according to Spinoza? Interestingly enough, at least in certain cases, Spinoza identifies miracles as signs. For instance, in chapter 2, it reads:

> Indeed, this Prophetic certainty was not mathematical, but only moral, as is evident from Scripture itself. For in Deuteronomy 13[:2] Moses warns that any Prophet who wants to teach new Gods should be condemned to death, even though he confirms his teaching with signs and miracles. For as Moses himself goes on to say, God also uses signs and miracles to test the people. (*TTP*, 2 [7])[14]

Moreover, later in the chapter Spinoza says:

> Similarly, the sign of the backward motion of the shadow was revealed to Isaiah according to his power of understanding, viz. as a backward motion of the sun [cf. 2 Kings 20:8–12 with Isaiah 38:7–8]. For he too thought that the sun moves and that the earth is at rest. As luck would have it, he never thought of *parhelia*, not even in a dream. We are permitted to maintain this without any hesitation because the sign could really happen, and be predicted to the king by Isaiah, even though the Prophet did not know its true cause. (*TTP*, 2 [28])

Spinoza notes that having to explicate 'the backward motion of the sun' in terms of imagination does not necessarily mean that it could not be explained by reason. However, in chapter 6, Spinoza refers to the same event, saying:

> We ought not doubt that many things are related as miracles in the Sacred Texts whose causes can easily be explained according to known principles of natural things. We already hinted at this in Ch. 2 when we spoke about the sun's standing still in the time of Joshua, and its going backward in the time of Ahaz. But we'll soon treat this more fully, when we discuss the interpretation of miracles, as I've promised to do in this chapter. (*TTP*, 6 [15])

Here, Spinoza discusses the same event, but in terms of miracle. So, if miracles can be a sign, I suggest we turn now to discuss the place of miracles in revealed knowledge.

---

14 Cf. *TTP*, 6 [31]: 'For he says that (even if) a sign and a wonder he has predicted to you should happen, etc., do not (nevertheless) assent to the words of this Prophet etc., because the Lord your God tests you etc. (Therefore) let that Prophet be condemned to death etc. From this it clearly follows that even false Prophets can perform miracles, and that unless men are well protected by the true knowledge and love of God, miracles can lead them to embrace false Gods as easily as the True God. For Moses adds since the Lord your God is testing you, to know whether you love him with all your heart and all your soul.'

Miracles as Signs: the First Problem

A miracle can serve as a sign, but what is a miracle? I think we are now in a position to see the difficulties that miracles create in Spinoza's dual commitment, namely to both literal sense hermeneutics and his *separation thesis*.

If we return to the scholars previously discussed, I think we can say that a miracle is an event perceived by both the Bible and the prophet as violating the law of nature. Now, if we say that a sign is a miracle, how does it contribute to theology? To answer this question, we would have to explore how a miracle can endow the prophet's revelation (or his audience) with certainty that the sign is indeed a miracle. A miracle shows that providence can violate the natural order; providence's interference with the natural order is a sign that adds certainty to the content of revelations.

If we are correct in our interpretation of Spinoza as being committed to a strong version of the *separation thesis*, which requires (as we have suggested) a revelation to be explained without any reference to reason, then a miracle qua sign will not be very helpful. After all, the prophet's entire conviction is based on an argument of reason which roughly claims: you have seen an event, and you know that events generally follow the natural law, the laws of reason. However, what you have seen here is a miracle, which means that providence can bend the laws of nature; this is a sign telling you that prophetic revelation is true. If we accept this explication of miracle and sign, we see that miracles—when interpreted according to the literal sense method—present a serious difficulty to Spinoza: this kind of certainty would be explicitly informed by an argument from reason.

However, there is one good reason to reject my interpretation, because by adopting dogmatic hermeneutics, Spinoza falls down yet another pit. Let me elaborate: if we accept Spinoza's position on miracles, then the Bible and the prophet agree with him and miracles are not events which are bent by providence to violate laws of nature. So, what is the contribution of non-existent miracles to prophetic certainty? Let me suggest a revised version of this refuted interpretation of mine.

The Sceptic and the Dogmatic

Spinoza posits his critical hermeneutics in opposition to two hermeneutical schools. We have already discussed the opposition to dogmatic hermeneutics. In chapter 15, Spinoza posits critical hermeneutics against sceptical hermeneutics.

Spinoza depicts the sceptic's reading of the Bible in the following way:

> Those who don't know how to separate Philosophy from Theology debate whether Scripture should be the handmaid of reason, or reason should be the handmaid of Scripture—that is, whether the meaning of Scripture ought to be accommodated to reason, or reason ought to be accommodated to Scripture. The skeptics, who deny the certainty of reason, defend the accommodation of reason to Scripture. (*TTP*, 15 [1])

Spinoza is aware of the fact that the sceptic is following literal sense method to a certain extent. In chapter 15, he makes the following comment on the sceptic:

> Insofar as he wants to explain Scripture by Scripture, I praise him. But I'm amazed that a man endowed with reason should be so eager to destroy reason. It's certainly true that Scripture ought to be explained by Scripture, so long as we're only working out the meaning of the statements and the Prophets' intention. (*TTP*, 15 [8])

Before I turn to discuss Spinoza's objection to the sceptic, let me just point out that Spinoza's adversary in his discussion of miracles is very likely a sceptic. Spinoza describes the common people as those who have the tendency to claim that miracles are God's actions that violate the natural order (*TTP*, 6 [2–5]). Spinoza explains the motivation driving them in the following manner:

> So the common people call unusual works of nature miracles, or works of God. Partly from devotion, partly from a desire to oppose those who cultivate the natural sciences, they don't want to know the natural causes of things. They long to hear only the things they're most ignorant of, which they're most amazed by. (*TTP*, 6 [3])

The desire to 'oppose those who cultivate the natural sciences' is quite similar to the depiction of the sceptic's madness in chapter 15:

> Who but someone desperate and mad would want to recklessly say goodbye to reason, or to scorn the arts and sciences, and deny the certainty of reason? (*TTP*, 15 [38])

In fact, the sceptic's resemblance to the miracle advocate comes up in a context that is more significant to our discussion. In chapter 15, Spinoza says:

> Who but someone desperate and mad would want to recklessly say goodbye to reason, or to scorn the arts and sciences, and deny the certainty of reason? [...] They want to call upon reason to repudiate reason, and by a certain reason make reason uncertain. While they're trying to show the truth and authority of Theology by mathematical demonstrations, and to take away the authority of reason and the natural light, all they're doing is dragging Theology under the control of reason. They clearly seem to suppose that Theology has no brilliance unless it's illuminated by the natural light. (TTP, 15 [38–9])

The sceptic in chapter 15 is actually the one who 'calls upon reason to repudiate reason.' If we return to Spinoza's miracle adversary, we see that he meets the sceptic's criteria. In chapter 6, Spinoza depicts the miracle advocate:

> Next, we know that nothing agrees with nature (or is contrary to it) except what we have shown to agree with those principles (or to be contrary to them). So if we could conceive that by some power (whatever in the end it was) something could happen in nature which was contrary to nature, that would be contrary to those first notions, and we would have to reject it as absurd—either that, or we would have to doubt the first notions (as we have just shown) and consequently, doubt God and all things, however they might have been perceived. (*TTP*, 6 [18])

Thus, Spinoza states here that anyone who claims that miracles are events that violate the laws of nature (i.e. the miracle advocate) is actually claiming that reason refutes reason (i.e. the sceptic). We see, then, that according to Spinoza, when someone claims that miracles are contrary to the natural order, what he is saying is actually a statement about knowledge.

Critical Hermeneutics and the Sceptic's Argument from Miracles

Is Spinoza's thesis regarding the compatibility between literal sense hermeneutics and the *separation thesis* in danger, if Spinoza's miracle adversary is indeed the sceptic? As Spinoza grants, the sceptic's approach is quite similar to his own when it comes to the literal sense interpretation. (*TTP*, 15 [8]) So, let us reconstruct the sceptic's argument and review Spinoza's answer.

Let us first a compare Spinoza's answer to the sceptic concerning prophecy with his answer concerning miracles. In the case of prophecy, the sceptic's argument would be the following: the literal sense implies that prophecy is true, and since prophetic knowledge is different from natural knowledge, accepting prophetic truth implies that natural knowledge is subordinate to natural knowledge. Spinoza's answer to this is that critical hermeneutics indeed confirms that prophetic knowledge is valid. However, it also confirms that revealed knowledge is made valid by imagination; hence it does not imply anything concerning reason. As long as we can keep the domains of theology and philosophy separate, namely as long as they do not inform each other, then there is no basis for the sceptic's position, just as there is no basis for the dogmatic one.

What is the case for miracles? The sceptic's argument would be that the certainty of the revelation is endowed by the sign or the miracle. If we go back to Spinoza's claim that a miracle is an action on the part of providence against the order of nature—which is tantamount to the claim that *reason refutes reason*—then the biblical teaching supports scepticism.

Can Spinoza refute the sceptic's argument by arguing from the *separation thesis*? In contrast to the case of prophecy, in the case of miracles, the answer seems to be no. It seems to be the case that theological knowledge is informed by reason, and since certainty of revealed knowledge is dependent on the insight that knowledge of reason is invalid, the *separation thesis* cannot hold.

Now we can return to our original difficulties: does Spinoza have a reason to adopt dogmatic hermeneutics in his interpretation of miracles? The answer is yes; if he does not adopt this kind of hermeneutics, the literal sense method is in support of the sceptic.

– Does Spinoza have a reason to claim that the prophets hold the same views as he does concerning miracles? Yes: if theology admits that miracles imply an interruption of the natural order, then the *separation thesis* is disproved (remember that in order to refute the *separation thesis*, we only need to show that theology is not supported by its own means).

— Does Spinoza have a good reason to distinguish between miracles and prophecy, stating that the question of miracles is philosophical, whereas the question of prophecy is a purely theological? Yes: prophetic knowledge can be entirely explained as proceeding from the foundations of theology, hence investigating its teaching in accordance with the literal sense method makes sense; however, since miracles cannot explain theology without relying on natural knowledge, they cannot qualify as revealed knowledge.

— Does Spinoza have a good reason to suggest applying censorship in case the Bible implies that miracles support theology? Yes, otherwise we would have to agree with the sceptic that biblical teaching is dependent on knowledge of reason.

Should We Accept that Spinoza's Analysis of Miracles is a Dogmatic One?

Our interpretation challenges the scholars' claim that Spinoza had no good reason to adopt a dogmatic hermeneutics in his interpretation of miracles. In contrast, our interpretation shows that he had very good reasons for adopting dogmatic hermeneutics. Contrary to the scholars' claim that the reason for adopting a dogmatic hermeneutics has nothing to do with Spinoza's own hermeneutics, we have seen that Spinoza's reason for doing so was his own literal sense method.

As appealing as our interpretation may be for explaining Spinoza's reason for his deviation from the literal sense method, it remains very weak: what kind of answer would that be on Spinoza's part? Merely claiming that the literal sense method should not be used in that particular case just because it violates another thesis is an interpretation which could perhaps sound convincing to certain historians of philosophy, but would Spinoza qua philosopher also be convinced?

If we wish to interpret Spinoza qua philosopher, we have to address the following two challenges to our interpretation:
1. Can Spinoza's explication of biblical miracles be supported from his critical hermeneutics?
2. Does Spinoza have an answer to the sceptic's challenge from miracles which does not suspend the literal sense method when it comes to miracles?

Spinoza's Explication of Miracles Reconsidered

Up until now, we have accepted the scholars' premise that Spinoza's interpretation of miracles is indeed a dogmatic one. Yet our interpretation, which identifies Spinoza's miracle adversary as the sceptic, can serve as the pivotal point for turning our perception of Spinoza's view of miracles upside down. I will argue that using our interpretation, we can show that Spinoza's analysis of miracles does not necessitate the suspension of the literal sense method; rather, Spinoza has a good answer to the sceptic which keeps the literal sense method in effect.

The philosophical challenge that Spinoza faces is how to show that a miracle can support the certainty of revealed knowledge from its own domain. Another question is: how can miracles support theology if we do not assume that they violate the natural order?

Miracles and Certainty of Revealed Knowledge

Philosophically speaking, our interpretation of Spinoza will be more solid if we show that miracles can be signs which endow prophetic knowledge with certainty. Now, even if we accept the common reading, namely that Spinoza's interpretation of miracles is a dogmatic one, we still have to explain how miracles qua signs create certainty in the prophet's (or the believer's) mind.

Now, even if we do accept this view, we should keep in mind Spinoza's firm theses that 1) the prophets themselves believed that miracles were not an interruption to the natural order, and 2) biblical teaching or theology agrees with philosophy in rejecting miracles (assuming that the meaning of the latter is an action of providence which interrupts the natural order). Yet what could a miracle be, if we reject the latter understanding of miracles? Can a miracle have any theological meaning (in terms of imagination) which would not imply a violation of the natural order?

Spinoza suggests a certain mental affect caused by miracles. In chapter 1, the text reads:

> That's also why they called miracles works of God, i.e., works to be astonished at. For of course, all natural things are God's works, and exist and act only through the divine power. It's in this sense that the Psalmist calls the miracles of Egypt God's powers, because in a situation of extreme danger they opened up the way to deliverance for the Hebrews, who were expecting nothing like them, and hence were amazed by them. (*TTP*, 1 [30])

Thus, *astonishment* or *amazement* are affects that can be triggered by miracles. Yet the fact that a miracle causes astonishment and amazement does not bring us much further: it is possible that the effect of amazement is actually the result of reasoning that providence is interfering with the natural order. But if we can show that miracles can be understood to support theology without having to depend on reason, our interpretation will not violate the separation principle.

In fact, Spinoza explicitly claims that when we refer to 'amazement', we are not in violation of the separation principle. In chapter 6, he says:

> Though the voice the Israelites heard [on Mount Sinai] could not give them any philosophical or mathematical *certainty* about God's existence, still, it was enough to make them *wonder* at God, insofar as they had previously known him, and to motivate them to *obedience*. That was the pur-

pose of that manifestation. God did not want to teach the Israelites the absolute attributes of his essence. (He did not reveal any of them at that time.) He wanted to break their stubborn heart and win them over to *obedience*. So he addressed them with the sound of trumpets, with thunder, and with lightning, *not with arguments*. (*TTP*, 14 [36]; my italics)

Spinoza's argument here gives us several clues which could be helpful in our analysis of miracles. He begins by noting that we should not assume that arguments play any role in the way in which miracles are related to revealed knowledge. In accordance with the latter claim, Spinoza is using 'amazement' to mean 'that which connects the imaginary mind to revealed knowledge.' In addition, Spinoza explains the role of miracles on Mount Sinai in the following way: the people already knew God, namely miracles were in no way supposed to convey the knowledge of God. However, the fact that they already knew that God existed did not make them ready to accept the knowledge revealed on Mount Sinai or to follow it; the miracles on Mount Sinai, then, were supposed to connect the people to the revealed knowledge.[15]

To recapitulate what we have just unpacked from chapter 6: we can keep the domains of philosophy and theology entirely distinct if we understand miracles only in terms of imagination (the affect of wondering). Miracles connect a person's mind to the content of the revelation by the affect of amazement (imagination).

Now, let us see how the aforementioned insight can help us to understand the prophet's certainty in revealed knowledge. Certainty, or the prophet's readiness to commit himself to the knowledge revealed to him, is achieved through the amazement which accompanies the miracle.

We still have to account for two points:
1. What is it about the affect of amazement which accompanies miracles that connects the beholder to revealed knowledge?
2. Can we account for the role of miracles in achieving certainty when the prophet conceives a miracle as merely a natural event (as we explained with reference to Nadler, Spinoza states that the prophets agreed with him that miracles are natural events).

Is the Mind Capable of Perceiving an Event as Both Natural and Miraculous?

Spinoza claims that miracles are events which cause us to be amazed, yet the prophet can wonder at the event and simultaneously hold the view that it is entirely natural. However, is this not an empty formula? Can we really wonder at an event, see it as a sign, and the same time perceive it as being entirely natural?

---

15 Spinoza's preference for the term 'sign' over 'miracle' will also get clearer by our interpretation.

In fact, I would argue that Spinoza is referring to a very common state of mind. Think of the following two examples. In the first case, I win the lottery, I feel really fortunate, and I say: 'God really loves me. I am blessed.' Now consider the second case, which conveys an opposite view of myself: I am an academic and all my efforts over many years to obtain a professorship at the university have been futile. I am unemployed and I say: 'I am so unlucky, God really hates me, I am cursed.' Can I not think, in the first case, both that my winning the lottery may be explained by the laws of causality which govern the lottery machine and yet at the same time feel that I am lucky, that I am blessed, and that God loves me? Consider now the second case: can I not admit that the reason I did not obtain a professorship is because—in accordance with the natural order—only those who are endowed with *professorial wisdom* obtain this position, and I am not one of them? And can I not think at the same time that I am unlucky, unfortunate, and cursed by God?

Let us now apply that state of mind to the prophet: knowledge is revealed to the prophet through imagination, but he still lacks certainty. He then wins the lottery; he sees it as a sign that God is in direct contact with him, that God is interested in him, that God loves him, that he is very special to God, etc. If this is the prophet's state of mind, it is possible for him to consider the event as both something which does not violate the natural order and yet as a sign that God has a special relationship with him.

Re-examination of Spinoza's Dogmatism

Let us now proceed to re-examine Spinoza's analysis of miracles in chapter 6 in light of our interpretation. Spinoza's theses—1) that the prophets consider miracles to be natural events and 2) that the Bible must teach that miracles are natural events—are defendable if Spinoza is committed to the strong version of the *separation thesis*; accordingly, the contribution of *miracles* qua signs to the certainty of revealed knowledge can be accounted for only from the realm of imagination. Thus, if we account for the certainty of prophecy by assuming that a miraculous event provides evidence for the superiority of revealed knowledge over natural knowledge, we violate the *separation thesis*.

The aforementioned theses are in perfect accordance with Spinoza's literal sense method. As we have seen, at the end of chapter 2, Spinoza claims that his analysis of prophecy in chapters 1 and 2 supports the *separation thesis*. We therefore concluded that the *separation thesis* is derived from the biblical text in accordance with the literal sense method.[16] For that very reason, the certainty of the sign must be accounted

---

[16] This claim does not entail that a derivation of the *separation thesis* from reason is excluded according to Spinoza; our claim here is only the following: the *separation thesis* can be derived—and Spinoza does in fact derive it—from theological principles, independently of its derivation from reason, and vice versa.

for from theological theses only. We have shown that Spinoza indeed accounts for the certainty a sign lends to revealed knowledge exclusively from the principles derived from prophetic revelation.

In his *apology*, Spinoza states that miracles are the object of philosophy alone and that therefore they should be addressed with reason alone. We reviewed two difficulties:
1. Nadler's objection:—is that thesis not a violation of Spinoza's literal sense method?
2. Harvey raised the following difficulty:

> Spinoza claims that the subject of prophecy is 'theological' because it 'surpasses human knowledge' (*captum humanum superat*), whereas that of miracles is 'philosophical' because it involves the philosophical question of 'whether we can concede that something may happen in Nature that contravenes its Laws.' However, he might just as easily have said: the subject of prophecy is 'philosophical', for it involves the philosophical question of whether there can be suprarational knowledge, whereas that of miracles is 'theological'.[17]

A careful examination of Spinoza's *apology* in light of our interpretation resolves both Nadler's and Harvey's questions. It is worthwhile to quote Spinoza's *apology* once again:

> I've proceeded regarding miracles according to a method completely different from the one I followed regarding Prophecy. Concerning Prophecy I affirmed nothing but what I could infer from foundations revealed in the Sacred Texts. But here I've elicited the main points only from principles known to the natural light. I did this deliberately. For since Prophecy surpasses man's power of understanding, and is a purely Theological question, I could affirm nothing about it, nor even know in what it chiefly consisted, except from the foundations which have been revealed. I was compelled to put together a history of Prophecy, and to formulate certain doctrines from it, which would teach me the nature and properties of Prophecy, as far as this can be done. [66] But concerning miracles what we are asking is completely philosophical: can we grant that something happens in nature contrary to its laws, or something which couldn't follow from them? So I didn't need anything like that. Indeed, I thought it wiser to unravel this question according to foundations known to the natural light, as those which are most known. I say that I thought it wiser, for I could easily have resolved it solely from the doctrines and foundations of Scripture. (*TTP*, 6 [65–6])

We have shown that 1) Spinoza's claim that *a miracle is the result of providence's interruption of the law of nature* is actually the sceptical claim that natural knowledge is inferior and should therefore be corrected by revealed knowledge. We have also claimed that 2) the sceptic's argument is to use reason to counter reason. Now, in the *apology*, Spinoza says: 'But concerning miracles *what we are asking* is completely philosophical: *can we grant that something happens in nature contrary to its laws*, or something which couldn't follow from them?' (*TTP*, 6[66]; my italics). Thus, the thesis

---

[17] Harvey, "Spinoza on Biblical Miracles," 666–667.

of Spinoza's adversary regarding the 'interruption of the natural order' would indeed be the sceptic's thesis. As we have shown, the sceptic's thesis is one that is derived from reason, and hence Spinoza is entirely justified in claiming that such an understanding of miracles—'that something happens in nature contrary to its laws'—should in fact be approached and answered from reason. This is precisely what Spinoza is doing when he examines the theses which are apparently derived from this understanding of miracles.

Our interpretation ultimately resolves both Nadler's and Harvey's objections: Spinoza does not violate the literal sense method, but rather refutes the sceptic's theses with philosophical arguments, and this approach is in fact the proper one, because the sceptic's understanding of miracles is derived 'from reason.' This would also explain why he says that in this respect, the issue of miracles is a philosophical matter, whereas the issue of prophecy is a theological one.

The interpretations we have reviewed and rejected consider Spinoza's stance on miracles to be a dogmatic one. I think we have explained our objections. As a matter of fact, our interpretation yields an interesting result: Spinoza's explication of miracles in chapter 6 is anti-dogmatic. His argument against the sceptic shows that the sceptic's explication of miracles only makes sense if we assume that 'something happens in nature contrary to its laws,' but in Spinoza's terms, this would be a philosophical claim. Thus, the sceptic is, in fact, the one who is committed to dogmatic hermeneutics. This might seem like a purely formal claim, but I think that our interpretation proves that this is exactly the case in terms of actual biblical interpretation. The sceptic's dogmatic understanding of miracles actually imposes an anachronistic interpretation of the Bible. In other words, by adopting the dogmatic view that miracles are 'something that happens in nature contrary to its laws,' the sceptic subjects the Bible to a philosophical problematic which is mostly a medieval one; from the critical point of view there is no reason to attribute such a view to the prophets. Conversely, we have shown that Spinoza's claim that the prophets are in agreement with the view that miracles are not an interruption of the natural order is what ultimately liberated him from the view that miracles should be regarded as biblical teaching. Once free from this view, we are able to grasp the difference between prophecy and miracles; only then is it possible to examine the role miracles play in the Bible, to understand the difference between signs and revealed knowledge, etc.

Diego Lucci
Political Scepticism, Moral Scepticism, and the Scope and Limits of Toleration in John Locke

1 Introduction

In *A Letter concerning Toleration*, written in late 1685 and published in 1689, John Locke argued for the separation between the state and religious organizations.[1] He advocated toleration of all those subscribing to organized religion, be they Christians, Jews, Muslims, or pagans. Nevertheless, as Jonathan Israel has noted, in Locke's *Letter* 'those who subscribe to no organized religion, be they agnostics, Deists or *indifferenti*, in confessional matters while not explicitly excluded are left in a vague

---

This essay is one of the results of a study period I spent in Hamburg from February to July 2018, when I was a Senior Research Fellow of the Maimonides Centre for Advanced Studies (MCAS) at the University of Hamburg. Before finalizing this essay, I presented its thesis at the 2018 Conference of the International Society for Intellectual History (ISIH), which took place at the University of St Andrews on June 10 to 13, 2018. I would like to express my deepest gratitude to the Director of the MCAS, Prof. Giuseppe Veltri, for his support, friendship, and sincere interest in my research. I would also like to thank all the administrators, staff members, research associates, and research fellows of the MCAS for their assistance, encouragement, and attention to my scholarly activities. Concerning this article, I am very grateful to Dr. Bill Rebiger, Dr. Raffaele Russo, Dr. Jeffrey R. Wigelsworth, and an anonymous reviewer for their precious suggestions and assistance. I would finally like to thank Prof. Peter Anstey, Prof. Teresa Castelao-Lawless, Prof. Mark Goldie, Prof. Michael Hunter, and Dr. Adam Sutcliffe for the feedback and advice they gave me at the 2018 ISIH Conference.

1 [John Locke], *Epistola de Tolerantia* (Gouda: Justum ab Hoeve, 1689). The *Letter* was promptly translated into English: [John Locke], *A Letter concerning Toleration*, [trans. William Popple] (London: Churchill, 1689). After publishing the *Letter*, Locke engaged in a debate with the Oxford chaplain Jonas Proast. In responding to Proast in three more letters written in 1690, 1692, and 1704, Locke reaffirmed and further clarified his views on toleration. This article concentrates on Locke's first letter, while referring to the other letters when necessary. On the Locke–Proast controversy, see Mark Goldie, "John Locke, Jonas Proast, and Religious Toleration, 1688–1692," in *The Church of England, c.1689–c.1833: From Toleration to Tractarianism*, eds. John Walsh, Colin Haydon, and Stephen Taylor (Cambridge: Cambridge University Press, 1993): 143–171; Richard Vernon, *The Career of Toleration: John Locke, Jonas Proast, and after* (Montreal–Kingston: McGill–Queen's University Press, 1997); *Locke on Toleration*, ed. Richard Vernon (Cambridge: Cambridge University Press, 2010); Adam Wolfson, "Toleration and Relativism: The Locke–Proast Exchange," *The Review of Politics* 59 (1997): 213–232; Adam Wolfson, *Persecution or Toleration: An Explication of the Locke–Proast Quarrel, 1689–1704* (Lanham: Lexington, 2010); John W. Tate, *Liberty, Toleration and Equality: John Locke, Jonas Proast and the Letters Concerning Toleration* (New York: Routledge, 2016).

OpenAccess. © 2018 Diego Lucci, published by De Gruyter. This work is licensed under the Creative Commons Attribution-NonCommercial-NoDerivatives 4.0 License.
https://doi.org/10.1515/978-3-11-057768-6-007

limbo without any clear status or guaranteed freedom.'² In the *Letter*, Locke's main goal was indeed to prevent churches from gaining power from the political rulers and oppressing other religious groups. Thus, far from advocating complete freedom of conscience, he simply delineated the criteria regulating the relationships between political authorities and religious societies, as well as between different religious groups. This focus on merely the separation between the state and religious organizations is a significant shortcoming in the theory of toleration expounded in Locke's *Letter*—a theory much less inclusive than other seventeenth-century views on the matter, such as Spinoza's philosophical advocacy of freedom of conscience and Bayle's sceptical justification of wide toleration. However, Locke's later writings on religion imply different conclusions regarding toleration. In *The Reasonableness of Christianity* (1695), a theological book with significant irenic implications, Locke formulated a moralist soteriology based on what he took to be the fundamentals of Christianity—i.e. faith, repentance, and obedience, which he judged to be plainly revealed in Scripture, essential to morality and salvation, and hence placed at the core of the Christian Law of Faith.³ As Locke argued that every Christian had the right and duty to study Scripture by themselves, he admitted that more specific, non-fundamental beliefs might arise from different interpretations of biblical texts not dealing with the fundamentals of Christianity. However, to Locke, non-fundamentals are irrelevant to morality and salvation and, thus, must not hinder peace among Christians. Briefly, Locke's doctrine of the fundamentals implies that all those who try to live by the Christian Law of Faith ought to tolerate each other, regardless of non-fundamentals and confessional affiliation. Therefore, this position also allows for toleration of denominationally uncommitted Christians; and this is certainly a step beyond Locke's advocacy, in the *Letter*, of merely a separation between the state and religious societies.

In this essay, I reconsider the impact of Locke's moral and soteriological concerns on his approach to religious toleration and, thus, on the scope and limits of Locke's views on toleration in their development from the *Letter* to the *Reasonableness*. In doing so, I call attention to the sceptical dimension of Locke's thought. Although Locke devoted a good deal of Book IV of *An Essay concerning Human Understanding* (1690) to demonstrating that he was not a sceptic, several contemporaries considered his way of ideas as liable to lead to scepticism. Among Locke's critics who judged his epistemology to be essentially sceptic were the latitudinarian Bishop Edward Stillingfleet, the Catholic priest John Sergeant, the Church of England divine

---

[2] Jonathan I. Israel, "Spinoza, Locke and the Enlightenment Battle for Toleration," in *Toleration in Enlightenment Europe*, eds. Ole P. Grell and Roy Porter (Cambridge: Cambridge University Press, 1999): 103.

[3] In this article, where not indicated otherwise, I refer to the Clarendon edition of the *Reasonableness*: John Locke, *The Reasonableness of Christianity, as Delivered in the Scriptures*, ed. John C. Higgins-Biddle (Oxford: Clarendon Press, 1999).

Henry Lee, and such famous philosophers as Leibniz and Berkeley.⁴ Sam Black, investigating the sources of Locke's 'mitigated skepticism' in an article of 1998, contended that 'Locke is indebted for his ideas to the revival of New Academy skepticism.'⁵ In this respect, John Rogers has argued that, although Locke was definitely not a full-blown Pyrrhonian sceptic, the early modern revival of sceptical considerations informed his epistemology in a twofold sense.⁶ First, according to Locke we cannot expect to get behind ideas to things themselves, namely to the substance of things, which he defined as an unknown substratum or support of the qualities we perceive.⁷ Second, to Locke we cannot hope to attain certainty in most areas of inquiry, in which we can only aspire to rely on probabilities.⁸

While the sceptical aspects of Locke's epistemology are not the main subject of this article, it is important to stress that Locke's emphasis on the limits of knowledge significantly conditioned his approach to religious and moral matters. He believed that the amount of knowledge available to humankind in matters of religion and ethics was strictly limited, and he had serious doubts about the prospects for enlarging this stock of knowledge through the operation of natural reason alone.⁹ This awareness of the narrow scope of knowledge in religious and moral matters influenced Locke's conception of political authority. In this regard, some students of Locke—including, among others, Susan Mendus, David Wootton, and Richard Vernon—have contended that a sort of political scepticism inspired his arguments to exclude 'the Care of Souls' from the magistrate's purview.¹⁰ Locke's political scepticism involved

---

4 Edward Stillingfleet, *A Discourse in Vindication of the Doctrine of the Trinity* (London: Mortlock, 1697); John Sergeant, *Solid Philosophy Asserted, against the Fancies of the Ideists* (London: Clavil, 1697); Henry Lee, *Anti-Scepticism: or, Notes upon each Chapter of Mr. Locke's Essay concerning Human Understanding* (London: Clavel, 1702); Gottfried Wilhelm von Leibniz, *New Essays on Human Understanding* (1704), trans. and eds. Peter Remnant and Jonathan Bennett (Cambridge: Cambridge University Press, 1982); George Berkeley, *A Treatise Concerning the Principles of Human Knowledge* (Dublin: Pepyat, 1710). Stillingfleet was one of the major representatives of the English theological current known as latitudinarianism. *Contra* Calvinist predestination, the so-called 'latitude-men' upheld a moralist soteriology stressing the importance of human reason, free will, and morality. Moreover, they aimed to relax the terms of conformity in such a manner as to 'comprehend' at least the least radical Dissenters within the Church of England. See Martin I. J. Griffin, Jr., *Latitudinarianism in the Seventeenth-Century Church of England* (Leiden: Brill, 1992); William M. Spellman, *The Latitudinarians and the Church of England, 1660–1700* (Athens, GA: University of Georgia Press, 1993).
5 Sam Black, "Toleration and the Skeptical Inquirer in Locke," *Canadian Journal of Philosophy* 28 (1998): 475.
6 G. A. John Rogers, "John Locke and the Sceptics," in *The Return of Scepticism: From Hobbes and Descartes to Bayle*, ed. Gianni Paganini (Dordrecht: Kluwer, 2003): 37–53.
7 John Locke, *An Essay concerning Human Understanding*, ed. Peter H. Nidditch (Oxford: Clarendon Press, 1975), II.xxiii.1–6.
8 *Ibidem*, IV.xv.2, IV.xvi.6.
9 Black, "Toleration," 478.
10 Susan Mendus, "Locke: Toleration, Morality and Rationality," in *John Locke: "A Letter concerning Toleration" in Focus*, eds. John Horton and Susan Mendus (London: Routledge, 1991): 147–162; David Wootton, "Introduction," in John Locke, *Political Writings*, ed. David Wootton (London; Penguin,

not the existence of true religion, but the human ability to comprehend and, above all, communicate religious truth. In Locke, the limits of knowledge, especially in religious and moral matters, inform the scope of political power, as Black has explained:

> [T]here is a basic relationship between the *grounds* of state action and the limits of knowledge. This relationship is straightforward in Locke's case. The grounds of state action [...] conform to the boundaries of moral and religious knowledge. This implies, first, that the state is duty-bound to secure through coercive measures fundamental moral and religious truths. Second, the state is forbidden to pursue through force practical goals whose truth is inaccessible, at the expense of its citizens' basic interests. [...] [O]ne important reason why Locke advocates toleration is because Locke is a skeptic about *most* religious claims. It is a consequence of his mitigated skepticism that Locke advocates a duty of religious toleration.[11]

Although Locke called attention to the narrow scope of knowledge in religious and moral matters, his toleration did not extend beyond the boundaries of moral standards that he considered beneficial, or at least harmless, to the commonwealth and its members' civil interests. Surrendering to moral relativism, to Locke, would indeed be as dangerous as its opposite—namely, allowing religious fanaticism, enthusiasm, and dogmatism to influence civil life.[12] As Locke wrote in the *Letter*: 'No Opinions contrary to human Society, or to those moral Rules which are necessary to the preservation of Civil Society, are to be tolerated by the Magistrate.'[13] For this reason, the *Letter* expressly denied toleration to atheists, whom Locke considered devoid of morality, and Roman Catholics, who, in his opinion, held some moral views harmful to society. However, *A Letter concerning Toleration* and *An Essay concerning Human Understanding* denote a sort of moral scepticism that Locke brought to its logical conclusions, and attempted to overcome, in his later writings on religion, especially in *The Reasonableness of Christianity*. Locke's moral scepticism was not about the existence, rationality, and demonstrability of morality in itself; but he questioned the *actual* ability of natural reason to demonstrate moral ideas and, thus, to establish a thorough, convincing, flawless system of ethics.[14] Therefore, in his search for solid foundations for morality, Locke eventually turned to Christian revelation, particular-

---

1993): 100–106; Vernon, *Career*, 35–51, 124–144; Richard Vernon, "Introduction," in *Locke on Toleration*, xxiv–xxix; Black, "Toleration;" Alex Tuckness, "Rethinking the Intolerant Locke," *American Journal of Political Science* 46 (2002): 288–298; Richard H. Popkin, *The History of Scepticism: From Savonarola to Bayle* (Oxford: Oxford University Press, 2003), 257–261.
11 Black, "Toleration," 474.
12 Jerome B. Schneewind, "Locke's Moral Philosophy," in *The Cambridge Companion to Locke*, ed. Vere Chappell (Cambridge: Cambridge University Press, 1994): 208; Wolfson, "Toleration," 230; Wolfson, *Persecution*, 88–99.
13 John Locke, "A Letter concerning Toleration," in John Locke, *A Letter concerning Toleration and Other Writings*, ed. Mark Goldie (Indianapolis: Liberty Fund, 2010): 49–50.
14 Locke, *Essay*, IV.iii.18–20; Locke, *Reasonableness*, 148–150.

ly to Christ's assurance of otherworldly rewards and punishments—the only effective incentive to act morally.[15]

Locke's conviction that only the Christian Law of Faith can establish morality on solid grounds has controversial implications concerning the morality of believers who refuse this law—not only antinomians and deists, whom Locke openly criticized, but also post-biblical Jews and heathens. This urges some considerations regarding not only the salvation, but also the tolerability of non-Christian believers. However, whereas Locke's later religious writings describe eternal salvation as necessitating acceptance of the Christian Law of Faith, he never considered conversion to Christianity as a requirement for toleration, and he never proposed a Christian commonwealth as the proper way to do the business of morality. To the author of the *Reasonableness*, belief in a divine legislator and the consequent acceptance of and adherence to the divinely given Law of Nature were sufficient to make a person tolerable—even though unassisted reason in fact grasps the Law of Nature only partially and imperfectly, and even though rejecting the Law of Faith hinders the achievement of salvation. Yet, although the *Reasonableness* and Locke's other theological writings imply a tolerationism more inclusive than that of the *Letter*, Locke never went so far as to advocate complete freedom of conscience in matters of religion, since his views on toleration were always conditioned by a markedly religious conception of human life and morality.

2 Political Scepticism and the Struggle against Moral Scepticism in *A Letter concerning Toleration*

Whereas a detailed reconstruction of the development of Locke's approach to toleration from his early writings on the subject to *A Letter concerning Toleration* is beyond the scope of this article, it is worth pointing out that this issue attracted his attention since at least the early 1660s.[16] Locke's first work on toleration, the manuscript *Two Tracts on Government* (1660–1662), was occasioned by the publication of Edward Bagshaw's *The Great Question concerning Things Indifferent in Reli-*

---

[15] John T. Moore, "Locke on the Moral Need for Christianity," *Southwestern Journal of Philosophy* 11 (1980): 61–68; Takashi Kato, "The *Reasonableness* in the Historical Light of the *Essay*," *Locke Newsletter* 12 (1981): 55–56; Schneewind, "Locke's Moral Philosophy," 217–219; Nicholas Wolterstorff, "Locke's Philosophy of Religion," in *Cambridge Companion*, 185; Raffaele Russo, *Ragione e ascolto. L'ermeneutica di John Locke* (Naples: Guida, 2001), 168–174; Greg Forster, *John Locke's Politics of Moral Consensus* (Cambridge: Cambridge University Press, 2005), 40–83; Victor Nuovo, *John Locke: The Philosopher as Christian Virtuoso* (Oxford: Oxford University Press, 2017), 215–218.
[16] John W. Gough, "The Development of Locke's Belief in Toleration," in *John Locke: "A Letter concerning Toleration" in Focus*, 57–77.

gious Worship (1660).[17] Bagshaw argued, mainly on scriptural grounds, that individuals should be allowed to observe or disregard religious ceremonies (which he considered 'indifferent' to salvation) according to their conscience. Refuting Bagshaw's theory point by point, *Two Tracts* endorsed religious uniformity, thus expressing a position different to Locke's views in his later writings on this subject—starting with the manuscript *An Essay concerning Toleration* (1667), which advanced many of the arguments later refined and further developed in the *Letter*.[18] Locke highlighted the dangers of state-imposed religious uniformity and, on the other hand, the benefits of toleration of different religious societies in other manuscripts written before the *Letter*—most prominently in his *Critical Notes* (c.1681) on Stillingfleet's *The Mischief of Separation* (1680) and *The Unreasonableness of Separation* (1681).[19] In this manuscript, Locke advocated a separation between the state and religious societies, employing some of the arguments he later used in the *Letter* and arguing that 'a national Church [that] tends to the support of a national Religion' was unable to promote true religion, preserve civil peace, and prevent dangerous errors.[20] Locke was eventually prompted to write *A Letter concerning Toleration* by Louis XIV's revocation of the Edict of Nantes in October 1685—an event that led many French Huguenots to flee to surrounding Protestant countries. Locke attributed the causes of this and other intolerant policies to competition among churches aiming to gain power from the state. To Locke, the main cause of state-supported intolerance toward some religious groups was the rivalry among power-seeking churches themselves. In this regard, Locke also disapproved of the imprudence of civil magistrates whose willingness to favour a sect over another reflected a grievous failure properly to comprehend the origins, purpose, and limits of political authority. This is why the *Letter* begins with a plea for 'mutual toleration of Christians'[21] and gives arguments against undesirable alliances between the civil magistrate and one or more religious societies.

The *Letter* presents three arguments delineating the purview and aims of the commonwealth, which Locke defines as 'a Society of Men constituted only for the

---

[17] Edward Bagshaw, *The Great Question concerning Things Indifferent in Religious Worship* (London: s.n., 1660); John Locke, *Two Tracts on Government*, ed. Philip Abrams (Cambridge: Cambridge University Press, 1967).
[18] John Locke, "An Essay concerning Toleration," in Locke, *Political Writings*, 186–210.
[19] Edward Stillingfleet, *The Mischief of Separation* (London: Mortlock, 1680); Edward Stillingfleet, *The Unreasonableness of Separation* (London: Mortlock, 1681); John Locke, "Critical Notes upon Edward Stillingfleet's *Mischief* and *Unreasonableness of Separation*—Extracts," in John Locke, *Writings on Religion*, ed. Victor Nuovo (Oxford: Oxford University Press, 2002): 73–79. The 170-page manuscript *Critical Notes*, still unpublished in its entirety, is MS Locke c. 34 (Bodleian Library, University of Oxford). Several other manuscripts on toleration, written by Locke between the *Essay* of 1667 and the *Letter*, have been published in John Locke, *Political Essays*, ed. Mark Goldie (Cambridge: Cambridge University Press, 1997).
[20] Locke, "Critical Notes," 77–78.
[21] Locke, "Letter," 7.

procuring, preserving, and advancing of their own *Civil Interests*.'[22] By civil interests, Locke means 'Life, Liberty, Health, and Indolency of Body; and the Possession of outward things, such as Money, Lands, Houses, Furniture, and the like.'[23] It follows that the civil ruler's power does not extend to 'the Care of Souls,' as Locke argues in the first of his arguments—the argument from the mandate of the state:

> [T]he Care of Souls is not committed to the Civil Magistrate any more than to other Men. It is not committed unto him, I say, by God; because it appears not that God has ever given any such Authority to one Man over another, as to compel any one to his Religion. Nor can any such Power be vested in the Magistrate by the *Consent of the People;* because no man can so far abandon the care of his own Salvation, as blindly to leave it to the choice of any other, whether Prince or Subject, to prescribe to him what Faith or Worship he shall embrace.[24]

Consequently, to Locke 'there is absolutely no such thing, under the Gospel, as a Christian Commonwealth.'[25] Moreover, the political authorities cannot impose religious uniformity because of the nature of the power they exercise, as Locke explains in his second argument—the argument from belief:

> The care of Souls cannot belong to the Civil Magistrate, because his Power consists only in outward force: But true and saving Religion consists in the inward perswasion of the Mind; without which nothing can be acceptable to God. And such is the nature of the Understanding, that it cannot be compell'd to the belief of any thing by outward Force.[26]

Finally, Locke's third argument—the argument from error—states that, even 'though the rigour of Laws and the force of Penalties were capable to convince and change Mens minds, yet would not that help at all to the Salvation of their Souls.'[27] To Locke, there is only one true religion and many false ones. Therefore, in most cases, imposing the 'Religion of the Court' on the subjects would put them 'under an Obligation of following their Princes in the ways that lead to Destruction.'[28]

These arguments are far from being *positive* arguments in support of religious toleration. In the *Letter*, Locke supplied only a *negative* justification of a limited toleration on the part of the state, as he criticized several arguments for the magistrate's *complete* control of religious affairs.[29] Locke's negative justification of toleration relied on a sort of 'political scepticism,' which, nevertheless, was not about 'true reli-

---

[22] *Ibidem*, 12.
[23] *Ibidem*.
[24] *Ibidem*, 13.
[25] *Ibidem*, 42.
[26] *Ibidem*, 13.
[27] *Ibidem*, 14.
[28] *Ibidem*, 15. See, also, John Locke, "A Third Letter for Toleration," in *Locke on Toleration*, 123–124; Black, "Toleration," 488–490.
[29] David J. Lorenzo, "Tradition and Prudence in Locke's Exceptions to Toleration," *American Journal of Political Science* 47 (2003): 254.

gion' in itself. Locke never questioned the existence of true religion, which he identified with 'the truth of the Gospel,' containing all things 'necessary to salvation.'[30] Therefore, according to Locke, 'all charitable Admonitions, and affectionate Endeavours to reduce Men from Errors [...] are indeed the greatest Duty of a Christian.'[31] However, he argued that 'all Force and Compulsion are to be forborn' when 'one Man does not violate the Right of another, by his Erroneous Opinions, and undue manner of Worship, nor is his Perdition any prejudice to another Mans Affairs,' given that 'the care of each Mans Salvation belongs only to himself.'[32] Locke's rejection of 'force and compulsion' in religious matters not affecting others' civil interests is rooted in his scepticism about the human ability to correctly comprehend and, above all, to effectively communicate religious truth. Locke recognized that, although there can be but one true religion, differences in human understanding and the difficulties of communication had produced a plethora of divergent dogmas and ceremonies. As a result, 'every one is Orthodox to himself'[33] and believes that all others are heretics. This happens because most religious doctrines are simply a matter of opinion—not a matter of knowledge; but divergences in religious opinions should not hinder civil coexistence, as Locke argued in *An Essay concerning Human Understanding*:

> Since, therefore, it is unavoidable to the greatest part of men, if not all, to have several opinions, without certain and indubitable proofs of their truth; and it carries too great an imputation of ignorance, lightness, or folly for men to quit and renounce their former tenets presently upon the offer of an argument which they cannot immediately answer, and show the insufficiency of: it would, methinks, become all men to maintain peace, and the common offices of humanity, and friendship, in the diversity of opinions; since we cannot reasonably expect that any one should readily and obsequiously quit his own opinion, and embrace ours, with a blind resignation to an authority which the understanding of man acknowledges not. For however it may often mistake, it can own no other guide but reason, nor blindly submit to the will and dictates of another. [...] We should do well to commiserate our mutual ignorance, and endeavour to remove it in all the gentle and fair ways of information; and not instantly treat others ill, as obstinate and perverse, because they will not renounce their own, and receive our opinions, or at least those we would force upon them, when it is more than probable that we are no less obstinate in not embracing some of theirs.[34]

To facilitate coexistence between people holding different religious views, in the *Letter* Locke adopted the distinction between things indifferent and things necessary to salvation, and he maintained that toleration ought to apply to the latter. Nevertheless, Locke was aware that making a case for toleration based on the concept of

---

[30] Locke, "Letter," 66; John Locke, "A Second Letter concerning Toleration," in *Locke on Toleration*, 79.
[31] Locke, "Letter," 46.
[32] *Ibidem*, 45–46.
[33] *Ibidem*, 7.
[34] Locke, *Essay*, IV.xvi.4.

'things indifferent,' also called *adiaphora*, had two drawbacks. First, it was difficult to reach consensus about the boundary between things indifferent and things necessary to salvation. Second, the very notion of 'things indifferent' could lead to an argument for intolerance. Since some doctrines and rituals were indifferent to salvation, one might wish to impose them by authority, for the sake of decency and good order. This was the position of several latitudinarian divines who, as Mark Goldie has remarked,

> [...] were in fact intolerant, for their intention was to embrace moderate nonconformists, by softening the rigidities of the church's 'good order,' before penalizing the recalcitrant minority who refused to accept such revised terms.[35]

Moreover, Locke too, in his *Two Tracts* of the early 1660s, had used the distinction between *fundamenta* and *adiaphora* to show, *contra* Bagshaw, the necessity of the magistrate's complete authority over religion. However, by 1667—the year when Locke wrote *An Essay concerning Toleration*—he had already made a 180-degree turn on this issue. This change in perspective denotes Locke's shift to a greater optimism regarding human nature in the *Essay* of 1667 and in his later writings on political theory. Locke's political scepticism—originating in his recognition of the 'burden of incommunicability' and, hence, of the limits of civil communication and the limited scope of public reason—led him to conclude, in the *Letter*, that 'indifferent' beliefs and practices ought to be tolerated, even when the civil magistrate or other citizens consider these beliefs and practices erroneous.[36] In the *Letter* and in the second of the *Two Treatises of Government* (1690), the difficulties of communicative possibilities restrict the purview of political power to what can be publicly conveyed and largely agreed upon. To Locke, what can be largely agreed upon depends on practical reasoning, which leads human beings to take steps for preserving themselves and the rest of humankind while avoiding principles destructive of human interests and, hence, of society.[37] Adopting principles detrimental to life, property, and freedom would be inconsistent with the criteria of the divinely given faculty of reason— more specifically, with practical reasoning, which is at the basis of public reason. The proper use of practical reasoning leads to consensus about the necessity to procure, preserve, and advance the civil interests of the members of the commonwealth. Political power can thus be rightfully exercised for this purpose. Conversely, it is impossible to reach consensus on religious beliefs and practices that do not harm anyone's life, property, or freedom and that, therefore, are not relevant to worldly interests. Such beliefs and practices, which are indeed 'things indifferent,' are open to

---

[35] Mark Goldie, "Introduction," in Locke, *Letter*, xvii–xviii.
[36] Vernon, *Career*, 35–51, 124–144; Vernon, "Introduction," xxiv–xxix.
[37] John Locke, *Two Treatises of Government*, ed. Peter Laslett (Cambridge: Cambridge University Press, 1988), 285–302.

human choice.[38] Thus, Locke concludes that human beings cannot 'stipulate' about 'their spiritual and eternal Interest,' they cannot 'submit this Interest to the Power of the Society, or any Sovereign they should set over them,' and no one can undertake to provide salvation to another through authoritarian, paternalistic means.[39] In fact, truth does not need to be imposed, and true religion can only benefit from toleration. True religion

> [...] is not taught by Laws, nor has she any need of Force to procure her entrance into the minds of men. [...] [I]f Truth makes not her way into the Understanding by her own Light, she will be but the weaker for any borrowed force Violence can add to her.[40]

By 'truth,' Locke means the *Christian* truth, which, in his opinion, would better spread without 'force and compulsion' and, at the same time, without finding impediments:

> [T]he Christian religion [...] grew, and spread, and prevailed, without any aid from force or the assistance of the powers in being; and if it be a mark of the true religion that it will prevail by its own light and strength, but that false religions will not, but have need of force and foreign helps to support them, nothing certainly can be more for the advantage of true religion, than to take away compulsion everywhere.[41]

Briefly, the *Letter* suggests that every individual, left to their own devices and suitably encouraged (but not pressured) by friendly others, has the ability and the right (and the duty, under natural law) to seek religious truth for themselves. Therefore, neither the civil magistrate nor anyone else can impede the search for truth, which, if left free, might lead the searcher to find the true religion. Besides being useless and even detrimental to salvation, the imposition of religious conformity by the political authorities proves destructive to human society, in that it is likely to trigger widespread discontent and harm the civil peace. Consequently, practical reasoning disposes human beings to shun the imposition of religious uniformity as a principle destructive of their own interests, both spiritual and civil, and of the public good. Concerning Locke's notion of the public good, Alex Tuckness has correctly observed:

> [T]he public good and the fundamental law of nature which commands that as much as possible mankind is to be preserved are, for Locke, more or less interchangeable. When God issues such a commission, he takes into account the fact that fallible persons will have to interpret and carry out the commission. God, as a rational legislator, will not define the public good broadly if a narrower conception that would be misapplied less often would better promote the good.[42]

---

38 Wolfson, *Persecution*, 21–38; Tate, *Liberty*, 31–37.
39 Locke, "Letter," 75.
40 *Ibidem*, 45.
41 Locke, "Second Letter," 69. See, also, Adam Drozdek, "Locke and Toleration," *Studia Minora Facultatis Philosophicae Universitatis Brunensis* 44 (1997): 25–32.
42 Tuckness, "Rethinking," 291.

However, Tuckness's analysis of human fallibility in Locke's thought focusses not on the perspective of citizens disputing about true religion, but on 'the perspective of a legislator putting forward a principle that will guide' the disputants.[43] *Pace* Tuckness, I believe that Locke's concept of legislator or magistrate in the *Letter* ought to be considered in the wider context of his political thought. In Locke's *Second Treatise of Civil Government*, it is indeed up to the community to delegate the legislative function—'the supreme power of the common-wealth'—to magistrates representing the people and accountable to the people; thus, the magistrates' powers flow from the citizens' consent, natural law, and the tasks of government.[44] Moreover, when advocating toleration of different opinions in the above-cited passage from *An Essay concerning Human Understanding*, Locke considered relationships between individual citizens or persons in general, not between citizens and the magistrate.[45] Briefly, Locke stressed not simply the magistrate's fallibility, but something more basic—that is, human fallibility in general.

The tolerationist implications of Locke's political scepticism denote several similarities with the Socinians' discourse on religious freedom, especially with Johann Crell's *Vindiciae pro religionis libertate*, written in late 1632, first published in 1637, and translated into English in 1646.[46] According to the anti-Trinitarian and anti-Calvinist theologian Faustus Socinus and his followers, salvation depends on the individual's free will, which informs all human decisions and actions. Reaffirming Socinus's emphasis on free will, Crell argued that human beings voluntarily join in civil societies and establish political institutions for the sake of security and peace. To Crell, political authority does not extend to matters pertaining to eternal salvation. Therefore, the magistrate cannot forbid religious beliefs and practices that do not affect the civil interests or communal life. According to Crell, the magistrate has a duty to protect all citizens in their religious observances, which are an essential part of their liberty, exactly as he protects them in all other aspects of life. Moreover, the magistrate's duty to respect and protect the citizens' religious liberty must be ratified in civil agreements, covenants, and pacts, which both the magistrate and the subjects are bound to comply with. More than half a century before the publication of Locke's *Letter concerning Toleration*, Crell's *Vindiciae* envisaged a clear separation between the state and religious organizations.[47] There is, nevertheless, a significant point of

---

43 Ibidem.
44 Locke, *Two Treatises*, 355–363; Lorenzo, "Tradition," 254.
45 Locke, *Essay*, IV.xvi.4; Black, "Toleration," 500.
46 [Johann Crell], *Iuni Bruti Poloni Vindiciae pro religionis libertate* (Eleutheropolis [Amsterdam]: Typis Godfridi Philadelphi, 1637); [Johann Crell], *A Learned and Exceeding Well-Compiled Vindication of Liberty of Religion*, trans. N. Y. [John Dury] ([London]: s.n., 1646). The Polish-based Socinians' fear that King Wladislaw IV might disregard the terms of the Warsaw Confederation of 1573, a document granting religious freedom in the Polish-Lithuanian Commonwealth, urged Crell to write this book.
47 Sarah Mortimer, "Freedom, Virtue and Socinian Heterodoxy," in *Freedom and the Construction of Europe*, eds. Quentin Skinner and Martin van Gelderen, 2 vols. (Cambridge: Cambridge University Press, 2013), vol. 1, *Religious and Constitutional Liberties*: 84.

divergence between Socinian tolerationism and Locke's toleration in the *Letter*. Socinus, Crell, and their followers considered human beings primarily as individuals. To the Socinians, salvation depends on the individual's free choice to accept the assistance of divine grace and, thus, to have faith and behave accordingly. They claimed that every individual believer had the right to study Scripture and to choose their own way to salvation. Therefore, although the Socinians acknowledged the individual's right to create and join religious organizations, they did not consider affiliation to a religious society as necessary to salvation and to toleration as well. Socinus himself never officially joined the Minor Reformed Church of Poland, to which most of his disciples, the 'Polish Brethren,' belonged. Conversely, in the *Letter*, Locke talked of individual believers as members of religious societies. Concentrating exclusively on *organized* religion, he made a distinction between the civil commonwealth, which he envisioned as a *general* entity consisting of all citizens, and religious organizations, which he described as *particular* societies, each composed of people who had freely joined it for a precise purpose. 'The end of a Religious Society,' Locke wrote,

> [...] is the Publick Worship of God, and by means thereof the acquisition of Eternal Life. All Discipline ought therefore to tend to that End, and all Ecclesiastical Laws to be thereunto confined. Nothing ought, nor can be transacted in this Society, relating to the Possession of Civil and Worldly Goods.[48]

In this passage, Locke not only delineated the ends of religious societies as distinct from the state's aims: he also suggested that salvation could be pursued effectively only within the bosom of a religious society, by means of the public worship of God. However, to Locke, religious societies ought to be free and voluntary. For this reason, he maintained:

> [E]xcommunication neither does, nor can deprive the excommunicated Person of any of those Civil Goods that he formerly possessed. All those things belong to the Civil Government, and are under the Magistrate's Protection.[49]

Moreover, he clarified in which relation religious organizations must stand to each other and to private persons:

> No private Person has any Right, in any manner, to prejudice another Person in his Civil Enjoyments, because he is of another Church or Religion. [...] What I say concerning the mutual Toleration of private Persons differing from one another in Religion, I understand also of particular Churches; which stand as it were in the same relation to each other as private Persons among themselves; nor has any one of them any manner of Jurisdiction over any other, no not even

---

48 Locke, "Letter," 18.
49 *Ibidem*, 19.

when the Civil Magistrate (as it sometimes happens) comes to be of this or the other Communion.[50]

It is worth noting that, in this passage, by 'private persons' Locke means, in essence, *members of religious societies*. In fact, he argues that no one's civil rights can be limited 'because he is of another Church or Religion'—not because this person holds heterodox ideas, for instance, ideas that cannot be attributed to any church or religion. What counts, here, is only whether one belongs to one or another religious society —a factor that, to Locke, must have no impact on civil life. Accordingly, Locke limited the authority of ecclesiastical ministers to the boundaries of their churches and denied that such authority could 'be extended to Civil Affairs.'[51] To Locke, all these conditions applied to both Christian and non-Christian organizations, as he expressly advocated toleration of Jews, Muslims, and pagans.[52] However, in the *Letter*, those subscribing to no organized religion—be they deists, agnostics, *indifferenti*, denominationally uncommitted Christians, etc.—are left in a vague limbo. On the one hand, they are not expressly excluded from toleration; but, on the other, their status remains undefined and they are not explicitly guaranteed any rights or freedoms.[53] Moreover, Locke openly denied toleration to Roman Catholics and atheists, and he did so for moral reasons bearing significant political implications.

Locke's best-known argument against tolerating Catholics is of a prudential nature. He thought that the magistrate could not tolerate subjects who owed their primary allegiance to a foreign prince, such as the pope, and who were, therefore, untrustworthy members of the commonwealth.[54] Nevertheless, the *Letter* gave more reasons to exclude Catholics from toleration, repeating and expanding some of the points that Locke had made in *An Essay concerning Toleration*.[55] To Locke, some moral ideas that Protestant polemicists commonly ascribed to Catholics and that he mentioned in the *Letter* (i.e. *'that Faith is not to be kept with Hereticks,' 'that Kings excommunicated forfeit their Crowns and Kingdoms,'* and *'*[t]hat *Dominion is founded in Grace'*) were harmful to civil society.[56] Moreover, Locke certainly had the pope in mind when he stigmatized

---

50 *Ibidem*, 20.
51 *Ibidem*, 24.
52 *Ibidem*, 58–59.
53 Israel, "Spinoza," 103.
54 Locke, "Letter," 51–52.
55 Locke, "Essay concerning Toleration," 197, 202–203.
56 Locke, "Letter," 50–51. In *An Essay concerning Toleration*, Locke had also deplored Catholic intolerance: see Locke, "Essay concerning Toleration," 202. On representations of Catholics in England in Locke's time, see John Marshall, *John Locke, Toleration and Early Enlightenment Culture* (Cambridge: Cambridge University Press, 2006), 17–93.

> [...] the absolute Authority of the same Person; who has not only power to perswade the Members of his Church to whatsoever he lists, (either as purely Religious, or as in order thereunto) but can also enjoyn it them on pain of Eternal Fire.[57]

This passage confirms Mark Goldie's thesis that Locke intended to preclude not Catholicism as such, but the Catholics' 'antinomianism'—namely, the opinion that a sort of divinely given 'superiority' can take priority over ordinary moral rules and direct the faithful's conduct.[58] In the *Letter*, Locke indeed excluded Catholics from toleration *not* because of ceremonies and doctrines that Protestants deemed absurd, such as the doctrine of transubstantiation, and that, nevertheless, did not harm anyone.[59] The use of political coercion against some members of the commonwealth because of the (alleged) absurdity of their (indifferent) beliefs would indeed contradict Locke's political scepticism. Therefore, Locke did not exclude the theoretical possibility of tolerating Catholics, on condition that they discarded what rendered them undeserving of toleration—that is, morals destructive of society. It is finally worth noting that Locke's objections against the Catholics' 'antinomianism' can also apply to others who, like various Calvinistic factions in seventeenth-century England, claimed to be divinely inspired to rule or exempt from ordinary moral norms. On this point, I concur with Goldie's statement that '[t]here are hints that Locke had Puritan fanatics in mind as being also potentially intolerable.'[60]

Locke's moral concerns also led him to deny toleration to atheists. In *An Essay concerning Toleration,* he wrote:

> [T]he belief of a deity is not to be reckoned amongst purely speculative opinions, for it being the foundation of all morality, and that which influence the whole life and actions of men, without which a man is to be considered no other than one of the most dangerous sorts of wild beasts, and so incapable of all society.[61]

In the first of the two arguments against atheists in the *Letter*, Locke gave more details of why atheists are so dangerous to society:

---

[57] Locke, "Letter," 52.
[58] Goldie, "Introduction," xix–xx.
[59] Locke, "Letter," 44.
[60] Goldie, "Introduction," xix.
[61] Locke, "Essay concerning Toleration," 188. On belief in God as preferable to atheism, see, also, John Locke, "Atheism," in Locke, *Political Essays*, 245–246 (a journal note written in 1676). On the social harmfulness of atheism, see, also, John Locke, "A Vindication of the Reasonableness of Christianity" (1695), in John Locke, *The Reasonableness of Christianity, as Delivered in the Scriptures*, ed. Victor Nuovo (Bristol: Thoemmes, 1997): 162: '[A]theism being a crime, which, for its madness as well as guilt, ought to shut a man out of all sober and civil society.'

> Those are not at all to be tolerated who *deny the Being of a God*. Promises, Covenants, and Oaths, which are the Bonds of Humane Society, can have no hold upon an Atheist. The taking away of God, though but even in thought, dissolves all.[62]

Locke's definition of atheists as 'those [...] who *deny the Being of a God*' was quite specific, in a time when the epithet 'atheist' was utilized to define various sorts of religious heterodoxy. Locke's empiricist philosophy entailed a consideration of different ways of being an atheist, whereas most seventeenth-century English theologians judged the idea of God innate to human nature, hence deeming it impossible to genuinely deny God's existence and, thus, to be a 'speculative atheist.'[63] In their opinion, there were only 'practical atheists,' whom the Cambridge scholar Richard Bentley defined as 'them that, believing [God's] Existence, do yet seclude him from directing the Affairs of the World, from observing and judging the Actions of Men.'[64] Locke's rejection of innate ideas created the space for what Kei Numao has termed 'the "ignorant atheist," an atheist who has simply not yet developed the notion of a God,'[65] and contributed to raise the conceptual problem of the 'speculative atheist, [...] one who "rationally" reached the wrong conclusion that God does not exist, and obstinately held fast to this view.'[66] Locke considered the latter as the 'true' atheist and the truly intolerable one, not only because of the inherent irrationality of speculative atheism, but also because of its practical implications. Thus, Locke's first argument against atheism ought to be considered in light of his effort to overcome his moral scepticism.

For most of his life, starting with the manuscript *Essays on the Law of Nature* (1664),[67] Locke struggled to find rational grounds for morality. He was not sceptical about the existence, rationality, and demonstrability of morality in itself. In *An Essay concerning Human Understanding*, he deemed it correct to 'place morality amongst the sciences capable of demonstration.'[68] However, he doubted that natural reason alone could *actually* demonstrate moral ideas and, thus, find solid grounds for morality. This is why, in the *Essay*, he called attention to the difficulties that reason meets when trying to demonstrate moral ideas—difficulties like their unfitness for sensible

---

62 Locke, "Letter," 52–53.
63 Marshall, *John Locke, Toleration*, 256–263; David Berman, *A History of Atheism in Britain: From Hobbes to Russell*, 2nd edition (London: Routledge, 2013), 1–47; J. Kei Numao, "Locke on Atheism," *History of Political Thought* 34 (2013): 252–272.
64 Richard Bentley, *Eight Sermons Preach'd at the Honourable Robert Boyle's Lecture* (Cambridge: Crownfield, 1724), 4–5.
65 Numao, "Locke," 260.
66 *Ibidem*, 267.
67 John Locke, *Essays on the Law of Nature*, trans. and ed. Wolfgang von Leyden (Oxford: Clarendon Press, 1958). These eight essays were originally written in Latin. Von Leyden's edition also includes Locke's valedictory speech as censor of moral philosophy and some philosophical shorthand writings by Locke.
68 Locke, *Essay*, IV.iii.18.

representation and their complexity.⁶⁹ He argued that these difficulties 'may in a good measure be remedied by definitions, setting down that collection of simple ideas, which every term shall stand for: and then using the terms steadily and constantly for that precise collection.'⁷⁰ Nevertheless, he observed that the limits of human understanding and the weakness of human nature actually prevent us from demonstrating moral ideas in such an effective way as we can demonstrate, for instance, mathematical concepts.⁷¹ In fact, as Locke eventually noted in *The Reasonableness of Christianity*, unassisted reason had always proven unable to provide adequate foundations for morality.⁷² Briefly, as John Higgins-Biddle has observed, Locke's

> [...] whole analysis of human understanding was designed to show how little proper knowledge man has and how ineffectual that knowledge is in most matters of morality and religion. [...] Thus, he sought in the *Essay* to establish traditional revelation as the primary guide in that proper science and business of mankind, morality and religion.⁷³

According to Locke, a revelation having the discernible marks of being from God must take priority over the uncertain conjectures of unassisted reason.⁷⁴ Locke believed that, despite the limits of knowledge in religious matters, human beings could demonstrate God's existence through the operation of natural reason. To Locke, although no idea, including the idea of God, is innate, natural reason is able to deduce the idea of God's existence from the observation of Creation:

> [T]he visible marks of extraordinary wisdom and power appear so plainly in all the works of the creation, that a rational creature, who will but seriously reflect on them, cannot miss the discovery of a deity.⁷⁵

This means that atheism is irrational, because atheists do not accept a 'discovery' that 'carries such a weight of thought and communication with it.'⁷⁶ Locke also believed that, since God is a lawmaker, belief in God is crucial to establish morality: '[W]ithout a notion of a law-maker, it is impossible to have a notion of a law, and

---

69 *Ibidem*, IV.iii.19.
70 *Ibidem*, IV.iii.20.
71 *Ibidem*.
72 Locke, *Reasonableness*, 148–150.
73 John C. Biddle, "Locke's Critique of Innate Principles and Toland's Deism," *Journal of the History of Ideas* 37 (1976): 417. Locke distinguished 'traditional revelation'—including biblical revelation—from 'original revelation' in *Essay* IV.xviii.3.
74 Jonathan S. Marko, "The Promulgation of Right Morals: John Locke on the Church and the Christian as the Salvation of Society," *Journal of Markets & Morality* 19 (2016): 51.
75 Locke, *Essay*, I.iv.9. See, also, Locke, *Essays on the Law of Nature*, 109, 147–159; Locke, *Essay*, II.xxiii.12, IV.x.1–6.
76 *Ibidem*, I.iv.9.

an obligation to observe it.'[77] However, *An Essay concerning Human Understanding* neither provides a thorough description of this law, nor explains why human beings are obliged to observe it. In the *Essay*, Locke indeed fails to identify the source of moral obligation in a manner consistent with his way of ideas, as he does not clarify which simple ideas are combined to form the mixed-mode idea of moral obligation.[78] When working on the *Essay* in the 1680s, Locke actually attempted at a system of ethics consistent with his way of ideas in the manuscript *Of Ethick in General*, written around 1686 and originally intended as the final chapter of the *Essay*.[79] However, he eventually discarded this project and left the manuscript incomplete. Thus, the *Essay* does not explain how natural reason, albeit able to prove God's existence, can find reasons to act morally based on self-evident principles. Instead, the *Essay* argues that human beings should avail themselves of both reason and revelation, when considering matters of morality and religion:

> Reason is natural Revelation, whereby the eternal Father of Light and Fountain of all Knowledge, communicates to Mankind that portion of Truth which he has laid within the reach of their natural Faculties: Revelation is natural Reason enlarged by a new set of Discoveries communicated by God immediately, which Reason vouches the Truth of, by the Testimony and Proofs it gives, that they come from God.[80]

To Locke, revelation comes in where unassisted reason cannot reach:

> There being many things wherein we have very imperfect notions, or none at all; and other things, of whose past, present, or future existence, by the natural use of our faculties, we can have no knowledge at all; these, as being beyond the discovery of our natural faculties, and above reason, are, when revealed, the proper matter of faith.[81]

In such cases, reason can only recognize the *probability* of a revealed thing. To Locke, faith is, in fact, not a mode of *knowledge:* faith is assent to merely *probable* matters of fact. Far from being grounded on the premises of some demonstration, such assent is given based on one's belief that God has revealed these matters of fact:[82]

> Because the mind not being certain of the truth of that it does not evidently know, but only yielding to the probability that appears in it, is bound to give up its assent to such a testimony which, it is satisfied, comes from one who cannot err, and will not deceive. [...] For where the principles of reason have not evidenced a proposition to be certainly true or false, there clear revelation, as another principle of truth and ground of assent, may determine; and so it may be matter of faith,

---

77 *Ibidem*, I.iv.8.
78 Schneewind, "Locke's Moral Philosophy," 207.
79 John Locke, "Of Ethick in General," in Locke, *Writings*, 9–14. On this manuscript, see Nuovo, *John Locke*, 193–197.
80 Locke, *Essay*, IV.xix.4.
81 *Ibidem*, IV.xviii.7. On Locke's distinction between things according to reason, above reason, and contrary to reason, see *ibidem*, IV.xvii.23.
82 Wolterstorff, "Locke's Philosophy," 190.

and be also above reason. Because reason, in that particular matter, being able to reach no higher than probability, faith gave the determination where reason came short; and revelation discovered on which side the truth lay.[83]

Revelation indeed includes several things 'whose truth our mind, by its natural faculties and notions, cannot judge'—things that we, therefore, ought to accept as 'above reason.'[84] In the *Essay*, Locke gave the existence of an afterlife with reward and punishment as an emblematic example of truth above reason, unambiguously revealed in Scripture, in whose divine authority he firmly believed.[85] He also hinted at an afterlife with rewards and sanctions as the only effective incentive to act morally:

> For, since nothing of pleasure and pain in this life can bear any proportion to the endless happiness or exquisite misery of an immortal soul hereafter, actions in his power will have their preference, not according to the transient pleasure or pain that accompanies or follows them here, but as they serve to secure that perfect durable happiness hereafter.[86]

Moreover, in the *Essay*, Locke stated that God 'has power to enforce [the divine law] by rewards and punishments of infinite weight and duration in another life [...]. This is the only true touchstone of moral rectitude.'[87] Later, in the *Reasonableness*, Locke maintained that belief in reward and punishment in the afterlife, which he described as an essential part of faith (particularly of the Christian Law of Faith), provides a strong motivation to behave morally. Briefly, in his mature works, Locke stressed the importance of otherworldly sanctions as effective incentives for moral conduct.[88] Atheists, however, do not believe in a divine creator and legislator. Thus, to Locke, they are inherently immoral, in that they can neither understand their duties towards their creator, nor accept any divinely given law, nor appreciate otherworldly sanctions.

In his other argument against toleration of atheists, Locke maintained that 'those that by their Atheism undermine and destroy all Religion, can have no pretence of Religion whereupon to challenge the Privilege of a Toleration.'[89] The *Letter* indeed provides a theory of toleration for the benefit of those who have religion—namely, those who pursue eternal salvation and have voluntarily joined a church 'in order to the publick worshipping of God, in such a manner as they judge acceptable to him, and effectual to the Salvation of their Souls.'[90] However, atheists deny God's ex-

---

83 Locke, *Essay*, IV.xviii.8–9.
84 *Ibidem*, IV.xviii.9.
85 *Ibidem*, IV.xviii.7.
86 *Ibidem*, II.xxi.60.
87 *Ibidem*, II.xxviii.8.
88 Schneewind, "Locke's Moral Philosophy," 208.
89 Locke, "Letter," 53.
90 *Ibidem*, 15.

istence. Thus, they do not pursue salvation and do not belong to any church. In other words, they have no religion. Therefore, they cannot ask for toleration, which, in Locke's *Letter*, is a 'privilege' to be granted only to those who have religion.

Locke's denial of toleration to atheists is not an accidental deviation from the theoretical framework of the *Letter*. Locke's intolerance of atheists is the logical consequence of his notion of toleration in the *Letter* and shows the limitations of this notion, which is conditioned by a markedly religious conception of life and morality. Locke thought that only faith in a divine creator and legislator and, hence, in a divinely given moral law could enable human beings to behave in morally acceptable ways. Consequently, only faith in God could enable a person not only to pursue salvation, which the *Letter* nominated 'to be everyone's highest priority,'[91] but also to be a good member of society. This conclusion led Locke to expect from the members of the commonwealth the care of their own souls (which, in the *Letter*, entails not only compliance with a morality based on belief in God, but also membership to, and worship within, a religious society), if they wanted to enjoy the 'privilege' of toleration.

3 Christian Irenicism, the Pursuit of Salvation, and the Overcoming of Moral Scepticism in *The Reasonableness of Christianity*

Locke's major book of theology, *The Reasonableness of Christianity*, is widely considered a work aiming to find a common ground for peace and toleration among Christians. In this book, Locke pursued the so-called way of fundamentals, thus adhering to an important tradition in Protestant irenicism. This tradition included, among others, the Socinians and the Arminians (i.e. the followers of the anti-Calvinist Dutch theologian Jacob Arminius, also known as Remonstrants) besides several English scholars, including the members of the Great Tew Circle and various latitudinarian divines.[92] Although Locke always maintained that his theological ideas resulted exclusively from his own reading of Scripture, his writings on religion present many points in common with Socinianism, Arminianism, and other currents and thinkers pursuing the way of fundamentals.[93] According to this tradition, Christianity consists

---

[91] Marko, "Promulgation," 54.
[92] On Locke and the 'way of fundamentals,' see John C. Higgins-Biddle, "Introduction," in Locke, *Reasonableness*, lxii–lxviii; Russo, *Ragione*, 160–165; Victor Nuovo, *Christianity, Antiquity, and Enlightenment: Interpretations of Locke* (Dordrecht: Springer, 2011), 94–98.
[93] Although Locke always denied any connections with Socinianism, he referred to Socinian works in various manuscripts, he owned many Socinian books, and he was friends with several anti-Trinitarians. See John R. Harrison and Peter Laslett, *The Library of John Locke* (Oxford: Oxford University Press, 1965); Richard Ashcraft, "John Locke's Library: Portrait of an Intellectual," *Transactions of the Cambridge Bibliographical Society* 5 (1969): 47–60; Higgins-Biddle, "Introduction," lviii–lx; John Marshall, "Locke, Socinianism, 'Socinianism', and Unitarianism," in *English Philosophy in the Age of*

of few simple principles regarding God's existence and assisting grace, the divine authority of Scripture, the existence of an afterlife with reward and punishment, and the necessity of morality to achieve salvation. Disparate dogmas and practices may originate from different interpretations of Scripture, which every Christian is allowed to understand according to their intellectual capacities; but specific dogmas and practices are secondary in comparison with the fundamental tenets of Christianity. Therefore, divergences on secondary, non-fundamental doctrinal, ceremonial, and ecclesiological issues must not hinder peace among Christians. Peaceful coexistence among Christians should be attained through either mutual toleration between different churches (as the Socinians proposed) or comprehension of all denominations into one church admitting differences in secondary doctrines and practices (as most latitudinarians argued). Locke himself made a distinction between fundamental principles and secondary doctrines, as John Higgins-Biddle has noted:

> [Locke] distinguish[ed] consistently between beliefs necessary to make one a Christian and beliefs that a Christian might subsequently hold. He maintained that the former were so simple and readily discernible that all persons could discover and understand them, whatever their intellectual capacities. At the same time, by allowing Christians to pursue subsequent beliefs to the extent of their intellectual capacity and in the direction of their religious preference, he maintained the flexibility necessary for toleration, which was the goal of the way of fundamentals.[94]

Whereas I agree with Higgins-Biddle that Locke's doctrine of the fundamentals had important irenic implications, I believe that it was mainly Locke's preoccupation with morality and salvation to shape his approach to the way of fundamentals. Like Socinians, Arminians, and other Protestant irenicists, Locke refused the main tenets of Calvinist theology and, instead, upheld a moralist soteriology. He rejected predestination, believed in the power of the human will to accept or resist saving grace, and highlighted the role of good works in the pursuit of salvation. Locke's approach to saving belief, however, differs from the views of other representatives of the way of fundamentals in a significant respect. Arminian authors like Arminius himself and Locke's friend, the Dutch theologian Philipp van Limborch, and Socinian writers like Socinus and Crell limited the essence of the Christian religion to a few fundamental principles, while they left it to each Christian to infer non-fundamentals from their own reading of the Bible. Nonetheless, Arminians and Socinians developed complex systems of doctrine and, according to Locke, showed 'zeal for their orthodoxy.'[95] Conversely, other Protestant irenicists, especially in England, avoided any

---

Locke, ed. M. A. Stewart (Oxford: Clarendon Press, 2000): 111–182; Stephen D. Snobelen, "Socinianism, Heresy and John Locke's *Reasonableness of Christianity*," *Enlightenment and Dissent* 20 (2001): 88–125.
94 Higgins-Biddle, "Introduction," lxvi.
95 John Locke, "A Second Vindication of the Reasonableness of Christianity" (1697), in Locke, *Reasonableness*, ed. Nuovo, 295.

attempt to detail even the fundamentals of Christianity. For instance, in *The Religion of Protestants* (1638), the Great Tew Circle member William Chillingworth wrote that Christians should 'syncerely endeavour to finde the true sense of [Scripture], and live according to it.'[96] However, Chillingworth considered it undesirable, and actually impossible, to create a unique list of fundamentals to be followed by all Christians. Unlike Chillingworth, Locke embarked on identifying the fundamental articles of Christianity, as we will see below; but, unlike Arminians and Socinians, he refrained from endorsing a specific system of doctrine. Locke did not wish to endorse a particular system of doctrine to others because, in his opinion, saving belief does not result from the acceptance of some theological system: saving belief is rooted in Scripture alone. Therefore, the faithful ought to study Scripture to the best of their abilities in order to live the Christian life and pursue salvation. Locke even admitted the possibility of mistakes in interpreting Scripture, given the limits of human understanding. As John Marshall has pointed out, in the *Reasonableness* and its two vindications (written against the attacks on Locke's theology by the Calvinistic divine John Edwards), Locke 'was also accenting that much was not plain in Christianity and that the search for religious truth was more important than its maintenance, arguing that error held after sincere search was saving.'[97] Locke indeed acknowledged that

> [...] a great many of the Truths revealed in the Gospel, every one does, and must confess, a man may be ignorant of; nay, disbelieve, without danger to his Salvation: As is evident in those, who, allowing the Authority, differ in the Interpretation and meaning of several Texts of Scripture, not thought Fundamental.[98]

On the other hand, according to Locke, '[s]ome of the truths delivered in the holy writ are very plain: it is impossible, I think, to mistake their meaning; and those certainly are all necessary to be explicitly believed.'[99] These 'very plain' truths are what Locke identified as the three fundamentals of Christianity—namely, faith in Jesus as the Messiah, who had delivered a salvific message hitherto unknown to humankind, repentance for one's misdeeds, and obedience to the divine law, which only Christ had revealed completely and perfectly. Locke considered the acceptance of these fundamentals, which were clearly delivered in the Scriptures and had a prominently moral meaning, to be all that one needed to become a Christian. According to Locke, however, accepting and living by these fundamentals was necessary but not sufficient to salvation, given that the faithful also had to study the Bible conscientiously throughout their life. And Locke believed that disregarding the three fundamentals of Chris-

---

[96] William Chillingworth, *The Religion of Protestants a Safe Way to Salvation* (Oxford: Lichfield, 1638), 180.
[97] Marshall, "Locke, Socinianism," 172. See Locke, *Reasonableness*, 168–171; Locke, "Vindication," 164–165; Locke, "Second Vindication," 198, 234–235, 356–359, 376–377, 421–424.
[98] Locke, *Reasonableness*, 168.
[99] Locke, "Second Vindication," 356.

tianity, when reading the Bible, was likely to lead to either one of two equally extreme, albeit diametrically opposed, outcomes—antinomianism and deism.

In the *Second Vindication*, Locke declared that the antinomian controversy among Dissenters had prompted him to write the *Reasonableness*.[100] This controversy between Independent and Presbyterian ministers was occasioned by the republication, in 1690, of the Civil-War Independent divine Tobias Crisp's *Christ Alone Exalted* (1643) by his son Samuel.[101] To Locke, an incorrect, partial reading of Scripture was likely to lead to a radically predestinarian, antinomian soteriology, which he abhorred because all forms of antinomianism dismissed the importance of moral conduct for salvation. However, Locke's dislike of predestination denotes that he actually saw predestinarianism in itself—and not simply the extreme views endorsed by Crisp and his followers—as fundamentally antinomian and, hence, detrimental to the pursuit of salvation. According to Locke, the very concept of predestination—a concept essentially based on the doctrine of original sin, which he rejected[102]—was incompatible with God's justice and goodness. Moreover, the shortcomings of predestinarianism had led others to reach the opposite extreme in their reaction:

> For whilst some Men would have all *Adam*'s Posterity doomed to Eternal Infinite Punishment, for the Transgression of *Adam*, whom Millions had never heard of, and no one had authorized to transact for him, or be his Representative; this seemed to others so little consistent with the Justice or Goodness of the Great and Infinite God, that they thought there was no Redemption necessary, and consequently that there was none, rather than admit of it upon a Supposition so derogatory to the Honour and Attributes of that Infinite Being; and so made Jesus Christ nothing but the Restorer and Preacher of pure Natural Religion; thereby doing violence to the whole tenor of the New Testament.[103]

To Locke, the opinion that Jesus was merely a moral philosopher, who had solely reasserted a perfect Law of Nature already known to natural reason, without adding anything to it, was typical of deism.[104] This opinion implied that natural reason

---

[100] *Ibidem*, 186–187. Whereas Locke referred to this controversy, he never used the terms 'antinomian' and 'antinomianism' in the *Reasonableness* and its vindications.
[101] Tobias Crisp, *Christ Alone Exalted*, 2nd edition (London: Marshal, 1690).
[102] Locke, *Essay*, II.xxvii.22, II.xxvii.26; John Locke, "Peccatum originale," in Locke, *Writings*, 229–230; John Locke, "Homo ante et post Lapsum," in *ibidem*, 231. Locke wrote the manuscripts *Peccatum originale* and *Homo ante et post lapsum*, both of which deny original sin, in 1692 and 1693 respectively.
[103] Locke, *Reasonableness*, 5.
[104] Locke did not use terms like 'deism' or 'deist' in the *Reasonableness*, but he wrote the words 'deist' or 'deists' once in the first vindication and eight times in the second. Higgins-Biddle has persuasively argued that Locke's deist targets in these works were the heterodox Jewish intellectual Uriel Acosta and the Irish freethinker John Toland. See Higgins-Biddle, "Introduction," xxvii–xxxvii. Acosta had committed suicide in 1640, thus ending his conflictual relationship with the Jewish community of Amsterdam. Locke's friend, Limborch, published Acosta's biography in 1687: see Philipp van Limborch, *De Veritate Religionis Christianae, amica collatio cum erudito Judaeo; acced. Urielis Acosta Exemplar Humanae Vitae, cum Refutatione per Limborch* (Gouda: Justum ab Hoeve, 1687), 341–364. In a

alone was a sufficient guide to salvation. However, according to Locke, unassisted reason was actually unable to comprehend the ultimate truths in matters of religion and morality and, thus, to serve as a guide to salvation. Locke even argued that many ancient philosophers, relying on natural reason alone and showing an elitist attitude, had eventually fostered the spread of priestcraft:

> The Rational and thinking part of Mankind, 'tis true, when they sought after him, they found the One, Supream, Invisible God: But if they acknowledged and worshipped him, it was only in their own minds. They kept this Truth locked up in their own breasts as a Secret, nor ever durst venture it amongst the People; much less amongst the Priests, those wary Guardians of their own Creeds and Profitable Inventions. Hence we see that *Reason*, speaking ever so clearly to the Wise and Virtuous, had never Authority enough to prevail on the Multitude.[105]

This is why 'the Priests' ruled 'every where, to secure their Empire, having excluded *Reason* from having any thing to do in Religion.'[106] This was an indirect attack on deism, as Mark Goldie has pointed out: 'Contemporary deist claims for the great capacity of reason, Locke asserts, cannot be sustained in the face of history's evidence to the contrary.'[107] To Locke, only Jesus, revealing the divine law in its entirety, had reconciled religion and morality, thus avoiding the defects of '[t]he lives of pure idolatry and pure reason [which] were both failed projects.'[108]

Locke's sceptical attitude towards the actual capabilities of unassisted reason in matters of morality was another point of similarity with the Socinian tradition.[109] One of the main tenets of Socinianism is that God's Revealed Word is superior to the Law of Nature. This is a significant difference between the Socinians and the Magisterial Reformers, whose position on this subject is detailed in Philip Melanchthon's *Loci Communes* (1521). According to Melanchthon, human beings have an innate knowledge of God and of the divine law in its entirety—a knowledge not de-

---

manuscript note of 1695, Locke called Acosta 'the father and patriarch of the Deists;' see MS Locke d. 10, "Lemmata Ethica" (Bodleian Library, University of Oxford), 33. As to Toland, Locke first met him in 1693. In 1695, Toland sent some papers to Locke through the lawyer John Freke. These papers, which are lost, were probably the drafts of some sections of Toland's *Christianity Not Mysterious* (1696). See the letter by John Freke to John Locke, 28 March 1695, in *The Correspondence of John Locke*, ed. E. S. de Beer, 8 vols. (Oxford: Oxford University Press, 1979–1989), vol. 5, no. 1868; letter by John Freke and Edward Clarke to John Locke, 9 April 1695, in *ibidem*, no. 1874.
105 Locke, *Reasonableness*, 144.
106 *Ibidem*, 143.
107 Mark Goldie, "John Locke, the Early Lockeans, and Priestcraft," *Intellectual History Review* 28 (2018): 132.
108 *Ibidem*.
109 On Socinian ethics and soteriology, see Faustus Socinus, "De Jesu Christo Servatore," in *Bibliotheca Fratrum Polonorum quos Unitarios vocant*, 9 vols. (Irenopoli [Amsterdam]: Sumptibus Irenici Philalethii, post annum Domini 1656 [1665–1692]), vol. 2, *Fausti Socini Senensis Opera Omnia in duos tomos distincta* [1668], 115–246; Johann Crell, *Ad librum Hugonis Grotii quem de satisfactione Christi adversus Faustum Socinum Senensem scripsit* (Racoviae: Tipis Sternacianis, 1623). *De Jesu Christo Servatore* was written in 1576 and first published in 1594.

pendent on revelation. Melanchthon and the other Magisterial Reformers identified the divine law with a perfect Law of Nature, which Christian revelation had simply reaffirmed and clarified.[110] Socinus and his followers rejected this view. They maintained that religious belief proper does not depend on a natural instinct innate to all human beings and, thus, is unattainable by natural reason alone. According to the Socinians, faith results from one's free choice to accept the assistance of God's grace, which one can know of through biblical revelation. The acceptance of God's assisting grace entails a commitment to respect Christ's precepts, which the Socinians considered more coherent, convincing, and rewarding than the Law of Nature. To the Socinians, whereas the Law of Nature inclines human beings to the preservation of earthly goods, Christ's moral teachings offer a better prospect than merely worldly benefits —the prospect of eternal salvation. This means that, prior to Christian revelation, human morality was still imperfect, devoid of effective incentives to act morally, and flawed, in that it focussed on worldly interests alone. It was only after Christ's ministry on earth that humanity could comply with moral standards facilitating the pursuit of salvation and even clashing, in some cases, with the dictates of the Law of Nature.[111] This position was at the origin of the Socinians' radical pacifism and advocacy of non-resistance, which conflicted with the natural right to self-defence. While admitting that the Law of Nature disposes human beings to defend their lives when harmed by others, the Socinians inferred from the New Testament that doing violence to another human being, even for reasons of self-defence, would prevent one from attaining the supreme good—eternal beatitude.

Locke shared the Socinians' opinion that Christ's revelation was superior to the Law of Nature as discoverable, at least in theory, by unassisted reason. However, Locke disagreed with the Socinian idea that God's Revealed Word contradicted and invalidated some elements of the Law of Nature, such as our right of self-preservation and self-defence. To Locke, the Law of Nature gives us the right and duty to preserve the life that God has given us, the goods produced and acquired through our work, and the freedom to make use of our persons and possessions while respecting others' like rights.[112] According to Locke, Christ's precepts had neither nullified nor replaced any element of the Law of Nature. He thought that Christian revelation had fully disclosed, complemented, and completed the Law of Nature. It follows that, according to Locke, we still have a natural right and duty to preserve our life, property, and freedom, even when this means to resist a despotic political power.[113] To Locke, the Law of Nature is indeed a divinely established and, hence, eternally valid system

---

[110] Philipp Melanchthon, *On Christian Doctrine: Loci Communes 1555*, trans. and ed. Clyde L. Manschrek (New York: Oxford University Press, 1965), 51–53, 73–75.
[111] Sarah Mortimer, "Human Liberty and Human Nature in the Works of Faustus Socinus and His Readers," *Journal of the History of Ideas* 70 (2009): 197.
[112] Locke, *Two Treatises*, 269–272.
[113] *Ibidem*, 406–428.

of morality.[114] The Law of Nature is a law of convenience promoting utility, and most human beings know some of its elements in the form of prescriptions of civil law or moral principles formulated by philosophers.[115] However, Locke argued that, before Christ's revelation, unassisted reason had always failed to grasp the Law of Nature in its entirety:

> ['T]is too hard a task for unassisted Reason to establish Morality in all its parts upon its true foundation; with a clear and convincing light. [...] [H]umane reason unassisted, failed Men in its great and Proper business of *Morality*. It never from unquestionable Principles, by clear deductions, made out an entire body of the *Law of Nature*.[116]

Locke also thought that ecclesiastical tradition, priestcraft, and power politics had negatively affected the human capacity to grasp and respect the Law of Nature, because the defects of human nature make human beings prone to being misled by both their own mistakes and priestly frauds.[117] Due to these problems, God reaffirmed the Law of Nature through the covenant of works, establishing the Law of Moses, which consisted of a ceremonial part and a moral part—the Law of Works, identical to the Law of Nature.[118] The main advantage of the Law of Works over the Law of Nature was that the former was available in the Old Testament in terms comprehensible to everyone. Nevertheless, the Law of Moses was excessively rigorous and still did not offer effective incentives to act morally. This is why a new covenant, the covenant of grace or covenant of faith, was necessary. With this new covenant, Christ made the divine law known completely and perfectly, thus establishing the Law of Faith. To Locke, Christ revealed the Law of Nature in its entirety and complemented it with the assurance of rewards and punishments in the afterlife, thus providing a powerful incentive to act morally.[119] Locke emphasized this incentive, which was one of the main tenets of Socinian soteriology, not only in the *Reasonableness*, but also throughout the posthumously published *A Paraphrase and*

---

114 Locke, *Reasonableness*, 13–15.
115 Ibidem, 151–154.
116 Ibidem, 148–150.
117 Ibidem, 161–163. See, also, Locke, *Essay*, III.x.2, on the distortions of language deliberately made by 'the several sects of philosophy and religion.' Concerning Locke's anticlericalism and views on priestcraft, see John Marshall, *John Locke: Resistance, Religion and Responsibility* (Cambridge: Cambridge University Press, 1994), 353–357, 405–410; Richard Ashcraft, "Anticlericalism and Authority in Lockean Political Thought," in *The Margins of Orthodoxy: Heterodox Writing and Cultural Response, 1660–1750*, ed. Roger D. Lund (Cambridge: Cambridge University Press, 1995): 73–96; Goldie, "John Locke, the Early Lockeans;" James A. T. Lancaster, "From Matters of Faith to Matters of Fact: The Problem of Priestcraft in Early Modern England," *Intellectual History Review* 28 (2018): 145–165.
118 Locke, *Reasonableness*, 16–21.
119 Ibidem, 21–25, 110–112, 132. See, also, John Locke, "Voluntas," in Locke, *Political Essays*, 321 (a manuscript note written in 1693–1694).

Notes on the Epistles of St Paul.[120] However, Locke did not claim that accepting the Law of Faith and, thus, believing in an afterlife with reward and punishment leads, necessarily and unfailingly, to act morally. In *An Essay concerning Human Understanding*, which Locke revised multiple times until his death in 1704, and in his theological works, he acknowledged that even those who believe in otherworldly sanctions are still liable to commit evil deeds, given the limits of human understanding and the weakness of human nature.[121] Therefore, he shared another important tenet of Socinian soteriology—that is, belief in God's mercy. The Socinians thought that Christ had offered humanity a concrete hope of salvation, despite the limits and imperfections of human nature. In *De Jesu Christo Servatore* (1594), Socinus maintained that Christ had emphasized God's forgiveness. Socinus and his disciples rejected the opinion that God necessarily ought to punish sinners. They argued that God is merciful and omnipotent and, thus, not bound by any law—unlike human judges, who have to apply the laws of the state. To the Socinians, God could waive his right to punishment and, thus, forgive the sins of the repentant faithful who, during their life, had sincerely endeavoured to obey the divine law.[122] The importance that Locke attached to faith as one of the fundamentals of Christianity was in line with the Socinians' stress on God's forgiveness, as he wrote that '*by the Law of Faith, Faith is allowed* to supply the defect of full Obedience; and so the Believers are admitted to Life and Immortality as if they were Righteous.'[123] To Locke, Christ 'did not expect [...] a Perfect Obedience void of all slips and falls: He knew our Make, and the weakness of our Constitution too well, and was sent with a Supply for that Defect.'[124] This supply was faith. Nevertheless, Locke did not believe in salvation by faith alone. To Locke, human beings still ought to respect the eternally valid principles of the divinely given Law of Nature, which Christ, establishing the Law of Faith, had fully disclosed and had complemented and completed with two significant 'advantages'—a powerful incentive to act morally, in the form of an afterlife with reward and punishment, and an emphasis on God's forgiveness. According to the Law of Faith, the believer's faith compensates for their failure to perfectly comply with the divine law—a failure that, given the weakness of human nature, is inevitable, even when one is sincerely committed to obedience.[125] Thus, the faithful will receive 'the Pardon and Forgiveness of Sins and Salvation'[126] thanks to their faith,

---

[120] David Wootton, "John Locke: Socinian or Natural Law Theorist?," in *Religion, Secularization and Political Thought: Thomas Hobbes to J. S. Mill*, ed. James E. Crimmins (London: Routledge, 1989): 49.
[121] Locke, *Essay*, II.xxi.60–73, II.xxviii.12; Locke, *Reasonableness*, 19, 120, 130.
[122] Socinus, "De Jesu," 121–132; Crell, *Ad librum*, 164–167; Sarah Mortimer, "Human and Divine Justice in the Works of Grotius and the Socinians," in *The Intellectual Consequences of Religious Heterodoxy 1600–1750*, eds. John Robertson and Sarah Mortimer (Leiden: Brill, 2012): 75–94.
[123] Locke, *Reasonableness*, 19.
[124] *Ibidem*, 120.
[125] *Ibidem*, 130; Dewey D. Wallace, "Socinianism, Justification by Faith, and the Sources of John Locke's *The Reasonableness of Christianity*," *Journal of the History of Ideas* 45 (1984): 53–54.
[126] Locke, *Reasonableness*, 133.

but only on condition that, in their life, they repent for their misdeeds and wholeheartedly attempt to obey the divine law. It is in this sense that, in Locke's soteriology, faith 'justifies.' The justifying faith includes good works. Locke's views on justification distinguish him, on the one hand, from predestinarians and antinomians of different stripes and, on the other, from deists. Locke's position is actually in line with the Socinian and Arminian idea that human beings are able to accept or reject assisting grace. However, Locke thought that accepting divine assistance and, hence, adhering to the Law of Faith was the 'reasonable,' convenient option, given the above said advantages of Christ's Coming.

Briefly, to Locke, faith in Christ's Messiahship, repentance for one's misdeeds, and commitment to obey the divine law, along with a sincere and constant effort to study Scripture, are all that is required to achieve salvation. All those committed to pursuing salvation by these means should tolerate each other, instead of showing hostility to one another because of divergences about non-fundamentals. Therefore, the views on morality and salvation expressed in *The Reasonableness of Christianity* have important irenic implications. Locke's moralist soteriology even implies toleration of denominationally uncommitted Christians, although Locke lived and died a conforming member of the Church of England and although he never aimed at dissolving churches as formal associations with their specific doctrines, structures, norms, and ceremonies. In fact, Locke always granted churches the right to be uniformitarian. To Locke, there can be no forced church membership, but voluntary membership entails submission to the discipline of the religious society to which one has chosen to belong in order to perform the public worship of God. In the *Reasonableness*, Locke addressed public acts of worship, performed within religious societies, in the section concerning Jesus' attempt to reform the public worship among the Jews of his time. According to Locke, Christ had aimed at depriving '[t]he outward forms of *Worshipping the Deity*' of 'Stately Buildings, costly Ornaments, peculiar and uncouth Habits, And a numerous huddle of pompous, phantastical, cumbersome Ceremonies,' formerly, and mistakenly, 'thought the principal part, if not the whole of Religion.'[127] Locke maintained that Jesus had revealed the following:

> To be Worshipped in Spirit and in Truth; with Application of Mind, and sincerity of Heart, was what God henceforth only required. [...] Decency, Order, Edification, were to regulate all their publick Acts of Worship. [...] Praises and Prayer, humbly offered up to the Deity, were the Worship he now demanded; And in these every one was to look after his own Heart, And know that it was that alone which God had regard to, and accepted.[128]

To me, it seems that, while endorsing the renovation of public acts of worship advocated by Jesus in the name of 'Decency, Order, Edification,' this section does not describe public worship, and hence affiliation to a church, as essential to morality and

---

127 *Ibidem*, 159.
128 *Ibidem*, 160.

salvation. Here, Locke indeed stresses that God requires only 'Application of Mind, and sincerity of Heart' from those who 'humbly' offer up 'Praises and Prayer [...] to the Deity'—a form of worship demanded by God and practicable, publicly and collectively, by the members of a church, but not necessarily connected to public worship. Thus, in my opinion, the *Reasonableness* does not preclude the possibility of salvation to those who accept the Law of Faith but consider themselves as 'mere Christians'—as was, for instance, Locke's friend Benjamin Furly after renouncing Quakerism in the early 1690s. Whether Locke, in his theological works, conceived of unaffiliated Christians as simply 'traveling' in search of a church with doctrines and rites they could approve, or as believers who could remain denominationally uncommitted throughout their lives, is not crucial to my argument.[129] It is true that Locke suggests nowhere in the *Reasonableness*, or in his other later writings on religion, that an individual Christian might remain unaffiliated throughout their life. However, nowhere in the *Reasonableness*, or in Locke's other works written between the mid-1690s and his death in 1704, denominational affiliation is proposed as indispensable to moral conduct and the achievement of salvation.[130] As John Marshall has noted, Locke's later writings on religion actually show that he 'was opposed to dividing and denominating Christians on the basis of non-fundamentals, stressing the express words of Scripture and his status as a Christian, not the member of any sect.'[131] The *Reasonableness* and Locke's other later works on religion indeed extend the possibility of salvation to all those accepting the Law of Faith, regardless of non-fundamentals and confessional affiliation. Consequently, this position also allows for toleration of denominationally uncommitted Christians who adhere to the Law of Faith and the ethics it entails.

4 Non-Christian Believers in Locke's Later Writings on Religion

Locke's later theological works express the conviction that only the Christian Law of Faith can establish a coherent system of ethics and lead to salvation. As Locke put it in *A Paraphrase and Notes*, specifically in commenting on Ephesians 2:15:

---

129 Locke's use, in the *Reasonableness*, of the metaphor of the 'travel' is aimed at stressing the necessity of divine revelation (as facilitating our journey) in moral and religious matters and, on the other hand, at stigmatizing the unfortunate doctrinal conflicts among Christians: see *ibidem*, 156–159, 169–171.
130 I believe that Locke's manuscript *Sacerdos* (1698) does not require confessional affiliation as essential to salvation. In this manuscript, Locke stated that Christ, reuniting religion and morality, had reformed 'outward ceremonie' to fit with what 'decency & order requird in actions of publique assemblys.' Concerning ministers' right to regulate and perform public worship and 'to teach Men their dutys of Morality,' Locke was obviously talking of a right limited to the boundaries of their churches, which he always considered as voluntary societies. See John Locke, "Sacerdos," in Locke, *Writings*, 17–18.
131 Marshall, "Locke, Socinianism," 171.

> [T]he Subjects of [God's] Kingdom whereof this is now the Law, can be at no doubt or less about their Duty, if they will but read and consider the Rules of Morality, which our Saviour and his Apostles have deliver'd in very plain words in the holy Scriptures of the New Testament.[132]

In this regard, Victor Nuovo has observed that Locke's views on morality and salvation in his theological works imply that, 'if morality is the chief business of mankind, then the best way of pursuing it is to become a Christian'[133]—namely, to accept and live by the Law of Faith. Locke's moralist soteriology indeed implies a denial of the possibility of salvation for those refusing the Law of Faith and the ethics it entails— not only antinomians and deists, but also heathens, Muslims, and Jews unwilling to convert to Christianity.

Concerning pagans, the *Reasonableness* extended the possibility of salvation to those who had 'never heard of the Promise or News of a Saviour.'[134] Locke could not accept that God, in His goodness and mercy, would damn those people for not accepting a revelation they had never heard of. Therefore, he argued that God, 'by the Light of Reason,' had enabled them to grasp and respect the basic tenets of the Law of Nature and 'to find also the way to Reconciliation and Forgiveness' when they transgressed this law.[135] In Locke's words:

> [T]he Author of this Law, and God of Patience and Consolation, who is rich in Mercy, would forgive his frail Off-spring; if they acknowledged their Faults, disapproved the Iniquity of their Transgressions, beg'd his Pardon, and resolved in earnest for the future to conform their Actions to this Rule, which they owned to be Just and Right.[136]

Nevertheless, Locke abstained from extending the possibility of salvation to people who, having heard of Christian revelation, still preferred to profess other religions. Moreover, in *A Paraphrase and Notes*, Locke refrained from making any concession to the heathen world, including those who had 'never heard of the Promise or News of a Saviour.'[137]

As regards Muslims, Locke mentioned 'the *Mahometan* Religion' only once in the *Reasonableness*, when he observed that this religion had 'derived and borrowed' its monotheism from Christianity.[138] In the *Second Vindication*, he referred to the Islamic religion only in responding to John Edwards's charge of holding a non-Trinitarian,

---

132 John Locke, *A Paraphrase and Notes on the Epistles of St Paul to the Galatians, 1 and 2 Corinthians, Romans, Ephesians*, ed. Arthur W. Wainwright, 2 vols. (Oxford: Clarendon Press, 1987), vol. 2, 365.
133 Nuovo, *John Locke*, 245.
134 Locke, *Reasonableness*, 139.
135 *Ibidem*, 139–140.
136 *Ibidem*, 140.
137 Arthur W. Wainwright, "Introduction," in Locke, *Paraphrase*, vol. 1, 41–43; Marshall, *John Locke: Resistance*, 447–451.
138 Locke, *Reasonableness*, 145.

'Socinian,' 'Mahometan' view of Jesus as merely a prophet.[139] However, in his theological writings, Locke did not say anything about the possibility of salvation for Muslims.

Concerning Jews who lived before Jesus, Locke stated in the *Reasonableness:*

> [T]he *Faith* of those before *Christ*; (believing that God would send the *Messiah*, to be a Prince, and a Saviour to his People, as he had promised) [...] shall be accounted to them for Righteousness.[140]

However, in rejecting antinomian ideas and salvaging the importance of good works for salvation in the *Reasonableness*, Locke expressed views typical of supersessionism—that is, the Christian doctrine, also called 'replacement theology,' according to which the Christian Church has succeeded the Jewish people as the definitive people of God. Moreover, in *A Paraphrase and Notes*, he openly disparaged the Jewish religion. In order to counter antinomian readings of the New Testament, especially of Paul's epistles, Locke distinguished between the Christian concept of 'works' and the Mosaic notion of 'works of the law.' In the *Reasonableness*, Locke argued that Paul had not opposed good works. According to Locke, when Paul spoke against 'works,' he meant the 'works of the law,' namely the ceremonial part of the Law of Moses, which had only temporary validity, whereas its moral part, being identical to the Law of Nature, was eternally valid:

> [S]ome of God's Positive Commands being for peculiar Ends, and suited to particular Circumstances of Times, Places, and Persons, have a limited and only temporary Obligation by virtue of God's positive Injunction; such as was that part of *Moses's* Law, which concerned the outward Worship, or Political Constitution of the Jews, and is called the Ceremonial and Judaical law, in contradistinction to the Moral part of it; Which being conformable to the Eternal Law of Right, is of Eternal Obligation, and therefore remains in force still under the Gospel; nor is abrogated by the *Law of Faith*.[141]

Locke's view of the Mosaic Law is emblematic of the 'theory of condescension,' according to which, as Eldon Eisenach has put it, 'the Old Testament law is consigned to the dustbin of history.'[142] Several seventeenth-century latitudinarian theologians, including John Tillotson and Edward Stillingfleet, upheld this theory. In the early eighteenth century, the Newtonian scholar Samuel Clarke unambiguously formulated the basic tenet of this theory in a sermon entitled *The End and Design of the Jewish Law:* 'The Jewish Law was an Institution of Religion adapted by God in great conde-

---

139 Locke, "Second Vindication," 185, 283, 360, 362.
140 Locke, *Reasonableness*, 139.
141 *Ibidem*, 19.
142 Eldon J. Eisenach, "Religion and Locke's Two Treatises of Government," in *John Locke's Two Treatises of Government: New Interpretations*, ed. Edward J. Harpham (Lawrence: University Press of Kansas, 1992): 73. See, also, Raffaele Russo, "Locke and the Jews: From Toleration to the Destruction of the Temple," *Locke Studies* 2 (2002): 199–223.

scension to the weak apprehension of that people.'¹⁴³ Locke's remarks on Judaism in *A Paraphrase and Notes* are even more demeaning than Clarke's words and demonstrate why Locke's theological works do not contemplate the possibility of salvation for post-biblical Jews. In his paraphrase of Galatians 1:4, in which Paul states that Christ came to 'deliver us from this present evil world,' Locke maintained that by 'evil world' Paul means 'the Jewish nation under the Mosaical constitution.'¹⁴⁴ Accordingly, in commenting on Galatians 3:19–25, Locke argued that Christ's ministry on earth had marked the end of the Mosaic Law, which he considered superseded by the Law of Faith.¹⁴⁵ To Locke, 2 Corinthians 3:6 ('the letter killeth, but the spirit giveth life') indicates that 'the New Testament or covenant was also, though obscurely, held forth in the law [of Moses].'¹⁴⁶ However, the bulk of the Jewish people were unable to discard their literalist, legalistic reading of the Scriptures, and to accept Jesus as the Messiah, because a sort of hermeneutic 'veil' conditioned their biblical exegesis. Locke expressed this opinion in his paraphrase of 2 Corinthians 3:15 ('But even unto this day, when Moses is read, the vail is upon their heart'): in Locke's words, 'even until now when the writings of Moses are read, the veil remains upon their hearts, they see not the spiritual and evangelical truths contained in them.'¹⁴⁷ Even the Jews who converted to Christianity shortly after Christ's Coming were unwilling to abandon the 'works of the law,' thus causing tensions and divisions among the early Christians.¹⁴⁸ When talking of these Jewish converts to Christianity, Locke wrote in a note to 1 Corinthians 2:6 ('Howbeit we speak wisdom amongst them that are perfect: yet not the wisdom of this world, nor of the princes of this world, that come to nought'):

> St. Paul here tells the Corinthians that the wisdom and learning of the Jewish nation led them not into the knowledge of the wisdom of God, i.e. the Gospel revealed in the Old Testament, evident in this, that it was their rulers and rabbies, who, stiffly adhering to the notions and prejudices of their nation, had crucified Jesus, the Lord of glory, and were now themselves, with their state and religion, upon the point to be swept away and abolished.¹⁴⁹

In this passage, Locke claimed that Paul had foreseen the imminent destruction of the Jewish nation, state, and religion as a deserved punishment for having crucified Jesus. Locke even justified this 'destruction' in a note to Romans 3:8, in which Paul maintained that the 'damnation' of 'some' who had slandered him was 'just.' Locke thought that, by 'some,' Paul meant the Jews:

---

143 Samuel Clarke, "The End and Design of the Jewish Law," in Samuel Clarke, *Works*, 4 vols. (London: Knapton, 1738), vol. 2, 313.
144 Locke, *Paraphrase*, vol. 1, 121.
145 *Ibidem*, vol. 1, 138.
146 *Ibidem*, vol. 1, 278.
147 *Ibidem*, vol. 1, 280.
148 *Ibidem*, vol. 2, 483.
149 *Ibidem*, vol. 1, 174.

'Some.' It is past doubt that these were the Jews. But St. Paul, always tender towards his own nation, forbears to name them, when he pronounces this sentence, that their casting-off and destruction now at hand, for this scandal and their opposition to the Christian religion, was just.[150]

Briefly, Locke's later writings on religion depict the Jews as bound to their superseded law and hence incapable of pursuing salvation, like all those refusing the Christian Law of Faith. When focussing his attention on heathens and Jews in his theological works, Locke obviously had the issue of salvation in mind. On the other hand, explicit political considerations, concerning whether the religious and moral ideas of heathens and Jews make them tolerable or intolerable in a civil commonwealth, are absent from Locke's theological writings, although his moralist soteriology has powerful political implications, as Eisenach has noted:

> Only when the truth of morality is seen as part of a system of divine rewards and punishments will it attain both psychological force and historical reality. Only under these conditions will morality provide the basis for a civil law with teeth in it.[151]

In this regard, Victor Nuovo has observed that 'Locke's theology is a political theology at least in this respect, that the sovereign legislator of the moral law is God, or his viceregent Christ.'[152] However, Nuovo has correctly pointed out that Locke did 'not propose a Christian commonwealth as the proper way to do the business of morality.'[153] Locke actually laboured to ensure that the *Second Treatise*, with its advocacy of a *civil* commonwealth, would become part of his philosophical legacy. Moreover, he always opposed the institutionalization of Christianity as a national religion, which in practice, according to Locke, had done as much to disturb as to reinforce civil society and moral conduct. According to Nuovo, Locke never endorsed a Christian commonwealth for two main reasons—namely, his Christian view of history and the concept of the Law of Nature he had expressed in the *Second Treatise*:

> [A]ccording to the Scriptures, it was not God's intention to establish his kingdom or the kingdom of Christ—they are the same thing—until the history of redemption had run its course, until the resurrection and the last judgment. In the meantime, whether in a state of nature or in a civil state, the law of nature is the only proper rule to govern human behavior and civil institutions to safeguard human life and property.[154]

In the *Second Treatise*, Locke indeed described human beings as bound to the God-given Law of Nature, in that they are God's workmanship and, thus, they belong to

---

150 *Ibidem*, vol. 2, 506.
151 Eldon J. Eisenach, *Two Worlds of Liberalism: Religion and Politics in Hobbes, Locke, and Mill* (Chicago: The University of Chicago Press, 1981), 85.
152 Nuovo, *John Locke*, 246.
153 *Ibidem*.
154 *Ibidem*.

God.[155] Nevertheless, Locke's position on the Law of Nature in the *Reasonableness* makes things quite problematic, given that, in this book, Locke maintained that unassisted reason had never 'made out an entire body of the *Law of Nature*.'[156] Moreover, according to Locke, even when the Law of Nature became easily accessible through the Old Testament, given that the moral part of the Law of Moses (i.e. the Law of Works) was identical to the Law of Nature, the Law of Moses was still ineffective to establish morality on solid grounds. Locke eventually concluded that only Christ had revealed, perfectly and completely, the divine law, which comprises the Law of Nature in its entirety, besides the assurance of otherworldly rewards and punishments and an emphasis on God's forgiveness. Therefore, in order to achieve flawless, thorough, certain knowledge of the Law of Nature—'the only proper rule to govern human behavior and civil institutions,' in Nuovo's words—one needs to accept the Law of Faith revealed by Christ.

However, in the *Reasonableness* and his other theological writings, Locke did not invoke the civil power against pagans, Muslims, and Jews because of their weak, defective, imperfect morality. He actually ruled out any such use of the civil power in the *Two Treatises of Government*, in all his letters on toleration, and throughout his mature manuscripts, including those written between the mid-1690s and his death. Conversely, in *A Letter concerning Toleration*, he expressly excluded atheists and Roman Catholics from toleration, and he did so mainly for moral reasons, as I have explained above. So, why did he not deny toleration to heathens, Jews, and Muslims too for moral reasons? We can answer this question if we consider Locke's views on the different moralities of atheists, Roman Catholics, and non-Christian believers. Locke judged atheists intrinsically immoral, and hence socially dangerous, because of their failure to acknowledge the existence of a divine creator and legislator and their consequent failure to appreciate any (divinely given) moral law. Concerning Roman Catholics, Locke considered them intolerable only because of some of their moral ideas, which he judged harmful to society. Therefore, he did not exclude the theoretical possibility of tolerating Catholics, on condition that the latter renounce their antisocial ideas. When it comes to pagans, Jews, and Muslims, things are different, because they do believe in a divine creator and legislator. Thus, they are able to appreciate and grasp, albeit partially and imperfectly, the divine law and their duties towards their creator. For this reason, they are not intrinsically immoral and, thus, they are not comparable to atheists. Heathens of different stripes can indeed comprehend, by the light of reason, at least some basic elements of the Law of Nature. Jews can also know the Law of Nature in the form of the Law of Works accessible through their Scriptures. Briefly, the religious and moral views of non-Christian believers, although defective and imperfect, still enable them to meet at least minimally decent moral standards. Their failure to accept the Christian Law of Faith, with

---

155 Locke, *Two Treatises*, 271.
156 Locke, *Reasonableness*, 148–150.

the ethics it entails, certainly prevents them from achieving the salvation of their souls. However, as Locke argues in *A Letter concerning Toleration*, 'the Care of Souls' falls outside of the purview of political authority, as long as a religious opinion or practice is not destructive of the civil interests or communal life. Therefore, Locke's more or less explicit denial of the possibility of salvation to non-Christian believers in his theological works does not invalidate what the *Letter* states in this regard, namely that 'neither *Pagan,* nor *Mahumetan,* nor *Jew,* ought to be excluded from the Civil Rights of the Commonwealth, because of his Religion.'[157]

Finally, we need to consider the case of deists and antinomians—Locke's main polemical targets in his later works on religion. Although Locke questions the actual ability of unassisted reason to comprehend the Law of Nature entirely and perfectly, the deists' commitment to live by the Law of Nature, or at least by its basic tenets, should be enough to make them tolerable in a civil commonwealth. However, it might be argued that deists do not belong to any 'deistic church' and thus, given Locke's exclusive focus on *organized* religion in the *Letter*, they do not meet an essential requirement for being considered, and tolerated, as people who have 'religion.' In the *Letter*, deists are indeed left in a 'vague limbo,' as their status remains undefined. Nevertheless, Locke's irenicism in the *Reasonableness* does not require confessional affiliation as a necessary condition for salvation, and for toleration as well, when it comes to Christian believers. I believe that the scarce importance that Locke attaches to church membership in the *Reasonableness*, combined with his stress, in his political writings, on the Law of Nature as the only proper rule to govern human behavior in a state of nature or in a civil commonwealth, allows for toleration of deists too, although Locke criticized their reliance on natural reason alone as ineffective to salvation. As regards antinomians, Locke's exclusion of Roman Catholics from toleration because of their 'antinomian' moral ideas implies that other, if not all, forms of antinomianism are intolerable, at least in principle. Yet, whereas Locke opposed Calvinistic antinomianism as detrimental to salvation, he abstained from explicitly declaring Protestant antinomians 'intolerable' in any of his writings. I believe that Locke judged Protestant antinomianism to be not as socially dangerous as Roman Catholics' 'antinomian' moral ideas. In the *Letter*, he indeed attacked some specific antisocial ideas, commonly attributed to Roman Catholics, and he connected Catholic morals with the obedience that Catholics owed to their indisputable religious leader, the pope, who was also a foreign prince. Concerning Calvinistic antinomians, Locke was probably aware of their *potential* intolerability, as Mark Goldie has argued, given that their claims of divine inspiration could possibly lead them to act against ordinary moral rules and even against the civil commonwealth.[158] Nevertheless, this theoretical possibility, unlike the Catholics' antisocial convictions, was not

---

[157] Locke, "Letter," 58–59.
[158] Goldie, "Introduction," xix.

enough to make Protestant antinomians *actually* intolerable—as long as they did not engage in immoral, antisocial, illegal conduct.

5 Conclusion

Locke always argued for toleration within the boundaries of a morality that only religious belief could ground. His arguments in the *Letter* revolve around the separation between the state and religious societies. While Locke's political scepticism enabled him to effectively delineate the civil magistrate's purview, his preoccupation with the need for morality to construct a decent, stable society led him to expressly advocate toleration for only those who believed in God and pursued salvation within the bosom of a church (except Roman Catholics, as long as they held antisocial morals). In *The Reasonableness of Christianity* and other theological writings, Locke turned to Scripture with the purpose of overcoming his own moral scepticism and finding strong foundations for morality. He formulated an original doctrine of the fundamentals, extending the possibility of salvation and toleration to all those accepting the Law of Faith revealed by Christ, regardless of non-fundamentals and confessional affiliation. His conviction that the Law of Faith alone could establish a sound system of ethics and make salvation possible did not lead him to endorse a Christian commonwealth, or to recant his advocacy of toleration of pagans, Jews, and Muslims. In fact, although non-Christian believers refuse the Law of Faith and are hence unable to achieve salvation, they do believe in a divine creator and legislator. Therefore, they are able to appreciate and grasp, even if only partially and imperfectly, at least the divinely given Law of Nature and to behave accordingly. In conclusion, Locke's developing approach to toleration, from the *Letter* to his later theological writings, was always conditioned by his religious conception of life and morality. This enabled him to advance persuasive arguments against the civil magistrate's complete control of religious affairs and to play a significant role in the irenic Protestant tradition of the way of fundamentals. On the other hand, his religious conception of life and morality always prevented him from advocating proper freedom of conscience and, instead, led him to argue for only limited forms of religious toleration.

Guido Bartolucci
Jewish Scepticism in Christian Eyes: Jacob F. Reimmann and the Transformation of Jewish Philosophy

Introduction

Christian interest in the Jewish tradition in the modern age has long been recognised as an important field of research for understanding the history of European erudition, along with the study of Greek and Latin. Less investigated, however, is the relationship between this interest and the construction of definitions of Jewish tradition, culture and history that, built within the Christian field, ended up also becoming heritage of the field that had been the subject of these investigations, namely Judaism iseitself.[1] A particular case concerns the definition of 'Jewish philosophy.' This concept, in fact, has engaged scholars at least in the last century in attempts to reconstruct its history and to find a definition that would at last capture its 'essence', in a continuous oscillation between two extreme poles: the rejection of the existence of a Jewish philosophy at all and instead its centrality in understanding the history of Judaism itself.[2] Thus, in the introduction to an important volume on Jewish philosophy, the editor Daniel Frank writes:

This article is just a preliminary result of a research on Jewish scepticism and Jewish philosophy in the Lutheran world of the Early modern period undertaken during my fellowship at the Maimonides Centre for Advanced Studies, Universität Hamburg.

[1] On Christian Hebraism and the history of erudition, see François Secret, *Les kabbalistes chrétiens de la Renaissance* (Paris: Dunod, 1964); Jerome Friedman, *The Most Ancient testimony: Sixteenth-Century Christian-Hebraica in the Age of Renaissance Nostalgia* (Athens: Ohio University Press, 1983); Frank E. Manuel, *The Broken Staff: Judaism through Christian Eyes* (Cambridge, MA: Harvard University Press, 1992); Saverio Campanini, "Die Geburt der Judaistik aus dem Geist der Chrislichen Kabbalah," in *Gottes Sprache in der philologischen Werkstatt: Hebraistik vom 15. bis zum 19. Jahrhundert*, ed. Giuseppe Veltri and Gerold Necker (Leiden: Brill, 2004): 135–241; Anthony Grafton and Joanna Weinberg, *"I have always loved the Holy Tongue": Isaac Casaubon, the Jews, and a forgotten chapter in Renaissance scholarship* (Cambridge, MA: The Belknap Press of Harvard University Press, 2011); Theodor Dunkelgrün, "The Christian Study of Judaism in Early Modern Europe," in *The Cambridge History of Judaism*, vol. 7: *The Early Modern World, 1500–1815* (Cambridge: Cambridge University Press, 2017): 316–348. For a comprehensive bibliography, see Stephen G. Burnett, *Christian Hebraism in the Reformation Era (1500–1660): Authors, Books, and the Transmission of Jewish Learning* (Leiden: Brill, 2012).
[2] On this debate, see, e.g., in the present volume Dirk Westerkamp, "Quaestio sceptica disputata de philosophia judaeorum: Is there a Jewish Philosophy?," in *Yearbook of the Maimonides Centre for Advanced Studies 2018*, ed. Bill Rebiger (Berlin and Boston: De Gruyter, 2018): 3–14.

OpenAccess. © 2018 Guido Bartolucci, published by De Gruyter. This work is licensed under the Creative Commons Attribution-NonCommercial-NoDerivatives 4.0 License.
https://doi.org/10.1515/978-3-11-057768-6-008

Much the most important part of any answer we give to our initial query into the nature of Jewish philosophy is that Jewish philosophy is an academic discipline. It is an invention, for reasons important to ponder, of nineteenth-century historians, intent on bringing together certain thinkers, while simultaneously excluding others. Before the invention of Jewish philosophy as an academic discipline no one asked or wondered about the nature of Jewish philosophy, quite simply because the subject did not exist. [...] No one in premodern, indeed, in much of modern times understood Jewish philosophy as a subdiscipline of philosophy, as a way of philosophizing. No one felt the need to ascertain the essence of Jewish philosophy [...] distinguishing it from every other kind of philosophy or mode of theological interpretation.[3]

All these assertions could probably be applied to the Jewish world, starting at the beginning of the *Wissenschaft des Judentums*.[4] The Christian tradition, however, did not wait for the nineteenth century in order to reflect on Jewish philosophy. Its interest had begun far earlier, at the very least by the fifteenth century.[5] The question of Jewish philosophy in the history of Christian thought developed in a completely different way than what took place in the Jewish milieu. Jewish authors, such as Simone Luzzatto and Moses Mendelssohn, for example, envisaged their own philosophical thinking as something autonomous from religious tradition, whereas Christian authors attempted quite the opposite. Many Christian scholars were interested in Jewish philosophy for its alleged holiness, as we will see forthwith. But the history of this encounter is particularly significant in understand the interpretation of the meaning of Jewish Scepticism, because it was the Christian milieu (not the Jewish one) that first maintained the Jewish thought could be regarded as a sceptic philosophy.[6]

---

3 Daniel H. Frank, "What is Jewish philosophy," in *History of Jewish Philosophy*, eds. Daniel H. Frank and Oliver Leaman (London and New York: Routledge, 1997): 2–4.
4 On Jewish philosophy, see *The Cambridge History of Jewish Philosophy: From Antiquity through the Seventeenth Century*, eds. Steven H. Nadler and Tamar M. Rudavsky (Cambridge: Cambridge University Press, 2009); *The Cambridge Companion to Medieval Jewish Philosophy*, eds. Daniel H. Frank and Oliver Leaman (Cambridge: Cambridge University Press, 2003); *The Cambridge Companion to Modern Jewish Philosophy*, eds. Michael L. Morgan and Peter Eli Gordon (Cambridge: Cambridge University Press, 2007); Giuseppe Veltri, *Sapienza Alienata* (Rome: Aracne, 2015); Josef Stern, "What is Jewish Philosophy? A View from the Middle Ages," in *Yearbook of the Maimonides Centre for Advanced Studies 2017*, ed. Bill Rebiger (Berlin and Boston: De Gruyter, 2017): 185–204; Giuseppe Veltri, *Alienated Wisdom. Enquiry into Jewish Philosophy and Scepticism* (Berlin and Boston: De Gruyter, 2018).
5 On Jewish philosophy in Christian debate, see Dirk Westerkamp, *Die philonische Unterscheidung. Aufklärung, Orientalismus und Konstruktion der Philosophie* (München: Wilhelm Frank, 2009); idem, "The Philonic Distinction: German Enlightenment Historiography of Jewish Thought," *History and Theory* 47 (2008): 533–559; Haim Mahlev, "A Philosophy of the Patriarchs? The Agenda Behind Christoph August Heumann's Acta Philosophorum," *Journal of the History of Ideas* 76.4 (2015): 517–539.
6 On Jewish scepticism, see Giuseppe Veltri, "Principles of Jewish Skeptical Thought. The Case of Judah Moscato and Simone Luzzatto," in *Rabbi Judah Moscato and the Jewish Intellectual World of Mantua in 16th-17th Centuries*, eds. Giuseppe Veltri and Gianfranco Miletto (Boston and Leiden: Brill, 2012): 15–36; idem, "Maharal against Azaria de Rossi: The Other Side of Skepticism," in *Rabbinic Theology and Jewish Intellectual History: The Great Rabbi Loew of Prague*, ed. Meir Seidel (Ox-

Jacob Friedrich Reimmann (1668–1743), a Lutheran scholar, published a short essay in 1704 arguing under the provocative title "An Salomon fuerit scepticus?" ("Was Solomon a Sceptic?") that the essence of Jewish philosophy is scepticism.[7] To understand this fundamental passage, so decisive for the history of the reception of Jewish thought in the Christian culture of the early modern age, it is, however, necessary to carry out two preliminary steps: the first is to reconstruct the history of Christian interest in Jewish philosophy, the second is to understand the role played by the Lutheran world in this history.

1 Christian Discovery of Jewish Tradition

In the fifteenth century a phenomenon emerged in European culture—later to be defined as Christian Hebraism—this was the attempt to apply philological techniques, developed from the study of Latin and Greek texts, to the Hebrew text of the Bible and from there proceed to other sources of the Jewish tradition. This new approach profoundly changed the way of thinking about Judaism, widening the boundaries within which it had previously been understood. The new sources, studied in the original language, as far as this was possible at the time, not only helped to rethink the Christian tradition, but also gave access to previously unknown new texts and traditions. The use of philological instruments similar to those impemented for Greek and Latin sources also brought with it the need to use interpretative categories capable of bringing the Jewish tradition to the level of other Classical traditions. Until that time, the Hebrew tradition was not regarded comparable to the Greek and Latin cultures.[8] During this period a new instrument was introduced to interpret the Jewish tradition and legitimise its use. At the beginning of the fifteenth century, several authors borrowed a scheme from the works of the Greek Church Fathers, that divided the history of the Jews into two periods: the ancient, pure and primeval Hebraism of the patriarchs, and a modern Judaism corrupted by a literal interpretation of Mosaic law. This two-stage scheme was especially important in the second half of fifteenth century, for the development of a new idea of *Hebraica veritas*.[9] Several au-

---

ford: Oxford University Press, 2012): 65–76; idem, "Do/Did the Jews Believe in God? The Skeptical Ambivalence of Jewish Philosophy of Religion," in *Envisioning Judaism: Studies in Honor of Peter Schäfer on the Occasion of his Seventieth Birthday*, vol. 2, eds. Ra'anan Boustan *et alii* (Tübingen: Mohr Siebeck, 2013): 717–733; see also Veltri, *Alienated Wisdom*.
7 See note 32.
8 Cf. Jonathan Friedman, "The Myth of Jewish Antiquity: New Christians and Christian-Hebraica in Early Modern Europe," in *Jewish Christians and Christian Jews: From Renaissance to the Enlightenment*, eds. Richard H. Popkin and Gordon M. Weiner (Dordrecht, Boston and London: Kluwer Academic Publishers, 1994): 35–55.
9 Cf. Riccardo Fubini, *Storiografia dell'Umanesimo in Italia. Da Leonardo Bruni ad Annio da Viterbo* (Rome: Edizioni di Storia e Letteratura, 2003), 290–333; Jean Sirinelli, "Introduction générale," in Eu-

thors, such as Marsilio Ficino and Pico della Mirandola, justified their own interest in the Jewish tradition by maintaining that, for example, the Kabbalah was part of original Jewish wisdom, and not linked to modern Judaism.[10] This new attitude toward Judaism, which will not be analysed in depth here, contributed to the 'Judaisation' of European culture itself.[11] In using the term Judaisation I intend to refer to a process of increasing incorporation of Jewish works and authors into the myth of a single original ancient wisdom, where the Bible and Jewish literature (i.e. the part of it considered to be more ancient) came to be seen as sources that maintained their validity for all mankind.

This introduction was necessary to understand how the birth of interest in Jewish philosophy of the second half of the sixteenth century links to a Christian Hebraism that, in some aspects, was influenced by the *prisca theologia*, applying its approach to various fields of interest, within the framework of a genealogical construction of human knowledge rooted in ancient Jewish wisdom.[12] There are, however, different traditions that take the name *prisca theologia:* 1) one which saw in the Jewish tradition the only true pre-Christian revelation which reached the gentiles through the Egyptians who were instructed by Moses 2) a series of other pre-Christian revelations different and independent from the Jewish one. While the first was considered more orthodox, being approved by the fathers of the Church and maintaining a link with the Old Testament, the second was considered more dangerous as it implied that

---

sebius of Caesarea, *La préparation évangélique*, vol. 1, eds. Jean Sirinelli and Edouard des Places (Paris: Cerf, 1974), 7–62.

10 See Guido Bartolucci, *Vera religio. Marsilio Ficino e la tradizione ebraica* (Turin: Paideia, 2017); Flavius Mithridates, *Sermo de passione Domini*, ed. Chaim Wirszubski (Jerusalem: Academy of Science, 1963).

11 On this idea, see, e.g., Robert Dan, "'Judaizare': the Career of a Term," in *Antitrinitarianism in the Second Half of the 16th Century*, eds. Robert Dan and Antal Pirnat (Budapest and Leiden: Akademiai Kiado and Brill, 1982): 25–34.

12 See, e.g., Cesare Vasoli, "Il mito dei 'prisci theologi' come 'ideologia' della 'renovatio'," in idem, *Quasi sit Deus. Studi su Marsilio Ficino* (Lecce: Conte, 1999): 11–50. On prisca theologia, cf. Maria Muccillo, *Platonismo, Ermetismo e 'prisca theologia'. Ricerche di storiografia filosofica rinascimentale* (Florence: Olschki, 1996); Francis A. Yates, *Giordano Bruno and the Hermetic Tradition* (London: Routledge, 1964); Daniel P. Walker, *The Ancient Theology: Studies in Christian Platonism from the Fifteenth to the Eighteenth Century* (Ithaca, NY: Cornell University Press, 1972); Eugenio Garin, *Ermetismo del Rinascimento* (Rome: Editori riuniti, 1988); Charles B. Schmitt, "Prisca theologia e philosophia perennis," in *Il pensiero italiano del rinascimento e il nostro tempo*, Atti del V convegno internazionale del centro di studi umanistici Montepulciano, Palazzo Tarugi, 8–13 agosto 1968, ed. Giovannangiola Tarugi (Florence: Olschki, 1970): 211–236; Martin Mulsow, "Ambiguities of the Prisca Sapientia in Late Renaissance Humanism," *Journal of the History of Ideas* 65 (2004): 1–13; Wilhelm Schmidt-Biggemann, *Philosophia Perennis: Historical Outlines of Western Sprirituality in Ancient, Medieval and Early Modern Thought* (Dordrecht: Springer, 2004); Moshe Idel, "Prisca Theologia in Marsilio Ficino and in some Jewish Treatments," in *Marsilio Ficino: his Theology, his Philosophy, his Legacy*, eds. Michael Allen and Valery Rees (Leiden, Boston and Köln: Brill, 2002): 137–158.

some pagan philosophers had acquired knowledge of the truth equal to that of revealed religions.

In the history of *prisca theologia* these distinctions have a circumscribed value, since the different traditions intertwine and overlap each other, often preventing a clear distinction between ortodoxy and heresy or merely marking the differences between the various Christian confessions. However, it is important to note that such traditions succeeded in considering Jewish thought readable and interpretable with the tools of classical tradition. Also, in one of his most important works, Marsilio Ficino, one of the initiators of the *prisca theologia*, the *De Christiana religione*, maintained both positions, quoting the chain of wisdom that he had inherited from Gemisto Plethon on the one hand and introducing Eusebius' vision of a Jewish origin of Greek philosophical tradition on the other.[13]

I will report below some passages that best exemplify what we want to maintain here. One of the best known examples of this tradition is the debate on the origin of languages Guillaume Postel (1510–1581), hebraist, philosopher and self-acclaimed prophet, presented in his work *De originibus seu de Hebraismi antiquitate, linguarum affinitate*. Here he advocated the antiquity of the Hebrew language, using this argument to reconstruct the chain of human wisdom from the Jews to the Greeks.[14] The influence of this idea on sixteenth century culture is not limited to language but extends to other fields of knowledge, identifying, for instance, Moses as the inventor of poetry, an assumption that the first humanists, for reasons mentioned earlier, refused absolutely. The work of the French hebraist Gilbert Génébrard (1535–1597) is useful in understanding how the ideology of *prisca theologia* was able to take different forms. In fact, in his main work, the *Chronographia*, Génébrard refused the antiquity and the authority of Hermes Trismegistus, while, at the same time, used excerpts

---

13 Marsilio Ficino, *Opera quae hactenus extitere et quae in lucem nunc primum prodiere omnia* (Basel: Officina Henricpetrina, 1576), 25: 'Prisca gentilium theologia in qua Zoroaster Mercurius Orpheus Aglaophemus Pythagoras consenserunt tota in Platonis nostri voluminibus continetur;' *ibidem*, 30: 'Ex quibus apparet quod Clemens Alexandrinus et Atticus Platonicus et Eusebius et Aristobolus probant gentiles videlicet, siqua habuerunt egregia dogmata et misteria, a Iudeis usurpavisse. [...]. Plato usqueadeo Iudeos imitatus est, ut Numenius Pytagoricus dixerit Platonem nihil aliud fuisse quiquam Moysen actica lingua loquentem. Addit in libro de bono Pythagoram quoque iudaica dogmata sectatum fuisse. [...] Clearcus Peripateticus scribit Aristotelem fuisse Iudeum, Calanos quoque phylosophus apud Indos Iudeos fuisse. Megastenes insuper brachmanas Indiae phylosophos a Iudeis asserit descendisse. Ambrosius recte memini Pythagoram patre Iudeo natum ostendit.'

14 Guillaume Postel, *De originibus seu de Hebraismi antiquitate, linguarum affinitate* (Paris: Dyonisius Lescuier, 1538), Aiiiir-v: 'Primam [linguam] fuisse Chaldaeam seu Hebraeam constat et authoribus prophanis et sacris, ut ethnicis fiat fides Deo electis christianis amplificetur. Praeter illa antiquissima Graecorum de hac re testimonia, quae tam insignis author Iosephus, cui in civitate eloquentissima ob insignem peritiam, eruditionem, et in scrivendo candorem, statua donata est, quem veritatis odio supprimunt sui Iudei, in libris Antiquitatum Iudaicarum et contra Appionem Grammaticum adfert. Praeter etiam illa quae amplissima adducit Eusebius Caesariensis de Evangelico apparato, cognosces hic non levibus argumentis, hanc Hebraicam linguam sua vocabula insignoribus orbis terrarum provinciis olim per filios Noachi dedisse.'

from the Fathers of the Church, Eusebiusin particular, to maintain the dependence of Greek wisdom on the Jews. He identifies Moses as the first poet and initiator of this discipline.[15] Beyond the specific meaning of these statements, which certainly had polemical intent within the world of *Humanae litterae* in the second half of the sixteenth century, it is important to stress here the 'disciplinary' legitimation acquired by the Jewish tradition, to the point that in some milieus it challenges and sometimes exceeds the Greek and Latin traditions. Génébrard's short discussion of Jewish poetry is valid not only in itself, but it is also evidence of a peculiar interest in the Jewish tradition. Similarly, Henri Estienne (1528/31–1598), a Calvinist printer and editor of the first edition of the Orphic fragments, published an anonymous ancient tractate in 1580, the *Collatio legum Mosaicarum et Romanarum*, which developed a parallel between Mosaic laws and the laws of the twelve tables. Although the French lawyer François Pithou (1543–1621) had already published this work, Estienne wrote an introduction of particular salience to this discussion.[16] As already emphasised in the title of his work, Estienne wanted to distinguish between sources and rivers of the law, trying to reach the first ones. He identified these sources as the laws given by God to Moses, which the Egyptians then imitated and subsequently imparted to the Greeks.[17] The introduction of the Calvinist editor helps us see how the idea that Jewish laws were the source of Roman and Greek laws circulated in the European culture of the second half of the Sixteenth century, using precisely the patterns characteristic of the earlier *prisca theologia*.

In the same way, a century later, an identical scheme was used to build a genealogy that could legitimise scientific theories, which otherwise would have been hardly

---

15 Gilbert Génébrard, *Cronographiae libri quatuor* (Paris: Martinus Iuvenis, 1578), 78: 'Moses poëtis omnibus praeluxit. Nam Iobi historiam spondaicis versibus repraesentavit et Cantica seorsum illud Deut. 32 elegiaco carmine, ut versus alternatim senis et quinis constent pedibus. (Eus. Lib. 11 Praep. Cap. 3; Hieron. Ex Iosepho). Ad quos modos tria extant cantica apud Esaiam, vincae scilicet, urbis Sion et Ezechiae. (Isidor.) Quod aemulati Graeci veteres, hexametris suas cantiones et odas conficiebant.'

16 Pierre Pithou, "Collatio legum Mosaicarum et Romanarum," in *Observationes ad Codicem et Novellas Iustiniani Imperatoris*, eds. Pierre and François Pithou (Paris, 1689): 33. Petrus Pithou, a French jurist and a disciple of the jurist Jacques Cujas, published an edition of this anonymous work written around the fourth century which systematically compares the laws found in the Old Testament with those described by some ancient jurists in order to find common points between them. On the tradition of the Mosaic law, see Guido Bartolucci, *La repubblica ebraica di Carlo Sigonio* (Florence: Olschki, 2007), 177–184.

17 Henri Estienne, *Iuris civilis fonte set rivi, Iurisconsultorum veterum quidam loci, ex integris eorum voluminibus ante Iustiniani aetatem excerpti* (Basel, 1580), 1r: 'Atque hoc appello nomine rivos eos qui ex primariis potius rivis quam ex ipsis fontibus manasse videri queunt. Ita enim mea fert opinio, sicut primos legislatores Aegyptios ex Mosaica Politia pleraque (praesertimque ea quae legi naturae consentanea videbantur) ita Graecos ex Aegiptiis multa sumpsisse. [...] Quod si mihi de quapiam meorum etiam maiorum lege mentionem licet facere, nullam post Mosaicam (quae Deum ipsum autorem habuit not homines) inveniemus, quae peregrinos aeque commendatos habeat ac Celtica.'

sustainable. One of these attempts formulated the coincidence between the Epicurean theory of atoms and the Book of Genesis:

> We have also good historical probability for this Opinion, that this Philosophy was a thing of much greater Antiquity than either Democritus or Leucippus; and first, because Posidonius, an ancient and learned philosopher, did (as both Empiricus and Strabo tell us) avouch it for an old tradition, that the first Inventour of this Atomical Philosophy was one Moschus, a Phoenician, who, as Strabo also notes, lived before the Trojan War. [...] and Mr. Selden approves of the conjecture of Arcerius, the publisher of Iamblicus, that this Monchus was no other than the celebrated Moses of the Jews, with whose successors, the Jewish philosophers, priests, and prophets, Pythagoras conversed at Sidon.[18]

In this passage Ralph Cudworth (1617–1688), one of the most important Cambridge Platonists, uses themes and authors characteristic of the *prisca theologia*, clearly showing that, in mid-seventeenth century, this ideology still had a political and cultural implication. To infuse the atomistic theory with a mosaic *aurea* (without any philological and historical basis) gave him the opportunity to legitimise theories that were distant to any recognised orthodoxy.

These three cases are merely an example of the tranformation of the Christian perception of Jewish tradition. The framework developed by the humanists of the *prisca theologia* gave the European scholars an opportunity to think Judaism out of the traditional theological path. They now had the tools to interpret Jewish history as part of the history of language, poetry or law. Thus, this use of the sources of *prisca theologia* and of the interpretation of the Fathers of the Church and also gave them the chance to insert Judaism within the history of philosophy.

2 The Jewish Tradition in Germany in the Seventeenth Century and the History of Philosophy

At the same period in Germany, within the Lutheran world, we witness the diffusion of works whose main topic was the philosophical and political tradition of the Jews. Some of these treatises, published at the end of the seventeenth century, aimed to demonstrate not only that a Jewish philosophy existed, but also that it had influenced the Western philosophical tradition. The formulas and the sources used by these authors demonstrate their familiarity with the idea just outlined. On the other hand, other works, maintained the complete irrelevance of the Jewish tradition

---

18 Danton B. Sailor, "Moses and Atomism," *Journal of the History of Ideas* 25.1 (1964): 11. Cf. Ralph Cudworth, *The True Intellectual System of the Universe, wherein all the Reason and Philosophy of Atheism is Confuted, and its Impossibility Demonstrated* (London: Richard Royston, 1678), 12–13. On *philosophia perennis* and the history of philosophy in England in this period, see Dmitri Levitin, *Ancient Wisdom in the Age of the New Science: Histories of Philosophy in England, c. 1640–1700* (Cambridge: Cambridge University Press, 2015).

for the development of Greek and European philosophy, for its closeness to theology.[19]

The question of Jewish philosophy and its connection to the other philosophical traditions also became important for the first historians of philosophy who published their works in the second half of the seventeenth century. The Protestant world in particular was interested in the history of pagan philosophy: these authors were not attempting to trace an erudite history of human knowledge, but sought to implement this history in a polemical manner. From the second half of the seventeenth century, the Lutheran universities of the German States began to produce an ever-increasing number of small and large treatises concerned with both the history of philosophy and the history of theology.[20] From its foundation on, the Reformation had recognised the common path of these two disciplines, by composing either philosophical histories of theology (i.e. Christianity) or theological histories of philosophy (both Greek and 'Barbaric').[21]

At the outset (i.e. from the sixteenth century), Greek philosophy was recognised as one of the sources of the corruption of original Christianity. Soon, however, the confrontation with other confessions (Calvinism and Catholicism), forced Lutheranism to embrace philosophy and Aristotelian thought[22] in particular. The relationship between philosophy and theology was subjected to increasingly insistent and targeted attacks during the seventeenth century, when new methods of philosophy

---

[19] Cf. Valerio Marchetti, "Sulla degiudaizzazione della politica. In margine alla relazione di Horst Dreitzel," in *Aristotelismo politico e ragion di stato*, Atti del convegno internazionale di Torino 11–12 Febbraio 1993, ed. Artemio Enzo Baldini (Florence: Olschki, 1995): 349–358; idem, "An Pythagoras proselytus factus sit," *Dimensioni e problemi della ricerca storica* 2 (1996): 111–121; idem, "Aristoteles utrum fuerit Iudaeus. Sulla degiudaizzazione della filosofia europea in età moderna," in *Anima e paura. Studi in onore di Michele Ranchetti*, ed. Anna Scattigno (Macerata: Quodlibet, 1998): 249–266; Giuseppe Veltri, "Academic Debates on the Jews in Wittenberg. The Protestant Literature on Rituals, the Dissertationes and the Writings of the Hebraists Theodor Dassow and Andreas Sennert," *European Journal of Jewish Studies* 6 (2012): 123–146; Guido Bartolucci, "Jewish Thought vs. Lutheran Aristotelism: Johann Frischmuth (1619–1687) and Jewish Scepticism," in *Yearbook of the Maimonides Centre for Advanced Studies 2017*, ed. Bill Rebiger (Berlin and Boston: De Gruyter, 2017): 95–106.

[20] Cf., e.g., Jacob Thomasius, *Origines Historiae philosophicae et Ecclesiasticae* (Halle and Magdeburg: Johann Gottfred Renger, 1699).

[21] For these pages I refer to Luciano Malusa, "Renaissance Antecedents to the Historiography of Philosophy," in *Models of the History of Philosophy*, vol. 1: *From Its Origins in the Renaissance to the 'Historia Philosophica'*, eds. Giovanni Santiello *et alii* (Dordrecht: Kluwer Academic Publishers, 1993): 53–58; Giovanni Santiello, "The 'Historia Philosophica' in German Scholastic Thought," in *ibidem*, 373–442.

[22] Cf., e.g., Delio Cantimori, "Umanesimo e luteranesimo di fronte alla scolastica: Caspar Peucer," *Rivista di studi germanici* 2 (1937): 417–438.

emerged, inside and outside the Reformation, creating new conceptions of the history of Lutheranism and new theological challenges.²³

The history of philosophy, thus, acquired an important role in polemical debate within the Lutheran World. Studying the history of the different schools of philosophers involved reflecting on the different philosophical methods useful in understanding not only the history of thought, but also the history of the Church, and the history of the relationship between the two fields. From this perspective some authors of the period such as Christian Thomasius (1655–1728)—and later, as will be demonstrated, Johann Franz Budde (1667–1729)—developed a new way to study the history of philosophy.

From the 1660s, particularly after the foundation of the university in 1694, the city of Halle had been a location where opposition to Lutheran orthodoxy was growing. The presence of Thomasius and Budde (who moved to Jena in 1705), at the university and the Pietist community, in particular August Hermann Francke (1663–1727), in religious circles there, created an environment highly critical of the Lutheran tradition and promoted a new idea of religion and culture. The central point bonding men and perspectives often incompatible with one other was the need to rethink the Lutheran tradition, both from a theological and philosophical point of view. At the center of their reflection was the need to rethink Christianity and its relationship to pagan cultural tradition, through a careful study of the history of both the Church and philosophy. Studying the origins of philosophy and the various philosophical schools, also became a means to rethink the role of Lutheran theology and its relationship to the philosophical tradition, in particular the Aristotelian. In this new phase, the production of Lutheran universities, both within theological and philosophical faculties, focussed its attention precisely on these issues. The way the professors reflected on the various open questions took on different forms, literary genres and themes. In this debate the history of pagan philosophy and the role played by Jewish tradition in the transmission of human wisdom became the subjects for several works. Thomasius, for example, examined different philosophical methodologies, to find the best tool for challenging the dogmatism of Lutheran orthodoxy. By excluding sectarian, sceptical and syncretistic methodology he decided eclecticism was the best way to find an empirical method for his purposes.

According to Thomasius, the history of philosophy, gave scholars access to the different opinions of the philosophers of the past, stimulating the possibility to find the best solution to the problem of the present.²⁴ Despite his refusal of scepti-

---

23 See Francesco Bottin and Mario Longo, "The History of Philosophy from Eclecticism to Pietism," in *Models of the History of Philosophy*, vol. 2: *From the Cartesian Age to Brucker*, eds. Gregorio Piaia and Giovanni Santiello (Dordrecht, Heidelberg, London and New York: Springer, 2011): 302–385. See also Valerio Marchetti, *Saggi di storia della Chiesa evangelica tedesca. Tra XVII e XVIII secolo* (Bologna: Cisec, 1999).
24 Christian Thomasius, *Cautelae circa praecognita iurisprudentia* (Halle: Officina Libraria rengeriana, 1710), 57–58: '1. Historia et philosophia sunt duo oculi sapientiae, quorum uno, qui caret, mon-

cism in the interpretation of the history of philosophy, Thomasius was not insensitive to the contribution of scepticism to the struggle against dogmatism. He held history to be knowledge of the opinions of others, and thus more based on probability than certainty, and concluded thusly:

> Even if, when studying philosophy, one is really further from sceptical doubt than from the infallibility of the dogmatics, yet where historical matters are concerned, especially in political questions, one should not believe even the half of what is said. But one does not doubt without a good reason for doubting.[25]

But scepticism, according to Thomasius, was not confined to the realm of history, in his work on *Philosophia aulica*, he maintained scepticism was not a philosophical school similar to that of the past; but was the main antagonist to dogmatism.[26] The ambiguity of his statement mirrors the complexity of the debate in Germany toward scepticism. This Greek philosophy, in fact, was one of the topics on which several authors published short and long tractates, by defending or attacking his role within the history of pagan and Christian philosophy.[27]

Johann Franz Budde, student and then colleague of Thomasius, participated in the debate on the history of philosophy. Born in Anklam in 1667, he studied oriental languages, theology and philosophy at the University of Wittenberg. In 1693 he moved to Halle, where he met August Hermann Francke and Christian Thomasius.

---

oculus est ob summam utriusque connexionem [...] 9. Historia est de sensionibus alienis. Philosophia ratiocinatur de sensionibus propriis et alienis. 10. Utiles vero quam maxime sunt sensiones alienae ad studium sapientiae, quia partim adiuvant imperfectionem et insufficientiam propriam, partim quia multum prosunt ad emendationem.'

25 Ibidem, 68: 'Uti tamen in studio philosophico a dubio sceptico proprius abest, quam ab infallibilitate dogmaticorum, ita etiam circa historias, potissimum publicas, vix dimidiam partem credit. Interim tamen nunquam dubitat sine iuxta ratione dubitandi.' The English translation is in Mario Longo, "Christian Thomasius (1655–1728)," in *Models of the History of Philosophy*, vol. 2, 317.

26 Christian Thomasius, *Introductio ad philosophiam aulicam* (Halle: Officina Libraria rengeriana, 1702), 17–18: 'Pyrrhonii vero ne illud quidem comprehendi dicerent, quod aiebant, unde non tam sectam philosophorum constituerunt Sceptici, quam hostes communes omnis philosophiae, quae ab aliqua determinatione incipit (et propterea a philosophis dogmatica ad differentia sceptica dici solet) fuerunt.' On the use of scepticism in the debate on historical methodology, see Markus Völkel, *"Pyrrhonismus historicus" und "fides historica": die Entwicklung der deutschen historischen Methodologie unter dem Gesichtspunkt der historischen Skepsis* (Frankfurt am Main: Lang, 1987).

27 I list just few works on this topic: Heinrich Askan Engelken, Johann E. Udam (risp.), *Dissertatio de Scepticismi ortu et progressu* (Rostock: Nicolas Schwiegerovius, 1702); Johann Christian Wolff, *Programma de hodierno Scepticismo philosophico eiusdem causis* (Wittenberg: Christian Gerdesil, 1710); Johann Brucker, "De Pyrrhone a scepticismi universalis macula absolvendo," in *Miscellanea Lipsiensia ad incrementum rei litterariae edita*, vol. 5 (Leipzig: Haeredes Lanckisianorum, 1716); Sextus Empiricus, *Opera ... Graeca ex Mss. Codicibus castigavit, versiones emendavit supplevitque et toti operi notas addit J. Albertus Fabricius* (Leipzig: Johann Friderick Gleditsch, 1718). The history of scepticism in Germany in the seventeenth and eighteenth century has not received sufficient attention in the field of studies.

Budde was involved in the work of Thomasius and the Halle milieu in transforming Lutheran culture and published several tractates on different topics. Among the various works he wrote in this period, one is particular important for this analysis, the *Introduction to Jewish Philosophy*.[28] The treatise was part of a wider project on the general history of philosophy, its origin and link to the history of Christianity. He had already discussed the topic in other works: Firstly, in two short essays published in a journal edited in Halle from 1700 to 1704, and then in a tractate on the philosophy of Spinoza.[29] Budde developed a new idea of the history of human wisdom, by maintaining it to be possible to identify a common origin of the history of philosophy and theology. He discovers this in the first steps of the history of Hebrew wisdom, which Budde defines as *philosophia mystica* or *theosophia*, and then as Kabbalah. Budde's main task was to find a common origin of the two histories (philosophy and theology), for the purpose of reconsidering the relationship between Aristotelism and Lutheranism. By using the Jewish tradition, and inserting it in the wider history of ancient wisdom (*prisca theologia*) he was able to weaken the role played by Aristotlean philosophy and reinforce the effort of his group to reform Lutheran tradition.[30]

---

28 Johann F. Budde, *Introductio ad Historiam Philosophiae Ebraeorum* (Halle and Magdeburg: Orphanotrophius, 1702). On Budde's view of Jewish philosophy, see Wilhelm Schmidt-Biggemann, "Die Historisierung der 'Philosophia Hebraeorum' im frühen 18. Jahrhundert. Eine philosophisch-philologische Demontage," in *Historicization—Historisierung*, ed. Glenn W. Most (Göttingen: Vandenhoek & Ruprecht, 2001): 104–128; idem, *Geschichte der christlichen Kabbala*, vol. 3 (Stuttgart: Bad Cannstatt, 2013), 243–270; Valerio Marchetti, "Il teologo Johann Franz Budde (1667–1729) e la filosofia ebraica," in *L'interculturalità dell'ebraismo*, ed. Mauro Perani (Ravenna: Longo, 2008): 299–314; Haim Mahlev, "Kabbalah as Philosophia Perennis?: The Image of Judaism in the German Early Enlightenment: Three Studies," *Jewish Quarterly Review* 104.2 (2014): 234–257. On the debate on Kabbalah and Jewish Philosophy, especially between Budde and Johann Georg Wachter, see Schmidt-Biggemann, *Geschichte der christlichen Kabbala*, vol. 3, 214–242.

29 Johann F. Budde, "Observatio I. Origines philosophiae Mysticae, sive Cabbalae Veterum Ebraeorum brevis delineatio," *Observationum selectarum ad rem litterariam spectatium* 1 (1700): 1–26; idem, "Defensio Cabbalae Ebraeorum contra auctores quosdam modernos," *ibidem*, 207–231; idem, *Dissertatio philosophica de Spinozismo ante Spinozam [...] submittit Ioannes Fridericus Werder* (Halle: Ch. Henckel, 1706). This last work, a dissertation discussed at the University of Halle, was a response to Johann Georg Wachter, *Der Spinozismus im Jüdenthumb* (Amsterdam: Wolters, 1699). The debate on Spinoza's philosophy was of course linked to the discussion on Jewish philosophy; see, e.g., David Bell, *Spinoza in Germany from 1670 to Age of Goethe* (London: Institute of Germanic Studies, University of London, 1984); Winfried Schröder, *Spinoza in der deutschen Frühaufklärung* (Würzburg: Königshausen & Neuman, 1987).

30 The inclusion of Jewish tradition within the history of philosophy was also present in the work of a scholar close to the Pietist milieu, Johan Wilhelm Zierold (1669–1731); see Mario Longo, "Johan Wilhelm Zierold (1669–1731)," in *Models of the History of Philosophy*, vol. 2: 323–331. On the links between history of philosophy and Pietism, see Martin Gierl, *Pietismus und Auklärung. Theologische Polemik und die Kommunikationsreform der Wissenschaft am Ende des 17. Jahrhunderts* (Göttingen: Vandenhoeck & Ruprecht, 1997); Jean-Marie Carré, "Le piétisme de Halle et la philosophie des Lumières (1690–1750)," *Revue de synthèse historique* 37.3, n. 81 (1913): 279–308.

As has been observed, the first attempt to analyse Jewish philosophy was published in the journal *Observationes selectae* edited in Halle by Budde and Thomasius. All the works in this collection appeared anonymously and encapsulated the thought of the school of Halle. The school was based on the principles already mentioned: anti-Aristotelism, anti-dogmatism both in the cultural and religious domain, and a harsh criticism of Lutheran orthodoxy.[31]

3 Jacob Reimmann and Jewish Scepticism

In the eighth volume of this journal, another work on the history of Jewish philosophy was published. Its author was Jacob Friedrich Reimmann, and the essay bore the provocative title: "Was Salomon a Sceptic?".[32]

Reimmann was born in Gröningen near Halberstadt in 1668, and studied theology and philosophy for two years at the University of Jena. He then became director of the school of Halberstadt, and continued to work in the school system of his town. He was also involved in religious life: he became a deacon in 1714 and preacher at Halberstadt, and went on to become superintendent of the churches at Hildesheim. He died in the same town in 1743. Throughout his life, he remained in contact with the most eminent figures of the time, such as Thomasius and Gottfried Wilhelm Leibniz (1646–1716) and published several works on a variety of subjects both in Latin and in German. Influenced by Halle's milieu, he saw his main task to be combining rational thought and Lutheranism, which incurred going beyond traditional German scholasticism.[33]

He dealt with the Jewish tradition and its theology and philosophy in various works, both in Latin and German. He published a long and articulate treatise entitled *Versuch einer Enleitung in die Historie der Theologie insgemein und Juedischen Theologie ins besondere* (*Attempt at an Introduction to the History of Theology in General*

---

[31] On the authorship of the different essays published in this collection, see Christoph August Heumann, "Revelatio auctorum Observationum Halensium Latinarum," *Miscellanea Lipsensia Nova* 1 (1742): 292–318. In addition to Budde's essays published in the first volume there is also Christian Thomasius, "Observatio II. Scholae quid? Et Quomodo ab Academiis differant?," *Observationum selectarum* 1 (1700): 26–35.

[32] Jacob F. Reimmann, "An Salomon fuerit Scepticus," *Observationum selectarum* 8 (1704): 327–367.

[33] On Reimmann, see Theodor Günther, *Jacob Friedrich Reimmann (1668–1743). Mühsal und Frucht* (Köln: Günther, 1974); Ralph Häfner, "Das Erkenntnisproblem in der Philologie," in *Philologie und Erkenntnis. Beiträge zu Begriff und Problem frühneuzeitlicher Philologie*, ed. Ralph Häfner (Tübingen: Max Niemeyer, 2001): 93–128; Martin Mulsow and Helmut Zedelmaier, eds., *Skepsis, Providenz, Polyhistorie. Jakob Friedrich Reimmann (1668–1743)* (Tübingen: Max Niemeyer Verlag, 1998); Winfried Schröder, "Einleitung," in Jacob F. Reimmann, *Historia Universalis atheismi et atheorum falso et merito suspectorum*, ed. Winfried Schröder (Stuttgart and Bad Cannstatt: Frommann-Holzboog, 1992): 7–37.

and Jewish Theology in Particular), published in Magdeburg in 1717.[34] Reimmann dedicated an entire work to the study of atheism, a topic very much *en vogue* at the time, with a chapter specifically devoted to the atheism of the Jews, leading, inevitably, to a discussion of Jewish philosophy itself.[35] But in other short tractates, such as the essay dedicated to the four elements, he always made reference to the Jewish tradition.[36]

Reimmann was, therefore, well aware of the importance of the discussion on Jewish tradition for the debate on the history of philosophy and for the history of theology, however, he developed his idea of Jewish philosophy through a completely different approch. He decided to combine this topic with another theme discussed in that period; scepticism and in so doing combined them in an original way. Reimmann chose the figure of Solomon primarily because traditionally, and especially in the book of Ecclesiastes, the Jewish king had expressed doubts about the ability of the human mind to know. Clearly Reimmann is to use his figure to support his model of philosophy, as will be demonstrated. It is interesting to note that from now on the figure of Solomon becomes important for the debate on scepticism in Germany.[37]

Reimmann divided his essay on Solomon into two parts. In the first he discusses the 'nature' of Jewish philosophy, and its link to sceptical tradition. In the second he defends his statement against the critique of his opponents, in particular from the accusations of Protestant theologian Joachim Lange (1670–1744).

From the very beginning, Reimmann criticised the uses several scholars had made of the Jewish philosophical tradition. He underlined three aspects in particular: 1) Many scholars, especially the historians of philosophy, have maintained that all the patriarchs, leaders and kings of the Jews have been philosophers (even in

---

[34] Jacob F. Reimmann, *Versuch einer Enleitung in die Historie der Theologie insgemein und Juedischen Theologie ins besondere* (Magdeburg: Christoph Seidel, 1717). In this work, for example, he discussed the interpretation of Kabbalah in Budde's work; cf. *ibidem*, 333–459 on kabbalistic theology and 350–351 on Budde's interpretation. On Reimmann's interpretation of Kabbalah, see Mahlev, "Kabbalah as Philosophia Perennis?," 249–255.

[35] Cf. Jacob F. Reimmann, *Historia Universalis atheismi et atheorum falso et merito suspectorum* (Hildesheim: L. Schröder, 1725), 24–50.

[36] See, e.g., Jacob F. Reimmann, "Observatio III. Nescire Philosophos adhuc quid sit aer," in *Observationum selectarum* 5 (1700): 85: 'Etenim ut ab Hebraeis quorum philosophia procul dubio est antiquissima faciamus initium, hi aeris naturam usque adeo ignorarunt, ut ne nomen quidem habuerit cognitum;' idem, "Observatio IV. Nescire Philosophos quid sit aqua, in Observationum selectarum," *ibidem*, 109: 'Etenim si Hebraeorum Cryptas philosophicas, qua fas est diligentia perreptamus, de divisione quidem aquarum hinc atque hinc quaedam vestigia deprehendimus, sed de definitione earundem, ne *gru* quidem. Et ipsae quoque divisiones sic comparatae sunt, ut nobis ignorantiam nostram exprobrare videantur. Ut enim de divisione rabbinica et kabbalistica nil dicam in praesenti, qua aquas in masculas et foeminas disponere consueverunt.'

[37] On Salomon and scepticism, see, e.g., Stuart Weeks, *Ecclesiastes and Scepticism* (New York: T & T Clark International, 2012).

the absence of any evidence).[38] 2) The Hebrew patriarchs were often seen as dogmatic philosophers.[39] 3) Their philosophy had been interpreted in different ways according to the thought of their interpreters. (e. g. Reimmann noted, Moses was seen at the same time as a Cartesian philosopher, an Aristotelian, and so on).[40] The first critique was addressed to all the previous traditions that, as seen above, have used Jewish wisdom to legitimise differing philosophical ideas. He probably had Budde's work in mind too for, as already mentioned, Budde presented Judaism as the space where it would be possible to find the common origin of philosophy and theology.

Reimmann distances himself from previous tradition on the one hand, but on the other, he decided to follow the strategy of the historians of philosophy in using Jewish wisdom to legitimise his philosophical ideas. He maintains that after Job, King Solomon was the only Jewish man possible to be considered a true philosopher.[41] Reimmann analyses Solomon's thought by using different sources, and outlines the

---

38 Reimmann, "An Salomon," 328–329: 'Cum multi omnino sint qui magno conatu nihil agere, et, uti Latinorum habet proverbium, "Tellenas conduplicare tricas," soleant. Tum illi cumprimis ad hanc κατηγορίαν referri merentur, qui antiquorum Hebraeorum Antistites, Patriarchas videlicet Ducesque et Judices, imo etiam Reges, Pontifices aliosque etc. ad Philosophorum Dogmaticorum censum revocare eosque volentes nolentesque Magistros totius Encyclopaediae Philosophicae salutare consueverunt. Etenim ut non dicam, eos interdum ne per somnum quidem de iis scientiis ac disciplinis cogitasse, quas didicisse solicite, et posteros suos docuisse a nobis creduntur. Quam imbecillia ea sunt argumenta, quibus οἱ ἐξ ἐναντίας causam sua colorare, et Hebraeorum Principes Doctores Philosophiae creare annituntur?'
39 Ibidem, 330–331: 'Nam licet omnes, qui historiam Philosophicam contexuere adhuc, eosdem fecerint Dogmaticos, tamen recogitandum est, hoc factum esse a Dogmaticis, adeoque exinde non consequi revera fuisse tales. Siquidem hic mos est eorum qui partibus addicti sunt, ut describant homines, non ut fuerunt, sed ut fuisse cupiunt, fingantque sibi interdum et suo ingenio assentatores quosdam, quo sectam suam antiquiorem caeteris augustioremque efficiant.'
40 Ibidem, 331: 'Plane sicut experientia edocti sumus, *Mosen* jam Cartesianum, jam Aristotelicum, mox Atomisticum et Eclecticum factum esse, prout lectorem huic vel isti haeresi addictus indeptus fuerit.'
41 Ibidem, 332–333: 'Sed quid, ais, ille omnium Hebraeorum sapientum sapientissimus Rex Salomo istane ἀκαταληψία Sceptica, quam tu laudibus tantopere effers, excelluit? An putas enim fuisse Aporeticum, qui etiam in rebus naturalibus fuit θεοδίδακτος? Qui sua sibi δενδρολογία et ζωολογία tantam lucem circumfudit? Qui prosa juxta et versa oratione in toto orbe inclaruit, nihilque ignoravit eorum, quae ad dogmaticum eruditionis circulum requiruntur? Equidem fateor, haec non sine magno colore nobis objici posse a Dogmaticis; sed an pari soliditate objiciantur, adhuc animi vehementer pendeo. Nam primum nulla prorsus est consequentia, "Salomon in rebus naturalibus fuit θεοδίδακτος, equidem fuit Dogmaticus." Siquidem et in rebus naturalibus potest esse θεοδίδακτος qui a Deo edoctus est, "nos in rebus naturalibus nil scire," adeoque nil affirmare certo de iis nec negare posse. Tum et Scepticus sibi δενδρολογίᾳ et ζωολογίᾳ potest famam acquirere, si ostendat; Dogmaticos in his scientiae naturalis partibus eneptivisse adhuc, et nil nisi fumos suis discipulis vendidisse. Ac tandem in prosa juxta et versa oratione potest Scepticus inclarescere, nosseque omnia quae in Scholis Dogmaticorum proponuntur, non quidem ut pro veris certisque ea habeat, sed ut falsitatem et incertitudinem penitius cognoscat, eamque suis adversariis ostendat.'

king's philosophy as anti-dogmatic thought linked to the sceptical tradition.⁴² He describes three qualities of Solomon's philosophy, and compares it with the philosophy of his own time. According to him, Solomon's thought had its origin in divine revelation, and not in natural illumination.⁴³ Its object was the distinction between good and bad, and not, like the philosophy of Reimmann's time, between true and false,⁴⁴ and it was a practical philosophy and not a theoretical one.⁴⁵ He seems to adopt a traditional (conservative) attitude toward the new rationalistic philosophy of his day, by comparing, for example, divine and natural efficient cause.⁴⁶ Indeed, throughout the history of its discovery during the early modern age, scepticism was often used as a tool against pagan philosophy, for example, in the work of Giovanfrancesco Pico della Mirandola.⁴⁷

Reimmann, however, had a different plan in mind. When he describes the nature of Solomon's wisdom he underlines that the Jewish king was taught by God himself.⁴⁸ This statement, he maintains, could be seen as evidence of the dogmatic nature of his thought, while it is the opposite. Reimmann writes:

> First of all there is absolutely no consequentiality here: 'Solomon was taught by God in natural causes, therefore he was a dogmatic.' For even with regard to natural causes it can happen that the person who has been taught by God has been instructed by God that we know nothing about natural causes, or even that nothing certain can be affirmed or denied about them.⁴⁹

---

42 *Ibidem*, 334: 'Plane sicur Rex sapientissimus Salomo c. I v. 17 scribit, se adjecisse animum non solum ad cognoscendam (Scepticorum) sapientiam (לדעת חכמה) sed etiam ad perspiciendam omnem (Dogmaticorum) insaniam et stoliditatem לדעת הללת ושכלות Conf. cap. VII v. 26.'
43 *Ibidem*, 334–335: 'Postea vero suspiriis devotis a Deo indeptum quidem sapientiam et Philosophiam, sed toto coelo a nostra, qua mundus hodie decipitur, diversam. Etenim quod ad ejus causam efficientem attinet, non a lumine naturae, nec ab institutione, nec ab exercitatione eadem manaverat, siquidem haec tria principia (φύσις, μάθησις, ἄσκησις) peccati originalis diritate ita corrupta sunt, ut non nisi eruditio superficiaria et falsa ab iis exspectari possit, sed a lumine supernaturali et divino duxerat originem.'
44 *Ibidem*, 336: 'Quamobrem mirandum etiam non est, quod nostra Philosophia a Solomonaea objecto etiam differat. Cum enim illa in veritate et falsitate rerum eruenda occupetur cumprimis, haec in bonitate et malitia detegenda solummodo districta est, ut patet ex 1 *Reg.* III v. 9 ubi petit siti Salomo sapientiam non quidem ad discernendum verum a falso, sed tantum bonum a malo.'
45 *Ibidem*, 337: 'Porro quod ad formam Philosophiae Salomonaeae est, consistit illa tantum in praxi, i.e. ut *Proverb.* IX v. 6 dicitur, "in omittendis stultorum vitiis et perpetrandis prudentum virtutibus," quo nomine non parum a nostra philosophandi ratione distat. Nam licet nos in disciplinis practicis eundem cum eo finem habere videri discupiamus; revera tamen longe ab eo absumus, quia nostrae disciplinae non re, sed nomine tantum sunt practicae, dum a principio ad finem usque otiosis speculationibus de virtutum definitionibus, divisionibus, axiomatis, etc. refertae sunt et constipatae.'
46 See note 39.
47 On fideistic scepticism, see, e.g., Richard Popkin, *The History of Scepticism: From Savonarola to Bayle* (Oxford: Oxford University Press, 2003): 20–24.
48 Reimmann uses the Greek word θεοδίδακτος.
49 Reimmann, "An Salomon," 333: 'Nam primum nulla prorsus est consequentia, "Salomon in rebus naturalibus fuit θεοδίδακτος, equidem, fuit Dogmaticus." Siquidem et in rebus naturalibus potest

Thus, he seems to strengthen the definition of fideistic scepticism, but, on the other hand he goes further and presents this divine scepticism as the only useful critical tool of dogmatic thought in the philosophical debate of his time. In the confrontation between the old philosophy of Salomon and the thought of his time, a new philosophy emerges using Aristotelian categories, but entirely different to the scholastic thought in the Lutheran Universities. Reimmann discusses Aristotle's definition of the intellect and his distinction between theoretical and practical intellect. Aristotle himself and his commentators considered theoretical intellect to be superior to the practical, but Reimmann overturns this hierarchy: he uses scepticism to attack Aristotelian theoretical intellect, and exalt the practical.[50] He shows that Jewish tradition could be used in a completely different way. In his view, Jewish philosophy was not a tool to legitimise a philosophical system, but a strategy or instrument to criticise the other dogmatic philosophies.

In the second part of his tractate, Reimmann defends his interpretation from the critique of theologian Jacob Lange. It has been recorded that Reimmann told Lange of his interpretation of Solomon's philosophy during a private conversation in 1704, and the latter went on to attack him in his book *Medicina mentis*, published the same year in Berlin.[51] Lange was one of the most important Pietist theologians of the time, he grew up in the Halle milieu, together with Francke and Thomasius, and then lived in Berlin contemporary to Spener.[52] Lange's tractate attempted to rethink the history of philosophy in the light of the Pietistic critique of the traditional orthodox Lutheranism. Thus, Reimmann's idea that the holy philosophy of Solomon corresponded to scepticism was unacceptable and, for Lange, clear evidence of atheism.[53] Reimmann,

---

esse θεοδίδακτος qui a Deo edoctus est, "nos in rebus naturalibus nil scire," adeoque nil affirmare certo de iis nec negare posse.'

50 On this topic, as well as the Jewish philosophical debate in the Middle Ages, see Shlomo Pines, "Truth and Falsehood versus Good and Evil: A Study in Jewish and Genral Philosophy in Connection with the Guide of the Perplexed I, 2," in *Studies in Maimonides*, ed. Isadore Twersky (Cambridge, MA: Harvard University Press, 1990): 95–127. I am grateful to Daniel Davis for drawing my attention to this article.

51 Joachim Lange, *Medicina mentis, qua praepostera philosophandi methodo ostensa ac reiecta, secundum sanioris philosophiae principia, aegrae mentis sanatio ac sanatae usus in veri rectique investigatione ac communicatione* (Berlin: Wessel, 1704). On the debate between Reimmann and Lange, see Martin Mulsow, "Die Paradoxien der Vernunft. Rekonstruktion einer verleugneten Phase in Reimmanns Denken," in *Skepsis, Providenz, Polyhistorie. Jakob Friedrich Reimmann (1668–1743)*, eds. Martin Mulsow and Helmut Zedelmaier, 26–32. Cf. Reimmann, "An Salomon," 344: 'Et quia Auctori huic, quem alias ob pietatem et eruditionem magni facio, paneque ita rationem duco, eum non malo animo hunc paragraphum Historiae suae inseruisse; Ita collubuit hanc nostram sententiam, quam eidem privatim communicaveramus, publicere rejicere, eamque ceu impiam et praeposteram condemnare, fas erit, opinor, ad haec ejus dubia jam publice respondisse.'

52 On Lange's biography, see Jendris Alwast, "Lange, Joachim," *Neue Deutsche Biographie* 13 (1982): 548 f. [Online-Version]; URL: https://www.deutsche-biographie.de/pnd118569376.html#ndbcontent.

53 Lange, *Medicina Mentis*, 393: 'Videtur laudatae sapientiae Salomonaeae hominisque sapientis officio obstare quae ejus tradit Ecclesiastes? Ita quidem judicant, qui citra Salomonaeum principium,

thus, spends the last part of his tractate defending not only his interpretation of Solomon's philosophy, but largely scepticism itself. At the end of his work he openly quotes Sextus Empiricus to make clear to his adversaries scepticism was not a philosophy which 'did not doubt all beliefs generally,' rather it 'doubted only uncertain or dubious things, which were investigated and disputed by the sciences of the dogmatics.'[54] Finally, he concludes that scepticism was not addressed to theological wisdom:

> [...] so, far be it from me to place all of Solomon's doctrine within the framework of *akatalepsia*; rather, I will distinguish as carefully as possible theological questions from philosophical ones, theory from praxis, dogmas about the existence of things from dogmas about the essence of things.[55]

Surely Reimmann was influenced by Halle's Enlightment. But his idea of scepticism cannot be traced exclusively to the 'rationalistic' use of scepticism at the time. The sources he uses refer, on the one hand, to the French tradition: two long quotations taken from the philosopher François de La Mothe Le Vayer (1588–1672).[56] While on the other, mystic and anti-Cartesian Pierre Poiret (1646–1719) is mentioned at the end of the treatise.[57] The reference to his work, which had been re-edited only a

---

quod ille in timore Dei collocat, e Salomone impie et praepostere philosophantur. Ex horum numero sunt, qui ad hujus libri ductum non dubitant, e Salomone alterum quasi Pyrrhonem seu Scepticum facere ejusque doctrinam ἐν ἀκαταληψίᾳ seu ignorantia et fluctuatione Sceptica ponere. Qui ubi principium suum: "Nos scire nihil," in hoc libro inveniant, et quid e nihilo suo derivari velint, equidem non deprehendo. Si quis vero principia et indolem Philosophiae Salomonaeae ex hoc praecipue libro eruere voluerint, inter alia secreta meditatione excutiat sequentia loca, in quibus simul caeterorum clavis est c. 1 v. 2; c. VII v. 13, 20, 30; VIII 12, 13; IX v. 18; XI v. 9, 10; XII v. 7, 13, 14.'

54 Reimann, "An Salomon," 361–362: 'Etenim ut ipsi olim Sceptici non generatim de omnibus dubitabant dogmatis et v. g. calefacti vel frigefacti non dicebant, puto me non calefieri vel frigefieri; sed, ut expresse habet Sextus Empiricus l. 1 hypothes. Pyrrhon. c. VII p. m. 12 de iis tantum, quae erant de rebus incertis ac dubiis, de quibus in Dogmaticorum scientiis quaeritur, et ambigitur.'

55 *Ibidem*, 362: 'Ita tantum abest, ut omnem doctrinam Salomonis ἐν ἀκαταληψίᾳ reponamus, ut potius Theologica a Philosophicis, theoretica a practicis, et dogmata de rerum existentia a dogmatis de rerum essentia, quam solicitissime distinguamus.'

56 See Reimmann, "An Salomon," 348–350 and 353–360. Both are quotations from François La Mothe Le Vayer, *De la Vertu des Payens*, in idem, *Oevres* (Paris: Augustin Courbe, 1662): 662. On La Mothe Le Vayer, see René Pintard, *Le Libertinage érudit dans la première moitié du XVIIe siècle* (Geneve: Slatkine, 1983), 505–538; Popkin, *The History of Skepticism*, 82–87. As Martin Mulsow has pointed out, the history of Pyrrhonism and of scepticism in general has opened the door to the reception of the *Libertinage érudite* in Germany during the first Enlightenment; see Mulsow, "Die Paradoxien der Vernunft. Rekonstruktion einer verleugneten Phase in Reimmanns Denken," 32; idem, "Appunti sulla fortuna di Gabriel Naudé nella Germania del primo illuminismo," *Studi filosofici* 14/15 (1991–1992): 145–156.

57 See Reimmann, "An Salomon," 366: 'Unicum tantummodo locum de commodis Philosophiae scepticae adjiciam, quem habet Cl. Auctoris nostri dux et Coryphaeus Petrus Poiretus in praefat. Tom. 1 de Oeconomia divina Edit. Amestelod. in 12mo 1687. Ubi ita infit: "Cette sentence peut assi servir aux bonnes ames pour les porter à l'admiration des grandeurs adorables de Dieu à la recherche

few years earlier by Thomasius, shows us the complexity of the sources of his thought, which certainly require further inverstigation.⁵⁸

Conclusion

Reimmann's involvement in Thomasius and Budde's *Observationes selectae* project shows that he agreed with the attempt the Halle school made to attack dogmatism, and re-think Lutheran orthodoxy. However, he believed that Thomasius and Budde's tools, and particularly eclectic philosophy, were insufficient.⁵⁹

Reimmann argues that Solomon was the best example of the Jewish philosophical tradition, and as the Jewish king lived centuries before Pyrrhon, it would be fair to claim him as the real founder of scepticism.⁶⁰ The relationship between scepticism and the Jewish tradition, for Reimmann, served to strengthen the main characteristic of that kind of Greek philosophy—that being its acknowledgement of human ignorance and doubt. Reimmann, however, uses fideistic garb to legitimise the sceptic strategy against dogmatism and traditional knowledge.

In so doing, he transforms the idea of Jewish philosophy in the eyes of Christians. As we have seen, from the beginning of the early modern age, Christian culture used the Jewish tradition for the purpose of legitimising particular philosophical systems—e.g. Platonism, Atomism, or Cartesian thought—and also to give them a holy veneer. This scheme established a strong relationship between the Jewish tradition and pagan philosophy: it regarded the former as possessing a philosophical system and attributed an aura of holiness to the latter.

Reimmann went further in establishing a connection between the pagan tradition and the Jewish one, but he refused to attribute a given philosophical system to Jewish philosophy. According to him, thanks to their unique relationship with

---

de son amour, et en meme tems mettre à fond leurs coeurs en repos sur une infinité de difficultes dont on se tourmente l'Esprit sur autres choses.'" Cf. Pierre Poiret, *L'Oeconomie Divin ou Systeme Universel et Demontré des Oeuvres et des Desseins de Dieu envers les Hommes* (Amsterdam: Henry Wetstein, 1687). On Poiret, see Marjolaine Chevallier, *Pierre Poiret (1646–1719). Du protestatisme à la mystique* (Geneve: Labor et Fides, 1994).

58 See Pierre Poiret, *De eruditione triplici, solida superficiaria et falsa libri tres [...] accedit Christiani Thomasii nova praefatio* (Frankfurt and Leipzig: Johann Friedrich Zeitler, 1708).

59 Martin Mulsow, "Eclecticism or Skepticism? A Problem of the Early Enlightenment," *Journal of the History of Ideas* 58.3 (1997): 468. See this article also for the influence that the work of Georg Struve had on Reimmann's thought; cf. Burcard Gotthelff Struve, Johann Christoph Dorn (resp.), *Dissertatio de doctis impostoribus* (Jena: Litteris Mullerianis, 1703).

60 Reimmann, "An Salomon," 361: 'Tertio nec illud bene dicitur, quod ait, hos homines e Salomone *alterum* quasi Pyrrhonem vel Scepticum facere. Qui enim illi alterum e Salomone possent facere Pyrrhonem, cum *alter* ratione ordinis priori sit posterior, et Salomon Pyrrhonem fere octingentos annos antecesserit? Equidem ex Pyrrhone facere *Salomonem alterum*, quoad in ἀκαταληψίᾳ conveniunt, non prorsus esset impossibile; Sed enim ex Salomone fingere Pyrrhonem alterum tam est ἀδύνατον, quam ipsum archetypum ex ectypo exprimere.'

God, the Jewish philosophers (Job and Solomon), were the only ones aware of the weakness of the human mind. The German scholar, therefore, used the Jewish tradition to legitimise not so much a philosophical system, as a philosophical strategy that was to undermine traditional knowledge. Jewish philosophy, for Reimmann's intentions, had to lose its legitimising role and transform itself into its opposite, that is to say, into an instrument for criticising all dogmatic philosophical systems.

Reimmann's idea of Jewish philosophy was not developed any further, nor did it influence subsequent reflections on the topic. On the contrary, it provoked several opposing reactions. Largely he was accused of wanting to transform Solomon into an atheist.[61] Despite this, however, the recognition of Jewish philosophy as a sceptical philosophy, and the justification of sceptical doubt as the only tool for philosophical knowledge, was bound to have significant consequences, not only for the history of Jewish philosophy in the Lutheran world, but above all, for the history of philosophy in general.

After Reimmann, Jewish philosophy began to be seen in a different way by Christian eyes: it became less important as a means to defend specific philosophical systems, or to understand the relationship between philosophy and theology. It was 'normalised' and became equal to all other non-Greek philosophical traditions. Reimmann's work may not have played a role in this process, but it almost certainly stands as evidence of this transformation.

---

61 Reinhard H. Roll, *Salomo Scepticismi crimine contra iniustam observatoris Halensis imputationem* (Rostock: Impensis Wepplingianis, 1710); Johann Cristoph Ortlob, Georg Stisser (resp.), *Dissertatio processum Salomonis contra Simei* (Leipzig: Literis Immanuelis Titii, 1719).

Lukas Lang
Reidian Common Sense: An Antidote to Scepticism?

1 Common Sense and Scepticism

Scepticism is in most cases disliked. Much of contemporary epistemology can be construed as a response to the modern incarnation of scepticism, i.e. the view that justification is impossible or that nothing is known, either in general or about a certain area of discourse (say, unperceivable objects).[1] In contrast to this, its ancient relative did not preach theory or rely on dubitable premises. The Pyrrhonists[2] were concerned with a way of life, the aim of which was *ataraxia*—tranquility of mind—and its method *epoché*—suspension of judgement. Whereas it had much influence in the early modern period (due to translations that made the works of Sextus Empiricus, the Pyrrhonist's chief author, available to scholars at the time), it had not been taken seriously by contemporary scholars of ancient philosophy until a few decades ago, 'because it was regarded as a patently absurd or far-fetched form of skepticism,'[3] and the attention it received outside the ancient philosophy classroom was practically non-existent.

One reason for the neglect of Pyrrhonian scepticism is the *apraxia* objection,[4] which states in its evidential mode that sceptical life is impossible and in its pragmatic mode that sceptical life is impractical. The pragmatic mode presupposes that sceptical life (i.e., life without opinion or beliefs) is possible, but argues that

---

This article was written during my time as a Junior Fellow at the Maimonides Centre for Advanced Studies. I am especially thankful for the comments to versions of this paper presented at the Internal Workshop and at the Reading Evening on Common Sense and Scepticism. Many thanks also to Máté Veres, whose feedback was very helpful.

1 Cf. Peter Klein, "Skepticism," *The Stanford Encyclopedia of Philosophy* (Summer 2015 Edition), ed. Edward N. Zalta, URL = <https://plato.stanford.edu/archives/sum2015/entries/skepticism/>.
2 Ancient Scepticism encompasses two broad traditions, each of which was subject to transformations and different proponents with varying views on scepticism. For the first tradition, Academic Scepticism, see Diego Machuca, "Ancient Skepticism. The Skeptical Academy," *Philosophy Compass* 6 (2011): 259–266. For the second tradition, Pyrrhonian Scepticism, see idem, "Ancient Skepticism. Pyrrhonism," *Philosophy Compass* 6 (2011): 246–258. I will use 'Pyrrhonian scepticism' and 'scepticism' interchangeably on most occasions. Context makes clear where I intend to distinguish Pyrrhonian scepticism from the modern versions of scepticism.
3 Diego Machuca, "Ancient Skepticism. Pyrrhonism," 248.
4 Cf. Katja M. Vogt, "Scepticism and Action," *Cambridge Companion to Ancient Scepticism*, ed. Richard Bett (Cambridge: Cambridge University Press): 165–180, and Gisela Striker, "Sceptical Strategies," *Doubt and Dogmatism*, eds. Malcom Schofield, Myles F. Burnyeat and Jonathan Barnes (Oxford: Oxford University Press, 1980): 54–83.

we *should not* be sceptics, on the grounds that it would be imprudent, dangerous, or bad to be so. According to the evidential mode, sceptical life is impossible. It claims that in order to act, we need beliefs. For example, the action of reaching for my mug requires belief in it being there, or, to echo a common accusation, alluding to fellow philosophers requires the belief that they exist. The idea is that addressing, quoting, or meeting people requires belief in their existence, their qualities, and so on.[5] Given that the self-proclaimed sceptic does drink his coffee and does argue with other philosophers, the evidential mode concludes that we *are not* and that we *cannot* be sceptics.[6] As readers of Sextus' works will know, this objection misses its target by miles. Given that we will discuss his reply in detail below, a very short summary of the Pyrrhonian reply to the *apraxia* objection is adequate. According to Sextus, the sceptic acts in line with those appearances that force their assent upon him. That is, he drinks because he is thirsty, but suspends any opinion as to whether the mug is *really* there, or whether it is just an idea, an illusion and so on.

In this paper, I discuss Thomas Reid's (1710–1796) common-sense-based version of the *apraxia* objection, because it appears to be immune to Sextus' reply and so still has a chance to succeed. It is much more radical, in that it is not based on action, but on life and the human condition. Thus, it is not only by acting that the sceptic betrays his philosophy, but in fact merely by being human.

Basing his objection on common sense, Reid makes his objection far more threatening by comparison with other attacks on (ancient and modern) scepticism. Most philosophical arguments against scepticism make use of heavy-weight assumptions which are easy for the sceptic to avoid.[7] The common-sense strategy purports to overcome this by shifting the discussion to a pre-theoretical point. As with the sceptic, the common-sense-based attack depends on no theoretical assumptions, and so it appears the sceptic is forced to agree. If scepticism is ruled out by something that is a precondition for the discussion, for action in general, or even more broadly, life, and we only need common sense to see this, there appears to be no way out for scepticism.[8] And while this seems like the version of the *apraxia* objection we just dis-

---

[5] This polemic accusation is made by George E. Moore in his discussion of philosophers who disagree with his list of common sense propositions. He also mentions that their use of 'we' betrays their position, because clearly such usage implies the existence of other human beings. Cf. George E. Moore, "A Defence of Common Sense," in *Philosophical Papers*, Muirhead Library of Philosophy, ed. George. E. Moore (London: George Allen & Unwin Ltd., 1958): 40–41.

[6] Cf. Suzanna Obdrzalek, "From Skepticism to Paralysis," *Ancient Philosophy* 32 (2012): 370.

[7] A fitting example for a popular heavy-weight defence against scepticism is externalism, both in its semantic form or as a claim about mental content. For semantic externalism, see Hilary Putnam, "The Meaning of 'Meaning'," *Minnesota Studies in Philosophy of Science* 7 (1975): 131–193. For externalism about mental content, see Colin McGinn "Charity, interpretation, and belief," *Journal of Philosophy* 74 (1977): 521–535.

[8] The similarities to Wittgenstein and contemporary hinge-epistemology are no surprise, given Reid's influence on Moore, and Moore's influence on Wittgenstein. For the presence of Reid in the circles of

carded, it has to be observed that it did not fail for structural reasons, but for making an assumption Sextus did not share. As Reid's version is grounded on common sense, the idea is that there is no assumption involved that Sextus cannot share. So, if we find something that really is a precondition for discussion, action or life (and according to Sextus there appear to be such things: without appearances that force our assent we would be inactive, see section 3), that contradicts something to which Sextus is committed, the *apraxia* objection would be successful.

However, the shift to a pre-theoretical point is faced with a dilemma. Either the ability to engage with the sceptic is lost, or the strategy risks forfeiting its advantage. If the sceptic refuses to acknowledge that which is impossible not to acknowledge (according to common sense), there is no common ground left between the disputants. Historically, this leads either to ignorance towards or ridicule of the sceptic. On the other hand, any bit of theory that is endorsed can be used by the sceptic again. Later in the paper (section 4) we will see a version of this dilemma, and how it endangers Reid's argument against the sceptic.

Another reason for discussing Reid in this context is that common-sense-based arguments are still being performed to this day. The following passage from Kit Fine's article "The Question of Realism" published in 2001 is a vivid example of the relevancy of common sense as a strategy against scepticism:

> However, in this age of post-Moorean modesty, many of us are inclined to doubt that philosophy is in possession of arguments that might genuinely serve to undermine what we ordinarily believe. It may perhaps be conceded that the arguments of the skeptic appear to be utterly compelling; but the Mooreans among us will hold that the very plausibility of our ordinary beliefs is reason enough for supposing that there must be something wrong in the skeptic's arguments, even if we are unable to say what it is. Insofar, then, as the pretensions of philosophy to provide a world-view rest upon its claim to be in possession of the epistemological high ground, those pretensions had better be given up.[9]

According to Fine (who echoes what has become dogma in some circles of philosophy),[10] no matter how good or convincing the sceptic's argument is, we should retain all our ordinary beliefs in response, even if we are unable to find any fault in the sceptic's arguments due to the high plausibility of our ordinary beliefs. The term 'common sense' does not appear in Fine's proclamation, but both his talk of ordinary beliefs and his reference to George E. Moore (1873–1958)—who famously attempted

---

Moore and Russell, see Ronald Beanblossom, "Russell's Indebtedness to Reid," *The Monist* 61 (1978): 192–204.

9 Kit Fine, "The Question of Realism," *Philosopher's Imprint* 1 (2001): 2.

10 Other contemporary examples include David M. Armstrong, "A Naturalist Program: Epistemology and Ontology," *Proceedings and Addresses of the American Philosophical Association* 73 (1999): 77–89; David Lewis, "Elusive Knowledge," *Australasian Journal of Philosophy* 74 (1996): 549–567, and Jonathan Schaffer, "On What Grounds What," *Metametaphysics. New Essays on the Foundations of Ontology*, eds. David Chalmers, David Manley, and Ryan Wasserman (Oxford: Oxford University Press, 2009): 347–383.

to refute idealism by merely holding up his hands, and wrote the *Defence of Common Sense* in 1925—suffices for us to take this as an instance of a classic appeal to common sense.

Reid, in contradistinction to Moore, developed a theory that attempts to put this attack on firm ground. In other words, Reid attempted to move the appeal to common sense away from a rhetorical device (used as a last resort in the face of glaring objections) to a sensible and philosophically sound method.

The paper proceeds as follows. I will show in section 2 that we can plausibly assume that Reid did in fact put forward a common-sense-based *apraxia* objection in the evidential mode against Pyrrhonian scepticism (and one that goes beyond mere polemics). Section 3 explores the relationship between Reid's notion of belief and Sextus' notion of assent and finds that they are closely connected. Given this close connection, in the fourth section, after dealing with two objections, I will argue that Reid's *apraxia* objection is either not threatening Pyrrhonian scepticism or not sharing enough common ground with Pyrrhonian scepticism to be successful. In section 5, I conclude that Reid's common-sense-based *apraxia* objection fails.

2 Reid's Attack on Pyrrhonian Scepticism

Most of Reid's work is directed against the way of ideas and its proponents, such as Hume, Locke, Berkeley or Descartes. According to the way of ideas, the direct objects of perception are ideas, rather than external objects. From this point on it is but a short step before one descends into sceptical concerns that knowledge of external objects is impossible if ideas are our only source of information. According to Reid, Hume deserves credit for having exposed the scepticism that was already implicit in the way of ideas' first formulations. Both Berkeley and Reid found this scepticism to be unacceptable. But where Berkeley preserved the way of ideas, and instead rejected the external objects, Reid preserved the external objects and rejected the way of ideas.

Nevertheless, I shall argue that we can also find arguments in Reid against other forms of scepticism, such as Pyrrhonian scepticism. Although I do think that Reid was aware of Pyrrhonian scepticism and that he aimed at refuting it on some occasions, I don't want to rely on a historical argument, nor do I aim for a purely historical claim.[11] Rather, I think that Reid appears to have a theory that sustains his argument against Pyrrhonian scepticism, and so we should read it as such (even though

---

[11] Hume scholars have long since sought to find out which editions, if any, of Sextus' writing were available to scholars in the early modern period and to Hume in particular. A good summary of these findings are presented in Peter S. Fosl, "Skepticism and the Possibility of Nature," in *Pyrrhonism in Ancient, Modern, and Contemporary Philosophy*, ed. Diego E. Machuca (Dordrecht: Springer, 2011): 145–170.

he ignored, or perhaps was not aware, of some of the subtleties of Pyrrhonian scepticism).

For us, the most relevant discussion of Reid's anti-sceptical arguments is that of Philip de Bary. De Bary claims the four arguments he discusses (labelled A-D below) are mere polemics, however, I feel A and B are serious and threatening, while only C and D can be termed polemics. The four arguments are as follows:[12]

> A. I never heard that any sceptic run his head against a post, or stepped into a kennel, because he did not believe his eyes. (EIP 234a)
>
> B. If a man pretends to be a sceptic with regard to the informations of sense, and yet prudently keeps out of harm's way as other men do, he must excuse my suspicion, that he either acts the hypocrite, or imposes upon himself. (IHM 170)
>
> C. Pyrrho the Elean, the father of this philosophy, seems to have carried it to greater perfection than any of his successors [...] And therefore, if a cart run against him, or a dog attacked him, or if he came upon a precipice, he would not stir a foot to avoid the danger, giving no credit to his senses. But his attendants, who, happily for him, were not so great sceptics, took care to keep him out of harm's way; so that he lived till he was ninety years of age. (IHM 20)[13]
>
> D. If a sceptic should build his scepticism upon this foundation, that all our reasoning and judging powers are fallacious in their nature, or should resolve at least to withhold assent until it be proved that they are not, it would be impossible by argument to beat him out of this stronghold. And he must even be left to enjoy his scepticism. (EIP 447b)

De Bary argues that all these should be read as mere polemics, because (i) Reid's chief aim is Hume, and (ii) these arguments mischaracterise Hume. Additionally, (iii) it is implausible that Reid is serious here, given that elsewhere he gives a correct picture of Hume.[14] From the viewpoint of de Bary, Reid is either inconsistent or the arguments are polemics, and so he chooses the latter option.

I agree with the second and third claim, the arguments do mischaracterise Hume and Reid is aware of this. For example, right before the first argument (A) Reid ac-

---

[12] The passages from Reid's Inquiry are cited from Thomas Reid, *An Inquiry into the Human Mind on the Principles of Common Sense*, The Edinburgh Edition of Thomas Reid, ed. Derek R. Brookes (Edinburgh: Edinburgh University Press, 1997) = (IHM). The rest of Reid's work is cited from the eighth edition of the Hamilton edition: Thomas Reid, *Essays on the Intellectual Powers of Man*, ed. Sir William Hamilton (Hildesheim: Georg Olms, 1983) = (EIP), Thomas Reid, *Essays on the Active Powers of the Human Mind*, ed. Sir William Hamilton (Hildesheim: Georg Olms, 1983) = (EAP), Thomas Reid, *Reid's Letters*, ed. Sir William Hamilton (Hildesheim: Georg Olms, 1983) = (Letters). With regards to Sextus' works, I'm using Sextus Empiricus, *Outlines of Scepticism*, Cambridge Texts in the History of Philosophy, eds. Julia Annas and Jonathan Barnes (Cambridge: Cambridge University Press, 2000) = (PH).

[13] Brookes identifies this as a quotation from Diogenes Laertius, *Lives of Eminent Philosophers*, trans. Robert D. Hicks, Loeb Classical Library (Cambridge, MA: Harvard University Press, 1979): 475 (DL IX.62.). See the Explanatory Notes in Brookes' edition of Reid's Inquiry (p. 222).

[14] See Philip de Bary, *Thomas Reid and Scepticism: His Reliabilist Response*, Routledge Studies in Eighteenth-Century Philosophy 3 (London: Routledge, 2002), 7–19.

knowledges that Hume agrees that doubt with regard to the senses cannot be upheld (EIP 234a). But with regard to the first claim, I disagree with de Bary. As Louis Loeb pointed out, when Reid discusses the figures of the way of ideas, the chapter on Hume is the shortest.[15] Loeb also shows that only some passages of Hume are quoted by Reid (throughout his works) and that Reid ignored many features of Hume's theory, acknowledgement of which would have brought Reid—too close for comfort—to Hume. In place of viewing Reid mainly as an opponent of Hume, we should instead read him as an opponent of the way of ideas. This is supported by Reid's own self-perception, gained from sources such as the following letter from Reid to Dr. James Gregory (date unknown), in which he sums up his philosophical achievement as working against the way of ideas:

> The merit of what you are pleased to call my philosophy, lies, I think, chiefly, in having called into question the common theory of ideas, or images of things in the mind, being the only objects of thought. [...] I think there is hardly anything that can be called mine in the philosophy of mind, which does not follow with ease from the detection of this prejudice. (Letters 88b)

If we take de Bary's claim that the arguments misrepresent Hume along with Loeb's findings that Hume is not a central figure in Reid's writings, we are no longer required to see these arguments to be directed against Hume. As a result, I am rejecting de Bary's first claim that Hume is the primary target, and instead propose that the primary target is the alleged Pyrrhonian sceptic, for the following two reasons.[16]

Firstly, arguments A, B and C are instances of the *apraxia* objection (A and B of the evidential, C of the pragmatic mode), which Pyrrhonian scepticism has been confronted with from its inception. The *apraxia* objection and its two modes has already been discussed, so we can content ourselves with this rough reconstruction of the evidential *apraxia* objection (to be referred to later):

(1) If you are a sceptic, you have no beliefs.
(2) If you have no beliefs, you cannot act.
(3) You can act.
(4) It is not the case that you have no beliefs.
(5) It is not the case that you are a sceptic.

The first premise sums up the sceptic's claim that he lives without beliefs (PH I 8), while the second premise is the core of the *apraxia* charge, namely, that beliefs are necessary for action. Coupled with the observation that sceptics do act and conduct their lives in an orderly fashion (3), we can reason via *modus tollens* and conclude that the sceptic must have beliefs (4) and is therefore not a sceptic at all (5).

---

15 See Louis E. Loeb, "The Naturalisms of Hume and Reid," *Proceedings and Addresses of the American Philosophical Association* 81 (2007): 66.
16 For if the argument is successful, there are no Pyrrhonian sceptics.

Secondly, there is an inconsistency between the four arguments and between some of the arguments and Reid's broader work. The last argument (D) recommends not to engage with the sceptic, while the first three (A-C) do engage with the sceptic. The story about Pyrrho suggests sceptical life is possible, while arguments A and B suggest that scepticism is actually impossible and every self-proclaimed sceptic a fraud. This could be taken as evidence for the claim that his attitude is merely polemical, but the other inconsistency is, I think, more important, i.e. that between arguments C and D and Reid's philosophy of mind. Given this inconsistency, I suggest that only arguments C and D are polemics and that A and B remain as serious attacks on alleged Pyrrhonian sceptics.

If we take Reid's writing at face value it seems that he denies the actual and possible existence of Pyrrhonian sceptics. With regard to the modality in play, I assume Reid would say that God could have constituted us in such a manner that we are able to live without beliefs, but he has not and therefore such sceptics cannot exist. Pyrrhonian sceptics live without beliefs, but according to Reid's philosophy of mind there are at least two sources of beliefs we cannot resist: Immediate beliefs caused by our constitution and beliefs that arise from the workings of our mental faculties. In terms of the first category, Reid postulates that our constitution forces some beliefs upon us e.g. the belief that we are conscious:

> Can any man prove that his consciousness can't deceive him? No man can: nor can we give a better reason for trusting to it, than that every man, while his mind is sound, is determined, by the constitution of his nature, to give implicit belief to it, and to laugh at, or pity the man who doubts its testimony. (IHM 17)

An example for the other source is perception, where Reid holds that:

> [W]e shall find in [perception] these three things: First, Some conception of notion of the object perceived; Secondly, a strong and irresistible conviction and belief of its present existence; and, Thirdly, That this conviction and belief are immediate, and not the effect of reasoning. (EIP 258a)

Both our mind and the employment of our senses already force beliefs upon us. This, I take it, rules out the Pyrrhonian life without beliefs, as does the conclusion of the evidential *apraxia* objection. Thus, it makes no sense for Reid to engage with the sceptic by using arguments that presuppose that the sceptic can act (as do arguments C and D). The 'stronghold' of argument D is a paper castle at best, because as soon as the sceptic becomes hungry, he has to crawl out. All that is left to Reid is to engage with those who still claim to be sceptic and rub it into their faces how life involves immediate beliefs forced upon us by nature (and Reid rarely misses out on such an opportunity).

3 Reidian Belief and Pyrrhonian Assent

Thus far, we have seen that Reid's engagement with scepticism can be taken seriously by his formulating an instance of the *apraxia* objection in the evidential mode that is anchored in his theory of the mind (which, in turn, is based on his methodology of common sense). In this section, I wish to consider the potentially undermining parallels between Reidian belief and Pyrrhonian assent.[17] Reid's *apraxia* objection does not function when Pyrrhonian assent is taken as the key mental state. But it is not clear whether there really is a substantial difference between Pyrrhonian assent and Reidian belief. Both Reid and Sextus characterise their mental state phenomenologically and functionally. By showing how these characterisations are almost identical, I hope to cast doubt on the idea that Reidian belief differs (sufficiently enough) from Pyrrhonian assent.

Reid's philosophy of mind is revolutionary in many ways, and it is what truly distinguishes his attack on the way of ideas. Instead of merely concluding that the way of ideas is wrong (given that it leads to scepticism), he puts something in its place that, according to Reid, comprises less flaws and greater explanatory power. The first notable feature of Reid's philosophy of mind is his faculty psychology. Instead of trying to reduce all mental activities to a single source, Reid finds, based on his own introspection, many mental faculties that exist independently, although closely connected with each other. Belief is mostly associated with the faculty of judgement,[18] but accompanies many mental processes.

On the Reidian philosophy of mind, belief is simple and cannot be defined any further.[19] Although there is no systematic discussion of belief, given that it plays an important role in perception and in his reply to the sceptic, we can still reconstruct his theory of belief from the relevant passages. The feature he gives the most credit to is its irresistibility. For example, Reid cites this feature in response to the sceptic who advises suspending judgement on the existence of the external world, for objects can exist without perception, just as perception can exist without the object. Reid replies:

> [I]t is not in my power [to get rid of my belief in external objects]: why then should I make a vain attempt? It would be agreeable to fly to the moon, and to make a visit to Jupiter and Saturn; but when I know that Nature has bound me down by the law of gravitation to this planet which I inhabit, I rest contented, and quietly suffer myself to be carried along in its orbit. My belief is carried along by perception, as irresistibly as my body by the earth. And the greatest sceptic will find himself to be in the same condition. (IHM 169)

---

17 For the time being, I'm only focussing on Sextus' notion of forced assent. As Katja M. Vogt points out, there is also 'a kind of assent […] that is not necessitated but is yet sufficiently passive in order to differ from assent or judgement as the dogmatists envisage it. Involuntary and non-doxastic assent play this role;' see Katja M. Vogt, "Appearances and Assent: Sceptical Belief Reconsidered," *Classical Quarterly* 62 (2012): 661.
18 See EIP 414b.
19 See IHM 28.

Turning to how belief originates, Reid alternates between belief being suggested by sensation or being created by natural signs. The reason why belief arises in these cases is unknown to us, or it happens 'by a natural kind of magic.'[20] Alternatively, and this has both a phenomenological and an abductive reading, it is a result of our constitution or of nature.[21] It might be that these are still expressions of the irresistibility of belief, in the sense that it feels as if nature, or our constitution, forces the belief upon us. If that is not the case, however, these expressions could also be inferences toward the best explanation. It may be a law of human nature that when we perceive an apple, a belief that the apple exists, as we see it, is created alongside the perception. This law, together with the information that a subject perceives an apple, permits us to deduce that the subject also has the corresponding belief. A third option here is Reid distinguishing speculation from proper science.[22] All that can be said is that it is caused by our constitution, and nothing more can, or should, be said. This line of interpretation is supported by the following passage in which Reid talks about the information that is suggested by vision, namely colour and position, and nothing else:

> Now, this material impression, made upon a particular point of the retina, by the laws of our constitution, suggests two things to the mind, namely, the colour, and the position of some external object. No man can give a reason, why that same material impression might not have suggested sound, or smell, or either of these along with the position of the object. That it should suggest colour and position, and nothing else, we can resolve only into our constitution, or the will of our Maker. (IHM 100)

The next feature of Reidian belief is its immediacy. Belief is often not a result of reasoning but occurs immediately:

> When I hear a certain sound, I conclude immediately, without reasoning, that a coach passes by. There are no premises from which this conclusion is inferred by any rules of logic. It is the effect of a principle of nature, common to us with the brutes. (IHM 50)

> How a sensation should instantly make us conceive and believe the existence of an external thing altogether unlike to it, I do not pretend to know; and when I say that the one suggests the other, I mean not to explain the manner of their connection, but to express a fact, which every one may be conscious of; namely, that by a law of our nature, such a conception and belief constantly and immediately follow the sensation. (IHM 74)

> I know moreover, that this belief [in a perceived object's present existence] is not the effect of argumentation and reasoning; it is the immediate effect of my constitution. (IHM 168)

---

20 See IHM 36.
21 See IHM 70.
22 Ryan Nichols, *Thomas Reid's Theory of Perception* (Oxford: Oxford University Press: 2007), 26.

Finally, Reid maintains that belief plays a pivotal role in guiding action. Further to the point that we cannot suspend judgement, he adds that even if we could suspend judgment, we should not:

> I resolve not to believe my senses. I break my nose against a post that comes in my way; I step into a dirty kennel; and, after twenty such wise and rational actions, I am taken up and clapt into a mad-house. Now, I confess I would rather make one of the credulous fools whom Nature imposes upon, than of those wise and rational philosophers who resolve to with-hold assent at all this expence. (IHM 170)

Besides this being an instance of the pragmatic mode of the objection, we can see what role belief plays in action. Belief keeps us out of harm's way and it guides our actions. In his *Essays on the Active Power of Man*, Reid distinguishes between three kinds of action: voluntary, involuntary and mixed actions. There are three classes of principles of action, which belong to the three kinds of action. Mechanical principles determine the involuntary actions, animal principles determine the mixed actions, and rational principles determine the voluntary actions.[23] In contemporary parlance, we would only call the voluntary actions proper actions (where involuntary sneezing, sleep-walking and breathing are not considered actions at all).

Belief is essential for voluntary actions (that are guided by the rational principles), but even the animal principles require associated beliefs. Without the beliefs that are formed in perception (that the perceived object is like it seems to be) we cannot explain why someone moves towards the perceived object. If I know that there is merely the illusion of an apple in front of me, I would not, despite my hunger, attempt to eat it (and here we can also argue that it is my belief that the apple is an illusion that forms part of my refusal to grab the apple). But if I believe that it is a real apple, I would reach for it, and so we see that belief plays an important role for action.

Before turning to Sextus' account of assent, I will summarise the findings. On the phenomenological side of the Reidian account of belief, belief is irresistible and immediate. On the functional side of his account, belief is a necessary constituent of action. The same three features are present in the following passages from Sextus, in which he replies to accusations not dissimilar to those Reid has voiced against him in his *apraxia* objection:

> Those who say that the Sceptics reject what is apparent have not, I think, listened to what we say. As we said before, we do not overturn anything which leads us, without our willing it, to assent in accordance with a passive appearance—and these things are precisely what is apparent. When we investigate whether existing things are such as they appear, we grant that they appear, and what we investigate is not what is apparent but what is said about what is apparent—and this is different from investigating what is apparent itself. (PH I 19)

---

[23] EAP 543.

Thus, we find that Sextus' key mental state is assent to the appearance, which we can neither control nor resist. Although not expressed verbally, the assent is also immediate, rather than the product of reasoning. Sextus' entire point is that suspension of judgement is not exercised over the appearances. If assent to them were the product of reasoning, one would be able to reason against them to reach *epoché* again. I therefore conclude that Pyrrhonian assent is both irresistible and immediate.[24] Does it thus also play a role similar to Reidian belief with regard to action?

> Thus, attending to what is apparent, we live in accordance with everyday observances, without holding opinions—for we are not able to be utterly inactive. These everyday observances seem to be fourfold, and to consist in guidance by nature, necessitation by feelings, handing down of laws and customs, and teaching of kinds of expertise. By nature's guidance we are naturally capable of perceiving and thinking. By the necessitation of feelings, hunger conducts us to food and thirst to drink. By the handing down of customs and laws, we accept, from an everyday point of view, that piety is good and that impiety is bad. By teaching of kinds of expertise we are not inactive in those which we accept. And we say all this without holding any opinions. (PH I 23, 24)

I take the answer to be 'Yes'. This, in effect, fits neatly with Reid's account of action, and even goes beyond the mere minimum by including the acknowledgement of custom, laws and expertise. It can be concluded that all three features which characterise Reid's mental state, that he calls 'belief', namely irresistibility, immediacy and its role in action, are also true of Sextus' mental state, which he calls 'assent'.[25] Now turning to the *apraxia* objection and applying it to Sextus' notion of assent in the place of Reidian belief, it is clear Sextus would disagree with (1): Being a sceptic does not mean resisting assenting to the appearances that are forced upon us. But he would agree with (2): If we were able to resist assenting, we would have no guidance for our actions. Something crucial would be missing for living life, sceptical or otherwise. Sextus also agrees with (3), naturally, because he thinks that he can act. The first conclusion, that it is not the case that we do not assent, follows. Only the second conclusion, which hinges on the first premise (the one Sextus disagrees with), does not follow, for in Sextus' account the sceptic does assent to the appearances.

In order not to equivocate, the other option is to read the argument in such a way that (1) is true on Sextus' account, and as a consequence the rest of the argument fails—(2), (4) and (5) would be rendered false. On the other hand, if we want (2) to be true, a part of the argument can function, namely (2) to (4), but that only

---

[24] An objector might cite PH I 9, in which Sextus says that the sceptic opposes what appears to be both with what appears to be and what is thought of, but PH I 19 makes clear that the arguments against the appearances serve the aim to 'display the rashness of the dogmatics,' and not to suspend judgement about the appearances.
[25] This is also supported by the other passages in which Sextus discusses assent, see PH I 113, 193, 230, 233 and PH II 10, 251–2.

shows how important the mental state is that Sextus calls 'assent'. It does not demonstrate that scepticism is impossible.

4 Two objections

Before moving to the conclusion and determining where these parallels leave Reid's *apraxia* objection, two objections are to be considered. Both of which depend on features of Reid's account of belief which have hitherto not been touched upon.

The first feature is that '[b]elief admits of all degrees, from the slightest suspicion to the fullest assurance.'[26] At the same time, Sextus appears to directly negate the corresponding thesis of degrees of assent, when he says 'that appearances are equal in convincingness or lack of convincingness' (PH I 227). Although this is far from a full answer (which would require an entire paper in itself), I do not think this to be Sextus' final position on this matter. The passage that most clearly speaks against this is the very last section of the *Outlines* titled "Why do Sceptics sometimes propound arguments that are of feeble plausibility?" Here, Sextus, comparing the sceptic with a doctor, states that, for philanthropic reasons, the sceptic will use weighty arguments for some 'patients', but weak arguments for others, for everyone to reach *ataraxia*. That is, this section presupposes that arguments differ in convincingness. Having established that a difference in convincingness is possible at all, the next step would be to subsume arguments under appearances to conclude that at least some appearances differ with respect to convincingness. A second line of defence can be based on (at least, my) psychological reality. If assent is to be a state that does not allow for degrees, I have no idea what Sextus' assent is. The only notion one can be aware of introspectively that comes close to Sextus' assent is forced upon one with various degrees of strength, depending on the phenomena, time, place, and so on. Thirdly, if all things are equally strong with regard to forcing assent to them, it trivialises the ability of the sceptic Sextus is talking about in the fourth section of the first Book, i.e. the ability to 'set out oppositions of things which appear and are thought of in any way' (PH I 8). He himself says that by 'ability' he means nothing fancy, but still, it seems it would make things much too easy. The worst counterexample could endanger belief in the best theory, for 'worst' and 'best' are already categories that presuppose that some things are more convincing than others. As this is far from sufficient as an argument, I choose to read PH I 8 as speaking of the ability to have, even for belief in very convincing theories, the right countermeasure.

The second feature of Reidian belief that is missing from Pyrrhonian assent is the content of Reidian beliefs. While Sextus' assent is supposed to be non-committal in every conceivable sense, Reidian beliefs are, among other things, beliefs that the perceived objects are in reality as they seem to be, existing mind-independently and ex-

---

26 EIP 327b.

ternally from us, and so on.[27] This goes far beyond Sextus' account of assent and also seems to contradict it. Does this mean that Reid's *apraxia* objection is successful after all?

Although we have seen that there is a difference between Reidian belief and Pyrrhonian assent in terms of its alleged content, Sextus could actually be too close to Reid for the objection to be successful. Consider the situation from the point of view of Sextus. He hears of this mental state that feels a certain way, it is forced upon us, we cannot resist it, it occurs immediately, it guides our actions, it helps us crossing the street. 'All this,' Sextus may say, 'I find, too, when I introspectively observe the goings on of my mind. Surely, he must speak about that assent that is forced upon us by the appearances.' Only at this point does Reid say: 'No, because this belief is a belief in the mind-independent existence of the external objects of our perception.' It is only this last step that Sextus cannot take. But Sextus is not constituted differently. Hence, the dilemma from the introduction appears again. Either Sextus agrees to everything that is found in introspection or not. If he does, then there is no belief in the external existence of the objects of perception, for this does not appear to Sextus, and we have to read Reid differently. Perhaps it is not actually the content of the beliefs, but an expression of how the appearances feel. Surely the appearances are such that things appear to be independent of our minds and in a certain distance from us (i.e., they seem to be external). In this case, Reid's *apraxia* objection fails, as in this interpretation it does not contradict Pyrrhonian scepticism. A successful *apraxia* objection requires a theory of belief that goes beyond what we find in introspection. According to the other horn of the dilemma, Sextus and Reid disagree about what is found in introspection. In this case there is no more room for debate. The common ground the *apraxia* objection requires does not exist. Thus, Reid, in this reading, thinks scepticism is wrong, but there is no way to ever communicate this to the sceptic successfully. Additionally, we all have the power of introspection, and I personally do not find my perceptual beliefs to be committed to mind-independent objects. We also would have to explain the attractiveness of non-realist philosophies, when everyone always believes, as part of how perception works, that these non-realist philosophies are wrong. Be that as it may, both options have their problems, and so this qualifies as a true dilemma: Either one is forced to perform mental gymnastics in our interpretation of Reid, or we are left with an implausible and problem-burdened view of beliefs.

---

27 Reid's first principle number five captures this: 'That those things do really exist which we distinctly perceive by our senses, and are what we perceive them to be' (EIP 445).

5 Conclusion

If Reid bases his *apraxia* argument merely on introspection, it does not succeed. The only route to success would be to claim that Sextus is confused or lying, or that Sextus and Reid are constituted differently. Both these routes are not particularly promising. If he goes beyond introspection, Sextus is not obliged to follow. For every reason Reid adds as a premise to his case, Sextus can find a reason that speaks against it. This is especially easy given that the other big common-sense philosopher, Moore, embraces the way of ideas as part of his common sense philosophy:

> I hold it to be quite certain that I do not directly perceive my hand; and that when I am said [...] to 'perceive' it, that I 'perceive' (in a different and more fundamental sense) something which is (in a suitable sense) representative of it.[28]

I conclude, therefore, that no matter what route Reid is taking, he cannot beat the Pyrrhonian sceptic with his version of the *apraxia* objection.

---

[28] Moore, "A Defence of Common Sense," 55.

Ze'ev Strauss

The Ground Floor of Judaism: Scepticism and Certainty in Moses Mendelssohn's *Jerusalem*

Introduction

One of the central themes that Moses Mendelssohn's *Jerusalem oder über religiöse Macht und Judentum* (*Jerusalem or on Religious Power and Judaism*) is predicated upon is the notion of doubt. Yet in *Jerusalem*, Mendelssohn seems to employ not just one type, but rather a wide array of varying modes of doubt. The following paper will set out to explore Mendelssohn's equivocal application of doubt in *Jerusalem*, and in so doing endeavour to demonstrate that he, despite his rather unfavourable view of scepticism as a 'disease of the soul' ('Krankheit der Seele'),[1] nonetheless draws heavily on it. Indeed, this is by no means a foreign topic to Jewish thought: Already in the first century CE, the Jewish Platonist Philo of Alexandria resorted to Neo-Pyrrhonian and New Academic scepticism to substantiate the ultimate metaphysical truth of Jewish Scripture.[2] Similarly, we also find references to philosophical scepticism in the work of the medieval Jewish thinker Judah Halevi (1075–1141) and the Venetian Rabbi Simone Luzzatto (?1582–1663).[3] Furthermore, the Jewish intellectual tradition can be understood as a constant interplay between scepticism and dog-

---

[1] Moses Mendelssohn, *Jerusalem or on Religious Power and Judaism*, trans. Allan Arkus, Introduction and Commentary by Alexander Altmann (New England: University Press of New England, 1983): 66–67; idem, *Jerusalem oder über religiöse Macht und Judentum*, in, idem, *Gesammelte Schriften. Jubiläumsausgabe* (JubA), vol. 8, eds. Ismar Elbogen, Julius Guttmann, Eugen Mittwoch, Alexander Altmann, Eva J. Engel and Daniel Krochmalnik (Bad Cannstatt: Frommann-Holzboog, 1983): 134. Gideon Freudenthal has already pointed this out in his *No Religion without Idolatry* (Indiana: University of Notre Dame Press, 2012): 22, 41–42. Cf. also Jeremy Fogel, "Scepticism of Scepticism: On Mendelssohn's Philosophy of Common Sense," *Melilah* 12 (2015): 61. Mendelssohn doesn't refer to scepticism as 'Seelenkrankheit' only in his *Jerusalem*, but also in his *Morgenstunden oder Vorlesungen über das Daseyn Gottes* (Berlin: Christian Friedrich Voß, 1785): 144 (JubA 3.2, 72): 'Atheismus und Aberglaube, Zweifelsucht und Schwärmerey, sind beides Krankheiten der Seele, die ihr den sittlichen Tod androhen.'
[2] For a detailed analysis of Philo's scepticism, see Carlos Lévy, "La conversion du scepticisme chez Philon d'Alexandrie," in *Philo of Alexandria and Post-Aristotelian Philosophy*, ed. Francesca Alesse (Leiden and Boston: Brill, 2008): 103–120.
[3] For Luzzatto's use of sceptical strategies, see Bill Rebiger, "Sceptical Strategies in Simone Luzzatto's Presentation of the Kabbalists in his *Discorso*," in *Yearbook of the Maimonides Centre for Advanced Studies 2017*, ed. Bill Rebiger (Berlin and Boston: De Gruyter, 2017): 51–69; Giuseppe Veltri, *Renaissance Philosophy in Jewish Garb: Foundations and Challenges in Judaism on the Eve of Modernity* (Leiden and Boston: Brill, 2009): 33–36, 107–108; David B. Ruderman, "Science and Skepticism. Simone Luzzatto on Perceiving the Natural World," in idem, *Jewish Thought and Scientific Discovery in Early Modern Europe* (Detroit: Wayne State University Press, 1995): 153–184 (5th Chapter).

OpenAccess. © 2018 Ze'ev Strauss, published by De Gruyter. This work is licensed under the Creative Commons Attribution-NonCommercial-NoDerivatives 4.0 License.
https://doi.org/10.1515/978-3-11-057768-6-010

matism. However, the idea of philosophical doubt has led Mendelssohn—in contrast to the aforementioned Jewish thinkers—in a completely different direction: to an outright repudiation of the pivotal premise of Jewish philosophy, which claims that the Holy Scriptures of Judaism entail eternal philosophical truths ('ewige Vernunftwahrheiten'):

> Judaism boasts of no exclusive revelation of eternal truths that are indispensable to salvation, of no revealed religion in the sense in which that term is usually understood. Revealed religion ['geoffenbarte Religion'] is one thing, revealed legislation ['geoffenbarte Gesetzgebung'], another. The voice which let itself be heard on Sinai on that great day did not proclaim, 'I am the Eternal, your God, the necessary, independent being, omnipotent and omniscient, that recompenses men in a future life according to their deeds.' This is the universal religion of mankind, not Judaism; [...].[4]

In the following article, I wish to argue, both systematically und historically-philologically, that Mendelssohn's basic motivation for resorting to sceptical stances is essentially twofold: He attempts to isolate the core of Jewish *belief* from philosophical doubt and at the same time expose the conceptual vulnerability of the dogmas of Christianity. The main assertion I will thus develop is that Mendelssohn's exploitation of sceptical concepts comes from the general *apologetic* impulse for writing *Jerusalem*. As is known, Mendelssohn formulated this treatise as a reaction against the polemical ultimatum posed anonymously by August F. Cranz (1737–1801) in *Das Forschen nach Licht und Recht*[5] to either convert to Christianity or to account for his staying loyal to his Jewish faith while taking his 'enlightened' viewpoint of natural religion into account.[6] In light of this apologetic and interreligious discourse within which *Jerusalem* is situated, I will maintain that Mendelssohn endeavours to delineate the crucial differences between Judaism and Christianity *through* the idea of scepticism. In the process, I will set out to answer two questions: (1) To what aim does Mendelssohn utilise sceptical strategies in *Jerusalem* for his fundamental understanding of religion and philosophy, revelation and reason? (2) What *kind* of dif-

---

4 Mendelssohn, *Jerusalem*, 97 (JubA 8, 165).
5 August F. Cranz, *Das Forschen nach Licht und Recht in einem Schreiben an Herrn Moses Mendelssohn auf Veranlassung seiner merkwürdigen Vorrede zu Manasseh Ben Israel* (Berlin, 1782): 9–11.
6 *Ibidem*, 41: 'So lange Sie diesen Schritt nicht thun, nachdem Sie iezt den ersten gethan haben, steht das Publikum in der allergerechtesten Erwartung, entweder eine Rechtfertigung von Ihnen zu lesen, wie Sie eine so wichtige Abweichung mit der Religion Ihrer Väter vereinbaren wollen, oder—Gründe, die Sie einem öffentlichen Uebergang zu dem Glauben der Christen und dem eigentlichen Christentum selbst entgegen zu setzen haben.' Cf. *ibidem*, 9. Mendelssohn himself addresses this point explicitly; see his *Jerusalem*, 86–87 (JubA 8, 152–153). For a more detailed discussion, see Micha Gottlieb, *Faith and Freedom: Moses Mendelssohn's Theological-Political Thought* (Oxford and New York: Oxford University Pres, 2011): 34 and 51; Shmuel Feiner, *Moses Mendelssohn: Sage of Modernity* (New Haven and London: Yale University Press, 2010): 150 and 159–176; Elias Sacks, *Moses Mendelssohn's Living Script: Philosophy, Practice, History, Judaism* (Bloomington and Indianapolis: Indiana University Press, 2017): 25–28, 98 and 176–178.

ferent sceptical stances does Mendelssohn make use of in *Jerusalem?* The answer to these questions will unfold in three essential stages. In the first part, I will elaborate on Mendelssohn's understanding of what 'the spirit of true Judaism'[7] is as it pertains to his harsh critique (if not sceptical undermining) of Maimonides' dogmatic and philosophical distortion of its 'ancient, original' meaning.[8] In the second part—drawing on the perceptive and innovative research conducted by Gideon Freudenthal in his *No Religion without Idolatry* (2012)—I will suggest that Mendelssohn entertains sceptical doubt concerning the nature of language as an effective epistemic vehicle to emphasise the merits of 'the old Judaism' ('das alte Judentum'), which is primarily construed as a system of ceremonial laws ('Zeremonialgesetze'). In this part, light will be shed on a number of theological and philosophical sources that constitute points of departure for Mendelssohn's own stances and discussions. Several of these sources are by no means sceptical in nature, but they still share one unifying feature: They all entail critical inclinations in one way or another towards language and signs. Exactly this common thread seemed to have been cleverly exploited by Mendelssohn and incorporated into his systematic sceptical stance towards language in *Jerusalem*. In the concluding part, I turn to his employment of a sceptical viewpoint in the framework of his critical analysis of ecclesiastical law ('Kirchenrecht') in the Kingdom of Prussia and the intolerance of the law towards the Jewish population. I will show that Mendelssohn's description relies, in this instance, not so much on ancient scepticism, nor on the Jewish philosophical account of ancient scepticism, but rather specifically on Johann M. Schröckh's fourth volume of his *Christliche Kirchengeschichte* (1777).[9]

1 The Non-Speculative Nature of Ancient Judaism

In one of the central sections of the second part of *Jerusalem*, Mendelssohn seems to grapple with Cranz's supposition that Judaism has determined articles of faith ('Glaubensartikel der jüdischen Religion').[10] The way he proceeds is not by straightforwardly criticizing Cranz, but rather by disputing Maimonides' dogmatic understanding of Judaism. The specific notion he casts doubt on is Maimonides' contention

---

[7] Mendelssohn, *Jerusalem*, 100 (JubA 8, 167): 'Geist [...] des ächten Judentums.'
[8] JubA 8, 168: 'd[as] alte, ursprüngliche [...] Judentum [...].'
[9] Johann M. Schröckh, *Christliche Kirchengeschichte*, vol. 4 (Leipzig: Engelhart Benjamin Schwickert, 1777).
[10] In this context, Cranz refers to the negative article of belief that keeps God's chosen people away from gentiles so their holiness would not be desecrated: 'ist ein Glaubensartikel der jüdischen Religion, nach welchem alle andere Völker, wie eine Art unreiner Geschöpfe angesehen werden, durch deren nähern Umgang das Volk Gottes entheiliget würde;' see idem, *Das Forschen nach Licht und Recht*, 36. Cranz also alludes to the *principles* of the Jewish 'church': 'Grundsätze [...] der Kirche;' see *ibidem*, 13.

that Jewish faith can at bottom be summed up in thirteen simple principles (שלוש
עשרה עקרים):

> Maimonides was the first to conceive of the idea of reducing the religion of his fathers to a certain number of principles, in order that, as he explains, religion, like all other sciences, would have its fundamental conceptions, from which all the others are deduced. This merely accidental idea gave rise to the *thirteen articles* of the Jewish catechism, to which we owe the morning hymn *Yigdal*, as well as some good writings by Chasdai, Albo, and Abrabanel. These are all the results they have had up to now. Thank God, they have not yet been forged into shackles of faith. Chasdai disputes them and proposes changes; Albo limits their number and wants to recognize only three basic principles which correspond rather closely to those which Herbert of Cherbury, at a later date, proposed for the catechism; [...].[11]

The tone of Mendelssohn in the quoted passage towards the most celebrated rabbinic authority and Jewish philosopher of the Middle Ages is remarkably critical: He accuses him of advocating nothing short of a reductionist and completely falsified account of Judaism as a set of theoretical beliefs.[12] Mendelssohn suggests that the historical repudiation of the Maimonidean precepts of faith by major medieval Jewish thinkers, such as Ḥasdai Crescas (c. 1340–1410), Joseph Albo (1380–1440) and Isaac Abrabanel (1437–1508), strongly attest to their inauthentic core. With reference to this very passage, Warren Zev Harvey has insightfully pointed out the similarity between Mendelssohn and these medieval anti-Maimonidean thinkers, first and foremost Ḥasdai Crescas, with respect to their undogmatic conception of Judaism.[13] A speculative mindset that poses an even greater threat to authentic Judaism is the kabbalistic one, which, according to Mendelssohn, reduces the entire Scripture to 'fundamental doctrines' ('Fundamentallehren') of an utterly speculative nature.[14]

However, my reading of this central passage emphasises another aspect: These important thinkers demonstrated to Mendelssohn exactly how a metaphysical understanding of Holy Scripture not only fails to underpin the absolute truth of Jewish belief, but has the quite counterproductive effect of making Judaism susceptible to philosophical doubt and thus jeopardizing the whole conceptual construct of its

---

11 Mendelssohn, *Jerusalem*, 101 (JubA 8, 167). For a more detailed analysis, see Gottlieb, *Faith and Freedom*, 34–56.
12 Freudenthal, *No Religion without Idolatry*, 153–154.
13 Warren Zev Harvey, "Ḥasdai Crescas and Moses Mendelssohn on Beliefs and Commandments," in *Moses Mendelssohn: Enlightenment, Religion, Politics, Nationalism*, ed. Micha Gottlieb and Charles H. Manekin (Bethesda: University of Maryland Press, 2015): 79–89.
14 Mendelssohn, *Jerusalem*, 101 (JubA 8, 167). See Harvey, "Ḥasdai Crescas and Moses Mendelssohn on Beliefs and Commandments," 85. On anti-Kabbalistic tendencies in the Haskalah and preceding, see Bill Rebiger, "The Early Opponents of the Kabbalah and the Role of Sceptical Argumentations: An Outline," in *Yearbook of the Maimonides Centre for Advanced Studies 2016*, eds. Giuseppe Veltri and Bill Rebiger (Berlin: De Gruyter, 2016): 39–57; Christoph Schulte, "Kabbala in Salomon Maimons Lebensgeschichte," in *Kabbala und die Literatur der Romantik: Zwischen Magie und Trope*, eds. Eveline Goodman-Thau, Gert Mattenklott and Christoph Schulte (Tübingen: Max Niemeyer Verlag, 1999): 33–66.

tradition. This reading is strongly reinforced when we take, for example, Mendelssohn's own reiteration of the main thesis of *Jerusalem* into consideration—Judaism is not a revealed religion ('geoffenbarte Religion'), but rather revealed legislation ('geoffenbarte Gesetzgebung')—[15] in *An die Freunde Lessings* (1786), which he emphasises in conjunction with scepticism and common sense:

> When I talk of rational conviction, however, and I want to presuppose this as undoubted in Judaism, the talk is not about metaphysical argumentation as we are used to carrying it on in books, not about pedantic demonstrations that all meet the test of the subtlest skepticism, but about the claims and judgments of a simple, sound commonsense, which looks things right in the eye and reflects calmly.[16]

Mendelssohn makes it abundantly clear that he wishes to establish the Jewish religion as a position that is beyond doubt ('unbezweifelt'); i.e. a stance that, in contrast to metaphysical reasoning ('metaphysische Argumentation'), does not have to withstand the penetrating attacks of philosophical scepticism.[17]

Spinoza's unrelentingly harsh critique in his *Tractatus Theologico-Politicus* (TTP) of Maimonides' unscientific exegetical method might also have had an effect on this view held by Mendelssohn.[18] Moreover, the scientific approach applied to biblical exegesis advocated by Spinoza in the TTP—to attempt, through newly developed phi-

---

15 Mendelssohn, *Jerusalem*, 97 (JubA 8, 157).
16 I used the English translation found here: *Leo Strauss on Moses Mendelssohn*, trans. and ed. Martin D. Yaffe (Chicago and London: University of Chicago Press, 2012): 117. *Moses Mendelssohn an die Freunde Lessings* (Berlin, 1786): 30 (JubA 3.2, 197): 'Wenn ich aber von vernunftmäßiger Ueberzeugung rede, und solche im Judenthum als *unbezweifelt* voraus setzen will; so ist die Rede nicht von metaphysischer Argumentation, wie wir sie in Büchern zu führen gewohnt sind; nicht von schulgerechten Demonstrationen, *die alle Proben des subtilsten Zweifelmuths bestanden sind;* sondern von den Aussprüchen und Urtheilen eines schlichten gesunden Menschenverstandes, der die Dinge gerade ins Auge faßt und ruhig überlegt.' To the best of my knowledge, Leo Strauss, in his *Einleitung zu 'Morgenstunden' und 'An die Freunde Lessings'*, is the first to point this out with reference to this specific passage (JubA 3.2, LXVII): 'The connection between his increased inclination toward the philosophy of sound commonsense and his defense of Judaism becomes fully distinct in the following statement in *To the Friends of Lessing*: [...]. [Der Zusammenhang zwischen seiner verstärkten Neigung zur Philosophie des gesunden Menschenverstandes und seiner Verteidigung des Judentums wird vollends deutlich in folgender Äußerung in dem Schreiben "An die Freunde Lessings"];' see *Leo Strauss on Moses Mendelssohn*, 117; the original German, see Leo Strauss, *Gesammelte Schriften*, vol. 2: *Philosophie und Gesetz – Frühe Schriften*, ed. Heinrich Meier (Stuttgart and Weimar: J. B. Metzler, ²2013): 579. Cf. Freudenthal, who develops this point much further and was the first to link it to Mendelssohn's scepticism regarding language; see idem, *No Religion without Idolatry*, 28–29.
17 Freudenthal elucidates this important aspect of Mendelssohn's thought in a very systematic manner: *No Religion without Idolatry*, 21–64 (Ch. 1. *Mendelssohn: Common Sense, Rational Metaphysics, and Skepticism*).
18 For a more detailed analysis, see Julius Guttmann, "Mendelssohns Jerusalem and Spinozas Theologisch-Politischer Traktat," in *Achtundvierzigster Bericht der Hochschule für die Wissenschaft des Judentums in Berlin N. 24, Artilleriestraße 14* (Berlin: 1931): 31–67; Micha Gottlieb, *Faith and Freedom*, 9–12 and 24–54.

lological tools, to unearth the original meaning of Scripture, unfiltered by theological premises—gained a strong foothold in the intellectual Protestant circles in the German-speaking world of the eighteenth century and was further cultivated. Protestant philologists of Biblical Hebrew, such as Johann W. Meiner (1723–1789), Robert Lowth (1710–1787), Johann D. Michalis (1717–1791), Johann G. Herder (1744–1803) and Johann G. Eichhorn (1752–1827), seem to have had a great impact on Mendelssohn's perception of the Hebrew Bible as an aesthetic piece of writing.[19] The progress in the field of Biblical Hebrew could have facilitated Mendelssohn's uncovering of the philological shortcomings of the presuppositions upon which much of Jewish philosophy is grounded. Mendelssohn was not only familiar with Spinoza's critique of Maimonides, but also with that of Protestant authors. If we take, for example, the first volume of Heinrich Corrodi's *Kritische Geschichte des Chiliasmus* (1781), a book Mendelssohn was familiar with,[20] we find a fierce critique of Maimonides' as nothing less than a 'fraudulent' Aristotelian exegesis of Jewish Scripture:

> Maimonides deceives himself, insofar as he does not derive his philosophy from Jewish Scriptures, but from Aristotle; this was also done by those, who solely recognised a reasonable system of philosophy and not that of the sinister kabbalistic web of dreams. For they didn't find what they were looking for in the philosophy of their nation.[21]

The attitude of these theologians of the German-speaking world towards the exegetical rabbinic tradition as a whole was very deprecatory, since it made speculative assumptions superimposed on Jewish Scripture. In the section "Talmud und Rabbinen" (III. § 341: "Schriften der Rabbinen") of Eichhorn's pioneering three-volume *Einleitung ins Alte Testament* (1780–1783), which Mendelssohn possessed in its entirety in his library,[22] he assesses their Scriptural interpretation as unscientific. For this reason, he emphasises that his analysis of the Biblical corpus will not depend on their *uncritical* judgments.[23] It is, of course, plausible that the 'nervensaftverzehrende' *Kri-*

---

19 See *Verzeichniß der auserlesenen Büchersammlung des seeligen Herrn Moses Mendelssohn* (Berlin: 1786): 13 (N⁰ 198), 14 (n⁰s 215–216, 219–231),25 (N⁰ 81), 27 (n⁰s 166–168), 30 (N⁰ 227), 33 (N⁰ 272), 36 (N⁰ 321), 33 (N⁰ 272), 44–45 (n⁰s 501–511, 530).
20 See *Verzeichniß*, 23 (n⁰s 97–99).
21 Heinrich Corrodi, *Kritische Geschichte des Chiliasmus*, vol. 1 (Frankfurt and Leipzig, 1781): 26–27 (fn. *; my translation): 'Maimonides straft sich auch dadurch selbst Lügen, daß er seine Philosophie nicht aus den jüdischen Schriften, sondern aus Aristoteles schöpft, auch haben das alle gethan, die ein erträgliches System der Philosophie und nicht das finstere kabbalistische Geweb von Träumereyen allein kannten. Denn sie fanden in der Philosophie ihrer Nation nicht was sie suchten.' Corrodi characterises the exegetical method of Philo of Alexandria, 'der platonisierende Jude,' in analogous terms; see *ibidem*, 42: 'Philo [...] hat ein System, das offenbar aus dem Platonischen entstanden ist.'
22 *Verzeichniß*, 27 (n⁰s 166–168).
23 Johann G. Eichhorn, *Einleitung ins Alte Testament*, vol. 2 (Leipzig: Weidmanns Erben und Reich, 1781): 8: 'Nicht auf ihre Urtheile bauen wir unsre Vorstellungen von der jetzigen Beschaffenheit des Hebräischen Textes, sondern auf das, was Erfahrung und kritische Untersuchung desselben uns gelehrt hat.'

tik der reinen Vernunft (KrV)²⁴ 'des alles zermalmenden Kants,'²⁵ published only two years prior to *Jerusalem* in 1781, illustrated to Mendelssohn the striking epistemological limitations of speculative metaphysics and the implications this insight might have on *a* Judaism that is strongly premised on theoretical notions.²⁶

2 Scepticism and the Non-Verbality of Mosaic Law

Subsequently, Mendelssohn considerably widens the scope of the problem concerning theological dogmatism within the framework of Judaism: He proceeds to doubt entirely the capacity of the fixed written and spoken word as a symbol for mediating the true lively essence of Judaism and metaphysical truth. The immediate reason for his addressing this issue seems to be rooted in the following statement Cranz made in the opening of *Das Forschen nach Licht und Recht*:

> This figurative expression [i.e. of Moses covering his radiant face] probably signifies nothing more than that there was a time when the eyes of as-yet-unenlightened nations were still unable to bear the truth pure and whole, and that there came another time when people dared to take a longer glimpse at the bright sun and considered themselves strong enough to throw away the veil, and, speaking frankly, to teach in an unconcealed manner what had otherwise only been cloaked in hieroglyphics and more than halfway veiled in figurative expressions.²⁷

In this quotation, Cranz attempts to describe the conceptual progression Christianity has made with respect to Judaism, the belief system it evolved from: 'In the period of the so-called New Testament, the Christians boasted of seeing Moses with his face uncovered.'²⁸ This passage revolves around the New Testament metaphoric ('bildli-

---

24 JubA 13, 100.
25 Mendelssohn, *Morgenstunden*, IV. Fogel also alludes to this specific characterisation of Kant by Mendelssohn: "Scepticism of Scepticism: On Mendelssohn's Philosophy of Common Sense," 62. It should be noted that Mendelssohn did not possess the KrV in his library, but the *Prolegomena zu einer jeden künftigen Metaphysik, die als Wissenschaft wird auftreten können*, which was published like *Jerusalem* in 1783. See *Verzeichniß*: 29, № 205; see also *ibidem*, n°s 38–41, n°s 353–355).
26 Freudenthal, *No Religion without Idolatry*, 32 and 38–40.
27 August F. Cranz, "The Search for Light and Right in a Letter to Mr. Moses Mendelssohn, on the Occasion of his Remarkable Preface to Menasseh ben Israel," in *Moses Mendelssohn: Writings on Judaism, Christianity & the Bible*, ed. Micha Gottlieb (Waltham: Brandeis University Press 2011): 55–56; Cranz, *Das Forschen nach Licht und Recht*, 5–6. Attention has already been drawn to this important link by several researchers, cf. Jeffrey S. Librett, *The Rhetoric of Cultural Dialoge: Jews and Germans from Moses Mendelssohn to Richard Wagner and Beyond* (Stanford: Stanford University Press, 2000): 48–50; Christiane Frey, "Gramma Hieroglyphe und jüdisch-hebräische Kultur (Herder, Dohm, Mendelssohn)," in *Die Ordnung der Kulturen: zur Konstruktion ethnischer, nationaler und zivilisatorischer Differenzen 1750–1850*, eds. Hansjörg Bay and Kai Merten (Würzburg: Königshausen & Neumann, 2006): 149–151.
28 Cranz, "The Search for Light and Right in a Letter to Mr. Moses Mendelssohn," 55; idem, *Das Forschen nach Licht und Recht*, 5.

che Vorstellungsart') in 2 Corinthians 3:13–18, which is in turn an allusion to the radiant face of the Jewish lawgiver depicted in Exodus 34:29–35 – the point being that Jewish belief has only an oblique access to the Godly mysteries, in contrast to the Christian faith, which gains unmediated insight into these revealed truths.[29] Cranz seems to explicate this metaphor, which he regards as an insinuation of the spiritual backwardness of Judaism, which can grasp God only in his concealment (*Deus absconditus*), in terms of the *semiotic* notion conveyed in 2 Corinthians 3:6: *For the letter kills, but the Spirit gives life* (τὸ γὰρ γράμμα ἀποκτέννει, τὸ δὲ πνεῦμα ζῳοποιεῖ).[30] Cranz implies that Jewish faith is by definition reliant upon the intermediation of signs in the form of the figurative Biblical Hebrew language ('in Hieroglyphen kleidete, und in figürlichen Vorstellungsarten'). It is quite apparent that Mendelssohn's *Jerusalem* directly quarrels with Cranz's Christocentric apprehension of Judaism as conveyed in the above-mentioned passage on the veiled face of the Jewish lawgiver. Two reasons present themselves for this claim: (1) Mendelssohn also alludes to *hieroglyphs* in juxtaposition with Biblical Hebrew as an epistemological obstacle to the original unmediated truths of the Sinaitic revelation.[31] (2) He employs the Pauline symbols of dead letter ('toter Buchstabe') and lively spirit ('lebendiger Geist') in 2 Corinthians 3:6 at the centre of his depiction of the true nonverbal, spiritual nature of Judaism as ceremonial law ('Zeremonialgesetz').[32]

It seems, however, to be a bit perplexing that Cranz juxtaposes the Biblical Hebrew, spoken by the veiled Moses to the Israelites, with hieroglyphs. A possible explanation can be traced back to *De vita Moysis* I 23 of Philo of Alexandria, which describes how Moses in his adolescence was instructed by knowledgeable Egyptians in the philosophy expressed in symbols (ἡ διὰ συμβόλων φιλοσοφία), as exhibited in the pictorial characters commonly referred to as hieroglyphs (ἱερὰ γράμματα). Cranz, a trained theologian from the University of Halle,[33] was surely acquainted to some extent with the body of thought of the Jewish Alexandrian. Moreover, in 1778, just four years prior to Cranz's response to Mendelssohn's *Preface to Menasseh*

---

[29] Cf. Librett, *The Rhetoric of Cultural Dialoge*, 48–50; Frey, "Gramma Hieroglyphe und jüdisch-hebräische Kultur (Herder, Dohm, Mendelssohn)," 149–151.

[30] See Daniel Krochmalnik, "Das Zeremoniell als Zeichensprache: Moses Mendelssohns Apologie des Judentums im Rahmen der aufklärerischen Semiotik," in *Fremde Vernunft. Zeichen und Interpretationen*, vol. 4, eds. Josef Simon and Werner Stegmaier (Frankfurt am Main: Suhrkamp, 1998): 274–275 and 278; Librett, *The Rhetoric of Cultural Dialoge*, 49; Frey, "Gramma Hieroglyphe und jüdisch-hebräische Kultur (Herder, Dohm, Mendelssohn)," 150.

[31] Mendelssohn, *Jerusalem*, 108–111 (JubA 8, 184–185). See Freudenthal, *No Religion without Idolatry*, 105–134 (Ch. 5: *Idolatry: Egyptian and Jewish*); Veltri, *Renaissance Philosophy in Jewish Garb*, 169–194 (Ch. 8 Ceremonial Law: History of a Philosophical-Political Concept); Sacks, *Living Script*, 11–12 and 22–60.

[32] Mendelssohn, *Jerusalem*, 108 (JubA 8, 184).

[33] See Dieter Reichelt, *August Friedrich Cranz: Ein Kgl. Preußischer Kriegsrath als Schriftsteller von Profession. Zeugnisse aus seinem merkwürdigen Leben und Wirken in Berlin* (Bargfeld: Luttertaler Händedruck 1996): 60.

Ben Israel (*Vorrede zu Manasse ben Israel: Rettung der Juden*), *De vita Moysis* I-II (*Mos.*) was published anonymously in a German translation under the title *Philo vom Leben Moses*,³⁴ where he could have encountered this passage, which reads as follows:

> These [i.e. the learned Egyptians] further instructed him [i.e. Moses] in the philosophy conveyed in symbols, as displayed in the so-called holy inscriptions and in the regard paid to animals, to which they even pay divine honours.³⁵

This suggestion doesn't seem farfetched at all if, for example, we take into consideration that this topic, with reference to this very Philonic account of Moses' intellectual formation, was mentioned in Schiller's *Die Sendung Moses* from 1790.³⁶

---

34 *Philo vom Leben Moses, das ist: von der Gottesgelahrheit und dem prophetischen Geiste* (Dresden: Waltherische Hofbuchhandlung, 1778).
35 *Philo. In Ten Volumes* (PLCL), vol. 6, trans. Francis H. Colson (Cambridge, MA: Harvard University Press, ⁵1984): 287–289. For this passage in the German translation used by Mendelssohn, see: 'Es brachten ihm aber die Aegyptischen Gelehrten […] die symbolische Weltweisheit, welche in den sogenanten heiligen Schriften durch Bilder gewisser vorzüglicher Thiere, welche sie auch göttlich verehren, gelehrt wird.' (*Gottesgelahrheit*, 12–13)
36 Friedrich von Schiller, *Sämmtliche Werke*, vol. 7 (Stuttgart and Tübingen: J. G. Cotta'sche Verlagsbuchhandlung, 1819), 70: 'Der Geschichtschreiber Philo sagt, Moses sei von den ägyptischen Priestern in der Philosophie der Symbolen und Hieroglyphen wie auch in den Geheimnissen der heiligen Tiere eingeweihet worden. Eben dieses Zeugnis bestätigen mehrere, und wenn man erst einen Blick auf das, was man ägyptische Mysterien nannte, geworfen hat, so wird sich zwischen diesen Mysterien und dem, was Moses nachher getan und verordnet hat, eine merkwürdige Aehnlichkeit ergeben.' For an analysis of this motif in Schiller's *Die Sendung Moses*, see Frey, "Gramma Hieroglyphe und jüdisch-hebräische Kultur (Herder, Dohm, Mendelssohn)," 151 and 157–158. Cf. William Warburton, *Die göttliche Sendung Mosis, aus den Grundsätzen der Deisten bewiesen*, vol. 3 (Frankfurt and Leipzig: Johann Gottlieb Vierling, 1753): 104 (fn. i): 'Philo führt in seiner Lebensbeschreibung Mosis, die Egyptischen Priester ein, und lasset sie nach Platonischen Grundsätzen von der Seele, welche den Leib Mosis belebt, sich bei sprechen; welches eben so klug geurtheilet heißt, als wenn ein neuer Scribent, welcher das Leben des Ptolomäus, des Sternsehers, schriebe, ihn die Grundsätze des Herrn Isaac Newtons erklären ließe.' Mendelssohn mentions the German translation of *The Divine Legation of Moses Demonstrated* in his recension of Joseph Warton's *An Essay on the Writing and Genius of Pope*; see JubA 4, 323. For the significance of Warburton, see Freudenthal, *No Religion without Idolatry*, 94–95, 106, 116–117, 121–124, 250, 273–275, and 278–279; cf. Krochmalnik, "Das Zeremoniell als Zeichensprache," 263 and 279–284. Cf. Paul E. Jablonski's *Pantheon Aegyptiorum*, a work Mendelssohn was well familiar with; see JubA 5.2, 113. Jablonski mentions Philo's understanding of the sin of the golden calf in *Mos.* 2.161–162 as a regression to Egyptian *idolatry*; see idem, *Pantheon Aegyptiorum, Sive de Diis Eorum Commentarius: Cum Prolegomenis de Religione Et Theologia Aegyptiorum*, vol. 1 (Frankfurt an der Oder: 1750), 180: '[…] ubi de idolataria israelitarum, vitulum aureum in deserto adorantium […]: ζηλωταὶ τῶν αἰγυπτιακῶν γίνονται πλασμάτων. εἶτα χρυσοῦν ταῦρον κατασκευασάμενοι, μίμημα τοῦ κατὰ τὴν χώραν ἱερωτάτου ζῴου δοκοῦντος εἶναι, θυσίας ἀθύτους ἀνῆγον.' Cf. Mendelssohn's depiction in *Jerusalem*: 'Schon in den ersten Tagen der so wundervollen Gesetzgebung fiel die Nation in den sündlichen Wahn der Aegyptier zurück, und verlangte ein *Thierbild*' (emphasis in original).

With respect to Mendelssohn, we can easily establish his well-founded familiarity with this specific Philonic writing: He not only possessed the German translation in his library[37] but even alludes, in three significant instances, in his *Bi'ur* (ספר נתיבות השלום) to themes directly stemming from *Mos*.[38] In his introduction to the *Bi'ur*, he twice refers to Philo's depiction of the Greek translation of Hebrew Scripture:

> And also Yedidia ha-Alexandroni, who is called Philo, [together with Josephus Flavius] describe this event in accordance with the abovementioned account of Aristeas, with some slight modifications and a more succinct description, in such a manner indicating that what they said was from this Greek book [i.e. *Letter of Aristeas*] [...]. [...]: *it would thus appear that we mustn't deny the testimony of the ancients in regard to this, in particular the testimony of Philo, who was one of the citizens of Alexandria itself, the city in which the elderly completed this translation work three hundred years before him, and the testimony of several Christian scholars that lived at the times of the first Tannaim, for they all agree about the entire story of Aristeas*, [...].[39]

In his commentary to Exodus 25:4, he mentions the understanding of the 'wise Philo' (!) of the colour ארגמן as πορφύρα in *Mos*. 2.84–88: 'And also Josephus in his *Antiquities* [i. e. *Antiquitates Judaicae*] and the wise Philo in his book *The Life of Moses* refer to it as purple-red [...].'[40] Mendelssohn could have also been confronted with the significance of Philo's depiction, in *Mos*. 1.23, of Moses' Egyptian educational for-

---

37 *Verzeichniß*, 34 (№ 275).
38 For a more detailed analysis of the reception of Philo of Alexandria in the Haskalah, see Ze'ev Strauss, *Rabbi Jedidjah ha-Alexandri. Die Wiederentdeckung der Religionsphilosophie des Philon von Alexandria in der osteuropäischen Haskala* (Berlin and Boston: De Gruyter, forthcoming 2019).
39 JubA 15.1, 36 (German translation: JubA 9.1, 49) (my translation): "וכן ידידיה האלכסנדרוני, המכונה פילון, ספרו את המאורע ההוא כדברי אריסטיאה הנ"ל, בשנוי מעט וקצור הדברים, עד שכפי הנראה לקחו את רוב דבריהם מעל הספר היוני ההוא [...]. ופרט עדות ידידיה מתושבי אלכסנדריאה עצמה, העיר אשר בה נעשה מלאכת ההעתיקה ההוא, אחרי הזקנים ההם כשלש מאת שנה, ועדות כמה חכמי נוצרים שהיו בימים התנאים הראשונים, שכלם מסכימים בכללות הספור של אריסטיאה, [...]."
40 JubA 16, 240 (my translation). Mendelssohn's translation reads accordingly as follows: 'Auch himmelblauen, *purpurrorthe* und hochrothe Wolle, und Leinengarn und Ziegenhaare.' (my emphasis) He also refers to Philo's *Mos*. 1.256–257 in his allegorical interpretation of Numbers 21:18 ("בְּאֵר חֲפָרוּהָ שָׂרִים"; see idem, (במדבר) ספר נתיבות שלום והוא חבור כולל חמשה חומשי תורה (Prague: Verlag des S. Freund, 1860): 121: "והנה ידידיה המכונה פילון בספרו חיי משה כתב שהוציאו מלכי הארץ ההיא ויושביה הוצאת רבות לחפור את הבאר ההיא, והיא תוכה רצוף אבנים והוא בנין מפואר ויקר עד מאוד מורה על עושר כבוד המלכים ההם, ויתכן על זה לאמר, דרך מליצת השיר שחפרוה שרים כרוה נדיבי עם במחקק במשענותם." It is also worth mentioning that Johann B. Kölbele, in his polemic letter to Mendelssohn (1770), implicitly endeavours to identify Mendelssohn with Philo: 'Die Gottheit Christi und die damit genau verbundene Lehre von der Heiligen Dreyeinigkeit solten wenigstens einen Platonisierenden, Philonisierenden, und Kabalistischen Juden nicht sehr befremden [...];' see idem, "Zweites Schreiben an Herrn Moses Mendelssohn insonderheit über den ehemaligen Mendelssohnischen Deismus, über das Mendelssohnische Kennzeichen einer Offenbarung, und kürzlich über die Glaubwürdigkeit der Evangelischen Geschichte," in Carl Bonnet, *Philosophische Untersuchung der Beweise für das Christenthum. Samt desselben Ideen von der künftigen Glückseligkeit des Menschen*, Teil 2: *Sammlung derer Briefe, welche bey Gelegenheit der Bonnetschen philosophischen Untersuchung der Beweise für das Christenthum, zwischen Hrn. Lavater, Moses Mendelssohn, und Hrn. Dr. Kölbele gewechselt worden* (Frankfurt am Main: Johannes Bayrhoffer, 1774): 131.

mation in John Spencer's *De Legibus Hebraeorum Ritualibus et Earum Rationibus Libri Quatuor* (1732), a work he possessed in folio format in his library.⁴¹ Spencer took it upon himself, in the words of Jan Assmann, to prove the 'Egyptian origin of the ritual laws of the Hebrews.'⁴² Assmann regards this short Philonic passage as decisive for Spencer's Egyptian portrayal of Moses:

> Moses certainly knew hieroglyphic writing, which Spencer takes to be a secret code by which the Egyptian priests transmitted their wisdom to the initiated. His sources include Philo of Alexandria, De Vita Mosis, book 1, where we read that Moses learned from his Egyptian masters, among other subjects, ten dia symbolon philosophian.⁴³

Our proposed reading is substantiated even further if we account for the fact that Cranz probably reacted not only to Mendelssohn's *Vorrede*, the German translation of Menasseh Ben Israel's *Vindicia Judaeorum* (1656), but also to the contents of the translated essay itself. This is due to the fact that Philo occupies a crucial position in *Rettung der Juden*, written by Spinoza's Amsterdam rabbi, which makes numerous references to the historical descriptions of the Jewish Alexandrian to illustrate the hardships Jews endured under the rule of the Roman Empire.⁴⁴ For precisely this reason, Mendelssohn makes the following observation regarding Ben Israel's drawing on Philo (and Josephus Flavius):

---

41 *Verzeichniß*, 4 (№ 58).
42 Jan Assmann, *Moses the Egyptian: The Memory of Egypt in Western Monotheism* (Cambridge, MA and London: Harvard University Press, 1997): 56.
43 *Ibidem*, 73. See also *ibidem*, 56: 'For Spencer's project, this short sentence [i.e. that, according to St. Stephanus, 'Moses was well versed in all the wisdom of the Egyptians'] was absolutely crucial. It was the one foundation on which he could build his entire edifice, and it was the one testimony that could save him from being accused of heresy. Serving as leitmotifs throughout the whole line of the Moses debate, which started with Spencer [...], are this sentence and a short passage from Philo of Alexandria in *De Vita Mosis* in which he says that Moses was initiated into the "symbolic" philosophy of the ancient Egyptians.' Spencer's reliance upon Philo is very striking; in this work, the Jewish Platonist seems to hold the most important position by far amongst Jewish thinkers. Another book that is worth drawing attention to in this context is Ralph Cudworth, *The True Intellectual System of the Universe: Wherein all the Reason and Philosophy of Atheism is Confuted and its Impossibility Demonstrated with a Discourse concerning the True Notion of the Lords Supper* (New York: Gould & Newman, 1837), which Mendelssohn possessed in folio and in Mosheim's Latin translation (*Verzeichniß*, 4: nºs 67–68); see *ibidem*, 416: 'For which cause, we can by no means give credit to that of Philo, in the life of Moses, that besides the Egyptian priests, learned men were sent by Pharaoh's daughter out of Greece to instruct Moses.' Cf. Ludwig Holberg, *Jüdische Geschichte: von Erschaffung der Welt bis auf gegenwärtige Zeiten*, vol. 1 (Altona and Flensburg: Verlag der Gebrüder Korte, 1747): 109: 'Moses wird an dem ägyptischen Hofe erzogen: Nach einigen Jahren lies die Fürstin Mosen zu sich kommen, und nahm denselben nicht aus nur als ihr eignes Kind auf, sondern sie lies ihn auch in allen ägyptischen Künsten und Wissenschaften aufs sorgfältigste unterrichten. Das beste aber, nämlich die Erkenntnis des wahren Gottes hatte er bereits durch den Unterricht seiner Eltern gefaßt.'
44 Mendelssohn, *Menasseh Ben Israel. Rettung der Juden: Aus dem Englischen übersetzt nebst einer Vorrede von Moses Mendelssohn* (Berlin and Stettin: Friedrich Nicolai 1782): 36–39 and 47.

> If in this passage we should understand by empire of honour a certain empire in the world, then the only possible thing that could be meant is the reign of the Roman Empire, under which the Jews in those days lived and during which this prayer was introduced. How can this, however, be reconciled with the assertion of our Rabbi [i.e. Menasseh Ben Israel], which demonstrates this from passages of Josephus and Philo, namely that the Jews sacrificed and prayed for the well-being of the Roman emperor? Indeed, according to the dictum of the rabbis the sin altogether, but not the sinner, should be anathematised[45].[46]

Mendelssohn does not merely reaffirm Cranz's theological critique concerning the metaphorical language of ancient Hebrew, but further develops this line of thought into a well-thought-out sceptical stance in regard to the epistemic status of language altogether:

> Doctrines and laws, convictions and actions. The two former were not connected to words or written characters which always remain the same, for all men and all times, amid all the revolutions of language, morals, manners, and conditions, words and characters which invariably present the same rigid forms, into which we cannot force our concepts without disfiguring them. [...] The ceremonial law itself is a kind of living script, rousing the mind and heart, full of meaning, never ceasing to inspire contemplation and to provide the occasion and opportunity for oral instruction. [...] We teach and instruct one another only through writings; we learn to know nature and man only from writings. We work and relax, edify and amuse ourselves through overmuch writing. [...] Everything is dead letter ['toter Buchstabe']; the spirit of living conversation has vanished. [...] In a word, we are *literati*, *men of letters* ['Buchstabenmenschen']. Our whole being depends on letters; and we can scarcely comprehend how a mortal man can educate and perfect himself without a *book*.[47]

Gideon Freudenthal has convincingly shown that this sceptical position towards language advocated for by Mendelssohn is not only unique to his *Jerusalem* but constitutes a systematic philosophical viewpoint of his later years which also correlates with his common-sense tendency:

---

45 See Babylonian Talmud, *Berakhot* 10a. Cf. Mendelssohn, *Jerusalem*, 124–125 (JubA 8, 190): 'And if this is the case, I cannot fear such a condition; nor can I wish for a revelation [assuring me] that I shall never be placed in this condition of magnanimous benevolence which brings felicity to my fellow creatures and myself. What I have to fear is sin itself.'
46 *Ibidem*, 30–31 (fn. *; my translation and emphasis). Cf. JubA 8, 48: 'Wenn in dieser Stelle unter Reiche des Stoltzes ein gewisses Reich auf Erden verstanden werden soll; so kann wohl kein anderes, als das Römische gemeinet seyn, unter dessen Drucke die Juden damals lebten, als dieses Gebet eingeführet worden. Wie räumt sich dieses aber mit dem, was unser Rabbi in der Folge behauptet, und *durch Stellen aus* dem Josephus *und Philo beweiset*, daß nehmlich die Juden für das Wohl der römischen Kaiser und des Reichs geopfert und Gebete angestellet? Ja, nach dem Ausspruch der Rabinen überhaupt soll der Sünde, aber nicht dem Sünder gefluchet werden' (my emphasis).
47 Mendelssohn *Jerusalem*, 102–104 (original emphasis) (JubA 8, 169–170). Cf. Julius Guttmann, *Die Philosophie des Judentums* (Wiesbaden: Fourier Verlag, 1985): 314. Krochmalnik, "Das Zeremoniell als Zeichensprache," 270–274; Ulrich Ricken, "Mendelssohn und die Sprachtheorien der Aufklärung," in *Moses Mendelssohn im Spannungsfeld der Aufklärung*, eds. Michael Albrecht and Eva J. Engel (Stuttgart: Frommann-Holzboog, 2000): 228–229.

And yet readers cannot ignore his repeated advocacy of common sense or sound reason and his reservations concerning metaphysics as such. Scholars wished to attenuate this inconsistency and suggested that at first Mendelssohn was a Wolffian metaphysician but that he grew ever more sceptical regarding metaphysics and more inclined to common sense.[48]

As Freudenthal argues, Mendelssohn is to be regarded as 'a common-sense philosopher and sceptic in metaphysics,'[49] who became increasingly doubtful of 'the ability of language to adequately represent and to help generate truth transcending common-sense knowledge of the empirical world.'[50] Mendelssohn's apprehension of Judaism is nothing short of puzzling: Hebrew Scripture, when taken for the absolute truth, leads to idolatry.[51] I would like to make five observations regarding the quotation at hand:

1) Mendelssohn's sceptical evaluation of language, in all likelihood, draws upon Plato's *Schriftkritik* in the *Phaedrus* (274b-278e), where Plato puts the following statement into the mouth of Socrates:

> Writing, Phaedrus, has this strange quality, and is very like painting; for the creatures of painting stand like living beings, but if one asks them a question, they preserve a solemn silence. And so it is with written words; you might think they spoke as if they had intelligence, but if you question them, wishing to know about their sayings, they always say only one and the same thing. And every word, when once it is written, is bandied about, alike among those who understand and those who have no interest in it, and it knows not to whom to speak or not to speak; when ill-treated or unjustly reviled it always needs its father to help it; for it has no power to protect or help itself. (*Phdr.* 275d4-e5)[52]

---

[48] Freudenthal, *No Religion without Idolatry*, 13. Fogel also follows this line of interpretation: "Scepticism of Scepticism: On Mendelssohn's Philosophy of Common Sense," 54 and 58–67.
[49] Freudenthal, *No Religion without Idolatry*, 17.
[50] Ibidem, 16.
[51] In this context, Mendelssohn refers explicitly to Christoph Meiners' *Versuch über die Religionsgeschichte der ältesten Völker, besonders der Egyptier* (Göttingen: Johann Christian Dietrich, 1775): 'Mr. Meiners's remark would accordingly be a sort of confirmation of my hypothesis that the need for written characters was the first cause of idolatry. In judging the religious ideas of a nation that is otherwise;' see Mendelssohn, *Jerusalem*, 113 (JubA 8, 179); see Alexander Altmann's commentary, *Jerusalem*, 27. I believe Mendelssohn is alluding to another passage of Meiners than the one suggested by Alexander Altmann: '[...]: dringt man aber tiefer ein, so findet man den vollständigsten Stammbaum der Abgötterey, eine ununterbrochene Folge, und leicht begreiflich Zeugung aller Arten von Irrthümern, die so wie sie sind, nothwendig auseinander entstehen mußten. Die Grundbegriffe dieser ganzen Irr-Theorie gründeten sich in der Lage und Beschaffenheit des Landes, in der Lebensart der Einwohner. [...]: diese verbunden mit den Hieroglyphen konnten keinen andern, als einen solchen Zustand der Gelehrsamkeit erzeugen;' see Meiners, *Versuch über die Religionsgeschichte der ältesten Völker*, 62.
[52] Plato, *Euthyphro, Apology, Crito, Phaedo, Phaedrus*, trans. Harold N. Fowler (Cambridge, MA and London: Harvard University Press, 2005): 565–567. Mendelssohn refers to Plato's distinction of earthly and heavenly ἔρως and exploits it for his own differentiation between worldly and otherworldly politics; see Mendelssohn, *Jerusalem*, 131 (JubA 8, 196).

The main similarity in this respect between Mendelssohn and Plato is grounded on the almost identical dichotomy between the living word (spoken) and the inanimate one (written), which both equate with an image. In *Phdr.* 276a, we read: 'You mean the living and breathing word [λόγον ... ζῶντα καὶ ἔμψυχον] of him who knows, of which the written word may justly be called the image [εἴδωλον].'[53] In an analogous manner, Mendelssohn juxtaposes written language as 'permanent signs' ('fortdauernde Zeichen') with the notion of an image:

> We have seen how difficult it is to preserve the abstract ideas of religion among men by means of permanent signs. Images and hieroglyphics ['Bilder und Bilderschrift'] lead to superstition and idolatry, and our alphabetical script makes man too speculative. It displays the symbolic knowledge of things and their relations too openly on the surface; it spares us the effort of penetrating and searching, and creates too wide a division betwe[e]n doctrine and life.[54]

Mendelssohn's explicit and overtly approving references, in this very section, to Meiners' *Versuch über die Religionsgeschichte der ältesten Völker, besonders der Egyptier* (1775)[55] solidifies our hypothesis further, since the author makes recourse in this work to Plato's critique of written language. The philosopher and historian Christoph Meiners (1747–1810) partially translates and then comments on Socrates' portrayal of Thamus' condemnation of Theuth's invention of letters (γράμματα) (*Phdr.* 274c5–275b2).[56]

2) Mendelssohn's innovative solution to this problem, the ceremonial law perceived as 'living script,' could also be linked to the Platonic *Schriftkritik* in the *Phaedrus*: If our earlier suspicion is correct as to the impact Philo's *De vita Moysis* had on Mendelssohn's perception of Judaism, then one should at this juncture bear in mind Philo's Platonic depiction of Mosaic law, which is unequivocally predicated on Plato's

---

53 Plato, *Euthyphro, Apology, Crito, Phaedo, Phaedrus*, 567. Cf. Krochmalnik, "Das Zeremoniell als Zeichensprache," 274–275; Grit Schorch, *Moses Mendelssohns Sprachpolitik* (Berlin and Boston: De Gruyter, 2012): 228, n. 52.
54 Mendelssohn, *Jerusalem*, 118 (JubA 8, 184).
55 Mendelssohn, *Jerusalem*, 112–113 and 121 (JubA 8, 177–179 and 186). The influence of this document on Mendelssohn's *Jerusalem* has been already pointed out by Alexander Altmann in the commentary to the English translation: 223–224. See also the insightful remarks on the subject in Freudenthal, *No Religion without Idolatry*, 106 and 273.
56 Meiners, *Versuch über die Religionsgeschichte der ältesten Völker*, 208–209: 'Ich habe von einem alten Gotte in Naukraties [Ναύκρατιν] gehört, dessen (δαιμονος) Nahme Theuth heist, daß er nicht nur die Kunst zu zählen, sondern auch die Kunst zu rechnen, die Geometrie, Astronomie, Schriftzeichen, nebst vielen Arten von Spielen erfunden habe. Er soll zu den Zeiten des in Theben wohnenden, und über ganz Egypten herschenden Königs Thamus gelebt, und ihm in einer Unterredung, ausser seinen übrigen Künsten, d*ie Kunst zu schreiben, als eine der heilsamsten Hülfsmittel und Unterstützungen des Gedächtnisses, empfohlen haben, gegen welche letztere der König aber mehrere Einwürfe machte*. Sokrates rückt die Disputation des Theuths und Thamus, und die Gründe von beyden Seiten ein; es ist sonderbar, was man in diesen beyden Stellen alles übersehen hat' (my emphasis). For a more detailed discussion, see Thomas A. Szlezák, *Platon und die Schriftlichkeit der Philosophie: Interpretationen zu den frühen und mittleren Dialogen* (Berlin and New York: De Gruyter, 1985).

λόγος ζῶν καὶ ἔμψυχος (*Phdr.* 276a8). In *Mos.* 1.162, Philo designates the Jewish Lawgiver as the personification of the rational and living law (νόμος ἔμψυχός τε καὶ λογικὸς).[57] The ideal figure of Moses serves the Jewish Platonist as the prime example, through which he illustrates this aspect:

> They know this well who read the sacred books, which, unless he was such as we have said, he would never have composed under God's guidance and handed on for the use of those who are worthy to use them, to be their fairest *possession, likenesses and copies of the patterns enshrined in the soul, as also are the laws set before us in these books, which shew so clearly the said virtues.* (*Mos.* 2.11)[58]

Philo applies Plato's critical analysis of literal language to his spiritual conception of Jewish law. This motif is quite a common one in Philo's Jewish Platonism. Accordingly, the biblical patriarchs, Abraham, Isaac and Jacob, also didn't require the written laws (νόμων γραφή), since they all embodied the ἔμψυχοι καὶ λογικοὶ νόμοι in their souls.[59] We find a similar explanation in Mendelssohn's *Jerusalem*:

> And now I am able to explain more clearly my surmise about the purpose of the ceremonial law in Judaism. The forefathers of our nation, Abraham, Isaac, and Jacob, remained faithful to the Eternal, and sought to preserve among their families and descendants pure concepts of religion, far removed from all idolatry.[60]

Philo strives *ipso facto* to accentuate the *aliveness* of the Godly *unwritten* law (ἄγραφος νόμος), in order to unearth its rational and *undoubtable* core as rational content intrinsic to the human soul. This is very similar to the conceptual move made by Mendelssohn in *Jerusalem* with regard to the spiritual and dynamic *Zeremonialgesetze*. In his important article "Das Zeremoniell als Zeichensprache," Daniel Krochmal-

---

[57] The German translation of Mendelssohn's edition of *De vita Moysis* reads as follows: 'Vielleicht aber hat auch die göttliche Vorsehung Mosen lange vorher *zu einem lebendigen und vernünftigen Gesetze* gemacht, weil er einst ein Gesetzgeber werden sollte, und ihn im Voraus, ehe er es sich noch selbst in die Gedanken kommen ließ, dazu bestimmte;' see *Gottesgelahrheit*, 70–71 (my emphasis). Cf. *Mos.* 2.4 (νόμον ἔμψυχον) translated in *Gottesgelahrheit*, 146: 'ein lebendiges Gesetz.'

[58] PLCL 6.455–457 (my emphasis). For the German translation of this passage read by Mendelssohn, see: 'Es wissen aber diejenigen, welche die heiligen Bücher lesen, daß er diese nicht durch göttlichen Eingebung würde haben schreiben, noch denen, die sich dergleichen Güter zu bedienen wissen, das schönste Bild des vollkommensten Wesens, *das jemals eine Seele gezieret hat, von welchem die bekannt gemachten Gesetze Abrisse und Nachahmungen sind, in denen man die vorher genannten Tugenden deutlich erblicket*, hinterlassen können, wenn er nicht ein so vollkommener Mann gewesen wäre.' (*Gottesgelahrheit*, 149–150; my emphasis). Cf. Mendelssohn, *Jerusalem*, 128 (JubA 8, 191): 'Das allerhöchste Wesen hat sie [i.e. ewige Wahrheiten] allen *vernünftigen* Geschöpfen durch Sache und Begriff geoffenbaret, *mit einer Schrift in die Seele geschrieben*, die zu allen Zeiten und an allen Orten leserlich und verständlich ist' (my emphasis). Cf. Krochmalnik, "Das Zeremoniell als Zeichensprache," 267–273.

[59] *Abr.* 5–6; *Decal.* 1.

[60] Mendelssohn, *Jerusalem*, 117–118 (JubA 8, 183).

nik stresses the rationality at the bottom of Mendelssohn's idea of ceremonial law as a distinct type of sign language of the religion of reason ('besondere Zeichensprache der Vernunftreligion'):⁶¹

> Mendelssohn spricht dem Judentum einen religiösen Lehrgehalt nicht ab; nur daß es sich dabei nicht um eine besondere Doktrin handelt, sondern um eine vernünftige Weisung, die durch besondere Zeremonien und die an sie anknüpfende maieutische Unterweisung vermittelt wird. Das Judentum zeichnet sich nicht durch eine besondere Lehre, sondern durch ein besonderes Medium der Vernunft aus.⁶²

Thus, this Platonic rationalisation of Mosaic law underlying Mendelssohn's *Zeremonialgesetz* resembles, in its objective, that of Philo. Freudenthal aptly elucidates this aim as it pertains to Mendelssohn: 'The ceremonies of Judaism have a practical function similar to philosophy: they help buttress truths of reason against doubts.'⁶³

3) As previously mentioned, Mendelssohn's employment of the dichotomy between the inanimate word ('toter Buchstabe') and the living spirit ('lebendiger Geist') not only corresponds to Plato, but also and *a fortiori* to Paul according to 2 Corinthians 3:6.⁶⁴ This can be demonstrated by juxtaposing a passage by Mendelssohn with an excerpt from Lessing's German translation of Juan Huarte de San Juan's *The Examination of Men's Wits* (*Prüfung der Köpfe zu den Wissenschaften*; 1752), a work that Mendelssohn apparently used for his own depiction:

Wir lehren und unterrichten einander nur in Schriften; lernen die Natur und die Menschen kennen, nur aus Schriften; [...] Alles ist **toter**	**Wir** schämen uns wollen sie sagen, unsre Entscheidung oder unsern Rath ohne Anführung eines Gesetzes zu geben, welches das was wir

---

61 Krochmalnik, "Das Zeremoniell als Zeichensprache," 242.
62 *Ibidem*, 272; Guttmann, *Philosophie des Judentums*, 314–135. See Mendelssohn, *Jerusalem*, 118–119 and 127–128 (JubA 8, 166 and 184).
63 Freudenthal, *No Religion without Idolatry*, 149.
64 See further Christiane Frey, "Geist und Buchstabe: Ideologeme der Darstellbarkeit bei Hamann, Mendelssohn und Kleist," in *Darstellbarkeit: Zu einem ästhetisch-philosophischem Problem um 1800*, eds. Claudia Albes and Christiane Frey (Würzburg: Königshausen & Neumann, 2003): 143–156.
65 JubA 8, 170 (my emphasis).
66 Johann Huart (= Juan Huarte), *Prüfung der Köpfe zu den Wissenschaften: Worinne er die verschiedenen Fähigkeiten die in den Menschen liegen zeigt einer jeden den Theil der Gelehrsamkeit bestimmt der für sie eigentlich gehöret und endlich den Aeltern Anschläge ertheilt wie sie fähige und zu den Wissenschaften aufgelegte Söhne erhalten können. Aus dem Spanischen übersetzt von Gotthold Ephraim Leßing* (Zerbst: Zimmermannische Buchhandlung, 1752): 203–204 (my emphasis). It is noteworthy that Huarte makes use of Plato's understanding of the solicitor in this context; see *ibidem*, 206–207 and 212–213. Cf. further Stephanie Catani, "Prüfung der Köpfe zu den Wissenschaften: Lessings Huarte-Übersetzung im Kontext poetologischer und anthropologischer Diskurse der Aufklärung," in *'ihrem Originale nachzudenken': Zu Lessings Übersetzungen*, ed. Helmut Berthold (Tübingen: Niemeyer, 2008): 29–46. Cf. Gotthold E. Lessing, *Lessing: Philosophical and Theological Writing*, ed. Hugh B. Nisbet (Cambridge: Cambridge University Press, 2005), 63: 'In short, the letter is not the spirit, and the Bible is not religion. Consequently, objections to the letter, and to the Bible, need not also be objections to the spirit and to religion. For the Bible obviously contains more.'

Buchstabe; nirgend **Geist** der **lebendigen** Unterhaltung. [...] **Wir** brauchen des erfahrenen Mannes nicht, wir brauchen nur seine Schriften. Mit einem Wort, wir sind ***litterati***, **Buchstabenmenschen**. Vom **Buchstaben** hängt unser ganzes Wesen ab, und **wir** können kaum begreifen, wie ein Erdensohn sich bilden, und vervollkommnen kann, ohne *Buch*.[65]

entscheiden oder rathen ausdrücklich bestimmt. Dieser Bedeutung nach können die Gottesgelehrten keine **Litterati** heissen, weil in der h. Schrift ([II] Cor. III) der **Buchstabe tödtet**, der **Geist** aber **lebendig** macht. Ihr **Buchstabe** ist geheimnißvoll, voller Figuren und Bilder, dunkel und nicht einem jeden verständlich. Auch die Aertze haben keinen Buchstaben dem sie sich unterwerfen müßten. [...]; weil in der Medicin Vernunft und Erfahrung von weit grösserm Gewichte sind als das Ansehen.[66]

It seems almost beyond doubt that Mendelssohn relies, in these central passages out of *Jerusalem*, on Lessing's translation of Huarte's characterisation of the solicitor ('Rechtsgelehrter') in the eleventh section of his book.[67] The main feature of the solicitor is his strong dependency on the *literal* letters of the law. These 'Rechtsgelehrten' as literalists (*Litterati*) are then contrasted by Huarte to biblical exegetes ('Gottesgelehrten'), who have the lively spirit as the guiding principle of their enquiry. Huarte goes on to make a distinction between incompetent legal scholars and competent ones, the former more reliant on the faculty of memory ('Gedächtnis'), the latter predominantly on the faculty of reason ('Verstand').[68] He then turns to implicitly equate the incompetent 'Gottesgelehrten' that constrain their whole being to the prosaic letters of the law with the negative mindset of Jews as a prime example of *Litterati*:

> All which breedeth an alteration in the decision of the law, and if the judge or pleader be not endowed with discourse, to gather out of the law, or to take away or adjoine that which the law selfe doth not express in words, he shall commit manie errors in following the letter: for it hath been said that the words of the law are not to be taken after the Jewish manner, that is, to construe onely the letter, and so take the sense.[69]

Stumbling upon such a passage written by none other than his close friend Lessing, who, according to his own account, revered Huarte's scientific method of exploration

---

[67] The title of this section, Huarte, *Prüfung der Köpfe*, 200, reads as follows: 'Worinne erwiesen wird, daß der theoretische Theil der Rechtsgelahrsamkeit dem Gedächtnisse, der practische Theil, das Amt nämlich der Advocaten und Richter, dem Verstande, die Regierung, aber des Staats der Einbildungskraft zugehöre.'

[68] *Ibidem*, 210–211 and 213.

[69] Juan Huarte de San Juan, *The Examination of Mens Wits*, trans. Richard Carew (London: Adam F. Slip, for Richard Watkins, 1594): 157–158 (my emphasis). For the German translation Mendelssohn used, see: 'thereof *verba legis non sunt capienda iudaice*. Das ist: die Worte des Gesetzes müssen nicht auf jüdische Art erklärt werden. Diese jüdische Art aber bestehet darinne, daß man eine grammatikalische Zergliederung damit anstellt und *den buchstäblichen Sinne herauszieht*;' see Huarte, *Prüfung der Köpfe*, 211 (my emphasis).

by means of unbiased free thought alone,[70] must have left a deep impression on Mendelssohn as he saw how his Jewish faith was being misrepresented. Certainly, this was not the first time Mendelssohn encountered such a critical evaluation of Judaism with respect to the Pauline distinction between the dead letter and the living spirit. For example, in *Kritische Geschichte des Chiliasmus* of Corrodi, a renowned Leibniz-Wolffian adherent to the enlightened 'Vernunftreligion', we find a similar negative assessment regarding Judaism as solely a spiritless 'Zeremonialreligion':

> The Jewish rights, and constitutions do not, however, convey us a favourable opinion of this nation. We marvel at the appearance of legal scholars who constantly ignore the *spirit of the law*, and solely want to acknowledge its *letter*; who treat seriously and extensively the frivolities and wretched trifles, for which no law giver in the whole world cares; who issue prescriptions about unending improbable cases, of which no reasonable human being would conceive. We are surprised to find moral teachers which they follow who constantly ignore the eternal laws of nature, and decrees and constitutions of a very *arbitrary* essence, which seem to have no influence whatsoever on human happiness, and which have neither real morality nor immorality; were there ever teachers of religion, who took customs and *ceremonies to be the sole essence of that religion*, and were used to taking the outer shell and shadow of the virtue for the virtue itself, and perceiving the externality of religion for the interiority thereof [...] such teachers are the Jews.[71]

Mendelssohn's manner of dealing with these Christian prejudices is innovative. He inverts the Christocentric reading of 2 Corinthians 3:6 completely and gives it a Jewish twist: Henceforth, it is Judaism in its ancient original meaning that is the undogmatic religion of spirit, which does not rest on inanimate letters. Mendelssohn also does not retreat from the notion of Mosaic law. On the contrary: The dynamic nature of Mosaic 'Zeremonialgesetze' is precisely what gives Judaism its aliveness and frees it from being dependent upon the *literal sense* of Hebrew Scripture.[72] In the closing

---

70 Gotthold E. Lessing, "Vorrede des Uebersetzers," in Huarte, *Prüfung der Köpfe zu den Wissenschaften*, [6b]: '[...] er beurtheilt und treibt alles auf eine besondere Art, er endtecket alle seine Gedanken frey und ist sich selbst sein eigner Führer.' Cf. Catani, "Prüfung der Köpfe zu den Wissenschaften," 31–32.

71 Corrodi, *Kritische Geschichte des Chiliasmus*, 92–93 (my translation): 'Die jüdischen Rechte, und Satzungen bringen uns indeß keine günstigere Meinung vom Charakter dieser Nation bey. Wir wundern uns, Rechtsgelehrte zu sehen, die den *Geist des Gesetzes* beständig aus den Augen setzen, und seinen *Buchstaben* allein gehalten wissen wollen, die Frivolitäten, und nichtswürdige Kleinigkeiten, um die sich kein Gesetzgeber in der Welt bekümmert, ernsthaft und weitläufig abhandeln, die über unendlich unwahrscheinliche Fälle, an die kein vernünftiger Mensch denken wird, Verordnungen machen. Wir wundern uns Sittenlehrer zu finden, die die ewigen Naturgesetze unaufhörlich aus den Augen setzen, und Verordnungen, und Satzungen, die ganz *willkürlich* sind, und von ganz keinem Einfluß auf die menschliche Glückseligkeit scheinen, keine würkliche Sittlichkeit, oder Unsittlichkeit haben, an ihre Stelle setzen; gab es jemals Lehrer der Religion, welche Gebräuche und *Ceremonien für das Wesen derselben nehmen*, und sich gewohnt haben, die Schaale und den Schatten der Tugend für die Tugend selbst, und die äußere Seite für das Innwendige der Religion anzusehen, [...]; so sind die Juden solche Lehrer' (my emphasis).

72 For the influence of Wolffian philosophy on Mendelssohn's conception of the ceremonial law, see Krochmalnik, "Das Zeremoniell als Zeichensprache," 255–259.

part of *Jerusalem*, Mendelssohn places Jesus of Nazareth in the Jewish tradition of Halakha, for he 'is in complete agreement not only with Scripture, but also with the tradition.'[73] Mendelssohn would scarcely have a problem making the same conceptual move with the founding figure of Christianity, Paul, who does not speak of the abolition of Mosaic law, but rather, like Jesus (Matthew 5:17: πληρῶσαι), of its spiritual fulfilment (Romans 13:10: πλήρωμα ... νόμου). In sum, Mendelssohn attempts to break the reductionist equation of Jewish religion (spirit) with its Scriptural texts (letters), a stance he was already familiar with from Lessing's famous theological axiom for Christianity (1778): 'The letter is not the spirit, and the Bible is not religion.'[74]

4) Johann G. Herder has not been paid sufficient attention to his influence on Mendelssohn's growing scepticism towards language and its innate shortcomings.[75] As Freudenthal has persuasively shown, Mendelssohn's growing doubt concerning the aptness of language for articulating metaphysical truths is not merely a transitional position we accidentally come across in *Jerusalem*, but rather constitutes a systematic philosophical stance of his later years that is also elaborated on in his *Morgenstunden oder Vorlesungen über das Daseyn Gottes* (1785).[76] Herder's special appeal to Mendelssohn in this regard probably stems from the fact that he not only dealt with the pure theoretical elements of language, but also with an aesthetic analysis of Biblical Hebrew.[77] He even personally reviewed in a very favourable manner Herder's work on language theory, *Abhandlung über den Ursprung der Sprache* (1772), in Friedrich Nikolai's *Allgemeine deutsche Bibliothek* 19.2 (1773).[78] In Herder's *Abhandlung über den Ursprung der Sprache*, where he evaluates language as a profane

---

73 Mendelssohn, *Jerusalem*, 134 (JubA 8, 199). See Alexander Altmann's commentary: *Jerusalem*, 239. Cf. Oswald Bayer, "Der Mensch als Pflichtträger der Natur Naturrecht und Gesellschaftsvertrag in der Kontroverse zwischen Hamann und Mendelssohn," in *Mendelssohn und die Kreise seiner Wirksamkeit*, eds. Michael Albrecht, Eva J. Engel and Norbert Hinske (Tübingen: Max Niemeyer Verlag, 1994): 184– 189.
74 Lessing, *Lessing: Philosophical and Theological Writing*, 63 and 127.
75 Cf. Ricken, "Mendelssohn und die Sprachtheorien der Aufklärung," 213 and 224–225.
76 Freudenthal, *No Religion without Idolatry*, 38–45.
77 Mendelssohn possessed, in his library, both Herder's *Abhandlung über den Ursprung der Sprache* (Berlin: Christian Friedrich Voß, 1772) as well as his *Vom Geist der Ebräischen Poesie. Eine Anleitung für die Liebhaber derselben und der ältesten Geschichte des menschlichen Geistes* (Dessau: Verlagskasse and Buchhandlung der Gelehrten und Künstler, 1782); see *Verzeichniß*, 22 (n°s 81–82), 53 (N° 655). Cf. Eva J. Engel, "'Die Freyheit der Untersuchung': Die Literaturbriefe 72–75 (13. und 20. Dezember 1759)," in *Mendelssohn und die Kreise seiner Wirksamkeit*, eds. Michael Albrecht, Eva J. Engel and Norbert Hinske (Tübingen: Max Niemeyer Verlag, 1994): 252 and 268.
78 JubA 5.2, 176: 'Ueberhaupt unterscheidet sich das philosophische Genie des Herrn Herders durch die Geschicklichkeit, alles was ihm seine ausgebreitete Kenntniß in der Philosophie, Naturkunde und der ganzen Litteratur darbot, zu seinem Vortheil anzuwenden, daher ist er auch vermögend, seine Materie in ein helleres Licht zu setzen, sie von mehrern Seiten zu betrachten, und mehr darinn zu entdecken, als es dem andern Verf. [i.e. D. Tiedemann] möglich war. [...] Herrn Herders Schreibart ist freylich stärker, aber auch geschmückter und glänzender; [...].'

and animalistic product of human spirit ('überall Spuren vom Gange des menschlichen Geistes!'),[79] he voices considerable doubt regarding the adequacy of artificial philosophical language, given its arbitrariness, for conveying absolute truths.[80] The animalistic origin ('tierischer Ursprung') of language also pertains, as Herder argues, to the so-called Godly language of Biblical Hebrew. The writing style of this ancient language intuitively indicates this very fact, since it entirely contradicts the demands of common sense:

> This manner of writing is so contrary to the course of sound reason—of writing the nonessential and omitting the essential—that it would be incomprehensible to the grammarians, if the grammarians were accustomed to comprehend.[81]

This sceptical attitude towards Biblical Hebrew as a language could account for Herder's shifting to explore the aesthetic dimensions of Hebrew Scripture. In his poetological analysis of the Hebrew Bible in *Vom Geist der Ebräischen Poesie* (1782), he constantly highlights sublimeness as a key feature of biblical poetic language ('Erhabenheit der Poesie'). This line of interpretation seems to mainly be a result of the preliminary study *De sacra poesi hebraeorum praelectiones academicae oxonii habitae* (1753), conducted by Robert Lowth, and of the extensive reception in the Enlightenment of Pseudo-Longinus' ancient poetological essay *On the Sublime* (περὶ ὕψους).[82] Very similar observations were already made by Mendelssohn between 1757 and 1758 in his review articles *Betrachtungen ueber das Erhabene und Naive in den schönen Wissenschaften* (1758)[83] and *De sacra poesi Hebraeorum, praelectiones academicae Oxonii habitae, a Roberto Lowth* (1757),[84] in which he favourably evaluates both Pseu-

---

79 Herder, *Abhandlung über den Ursprung der Sprache*, 133. Cf. to Karl W. Jerusalems essay: "Daß die Sprache dem ersten Menschen durch Wunder nicht mitgetheilt seyn kann," in *Philosophische Aufsätze*, ed. Gotthold E. Lessing (Braunschweig: Buchhandlung des Fürstlichen Waisenhauses, 1776): 1–12. See *Verzeichniß*, 51 (№ 635).
80 Herder, *Abhandlung über den Ursprung der Sprache*, 43–44. See also *ibidem*, 60–61, 93 und 124–125: 'Man weiß, auf welchen Wegen die meisten Abstraktionen "in unsre wissenschaftliche Sprache" gekommen sind, in Theologie und Rechtsgelehrsamkeit, in Philosophie und andre. Man weiß, wie oft die Scholastiker und Polemiker nicht einmal mit Worten ihrer Sprache streiten konnten und als Streitgewehr (Hypostasis und Substanz, ὁμοούσιος und ὁμοιούσιος) aus denen Sprachen herüberholen mußten, in denen die Begriffe abstrahirt, in denen das Streitgewehr geschärft war!,' as well as 133–134 and 140.
81 *On the Origin of Language: Jean-Jacques Rousseau Essay on the Origin of Languages, Johann Gottfried Herder Essay on the Origin of Language*, trans. John H. Moran and Alexander Gode (Chicago and London: University of Chicago Press, 1986): 95; Herder, *Abhandlung über den Ursprung der Sprache*, 17; cf. *ibidem*, 111.
82 See Martin Fritz, *Vom Erhabenen: der Traktat "Peri Hypsous" und seine ästhetisch-religiöse Renaissance im 18. Jahrhundert* (Mohr Siebeck: Tübingen, 2011); Schorch, *Moses Mendelssohns Sprachpolitik*, 106–109; Libera Pisano, "Judentum, Entfremdung, Sprache. Der vergessene Zusammenhang zwischen Mendelssohn und Hegel," *Judaica* 4 (2016): 482–483.
83 JubA 1, 191–218.
84 JubA 4, 20–62.

do-Longinus' *On the Sublime* as well as Lowth's Latin lectures on the poetical nature of Scriptural Hebrew.[85] Having said that, Herder's stance towards language in general and Biblical Hebrew in particular could have still helped form some of Mendelssohn's critical tendencies in *Jerusalem:* Like Herder, he was critical of language and saw an unbridgeable gap between arbitrary linguistic signs and that which they aim to signify.[86] Herder's treatment of Biblical Hebrew as a deficient language with clear limitations and a mere derivative of the human spirit could have also led him to rule out the possibility of Holy Scripture entailing absolute philosophical truths. Mendelssohn also considered language in all its relativity as a criterion for evaluating the varying *Bildungsniveaus* of nations:

> The Greeks had both culture and enlightenment. They were an educated nation just as their language is an educated language. – Generally, the language of a people is the best indication of its education, of its culture as well as its enlightenment, in terms of both its extent and its strength.[87]

It is therefore hardly surprising that Mendelssohn juxtaposes the *sublime* poetical language of Biblical Hebrew with the classic literature of ancient Greek and Roman poets of the stature of Homer and Virgil and implies the moral superiority of the former.[88] The aesthetic approach is the manner in which Mendelssohn attempted to exhaust much of the lost meaning of the Hebrew Bible without resorting to unsubstantiated presuppositions of wishful thinking.[89]

5) Mendelssohn's sceptical analysis of semiotics may very well also be directly influenced by the Neo-Pyrrhonian critique of the Stoic theory of signs, which

---

85 Schorch, *Moses Mendelssohns Sprachpolitik*, 112–114; Pisano, "Judentum, Entfremdung, Sprache," 482–483.
86 Mendelssohn, *Jerusalem*, 108–112 (JubA 8, 173–177). See Herder, *Abhandlung über den Ursprung der Sprache*, 211.
87 Moses Mendelssohn, "On the Question: What Does 'to Enlighten' Mean?," in idem, *Philosophical Writings*, trans. and ed. Daniel O. Dahlstrom (Cambridge: Cambridge University Press, 1997): 314; Moses Mendelssohn, "Über die Frage: was heißt aufklären," in *Was ist Aufklärung? Thesen und Definition*, ed. Ehrhard Bahr (Stuttgart: Reclam, 2004): 5 (JubA 6.1, 116).
88 Mendelssohn, *De sacra poesi Hebraeorum*, 171 (JubA 4, 20): 'Man liest den Homer, Virgil und die übrigen Schriften der Alten; man zergliedert alle Schönheiten, die darin enthalten sind, mit der größten Sorgfalt, und giebt sich alle Mühe, unsern Geschmack nach ihrem Muster zu bilden; aber selten bekümmert man sich um die Regeln der Kunst, nach welchen jene göttlichen Dichter unter den alten Hebräern die erhabensten Empfindungen in uns rege machen, und unmittelbar den Weg nach unserm Herzen zu treffend wissen. Der feine attische Geschmack, den wir aus den Schriften der alten Griechen und Römer schöpfen, kann sehr leicht in Weichlichkeit ausarten; aber der ächte orientalische Geschmack, der in den Schriften der heiligen Dichter herrscht, ist allzu männlich, allzu edel, als daß er uns je zu unwürdigen Gesinnungen verleiten könnte.'
89 For a more detailed discussion of Mendelssohn's aesthetic approach, see Daniel Krochmalnik, "Zeichen der Kunst, Zeichen der Moral, Zeichen der Religion," in *Zur Religionsästhetik und -semiotik der Aufklärung, in Zeichen-Kunst. Zeichen und Interpretation*, ed. Werner Stegmaier (Frankfurt am Main: Suhrkamp, 1999): 101–111.

makes up a central part of the second book of Sextus Empiricus' *Outlines of Pyrrhonism* (*PH* II 97–133).⁹⁰ In these two following chapters x and xi of book II, Sextus presents the Stoic distinction between the recollective sign (σημεῖον ὑπομνηστικόν) and the indicative sign (σημεῖον ἐνδεικτικόν), casting doubt on the provability of the existence of the latter as a mental representation of the inherently ambiguous object of knowledge being signified (σημαινόμενον):⁹¹ 'Thus, since such plausible arguments are adduced both for there being signs and for there not being, we should no more say that there are signs than that there are not.'⁹² Indicative signs here are also strongly linked with *discursive* thought as they are defined as a sort of preposition (λεκτόν), which is 'a pre-antecedent statement in a sound conditional, revelatory of the consequent.'⁹³ Mendelssohn's critical account of signs as irreal and arbitrary abstractions of human reason resembles Sextus' sceptical evaluation of Stoic semiotics:

> [...]; for without the aid of signs, man can scarcely remove himself one step from the sensual. In the same way in which the first steps toward rational knowledge must have been taken, the sciences are still being expanded and enriched by inventions; this is why the invention of a new scientific term is, at times, an event of great importance. The man who first invented the word nature does not seem to have made a very great discovery. Nevertheless, his contemporaries were indebted to him for enabling them to confound the conjurer who showed them an apparition in the air, and to tell him that his trick was nothing supernatural, but an *effect of nature*.⁹⁴

Three facts immediately suggest that Mendelssohn was acquainted with this specific section of Sextus' *Outlines of Pyrrhonism:* (i) Mendelssohn possessed the 1718 folio edition of Sextus' writings in his library, edited by Johann A. Fabricius on the basis of the original commentated edition of Henry Etienne from 1562.⁹⁵ (ii) In addition, we also know that Mendelssohn was well familiar with Johann J. Bruckers *Historia critica philosophiae*, a five-volume work that he had its first edition (1742–1744) in his library⁹⁶ and also reviewed its supplemented appendix published in 1767 in the *Allgemeine deutsche Bibliothek* 11.1 (1770).⁹⁷ In Brucker's portrayal of the history of

---

90 Cf. Fogel, "Scepticism of Scepticism: On Mendelssohn's Philosophy of Common Sense," 58–60.
91 *PH* II 99–101.
92 The translation used is Sextus Empiricus, *Outlines of Scepticism*, eds. and trans. Julia Annas and Jonathan Barnes (Cambridge: Cambridge University Press, 2000), 101 (*PH* II 133).
93 Sextus Empiricus, *Outlines of Scepticism*, 93 (*PH* II 101).
94 Mendelssohn, *Jerusalem*, 105–106 (emphasis in original; JubA 8, 171).
95 *Verzeichniß*, 3 (№ 35): *Sextus Empiricus: Opera graece & latine* (Leipzig: Johann Friedrich Gleditsch und Sohn, 1718): 88–96 (*PH* II 10–11).
96 *Verzeichniß*, 8 (nºs 59–64). Mendelssohn apparently had six volumes of this work, which might suggest that he also possessed the additional appendix (1767) of the second edition. Johann J. Brucker, *Historia critica philosophiae*, 5 vols. (Leipzig: Bernhard Christoph Breitkopf, 1742–1744).
97 JubA 5.2, 113–116.

philosophy Sextus' critique of Stoic semiotics is discussed.[98] (iii) Mendelssohn also had in his possession Dietrich Tiedemann's *System der stoischen Philosophie*,[99] where attention, in the section 'Von den Worten, und Ausdrücken der Gedanken' (143–172), is drawn to Sextus Empiricus' sceptical account of Stoic semiotics and conception of language.[100]

3 Doubting Pythagoras' Golden Thigh

Let us now turn to an important passage from the first part of *Jerusalem*, concerning scepticism, that is generally overlooked:

> But should there be an end to all dispute on account of this? Must one never doubt principles? If so, men of the Pythagorean school could dispute forever how their teacher happened to come by his golden hip ('güldene Hüfte'), and no one would dare to ask: Did Pythagoras actually have a golden hip? Every game has its laws, every contest its rules, according to which the umpire decides. If you want to win the stake or carry away the prize, you must submit to the principles. But whoever wishes to reflect on the theory of games may certainly examine the fundamentals. Just as in a court of law.[101]

In this citation, Mendelssohn grapples with the vicious prejudiced critique of the reviewer of his *Vorrede* to Menasseh Ben Israel's *Rettung der Juden* in *Göttingische Anzeigen von gelehrten Sachen*, published on the 14th of September 1782. The central point of the dispute, from the perspective of the reviewer, was that Mendelssohn calls into question the right to apply Prussian ecclesiastical law, predicated on Christian doctrines,[102] to Jewish communities.[103] The reviewer does not refrain from exhibiting his negative sentiments towards the Jewish people,[104] which he tries to validate with reference to anti-Judaic works such as Johann A. Eisenmenger's *Entdecktes Judenthum*.[105] The sudden dogmatic conclusion of the reviewer ('all this is new and harsh. First principles are negated, and all dispute comes to an end')[106] is exactly the point of departure for Mendelssohn. 'Die ersten Grundsätze' of the ecclesiastical

---

98 Brucker, *Historia critica philosophiae*, 1.1338–1339.
99 *Verzeichniß*, 48 (nºs 578–581); Dietrich Tiedemann, *System der stoischen Philosophie*, 3 vols. (Leipzig: Weidmanns Erben und Reich, 1776).
100 Ibidem, vol. 1, 167–169.
101 Mendelssohn, *Jerusalem*, 81 (JubA 8, 148–149).
102 *Göttingische Anzeigen von gelehrten Sachen* (III. Stück) (14.09.1782): 893: 'Recht [...], das mit Lehrmeinungen zusammenhängt und auf demselben beruht.'
103 Ibidem: 'Aus dieser Insinuation mußten wir nothwendig schliessen, daß man dem königl. Preuss. Justizdepartement eigentlich begreiflich machen wollte, kein christl. Justizcollegium könne die Juden richten; dies sey die Sache der Rabbiners; [...].'
104 Ibidem, 892: 'die gemeinschädlichen Grundsätze der Juden [...] Unarten ihrer Väter' etc.
105 Mendelssohn was familiar with this work; see *Verzeichniß*, 18 (Nº 301); JubA 13, 49–50.
106 Mendelssohn, *Jerusalem*, 81 (JubA 8, 148).

authority by definition, as Mendelssohn argues, cannot be proven. He then goes on to implicitly identify this attitude with the dogmatism of the Pythagorean school. Similarly, in the fourth part of Judah Halevi's *Kuzari*, the Pythagorean school of thought is referred to in the context of the impossibility for philosophy to reach a final verdict on metaphysical principles:

> Neither do two philosophers agree on this point, *unless they be disciples of the same teacher.* But Empedocles, *Pythagoras*, Aristotle, Plato, and many others entirely disagree with each other.[107]

Like Mendelssohn, Halevi points to the dogmatic and tribal nature of different philosophical schools, whose disciples agree solely with their own philosophical masters. Mendelssohn was also well acquainted with Diogenes Laërtius' *Lives and Opinions of Eminent Philosophers*,[108] where the myth of Pythagoras' golden thigh is mentioned.[109] With that said, I want to advance the argument that Mendelssohn's depiction is actually derived from Johann M. Schröckh's fourth volume of his monumental work *Christliche Kirchengeschichte* (1777), where we find the following description:

> These are rumors and tales of the later Pythagoreans; many of them unreasonable and suspicious, many of them cannot even be traced back, with certainty, to a specific time, and the seeming imitation of the evangelical history takes away its entire full worth and true usage. [...] He [i.e. Pythagoras] cured diseases of the body and the soul with magical sayings and was regarded because of his *golden thigh* to be Apollo. Had the Christians propagated similar *tales*, with so *little believability*, about the founders of their religion: then they would have been rightly ridiculed. Apart from that, they were not yet entitled to designate Pythagoras as a deceiver, insofar as one cannot longer establish anything in regards to this otherwise wise and virtuous man other than, at the utmost, the fact that he concealed a great deal of his doctrines and employed them against the large heap of artificial conceptions, which he might have perceived as necessary. But the Christians could have then even further advanced their accusation of the credulity against his adorers.[110]

---

107 Judah Halevi, *The Kuzari. An Argument for the Faith of Israel*, trans. Hartwig Hirschfeld (New York: P. Shalom, 1969): 239 (my emphasis; the Hebrew translation used by Mendelssohn reads as follows: 'אין שנים מן הפילוסופים מסכימים זה עם זה, אם לא שהם בני סיעה אחת הסומכת על מסרת שקבלו מפי פילוסוף אחד: אמפידוקלס או פיתגורס, אריסטו או אפלטון, או אחד משאר הפילוסופים, שאף הם אין אחד מהם מסכים לדעת חברו.'). Cf. Sacks, who quotes the very same passage of Halevi with reference to Mendelssohn's *Jerusalem*. But he does this in order to show that 'Mendelssohn [...] diverges significantly from Halevi regarding philosophical change,' see Sacks, *Living Script*, 207–208. For the influence of Simone Luzzatto on Mendelssohn's *Jerusalem*, see Veltri, *Renaissance Philosophy in Jewish Garb*, 221.
108 See *Verzeichniß*, 26 (№ 149).
109 Diogenes Laërtius, *The Lives and Opinions of Eminent Philosophers* (London: Bohn's Classical Library, 1853): 342: 'He is said to have been a man of the most dignified appearance, and his disciples adopted an opinion respecting him, that he was Apollo who had come from the Hyperboreans; and it is said, that once when he was stripped naked, he was seen to have a golden thigh [τὸν μηρὸν ὀφθῆναι χρυσοῦν].'
110 My translation of Johann M. Schröckh, *Christliche Kirchengeschichte*, vol. 4 (Leipzig: Engelhart Benjamin Schwickert, 1777), 348–349: 'Es sind Gerüchte und Erzählungen der spätern Pythagoräer;

The parallels to Mendelssohn's account are striking: Both descriptions exploit the myth of Pythagoras' thigh ('güldene Hüfte') to exemplify the problems of dogmatism. Schröckh tries to delineate the substantial difference between these implausible tales ('Erzählungen') about Pythagoras, passed on by the anti-Christian Porphyry, and the written transmission regarding the figure of Jesus. He claims that if the Christians propagated such farfetched rumours about the founders of their religion, they would have deserved much ridicule. Mendelssohn, on the other hand, attempts to show that this is already, to some degree, the case concerning ecclesiastical authority ('Kirchenmacht') in the Prussian Kingdom, since its 'fundamental principles' are adhered to dogmatically by the majority of the Christian population without asking whether they are adequate and rational. If Mendelssohn really bases his passage on Schröckh's unfavourable characterisation of Pythagoreans, then his implicit statement against Prussian Christians is quite critical: They warrant mockery for their gullibility ('Leichtgläubigkeit'). The way Mendelssohn illustrates the ludicrousness of the assessment of his reviewer is through the sceptical metaphor of a game in which rules can be arbitrarily made up. It should be noted that the correlation between sceptical doubt and the contingency of the predetermined rules of a game is not foreign to Jewish thought. Already in Simone Luzzatto's treatise *Socrates or on Human Knowledge* (1651) we find a very similar sceptical observation with recourse to the arbitrarily defined 'first positions' of a chess game:

> Hence, I likewise started to suspect that as human beings we are indeed not endowed with sufficient organs and faculties to apprehend and acknowledge the truth. Besides, the early bases and foundations from which the edifice of human knowledge rises are indeed not fixed and stable, but arbitrary and laid at our whim, as is usually the case with games, especially with chess, where similarly, while deductions and consequences are necessary, the first positions are indeed contingent and voluntary.[111]

---

viel Ungereimtes und Verdächtiges, vieles das nicht einmal auf eine sichere Zeitrechnung zurück geführt werden kann, und die augenscheinliche Nachahmung der evangelischen Geschichte benimmt ihren vollends allen Werth und wahren Gebrauch. [...] Krankheiten des Leibes und der Seele heilte er durch Zaubersprüche, und wurde wegen seiner *güldenen Hüfte* vor den Apollo gehalten. Hätten die Christen solche *Erzählungen*, und mit so geringer *Glaubwürdigkeit*, von den Stiftern ihrer Religion ausgebreitet: so würden sie mit Recht verspottet worden seyn. Im übrigen waren sie zwar dadurch noch nicht berechtigt, den Pythagoras einen Betrüger zu nennen, weil man von diesem sonst weisen und tugendhaften Manne höchstens nicht mehr beweisen kann, als daß er viele seiner Lehrsätze verheimlicht, und gegen den großen Hauffen Kunstbegriffe, die er vielleicht vor nothwendig hielt, angewandt habe. Aber seinen Bewunderern konnten die Christen desto mehr eine unwürdige Leichtgläubigkeit vorwerfen' (my emphasis). The fifth volume was, for example, reviewed in Friedrich Nicolai's journal *Allgemeine deutsche Bibliothek* 40.1 (1780): 536–540, where Mendelssohn reviewed numerous works between 1765 and 1784; see JubA 5.2. Cf. *AdB* 23 (1774), 375: 'Aristoteles, der in seinen exoterischen Schriften gemeinnützige Materien für den Bürger gemeinnützig vortrug, war ein weiser Mann; aber der Pythagoras, der eine goldene Hüfte vorgab, aus der Hölle zurückkam und sich die Rüstung des Euphorbus zueignete, war ein Charlatan.'

111 The translation of this passage used here is taken from Giuseppe Veltri, "Negotiating the Principle of (Non)-Contradiction: Johann Frischmuth on the Rabbinic Dialectic Discussion," in *Yearbook*

To a Prussian Jew such as Mendelssohn, looking at mainstream Christian society from the outside, these rules are extraneous and can be randomly modified. And it seems quite evident that he is not only interested in tackling the ecclesiastical laws ('Kirchenrechte'), but also that which is at their core: Christian doctrines ('Lehrmeinungen'). With this example, one can see how sceptical thought patterns also entered Mendelssohn's practical *Weltanschauung*.

Summary

In conclusion, it can be said that Mendelssohn's perspective underlying the main apologetic contentions of his *Jerusalem* is a philosophical, sceptical one: He assumes that religion cannot withstand the scrutinizing assaults of philosophy and for that reason attempts to secure his own Jewish belief as a non-theoretical religion based primarily on the practical notion of ceremonial law. In order to ward off these threats, Mendelssohn has to compromise on a very central and common premise of traditional Jewish belief: The view that the Hebrew Bible manifests absolute truth. Hebrew Scripture can, at most, facilitate the attainment of common-sense knowledge regarding natural religion. But Mendelssohn did not seem much discouraged by this fact, as he also appreciated the aesthetic dimensions of poetical Biblical Hebrew, a field that was rapidly gaining ground in the second half of the eighteenth century in German-speaking Europe. At the same time, the critical analysis of Biblical texts was emerging as a very promising method; it certainly also had an effect on Mendelssohn's unconditioned refutation of both Maimonidean as well as kabbalistic understanding of Scripture as speculative texts.

I then turned to uncovering Mendelssohn's intricate usage of numerous philosophical and theological sources, which he seems to utilise for his sceptical account of language. It was demonstrated that Mendelssohn's critical discussion takes for its starting point Cranz's employment of Pauline metaphor (2 Corinthians 3), through which he distinctively demarcates Judaism from Christianity by highlighting the mediatory role of symbolic language taken at face value. Mendelssohn then proceeds to philosophically develop his sceptical attitude towards language, drawing upon the Platonic *Schriftkritik* in the *Phaedrus*. Subsequently, I went on to suggest that Mendelssohn's preferred solution for the problem of dependency upon Hebrew Scripture, the ceremonial law, can also be linked to Plato's critical analysis of the written word. As shown above, Mendelssohn had first-hand knowledge of Philo's *De vita Moysis*, to which he refers a number of times in his *Bi'ur*. In this allegorical exegesis, Philo incorporated Plato's *Schriftkritik* and appraisal of the dynamic aliveness of spoken lan-

---

of the Maimonides Centre for Advanced Studies 2017, ed. Bill Rebiger (Berlin and Boston: De Gruyter, 2017): 114. I would like to thank Giuseppe Veltri for drawing my attention to this insightful passage of Simone Luzzatto. The first English translation of *Socrates*, a project undertaken both by Giuseppe Veltri and Michela Torbidoni, is expected to be published soon.

guage (λόγον ... ζῶντα καὶ ἔμψυχον, *Phdr.* 276a8) into his own understanding of Mosaic law and accordingly conceptualises it as not being confined to inanimate written language, but rather as animate and rational (νόμος ἔμψυχός τε καὶ λογικὸς, *Mos.* 1.162). Additionally, it was shown that Mendelssohn, within the context of his critique of language, elaborates on 'das echte Judentum,' based on the idea of ceremonial law, by apologetically appropriating the well-known Pauline dichotomy of letter and spirit. However, he does not do so directly, but through the mediation of Lessing's German translation of Juan Huarte de San Juan's *The Examination of Men's Wits*, where legal scholars and Jewish exegetes of the Bible are both depicted as *Litterati*. Mendelssohn simply semantically inverts this anti-Judaic understanding of the Pauline dichotomy of the inanimate letter and the animate spirit: Judaism in its 'ancient, original' sense orients itself by the lively spirit of the ceremonial acts ('Zeremonialhandlungen') of Mosaic law; it is Christianity as a revelatory religion ('geoffenbarte Religion') that relies heavily on the inanimate letters of its various speculative 'Heilswahrheiten' and is to be regarded as 'a yoke in spirit and in truth'[112] for its followers. Moreover, I attempted to point to the plausible impact that both Herder's philosophy of language as well as the Neo-Pyrrhonian scepticism of Sextus Empiricus might have had on Mendelssohn's critical attitude towards signs and language.

Lastly, I illustrated how Mendelssohn uses sceptical strategies to call the ecclesiastical laws and the Christian doctrines upon which they are grounded into question. He challenges them by presenting the distinctive example of the myth of Pythagoras's golden thigh, which the Greek philosopher's dogmatic devotees don't dare to doubt. In so doing, Mendelssohn wishes to reveal the vulnerability of Christian dogmatism to philosophical scepticism. Analogous to the rules of a game, the starting points, the fundamental Principles ('die ersten Grundsätze'), are selected arbitrarily and can for that very reason be superseded and substituted at any time. I pointed out the possible influence the fourth part of Judah Halevi's *Kuzari* might have had on Mendelssohn at this point, since he portrays Pythagoras' adherents as dogmatic within the wider context of metaphysical abeyance between the various philosophical schools. I ultimately presented the fourth volume of Schröckh's *Christliche Kirchengeschichte* as a more plausible source for this particular passage, since it also mentions Pythagoras' golden thigh in conjunction with both unfounded dogmatism and the question of the authenticity of Christian doctrines.

Mendelssohn's metaphorical portrayal of the asymmetrical relation between Judaism and Christianity as a somewhat unstable, multi-story building is quite illustrative for our theme at hand.[113] In this simile, Judaism is placed on the solid ground floor, while speculative Christianity inhabits one of the upper floors of the same

---

112 Mendelssohn, *Jerusalem*, 248 (Appendix: *Draft of Jerusalem*).
113 This simile is, of course, an allusion to Cranz: *Das Forschen nach Licht und Recht*, 23–24. See Alexander Altmann's introduction for commentary on this simile: *Jerusalem*, 10, 203–204.

building. The advantage of undogmatic Judaism resides in its secure position and, as a result, its protection from attacks by sceptical philosophy.[114] The chief aim of Mendelssohn's *Jerusalem* can be derived from this particular point of view: it is an attempt to conceptually fortify the Jewish *Religionsgebäude*[115] against persistent sceptical doubt. But one should not be so mistaken as to believe Jesus or Paul occupy the upper floor.

---

114 Cf. Mendelssohn, *Jerusalem*, 248 (Appendix: *Draft of Jerusalem*).
115 Cranz, *Das Forschen nach Licht und Recht*, 26.

Andreas Brämer

Abraham Geiger—skeptischer Pionier einer Glaubenslehre des Reformjudentums?

Die Wissenschaft des Judentums brachte sich seit den 1820er Jahren zunächst vor allem im deutschsprachigen Raum in Stellung, wo sie mit autoritativem Anspruch als neues Deutungsmodell jüdischer Religion, Geschichte und Kultur auftrat, die sie mit dem methodischen Rüstzeug der Philologie, Historiographie und Philosophie zu erschließen suchte.[1] Die Genese und Entwicklung einer an akademischen Standards ausgerichteten jüdischen Forschung bezeichnete einen Paradigmenwechsel gegenüber den Auslegungstraditionen der Vormoderne, in denen sich das Judentum als sinnvermittelndes Handlungssystem präsentiert hatte, das auf der Grundlage einer ewig gültigen göttlichen Selbstmitteilung fußte. In einem programmatischen Aufsatz hatte Leopold Zunz (1794–1886), profilierter Wegbereiter einer kritischen jüdischen Gelehrsamkeit, bereits 1818 die Parole ausgegeben, dass

> die ganze Litteratur der Juden, in ihrem größten Umfang, als Gegenstand der Forschung aufgestellt [werden solle], ohne uns darum zu kümmern ob sämmtlicher Inhalt auch Norm für unser eigenes Urtheilen sein soll oder kann.[2]

Die Wissenschaft des Judentums sollte also über etwaige sakrale Geltungsansprüche der Texte hinwegsehen, denen vielmehr als Zeugnissen geistiger Produktivität Aufmerksamkeit zuteil wurde. Von dieser Perspektive aus betrachtet, konnte Gott weder Gegenstand der wissenschaftlichen Untersuchung sein noch ihm die Urheberschaft

---

Dieser Aufsatz präsentiert Ergebnisse von Forschungen, die ich 2014–2015 als Charles W. and Sally Rothfield Fellow am Herbert D. Katz Center for Advanced Judaic Studies, University of Pennsylvania, Philadelphia, und 2017–2018 als Fellow am Maimonides Centre for Advanced Studies—Jewish Scepticism an der Universität Hamburg durchführen konnte. Für eine kritische Durchsicht des Textes danke ich Michael A. Meyer, Cincinnati.

1 Zur Wissenschaft des Judentums vgl. z. B. die Sammelbände: Kurt Wilhelm, Hrsg., *Wissenschaft des Judentums im deutschen Sprachbereich. Ein Querschnitt*, 2 Bde. (Tübingen: Mohr, 1967); Julius Carlebach, Hrsg., *Wissenschaft des Judentums. Anfänge der Judaistik in Europa* (Darmstadt: Wissenschaftliche Buchgesellschaft, 1992); Ismar Schorsch, *From Text to Context: The Turn to History in Modern Judaism* (Hanover und London: Brandeis University Press, 1994); Michael Brenner und Stefan Rohrbacher, Hrsg., *Wissenschaft vom Judentum. Annäherungen nach dem Holocaust* (Göttingen: Vandenhoeck & Ruprecht, 2000); Thomas Meyer und Andreas Kilcher, Hrsg., *Die „Wissenschaft des Judentums". Eine Bestandsaufnahme* (Paderborn: Wilhelm Fink, 2015).
2 Leopold Zunz, *Etwas über die rabbinische Literatur, nebst Nachrichten über ein altes bis jetzt ungedrucktes hebräisches Werk* (Berlin: In der Maurerschen Buchhandlung, 1818), 5.

des kulturellen Erbes zugeschrieben werden, das vielmehr als menschlich Gestaltetes und sich in der sowie durch die Geschichte Veränderndes zum Vorschein trat.³

Unbeschadet ihrer betont überlieferungskritischen Ambitionen entwickelte sich die jüdische Forschung aber durchaus nicht als „unabhängig von jüdischen Bindungen zu betreibende, säkulare Disziplin", sondern entfaltete sich im Laufe des zweiten Jahrhundertdrittels vornehmlich als bekenntnisgebundene Wissenschaft, in der das ergebnisoffene Erkenntnisstreben in einem konstanten Spannungsverhältnis zu den systematisch-normativen Ansprüchen der Religionsgemeinschaft verblieb.⁴ Insofern die jüdische Religion sowohl den objektiven als auch den subjektiven Referenzrahmen der Wissenschaft des Judentums bezeichnete, beabsichtigte diese keine antiquarische Vermessung der Vergangenheit, sondern definierte sich als interessengeleitete „jüdische Theologie", als positive Wissenschaft des jüdischen Glaubens in Geschichte und Gegenwart, die an die religiöse Orientierungskrise einer zunehmend mit den Herausforderungen der Moderne konfrontierten Minderheit anknüpfte. Zeugte die *jüdische Wissenschaft*⁵ von der produktiven Teilhabe von Juden an den allgemeinen Wissenschaftsbestrebungen, die sich freilich weitgehend außerhalb der Hochschulen unter staatlicher Aufsicht entfalten musste, so zielte die Wissensproduktion nicht zuletzt auch auf eine defensive Modernisierung jüdischer Religion, die als bürgerliche Konfession ihren Platz in der Gesellschaft einforderte.⁶

Keine Geschichte der Wandlungen der Wissenschaft des Judentums im 19. Jahrhundert ließe sich erzählen, ohne hierin Abraham Geiger (1810–1874) einen prominenten Platz einzuräumen. Dass Geiger, Rabbiner zunächst in Wiesbaden, dann in Breslau, Frankfurt am Main und Berlin, zum Namenspatron des 1999 eröffneten Potsdamer Rabbinerkollegs avancierte, lässt erahnen, welches Ansehen er als Schrittmacher und Meisterdenker einer progressiven Theologie des Judentums noch

---

3 Vgl. dazu z. B. Leon Wieseltier, „Etwas über die jüdische Historik: Leopold Zunz and the Inception of Modern Jewish Historiography", in *History and Theory* 20 (1981): 135–149; Richard S. Sarason, „Rabbinic Literature, Rabbinic History, and Scholarly Thinking: *Wissenschaft* and Beyond", in *Modern Judaism and Historical Consciousness: Identities-Encounters-Perspectives*, hrsg. von Andreas Gotzmann und Christian Wiese (Leiden: Brill, 2007): 93; Nils Roemer, *Jewish Scholarship and Culture in Nineteenth-Century Germany: Between History and Faith* (Madison, Wis.: University of Wisconsin Press, 2005), 24; Christoph Schulte, „Kritik und ‚Aufhebung' der rabbinischen Literatur in der frühen Wissenschaft des Judentums", in *„Im Vollen Licht der Geschichte". Die Wissenschaft des Judentums und die Anfänge der kritischen Koranforschung*, hrsg. von Dirk Hartwig, Walter Homolka, Michael Marx und Angelika Neuwirth (Würzburg: Ergon-Verlag, 2008), 102.

4 Vgl. Christian Wiese, *Wissenschaft des Judentums und protestantische Theologie im wilhelminischen Deutschland. Ein Schrei ins Leere?* (Tübingen: Mohr Siebeck, 1999), XI.

5 Der in der Literatur des 19. Jahrhunderts weit verbreitete Terminus „jüdische Wissenschaft" wird in diesem Aufsatz synonym zum Begriff „Wissenschaft des Judentums" verwendet.

6 Vgl. auch Michael A. Meyer, „Two Persistent Tensions in Wissenschaft des Judentums", in *Modern Judaism* 24.2 (2004): 105–110. Zum Begriff der bürgerlichen Konfession(alität) vgl. Andreas Gotzmann, „Zwischen Nation und Religion: Die deutschen Juden auf der Suche nach einer bürgerlichen Konfessionalität", in *Juden, Bürger, Deutsche. Zur Geschichte von Vielfalt und Differenz 1800–1933*, hrsg. von Andreas Gotzmann, Rainer Liedtke und Till van Rahden (Tübingen: Mohr Siebeck, 2001): 241–261.

heute bzw. heute wieder genießt.[7] Aber bereits liberale Zeitgenossen und die ältere Historiographie erkannten Geiger als Speerspitze einer gelehrten Avantgarde, deren Forschung nicht nur die Vergangenheit abbildete, sondern auch auf eine Neugestaltung der Gegenwart und Zukunft zielte.[8] Dieser Aufsatz will Abraham Geigers Bedeutung als Pionier einer jüdischen Theologie auf wissenschaftlicher Basis nicht grundsätzlich neu bewerten, nimmt dessen Werk aber vor allem im Kontext der Suche nach einer systematischen Theologie in den Blick. Die zeitgenössische Sehnsucht nach einer methodisch reflektierten Darstellung des Glaubensinhalts des Judentums durchzieht die deutsch-jüdische Publizistik des 19. und frühen 20. Jahrhunderts.[9] Die Untersuchung unternimmt es deshalb vor allem, danach zu fragen, inwieweit und in welcher Form Geigers Schriften diesem Bedürfnis nach Orientierung im Glauben Rechnung trugen.

Wie unscharf sich das Bild in dieser Hinsicht bislang präsentiert, veranschaulicht wiederum eine Durchsicht der älteren Geschichtsschreibung. 1910 erschien die als Sammelband konzipierte Biographie Geigers, die sein Sohn Ludwig (1848–1919) unter Mitwirkung namhafter liberaler Rabbiner anlässlich des 100. Geburtstags des Vaters herausgab. Hier unternahm es Heinemann Vogelstein (1841–1911), langjähriger Vorsitzender der Vereinigung der liberalen Rabbiner, in einem mehr als dreißigseitigen Beitrag, Abraham Geiger nicht nur als den „wissenschaftliche[n] Theologe[n] des neunzehnten Jahrhunderts" zu bestätigen, sondern ihm auch als dem „Begründer der systematischen Theologie" ein Denkmal zu setzen. Dass Kaufmann Kohler (1843–1926), Präsident des Hebrew Union College in Cincinnati (Ohio), wenige Monate zuvor seinen *Grundriss einer systematischen Theologie des Judentums auf geschichtlicher Grundlage* publiziert hatte, die Vogelstein zudem als erste „zusammenhängende, von einem jüdischen Gelehrten bearbeitete Darstellung des Glaubensinhaltes der jüdischen Religion" würdigte, liefert aber bereits Anhaltspunkte, dass Geigers Beitrag zur

---

[7] Informationen zum Abraham Geiger Kolleg an der Universität Potsdam: http://www.abraham-geiger-kolleg.de (Datum); siehe auch Jakob J. Petuchowski, Hrsg., *New Perspectives on Abraham Geiger, An HUC-JIR Symposium* (New York: Ktav Publishing House, 1975); Christian Wiese, Walter Homolka und Thomas Brechenmacher, Hrsg., *Jüdische Existenz in der Moderne. Abraham Geiger und die Wissenschaft des Judentums* (Berlin und Boston: de Gruyter, 2013).

[8] Sigismund Stern, *Geschichte des Judenthums von Mendelssohn bis auf die Gegenwart. Nebst einer einleitenden Überschau der älteren Religions- und Kulturgeschichte* (Frankfurt am Main: Rütter, 1857), 232; Leopold Löw, „Literarische Anzeige zu Geigers Urschrift", in *Ben Chananja* 1 (1858): 93 f.; Emanuel Schreiber, *Abraham Geiger als Reformator des Judenthums* (Loebau: R. Skrezeczek, 1879); „Rede des Dozenten Dr. Ismar Elbogen", aus „Reden bei der Abraham Geiger-Feier der Lehranstalt für die Wissenschaft des Judentums am 22. Mai 1910", in *Neunundzwanzigster Bericht der Lehranstalt für die Lehranstalt für die Wissenschaft des Judentums in Berlin* (Berlin: H. Itzkowski, 1911): 54; Caesar Seligmann, *Geschichte der jüdischen Reformbewegung von Mendelssohn bis zur Gegenwart* (Frankfurt am Main: Kauffmann, 1922), 91–94; vgl. außerdem Wiese, Hrsg., *Jüdische Existenz in der Moderne*; Imke Stallmann, *Abraham Geigers Wissenschaftsverständnis. Eine Studie zur jüdischen Rezeption von Friedrich Schleiermachers Theologiebegriff* (Frankfurt am Main: Lang, 2013).

[9] Vgl. Hans-Joachim Schoeps, *Jüdischer Glaube in dieser Zeit. Prolegomena zur Grundlegung einer systematischen Theologie des Judentums* (Berlin: Philo Verlag, 1932).

systematischen Theologie sich einer pauschalisierenden Einordnung entzog.[10] Dass es eben nicht möglich war, Texte zu benennen, in denen schon Geiger eine umfassende Glaubens- und Sittenlehre des Judentums in geordneter Form präsentiert hätte, musste auch Vogelstein einräumen.[11]

Auch ein Blick auf seinen Sohn, Rabbiner Hermann Vogelstein (1870–1942), bestätigt diese Wahrnehmung einer Uneindeutigkeit: Bekräftigte er als Mitarbeiter an der Sammelbiographie noch die Sicht seines Vaters, indem er den Theologen Geiger ebenfalls als Systematiker vorstellte, so fiel sein Urteil 1927 nachdenklicher aus. Mit der Einschätzung, dass eine jüdische Theologie immer noch ein dringendes Desideratum der Gegenwart bezeichne, gab er jetzt der Überzeugung Ausdruck, dass Geiger mit dem Prinzip der geschichtlichen Entwicklung lediglich die methodischen Grundlagen einer wissenschaftlichen Theologie entwickelt, er aber „so recht eigentlich nicht die theologischen Inhalte" herausgearbeitet habe.[12] Seither hat die Geigerforschung diesen Faden nicht wieder aufgenommen. Es lohnt sich aber, der Ambivalenz in Geigers Oeuvre nachzuspüren, zumal, wenn man vermutet, dass sie nicht dem Zufall geschuldet ist, sondern sich aus dem religiösen Weltbild herleiten lässt und als spezifische Antwort des Theologen Geiger auf die Moderne zu verstehen ist.[13] Es gilt mithin sowohl danach zu fragen, welche Funktion und Bedeutung Abraham Geiger der systematischen Theologie zumaß, als auch zu untersuchen, welchen Platz diese Disziplin in seiner eigenen Forschungsagenda einnahm, um „die jüdische Welt sich selbst vorstellig zu machen" (Eduard Gans).

---

10 Heynemann [sic] Vogelstein, „Systematische Theologie", in *Abraham Geiger. Leben und Lebenswerk*, hrsg. von Ludwig Geiger (Berlin: Reimer, 1910), 243–276; vgl. Kaufmann Kohler, *Grundriss einer systematischen Theologie des Judentums auf geschichtlicher Grundlage* (Leipzig: Fock, 1910); englisch: *Jewish Theology. Systematically and Historically Considered* (New York: Macmillan, 1918).
11 Dass es Rabbiner Ludwig Philippson (1811–1889) war, der anknüpfend an die Offenbarungstexte sowie auf der Grundlage der Geschichte Glaube und Ethik des Judentums für ein gebildetes bürgerliches Publikum systematisch zusammenfasste, ist in der jüdischen Geschichtsschreibung bislang noch nicht ausreichend gewürdigt worden; siehe Ludwig Philippson, Jüdische Religionslehre, 3 Bde. (Leipzig: Baumgärtner, 1861–1865); vgl. „Rede des Dozenten Dr. I. Elbogen bei der Ludwig Philippson-Feier der Lehranstalt für die Wissenschaft des Judentums am 8. Januar 1912", in Dreissigster Bericht der Lehranstalt für die Wissenschaft des Judentums (Berlin: H. Itzkowski, 1912), 63; Andreas Brämer, „Überlegungen zur Gebietsmarkierung der Wissenschaft des Judentums—Das Beispiel Ludwig Philippson als zentrale Randfigur (1811–1889)", in *Judaica* 74.1–2 (2018): 1–22.
12 Hermann Vogelstein, „Der Theologe. Einleitung", in *Abraham Geiger*, hrsg. von Geiger, 235; idem, „Gotteserkenntnis. Eine theologische Skizze", in *Festschrift zum 70. Geburtstage von Moritz Schaefer. Zum 21. Mai 1927 herausgegeben von Freunden und Schülern* (Berlin: Philo-Verlag, 1927): 258. Es sei an dieser Stelle auch angemerkt, dass der Religionshistoriker Hans-Joachim Schoeps (1909–1980) in seiner Dissertation *Jüdischer Glaube in dieser Zeit* Abraham Geiger unerwähnt lässt.
13 Vgl. Michael A. Meyer, *Antwort auf die Moderne. Geschichte der Reformbewegung im Judentum* (Wien, Köln und Weimar: Böhlau, 2000); Zur Vernachlässigung der Metaphysik durch die Wissenschaft des Judentums vgl. Zeev Falk, „Jüdisches Lernen und die Wissenschaft des Judentums", in *Judentum im deutschen Sprachraum*, hrsg. von Karl E. Grözinger (Frankfurt am Main: Suhrkamp, 1991): 350.

I

Die zeitgenössischen Benennungen *Wissenschaft des Judentums*[14] oder *jüdische Wissenschaft* suggerieren zunächst eine homogene Geschlossenheit, die dem methodischen und konzeptuellen Facettenreichtum der Disziplin nicht ausreichend Rechnung trägt. Das verdeutlichen die Entwicklungen insbesondere im zweiten Drittel des 19. Jahrhunderts, als sich die jüdische Forschungslandschaft signifikant vervielfältigte und nicht zuletzt Rabbiner mit Universitätsbildung mit wichtigen philologischen, historischen und philosophischen Arbeiten auf den Plan traten. Abraham Geiger beanspruchte bereits in jungen Jahren einen Platz in der ersten Reihe dieser neuen Gelehrtengeneration, den er zeitlebens mit intellektueller Brillanz ebenso wie mit großem Selbstbewusstsein zu verteidigen wusste.[15] Gegen den Begriff „Wissenschaft des Judentums" brachte Geiger keine grundsätzlichen Einwände vor, doch bevorzugte er im Grunde das Etikett „jüdische Theologie", um die eigene Forschung schlagwortartig zu beschreiben.[16]

Nähert man sich Geigers Leitbild einer wissenschaftlichen Theologie in Abgrenzung von anderen Lesarten jüdischer Wissenschaft, dann ist es zunächst hilfreich, dessen zum Teil sachliche, zum Teil aber auch polemische Auseinandersetzung mit dem zeitgenössischen Schrifttum zu beleuchten. Denn Geiger kommentierte die jüdische Literatur seiner Gegenwart mit spitzer Feder, die auch vor Freunden und Vertrauten nicht Halt machte, wenn es galt, sein Plädoyer für ein Forschungsethos auf der Höhe der Zeit zu untermauern. Besonders aufschlussreich ist seine ambivalente Haltung zu Leopold Zunz, dessen kompromissloses Wissenschaftsideal ja ebenfalls schulbildend wirkte und Generationen von Gelehrten als Inspiration diente. Geiger war mit Zunz erstmalig als 20jähriger Student in Kontakt getreten, der sich dann über Jahrzehnte fortsetzen sollte und neben dem brieflichen Austausch auch persönliche Besuche einschloss. Unbeschadet seiner Wertschätzung für Zunz, der ihm ja die Er-

---

[14] Der Begriff „Wissenschaft des Judenthums" war erstmals im Kreis des 1819 gegründeten Berliner „Vereins für Cultur und Wissenschaft der Juden" aufgetaucht, der 1822–23 auch die von Leopold Zunz redigierte *Zeitschrift für die Wissenschaft des Judenthums* herausgab; siehe dazu z. B. Ismar Schorsch, „Breakthrough into the Past: The Verein für Cultur und Wissenschaft der Juden", in *Leo Baeck Institute Year Book* 33 (1988): 3–28; Siegfried Ucko, „Geistesgeschichtliche Grundlagen der Wissenschaft des Judentums (Motive des Kulturvereins vom Jahre 1819)", in *Zeitschrift für die Geschichte der Juden in Deutschland* 5 (1935): 1–34.

[15] Vgl. Wiese, Homolka und Brechenmacher, Hrsg., *Jüdische Existenz in der Moderne*.

[16] Vgl. etwa Abraham Geiger, „Einleitung in das Studium der jüdischen Theologie (1849)", in *Abraham Geiger's Nachgelassene Schriften*, hrsg. von Ludwig Geiger, Bd. 2 (Berlin: Gerschel, 1875), 1–32; idem, „Allgemeine Einleitung in die Wissenschaft des Judenthums", in *ibidem*, 33–245; vgl. außerdem Ismar Elbogen, *Ein Jahrhundert Wissenschaft des Judentums* (Berlin: Philo Verlag, 1922), 40 f.; Stallmann, *Abraham Geigers Wissenschaftsverständnis*; Ismar Elbogen, „Abraham Geiger", in *Jahrbuch für Jüdische Geschichte und Literatur* Nr. 14 (1911): 75; Karl Erich Grözinger, *Jüdisches Denken. Theologie–Philosophie–Mystik, Bd. 3: Von der Religionskritik der Renaissance zu Orthodoxie und Reform im 19. Jahrhundert* (Frankfurt und New York: Campus-Verlag, 2009), 578–616.

fahrung eines Vierteljahrhunderts voraushatte, betrachtete er dessen umfangreiches Werk bereits früh mit einer kritischen Distanz, die auf den unterschiedlichen Forschungsperspektiven gründete. Seine eigene Forschung schlug eine neue Richtung ein, die Abhilfe versprach gegen jene Unzulänglichkeiten, die Geiger der bisherigen Forschung anlastete.[17]

Im Zentrum der Kritik an Zunz stand dessen dezidiertes Desinteresse an theologischen Inhalten. Was war darunter zu verstehen? Wie Geiger bereits 1836 in einem Privatschreiben an den Mathematiker Moritz Abraham Stern (1807–1894) bemängelte, vertrat Zunz eine Gelehrsamkeit, die der inneren Entwicklung des jüdischen Glaubens zu wenig Aufmerksamkeit schenkte.[18] Damit zusammen hing auch seine Beobachtung, dass Zunz das jüdische Schrifttum nicht als eine religiöse, sondern als eine Volksliteratur präsentierte. Zunz' Version einer Wissenschaft des Judentums beschränke sich demnach auf eine bloße Altertumswissenschaft, die zwar die Erscheinungen der Zeiten in den Blick rücke, jedoch weder ein Verständnis der Vergangenheit selbst schaffe noch die Frage nach deren Bedeutung in ihrem Bezug zur Gegenwart stelle. Von diesem Blickwinkel aus betrachtet lieferten Zunz und seinesgleichen lediglich akribisch gefertigte Bausteine zu einer Geschichte des Judentums, deren leitende Ideen sie aber außer Acht ließen.[19]

Vehementen Einspruch erhob Geiger vor allem gegen das viel diskutierte Buch *Zur Geschichte und Literatur*, eine Sammlung von Abhandlungen zur jüdischen Geschichte, Literaturgeschichte und Bibliographie, die Zunz 1845 im Druck vorlegte. In dem radikalen Reformblatt *Der Israelit des neunzehnten Jahrhunderts*, das der sächsisch-weimarische Landrabbiner Mendel Hess (1807–1871) herausgab, platzierte Geiger eine mehrteilige Besprechung der Veröffentlichung. Wer Geigers Nichteinverständnis mit Zunz' Wissenschaftsideal verstehen will, muss sich auch in Erinnerung rufen, dass Zunz ausdrücklich die Maxime ausgegeben hatte, die jüdische Wissenschaft müsse sich „zunächst von der Theologie emanzipieren und zur geschichtlichen Anschauung erheben", d. h. von einer religiösen Verwertung der Forschung absehen, die er insbesondere dem Reformjudentum anlastete.[20] Dass sich Geiger am Schluss dieser Rezension als Zunz' „treu aufhorchenden und begierig lauschenden Schüler"

---

[17] Geiger, *Abraham Geiger*, 16 f.; Ismar Schorsch, *Leopold Zunz: Creativity in Adversity* (Philadelphia: University of Pennsylvania Press, 2016), passim; Michael A. Meyer, „Jewish Religious Reform and Wissenschaft des Judentums. The Positions of Zunz, Geiger and Frankel", in *Leo Baeck Institute Year Book* 16 (1971): 19–32.

[18] „Abraham Geiger an Leopold Zunz, 31. März 1836", in *Abraham Geiger's Leben in Briefen*, hrsg. von Ludwig Geiger (Berlin: Gerschel, 1878): 90.

[19] Abraham Geiger, „Literarisch-kritische Uebersicht", in *Wissenschaftliche Zeitschrift für jüdische Theologie* 6 (1847): 95; vgl. auch idem, „Jüdische Zeitschriften", in *Wissenschaftliche Zeitschrift für jüdische Theologie* 4 (1839): 288 f.; idem, „Einleitung in das Studium der jüdischen Theologie", 27; idem, „Jüdische Geschichte von 1830 bis zur Gegenwart (Vorlesungen gehalten zu Breslau, Winter 1849/50)", in *Abraham Geiger's Nachgelassene Schriften*, hrsg. von Geiger, Bd. 2, 261.

[20] Dass auch Leopold Zunz eine Forschung betrieb, die von religiösen Interessen geleitet wurde, kann hier nur angedeutet, aber nicht ausführlich erläutert werden; siehe dazu Schorsch, Leopold Zunz.

bekannte, mochte sich auf dessen philologische Sorgfalt beziehen. Als Anschauungsobjekt diente ihm die von Zunz dargebotene Forschung aber zugleich, um sie als radikales wissenschaftliches Gegenmodell zu entwerten: In ihrer positivistischen Fixierung produzierte sie zwar überprüfbares Wissen, die den Phänomenen der jüdischen Vergangenheit als solchen bereits von vornherein Bedeutung zumaß, ohne die Fakten auch kritisch auf ihre religiöse Gegenwartsrelevanz hin zu befragen.[21]

II

Es bleibt unklar, warum die Rezension nicht in der *Wissenschaftlichen Zeitschrift für jüdische Theologie* abgedruckt wurde, die Geiger seit 1835 („in Verbindung mit einem Vereine jüdischer Gelehrter") herausgab und idealerweise als Forum einer von zeitgenössischen religiösen Erkenntnisinteressen geleiteten Forschung dienen sollte.[22] Das Periodikum, das – teilweise unregelmäßig – bis 1847 erschien, brachte insbesondere Studien zu historischen und philosophischen Themenfeldern sowie zeitgenössische Reflexionen. Beiträge zu einer Glaubenslehre des Judentums sind in den insgesamt sechs Jahrgängen allerdings fast gar nicht zu finden. Immerhin gelang es dem Pädagogen Michael Creizenach (1789–1842) sowie dem Orientalisten Joseph Dernburg (Dérenbourg, 1811–1895), mit Geigers Billigung zaghafte Versuche einer systematischen Annäherung an die Grundlehren der jüdischen Religion unterzubringen.[23] Doch im Allgemeinen ging es in dem Periodikum nicht darum, Aussagen

---

21 Abraham Geiger „Recension. Zur Geschichte und Literatur. Von Dr. Zunz. Erster Band. Berlin, Veit & Comp. 1845. VIII u. 607 S. gr. 8., S."; in *Literaturblatt zum Israeliten des neunzehnten Jahrhunderts* 1 (1846): 82; vgl. „Geiger an Zunz, 26. Dezember 1845", in *Abraham Geiger's Leben in Briefen*, hrsg. von Geiger, 186; Leopold Zunz, „Zur Geschichte und Literatur", in idem, *Gesammelte Schriften*, Bd. 1 (Berlin: Gerschel, 1875): 57; Michael A. Meyer, „Abraham Geiger's Historical Judaism", in *New Perspectives on Abraham Geiger*, hrsg. von Petuchowski, 10 f.; Kerstin von der Krone, *Wissenschaft in Öffentlichkeit. Die Wissenschaft des Judentums und ihre Zeitschriften* (Berlin u. a.: de Gruyter, 2012), 173, Anm. 33; Ismar Schorsch, „Ideology and History in the Age of Emancipation", in idem, *From Text to Context*, 276–278; und vor allem idem, *Leopold Zunz*, 131–141.
22 Barbara Suchy, „Die jüdischen wissenschaftlichen Zeitschriften in Deutschland von den Anfängen bis zum Ersten Weltkrieg. Ein Überblick", in *Wissenschaft des Judentums*, hrsg. von Carlebach, 184–186; von der Krone, *Wissenschaft in Öffentlichkeit*, 58–61. Möglicherweise fürchtete Geiger, Zunz als Mitarbeiter an der *Wissenschaftlichen Zeitschrift für jüdische Theologie* zu verlieren. Dieser hatte aber bis dahin ohnehin nur Analekten und kürzere Beiträge geliefert; siehe die Bibliographie des Leopold Zunz Archivs in http://www.jewish-archives.org/nav/classification/11214 (29. Mai 2018); sowie Schorsch, *Leopold Zunz*, 92–94.
23 Michael Creizenach, „Grundlehren der israelitischen Religion", in *Wissenschaftliche Zeitschrift für jüdische Theologie* 1 (1835): 39–51 und 327–339 sowie in *Wissenschaftliche Zeitschrift für jüdische Theologie* 2 (1836): 68–77 und 436–445; Joseph Dernburg, „Das Wesen des Judenthums nach seinen allgemeinsten Grundzügen", in *Wissenschaftliche Zeitschrift für jüdische Theologie* 4 (1839): 12–18; vgl. auch den Brief von A. Geiger an J. Dernburg, vom 10. April 1837, in Ludwig Geiger, Hrsg., „Abraham Geigers Briefe an J. Dérenbourg (1833–1842)", in *Allgemeine Zeitung des Judenthums* 60 (1896): 190.

über Gott oder über jüdische Gotteserfahrungen zu machen. In zahlreichen Aufsätzen unter die Lupe genommen wurden die Religionspraxis und deren Reform („Ueber die synagogische Zulässigkeit und Einrichtung der Confirmation"; „Ueber die Abschaffung bestehender Gebräuche"; „Ueber Trauungen in der Synagoge"; „Ueber die jüdischen Trauergebräuche"; „Ueber die Leviratsehe und die Ceremonie des Schuhausziehens"; „Ueber das Entbehren lederner Schuhe am Versöhnungstage"; „Ueber die jüdischen Fasttage"; „Noch ein Wort über das Haartragen der Frauen"; „Ueber religiöse Trauung"; „Materialien zu einem Commissionsbericht über die Speisegesetze"). Die Stoßrichtung dieser Texte war offensichtlich: „Das Bewußtsein des guten Rechts der Reform", so Geiger im letzten Jahrgang der *Wissenschaftlichen Zeitschrift*, „soll nun auch in die Lebensverhältnisse eindringen und den religiösen Boden umpflügen."[24]

Wichtige Einblicke in seine Agenda gab Abraham Geiger auch in seiner *Einleitung in das Studium der jüdischen Theologie*, die Ludwig Geiger postum edierte. Das Buch beruhte auf dem Manuskript einer Vorlesung, die der Vater 1849 in Breslau vor jüdischen Studenten gehalten hatte. Die „Theologie als jüdische", so stellte dieser hier klar, drehe sich um „die Erkenntnis der religiösen Wahrheiten und des ihnen entsprechenden Lebens nach der Lehre des Judenthums".[25] Der Text erlaubt Rückschlüsse, welche Anregungen der Autor Friedrich Schleiermacher (1768–1834) verdankte, der sich ja wie Geiger gegen die Dichotomie von Religion und Wissenschaft ausgesprochen hatte. Die Theologie bezeichnete demnach eine handlungsleitende Disziplin, die ihre funktionale Einheit aus dem Bezug auf das Betätigungsfeld der religiösen Leitung bezog. Wenn Geiger der jüdischen Theologie mit Philosophie, Geschichte und Praxis drei verbundene Gebiete zuwies, übertrug er wiederum Überlegungen des protestantischen Kirchenlehrers, dessen *Kurze Darstellung des theologischen Studiums* ihm unzweifelhaft vertraut war.[26]

---

[24] Abraham Geiger, „Die religiösen Thaten der Gegenwart im Judenthume", in *Wissenschaftliche Zeitschrift für jüdische Theologie* 6 (1847): 1.
[25] Geiger, „Einleitung in das Studium der jüdischen Theologie", 4.
[26] Vgl. Friedrich Schleiermacher, *Kurze Darstellung des theologischen Studiums zum Behuf einleitender Vorlesungen. Zweite, umgearbeitete Ausgabe* (Berlin: Reimer, 1830); Christoph Schwöbel, Art. „Theologie", in *Religion in Geschichte und Gegenwart*, hrsg. von Hans Dieter Betz, Bd. 8, 4. Aufl. (Tübingen: Mohr Siebeck, 2008): 265 und 302f.; Zu Geiger und Schleiermacher siehe z.B. Stallmann, *Abraham Geigers Wissenschaftsverständnis*; Carsten Wilke, „Abraham Geigers Bildungsutopie einer jüdisch-theologischen Fakultät", in *Jüdische Existenz in der Moderne*, hrsg. von Wiese, Homolka und Brechenmacher, 380; Grözinger, *Jüdisches Denken*, 589f.; sowie Ulrich Steuer, *Schleiermachers Religionsphilosophie in ihrer systematischen und historischen Bedeutung für die jüdische Religionsphilosophie* (Köln: Typoskript Dissertation, 1969), 122–131; Vermutungen über den Einfluss Schleiermachers auf Geiger hatte bereits 1843 der preußische Kultusminister Johann Albrecht Friedrich von Eichhorn geäußert, als er in dem Streit um die Berufung Geigers nach Breslau diesem eine Audienz gewährte; vgl. *Abraham Geiger's Leben in Briefen*, hrsg. von Geiger, 121f.; Emanuel Schreiber, *Abraham Geiger als Reformator des Judenthums* (Loebau/Westpreußen: Richard Skrzeczek, 1879), 105.

Den Vorwurf, Schleiermacher auch inhaltlich kopiert und auf diese Weise quasi christliche Ideen auf das Judentum übertragen zu haben, wusste Geiger freilich weit von sich zu weisen.[27] Im Zusammenhang mit der zentralen Fragestellung dieses Aufsatzes ist jedenfalls eine Beobachtung frappierend: Während Schleiermacher seine Stellung als wichtigster evangelischer Theologe des 19. Jahrhunderts auch durch eine zweibändige Glaubenslehre des evangelischen Christentums untermauerte, liegt von Geiger eben keine Darstellung der jüdischen Glaubensinhalte in zusammenhängender Form vor.[28] Auch seine *Einleitung* sparte dieses Themenfeld komplett aus.[29]

III

Die private Korrespondenz, deren vertrauliche Diktion ja im Regelfall nicht auf ein öffentliches Publikum zielte, liefert erste Anhaltspunkte über Gründe einer skeptischen Zurückhaltung, mit der sich Geiger über das eigene religiöse Weltbild ausließ. Aus seinen Briefen an den frühen Weggefährten Joseph Dernburg entsteht das Bild eines noch jungen Rabbiners, der seit 1832 in Wiesbaden bereits die Verantwortung für eine eigene Gemeinde trug, der aber im Angesicht einer desorientierenden Moderne den eigenen Glauben erst selbst noch befestigen musste. Kritisierte er 1833 das zeitgenössische Judentum zunächst als abstrakte Religion, der es an erbaulichen Ideen mangele und in der Gott den Menschen zu fern stehe, wusste er sich drei Jahre später mit jenem versöhnt. Enthusiastisch berichtete er, inzwischen ein Judentum gefunden zu haben, das ihn befriedige,

> einen Glauben, dessen Grundlagen das Vertrauen auf einen Weltenlenker und die an uns gestellte Anforderung der Gerechtigkeit und Milde ist, der sich in Werken die diesem Anspruche genügen, ausspricht und mit erhebenden Formen zur Erweckung dieser Gesinnungen umgiebt.[30]

---

27 Vgl. Abraham Geiger, „Offenes Sendschreiben an Herrn Professor Dr. H.A. Holtzmann", in idem, *Das Judenthum und seine Geschichte von der Zerstörung des zweiten Tempels bis zum Ende des zwölften Jahrhunderts* (Breslau: Schletter, 1865): 190–193; idem, „Allgemeine Einleitung in die Wissenschaft des Judenthums", 63.
28 Friedrich Schleiermacher, *Der christliche Glaube nach den Grundsätzen der evangelischen Kirche im Zusammenhange dargestellt*, 2 Bde., 2. Ausgabe (Berlin: Reimer, 1830/31).
29 Geiger erwähnt allerdings Metaphysik und Ethik als Disziplinen einer Religionsphilosophie, die der jüdische Theologe nicht völlig voraussetzungslos betreiben kann; siehe Geiger, „Einleitung in das Studium der jüdischen Theologie", 7 f.; siehe außerdem Geigers kritische Zeilen zur Schleiermacherrezeption in *Jüdische Zeitschrift für Wissenschaft und Leben* 7 (1869): 211–215; dort bezieht sich Geiger auch auf Schleiermachers kritisches Verhältnis zum Judentum; siehe dazu auch Matthias Blum, „Ich wäre ein Judenfeind". Zum Antijudaismus in Friedrich Schleiermachers Theologie und Pädagogik (Köln, Weimar und Wien: Böhlau, 2010).
30 „A. Geiger an J. Dernburg, 23. Februar 1836", in Geiger, „Abraham Geigers Briefe", 115; vgl. „A. Geiger an J. Dernburg, 15. Juli 1833", in *ibidem*, 91; vgl. Schleiermacher, *Der christliche Glaube*, § 4.

Auch in späteren Bekenntnissen, in denen der ethische Monotheismus als Gewissheit aus der Innerlichkeit des Individuums hervorging, machte Schleiermacher seinen Einfluss geltend. Gegenüber Moritz Abraham Stern distanzierte sich Geiger 1843 ausdrücklich von den Ideen des Pantheismus, um stattdessen – in deutlicher Anlehnung an Schleiermachers Deutung der Frömmigkeit als Gefühl der „schlechthinnigen Abhängigkeit" – zu bekräftigen,

> dass ich einen Ueberschuss über die Immanenz statuire, dass ich ein Unbegreifliches über uns anerkenne, dass ich dem Gefühle, das sich zum Abhängigkeitsbewusstsein steigert, sein Recht einräume und nicht verkümmert wissen will, dass ich die Leugnung der Religion als einen Irrthum, als einen gefährlichen Irrthum verwerfe.[31]

Unbeschadet solcher Konfessionen widerstrebte es Geiger aber selbst im Austausch mit engen Vertrauten, ausführlichere Auskünfte über sein Credo zu erteilen. Dass Stern Geiger auch in späteren Jahren hartnäckig über dessen Glauben befragte, illustriert zunächst, dass er in Geigers Schriften keinen hinreichenden Aufschluss über diesen Gegenstand zu finden glaubte. Gegenüber seinem Freund bekannte sich Geiger im Sommer 1858 zu einem Theismus, für den er aber als Privatmeinung nicht öffentlich Partei ergreifen wollte. Stern freilich gab sich mit dieser Antwort noch nicht zufrieden, möglicherweise, weil Geiger es zu vermeiden gewusst hatte, Gott als solchen konkret zu benennen. Ungehalten über Sterns Beharrlichkeit, zögerte Geiger monatelang, bis er endlich doch eine weitere Antwort verfasste, in der er nun auch einem personifizierten Gottesgedanken Platz einräumte:

> Es ist die unerquickliche Discussion über Gott, auf der Du beharrst. Ich trage seine Ahnung in mir; mein eigner Geist, dessen volle selbständige, vom Körper unabhängige, wenn auch gegenwärtig mit ihm verbundene Persönlichkeit mir eine gewisse Thatsache innerer Erfahrung ist, bürgt mir für die Existenz eines gleichfalls persönlichen Allgeistes, eines Gottes, der wie es das Bedürfniss, das höchste Bedürfniss des Geistes, liebend überströmt. In dieser Ahnung liegt freilich nicht der volle, mit aller Klarheit umschriebene Gedanke, es liegt eine gewisse, sehr wohlthuende Poesie darin, eine Poesie jedoch, deren beraubt die Welt nicht minder als ich selber gar nüchtern würde. [...] Dass bei solcher vollen Anerkennung eines persönlichen Gottes und seines eingreifenden Waltens, aber als eines Geistes, der die vorigen, auch in unserem Geiste sich offenbarenden Gesetze des Geistes in sich trägt, dass es dabei – sage ich – an einzelnen vermenschlichenden Ausdrücken nicht fehlen wird – zumal in Stimmungen, wo eine tiefere Anregung das Herz durchwühlt und dieses seinen Ausdruck verlangt –, will ich nicht in Abrede stellen; es wird jedoch kaum einer Nachsicht dazu bedürfen, solche Ausdrücke entschuldbar zu finden. Lass uns daher über diese philosophische Discussion hinwegkommen. Soweit ich vordringen kann, thue ich es mit aller Unbefangenheit; über meinen eigenen Geist hinaus und gar über die Wurzel hinaus, aus der er Nahrung zieht, kann ich nicht, da glaube ich es beim freudigen Bewusstsein von dem einen, bei der Verehrung der andern wohl bewenden lassen zu dürfen.[32]

---

[31] „A. Geiger an M.A. Stern, 25. August 1843", in *Abraham Geiger's Leben in Briefen*, hrsg. von Geiger, 167 f.; sowie anonym in *Zur Judenfrage in Deutschland* 2 (1844): 114 f.
[32] „A. Geiger an M.A. Stern, 28. Dezember 1858", in *Abraham Geiger's Leben in Briefen*, hrsg. von Geiger, 229 f.; auch in Geiger, *Abraham Geiger*, 226; Vogelstein, *Systematische Theologie*, 248 f.; vgl. auch

Geigers Widerstreben, detaillierte Angaben über die persönliche religiöse Weltanschauung zu machen, hing folglich weniger mit eigenen Zweifeln zusammen, sondern gründete auf der Einsicht des Unvermögens, Glaubensüberzeugungen als überprüfbare Gewissheiten zu präsentieren. Hier spielte auch eine Rolle, dass Geiger in der Erkenntnis der religiösen Wahrheiten des Judentums als positive Religion nicht eine „Aufgabe des Denkens, der philosophischen Betrachtung" erkennen wollte, sondern sie der Historiographie zuwies, also vornehmlich empirisch aus der Rekonstruktion der Vergangenheit ermitteln zu können glaubte.[33] Als Schriftsteller und Rabbiner sah sich Geiger aber zugleich vor die Aufgabe gestellt, geistliche Orientierung in einer Epoche zu ermöglichen, die eben auch durch eine Vervielfältigung jüdischer religiöser Selbstpositionierungen bestimmt war. Seine Schriften sowohl zur theoretischen als auch zur praktischen Theologie spiegeln dieses Dilemma wider.

IV

Geigers Theologie fußte auf einem romantischen Begriff der Religion, der diese nicht objektiv, also als ein gegebenes System von Wahrheiten, sondern subjektiv, vom Individuum her erklärte. Als anthropologische Konstante bezeichnete Religion ein sowohl ubiquitäres als auch unvergängliches Phänomen. Dem Menschen eigen war demnach eine Doppelnatur, die das Bewusstsein einer höheren Weltordnung und das enthusiastische Streben zur sittlichen Selbstvervollkommnung mit der demütigen Einsicht der eigenen Unvollkommenheit verknüpfte. Das universale Sehnen des Menschen nach dem Unendlichen trotz der Unfähigkeit, das Endliche und Begrenzte zu überwinden, galt Geiger zugleich als Bürgschaft für die Wirklichkeit dieses Strebens, das in den verschiedenen Religionen zugleich unterschiedliche Formen annahm.[34] So wurde der Gottesbeweis quasi aus der Geschichte abgeleitet. Auf die jüdische Religion schauend, bemerkte er:

„A. Geiger an M.A. Stern 9. August 1858", in *Abraham Geiger's Leben in Briefen*, hrsg. von Geiger, 227 f.; siehe außerdem Arnulf von Scheliha, „Schleiermachers Deutung von Judentum und Christentum in der fünften Rede ‚Über die Religion' und ihre Rezeption bei Abraham Geiger", in *Christentum und Judentum. Akten des Internationalen Kongresses der Schleiermacher-Gesellschaft in Halle, März 2009*, hrsg. von Roderich Barth, Ulrich Barth, Claus-Dieter Osthövener (Berlin und Boston: De Gruyter, 2009): 223.
33 Geiger, „Einleitung in das Studium der jüdischen Theologie", 4.
34 Abraham Geiger, *Das Judentum und seine Geschichte. In vierunddreißig Vorlesungen* (Breslau: Jacobsohn, 1910), 9–11; vgl. idem, „Der Mangel an Glaubensinnigkeit in der jetzigen Judenheit. Bedenken eines Laien (1835)", in *Abraham Geiger's Nachgelassene Schriften*, hrsg. von Geiger, Bd. 1, 457; Abraham Geiger, „Abhandlungen aus den Programmen der jüdischen Religionsunterrichtsanstalt in Breslau 1844–1863", in *ibidem*, 349; siehe auch Karl E. Grözinger, „Abraham Geigers theologische Wende vor dem Hintergrund der neuzeitlichen Debatte um Religion und Vernunft", in *Jüdische Existenz in der Moderne*, hrsg. von Wiese, Homolka und Brechenmacher, 32f.

> Das Judenthum wird eine [...] kritische Prüfung auch nicht zu scheuen haben, denn wenn wir auch nicht den Schleiermacher'schen Grundsatz in seiner vollen Ausdrucksweise annehmen können, dass eine vorhandene einflussreiche Stiftung für die Dignität des Stifters oder gar für den unmittelbaren göttlichen Ursprung zeugt, so müssen wir doch eingestehen, dass die Thatsache einer weltgeschichtlichen Institution, die ihren Einfluss gebieterisch ausübt, die Bürgschaft gibt für die Macht des Gedankens, der in ihr waltet, für die Wahrheit der Idee, die sie trägt und Geschichte und Sage erzeugt hat.[35]

Die Pluralisierung der religiösen Ideologien im deutschen Judentum des 19. Jahrhunderts lässt sich nicht zuletzt auch als Konsequenz der Suche nach zeitgemäßen Ausdrucksformen gelebter Frömmigkeit sowohl im Kultus als auch im Alltagsleben der Gläubigen beschreiben. Die Vielfalt im Glauben gründete aber auch auf unterschiedlichen Auslegungen von Offenbarung und Tradition als konstituierenden Faktoren des Judentums. Abraham Geiger hatte bereits 1835, im ersten Jahrgang seiner *Wissenschaftliche Zeitschrift für jüdische Theologie*, angemahnt, dass die jüdische Literatur sich dringend diesen Hauptfragen zuwenden müsse, um sie sowohl historisch als auch philosophisch zu erörtern. Geigers Theologie ist denn auch ohne seine eigene Deutung des Offenbarungsgeschehens gar nicht zu verstehen. Dabei sollte es ihm gelingen, das Judentum als positive Religion zu präsentieren, in der das allgemeinmenschliche „Ahnen" einer höheren Macht in einen spezifischen religionshistorischen Kontext gestellt wurde, ohne sich jedoch auf ein konkretes Bild von Gottes eingreifendem Walten zu beziehen.[36]

Geiger konnte und wollte keine voraussetzungslose jüdische Wissenschaft betreiben, die ja die Religion sowohl zum ausschließlichen Gegenstand der Forschung machte als auch eine religiöse Agenda zur Gestaltung der Gegenwart und Zukunft verfolgte. Der Offenbarungsglaube, den er als *conditio sine qua non* der theologischen Forschung formulierte, unterschied sich freilich signifikant von traditionellen Auslegungen, indem er das Offenbarungsgeschehen weniger als göttliche Intervention, herablassende Zuwendung, und Übergabe von Weisungen und Belehrungen schilderte, die mit einer sinnlichen Wahrnehmung der Empfänger einhergingen, sondern es als einen inneren Vorgang plötzlicher Einsicht ewiger Wahrheiten beschrieb, die also letztlich vom Menschen selbst ausging.[37] Die besondere weltgeschichtliche

---

[35] Abraham Geiger, „Allgemeine Einleitung in die Wissenschaft des Judenthums", 62.
[36] Abraham Geiger, „Heuchelei, die erste Anforderung an den jungen Rabbiner unserer Zeit", in *Wissenschaftliche Zeitschrift für jüdische Theologie* 1 (1835): 299; vgl. Nathan Rotenstreich, *Tradition and Reality: The Impact of History on Modern Jewish Thought* (New York: Random House, 1972), 7–18; Gershom Scholem, *Über einige Grundbegriffe des Judentums* (Frankfurt am Main: Suhrkamp 1970), 90–105; Michael A. Meyer, „Ob Schrift? Ob Geist?—Die Offenbarungsfrage im deutschen Judentum des neunzehnten Jahrhunderts", in *Offenbarung im jüdischen und christlichen Glaubensverständnis*, hrsg. von Jacob J. Petuchowski und Walter Strolz (Freiburg, Basel und Wien: Herder, 1981): 175–179; Grözinger, *Jüdisches Denken*, Bd. 3, 593–604.
[37] Allerdings deutete Geiger mehrfach an, dass sein Offenbarungsglaube partiell an die jüdische Philosophie des Mittelalters anknüpfe, also etwa bei Jehuda Halevi und Moses ben Maimon; vgl. Geiger, *Das Judentum und seine Geschichte*, 37 und 319 f.

Stellung des Judentums hing nun mit dem religiösen Genie der Juden zusammen, denen als Volk die besondere Befähigung eigen war, neue intellektuelle Anschauungen im Sinne einer Offenbarung zu gewinnen. Bezeichnete dieses Genie zunächst eine kollektive geistige Anlage in Form einer besonderen Empfänglichkeit, so blieben der Gesamtheit dennoch konkrete Offenbarungserfahrungen verwehrt. Individuelle Träger und Verkünder der „höheren Erleuchtung" waren vielmehr die Propheten, deren geläutertes religiöses Bewusstsein mit einer klareren sittlichen Anschauung einherging und sich, verdichtet zur Lehre des Judentums, allmählich im Volk Geltung verschaffte.[38]

Wusste Geiger bereits die Offenbarung als dynamisches menschlich-geistiges Schöpfungswerk, wenngleich göttlicher Abstammung, auch in einen geschichtlichen Bezugsrahmen zu stellen, so endete diese formative Epoche mit der Rückkehr der Juden aus dem babylonischen Exil. Der in der Offenbarung sich ausprägende Geist sei aber, so Geiger, in veränderter Form auch in der Tradition weiter wirksam. Analog zur Natur, wo die gestaltende Kraft Gottes nach Vollendung des Schöpfungswerks sowohl erhaltend als auch als Evolution nachwirke, entfalte sich im Geistesleben die Tradition ebenfalls als Kraft der Entwicklung. Als Ausfluss des göttlichen Geistes wirke sie in der Gesamtheit, erwähle sich aber wiederum besondere Träger, die das Judentum in ihre jeweilige Gegenwart übersetzten und auf diese Weise dessen Lebensfähigkeit bewahrten. Nach Geigerscher Lesart war die jüdische Wissenschaft der Gegenwart nicht nur vor die Aufgabe gestellt, in der Überlieferung die religiöse Wahrheit in ihrer jeweils historischen Fassung und Entwicklung zu erkennen, sondern aus diesem Wissen und der Erkenntnis der Gegenwart auch Konsequenzen für die Fortbildung des Judentums zu ziehen. Als Fortsetzung der Tradition erhielt die wissenschaftliche Theologie damit eine zusätzliche religiöse Aufladung.[39]

V

Signifikant für Geigers Theologie war deren konfrontativer Gestus, der aus dem Widerspruch erwuchs und diesen sowohl ausdrücklich als auch implizit formulierte. In der Auseinandersetzung mit der Altertumswissenschaft und protestantischen Theo-

---

[38] Wie genau nun sich diese „Berührung der menschlichen Vernunft mit dem tiefen Urgrund aller Dinge" vollzogen hatte, wusste auch Geiger nicht völlig konsistent zu erklären; siehe Geiger, „Einleitung in das Studium der jüdischen Theologie", 6; idem, „Literaturbriefe aus dem Jahre 1853", in *Abraham Geiger's Nachgelassene Schriften*, hrsg. von Geiger, Bd. 2, 331; idem, *Das Judentum und seine Geschichte*, 36–38; vgl. Harvey Hill, „The Science of Reform: Abraham Geiger and the Wissenschaft des Judentum (sic)", in *Modern Judaism* 27.3 (2007): 332; Vogelstein, *Systematische Theologie*, 251–253.
[39] Abraham Geiger, „Der Boden zur Aussaat", in *Jüdische Zeitschrift für Wissenschaft und Leben* 1 (1862): 6 f.; idem, „Nothwendigkeit und Maass einer Reform des jüdischen Gottesdienstes. Ein Wort zur Verständigung", in *Abraham Geiger's Nachgelassene Schriften*, hrsg. von Geiger, Bd. 1, 203; idem, *Das Judentum und seine Geschichte*, 75 f.

logie konzipierte er seine religionshistorischen Forschungen als *counter history*, die er dazu benutzte, um die Deutungshoheit über wichtige Kapitel der jüdischen Vergangenheit zurückzugewinnen.[40] Seine wissenschaftliche Arbeit richtete sich aber noch mehr gegen den Hegemonialanspruch konservativer Strömungen des zeitgenössischen Judentums, deren theologische Gewissheiten er mit der und durch die Geschichte zu erschüttern suchte. Im Zentrum dieser teilweise auch polemisch ausgefochtenen Konflikte stand die Widerlegung des sakralen Statusanspruchs zentraler jüdischer Texte. An Dernburg schrieb Geiger im November 1836 die kämpferischen Zeilen:

> Der Talmud muß weg, die Bibel, jener Komplex von meistens so schönen und erhabenen, vielleicht den erhabendsten menschlichen Büchern, muß als Göttliches weg. [...] Um Himmelswillen, wie kann diese Lügenhaftigkeit fortdauern, immer und ewig auf den Kanzeln die Geschichten der Bibel als wahre Begebenheiten zu erklären, und an sie als an die höchsten Weltereignisse, an sie, die wir für uns in das Reich der Sage versetzt haben, Lehren anzuknüpfen und, wenn auch weiter gar nichts, Texte aus ihr zu entlehnen? Wie lange noch soll jene Verdrehung des kindlichen Geistes mit jenen Geschichten, die den natürlichen Sinn des zarten Menschenkindes entstellen, fortdauern? Wie dies wohl zu ändern? Je nun, eben durch das Hintreiben in die Enge, so daß es nicht mehr stattfinden kann, dadurch, daß man sich und anderen diesen Widerspruch aufdeckt, dadurch, daß man in alle Schlupfwinkel den Ausflüchte Suchenden verfolgt und so endlich den großartigen Einsturz mit bewirkt, der eine alte Welt unter seinen Trümmern begräbt, und eine neue uns öffnet.[41]

Die supranaturalistische Auffassung, dass es sich bei der schriftlichen und mündlichen Tora um Zeugnisse einer göttlichen Offenbarung ohne Verfallsdatum handelte, konnte in einer Theologie, die das Entwicklungsprinzip zur obersten Maxime erhob, keinen Platz haben. Die hebräische Bibel bezeichnete also die „Schriften der heiligen Gemeinschaft, der Heiligkeit oder des Heiligthums", aber eben keine heiligen Schriften. Geiger wollte Texte mit regulativem Anspruch durchaus als Urkunden anerkennen, die für den Geist des Judentums in der Zeit ihrer Entstehung und Bearbeitung zeugten. Aufgabe der Theologie sei es freilich, anknüpfend an die Erkenntnis eines ewigen Gehalts des Judentums, dessen Ausprägung sich im Zeitenlauf verän-

---

40 Susannah Heschel, *Der jüdische Jesus und das Christentum. Abraham Geigers Herausforderung an die christliche Theologie* (Berlin: Jüdische Verl.-Anst., 2001), 25–54; Amos Funkenstein, *Jüdische Geschichte und ihre Deutungen* (Frankfurt am Main: Jüdischer Verlag, 1995), 38 f.
41 „Geiger an Dernburg, 8. November 1836", in „Abraham Geigers Briefe", 165; vgl. auch „Geiger an Jakob Auerbach, 13. Januar 1846", in *Abraham Geiger's Leben in Briefen*, hrsg. von Geiger, 188; erste Zweifel am orthodoxen Glauben, so wusste sich Geiger in seinem Tagebuch zu erinnern, waren ihm im Alter von elf Jahren gekommen, ausgelöst durch die Lektüre von Beckers Handbuch der Weltgeschichte; vgl. Geiger, Hrsg., *Abraham Geiger's Leben in Briefen*, 7; siehe auch Michael A. Meyer, „Abraham Geiger—Der Mensch", in *Jüdische Existenz in der Moderne*, hrsg. von Wiese, Homolka und Brechenmacher, 5.

Es ist viel über den Einfluss von David Friedrich Strauss' und der Tübinger Schule auf Geiger geschrieben worden; siehe dazu Heschel, *Der jüdische Jesus*, 184–189; Meyer, *Antwort auf die Moderne*, 142 f.

dere, das religiöse Bewusstsein der Gegenwart zur Geltung zu bringen, „den religiösen Wahrheiten ihren Ausdruck zu geben, wie er der Zeit angemessen ist."[42] Hinzu trat die Erkenntnis, dass auch die Bücher der Bibel selbst in der vorliegenden hebräischen Fassung sowie in den Übersetzungen als das Ergebnis eines Tradierungsprozesses betrachtet werden müssen, in dem sich die inneren Wandlungen des Judentums in der Epoche seit der Rückkehr aus dem babylonischen Exil bis zum Abschluss des Talmud widerspiegelten. Sein Hauptwerk *Urschrift*, das Geiger 1857 herausbrachte, widmete sich dieser Überlieferungsgeschichte, die dem Glauben des gesetzestreuen Judentums an einen göttlichen Ursprung des masoretischen Textes also eine doppelte Absage erteilte, ohne aber damit auch dessen Bedeutung als Urkunde abzustreiten, in der sich die religiösen Lehren und Wahrheiten des Judentums als ethischer Monotheismus abbildeten.[43]

Welche Verachtung er für den „niedrigste[n] Standpunkt der Unmittelbarkeit" empfand, ließ Geiger auch in scharfen Besprechungen, so etwa in der Auseinandersetzung mit dem Vordenker der Neo-Orthodoxie Samson Raphael Hirsch (1808–1888), durchblicken.[44] Auch gegen die „Hirnlosigkeit" der Annahme, dass die mündliche Lehre unmittelbare Tradition sei,[45] schrieb Geiger in seiner *Urschrift* an, indem er das jüdische Sakralrecht aus jeglichem Offenbarungszusammenhang im Sinne einer göttlichen Inspiration herauslöste und ihm stattdessen einen Evolutionsprozess zumaß, den er im Wesentlichen aus dem Konflikt zwischen Pharisäern und Sadduzäern herleitete. Mit dem Abschluss des Talmud sei das Judentum dann in eine Epoche der „starren Gesetzlichkeit" eingetreten, in der das noch für die Offenbarung und Tradition gültige Entwicklungsprinzip ausgehebelt worden sei. Erst in der Gegenwart verschaffe sich mit der Kritik ein neues Zeitalter Geltung. Um das Judentum aus seiner vierzehn Jahrhunderte dauernden Umklammerung durch den Talmud zu befreien, gelte es nun, diesen nicht mehr als göttlichen Befehlskatalog von unbefristeter Validität zu betrachten, sondern als religionshistorisches Dokument menschlichen Ursprungs:

---

42 Vgl. Geiger, „Einleitung in das Studium der jüdischen Theologie", passim; idem, „Einleitung in die biblischen Schriften", in *Abraham Geiger's Nachgelassene Schriften*, hrsg. von Geiger, Bd. 4, 12; idem, „Jüdische Geschichte von 1830", 266.

43 Abraham Geiger, *Urschrift und Uebersetzungen der Bibel in ihrer Abhängigkeit von der innern Entwicklung des Judenthums* (Breslau: Hainauer, 1857); vgl. idem, „Einleitung in die biblischen Schriften", 132.

44 Abraham Geiger, „Recensionen", in *Wissenschaftliche Zeitschrift für jüdische Theologie* 4 (1839): 355–381, idem, „Das Verhältniß des natürlichen Schriftsinnes zur thalmudischen Schriftdeutung. Eine Skizze", in *Wissenschaftliche Zeitschrift für jüdische Theologie* 4 (1839): 53 f.; zu Hirsch siehe z. B. Roland Tasch, *Samson Raphael Hirsch. Jüdische Erfahrungswelten im historischen Kontext* (Berlin: De Gruyter, 2010).

45 Vgl. Abraham Geiger, „Die letzten zwei Jahre. Sendschreiben an einen befreundeten Rabbiner (1840)", in *Abraham Geiger's Nachgelassene Schriften*, hrsg. von Geiger, Bd. 1, 31.

Das Thalmudstudium muss von nun an, wenn es den Anspruch auf Wissenschaftlichkeit erheben will, sich ganz anders mit den Quellen befassen als bisher, es muss die arg hintangesetzten Werke zu Ehren bringen und die hoch überschätzte babylonische Gemara auf die Stufe versetzen, die ihr gebührt als dem jüngsten nach bestimmten Voraussetzungen umgewandelten Producte, als einem neuen Werke, das mit Unrecht den Anspruch erhebt, der treue Mund des grauesten Alterthums zu sein. [...] Die Erstarrung, der Tod eines jeden wahren religiösen Lebens, sich stützend auf die angebliche Abgeschlossenheit, welche einmüthig bezeugt werde, muss der Erkenntniss der geschichtlichen Bewegung weichen.[46]

VI

Wer die religiösen Auseinandersetzungen im deutschen Judentum im 19. Jahrhundert unter die Lupe nimmt, wird feststellen können, dass mit den unterschiedlichen Vorstellungen zeitgemäßer religiöser Lebensführung auch eine Konfessionalisierung einherging, die sich allerdings nicht als intrakonfessionelle Konsolidierung mit Tendenzen der Uniformierung, Klerikalisierung, Zentralisierung und Sozialreglementierung gestaltete. Konfessionalisierung im jüdischen Kontext beschrieb im Gegenteil eine innere Pluralisierung, d. h. die Entstehung von religiösen Bekenntnissen, deren Exklusivität sich an signifikanten theologischen Unterscheidungsmerkmalen festmachte.[47] Die zunehmende Vielfalt des jüdischen Glaubens befeuerte zudem eine Diskussion über die Existenz verbindlicher Glaubenslehren, in die auch Geiger eingriff, um seinem historisch-kritischen Standpunkt Gehör zu verschaffen.[48] Dass er sich so dezidiert gegen die Existenz jüdischer Dogmen aussprach, mag zum einen mit der apologetisch-polemischen Bemühung zusammenhängen, die Eigenheit und Vorzüge des Reformjudentums auch an grundsätzlichen Unterschieden zum christlichen Glauben festzumachen, in dem die Dogmatik ihren festen Platz in der Theologie be-

---

46 A. Geiger, *Urschrift*, IIIf.; vgl. idem, „Allgemeine Einleitung in die Wissenschaft des Judenthums", 127 et passim; siehe auch Ismar Schorsch, „Scholarship in the Service of Reform", in idem, *From Text to Context*, 318 f.

47 Zur Konfessionalisierung im Judentum vgl. Olaf Blaschke, „Bürgertum und Bürgerlichkeit im Spannungsfeld des neuen Konfessionalismus von den 1830er Jahren bis zu den 1930er Jahren", in *Juden, Bürger, Deutsche. Zur Geschichte von Vielfalt und Differenz 1800–1933*, hrsg. von Andreas Gotzmann, Rainer Liedtke und Till van Rahden (Tübingen: Mohr Siebeck, 2001): 33–66; Jacob Toury, „Die Revolution von 1848 als innerjüdischer Wendepunkt", in Das Judentum in der deutschen Umwelt 1800–1850, hrsg. von Hans Liebeschütz und Arnold Paucker (Tübingen: Mohr, 1977): 373; David Sorkin, „Religious Reforms and Secular Trends in German-Jewish Life. An Agenda for Research", in *Leo Baeck Institute Year Book* 40 (1995): 174.

48 Vgl. Schoeps, *Jüdischer Glaube in dieser Zeit*, 33; von der Krone, *Wissenschaft in Öffentlichkeit*, 427–429; dies., „Jüdische Wissenschaft und modernes Judentum: Eine Dogmendebatte", in *Die „Wissenschaft des Judentums"*, hrsg. von Meyer und Kilcher, 119 f.; siehe außerdem Leopold Löw, *Jüdische Dogmen. Offenes Sendschreiben an den Herrn Dr. Ignatz Hirschler, Eigenthümer des „Izraelita Közlöny"* (Pest: Aigner, 1871).

hauptete.⁴⁹ Zieht man seine Anstrengungen zur Dekonstruktion grundlegender Überzeugungen der Orthodoxie in Betracht, dann lässt sich Geigers Position aber zugleich in seinem innerjüdischen Bezugsrahmen einordnen. Geiger suchte seine progressive Theologie auch in Abgrenzung von anderen, konservativeren Strömungen zu definieren, denen er einen „unjüdischen" Dogmatismus nachweisen zu können glaubte.

Anlass zu einer klärenden Positionsbestimmung bot eine Kontroverse mit Manuel Joël (1826–1890), der 1864 als Breslauer Gemeinderabbiner Abraham Geiger ersetzt hatte, nachdem dieser einem Ruf nach Frankfurt am Main gefolgt war. Joël lebte bereits seit 1854 in Breslau, wo er vor seiner Wahl zum Rabbiner als Dozent am Jüdisch-Theologischen Seminar unterrichtet hatte – einem Rabbinerseminar, das unter der Leitung Zacharias Frankels (1801–1875) für eine moderate Modernisierung des Judentums eintrat.⁵⁰ Von dem Wunsch, einen Ausgleich zwischen reformkritischen und progressiven Positionen zu erzielen, zeugten vor allem Joëls Eingriffe in die Liturgie der Gemeinde. 1872 erschien seine tendenziell konservativere Revision jenes Siddurs, den Geiger 1854 mit deutlicher Reformabsicht publiziert hatte.

An Hinweisen, wie sehr Geiger mit der Überarbeitung haderte, mangelt es nicht. Bereits 1869 hatte er ein liturgisches Manifest Joëls zum Gegenstand einer scharfzüngigen Abrechnung gemacht.⁵¹ Seine Einlassungen gegen Joël liefern auch weitere Hinweise zu Geigers Skepsis gegenüber einer systematischen Theologie des Judentums. In seiner Broschüre *Zur Orientirung in der Cultusfrage* hatte Joël die Auffassung vertreten, dass das Judentum durchaus über Dogmen im Sinne von normativen Glaubensvorstellungen verfüge, zu denen sich auch der freisinnige Theologe *a priori* bekennen müsse, weil ihm andernfalls die innere Berufung für sein Amt fehle. Geiger glaubte, in der Festlegung eines verpflichtenden Glaubensbestandes vor allem das Bemühen der Orthodoxie sowie der „Vermittlungstheologie" erkennen zu können, ihre progressiven Gegner zu delegitimieren und auszugrenzen. Für das Judentum re-

---

49 Vgl. Geiger, „Die letzten zwei Jahre", 27; idem, „Das Verhalten der Kirche gegen das Judenthum in der neueren Zeit", in idem, *Das Judenthum und seine Geschichte. Dritte Abtheilung: Vom Anfange des dreizehnten bis zum Ende des sechszehnten Jahrhunderts* (Breslau: Schletter, 1871), 172.
50 Zu Manuel Joël vgl. Caesar Seligmann, „Rabbiner Dr. Manuel Joël zu seinem hundertjährigen Geburtstage 19. Oktober 1926. Sein Leben und seine Persönlichkeit", in *Monatsschrift für Geschichte und Wissenschaft des Judentums* 70 (1926): 305–315; Michael A. Meyer, „The Career of a Mediator. Manuel Joël, Conservative Liberal", in *Transversal* 14.2 (2016): 56–64. Zum Seminar vgl. Andreas Brämer, „Die Anfangsjahre des Jüdisch-Theologischen Seminars—Zum Wandel des Rabbinerberufs im 19. Jahrhundert", in *In Breslau zu Hause? Juden in einer mitteleuropäischen Metropole der Neuzeit*, hrsg. von Manfred Hettling, Andreas Reinke und Norbert Conrads (Hamburg: Dölling und Galitz, 2003): 99–112.
51 Manuel Joël, *Zur Orientirung in der Cultusfrage* (Breslau: Schletter'sche Buchhandlung, 1869); Abraham Geiger, *Etwas über Glauben und Beten. Zu Schutz und Trutz* (Breslau: Schletter'sche Buchhandlung, 1869); vgl. Max Freudenthal, „Manuel Joël und die Kultusfrage", in *Monatsschrift für Geschichte und Wissenschaft des Judentums* 70 (1926): 330–347; David Ellenson, „The Israelitische Gebetbücher of Abraham Geiger and Manuel Joël", in *Leo Baeck Institute Year Book* 44 (1999): 143–164.

klamierte er eine Freiheit, in der sowohl das Wissen um die geschichtliche Entwicklung als auch das persönliche Bewusstsein zur Geltung kam.[52]

Dass Geiger seinem Breslauer Nachfolger so vehement widersprach, überrascht allerdings insofern, als Joël durchaus keinen radikalen Gegenstandpunkt vertrat, sondern ebenfalls eine historisierende Anschauung präsentierte, in die er auch die Dogmen einbezog. Diese erfuhren nämlich, so Joël, zu keinem Zeitpunkt eine endgültige Fixierung, sondern seien in der Vergangenheit Gegenstand unterschiedlicher und sich verändernder Auslegungen gewesen, deren Schranken indes vom religiösen Schriftenkanon gesetzt wurden. Geiger war von dieser Position gar nicht so weit entfernt: Bereits in den 1840er Jahren hatte er die Ansicht verkündet, dass das Judentum zwar keine unveränderlichen Dogmen enthalte, deren Anerkennung Voraussetzung der Zugehörigkeit zur Glaubensgemeinschaft sei, dass es aber durchaus über einen Bestand von wesenhaften Grundsätzen verfüge, aus denen sich der Maßstab des jüdischen Handelns ableite. Jeder Gläubige stehe in der Pflicht, solche grundlegenden Wahrheiten des jüdischen Glaubens in sich zu befestigen, „und diese Wahrheiten gestalten sich ihm natürlich zu Grund- und Glaubenssätzen."[53]

Wie zu zahlreichen anderen Gelegenheiten präsentierte Geiger auch in der Auseinandersetzung mit Joël das Konzept der „religiösen Idee", die er dem Dogmenbegriff entgegenstellte. Gegen den Aufklärungsphilosophen Moses Mendelssohn (1729 – 1786), der ja das Judentum als offenbartes Religionsgesetz charakterisiert hatte, das die Wahrheiten der Vernunftreligion lediglich voraussetze, aber nicht enthalte, argumentierte Geiger, dass das positive Judentum mit neuen religiösen Ideen in die Geschichte eingetreten sei. Im Kern überzeitlich und unwandelbar, manifestierten sich diese Ideen aber im geschichtlichen Verlauf in unterschiedlicher Form und Gestalt. Geiger postulierte eine wissenschaftliche Theologie ohne Denkverbote, die ihm auch als Voraussetzung galt, um die religiösen Ideen im Judentum in noch reinerer Form zur Geltung zu bringen. Der religiöse Fortschritt, der sich insbesondere gegen den hegemonialen Anspruch des Religionsgesetzes richtete, beschrieb somit auch eine fortwährende und niemals abgeschlossene Annäherung der subjektiven Wahrheit an eine objektive Wahrheit, die aber letztendlich keine ausschließlich jüdischen Adressaten hatte, sondern universale Geltung beanspruchte.[54]

---

52 Geiger, *Etwas über Glauben und Beten*, 25 und 29 et passim.
53 Geiger, „Abhandlungen aus den Programmen der jüdischen Religionsunterrichtsanstalt", 322f.; vgl. idem, *Etwas über Glauben und Beten*, 2 – 10; Joël, *Zur Orientirung in der Cultusfrage*, 10 – 12; siehe auch idem, *Zum Schutz gegen „Trutz". Eine nothgedrungene Ergänzung der Schrift: „Zur Orientirung in der Cultusfrage"* (Breslau: Schletter, 1869); sowie Ken Koltun-Fromm, *Abraham Geiger's Liberal Judaism. Personal Meaning and Religious Authority* (Bloomington und Indianapolis: Indiana Univ. Press, 2006), 122f.
54 Geiger, *Etwas über Glauben und Beten*, 8 und 10 et passim; vgl. auch idem, „Die zwei verschiedenen Betrachtungsweisen. Der Schriftsteller und der Rabbiner", in *Wissenschaftliche Zeitschrift für jüdische Theologie* 4 (1839): 321 – 333; idem, „Jüdische Zeitschriften", in *Wissenschaftliche Zeitschrift für jüdische Theologie* 5 (1844): 374f. Zu Moses Mendelssohn vgl. z. B. Julius Guttmann, *Die Philosophie des Ju-*

Geigers vehemente Opposition gegen Joël hing wesentlich mit der zentralen Bedeutung des synagogalen Kultus zusammen, die er auch in Darlegungen zur Gebetbuchreform hervorhob. Anders als bei allen übrigen religiösen Handlungen, die er als Ausdruck einer individuellen Überzeugung in die Selbstverantwortung des Gläubigen stellte, wollte Geiger das gemeinschaftliche Gebet als kollektives Glaubensbekenntnis in den Mittelpunkt der Frömmigkeitspraxis platziert wissen, dem die Reform ihr besonderes Augenmerk zu widmen habe. Dabei ging es weniger um die Einhaltung eines Gebots, die Erfüllung einer Pflicht gegenüber Gott, sondern vielmehr darum, den religiösen Gefühlen und Bedürfnissen der Betenden ein Ventil zu verschaffen. Bei der Umgestaltung des Gottesdienstes, der als reinste Ausprägung des Gesamtbewusstseins den religiösen und ästhetischen Zeitgeist zum Ausdruck bringen sollte, sah sich Geiger aber mit bedeutenden Hindernissen konfrontiert. Hier kam wiederum zum Tragen, dass sich die Anschauungen des Glaubens als bloße Ahnungen einer exakten intellektuellen Erkenntnis entzogen. In einer Zeit, in der sich der Wunsch zur Umgestaltung der Liturgie langsam Bahn brach, aber noch auch auf bedeutenden Widerstand stieß, war die Suche nach einer Gebetsordnung, die formal und inhaltlich die Zustimmung der Gesamtheit der Gläubigen fand, ohnehin eine Illusion. Diese Erfahrung hatte Geiger bereits als Rabbiner in Breslau machen müssen.[55]

Seinen Widerspruch gegen Joëls Bekenntnis zum Dogma untermauerte Geiger vor allem mit Hinweisen auf solche Glaubensüberzeugungen, die zwar in der Geschichte des Judentums einst einen wichtigen Platz eingenommen hatten, aber im Zeitalter der Verbürgerlichung bei den Gläubigen keine Andacht mehr erzeugten. Zeigte sich Geiger in Fragen der Gebetsprache sowie der Gottesdienstdauer vermittlungsbereit, lehnte er in Angelegenheiten des Gebetsinhalts Kompromisse kategorisch ab. Der Reform wies er die Aufgabe zu, überholte religiöse Vorstellungen aus den Gebetstexten zu streichen, bzw. Formulierungen zu finden, die nicht im Widerspruch zu einer geläuterten Auffassung standen. Überlieferten Auffassungen, die in religiöser oder ästhetischer Hinsicht Empörung auslösten, wollte Geiger im Gebetdienst keinen Platz mehr eingeräumt wissen.[56]

---

dentums (München: Reinhardt, 1933), 312; vgl. auch Max Wiener, *Jüdische Religion im Zeitalter der Emanzipation* (Berlin: Philo Verlag, 1933), 175–257.

55 Abraham Geiger, *Unser Gottesdienst. Eine Frage, die dringend Lösung verlangt* (Breslau: Schletter, 1868), 1–3; idem, *Das Judentum und seine Geschichte*, 176; vgl. auch idem, *Grundzüge und Plan zu einem neuen Gebetbuche* (Breslau: Leopold Freund, 1849). Zu Geiger in Breslau siehe z. B. Andreas Brämer, „Ist Breslau „in vielfacher Beziehung Vorort und Muster für Schlesien"? Religiöse Entwicklungen in den jüdischen Gemeinden einer preußischen Provinz im 19. Jahrhundert", in *Jüdisches Leben zwischen Ost und West. Neue Beiträge zur jüdischen Geschichte in Schlesien*, hrsg. von Andreas Brämer, Arno Herzig und Krzysztof Ruchniewicz (Göttingen: Wallstein, 2014), 217–258.

56 Abraham Geiger, *Plan zu einem neuen Gebetbuche nebst Begründungen* (Breslau: Schletter'sche Buchhandlung, 1870), 5; *Israelitisches Gebetbuch für den öffentlichen Gottesdienst im ganzen Jahre. Im Einverständnisse mit der Gemeinde-Verwaltung in Frankfurt am Main, Erster Theil* (Berlin: Gerschel, 1870), VII; Geiger, *Etwas über Glauben und Beten*, 46.

Wo Bedarf zur Umgestaltung bestand, wusste Geiger insbesondere in seinem Plan für ein neues Gebetbuch in Frankfurt am Main (1870) konkret zu benennen. Seine Leitlinien zur Reform des Siddur zielten auf verschönernde Maßnahmen, nahmen aber vor allem theologische Revisionen der Liturgie vor, die sich vornehmlich auf die jüdische Gottesidee sowie das Verhältnis Gottes sowohl zu Israel als auch zur übrigen Menschheit bezog. Anthropomorphismen, die sich namentlich in den liturgischen Dichtungen des Mittelalters (*Piyyuṭim*) fanden, galt es ebenso zu beseitigen wie angelologische Vorstellungen sowie Erinnerungen an den Opfer- und Priesterkult. Der Glaube an die Unsterblichkeit sollte materielle Vorstellungen einer leiblichen Auferstehung der Toten in den Hintergrund rücken, um stattdessen die Idee einer unvergänglichen Seele hervorzuheben. Mit der Suche nach einer bürgerlichen jüdischen Konfessionalität ging zudem eine universale Umdeutung des Auserwähltseins Israels einher, das Geiger weniger als göttliche Bevorzugung und Absonderung eines Volkes denn als weltgeschichtlichen Auftrag an eine Religionsgemeinschaft zur Bezeugung, Verkündung und Verbreitung des Gottesglaubens auslegte. Göttliche Gnadenerweisungen durften sich somit nicht auf die Juden beschränken, sondern schlossen die gesamte Menschheit ein. Erteilte Geiger jeglichem Partikularismus der Juden eine Absage, dann mussten auch alle ethnisch-religiösen Zukunftshoffnungen in den Hintergrund rücken. Dazu zählten der Glaube an einen persönlichen Messias, das Heilsversprechen einer Sammlung der Zerstreuten in Zion oder die Hoffnung auf die Neuerrichtung des Tempels als Nationalheiligtum. So gesehen, bezeichneten Gebete für die Wiederherstellung Jerusalems, als „eine[r] durchaus gleichgültige[n] Stadt", keine religiöse Tat, sondern vielmehr „eine Gotteslästerung".[57]

Resümee

1854, kurze Zeit vor seiner Emigration nach Baltimore, veröffentlichte Reformrabbiner David Einhorn (1809–1879) seine Schrift *Princip des Mosaismus*, die er als Beitrag zu einer systematischen Darstellung des jüdischen Glaubens verstanden wissen wollte. Im Kontext dieses Aufsatzes aufschlussreich ist insbesondere das Vorwort des Buches, in dem der Autor seine Unzufriedenheit mit der jüdisch-theologischen Literatur seiner

---

[57] Geiger, *Etwas über Glauben und Beten*, 53 et passim; idem, *Plan zu einem neuen Gebetbuche*, 5–7; vgl. auch idem, „Nothwendigkeit und Maass", 207–209; Klaus Herrmann, „Liberale Gebetbücher von ‚Die Deutsche Synagoge' bis zum ‚Einheitsgebetbuch'", in *Liturgie als Theologie. Das Gebet als Zentrum im jüdischen Denken*, hrsg. von Walter Homolka (Berlin: Frank & Timme, 2005): 84 f.; K. Koltun-Fromm, „Historical Memory in Abraham Geiger's Account of Modern Jewish Identity", in *Jewish Social Studies* 7.1 (2000): 121–123; Jakob J. Petuchowski, *Prayerbook Reform in Europe. The Liturgy of European Liberal and Reform Judaism* (New York: World Union for Progressive Judaism, 1968), passim; allgemein zum jüdischen Messianismus in der Neuzeit: George Y. Kohler, Hrsg., *Der jüdische Messianismus im Zeitalter der Emanzipation. Reinterpretationen zwischen davidischem Königtum und endzeitlichem Sozialismus* (Berlin und Boston: de Gruyter, 2014).

Gegenwart zum Ausdruck brachte. Einhorn glaubte eine grundsätzliche Fehlentwicklung der wissenschaftlichen Kritik zu erkennen, die nämlich „eine einseitige und rein negative Stellung" einnehme, indem sie

> sich die Aufgabe gestellt [habe], zu zeigen, was das Judenthum nicht ist, und in dieser Hinsicht allerdings höchst beachtenswerte Materialien geliefert; auf die Frage aber, was das Judenthum ja sei, ist sie die Antwort bis auf die Stunde schuldig geblieben.[58]

Darüber, ob Einhorn auch Abraham Geiger in den Tadel einschloss, lässt sich nur mutmaßen. Immerhin fußte seine Beurteilung auf Beobachtungen, die auch auf seinen Kollegen und langjährigen Weggenossen zutrafen.[59]

Gewinnt man eine Anschauung davon, wie nachhaltig seine religionsgeschichtlichen Forschungen die traditionelle jüdische Glaubenswelt erschütterten, dann mag Geigers Argument überraschen, dass Fragen der systematischen Theologie im Streit der Gegenwart um die Modernisierung des Judentums allenfalls eine Nebenrolle spielten:

> Nicht ob die Welt aus Nichts geschaffen, nicht ob unmittelbare oder mittelbare Offenbarung anzunehmen sei, nicht ob Wunder geschehen oder nicht, ob Glaubenssätze in ihrer Strenge anzunehmen sind oder nicht, ist der wesentliche Differenzpunkt, wenn dieser auch manchmal auf der einen oder andern Seite mit hineinspielen mag.[60]

In das Zentrum seiner Kritik am gesetzestreuen Judentum stellte er dessen Orthopraxie, der er eine genuine Frömmigkeit des progressiven Judentums gegenüberstellte. „Legalität" und „Formglauben" beschrieben demnach eine konservative religiöse Praxis, der er zum Vorwurf machte, die Gültigkeit des jüdischen Regelkatalogs aus der normativen Kraft der Vergangenheit abzuleiten, ohne die Gebote auf ihr religiöses Moment hin zu befragen. Die „Gesetzlichen" huldigten also einer theonomen Willkür und forderten eine blinde Unterwerfung, die mit der Vorstellung der Vollkommenheit Gottes im Widerspruch stehe. Echter Gottesgehorsam hingegen bezeichne eine Geisteshaltung, die das sittliche Bewusstsein als Göttliches im Menschen zum Maßstab des Handelns erhob. Aus dieser Sicht besaß die Geschichte auch die Macht, der

---

[58] David Einhorn, *Princip des Mosaismus und dessen Verhältniß zum Heidenthum und rabbinischen Schriftthum*, Erster Theil (Leipzig: Verlag von E. L. Fritzsche, 1854), 6 f.; weitere Teile sind nicht erschienen.
[59] Zu Geiger und Einhorn siehe Christian Wiese, „Heros, Ikone, Gegenbild: Abraham Geiger aus der Perspektive der Reformbewegung in Amerika", in *Jüdische Existenz in der Moderne*, hrsg. von Wiese, Homolka und Brechenmacher, 213–242; sowie Michael A. Meyer, „German-Jewish Identity in Nineteenth-Century America", in idem, *Judaism within Modernity: Essays on Jewish History and Religion* (Detroit: Wayne State Univ. Press, 2001): 335–337.
[60] Geiger, „Die letzten zwei Jahre", 28.

Subjektivität jedes Zeitalters durch Veränderungen der religiösen Form Rechnung zu tragen.[61]

Paradigmatisch für Geigers ethischen Monotheismus stand dessen Auslegung der biblischen Erzählung von der ʿAqeda, der Bindung Isaaks, in der er die Erkenntnis der Unstatthaftigkeit des Menschenopfers nicht aus einer situativen Zuwendung Gottes, sondern aus der tieferen religiösen Einsicht Abrahams ableitete. Das Verdienst des biblischen Patriarchen wollte er gerade nicht in dessen Bereitschaft erkennen, einem göttlichen Befehl Folge zu leisten und den eigenen Sohn darzubringen. Der religiöse Fortschritt liege im Gegenteil darin begründet, dass der biblische Patriarch diese Versuchung, dem Beispiel der götzendienerischen Umwelt zu folgen, überwunden habe – in der geläuterten Einsicht, dass Gott ein solches Opfer niemals verlangen würde.[62]

1839 publizierte Geiger seinen Aufsatz über „Die zwei Betrachtungsweisen", in dem er die theoretische Arbeit des theologischen Schriftstellers und die praktische Wirksamkeit des Rabbiners gegenüberstellte. Dabei beschrieb er den Schriftsteller als unbequemen Mahner, dessen scheinbare Lust an der Zerstörung aber der Aufgabe geschuldet sei, die religiösen Ideen gegen das Übergewicht der Religionspraxis zur Geltung zu bringen.[63] Es mag daher nicht überraschen, dass solche Textpassagen, in denen Geiger positive Auskünfte zu den theologischen Grundlagen des jüdischen Glaubens erteilte, vor allem in dessen praktische Theologie eingebettet sind, in der die zeitgenössische Auffassung der religiösen Ideen zum Ausdruck kommen konnte. Es ist freilich bedauerlich, dass der talentierte Kanzelredner seine Predigten in der Regel nicht im Druck veröffentlichte.[64] Knappe, aber prägnante Aussagen zu den wesenhaften Grundlagen des jüdischen Glaubens in der Gegenwart finden sich in den Jahresberichten der jüdischen Religionsschule in Breslau, als deren Leiter Geiger 1846 die religiösen Prinzipien erläuterte, von denen sein Unterricht ausging:

> [...] und zwar 1. von dem Glauben an den einzigen heiligen Gott; 2. von dem Glauben, dass der Mensch eine höhere Würde, einen denkenden Geist, der ihn belebt, eine unsterbliche Seele besitzt, d. h. in dem Ebenbilde Gottes geschaffen ist, und endlich, 3. dass ein jeder einzelne Mensch in Verbindung mit allen übrigen zu dem hohen Ziele der Vervollkommnung der Gesammtmenschheit mitzuwirken habe, dass die Menschheit berufen sei, dem Ideale der gegenseitigen Verbrüderung, der Herrschaft der Gerechtigkeit, der Liebe und des Friedens immer entgegenzu-

---

[61] Idem, „Die Rabbinerzusammenkunft. Sendschreiben an einen befreundeten jüdischen Geistlichen", in *Wissenschaftliche Zeitschrift für jüdische Theologie* 3 (1837): 317 f.; idem, „Der Formglaube in seinem Unwerthe und seinen Folgen (aus der *Wissenschaftlichen Zeitschrift für jüdische Theologie* 1839)", in *Abraham Geiger's Nachgelassene Schriften*, hrsg. von Geiger, Bd. 1, 483–487; siehe auch „Geiger an Dernburg, 23. Februar 1836", in „Abraham Geigers Briefe", 115.

[62] Geiger, *Etwas über Glauben und Beten*, 41–43; Vogelstein, *Systematische Theologie*, 272–274.

[63] Abraham Geiger, „Die zwei verschiedenen Betrachtungsweisen", 323–332.

[64] Vgl. „A. Geiger an M.A. Levy, 2. September 1870", in *Abraham Geiger's Leben in Briefen*, hrsg. von Geiger, 332; siehe aber idem, „Gottesdienstlicher Vortrag gehalten in der grossen Synagoge zu Breslau am Sabbathe Matthot Massé 5598 (21. Juli 1838)", in *Abraham Geiger's Nachgelassene Schriften*, hrsg. von Geiger, Bd. 1, bes. 364.

streben, was der wahrhafte Gedankenkern des richtig verstandenen Messiasglaubens ist. Aus diesen Sätzen, der Einheit Gottes, der Gottähnlichkeit des Menschen, der Hoffnung auf die in Liebe vereinte Menschheit, welche überall in der heiligen Schrift wiederhallen, ergeben sich auf ganz einfache Weise die Pflichten gegen Gott, gegen uns selbst und gegen die Mitmenschen; sie sind die unerschütterlichen Grundlagen, welche das ganze Gebäude des religiösen und sittlichen Lebens tragen.[65]

Der systematische Ertrag dieser Erläuterungen ist zugegebenermaßen gering. Die wissenschaftliche jüdische Theologie, zu der sich Geiger enthusiastisch bekannte, konnte im Grunde nur religionsgeschichtliche Erkenntnisse zu Tage führen, musste aber die Antwort auf absolute religiöse Wahrheiten weitgehend schuldig bleiben. In seinen populären Vorträgen zur Frühgeschichte des Judentums, die er in den 1860er Jahren zunächst vor einem gebildeten Frankfurter jüdischen Publikum hielt, brachte Geiger auch begeisterte Beschreibungen der jüdischen Glaubenswelt, die er allerdings nicht als systematische Darstellung der geltenden Lehre präsentierte, sondern eben als historische Schilderungen eines ethischen Monotheismus, der in der Auseinandersetzung mit seiner heidnischen Umgebung in die Welt trat.[66] Gegenüber seinem Sohn Ludwig räumte Abraham Geiger 1866 freimütig ein, dass für die Grundlagen des Judentums („Gott, unsterblicher Menschengeist, Willensfreiheit, sittliche Anforderung und Veredlung") kein Beweis erbracht werden könne, diese aber dem menschlichen Bedürfnis nach Transzendenz Rechnung trugen und auch in der Zukunft universale Anerkennung beanspruchten. Seine Skepsis bezog sich also nicht allein auf die religiösen Wahrheiten selbst, sondern damit einher ging eine Zurückhaltung, die eigene Konfession in Wort und Schrift nach außen zu tragen. Belehrung über Glaubensinhalte mochte in der Kindererziehung probates Mittel sein, um die Grundlagen einer religiösen Identität der Heranwachsenden zu befestigen. Aufgabe und Freiheit jeder/ jedes erwachsenen Gläubigen war es aber, in der Kenntnis der jüdischen Religionsgeschichte die Bestätigung und konkrete Form der religiösen Ideen in sich selbst zu finden. Seiner Generation schrieb Geiger zugleich das Verdienst zu, diese Freiheit einer liberalen Anschauung des Judentums mühevoll errungen zu haben. Von einer solchen subjektiven Warte aus betrachtet, hatte die jüdische Theologie eine Gegengeschichte präsentiert und mit dieser die wissenschaftlichen Waffen für einen Befreiungskampf bereitgestellt, in dessen Verlauf die Orthodoxie ihren Hegemonialanspruch aufgeben musste. Das Reformjudentum trug einen Sieg davon, den Geiger aber durchaus nicht als Gelegenheit verstanden wissen wollte, eine progressive Fassung des jüdischen Glaubens auf Dauer normativ festzulegen.[67]

---

65 Geiger, „Abhandlungen aus den Programmen der jüdischen Religionsunterrichtsanstalt", 323 f.
66 Abraham Geiger, *Das Judenthum und seine Geschichte bis zur Zerstörung des zweiten Tempels. In zwölf Vorlesungen*, 2. Aufl. (Breslau: Schletter, 1865), 20–23.
67 „A. Geiger an Ludwig Geiger, 14. Januar 1866", in *Abraham Geiger*, hrsg. von Geiger, 179 f.

Asher Salah

Are Karaites Sceptics? The Jewish Perception of Karaism in Nineteenth Century Italy

In a note written by Sabato Morais (1823–1897), a rabbi native of Livorno and the founder of the *Jewish Theological Seminary* in the United States, and accompanying the text of Samuel David Luzzatto's *Autobiography*,[1] we find this hagiographical portrait of a man whom he considered his spiritual mentor:

> Nobody is more courageous than Luzzatto in expressing his opinions, so much courageous that sometimes he aroused against him a ruthless opposition. In all his writings Luzzatto, the believer, appears with a sharp sword to defend historical Judaism; piercing with his right hand the enemies of the traditions, repelling with his left hand the heretics who philosophize.[2]

While Morais is contributing to the transformation of Samuel David Luzzatto (1800–1865), also known by his Hebrew acronym ShaDaL, into a Jewish icon, making him a sort of archetypal Italian Jew,[3] it is less clear to whom he is referring when he mentions the 'enemies of the tradition' and the 'heretics who philosophise.' I have claimed elsewhere that the so called 'heretics who philosophise' should be identified with the advocates of Jewish Reform, who, in their writings and in their deeds, challenged the status of revelation, the power of the rabbis, and the observance of legal precepts.[4] For questioning the textual canon, religious authority, and shared practice of Judaism, orthodox antagonists, e.g. Luzzatto and to some extent also Sabato Morais, considered these reformers to be a threat undermining the legal, political, and social pact upon which Jewish life had relied for the previous two millennia, and were therefore accused of having been led astray by the 'sceptic spirit of the centu-

---

[1] Samuel David Luzzatto, *Autobiografia di Samuel David Luzzatto preceduta da alcune notizie storico-letterarie sulla famiglia Luzzatto a partire dal secolo decimosesto e susseguita da varie appendici* (Padua: Crescini, 1882). The editor of this posthumous autobiography was Samuel David Luzzatto's son, the notary Isaia (1836–1898) with the collaboration of friends and pupils, such as Sabato Morais from Philadelphia and Samuel Vita Zelman (1808–1885) from Melbourne.
[2] Luzzatto, *Autobiografia*, 70: 'Nessuno è più coraggioso di Luzzatto nell'espressione delle sue opinioni, coraggioso a tal segno ch'egli provocò talfiata contro di sé' un'opposizione spietata. In tutti i suoi scritti il credente [S. D. Luzzatto] apparisce con una spada tagliente, per difendere il Giudaismo storico; passando da parte a parte colla sua mano destra i nemici delle tradizioni, respingendo colla sinistra gli eretici che filosofeggiano.'
[3] Paraphrasing Alexander Altmann, "Moses Mendelssohn the Archetypal German Jew," in *The Jewish Response to German Culture: From the Enlightenment to the Second World War*, eds. Jehuda Reinharz and Walter Schatzberg (Hanover, NH: University Press of New England, 1991): 17–30.
[4] Asher Salah, "Jewish Reform in Italy," in *Wissenschaft des Judentums in Europe: Comparative and Transnational Perspectives*, eds. Christian Wiese and Mirjam Thulin (Berlin: De Gruyter, forthcoming).

ry.'⁵ To counter the spread of reformist stances within Italian Judaism, intense and unprecedented activities dedicated to dogmatic interpretations of Judaism were carried out via, for instance, the printing of countless catechisms,⁶ the composition of treatises under the heading *Dogmatic Theologies*,⁷ and attempting to ascertain what constitutes the essence of Judaism. The term essence became extremely popular subsequently, particularly in the German speaking states at the turn of the century, attracting both Reformers and the Orthodox, who produced countless books and booklets bearing the title of *Das Wesen des Judentums*.⁸

The so-called 'enemies of the traditions' were actually the great majority of the Jews in Italy after the Emancipation, now having become, allegedly, 'indifferent' toward religious questions in general and abandoning any bond with the Jewish community. Together with 'scepticism', 'indifferentism' was a recurring complaint registered in the writings of rabbis whose synagogues and schools had been deserted by their members and pupils. Conservative and liberal figures of the Italian rabbinate naturally proposed differing remedies to this situation but all shared a similar diagnose of the situation.

In Mantua, one of the most important Jewish communities of Northern Italy, Rabbi Salomone Nissim (1781–1864), a staunch orthodox, described what he deemed the greatest danger for his coreligionists in these terms: 'another plague of the century, that has its root in the ignorance, is the cold indifference.'⁹ His direct superior,

---

5 The expression 'spirito scettico del secolo' and similar ones are very common in Christian and Jewish works concerning religious and philosophical issues; cf., for instance, Salomon Munk, *Palestina: descrizione storica, geografica e archeologica* (Venice: Stabilimento nazionale, 1853), 1. It is important to stress that the term 'scepticism' does not refer only to an epistemology but concerns a general strategy to undermine authority and tradition and in some instances can be interpreted as atheism, agnosticism or even anarchism.

6 Cf. Gadi Luzzatto Voghera, "I catechismi ebraici tra Sette e Ottocento," in *Le religioni e il mondo moderno, II. Ebraismo*, ed. Davide Bidussa (Turin: Einaudi, 2008): 437–455.

7 The most important ones are written by Samuel David Luzzatto, *Lezioni di teologia dogmatica* (Trieste: Coen, 1863) and Elijah Benamozegh, *Teologia dogmatica ed apologetica* (Livorno: Francesco Vigo, 1877).

8 While in Germany this kind of literature was triggered mainly as a reaction to Adolf von Harnack, *Wesen des Christentums* (Leipzig: J. C. Hinrichs, 1900)—cf. the works of Isaac Breuer, *Lehre, Gesetz und Nation. Eine historisch–kritische Untersuchung über das Wesen des Judentums* (Frankfurt am Main: Verlag d. Israelit, 1914); Simon Mandel, *Das Wesen des Judentums* (Frankfurt am Main, 1904); Leo Baeck, *Das Wesen des Judentums* (Berlin: Nathansen und Lamm, 1905); Jacob Fromer, *Das Wesen des Judentums* (Leipzig: Hüpeden & Merzyn, 1905); Hermann L. Strack, *Das Wesen des Judentums. Vortrag gehalten auf der Internationalen Konferenz der Judenmission zu Amsterdam* (Leipzig: J. C. Hinrichs, 1906) –, in Italy it was popularised by Samuel David Luzzatto who titled the central chapter of his *Il giudaismo illustrato nella sua teorica, nella sua storia e nella sua letteratura* (Padua: Bianchi, 1848) as "Essenza del Giudaismo."

9 Salomone Nissim, *Appello di un rabbino nell'anno settuagesimo nono di sua età agli amati suoi correligionari* (Siena: Moschini, 1860): 'Altra piaga del secolo, che nell'ignoranza stessa ha radice, si è la fredda indifferenza.' On Nissim, see Mauro Perani and Gioia Liccardo, "Il testamento spirituale

the chief rabbi of Mantua, Marco Mortara (1815–1894), who unlike Nissim was favourable to the possibility of introducing certain reforms to Jewish practice, differed in his explanation of the phenomenon though was in agreement with the facts. In a letter to the Leghorn Jewish community, he writes: 'it is not because of the lack of the religious sentiment that people make transgressions, but to excuse the transgressions they affect religious indifference.'[10]

But in the theological debate in the nineteenth century there is a third category of Jews, related to the previous two, i. e. the Karaites, a religious movement founded in the eighth century in Babylon, who stirred considerable interest and preoccupation among Italian Jews as ambivalent objects of attraction and repulsion.[11] This article is dedicated to the attempt to understand who these Karaites are and why did they become a polemical target in the theological debate of the nineteenth century.

Karaites in the Early Modern Religious Debate

Obviously, Karaites have been a target of Jewish religious polemic not just in Italy and not only in the nineteenth century. From the early Middle Ages, Jewish authors occupied themselves a great deal with Karaism and were usually directed by an antagonistic mindset toward them. The Karaites were, accused of scripturalism, i. e. of a literal reading of the Hebrew Bible. Resentment between Rabbanites and Karaites has been particularly fierce in Eastern Europe and Islamic lands where the two communities lived at close quarters with one an another and became intimately acquainted with one another's laws and regulations. In Western Europe under Christian rulers, the presence of Karaites was extremely scant and sporadic, hence debates concerning this minority faith primarily came about in two different historical settings. The first from the sixteenth to the beginning of the eighteenth century, the second in the nineteenth century when the study of Karaism emerged as a fully-fledged field of academic scholarship.

---

del rabbino mantovano Salomone Nissim," in *Nuovi studi in onore di Marco Mortara nel secondo centenario della nascita*, eds. Mauro Perani and Ermanno Finzi (Florence: La Giuntina, 2016): 98–112.
10 See the letter of June 4, 1867, edited in Asher Salah, *L'epistolario di Marco Mortara (1815–1894), un rabbino italiano tra Riforma e Ortodossia* (Florence: La Giuntina, 2012), 211: 'Non è per mancanza di sentimento religioso che si trascorre alle trasgressioni, ma si' per iscusare le trasgressioni che si affetta l'indifferenza religiosa.' Already in his youth, Mortara had alerted against the dangers of 'religious indifferentism' in his sermon *Dell'indifferenza in fatto di religione* (Mantua, 1839), considering it a problem coming from France. He was probably influenced by the essay of the abbé Hugues-Félicité Robert de Lamennais, *Essai sur l'indifférence en matière de religion* (Paris, 1817), translated into Italian by the countess Ferdinanda Montanari Riccini, and published in Modena in 1824.
11 For a comprehensive bibliography on the subject, see Barry Dov Walfish and Mikhail Kizilov, *Bibliographia Karaitica: An Annotated Bibliography of Karaites and Karaism: Karaite Texts and Studies* (Leiden and Boston: Brill, 2010).

In the last two decades, much scholarly attention has been devoted to the instrumental role of the figure of the Karaite in early modern and modern European religious controversy.[12] From these studies emerges the importance of Protestant Hebraists in introducing Karaism within the range of European erudition in the early modern era. The considerable curiosity concerning Karaites among Christian scholars, particularly Protestants, was ostensibly due to the analogy between Karaism and Reformed Christianity on the one hand, and Rabbinic Judaism and Catholicism on the other. This correlation recurs in the writings of Leiden university professors, such as the antiquarian Joseph Justus Scaliger (1540–1609), the exegete Johannes Drusius (1550–1616), the theologian Johannes Hoornbeek (1617–1666), or Jacobus Trigland the Younger (1652–1705).[13] Karaism also became a central concern in millenarian circles all over Northern Europe, as in the works by the Scottish irenicist John Dury (1596–1680), correspondent of the Amsterdam rabbi Menasseh Ben Israel (1604–1657), and whose knowledge about the Karaites came mainly from the Christian kabbalist Johann Stephan Rittangel (1606–1652).[14] Missions were send to the Karaites residing in the Polish–Lithuanian commonwealth for the purpose of gathering information concerning their customs and writings, and probably also for converting them to Christianity, such as the mission organised by the Christian Orientalist Gustav Peringer (1651–1710) from Uppsala, under the aegis of king Charles XI of Sweden.

In the second period of revival of interest for the Karaites, in the nineteenth century, Karaism was invoked by some scholars of the incipient *Wissenschaft des Judentums*, such as Abraham Geiger (1810–1874), Isaak Markus Jost (1793–1860), Samuel Holdheim (1806–1860) or Isaac Hirsch Weiss (1815–1905), as the prototype of the

---

12 Cf. Jakob Petuchowski, "Karaite Tendencies in an Early Reform Haggada," *Hebrew Union College Annual* 31 (1960): 223–249; Johannes van den Berg, "Proto-Protestants? The Image of the Karaites as a Mirror of the Catholic-Protestant Controversy in the Seventeenth Century," in idem, *Religious Currents and Cross-Currents: Essays on Early Modern Protestantism and the Protestant Enlightenment*, eds. Jan de Bruijn, Pieter Holtrop, and Ernestine van der Wall (Leiden and Boston: Brill, 1999): 43–64; Daniel Lasker, "Ha-Qarai ke-Aḥer Yehudi" [Hebrew], *Peamim* 89 (2001): 96–106; idem, "Karaism and Christian Hebraism: a New Document," *Renaissance Quarterly* 59.4 (2006): 1089–1116; Valerio Marchetti, "The Lutheran Discovery of Karaite Hermeneutics," in *Una Manna buona per Mantova. Studi in onore di Vittore Colorni per il suo 92° compleanno*, ed. Mauro Perani (Florence: Olschki, 2004): 433–459; Marina Rustow, "Karaites Real and Imagined: Three Cases of Jewish Heresy," *Past and Present* 197 (2007): 35–74; Golda Akhiezer, *Historical Consciousness, Haskalah, and Nationalism among Eastern European Karaites* [in Hebrew] (Jerusalem: Ben Zvi Institute, 2016).
13 Cf. Berg, "Proto-Protestants? The Image of the Karaites," 43–64; Akhiezer, *Historical Consciousness*, 106–116. I would like to thank Hanan Gafni for sharing with me his observations on these sources in his forthcoming *Devarim she-be-'al-Peh, Devarim she-bi-Khtav: 'Al Tefisat ha-Torah she-be-'al-Peh ve-Toldoteah ba-Meḥqar ha-Yehudi ha-Moderni* [Hebrew] (Forthcoming).
14 Cf. Richard Popkin, "The Lost Tribes, the Karaites, and the English Millenarians," *Journal of Jewish Studies* 37.2 (1986): 213–228.

Jewish Reform they wanted to promote.[15] For many Jews, extolling Karaism became a means to stress the existence of an historical and allegedly more rational alternative to talmudic Judaism.

While this periodisation is undoubtedly correct, it suffers from its excessively Germano-centric and Protestant-centric perspective, in as much as a problem that concerns much of the scholarship regarding the *Haskalah* and the *Wissenschaft des Judentums* too, which conflates Jewish European modernity with the German model.[16] This has caused some scholars to underrate Catholic and Jewish interest in Karaites.[17]

However, Catholic scholars, such as Guillaume Postel (1510–1581), were the first to pave the way for greater European interest in the Karaites by other Christians and Jews. Later on, French Catholic intellectuals such as the Jesuit Nicolaus Serarius (1555–1609), the biblical scholar Jean Morin (1591–1659), Jacques Gaffarel (1601–1681)[18], and last but not least, Richard Simon (1638–1712), author of an important appendix on the Karaites,[19] published alongside his translation of Leon Modena's *Riti Hebraici*, admired the Karaites for their purportedly more critical approach to a tradition deemed to having been corrupted by rabbinic teachings. In Catholic polemics against Protestants it is not unusual to see the appropriation of the term Karaite by Catholics, attempting to demonstrate that Reform represented a deviate and later addition to the original evangelical message. [20] Finally, at the times of the French Revolution, the Abbé Grégoire (1750–1831), the revolutionary leader and

---

15 Cf. Richard Popkin, "Les caraïtes et l'émancipation des juifs," *Dix-huitième siècle* 13 (1981): 137–147.

16 For recent studies of *Wissenschaft* that aim at expanding on the Germano-centric narrative of the history of the academic study of Judaism and Jewish history beyond German lands, see the forthcoming volume, *Wissenschaft des Judentums in Europe: Comparative and Transnational Perspectives*, eds. Christian Wiese and Mirjam Thulin (Berlin: De Gruyter, 2019); Louise Hecht, "The Beginning of Modern Jewish Historiography: Prague: A Center on the Periphery," *Jewish History* 19 (2005): 347–373; Nils Roemer, "Outside and Inside the Nations: Changing Borders in the Study of the Jewish Past during the Nineteenth Century," in *Modern Judaism and Historical Consciousness: Identities, Encounters, Perspectives*, eds. Andreas Gotzmann and Christian Wiese (Leiden and Boston: Brill: 2007): 28–53.

17 For instance, in her fundamental work on Karaite historiography Golda Akhiezer stresses that with the exception of Protestant Hebraists in the seventeenth and eighteenth century, the Karaite movement did not have any significant impact upon early modern Jewish literature until the beginning of the Science of Judaism in the nineteenth century; see Akhiezer, *Historical Consciousness*, 25.

18 On these scholars relationships with Italian Jews, see Avner Ben Zaken, *Cross-Cultural Scientific Exchanges in the Eastern Mediterranean, 1560–1660* (Baltimore: Johns Hopkins University Press, 2010), in particular chapter three "Transcending Time in the Scribal East."

19 The author of this appendix was not Leon Modena as erroneously attributed in Ben Zaken, *Cross-Cultural Scientific Exchanges*, 98.

20 A later example of a catholic scholar presenting the Karaites has the true representatives of the original spirit of Judaism preserved intact by Roman Catholicism but altered and adulterated 'dallo spirito progressivo riformatore' ('the progressive reformist spirit') of rabbinism; see Niccolò C. Mariscotti, *Il clero cattolico e la civiltà*, vol. 2 (Florence: Galli, 1866), 150. Mariscotti mentions among the three main sects of Judaism at the times of Jesus the Pharisees, the Karaites, and the kabbalists.

Roman Catholic prelate, took the Karaites as a model of what he deemed modern Judaism should be.²¹ The second claim regarding the lack of attention to the Karaite phenomenon within Jewish communities before the nineteenth century, cannot be taken at face value, in the knowledge of the deep doctrinal stir caused the Karaism accusations addressed to heterodox members within the Sephardic communities of Amsterdam, Hamburg and London in the seventeenth and eighteenth century, studied by Yosef Kaplan and Shalom Rosenberg.²²

Oddly enough, contemporary scholarship seems to have overlooked the fact that, aside from the Northern European Sephardic communities, another important centre existed in the early modern era that produced a wide array of texts on the Karaites: Italy. In their appraisal of Karaism, Italian Jews, especially those gathered in Venice, differed from the Christian hebraists of their time and from Sephardic intellectuals living in the Netherlands. Not only was the first Karaite prayer book printed in Venice by Cornelius Adelkind in the Bomberg presses with the collaboration of local rabbanite Jews in 1528–1529,²³ but the Karaites also elicited much interest among the Venetian Jewish intellectual elite, such as Leon Modena (1571–1648), who wrote an entire tractate (now lost) on the Karaites,²⁴ Joseph Solomon Delmedigo (1591–1655) whose occupation with Karaism is attested by his *Sefer Elim* (Amsterdam, 1629),²⁵ and Simone Luzzatto (1580–1663), who devoted a few but significant paragraphs to Karaism in his *Discorso circa il stato degli Hebrei* (Venice: Giovanni Calleoni, 1638).²⁶

---

21 Cf. Popkin, "Les caraïtes et l'émancipation des Juifs," 137–147.
22 Yosef Kaplan, "Karaites in the Early Eighteenth Century," in idem, *An Alternative Path to Modernity: The Sephardi Diaspora in Western Europe* (Leiden and Boston: Brill, 2000): 234–279; Shalom Rosenberg, "Emunat Hakhamim," in *Jewish Thought in Seventeenth Century*, eds. Isadore Twersky and Bernard Septimus (Cambridge, MA: Harvard University Press, 1987): 285–295.
23 Cf. Giovanni Bernardo De Rossi, *Dizionario storico degli autori ebrei e delle loro opere*, vol. 1 (Parma: Dalla reale stamperia, 1802), 3, says without giving his source that the Karaites tried to print a new edition of this liturgic work in Venice in 1713.
24 Cf. Johann Christoph Wolf, *Bibliotheca Hebraea*, vol. 3 (Hamburg: Christophorus Felginer, 1727), 1150, who mentions this tractate, whose existence has been challenged by some modern scholars although it is substantiated by a letter of Modena himself; see Leon Modena, *She'elot u-Teshuvot Ziqnei Yehudah* [Hebrew], ed. Shlomo Simonsohn (Jerusalem: Mossad ha-Rav Kook, 1956), 16: letter 37. To this lost work we should add the possibility of Modena being the author of the provocative libel against rabbinic culture and associated by Modena himself to Karaite arguments, as claimed by Talya Fishman, *Shaking the Pillars of Exile: 'Voice of a Fool,' an Early Modern Jewish Critique of Rabbinic Culture* (Stanford: Stanford University Press, 1997). Omero Proietti defends the attribution of this pamphlet to Uriel da Costa in his *La città divisa: Flavio Giuseppe, Spinoza e i farisei* (Rome: Il Calamo, 2003).
25 Cf. Ben-Zaken, *Cross-Cultural Scientific Exchanges*, 98–102. On Delmedigo's personal acquaintance with Lithuanian Karaites, see Stefan Schreiner, "Josef Shelomo Delmedigos Aufenthalt in Polen-Litauen," in *An der Schwelle zur Moderne. Juden in der Renaissance*, eds. Giuseppe Veltri and Annette Winkelmann (Leiden and Boston: Brill, 2003): 207–232.
26 The *Discorso* is included in the edition of Luzzatto's two main Italian works; see Simone Luzzatto, *Scritti politici e filosofici di un ebreo scettico nella Venezia del Seicento*, ed. Giuseppe Veltri (Milan: Bompiani, 2013), 3–106.

While in Northern European Diaspora the label of 'Karaite' and the terms 'Sadducee' or 'Boethusian,' were used by rabbis such as Immanuel Aboab (1555–1628), Isaac Orobio de Castro (1617–1687), Moshe Hagiz (1671–1750), or David Nieto (1654–1728), to discredit those doubting the validity of the Oral Law, the Venetian rabbis appeared to have shared a less biased attitude towards Karaism.[27] While ridiculing its practices and contradictions, Modena, Delmedigo, and Luzzatto are sensitive to the critical attitude and intellectual integrity of Karaism, and were prone to considering this group a full-fledged component of the Jewish nation and not necessarily its antagonist. In the famous sixteenth "Consideratione" of his *Discorso*, Luzzatto lists the Karaites as the fourth class of Jews, after the talmudists, the philosophers ('teologi filosofanti'), and the kabbalists. He deems the Karaites, despite their small number and their rejection of tradition, to be praiseworthy for their piety and for their grammatical expertise. In particular, Luzzatto recognises that in comparison to ancient sects within Judaism they were closer to the fundamental principles of faith of the rabbanite Jews for believing in the immortality and immateriality of the soul and accepting the existence of the angels.[28]

This may explain why, in the context of the controversy regarding Sabbateanism, Italian Jews, such as Samson Morpurgo (1681–1740), a physician and rabbi in Ancona, appear to have been reluctant to endorse the equation between the heresy of Shabbatai Zevi (1626–1676) and Karaism, as prompted by Moshe Hagiz of Amsterdam.[29] It seems as if this ambiguous, and not entirely derogatory, appraisal of Karaism, so peculiar to the aforementioned Italian Jews, was due to their perception of the Karaites as a sort of sceptical sect that was wrong in its practical conclusions but correct in its intellectual challenges casting doubt on the conceit of reason. Certainly, much work remains to be done to ascertain the role of Italian Jews as intermediaries of information in early modern European debates of Karaism, exemplified by the case of the tobacco dealer and Sabbatean Jew Jonas Salvador of Pinerolo in Pied-

---

27 The image of Karaism in Italy seems to present some substantial differences from the way Marina Rustow describes the Sephardic diaspora in Northern Europe; see Rustow, "Karaites Real and Imagined," 36: 'more than any other type of deviation from rabbinic norms, Karaism came to represent the denial of rabbinic authority. This was true even in its absence: the label of Karaism served as a category into which rabbinic and communal authorities placed all manner of biblicizing error and of resistance to rabbinic authority.'
28 Luzzatto, *Discorso*, 84v-85r: 'sono più corretti che li antichi Saducei, admettendo essi l'incorporalità et immortalità dell'anima, come anco assentiscono che vi siano angioli immateriali.' A very similar description of the Karaites, though more attentive to the present condition of the Karaites in the diaspora can be found in Leon Modena, *Historia de gli riti hebraici* (Paris, 1637), fifth part, chapter one. Were the anonymous work *Qol Sakhal* ('The Voice of the Fool') to be attributed to Modena we would find a much more enthusiastic appraisal of Karaism considered to be the only one that preserved the correct revelation of Moses and did not fall into decline.
29 Cf. Elisheva Carlebach, *The Pursuit of Heresy: Rabbi Moses Hagiz and the Sabbatian Controversy* (New York: Columbia University Press, 1990), 136, 149, 195.

mont, who in 1670 became acquainted with Richard Simon in Paris, participated with him in an intense exchange of views on the Karaites.[30]

But where in Italy, a country where real Karaites have been absent at least since the vanishing of the last colonies in Sicily in the eleventh century, did Jews get their information from on Karaism?[31] The question is particularly relevant in understanding the position, both imaginary and real occupied by the Karaites in the writing of important representatives of the Science of Judaism in Italy in the nineteenth century.

Italian Jews' Knowledge on Karaism in the Nineteenth Century

Among the sources from which Italian Jews obtained their information on the 'Karaite question,' two were particularly popular in the nineteenth century, the *Kuzari* by Judah Halevi (c. 1075–1141) and the *Maṭṭeh Dan ve-ha-Kuzari ha-Sheni* ('The Staff of Dan and the Second Kuzari') by David Nieto.

Judah Halevi deals with the Karaites in the third chapter of his philosophical dialogue devoted to the refutation of the teachings of Karaism and to the history of the development of the oral tradition.[32] Not only the first editions of the Hebrew version of the *Kuzari* by Judah Ibn Tibbon were printed in Italy,[33] but also one of the most influential commentaries of Judah Halevi's work, the *Qol Yehudah* by Italian rabbi Judah Moscato (1530–1593), published posthumously in Venice in 1594 and since then frequently reprinted to accompany editions of the *Kuzari*.[34] Without doubt, Italian Jews were not the only readers of the *Kuzari* which was widely studied and debated by intellectual circles across Europe. In the early modern era, the *Kuzari* was, in fact, used as a major source and standard reference for the discussions of Jewish sects among Christians and Jews.

---

30 Gershom Scholem, *Sabbatai Ṣevi: The Mystical Messiah 1626–1676* (Princeton: Princeton University Press, 1973), 827–828.
31 According to Shmuel Spector, "The Karaites in Nazi-Occupied Europe as Reflected in German Documents" [in Hebrew], *Pe'amim* 29 (*1986*): 90–108, some Karaites are attested to have been in Italy in the first half of the twentieth century, mainly travelers passing through its ports e.g. the fifty Lithuanian Karaites mentioned by S. Zarhi, "Ha-'Olim ha-Rishonim mi-Polin higi'u Arṣah be-'Oniyyah" [Hebrew], *Davar*, December 2 (1949): 1, and the thirty-six refugees fleeing from Egypt in 1957 recorded in the Londonian *Jewish Chronicle*'s article "1000 Jewish Refugees arrive in Italy," on January 11, 1957.
32 On the possibility that the *Kuzari* was originally composed as a response to a Karaite, see Daniel Lasker, "Judah Halevi and Karaism," in *From Ancient Israel to Modern Judaism: Intellect in Quest of Understanding. Essays in Honor of Marvin Fox*, eds. Jacob Neusner, Nahum Sarna, and Ernst Frerichs (Atlanta: Scholars Press, 1989): 111–126.
33 See Fano, 1506, Venice 1547, and Venice 1594 containing Moscato's *Qol Yehudah*.
34 On Moscato intellectual background, see Giuseppe Veltri and Gianfranco Miletto, eds., *Rabbi Judah Moscato and the Jewish Intellectual World of Mantua in the 16th-17th Centuries* (Leiden and Boston: Brill, 2012).

After a period of relative neglect in the eighteenth century for its anti-rationalist stances, the *Kuzari* benefited from a resurge in interest in the following century. Adam Shear in his work on the *Rezeptionsgeschichte* of the *Kuzari* stresses 'the wide appeal of the book to all sides of the increasingly fragmented Jewish body politic' all over Europe in the age of the *Wissenschaft des Judentums*.[35] Mainly focussing on the Central and Northern European context, Shear's book sporadically refers to Italian Jews, but his observations concerning the importance of Halevi and the *Kuzari* in *maśkil* literature and among scholars of Judaism can be extended to Italy as well.

Aside from some rather marginal mentions of the *Kuzari* by the Mantuan *maśkil* and traveller Samuele Romanelli (1757–1814),[36] Judah Halevi became standard reading for educated Italian Jews, as demonstrated by the inclusion of the *Kuzari* in the educational programme for advanced students elaborated by Elia Morpurgo (c. 1731/40–1801) of Gradisca and published in the Berlin journal, *Ha-Meassef*, in 1786 under the title *Mikhtav mi-Eliyyahu*.[37] In the official curriculum of the *Collegio Rabbinico*, the rabbinic seminary of Padua, only the *Kuzari* with commentary by Moscato is featured as compulsory reading for students in theology classes, although the original programme made up by Isaac Samuel Reggio in the 1820s also referred to Maimonides' *Guide of the Perplexed*, later eliminated allegedly containing 'principles of Greek philosophy, now rejected.'[38] According to the 1867 program of studies of the rabbinical college of Leghorn, a rival institution to the seminar in Padua and more oriented toward mystical studies than to the spirit of the *Wissenschaft des Judentums*, students in theology were given the choice to be tested either on the *Kuzari*, or on Josef Albo's *Sefer ha-'Iqqarim* and Saadiah Gaon's *Sefer ha-Emunot ve-ha-De'ot*.[39]

---

[35] Adam Shear, *The Kuzari and the Shaping of Jewish Identity, 1167–1900* (Cambridge and New York: Cambridge University Press, 2008), 249.

[36] Samuele Romanelli, *Masa be-Arav* [Hebrew] (Berlin: Hinukh Nearim, 1792), thirteenth chapter, mentions the second essay, paragraph 26, of the *Kuzari* on sacrifices; idem, *Grammatica ragionata ebraica con trattato ed esempj di poesia* (Trieste: Stamperia Governiale, 1799), where he quotes extensively from Halevi's poetry. Shear, *The Kuzari*, 244, also mentions the possibility of Romanelli having served as one of the proofreaders of Joseph Hrashantsky's editon of the *Kuzari* (Vienna, 1795). On Romanelli and Haskalah, see my introduction to the Italian edition of Samuele Romanelli, *Visioni d'Oriente* (Florence: La Giuntina, 2006).

[37] Cf. Asher Salah, "'Bein Ghevule Ashkenaz VeItalia': Elia Morpurgo nel contesto delle riforme scolastiche nelle Unite Contee di Gradisca e Gorizia tra Sette e Ottocento," in *Cultura ebraica nel Goriziano*, ed. Marco Grusovin (Gorizia: Istituto di Storia Sociale e Religiosa, 2007): 101–123.

[38] 'Principi di filosofia greca in essa introdotti e presentemente obbliterati.' Cf. Nikolaus Vielmetti, "Das Collegio Rabbinico von Padua," in *Wissenschaft des Judentums: Anfänge der Judaistik in Europa*, ed. Julius Carlebach (Darmstadt: Wissenschaftliche Buchgesellschaft, 1992): 12–13, 54–57, and Maddalena Del Bianco Cotrozzi, *Il collegio rabbinico di Padova. Un'istituzione religiosa dell'ebraismo sulla via dell'emancipazione* (Florence: Olschki, 1995), 153.

[39] Cf. Alfredo S. Toaff, "Il collegio rabbinico di Livorno," *La Rassegna Mensile di Israel* 12 (1938): 188.

The popularity of the *Kuzari* is attested to by at least two Italian translations, one by the chief rabbi of Florence, David Maroni (1810–1888),[40] the second by Cesare Foà (1833–1907) in 1872.[41] Added to these two literary achievements are the numerous renditions of Halevi's poetry into Italian in the nineteenth century by towering figures of Italian Jewish intellectual life e.g. Cesare Rovighi (1820–1890),[42] Salvatore De Benedetti (1818–1891),[43] or Giuseppe Barzilai (1824–1902).[44] The most important representative of this Halevian revival is undoubtedly Samuel David Luzzatto whose affection for Halevi's poetry appears throughout his oeuvre, from the publication of a poetic anthology of Judah Halevi, with notes and an introduction, under the title of *Betulat Bat Yehudah* (Prague, 1840), to the vocalised and corrected edition of the *Diwan*'s eighty-six religious poems, with a philosophical commentary and introduction, published in Lyck in 1864.[45]

Erudite correspondences of Italian Jewish scholars shed light upon their obsessive search and interest for any extant commentary of the book, such as Judah Moscato's, *Qol Yehudah*, Nathanel Caspi's *'Edut le-Yiśrael*, or Salomon de Lunel's alias Salomon Vivas, *Ḥesheq Shelomo*.[46] The fact that personalities with radically different approaches to Judaism, such as the mystical Elijah Benamozegh (1822–1900) and the

---

[40] This manuscript translation is mentioned in Maroni's testament published in Lionella Viterbo, *Spigolando nell'archivio della comunità ebraica di Firenze* (Florence: La Giuntina, 1997), 132.

[41] *Il Cosarì: opera scritta in arabico da Giuda Levita, spagnuolo; recata in ebraico da Giuda ben Tibbón, e volgarizzata da Cesare Foà* (Casalmaggiore: Aroldi, 1872).

[42] Cesare Rovighi's translation of a hymn by Halevi from a manuscript belonging to the Paduan Giuseppe Almanzi was published in *Rivista Israelitica* 1.5 (1846): 285–287.

[43] Salvatore De Benedetti, *Canzoniere Sacro di Giuda Levita* (Pisa: Nistri, 1871). As a gift for the wedding Zabban-Pardo Roques, De Benedetti published *Un epitalamio ebraico di Giuda Levita* (Pisa: Nistri, 1891). A later version of selected poems was conducted by the rabbi of Soragna, Aldo Sorani, *Giuda Levita, poesie scelte*, preface by Hayim N. Bialik (Reggio: Riccardo Bondavalli, 1913).

[44] At the end of his translation of the Lamentations of Jeremiah, *I treni di Geremia, traduzione letterale dal testo ebraico in versi italiani con note originali* (Trieste: Coen, 1867), Barzilai included also his poetic version of the Sioneide, encouraged by Lelio della Torre who had already published his own version of this elegy by Halevi (Abul Hassan), now collected in the posthumous *Scritti Sparsi*, vol. 1 (Padua: Prosperini, 1908), 375–390.

[45] Cf. Irene Kajon, "The Problem of Divine Justice in Samuel David Luzzatto Commentary to the Diwan of Jehuda Ha-Levy," in *Jewish Studies at the Turn of the Twentieth Century, vol. 2: Judaism from the Renaissance to Modern Times*, eds. Judit Targarona Borrás and Angel Sáenz-Badillos (Leiden and Boston: Brill, 1999): 48–53.

[46] See, for instance, Marco Mortara's letters to Samuel David Luzzatto, June 27, 1855, July 15, 1855, August 6, 1856, and December 29, 1856, and to Moritz Steinschneider of September 8, 1859 and again May 7, 1862 and August 24, 1865, concerning the project of printing these two commentaries from the collection of the chief rabbi of Mantua; edited in Salah, *L'epistolario di Marco Mortara*, 95–98, 147–150. Luzzatto corresponded intensively with Gideon Brecher (1797–1873) on his works about the *Kuzari* published in Prague in 1838–1840.

anti-kabbalistic Samuel David Luzzatto,[47] shared an unblemished fondness for Judah Halevi's oeuvre, can be explained as a survival of a characteristic Italian desire from the late Renaissance on to harmonise a moderate Maimonidism with a fideistic approach to religion influenced by Halevi.[48]

However, Halevi's success among Italian Jews cannot be separated from his defence of the foundational value of the Oral Law and the traditional building of Jewish faith. This also explains the strong engagement of Italian Jewish scholars with the *Maṭṭeh Dan* written by David Nieto a Venetian rabbi, living in London.[49] This book was published simultaneously in Hebrew and Spanish in London in 1714, along with a separate edition in Hebrew and another exclusively in Spanish. While the first *Kuzari* was a defence of the Written Law, David Nieto's second *Kuzari* sets out to offer arguments in favour of the authenticity of the rabbinical tradition, against the attacks of the Karaites. Needless to say, these imaginary Karaites have little or nothing to do with the real Karaite communities living in Lithuania, Crimea and different parts of the Ottoman empire during that time. The Karaites David Nieto targets are none other than religious dissidents, mostly of Converso origin, influenced by a critical approach toward the Oral Law (*torah she-be-'al-peh*) of thinkers such as Uriel da Costa (c. 1585–1640), Juan (Daniel) de Prado (c. 1612–c. 1670), and most famously Baruch Spinoza (1632–1677). It is noteworthy that, although neither Spinozism nor Karaite communities in the East were apparently of great concern for Italian Jews in the following century, the *Maṭṭeh Dan*, which had been already partially translated by Aviad Sar Shalom Basilea (c. 1680–1743/9), rabbi of Mantua, in the first half of the eighteenth century,[50] was rendered into Italian in at least two integral translations; one by the aforementioned rabbi David Maroni in Florence, the other carried out between 1843 and 1845 under the title *Dissertazione e difesa della legge orale* ('Dissertation and Defence of the Oral Law') 1846 by Eliseo Pontremoli (1778–1851), at that

---

[47] Luzzatto's critical comments to the first volume of Gideon Brecher's 1838 edition of the *Kuzari* were deemed important enough by the editor to be included in the second volume published the next year.

[48] Elijah Benamozegh explicitly reminds the common ground of Maimonides' and Halevi's perception of Christianity and Islam in his *Teologia dogmatica ed apologetica* (Livorno: Vigo, 1877), 272, and *Israele e l'umanita. Il mio credo* (Pisa: ETS, 2002), 160: 'Credo come insegnano Giuda Levita e Maimonide che il cristianesimo e l'islamismo sieno grandi avviamenti all'organamento definitivo religioso dell'umanità, la quale sarà perfetta solo quando accetterà dalle mani dell'antico Israele la semplice religione laicale e razionale detta Noahide,' and see also his *Israël et l'Humanité* (Paris: Leroux, 1914), 176: 'Les rabbins, entre autres Maimonide et Juda Halevi, en ont jugé ainsi et ils nous disent qu'il existe à chaque epoque une aspiration messianique correspondant à la tendence universaliste qui ne cesse de travailler au sein de l'humanité.'

[49] The popularity of the book in the nineteenth century, outside Italy, is attested also by the versions into other European languages: in English by Louis Loewe, *The Rod of Judgment* (London: Wertheimer, 1842) and the manuscript version by Elias Hiam Lindo (1783–1865) made in 1853 and now preserved in the manuscripts Ms HUC JIR Cincinnati and Ms Montefiore 307. In the Jewish Theological Seminary, New York, there can be found a translation in Yiddish; see Ms New York, JTSL, 2390.

[50] A version of it is extant in a Cambridge manuscript.

time chief rabbi of Nice in the Kingdom of Piedmont.⁵¹ Both translations circulated in manuscripts. In 1819 the rabbi Avtalion Lampronti of Ferrara wrote a philosophical treaty and commentary of the *Maṭṭeh Dan* titled *Wikkuaḥ ʿal ʿOlam ha-Levanah ve-Shaʿar Kokhvei ha-Lekhet* ('Discussion on the Lunar World and on the other Planets'), devoted to the discussion of the relationship between science and faith, taking its cue from the fourth chapter of Nieto's work.⁵²

Aside from the work's status as a reference guide to Jewish thought, it is clear that the interest manifested by Italian Jews concerning Halevi and Nieto does not derive so much from the factual information concerning the Karaites in their oeuvre, but from the possibility of providing an apology of rabbinic Judaism. However, the malleability of the figure of the Karaite, cut off from any concrete reference to the real representatives of this community, allowed its appropriation and instrumental use in different historical contexts. In the nineteenth century, in a context of civil emancipation of the Jews and their progressive integration within society as a whole, Karaism reappears in the writings of Italian Jews attempting to define the characteristics and the role of Judaism in modernity. But while in the early modern era Jews tended to associate Karaism with deistic postures within the Jewish community and rationalist attacks against tradition, in the nineteenth century Karaites were increasingly singled out as a specular image of contemporary Jewish reform. Hence, Karaites are placed in the hot seat for the novelty of their doctrines and ignorance of Judaism, rather than for their alleged challenges against the Oral Law.

The Italian *Wissenschaft des Judentums*, the Reform and the Karaites

In the nineteenth century, the Karaites return to the fore in Jewish intellectual debate in a completely new context dominated by the opposition between Reform and Orthodoxy. Michael Meyer has noted that 'by reviving interest in Samaritans, Hellenizers, Essenes, Sadducees, and Karaites, Reformed Jews were able to challenge the association of Judaism with Pharisaism, whose extension was the rabbinism that reigned at the time.'⁵³ Therefore it is no surprise that the most often quoted works favourable to the Karaites are to be found among Reformers. Abraham Geiger, for instance, explicitly referred to the Karaites as the prototype of the Reformed Jew. Conversely, in the orthodox camps, Karaites are accused of all the evils of modernity, irreligiosity and assimilation. The Galician rabbi and scholar Solomon Judah Rapoport

---

51 See Ms Paris, Library of the Alliance Israélite Universelle, 254. On Pontremoli, see Asher Salah, "Judaism as a Moral Theology: the Work and the Figure of Elisha Pontremoli," *Zakhor*, nuova serie 1 (2017): 101–129.
52 Ms *Valmadonna* 156.
53 Michael Meyer, *Judaism Within Modernity: Essays on Jewish History and Religion* (Detroit: Wayne State University Press, 2001), 50.

(1786–1867) compared the strife and animosity of the Jewish reformers with the rift introduced within Judaism by Karaism and Sabbateanism.[54] Azriel Hildesheimer (1820–1899) reintroduced the use of writing the name of the followers of Karaism in Hebrew as *Qara'im* with an *'Ayin* instead of with an *Alef*, insisting by such of a device on the divisive nature of this sect within Judaism (the Hebrew root Q.R.A means 'to rip'). Examples of this attitude against and in favour of 'Karaism' are widespread to such an extent that the Karaites became what Daniel Lasker called the 'Jewish other' par excellence.[55]

Sometimes, the term 'Karaite' could be used by Reformed Jews as a double-edged polemical weapon against conservative rabbis. Therefore, reformers such as Joseph Aub (1804–1880) or the aforementioned Abraham Geiger, in whose writings the word 'Karaite' is a very ambivalent concept and depends on his polemical targets, sometimes accuse their orthodox counterparts of being Karaites for not being able to adapt to the changing situation of Jewish life and sticking to the letter of the Talmud.[56]

What all these uses of the word 'Karaite', pejorative or sympathetic, have in common, is that the Karaite has become the figure of a fractured Judaism in two opposite camps. It is worth quoting Marcus Jost's exemplary image of the Karaites: 'Die Karaiten [...] behaupten [...] gegen die übrigen Juden dieselbe Stellung, wie die Protestanten gegen die Katholiken, und die Schiiten gegen die Sunniten.'[57] In the German cultural domain, the Jewish world is therefore perceived to be as irremediably divided as Christianity and Islam, torn by an inner war of religions.

Without insisting or believing in an Italian *Sonderweg*, the Karaite question in Italy is posited in a quite different form than in German lands. At the turn of the nineteenth century, even prior to the mobilisation of the first and second *Kuzari* by the nascent Orthodoxy and Reformers in German speaking lands and in England,[58] Karaites elicited a good deal of curiosity among Italian Jews. This could well have been the background for the rumours widely circulated in Europe claiming Italian Jews were trying to implement substantial reforms of the Jewish law inspired by the spirit of Karaism. The rumours reached Abbé Henry Grégoire, and Italian rabbis were compelled to issue blunt disclaimers dismissing such allegations.[59] Nevertheless, Gré-

---

54 Solomon Judah Rapoport, *Tokhaḥat Megulla* [Hebrew] (Frankfurt am Main, 1845), 1.
55 Daniel Lasker, "Ha-Qarai ke-Aḥer Yehudi" [Hebrew], *Peamim* 89 (2001): 96–106.
56 Geiger defended himself against the charges of Karaism addressed to him by some Orthodox authors by labelling them as 'Talmud-Karaites'.
57 Marcus Jost, "Neue Berichte über die Karaiten und deren Geschichte," *Israelitische Annalen* 28 (1839): 217.
58 For these cultural areas the phenomenon has been analysed by Shear, *The Kuzari*, 257–261.
59 They were first published in the *Staats- und Gelehrte Zeitung des Hamburgischen unparteiischen Correspondenten* 57 (1796). On this episode, cf. Ulrich Wyrwa, *Juden in Toskana und in Preußen im Vergleich. Aufklärung und Emanzipation in Florenz, Livorno, Berlin und Königsberg i.Pr.* (Tübingen: Mohr Siebeck, 2003), 84. Cf. also Jacob Katz, *Out of the Ghetto: The Social Background of Jewish Emancipation, 1770–1870* (Syracuse, NY: Syracuse University Press, 1973), 153; Renzo De Felice, "Per una storia

goire's work praising the allegedly 'Karaite bent' of Italian Jews was translated into Italian by the Piedmontese Jew Salomon Isaac Luzzati titled *Osservazioni sullo stato degli ebrei in Francia e Germania* (Casale Monferrato: Zanotti Bianco, 1806),[60] and the Jewish press of the period reviewed it favourably.[61]

At around the same time Abraham Vita de Cologna (1755–1832), vice-president of the Napoleonic Sanhedrin in 1808 and Great Rabbi of France, a post he was to hold until 1826, wrote a self-defined 'anti-Karaite' treatise, that survived only in a 1820 translation from French into Hebrew, titled the *Qera ha-Gever* ('The Cockcrow'), by Elisha Pontremoli.[62] Posing as a history of the Karaites and their literature, which to a large degree it is, the *Qera ha-Gever* contains many anti-Christian remarks and constitutes a late offspring of a kind of apologetic literature in defence of the Oral Law against the criticism of Christian and Jewish sceptics. In choosing to translate this work into Hebrew clearly reveals Pontremoli's involvement in religious polemics, a subject to which he devoted a short text, *Wikkuaḥ Socrati be-'Inyanei ha-Emunah* ('Socratic Dialogue on Faith'), and his engagement in Jewish apologetics against those inclined to reform Judaism in the name of a restoration of the biblical purity, which the orthodox camp perceived as modern manifestations of Karaism. It is no coincidence that Pontremoli defines the despised Voltaire as 'a modern Sadducee.'

Despite this polemical attempt at disqualifying Karaism's claims to be the authentic representative of Judaism, Cologna's work in Pontremoli's translation makes a clear distinction between Karaism, as a sect of Judaism in the times of Geonim and contemporary Karaites, described in the eight chapter as 'much less distinct from rabbanite Jews today than they were in the past,' expressing the hope of a reconciliation with them in the near future, countering Christian attempts to increase the gap between the two Jewish groups. Cologna's treatise demonstrates a greater accuracy and deeper knowledge of real Karaism and the Karaite diaspora, and along with the traditional attacks to their faith present detailed description of their literature, their beliefs and their customs.

This is neither the first nor the only instance of an academic and less biased attitude concerning Karaism and Karaites. An earlier example of the curiosity attracted

---

del problema ebraico in Italia alla fine del XVIII e all'inizio del XIX. La prima emancipazione," *Movimento Operaio* 5 (1955): 681–727; Attilio Milano, *Storia degli ebrei in Italia* (Turin: Einaudi, 1963), 345; Lois C. Dubin, "Triest and Berlin: The Italian Role in the Cultural Politics of the Haskalah," in *Toward Modernity: the European Jewish Model*, ed. Jacob Katz (New York: Routledge, 1997): 207–208. See also the correspondence between Ricci and Grégoire in Maurice Vaussard, *Correspondence Scipione de Ricci–Henry Grégoire* (Florence: Sansoni, 1963).

60 Luzzati who also translated classics of Hebrew literature into Italian, such as the *Tofteh Arukh* by Moshe Zacut, *L'inferno preparato* (Turin, 1819), later converted to Catholicism took the name Amedeo Luzzati Valperga and published a periodical against the Talmud, *Osservatore talmudico: giornale periodico* (Turin: C. Sylva Tipografo, 1827).

61 As late as in 1880 we find positive reviews of this work. See, e.g. the Italian Jewish journal printed in Corfu but emanating from the Rabbinical College in Padua, *Mosé* 3 (1880): 297.

62 Ms Moscow, Russian State Library, Guenzburg 1440.

by this religious group is evidenced in the biblical studies inspired by the new methods of philology and textual criticism is inarguably the precious collection of Karaite manuscripts collected by the Venetian rabbi Jacob Raphael Saraval (1708–1782) in the course of his numerous travels throughout Europe.[63] Saraval provided the abbot Giovanni Bernardo De Rossi (1742–1831), professor of Oriental languages at the University of Parma, with the main body of information of Karaism that appeared in his encyclopaedic work on the history of Jewish literature. De Rossi was able to correct and add new sources to the classical textbooks on Karaism written by Jacobus Trigland, Johann Gottfried Schupart (1677–1730), Gustav Peringer and Johann Christoph Wolf (1683–1739) thanks to Saraval's erudite cooperation, from whose collection he purchased several Karaite manuscripts for the Palatine library in Parma.[64] Another bibliophile and book collector, Moise Beniamin Foà (1730–1822), an important Jewish scholar and merchant from Reggio well connected to the European academic networks, was able to bring part of Saraval's Karaite collection into the library holdings of the Duchy of Modena.[65]

A very positive assessment of Karaism can be found in the chapters thirteen and fourteen of the reform project designed by Aron Fernandez (1761–1828) (or Fernando —as he signed all of his works to Italianize his Iberian patronym) *Progetto filosofico d'una completa riforma del culto e della educazione politico-morale del popolo ebreo* (Tibériade, 1810; *vere* Florence: Marenigh, 1813) from Leghorn. Fernandez was convinced that 'Karaites agree with the rest of the Jews in what concerns the fundamental points of religion.'[66] He admired their faith unburdened of useless practices and dangerous superstitions that had entered into Judaism over centuries of wanderings among idolatrous cultures, but criticised Karaism for its 'austerity that makes it in many parts almost impracticable.'[67]

Despite a current image that is to be proven incorrect by recent Karaism scholarship, Fernandez was among the first scholars to understand that Karaites, were not adepts of a pure literal reading of the Bible for they accepted parts of the Masoretic interpretation of the Scriptures, and therefore could not be assimilated, based on the principle of *sola scriptura,* into Protestant hermeneutics. Fernandez is fully aware that Karaism is far from being a deistic and rational form of Judaism unlike the ver-

---

[63] A description of his travel to the Netherlands can be found in the seven letters included in Jacob Raphael Saraval, *Viaggi in Olanda* (Venice: Zatta, 1807).
[64] Cf. Giovanni Bernardo De Rossi, *Dizionario storico degli autori ebrei e delle loro opere* (Parma: Dalla reale stamperia, 1802), 121.
[65] Cf. Giovanni Bernardo De Rossi, *Annales hebraeo-typographici ab anno MDI ad MDXL digessit notisque hist.-criticis ab auctore instructi* (Parma: Carmignani, 1799), 34.
[66] Aron Fernandez, *Progetto filosofico d'una completa riforma del culto e della educazione politico-morale del popolo ebreo* (Tibériade, 1810; vere Florence: Marenigh, 1813), 184: 'I caraiti convergono in quanto riguarda i punti fondamentali della religione con gli altri ebrei.'
[67] *Ibidem*, 198: 'Austerità che la rende in moltissime parti pressoché impraticabile.'

sion of it he wishes to spread among his contemporaries and warns against an excessive idealisation of Karaism.[68]

Fernandez found an admirer of his radical project of reform in the otherwise moderate and observant rabbi of Gorizia, Isaac Samuel Reggio (1784–1855), a main figure of the *Wissenschaft des Judentums* in Italy and one of the founders of the rabbinical college of Padua. In 1852, Reggio published, under the title *Beḥinat ha-Qabbalah* ('Examination of the Tradition'), the work that he attributed to Leon Modena, the *Qol Sakhal* ('The Voice of the Fool'), a text that mentions the Karaites in highly favourable terms. According to Hanan Gafni, that very particular kind of Karaism found in Reggio's writings concerns the legal authority of the Talmud, considered by Reggio as purely theoretical, bearing no consequences for establishing the Halakhah.[69] The only binding text for Reggio was the Mishnah, thus relativizing the reverence the Talmud was given by Jews in the Middle Ages in the Diaspora. For this reason Solomon Judah Rapoport attacked Reggio dubbing him a 'Karaite'.[70]

Besides Reggio, another central figure of Italian Judaism in the nineteenth century, Samuel David Luzzatto, displayed an intense interest for Karaite scholarship and history. Like Reggio, Luzzatto corresponded with the Russian Karaite Abraham Leonowicz (1780–1851).[71] Luzzatto deals lengthily on the origins of the Karaites in his lessons of Jewish history, originally delivered during the academic year 1830–31 at the rabbinical college in Padua but published only two decades later.[72] His main goal is to demonstrate, against the *Kuzari* author's opinion and the seventeenth century Dutch reform theologian Jacob Trigland, that Karaism is posterior to the constitution of rabbinic Judaism. The question is not only a scholarly diatribe, but also who is to be considered the representative of the authentic and original Judaism and who is but a later, corrupted, reformed version of it. Luzzatto writes:

> [...] that the Karaites, not the Rabbanites, are to be identified with the new and reformed Jews. [...] The Karaites answer that the talmudists have often mentioned their sects, but that in their hatred they have confused it with the Sadducees. Consequently, some contemporary Rabbanites, influenced by their ignorance or by their hatred, still confuse the Karaites with the Sadducees.[73]

---

68 *Ibidem*, 196: 'Bisogna non lasciarsi trascinare dall'eccesso condannabile di deferire ciecamente a suoi errori nella ghisa medesima che approvate abbiamo le sue massime.'
69 Hanan Gafni, *Pshuṭah shel Mishnah. 'Iyyunim be-Ḥeqer Sifrut Ḥazal be-'Et ha-Ḥadashah* ("The Mishnah's Plain Sense. A Study of Modern Talmudic Scholarship") [Hebrew] (Tel Aviv: Hakibbutz Hameuchad, 2011), 104–118.
70 Cf. David Malkiel, "The Reggios of Gorizia: Modernization in Micro," in *The Mediterranean and the Jews*, ed. Elliott Horowitz (Ramat Gan: Bar-Ilan University Press, 2002): 73.
71 Akhiezer, *Historical Consciousness*, 222.
72 Samuel David Luzzatto, *Lezioni di Storia Giudaica* (Padua: Bianchi, 1852), 21, 83, 145–155 and 166–173.
73 *Ibidem*, 147: 'Che sono I caraiti, non già i rabbaniti, quelli che si debbono dire nuovi e riformati giudei. [...] Rispondono i Caraiti che i Talmudisti hanno soventi volte mentovata la loro setta, ma che per odio l'hanno confusa con quella dei Sadducei. Conche alcuni Rabbaniti moderni, spinti o dall'ignoranza, o dall'odio, hanno confusi i Caraiti coi Sadducei.'

In demonstrating his claim, Luzzatto puts forward four arguments. Firstly, that the Karaites are not mentioned in talmudic literature, secondly, the Karaites do not mention any scholar of their school before Anan in the eighth century, thirdly they have adopted the vocalic system of the rabbanite tradition of the Bible which Luzzatto believed was developed after the fifth century of the common era, and lastly they observe stricter rules than rabbanite Jews in their matrimonial law.

However, without sharing the sympathies of Fernandez and Reggio towards the Karaites, Luzzatto insists that Karaism does not necessarily contrast with what he deems the fundamental principles of faith of Judaism, to which he devotes his book *Lezioni di Teologica dogmatica* (Trieste: Coen, 1863). In line with his Italian predecessor, Luzzatto attempts to draw an historical portrayal of Judaism which in contradistinction to Christianity, has not been affected by religious schisms. Thus, he dismisses the Samaritans considering them as belonging to the Moabite nation and not to be Jews. Of the Sadducees and the Boethusians Luzzatto insists their weight in Judaism has been almost completely irrelevant. Writing of these sects, active in the Second Temple period he states they were 'always numerically feeble and did not have any public impact.'[74] And as for the last and still existing Jewish sect, the Karaites, after having demolished their claim to antiquity and allegedly superior adherence to the original meaning of the Scriptures, he concludes:

> [A]lthough they negate the rabbinical traditions, they do not do it in an absolute manner, since their opposition to the sacred text of the law is only apparent. In reality they admit the immortality of the soul, and in practice they are the most rigid observers of the Law and of the Moral.[75]

Rabbanite Jews and Karaites are united in their basic belief in a common faith and both reject the sceptic attitude of modernity against religion, which is Luzzatto's main polemical target.[76]

In the writings of Aron Fernando, Isaac Samuel Reggio, Samuel David Luzzatto, and others, the Karaite is not the figure of the classical schismatic, as say, the Protestant in the eyes of the Catholic, or the Reformed Jew in those of the Orthodox. In a country such as Italy, that had not experienced the religious divides of other European regions, the Karaites represented instead the fear of the possibility of such a division. Within Italian Judaism that was moving towards a more carefully defined doxology, the doctrinal differences between Karaism and Rabbinical Judaism had to be neutralized. Jews in Italy, reformist leaning or not, wished to maintain a façade of unity. In the words of one of the main political leaders of Italian Jews in the nine-

---

74 Luzzatto, *Il giudaismo illustrato*, 37: 'Furono sempre deboli di numero e di credito pubblico.'
75 *Ibidem*: 'I caraiti poi negano essi le tradizioni rabbiniche, ma non assolutamente, ma in quanto sembrano opporsi al sacro testo della legge; ammettono poi l'immortalità dell'anima, e sono nella pratica i più rigidi osservatori della Legge e della Morale.'
76 Luzzatto considers scepticism and not Karaism the main menace to the unity of the Jewish people and devotes different sections (24 to 27) of his *Lezioni di Teologica dogmatica* to undermining the spread of this dangerous attitude among his fellow Jews.

teenth century, Salvatore Anau (1807–1874): 'The world shall be Catholic for the universality of brotherly love!'[77] Giuseppe Levi, founder and director of the influential Jewish paper *l'Educatore Israelita*, gave voice to the same wish most precisely in a long article on the Karaites:

> Luckily enough in the bosom of Judaism [...] the word of God remained always one and uniform. [...] Therefore, Judaism in our times walks united, and the different opinions that strife within it, did not become, and we hope, will never become, a sect, distinct and opposed to it.[78]

Therefore, after summarizing its history and doctrines, Levi insists Karaism does not represent a schism within Judaism. On the contrary, 'not the principles, but only some rituals separate between us. [...] it would be nice and useful that the representatives of the great principle of God's unity, should all be united in beautiful harmony.'[79]

This also explains a reticence in using the word 'reform' which at the time was highly controversial. In Italy, even the most far-reaching Jewish reformers avoided it when describing their intended plans. Moderate or radical reformers, such as Mortara, Salomone Olper (1811–1877), Lelio Cantoni (1802–1857), and many others, preferred to designate themselves as progressives, or as moderate conservatives, and even as orthodox, inventing the category of ultra-orthodox to differentiate their views from the traditionalists they intended to disqualify. Undoubtedly, for Jews living in a Catholic environment, the word 'reform' evoked the schisms provoked within Christianity by Protestantism.

It is certainly worth noting that also in neighbouring Catholic France, the reform movement founded in 1907 adopted the name of *Union Libérale* and not *Union Reformée*.

Therefore, for Italian Jews, Karaites became the image of the threat to the Catholic, i.e. universalist, vocation of Judaism. To minimise their role in the historical de-

---

[77] Salvatore Anau, *Della emancipazione degli Ebrei* (Florence, 1847), 15.

[78] Giuseppe Levi, "Alcuni cenni popolari sui caraiti," *L'Educatore Israelita* 7 (1859): 290–291: 'Fortunatamente però nel seno proprio del Giudaismo [...] la parola di Dio rimase quasi sempre uniforme e sola. [...] Così il giudaismo ai nostri tempi cammina quasi uniforme ed unito, e le varie opinioni che si combattono ora nel suo seno non hanno pero ancora dato luogo e, speriamo, non lo daranno mai ad una setta pienamente distinta e contraria.' The main source of information concerning Karaism seems to be Samuel David Luzzatto, with some additions such as the possibility of the Karaites being the descendants of the lost tribes of Israel. He asks his young readers to imagine a synagogue and Karaite quarter and concludes that nobody would be able to tell the difference in Italian Jewish life, aside from the fact that Karaites are perhaps more rigid in their observance of the law than the descendants of Talmudic Jews, i.e. contemporary Italian Jews.

[79] Ibidem, *L'Educatore Israelita* 8 (1860): 10: 'Non sono principi, ma sono solo alcuni riti che ci separano. [...] sarebbe bello ed utile che i rappresentanti ed eredi del grande principio della Unità di Dio, fossero tutti uniti in bella armonia.' The same conclusion could be found in Fernandez, *Progetto*, 184: 'the Karaites agree with the other Jews in everything concerning the fundamental principles of religion' ('i caraiti convergono in quanto riguarda i punti fondamentali della religione con gli altri ebrei').

velopment of Judaism, stressing that the core of the dogmatic structure of Judaism, was shared by Karaites and Rabbanites, permitted Jews in Italy to find a common ground in fighting what Morais, in his literary portrait of Luzzatto, labelled 'the corrosive effects of indifferentism and scepticism.'

This too explains the transformation of Samuel David Luzzatto into a consensual Jewish icon for all emancipated Jews, notwithstanding their personal positions in the spectrum of attitudes toward religion, tradition, and practice. The strong drive to give a dogmatic foundation to Judaism, one of the major goals of Luzzatto's intellectual endeavour, resulted in a vision of the Jewish political and religious body as fundamentally unified and impermeable to change. In the process, the Karaites' differences to normative Judaism could be domesticated and transform their image from schismatics waiving the banner of scepticism against their fideistic antagonists (as was the case among Jews and Christians alike in a religiously divided Central and Northern Europe) into a branch of the people of Israel, exotic but innocuous, confirming the universality and eternity of the Jewish faith.

Libera Pisano
Anarchic Scepticism: Language, Mysticism and Revolution in Gustav Landauer

> *Even for the anarchist, language is the rope of the law bound around his neck;*
> *even the most free philosopher thinks with the words of philosophical language.*[1]

Gustav Landauer (1870–1919), a German-Jewish anarchist and a radical thinker, was brutally murdered by the *Freikorps* in Munich. He was an almost forgotten figure for a long time, even though his ideas exerted a crucial influence on the development of twentieth century Jewish thought and philosophy, particularly regarding the rehabilitation of utopian, messianic, anarchical and mystical elements. Landauer was one of very few Jewish authors permitting the word 'scepticism' to be included in the title of one of his works—namely *Skepsis und Mystik*[2]—in my view this very term is the *fil rouge* running through all his political and philosophical thought. However, this feature has not received the proper attention by scholars, which focus mainly on Landauer's singular account of anarchism and mysticism, alongside his conception of revolution and community.

In this essay, I will attempt to shed light on the connection between Fritz Mauthner's (1849–1923) linguistic critique and Landauer's anarchy, showing the political implications of sceptical thought. To this end, I will focus on the sceptical features of Landauer's anarchist socialism by analysing the connection between scepticism and mysticism, the role played by scepticism in his thought of community and in his account of revolution, history and time, and the definition of his anti-political attitude as sceptical *Lebensform*.

1 Anarchy as (Anti)political *Epoché*

There is an affinity between anarchism and scepticism, even if this binomial has not yet received proper attention. One can define anarchism as an (anti)political attitude whose main features are a radical critique towards authorities and a challenge to the system of representations, while scepticism could be broadly defined as a method as well as an attitude, which criticizes dogmatic assumptions and leads to a suspension of judgment. If anarchism could be interpreted as a rejection of political representation, it is possible to extend these particular critiques to any general forms of label-

---

[1] Cf. Fritz Mauthner, *Beiträge zu einer Kritik der Sprache*, 2nd edition, vol. 1 (Stuttgart and Berlin: J.G. Cotta'sche Buchhandlung, 1913), 221: 'Die Sprache legt auch dem Anarchisten den Strick des Gesetzes um den Hals und auch der freieste Philosoph denkt mit den Worten der philosophischen Sprache.'
[2] Gustav Landauer, *Skepsis und Mystik. Versuche im Anschluss an Mauthners Sprachkritik*, in idem, *Ausgewählte Schriften*, vol. 7, ed. Siegbert Wolf (Lich/Hessen: Edition AV, 2011).

ling representation or to any dogmatic systems of rule.³ Anarchy and scepticism share this ongoing criticism the aim of which is not a concrete systematisation transforming them into their contraries with anarchy becoming an institutional framework and scepticism turning into dogmatism. Indeed, the transformation of these terms into their contraries is, in both cases, a slippery slope. Is it possible to define a thinker, in the midst of an ongoing criticism not accepting any assumption, as being a dogmatic sceptic? Conversely, are we to define an anarchist, embedded in his criticism towards the state and the system, as representative of another form of authority and power? These open questions may help us to shed light on the special and controversial affinities between scepticism and anarchy.

As is well known, the etymology of 'anarchy' is 'absence of government' or 'of leader' (*archos*), but at the same time it is a lack of '*arche*', which is one of the key words of Greek ancient philosophy. '*Arche*' has a double meaning: on the one hand, it means 'origin', 'beginning' and 'principle of action', on the other, 'power', 'command', 'authorities'. If the word '*arche*' connects a temporal dimension to the authority, one can say that an anarchic thought par excellence has to take into account time and power, as Landauer did. Anarchy is not just an overthrowing of the '*arche*', but starts with a process of doubting and calling into question the *status quo*. As anarchy denies all forms of systematisation, it is a kind of suspension of authority, which, in my view, seems to be a form of (anti)political *epoché*.

2 Gustav Landauer at the Crossroad of Several Paths

As a political activist and writer, journalist and translator, Landauer was one of the most important thinkers combining Jewish messianism with anarchy, politics with mysticism, and a romantic philosophy of history with a belief in the urgency of change. His works comprises many articles, translations, fragments, reviews, and a number of discourses; important milestones are *Die Revolution* and *Aufruf zum Sozialismus*, but his only complete philosophical study, on which he worked for two years following his release from prison early in 1900, is *Skepsis und Mystik*.

The complicated intrigue of Landauer's anarchy concerns the conjunction of two levels: the mystical experience and the political action. The weave of these elements positions his thought at a crossroads of several paths, something quite unique in the history of philosophy. At least three reasons demonstrate how he is to be considered a complex thinker: firstly, his works are unsystematic; secondly, he mixes up different and—apparently—opposite elements; and thirdly he gives a singular definition to some key concepts. Scholars have used many adjectives in attempting to define his political socialist anarchism: mystical, anarchical, regressive, *Gemeindesozialismus*

---

3 See Jesse S. Cohn, *Anarchism and the Crisis of Representation: Hermeneutics, Aesthetics, Politics* (Selinsgrove: Susquehanna University Press, 2006).

to name but a few. His particular idea of socialism is based on an anarchic opposition toward any form of authority including political, social, ethical, and religious articulation of power. It is at the same time a project of liberation from all the forms of enslavement, interior and external, and a showing of the path required to take one from isolation to community—from theory to praxis.

At this point, I feel it pertinent to consider Landauer's biography. Born, 7th April, 1870, to a secular Jewish family in Karlsruhe, southern Germany, he studied German and English literature, philosophy and art history in Heidelberg, Strasbourg and Berlin. However, he completed none of these studies as his political militancy had him banned from all German universities. Stirner, Nietzsche, Ibsen, Spinoza and Schopenhauer are just a few of the many philosophers he was impressed by in that time. His first political commitments saw him rise to the top of German anarchist circles during the 1890s.[4] This political activity and anarchist commitment, led to his acquaintance with prominent activists such as Peter Kropotkin, Max Nettlau, and Errico Malatesta.[5] His biographer Ruth Link-Salinger tells us this period was devoted 'to a systematic definition of what anarchism was to be and was not to be,'[6] and this was arrived at also due to his collaboration with Fritz Mauthner.

In the first decade of 1900, Landauer withdrew almost entirely from public activity to engage in private study. He was to favour a more inner, philosophical and mystical idea of anarchism to the political manifestations of the time. This introspection was spurred by his translation of Meister Eckhart in prison and a deep affinity with the Mauthner's *Sprachskepsis*.[7] This new vein of Landauer's thought is sourced his "Durch Absonderung zur Gemeinschaft," a speech given at a meeting of the newly founded circle *Neue Gemeinschaft*—where he met Martin Buber and Erich Mühsam—and later was to serve as the first chapter of his *Skepsis und Mystik*. During these years Landauer and his second wife (the poet and translator, Hedwig Lachmann, whom he married in 1903) were extremely active translating Peter Kropotkin, Oscar Wilde, Walt Whitman, and Rabindranath Tagore.

---

[4] In the 1893 he participated in the Zurich congress of the second International as an anarchist delegate. The congress, dominated by German social democrats, expelled him along with the other anarchists. August Bebel—the leader of the social democrats—accused him of being a police informer. When Landauer returned to Berlin, he spent almost one year in prison for the writings he published in *Der Sozialist*. For Landauer's life, cf. Charles B. Maurer, *Call to Revolution: The Mystical Anarchism of Gustav Landauer* (Detroit: Wayne State University Press, 1971); Eugene Lunn, *Prophet of Community: The Romantic Socialism of Gustav Landauer* (Berkeley: University of California Press, 1973); Ruth Link-Salinger, *Gustav Landauer: Philosopher of Utopia* (Indianapolis: Hackett Publishing Co., 1977): 74–76.
[5] He travelled as an anarchist delegate to a second international congress in London where the anarchists were—once more—excluded and organised for themselves another conference. Landauer prepared a report for the occasion *From Zurich to London*, which became his most translated piece at that time.
[6] Link-Salinger, *Gustav Landauer: Philosopher of Utopia*, 48.
[7] Between 1893 and 1900 he spent a total of 18 months in prison on various charges of libel and defamation.

In 1906, Buber became editor in chief of a book series called *Die Gesellschaft* and asked his friend Landauer to write a book on the intriguing topic of revolution. Landauer's essay was published in 1907 and this year marked his return to political activism; in fact, he published "30 Socialist theses"[8] that anticipate his *Call to Socialism*, of 1911, which represents the peak of his political contribution. In May 1908, Landauer initiated the *Sozialistischer Bund* whose goal was to form small, independent communities or settlements as a material foundation for a new form of society and an embodiment of his notion of socialism. With the outbreak of war, Landauer and Hedwig Lachmann were isolated, being among the few pacifistic voices in Germany at that time. The majority of anarchists and leftist thinkers welcomed the war as an opportunity of political renovation.[9] Landauer was convinced the war was nothing but the extreme outcome of nationalism and imperialism. In 1917 he and his wife decided to move to Krumbach, southern Germany. In 1918 Hedwig died of pneumonia and his enormous loss has been interpreted by many biographers and friends as a point of no return in Landauer's life and justification for his 'sacrifice' or 'martyrdom' to the Munich Soviet Republic; in fact, in November 1918 he joined the Bavarian Revolution as one of its intellectual leaders. He was brutally murdered by the Freikorps (*Free corps*) on the 2nd of May in 1919.

Landauer's milieu was fin-de-siècle and pre-World War I. His generation, born in the nineteenth century living up to the outbreak of the war were faced with a great loss of structure and order and experienced great alienation that led many to a rejection of traditions. Two vital coordinates help understand Landauer's contribution: the *Sprachkrise* and the *Neue Mystik*. German Jews played a pivotal role in these particular German phenomena emerging at the beginning of the twentieth century.[10]

---

8 His essay entitled "Volk and Land: 30 Socialist theses"—published in *Die Zukunft* in January 1907—focussed on the problem of the state and voluntary cooperation and was simultaneously a programme for new, concrete organisation.
9 See Ulrich Sieg, *Jüdische Intellektuelle im Ersten Weltkrieg* (Berlin: Akademie Verlag, 2008): 145–150. Even Buber followed the general trend of German nationalism. In 1916, in the editorial "Die Losung" of the first issue of *Der Jude*, Buber took an ambiguous stand: on the one hand, he emphasised that Judaism had no connection with war, on the other he praised the individual commitment to the war as an effort to discovery community. Furthermore, in his essay "The spirit of the Orient and Judaism," Buber celebrated Germany for its spiritual affinity to the Eastern peoples and strong cultural interaction with Judaism, by defending the superiority of German spirit compared with other nations. Landauer was angry and disappointed by such arguments, rejecting the *Kriegsbuber* and his mere aestheticism and formalism. Community cannot be discovered in the midst of war and murder. Under Landauer's pressure, Buber later became hostile to the war. Landauer called his friend 'War Buber' in the letter of May 12, 1916. See Grete Schaeder, ed., *Martin Buber. Briefwechsel aus sieben Jahrzehnten*, vol. 1 (Heidelberg: Lambert Schneider, 1972), 433. This letter doesn't appear in the volume of Landauer's letter edited by Buber, Gustav Landauer, *Sein Lebensgang in Briefen*, 2 vols., ed. Martin Buber (Frankfurt am Main: Rütten & Loening, 1929).
10 Cf. Rolf Kauffeldt, "Anarchie und Romantik," in *Gustav Landauer im Gespräch. Symposium zum 125. Geburtstag*, eds. Hanna Delf and Gert Mattenklott (Tübingen: Max Niemeyer, 1997): 45; Adam

The so-called *Sprachkrise* was a complex critique of language discussed by poets and intellectuals in philosophical and literary debate during the years leading up to World War I (von Hofmannsthal, Schnitzler, Kraus, all the Jung-Wien members, etc.).[11] Its authors were beginning to doubt the role of language from many perspectives; the gap between language and reality renders the former into a defective tool presenting an insurmountable obstacle of grasping reality and revealing the truth. Even to this day the phenomenon of *Sprachkrise* has not been sufficiently focussed on in philosophical research, as it has been interpreted as a literal and cultural movement and not subject matter appropriate to the discourse of philosophy. However, in my view, it marks a turning point in the history of contemporary philosophy, as this sceptical-linguistic attitude, focussed special attention among German Jewish thinkers on language, anticipating the so-called 'linguistic turn'. In this constellation Mauthner and Landauer were crucial, with the former (in the wake of this sceptical approach) building a bridge between philosophy and literature, and the latter donating a political connotation.

The second coordinate, the *Neue Mystik*, was a reinterpretation by poets and writers of mysticism in Germany at the turn of the twentieth century.[12] This new kind of mysticism does not deal with the traditional idea of a mystical union between God and soul, but rather with a feeling of awareness of connection between individual and community, present and past. This kind of secularised mysticism combines aesthetic-linguistic aspects—it is no coincidence most involved were writers and poets—sharing a political and social idea of the regeneration of humankind.[13] Landauer plays an active role in many political attempts to rethink community on a social and mystical basis;[14] furthermore, his brilliant translation of Meister Eckhart's works significantly contributed to this new conception of mysticism.

M. Weisberger, *The Jewish Ethic and the Spirit of Socialism* (New York and Frankfurt am Main *et al.*: Peter Lang, 1997): 163.

11 See Gert Mattenklott, "Gustav Landauer. Ein Portrait," in *Gustav Landauer Werkausgabe*, eds. Gert Mattenklott and Hanna Delf, vol. 3 (Berlin: Akademie, 1997): XVII: 'Mauthner, Hugo von Hofmannsthal, Buber, Kraus oder Landauer die ihre Skepsis in ihrer Literatur oder—wie im Falle von Buber und Landauer—auch ihren Übersetzungen zugleich produktiv umzusetzen suchten—das Phänomen Sprachkrise zu beschreiben und erklären.'

12 For instance, Julius and Heinrich Hart, Wilhelm Bölsche, Willy Pastor, Rainer Maria Rilke, Alfred Mombert, Bruno Wille etc.

13 Cf. Walther Hoffmann, "Neue Mystik," in *Die Religion in Geschichte und Gegenwart*, eds. Friedrich Michael Schiele and Leopold Scharnack, vol. 1 (Tübingen: Mohr, 1913): 608–611; Uwe Spörl, *Gottlose Mystik in der deutschen Literatur um die Jahrhundertwende* (Paderborn: Schöningh, 1997); Martina Wagner-Egelhaaf, *Mystik der Moderne. Die visionäre Ästhetik der deutschen Literatur im 20. Jahrhundert* (Stuttgart: Metzler, 1989); Anna Wolkowicz, *Mystiker der Revolution. Der utopische Diskurs um die Jahrhundertwende* (Warsaw: WUW, 2007).

14 The connection between a new idea of community and a particular idea of language was also experienced at that time by the organisation *Neue Gemeinschaft*, formed by a group of artists and writers who shared the idea of the brothers Heinrich and Julius Hart known for their literary criticism. Their attempt was to offer a revitalisation of society in accordance with a reform of literature and

3 Linguistic Scepticism and Anarchist Thought: Mauthner and Landauer

Fritz Mauthner and Gustav Landauer were bound by a deep, lifelong intellectual friendship, evidenced by a huge epistolary.[15] The former's linguistic scepticism was used by Landauer as the tool for unmasking and smashing the oppressive idols hidden in language and its supposed truths.[16] Mauthner's treatment of language as a deceptive tool for human knowledge is at the root of Landauer's thought of anarchy. He used a linguistic-sceptical strategy to dismantle the power of the state and lead to a community based on a new idea of justice. While Mauthner focussed attention on the metaphorical and illusory value of language and human knowledge mediated by words, Landauer implemented linguistic scepticism to develop another political model.[17]

Fritz Mauthner was a philosopher and sceptic of language; he is an almost forgotten figure, who, nevertheless, produced a huge body of work: three volumes of *Contributions toward a Critique of Language*, a *Dictionary of Philosophy*, *History of*

---

the spiritual guide was the metaphysical and religious idea of Julius Hart explained in his works as *Der neue Gott* and *Die neue Welterkenntnis*. However, this kind of mystical environment was incapable —according to Landauer who left the organisation one year later— to change society. Furthermore, during World War I, he was active in some anti-militaristic circles—e.g. *Forte Kreis, Bund Neues Vaterland* and *Zentralstelle Völkerrechte*—whose goals were to create an alternative community.

15 See Gustav Landauer and Fritz Mauthner, *Briefwechsel 1890–1919*, eds. Hanna Delf and Julius H. Schoeps (München: Beck, 1994).

16 On linguistic scepticism, cf. Christian Mittermüller, *Sprachskepsis und Poetologie. Goethes Romane 'Die Wahlverwandtschaften' und 'Wilhelm Meister Wanderjahre'* (Tübingen: Niemeyer, 2008); Magdolna Orosz and Peter Plesner, "Sprache, Skepsis und Ich um 1900. Formen der belletristischen Ich-Dekonstruktion in der österreichischen und ungarischen Kultur der Jahrhundertwende," in '*…und die Worte rollen von Ihren Fäden fort…': Sprache, Sprachlichkeit, Sprachproblem in der österreichischen und ungarischen Kultur und Literatur der Jahrhundertwende*, eds. Magdolna Orosz, Amália Kerekes, and Katalin Teller (Budapest: ELTE, 2002): 355–368; Günter Saße, *Sprache und Kritik: Untersuchung zur Sprachkritik der Moderne* (Göttingen: Vandenhoeck & Ruprecht, 1977); Martin Kurzreiter, *Sprachkritik als Ideologiekritik bei Fritz Mauthner* (Frankfurt am Main: Lang, 1993), 25–80; Gerald Hartung, *Sprach-Kritik: Sprach- und Kulturtheoretische Reflexionen im deutsch-jüdischen Kontext* (Weilerswist: Velbrück Wissenschaft, 2012).

17 The connection between anarchy and language stems from Proudhon who considered the question of language connected to the idea of collective being. See Pierre Joseph Proudhon, "An Anarchist's View of Democracy," trans. Robert Hoffmann and S. Valerie Hoffman, in *Anarchism*, ed. Robert Hoffman (New York: Atherton Press, 1970): 52: 'Where and when have you heard the People? With what mouths, in what language do they express themselves?' According to him, nature and language produce associations and divisions through an ongoing articulation. Language is, on the one hand, a dispositive of power, on the other, the milieu in which socialism could happen as language avoids private property. However, it is a tool for identifying representation and creating associations or boundaries, it is not by chance that institutional power passes through language.

Atheism in the Western Society and numerous essays and novels.[18] The three volumes *Contributions toward a Critique of Language* are an example of thoroughgoing linguistic scepticism in the history of philosophy, coordinating linguistic doubt with epistemology. Mauthner's *Contributions* were written in an attempt to demonstrate how language is redundant as a means for the perception of reality and, insofar as knowledge is mediated by words, impossible. His originality lies in his anticipation of the linguistic turn in arguing that the philosophy of language sheds critical light on all philosophical questions.[19]

Thanks to Mauthner's intercession, Landauer translated some of Meister Eckhart's mystical writings into modern German, and these were used as materials aids for the writing of *Contributions toward a Critique of Language*. The two friends' cooperation in linguistic critique was deeply relevant; in prison Landauer edited Mauthner's *Contributions* and after publication of the first volume reviewed it for *Zukunft*. The ongoing discussion and confrontation between them led to a discussion on the limits of language and an exploration of the political effects of mysticism.

According to Mauthner, language deletes the uniqueness of our experience by transforming it into a series of tautologies and, although it can refer to reality only metaphorically, it is the only medium of human knowledge. Words exercise a social and political power; even if language is a collection of illusions, it is a dangerous weapon. All metaphysical abstractions are falsities, a mere trick of the language, which forces us to believe that each noun corresponds to a pre-existing substance. If the word is not representative of reality, the most important task of philosophy is the critique of language, i.e. the liberation from the superstitions and the tyranny of words (*Wortfetischismus, Wortaberglauben, Worttyrannei*).

Mauthner's *logos-scepticism* has many different features: a radicalisation of empiricism, the coincidence between thinking and speaking, the relevance of use and linguistic habits, the utopia of communication, the liberating task of philosophy, his controversial relationship with Judaism and silent mysticism. In my view, the practical aim of Mauthner's philosophy, i.e., the liberation from the superstitions of words is in accordance with the therapeutic value of ancient scepticism and, more-

---

18 Fritz Mauthner, *Beiträge zu einer Kritik der Sprache*; idem, *Wörterbuch der Philosophie. Neue Beiträge zu einer Kritik der Sprache*, 2nd edition, 3 vols. (Leipzig: Meiner, 1923); idem, *Der Atheismus und seine Geschichte im Abendlande*, 4 vols. (Stuttgart and Berlin: DVA, 1924).
19 On Mauthner's linguistic scepticism, see Luisa Bertolini, *La maledizione della parola di Fritz Mauthner* (Palermo: Supplementa, Aestetica, 2008); Gerald Hartung, ed., *An den Grenzen der Sprachkritik: Fritz Mauthners Beiträge zur Sprache- und Kulturtheorie* (Würzburg: Königshausen und Neumann, 2003); Joachim Kühn, *Gescheiterte Sprachkritik: Fritz Mauthners Leben und Werk* (Berlin and New York: De Gruyter, 1975); Elizabeth Bredeck, *Metaphors of Knowledge: Language and Thought in Mauthner's Critique* (Detroit: Wayne State University Press, 1992).

over, his mystical silence, arising from his critique, is a modern achievement of ancient *ataraxia*.[20]

Landauer interpreted the curative value of Mauthner's linguistic scepticism in a political way. In both perspectives there is an attempt at liberation from the tyranny of language and the chains of authority; however, while Mauthner develops a radical criticism, which leads him to a dismantling of language and solitary and elitist path of silence and mysticism, Landauer goes a step further and connects this introspective tendency emanating from scepticism with a liberation from isolation to experience a true community. Mauthner's attack on language as mere word superstitions, and in particular his questioning of belief in the empirically isolated self, provided Landauer with a useful basis for defending his own mysticism. He combined Mauthner's linguistic scepticism with an anarchic critique of society, by admitting the affinity between *Sprachkritik* and his account of anarchism and socialism.[21]

4 Active Scepticism and Social Mysticism

Landauer's philosophical work, *Skepsis und Mystik* is based on Mauthner's critique of language.[22] Its structure is puzzling, comprising of a collection of several essays, some of which appeared separately before the book. The first chapter, *Das Individuum als Welt* was initially a speech entitled *Durch Absonderung zur Gemeinschaft*, Landauer gave in 1901 for the *Neue Gemeinschaft*; the second chapter is made up of an article published 23rd November 1901 in *Zukunft* and a review of Julius Hart's book *Die neue Welterkenntnis* written by Landauer in 1902; the third chapter—*Die Sprache als Instrument*—had not been published previously.

In this book he recognises linguistic scepticism as the foundation for new political action, for it being a radical critique of human illusions. Landauer compares mysticism and scepticism in terms of their common power of negation and destruction of egoism.[23] According to him, scepticism exposes the world in all its nullity and is thus shows how the deepest scepticism engenders the highest mysticism. The act of doubting our knowledge, language, representations of the world and political in-

---

[20] Cf. Libera Pisano, "Misunderstanding Metaphors: Linguistic Scepticism in Mauthner's Philosophy," in *Yearbook of the Maimonides Centre for Advanced Studies 2016*, eds. Giuseppe Veltri and Bill Rebiger (Berlin and Boston: De Gruyter, 2016): 95–122.
[21] In a letter to Mauthner of May 17, 1911, Landauer wrote: 'Gewiss ist Sprachkritik untrennbar zu dem gehörig, was ich meinen Anarchismus und Sozialismus nenne.' Cf. Landauer, *Sein Lebensgang in Briefen*, vol. 1, 361.
[22] Landauer, *Skepsis und Mystik. Versuche im Anschluss an Mauthners Sprachkritik*, in idem, *Ausgewählte Schriften*, vol. 7, ed. Siegbert Wolf (Lich/Hessen: Edition AV, 2011). See Maurer, *Call to Revolution*, 67: '*Skepsis und Mystik* might be called Landauer's philosophic manifesto.'
[23] See Landauer, *Sein Lebensgang in Briefen*, vol. 2, 245: 'Die echte, klassische Mystik hat ja übrigens mit solchen egoistischen Wünschen nicht nur nichts zu tun, sondern zerstört sie so gründlich wie irgendein Skeptizismus.'

stitutions is not a mere theoretical exercise. Calling into question reality by doubting the power of language could lead to a new understanding and develop a new idea of community.[24] Thenceforth, he uses linguistic scepticism as a political strategy for an antiauthoritarian critique and a complex mystical thinking of community, in which the individual is indissolubly bound to the entire past and present of humanity.

Scepticism is not only unmasks the cult of the state, the very task of doubting leads to a political renewal of mankind. According to Landauer, mystical introspection—deeply connected with scepticism—is a form of deep, individual connection to the world and the key to the passage from isolation to community. The real innovation of his political thought is the connection between a theoretical mysticism and a 'terrestrial'[25] one. His singular account of mysticism does not deal with a separation from the world, but rather with a form of individual deep connection to the inner world and to the past.

In the introduction of *Skepsis und Mystik*, he underlined Eckhart's significance as the key to understanding his mystic anarchy.[26] Landauer emphasised that his metaphysical approach combining Christian dogma and pantheism should become the model for a political interpretation of mysticism; Eckhart proposed an idea of connection between the single entity and the whole world by going beyond the limits of language.[27] In fact, his thought—according to Landauer—was not only a *contemplatio mundi*, but was also rooted in an essential transformation of the relationship with the world: 'his mysticism is scepticism, but also vice versa.'[28] It is no coinci-

---

[24] The first philosopher who emphasised this aspect was undoubtedly Friedrich Nietzsche, who had been well studied by Mauthner as well as Landauer. As Paul Goodman, *Speaking and Language: Defense of Poetry* (New York: Vintage Books, 1971), 26, wrote: 'One of the most powerful institutions is the conventional language itself. It is very close to the ideology and it shapes how people think, feel, and judge what is functional.' The attack on signification is a kind of attack on an order that shaped human beings.

[25] Lunn, *Prophet of community*, 132.

[26] Between 1893 and 1900 Landauer spent almost 18 months in prison. During his six-month imprisonment in Tegel he translated Eckhart and wrote a part of his *Skepsis und Mystik*.

[27] Cf. Thorsten Hinz, *Mystik und Anarchie. Meister Eckhart und seine Bedeutung im Denken Gustav Landauer* (Berlin: Kramer, 2000); Christa Dericum, "Revolutionäre Geduld. Gustav Landauer," in *Christentum und Anarchismus. Beiträge zu einem ungeklärten Verhältnis*, ed. Jens Harms (Frankfurt am Main: Athenäum, 1988): 107: 'Der mittelalterliche Mystiker Meister Eckhart, dessen Werk Landauer während der Gefangenschaft ins Deutsche übersetzte, lehrte ihn, ganz zu sich zu kommen und bei sich zu verweilen.'

[28] Gustav Landauer, "Vorwort," in Meister Eckhart, *Meister Eckharts Mystische Schriften* (Berlin: Schnabel, 1903): 7. It is worth mentioning Fritz Brupbacher's (1874–1945) note here. He stated that a mystic should also be a sceptic and emphasised the relevance of Landauer's work, especially how he articulated the relationship between language and authority. This note of Brupbacher is recorded by Franz W. Seiwert, *Schriften. Der Schritt, der einmal getan wurde, wird nicht zurückgenommen*, eds. Uli Bohnen and Dirk Backes (Berlin: Kramer, 1978), 36: "Wer nicht zu wissen glaubt, wohin der Mensch zu gehen habe, wer skeptisch ist, ob es überhaupt einen für alle gültigen Sinn des Lebens gäbe oder wer von diesem Sinn aussagt, dass er nur im Gewissen eines jeden Einzelnen liege und nicht intellektuell formulierbar sei, wer also Mystiker ist, der muss Anarchist sein. Auf diese

dence that Landauer held the major exponents of scepticism in the history of philosophy to be mystics: from Dyonisius the Aeropagite to Boehme and Eckhart. Landauer offers a secularisation of mysticism by substituting 'God' with 'humanity', 'cosmos' with 'Volk' and by providing a new relation to the world. Community cannot be found initially in the external world but must be discovered in the interiority of the individual soul. Landauer sees in mysticism the way to overcome a violent account of anarchism and to think of a new form of community by crossing the atomisation of the individuals.[29]

5 From Abstractions to Community: Spiritualisation of Social Bounds

Landauer's controversial conception of mysticism, which leads to action, deals with his notion of *Geist*. Spirit is an ambiguous concept because it is both connection and independence, *Verbindung* and *Unabhängigkeit*. The binding power of spirit, synonymous of life, is an inner worldly feeling between man and man, man and earth, man and history that forges the real community; it is not an a priori principle, but rather its transcendence stems from men's action. This unity is not a form of dialec-

---

nahe Beziehung von Skepsis, Mystik und Anarchismus hat ja Landauer sehr klar hingewiesen. Es gibt gewiss viele Zwischenstufen zwischen Autoritäten und Anarchisten, Mischungen der Prinzipien; aber der Grundunterschied liegt eben darin, dass der Anarchismus die Besonderheit des Individuums in den Vordergrund rückt, während der Autoritär das Gemeinsame alle Individuen betont, die Notwendigkeit der Unterordnung des Besonderen unter das Gemeinsame. In der Sprache der mittelalterlichen Philosophie gesprochen: Der Autoritär ist Realist, der Anarchist Nominalist; der eine kennt ein aus den Produktionsverhältnissen zu bestimmendes allgemein gültiges Ziel, der andere erklärt alle solche allgemeinen Ziele für Schall und Rauch, das einmalige, irgendwohin wachsende Individuum ist ihm der Sinne des Lebens."

29 Thanks to the important works of Reiner Schürmann who reads Eckhart in an existential way, it is possible to define a form of mystic anarchy in Eckhart's thought, concerning two aspects in particular: the rethinking of time and the practical liberation from the concept of finality. In fact, in the *Mystische Schriften* translated by Landauer there is a redefinition of time, considered as an everlasting moment in which a spiritual union of the single and the whole takes place. This openness of time marks the divide because it leads to liberation from utilitarian dependence and seeking of God as a foundation. The second aspect deals with a transfiguration of all the relationships between man and man, man and world, man and God, which operates not as a final cause but as a suddenly irruption. These premises lead Eckhart to a rethinking of the abandonment and isolation from the outside word —*Abgeschiedenheit*—as the beginning of an ascetic exercise as an existential programme. In the *Sermons* the spiritual experience is not described as an ecstasy, but rather as a renewed and concrete form of a relationship with things and existence to forge reality and humankind. This practical *Bildung* is the revolutionary attempt of Eckhart mysticism to step back from causality, finality and spatiality. Cf. Reiner Schürmann, *Maitre Eckhart et la joie errante* (Paris: Rivages, 1972). On Landauer and Meister Eckhart, see the interesting contribution of Yossef Schwartz,"Gustav Landauer and Gershom Scholem: Anarchy and Utopia," in *Gustav Landauer: Anarchist and Jew*, eds. Paul Mendes-Flohr and Anya Mali (Berlin and Boston: De Gruyter, 2015): 172–190.

tical recognition, but a social mysticism which is at the core of Landauer's political thought. The heart of his idea of anarchist socialism is the attempt to render authority superfluous and unnecessary through a new kind of relationship and cooperation between men. His idea of an organic community and an authentic bond between individuals was a complete rejection of modern atomisation and the state. In his *For Socialism*, Landauer defined spirit in the following way: 'spirit is communal spirit, spirit is union and freedom, spirit is an association of men, soon we will see it even more clearly, spirit is coming over men.'[30] If spirit arises from an association of man, isolation is an epiphenomenon of its absence. The main task of anarchy is to fill this separation's gap among the individuals.

A critique toward any individuality seen as abstraction is at the core of Landauer's thought. This could be paradoxical from an anarchic point of view, but his social mysticism is based on an acknowledgment of every single person seen as an indissoluble bond:

> [I]t is time for the insight that there is no individual, but only unities and communities. It is not true that collective names designate only a sum of individuals: on the contrary, individuals are only manifestations and points of reference, electric sparks of something grand and whole.[31]

Landauer's emphasis on isolation is due to his personal experience and his interest in mysticism developed in prison.[32] Furthermore, according to him, the modern state is based on isolation and is an artificial surrogate for the spirit of the community. 'State' is nothing more than a word one uses in the attempt to project what is essentially an internal experience of dependence to a separate material construct; thence, state is a phantom and an idol. It is 'a social relationship; a certain way of people relating to one another. It can be destroyed by creating new social relationships; i.e., by people relating to one another differently.'[33] A violent overturning of the state is an illusion: 'those who believe that the state is also a thing or a fetish that can be overturned or smashed are sophists and believers in the Word.'[34]

Landauer's theory of power is sophisticated in that he combines liberation from authority with the word's capacity of hypostasise abstractions taken from Mauthner's linguistic scepticism. The word's superstition—*Wortaberglauben*—is the ground for Landauer's fetishist conception of state. In both perspectives there is an attempt of

---

30 Gustav Landauer, *For Socialism*, trans. David J. Parent (St. Louis: Telos, 1968), 30.
31 This passage taken by *Skepsis und Mystik* is translated by Maurer; see Maurer, *Call to Revolution*, 71.
32 See *ibidem*, 10–11: 'For most of his life Landauer lived and worked in isolation from the main political currents of his time; but his efforts were, nonetheless, rooted in a tradition of social philosophy established and perpetuated by some of the most original personalities of the eighteenth and nineteenth centuries.' See *ibidem*, 48: 'Gustav Landauer began this century in prison.'
33 Gustav Landauer, "Weak Statesman, weaker people," in idem, *Revolution and Other Writings: A political Reader*, ed. and trans. Gabriel Kuhn (Oakland: PM Press, 2010): 214.
34 Ibidem.

liberation from the tyranny of language and from the chains of authority. The famous sentence of Nietzsche—namely, 'Where the state ends, only there begins the human being who is not superfluous'[35]—is used by Landauer to perform the anarchic tension against state, which is an artificial bond, a false illusion and an absence of spirit. State is an irrational fetish which produces social inequality through hierarchy and domination, but on the other hand his power depends on the community of human subjects.

The switch from a conception of state seen as an abstraction or a fetish into an idea of state seen as a condition is one of the most original aspects of Landauer's political thought. This idea is deeply revolutionary, for it does not deal with a violent destruction of the state, but rather with new behaviour and a new relationship. The way to sabotage the state is by means of the institution of authentic bonds among people instead of the crystallisation of relationships.

Landauer's idea of power was deeply influenced by Etienne de la Boétie and his *Discourse on voluntary servitude*, quoted in the *Revolution*.[36] According to la Boétie, the tyrant's power is granted by the subjugated individuals who only need to refuse their support to overturn his power. Furthermore, it is worth noting that the de-transcendentalisation of the state in condition and relations anticipates Foucault's analysis of disseminated power and the following bio-political reflections of the twentieth century.[37]

Landauer's sceptical philosophy is not only a theoretical exercise, but is the foundation and the strategy for a particular idea of anarchy as *Gemeinschaftsleben*. At the outset of *Skepsis und Mystik* Landauer contends that scepticism has no value at all if it does not prepare the way for a newly created mysticism. Therefore, its function is to clear the ground for a new mysticism bound with a call to action. This kind of *contradictio in adjecto* of activism and mysticism is just one of the theoretical tensions in Landauer's thought. How could mysticism and scepticism—which generally lead to *apraxia*—be combined with a political action? How could a thought of community stem from a mystical attitude which is deeply elitist and individual?

---

35 Friedrich Nietzsche, *Thus Spoke Zarathustra*, eds. Adrian Del Caro and Robert Pippin (Cambridge: Cambridge University Press, 2006), 36.
36 In *Die Revolution*, Landauer—quoting La Boétie—admits: 'Where does the tremendous power of the tyrant derive from? It does not come from external power [...] no, its power comes from the voluntary servitude of men [...] It became a habit to be complacent in servitude; and habit is stronger than nature [...] tyranny is not a fire that has to be or can be extinguished. It is not an external evil. It is an internal flaw.' This message from La Boétie is at the core of Landauer's anarchy: 'human should not be united by domination, but as brother without domination: an-archy.' But he adds 'with spirit,' spirit that 'has to come over us.' At the end of the *Revolution*, Landauer compares La Boétie's notion of '*le contr'un*' with his notion of '*le contr'etat*': if the former is a group of individuals which recognise its servitude and rise above it, the second one is 'a community of people outside the state.' Cf. Landauer, *Revolution*, 151–173.
37 On this affinity, see Jesse S. Cohn, *Anarchism and the Crisis of Representation*, 69.

Landauer's answer is the spiritualisation of social relations as a synthesis between mysticism and socialism. The creation of a real community passes through an individual mystical experience which results in dismissing the illusion and false bonds. The regeneration of humankind is in no way a naïve and palingenetic exhortation, but presupposes a kind of a personal conversion. The way one must sabotage the state is via the creation of authentic bonds among people; however, the creation of this bond stems from an individual awareness and withdrawal that leads to a deeper and more authentic connection with the world and the past. Through these paths the spirit opens up and discloses the revolution as a cathartic renewal of humankind.

A personal *katabasis* and a symbolic suicide are needed as a face to face with a weird negativity and a self-liberation:

> So as not to be an isolate, lonely and God-forsaken, I recognise the world and sacrifice my ego to it, but only so that I might feel myself to be the world to which I have opened myself. Just as a suicide hurls himself into the water, so I crash precipitously into the world, but I find not death, rather life there. The ego kills itself so that the world ego might live.[38]

The social bounds are 'the bridges of light'[39] that connect people. Revolution should lead to a community working as a reparation—that we can call *tiqqun* as restoration in the Lurianic sense[40] of the fragments: 'because the world has fragmented into pieces and is divided and different from itself, we must flee into mystical seclusion to become one with the world.'[41]

6 Anarchic Time and the Sceptical Account of Revolution

In my view, it is possible to see in Landauer's work a triple idea of time connected deeply to his anarchy: the first is the mystical transformation of space in time arising from scepticism and as a premise for renewal of the community in *Skepsis und Mystik*; the second is his articulation of time in the *Revolution*, where history is an open process of becoming which resists any attempt of dogmatisation; the third is his idea of revolution—inspired by the Jewish Jubilee—as an exercise of interruption of the present power relations in *For Socialism*.

---

38 Landauer, *Skepsis und Mystik*, 48. This passage was translated into English by Weisberger, *The Jewish Ethic and the Spirit of Socialism*, 168.
39 Landauer, *Revolution*, 118.
40 On the Lurianic notion of *tiqqun* in contemporary Jewish thought, see Lawrence Fine, "Tikkun: A Lurianic Motif in Contemporary Jewish Thought," in *From Ancient Israel to Modern Judaism: Essays in Honor of Marvin Fox*, vol. 4, eds. Jacob Neusner, Ernest S. Frerichs, and Nahum M. Sarna (Atlanta: Scholars Press, 1989): 35–53.
41 Landauer, *Skepsis und Mystik*, 18. This passage was translated into English by Weisberger, *The Jewish Ethic and the Spirit of Socialism*, 166.

The relevance of the concept of time and the connection of the individual with his past are two important features of Landauer's thought. His idea of the regeneration of community—mainly in his *Skepsis und Mystik*—passes through an overcoming of the spatial and sensorial dimension to conceive a form of community based on a temporal dimension. In fact, according to Landauer, the spirit is not a spatial concept.[42] In terms of the connection between time and politics, one can argue that Landauer interpreted the external world as a mere sign of the internal one. Spatial development is nothing but a moment in the flow of time: 'space must be transformed into time.'[43] In this task there is the need to find new metaphors, or new language, for an authentic community. His account of time stems from a kind of mystical vision: 'Time is not merely perceptual, but it is the form of our experience of self; therefore it is real for us, for the conception of the world that we must form from out of ourselves.'[44] The effort of keeping together a social and an individual level is based on a new conception of time in which there is a perpetual bond between past, present and future generations.[45]

In *Skepsis und Mystik* he argued that time and historical change were actually rooted in internal experience, while in *Die Revolution* he developed what we should call a sceptical idea of history. *Die Revolution*, written in 1907 and republished posthumously in 1919, is a unique and sophisticated essay which embodies the spirit of the time and contains an attempt at a sceptical-anarchistic philosophy of history. This book, however, is not an easy read; mainly for Landauer's ambiguous usage of the word 'revolution', which has at least three meanings in the text: firstly, revolution is a permanent movement connected to his philosophy of history where it is to be interpreted as the threshold between *topia* and utopia; secondly, a long historical period that begun with the modern era and is the sum of different and partial revolutions or transformations;[46] thirdly, revolution is a realisation of the spirit which leads to the regeneration of the humankind and to the real community beyond state.

---

42 Gustav Landauer, "Die vereinigte Republiken Deutschlands und Ihre Verfassung, 25. November 1918," in *Gustav Landauer und die Revolutionszeit 1918/1919*, ed. Ulrich Linse (Berlin: Kramer, 1974): 63: 'Der Geist, meine Herren, ist keine Lokalität, wo es am Platz ist, sich vorzudrängen; eher ist er so etwas wie magisch erfüllte Zeit.'
43 Landauer, *Skepsis und Mystik*, 87.
44 *Ibidem*, 85.
45 According to him heredity is a force and a continuum which shapes ancestral life into a new form. This idea is also taken by the third volume of Mauthner's *Sprachkritik*, where there is a definition of heredity as a redefinition of Platonic eternal form. Cf. Mauthner, *Beiträge*, vol. 3, 71.
46 In these pages of *Die Revolution*, Landauer developed a philosophy of history from Middle Ages to his day. Landauer sees Middle Ages as completely different from the modern principle of centralism and state power; while the millennium from 500 to 1500 was marked by ordered multiplicity, and the era from 1500 until now by a lack of spirit, individualisation, state, violence and so on, he adds: 'This is the complexity in which we find ourselves, this is our transition, our disorientation, our search— our revolution' (135). The development of individualism during the Renaissance undermined the *Geist* which was completely defeated by the reformation and Luther's doctrine of salvation. The great individualism and the atomization of the masses arrived with Luther, according to Landauer: 'He rad-

Landauer's *Revolution* begins by calling into doubt any dogmatic and scientific conception of history. Doubting contains a political value and is a prelude to a new beginning connected to the formation of a new man and a new society; the rhythm of doubting is part of Landauer's philosophical style. He commenced his essay by admitting that history is not a science that requires scientific laws, because 'our historical data consist of events and actions, of suffering and relationships.'[47] At the outset of the book, Landauer adopted sceptical strategy to show the impossibility of a scientific definition of revolution; in fact, every scientific attempt cannot satisfy its understanding as a phenomenon. This is deeply connected to his idea of history as not fixed and unchanging, but in fact a sum of forces whose influence is permanent in our lives. In fact, whereas science creates theory and abstraction, history creates 'forces of praxis' in a process of *Vergegenwärtigung*, of becoming or of turning something into presence. However, Landauer tried to give a theoretical account of revolution connected to his conception of history, without any dogmatic presumption.

The entirety of history, according to him, is a sequence of *topias*—periods of order and fixed institutions—and utopias, which is moved by a desire for change, and 'consists of two elements: the reaction against the environment from which it emerges, and the memory of all known earlier utopias.'[48] He rejects a progressive idea of history. In fact, the past is not something finished, but always a process of becoming. History is not something already defined, everything is a result as well as a promise: 'there is only way for us, there is only future. The past itself is future. It is never finished, it always becomes. It changes and modifies as we move ahead.'[49] This historical becoming is both a passage from different phases as well as a permanent changing of the past at every stage of history. There is somehow a futurability of the past, and revolution is the period between of the old *topia* and the coming of the new one.[50]

According to Landauer, revolution is not the *telos*—ultimate aim—of the history, but a meta-historical threshold, which needs a systematic negation of the *topia* on the way to utopia. *Topia* is a stabile combination of state, economics, school, art, and so on, a combination of all the spheres of commonality. However, this gradual

---

ically separated life from faith and substituted organized violence for spirit' (142). This era is marked by an absence, a lack of spirit, but it does not disappear entirely, but it appears sometimes in some individuals. The revolution in which we live has to bring together a new common spirit. Since that time there has been a long revolution regarded as a struggle for the reestablishment of *Geist* as principle of human life.

47 Ibidem, 111.
48 Ibidem, 121.
49 Ibidem.
50 On Landauer's concept of revolution as *Zwischenzeit*, cf. Norbert Altenhofer, "Tradition als Revolution. Gustav Landauer 'geworden-werdendes' Judentum," in *Jews and Germans from 1860 to 1933: The problematic Symbiosis*, ed. David Bronsen (Heidelberg: Carl Winter Universitätsverlag, 1979): 183.

stability does not last for long. The changes are caused by utopia.⁵¹ Though it may appear dead, it is always a hidden force in history that resurrects whenever a *topia* reaches its limits. Therefore:

> Revolution is always alive, even during the time of relatively stable utopias. It stays alive underground. It is always old and new. While it is underground, it creates a complex unity of memories, emotions and desires. This unity will then turn into a revolution that is not merely a boundary (or a spate of time), but a principle transcending all eras (topias).⁵²

As stated by Landauer, anarchy is 'the expression for the liberation of man from the idols of the state, the church and capital,'⁵³ whereas scepticism as a systematic negation of every positive truth is the necessary strategy for anarchy. This negation is the heart of his (anti)political theory, particularly so in his famous conception of revolution. Revolution needs a negation of the *topia* on the way to utopia and this power of negation is the political translation of the act of doubting of all truths: 'Truth is, however, a completely negative word, it is the negation in itself, and therefore it is indeed the subject and aim of all science, whose long-lasting results are always of a negative nature.'⁵⁴ Scepticism and revolution have this need of negation in common which becomes a positive result, a creation that results from criticism.

In his conception of history Landauer challenged the very heart of the German-Hegelian conception of history as a self-realisation of the spirit, in a sceptical manner. He refuses any form of theorisation of history as a discipline and a Darwinian account of progress seen as inexorable and dogmatic historical tendencies. According to Landauer, a dogmatic idea of history—such as Marxism—impedes revolution. As scepticism engenders political action, dogmatism in contradistinction is an obstacle to change. His accusations against Marxism are at various levels. First of all, its view of a utopian project based on a scientific or rather a Darwinian idea of history, forwarding a mechanistic and deterministic view of history as self-driven progress,

---

51 It is fair to say that Landauer's interpretation of utopia is one of the most debated elements of his thought. Buber celebrated his friend in *Paths to Utopia* and, more broadly, Landauer has been defined as a thinker of contemporary utopia. In *Revolution* utopia plays a crucial role in his philosophy of history, however utopia should not be interpreted as a classic understanding of the term as a dream of a perfect society or as a rational political project. According to Landauer, utopia is the driving force of history seen as an alternation between *topia* and utopia, stabilisation and change. In the *Revolution*, Landauer deals with modern utopias, for instance Thomas More's work. Even if modern utopia was a rebellion and critique, it concerned a surrogate form of communality, namely the state. Furthermore, when Landauer speaks of Campanella's *City of the Sun*, he states: 'In Campanella's utopian system, the state has taken control of everything: love, family, property, education, religion. Campanella foresees the absolute democratic state, the state that knows neither society nor societies; the state that we call social democratic;' see Landauer, *Revolution*, 162. Also, in his *Aufruf*, Landauer clearly states that he does not offer any depiction of a utopian ideal.
52 Landauer, *Revolution*, 116.
53 Landauer, "Ethische Kultur," (March 7, 1896), reported by Lunn, *Prophet of Community*, 200.
54 Landauer, *Skepsis und Mystik*, 83.

postulating that capitalism will inevitably collapse and the communism will be inevitable. This optimistic and dogmatic trust in inevitable collapse is at the root of Marxist determinism that impedes the action, whereas Landauer's writings place a strong emphasis on the voluntary aspect and a call to action.

Landauer reads the Marxist conception of history as a necessary development;[55] it is a 'spiritless conception of history'[56] determined by providence. Landauer criticised the Marxist injunction of waiting for the 'supposed right moment,' which has

> postponed this goal further and further and pushed it into blurred darkness; trust in progress and development was the name of regression and this 'development' adapted the external and internal conditions more and more to degradation and made the great change ever more remote.[57]

Since revolution paves the way for something yet to come, rather than waiting for divine intervention, Landauer transposed the axis of hope to human *Tat* ('action') and human communities. This passage needs a sceptical attitude towards politics and institutions in order to create a different bond between individuals. He always emphasised the idea of beginning and underlined the need for action and the urgency of society's radical change, not to be postponed into a distant future, but to take place now.

Revolution can happen at any time and open the gate for the spirit. This idea was stressed by Landauer in a fascinating speech he gave as member of the work councils in Munich during the revolution: 'So anyone can help the revolution, anyone can heartily join it through any door, which is mostly already opened.'[58] The possibility of an overturning is possible anytime, hence there is a catastrophic—in the sense of the Greek word '*katastrophè*' which means 'overturn'—conception of history in

---

55 Cf. Landauer, *For Socialism*, 60–63. Landauer refused to consider the proletarian as the predestined and privileged revolutionary agent. In his vision, it is not a matter of class, or perhaps more precisely a matter of historically favoured social groups, for the radical transformation required the development of cooperation among all working members. Furthermore, the Marxist definition of the proletariat is given only as an economic factor not taking into account spiritual poverty, while the real change starts from a spiritual one. In the place of a dictatorship of the proletariat Landauer called for a democracy of the entire working community. Moreover, Landauer also saw a connection between Marxism and technology, which he asserted to be responsible for the process of depersonalisation and dehumanisation of relationships. Landauer's aversion to technology has to be understood as aligned to his idea of spirit as authentic bond between man and man, man and nature, man and history. Capitalism, the modern state and technology are all part of the same constellation.
56 *Ibidem*, 61.
57 *Ibidem*, 109.
58 Gustav Landauer, "Zur Frage der Deutschen Verfassung," in *Gustav Landauer und die Revolutionszeit*, ed. Linse, 58. This passage recalls Benjamin's narrow gate through which the Messiah could enter in his "Theses on the Philosophy of History;" see Walter Benjamin, "On the Concept of History," in idem, *Selected Writings*, vol. 4, eds. Howard Eiland and Michael W. Jennings, trans. Edmund Jephcott *et alii* (Cambridge: Harvard University Press, 2003): 389–400.

Landauer's thought. There is a tension between salvation and destruction at the very heart of his concept of revolution.[59] Against a progressive and evolutionist conception of history, Landauer formulated a different conception that we can define as an open and anti-dogmatic idea of history in which the messianic overturn can happen any time.

The third and last aspect of Landauer's anarchic conception of time deals with another account of revolution; in fact, at the end of his *For Socialism*, revolution is conceived as a permanent interruption of the order. In this essay Landauer quotes a passage from Leviticus (25:8–24) to emphasises the necessity of a revolution as a permanent interruption—*Durchbruch*—in order to redeem the whole of history. He interpreted this interruption on the basis of the Mosaic law, when the day of equalisation will come and 'every man is to regain what belongs to him.' This theological assumption gives more spiritual emphasis to Landauer's arguments:

> [T]he voice of the spirit is the trumpet that will sound again and again and again, as long as men are together. Injustice will always seek to perpetuate itself, and always as long as men are truly alive, revolt against it will break out. Revolt as constitution; transformation and revolution as a rule established once and for all; order through the spirit as intention; that was the great and sacred heart of the Mosaic social order. We need that once again: new regulations and spiritual upheaval, which will not make things and commandments permanently rigid, but which will proclaim its own permanence. The revolution must become an element of our social order, it must become the basic rule of our constitution.[60]

According to Landauer, revolution must be a part of a social order, as the basis of the constitution and the permanent work of the spirit. This interruption is a messianic interval, but it could be compared to a sceptical *epoché*, a suspension of the rhythm of the time and an overturning of authorities. Since revolution is a negation but also an interruption of authority and of power, it could be defined as the sceptical heart of community.

In contrast with a Marxist tradition positing revolution needs a 'right moment' to happen, Landauer place it as *Grundregel*—basic rule—of our constitution. In a wonderful mosaic he puts together the subversive features of Judaism and the socialistic-anarchistic tradition, as well as the restorative and utopian elements.[61] Even though the relationship between Landauer and Judaism is controversial,[62] I think that Lan-

---

59 At the outset of the Revolution, there is a passage from Maximus Tyrus: 'Here, now, you will see the road of passion, which you call destruction, because you make your judgment based on those who have already passed away on it—which I, however, call "salvation", basing myself on the order of those yet to come;' see Landauer, *Revolution*, 176.
60 Landauer, *For Socialism*, 130.
61 On the connection between anarchism and Jewish tradition, cf. Martin Buber, *Königtum Gottes* (Heidelberg: Schneider, 1956); Amedeo Bertolo, ed., *L'anarchico e l'ebreo. Storia di un incontro* (Milan: Eleuthera, 2001).
62 This is also one of the most discussed topics in secondary literature. For instance, according to Linse and Link-Salinger, the Jewish element is only one factor alongside the socialist and romantic

dauer as a German Jew, who conceived his identity as a complexity,[63] anticipated the feeling of the bifurcated soul of a whole generation of thinkers of the last century.[64] Thanks to his association with Martin Buber, Landauer became familiar with Jewish tradition and Jewish questions. Undoubtedly in the last years of his life, he was enthusiastic for Jewish national renaissance. After his death, Buber spoke of Landauer as the 'secret leader' of the Zionist movement and tried to translate his legacy from Germany to Israel.[65]

---

traditions in Landauer's thought; but Lunn points out that Jewish heritage played a pivotal role in Landauer's idea of redemption and the binding power of spirit. Cf. Link-Salinger, *Gustav Landauer: Philosopher of Utopia*, 74–76; Lunn, *Prophet of community*, 247. Hanna Delf, "'Prediger in der Wüste sein.' Gustav Landauer im Weltkrieg," in Gustav Landauer, *Werksausgabe. Gustav Landauer. Dichter, Ketzer, Außenseiter*, vol. 3, ed. Hanna Delf (Berlin: Akademie, 1997), XXIII-LI; Siegbert Wolf, "Einleitung," in Gustav Landauer, *Ausgewählte Schriften. Philosophie und Judentum*, vol. 5., ed. Siegbert Wolf (Lich/Hessen: Edition AV, 2012): 9–85.

[63] In one of his most important writings on Judaism—*Sind das Ketzergedanken?*—published in the volume *Vom Judentum* in 1913 and edited by the Zionist organisation in Prague Bar Kochba, Landauer wrote: 'I am, the Jew, a German. The expressions "German Jew or Russian Jew" are as obtuse as would be the terms "Jewish German" or "Jewish Russian". The relation is not one of dependency and cannot be described by means of an adjective modifying a noun. I accept my fate as it is. My Germanism and my Jewishness do each other no harm but much good. As two brothers, a first-born and a Benjamin, are loved by mother—not in the same way but with equal intensity—and as these two brothers live in harmony with each other whenever their paths proceed in common and also whenever each goes his own way alone, even so do I experience this strange and intimate unity in duality as something precious;' translated by Lunn, *Prophet of community*, 270. The special calling for humanity that characterised Judaism is that all Jews bear 'their neighbours in their own breasts;' see *ibidem*, 217. The Jewish *Volk* is free from the trap of the state which is also a threat to the integrity of Jewish identity. In his short lecture entitled "Judaism and Socialism" given to the Zionistische Ortsgruppe West Berlin on February 12, 1912, Landauer admitted the possibility of Jewish settlements but at the same time he supported the messianic feeling of *Galut* among the nations as chance of redemption for the humankind: 'The Galut, exile as an inner disposition of isolation and longing, will be that utmost calling that bonds them to Judaism and Socialism;' translated by Paul Mendes-Flohr, "Introduction," in *Gustav Landauer: Anarchist and Jew*, 1–2. The redemptive mission and the commitment of Jewish people of increasing brotherhood and justice is akin to socialism. His provocative idea was that *Galut* linked Judaism to Socialism, since Jewish people were particularly qualified for the task of helping to build socialist communities.

[64] See Paul Mendes-Flohr, *German Jews: A Dual Identity* (New Haven and London: Yale University Press, 1999), 1–2.

[65] See Martin Buber, "Der heimliche Führer," in *Gustav Landauer Gedenkheft*, in *Die Arbeit* (1920): 35: 'Gustav Landauer was an awakener for us; he has transformed our lives, and he has given our Zionism—which he never mentioned by name—a new meaning, a new intensity, a new direction;' see also Martin Buber, "Landauer und die Revolution," *Masken: Halbmonatsschrift des Düsseldorfer Schauspielhauses* 14.18–19 (1919): 291; Bar Kochba, ed., *Vom Judentum* (Leipzig: Kurt Wolff, 1913).

7 Scepticism as Anti-Political Form of Life

Landauer's idea of revolution deals with the power of negation, with his conception of history and with a politicisation of time to provide a regeneration of humankind. As noted above, he proposed a qualitative conception of historical time: the revolution is a meta-historical element that could happen in a sudden eruption and historical metamorphosis of an abrupt moment, *Durchbruch*. At the same time, revolution is a renewal of humankind and a process taking place in the individual's interiority. In his preface to the second edition of the *Aufruf* Landauer talks of the transformative feature of the revolution, stating that in the revolution 'the incredible miracle is brought into the realm of possibility.'[66] This aesthetic and ethic renovation of the spirit involves joy, love, transcendence, religion.[67] The conversion of the greatest difficulty and necessity into the highest virtue, of the crisis into socialism is the hardest task of revolution.

Thence, revolution is not just a political event, but rather it is a *metànoia*—a conversion, an exercise of becoming and an interior transformation in order to create new relationships between men. I think that this conception of revolution as conversion is also the key to understanding his initial participation in the Bavarian Soviet Republic; in fact, he enthusiastically participated in this revolution as a spiritual guide, following Eisner's suggestion to join it for a 'transformation of the souls' ('Umbildung der Seele').[68]

---

[66] Landauer, *For Socialism*, 21.
[67] In the preface of his *For Socialism*, Landauer speaks of true socialism and social change as a religion of action and love. His religious and prophetical vein is also the element that his friends—after his death—will take to save his memory and celebrate Landauer as a martyr of revolution; see, *ibidem*, 26: 'May the revolution bring rebirth. May, since we need nothing so much as new, uncorrupted men rising up out of the unknown darkness and depths, may these renewers, purifiers, saviours not be lacking to our nation. Long live the revolution, and may it grow and rise to new levels in hard, wonderful years. May the nations be imbued with the new, creative spirit out of their task, out of the new conditions, out of the primeval, eternal and unconditional depths, the new spirit that really does create new conditions. May the revolution produce religion, a religion of action, life, love, that makes men happy, redeems them and overcomes impossible situations.' Furthermore, at the end of his *Revolution*, he underlines this idea of joy and revolution as a kind of divine or mystic ecstasy; see Landauer, *Revolution*, 171–172: 'The joy of revolution is not only a reaction against the former oppression. It lies in the euphoria that comes with a rich, intense, eventful life. What is essential for this joy is that humans no longer feel lonely that they experience unity, connectedness, and collective strength.'
[68] Gustav Landauer, *Sein Lebensgang in Briefen*, vol. 2, 296 note 1: 'Kurt Eisner hatte am 14. November an Landauer geschrieben: "Kommen Sie, sobald es Ihre Gesundheit erlaubt. Was ich von Ihnen möchte, ist, daß Sie durch rednerische Betätigung an der Umbildung der Seelen mitarbeiten."' In the Munich Revolution, Landauer saw a prophetical realisation of the spirit. He was deeply convinced of a spirituality transforming of revolution. It is worth noting that in his speeches and writings during the *Räterepublik*, Landauer spoke or wrote as a spiritual guide or as a prophet of the spirit that is yet to come.

According to Landauer, anarchy is based on a deep scepticism towards political dogma, institutions and authority. It is in no way an abstract model or doctrine, but an ethic and spiritual form of life whose aim is the *Bildung* of a new man ('der werdende Mensch') and a new community based on an authentic social justice. In Landauer's view the libertarian approach is radically rethought in a holistic harmony in which there is a kind of *anarchic poiesis*.

One of the most innovative aspects in his thought is the distinction between an idea of politics as artificial device of power—also to found in Marxism—and an anti-political approach. In his *Anarchic Thoughts about Anarchism* Landauer writes: 'Anarchy is not a matter of the future; it is a matter of the present. It is not a matter of making demands; it is a matter of how one lives.'[69] Anarchy is seen in psychological terms and is described as a radical transformation of human being. This is also the reason why his revolutionary activity was a kind of *Lebensform*, as it concerns all dimensions of life.

Landauer's *Anti-Politik* arises from his criticism of modern political thought. He barely distinguished his idea of socialism from politics in general: 'socialism is a cultural movement, a struggle for beauty, greatness, abundance of the peoples.'[70] Whereas the politician is interested only in a partial aspect of the human life, socialist thinks holistically: 'whether he is a thinker or a poet, a fighter or a prophet: the true socialist will always have a vital element of the universal in him.'[71] Whereas socialism concerns all aspects of human life, politics is surrogate and a device which deals with but partial aspects. Politics is a technique related to state, representation and institution, while anti-politics could be interpreted as a sceptical attitude against power; in fact, as it is a *Gegenmacht* ('counter power') that refuses to become power, it could be interpreted as a sceptical stand which avoids dogmatic conclusion and ruling institutions.

Anti-politics is a strategy to discard doctrine or assumptions from the flux of life which is impossible to define in scientific terms. In the work and in the biography of Landauer one can see a lively exemplum of anarchy as a sceptical refusal of political dogmatism. He uses sceptical argumentations in his philosophical political thought and in his anti-political praxis as well. Scepticism has many different features in his thought: it is a radical critique towards state, dogmatism and progress; the way to follow in order to discover a lively idea of community based on a particular idea of time and history; a critique towards idols and authorities, and a living praxis which is an ongoing challenge to dogmatic power.

In a compelling puzzle of many elements his thought provides both warnings and the pathway for a radical challenge to politics. His immolation as a martyr of community symbolised his radical attempt to connect an open revolution to a scep-

---

69 Gustav Landauer, "Anarchic Thoughts about Anarchism," in idem, *Revolutions and Other Writings*, 87.
70 Landauer, *For Socialism*, 64.
71 *Ibidem*, 45.

tical form of life; on the other hand, however, his death shows the controversial consequences of an anti-political attitude that later became a tragic constant in the history of the last century. Landauer was a medieval mystic, an old-fashioned socialist-anarchist, a linguistic sceptic, and a tormented spirit from the beginning of the twentieth century. In this regard, he was the first thinker who combined a thinking of community with the breakdown of certainty; as a result, he demonstrated the extreme consequences of a sceptical definition of politics and an anarchic conception of time. I believe this to be the very heart of his legacy through which it could be possible—even to this day—to develop a more philosophical thinking of community as a bond between human beings, beyond dogmatic assumptions and technical accounts of politics.

Part II **Reports**

Activities and Events

9 November, 2017
Opening of the 3rd Academic Year

Katja Maria Vogt, Columbia University, New York/USA
The Nature of Disagreement: Ancient Relativism and Scepticism

Pyrrhonian scepticism has roots in metaphysical discussions relevant to relativism. The lecture reconstructed these discussions in Plato's *Theaetetus* and explored how different versions of Pyrrhonian scepticism—the scepticism of Pyrrho, Aenesidemus, and Sextus Empiricus—compare to Protagorean relativism. It began with a sketch of why Plato interprets Protagoras' 'Measure Doctrine' as global relativism rather than relativism about a particular domain. Pyrrhonian scepticism, it was argued, inherits this global scope. But Pyrrhonian responses to disagreement have important differences from the responses envisaged by Protagorean relativism. Scepticism suggests that, when encountering disagreement, it is rational to step back from one's view and investigate, rather than simply to hold on to one's view, as the relativist presumably does. The lecture defended scepticism's response to disagreement as construed by Sextus Empiricus as being superior to earlier proposals.

Regular Events

Dialectical Evenings

The Dialectical Evening is an informal meeting every four weeks (in fortnightly rotation with the Reading Evening) for discussions and readings, which is designed to promote dialectical culture and sceptical thought within the research unit. Members of the Maimonides Centre and occasional guests convene to challenge, doubt, and explore theses in various subject areas.

[DE 17] 21 November, 2017
Giada Coppola and Michael Engel: **On the Eternity of the Movement of Generation and Destruction**

The Jewish thinker Obadiah ben Jacob Sforno (c. 1475–1550) is considered to be the last Jewish scholastic author. He is best known for his biblical commentaries and exegetical activity, although he also wrote a philosophical treatise entitled *The Light of the Nations*. The work was published in Hebrew in 1537 with the title *Or 'Ammim*. The author himself then translated it into Latin, revising it significantly in order to address its content to the Christian humanist audience (*Lumen Gentium*, 1548). The text strives to reproduce the classical scholastic form of argument (*summa*) and attempts to refute Averroes' Aristotelianism by using the Aristotelian method to subvert and undermine its own doctrines in order to elevate the Jewish religious dogmatic concepts.

The opening *quaestio* of *The Light of the Nations* aimed to confute the eternity of the movement of generation and destruction (also known as the coming-to-be and ceasing-to-be). Sforno presents three arguments in favour of the eternity of generation and destruction (*pro*) and five (four in the Latin version) counterarguments (*contra*). As expected, the *quaestio* is solved with a negative answer: the movement of generation and destruction is not eternal, but Sforno's conclusion gives rise to a new difficulty.

[DE18] 23 January, 2018
Friedhelm Hartenstein and Hanna Liss: **The Torah as a Material and Verbal Medium of the Divine Presence**

This Dialectical Evening asked how the ritual practices of ancient and modern Judaism reflect on the fundamental human need for images from two different points of view (Protestant biblical exegesis and Jewish studies). In the light of the explicit biblical prohibition of cultic images, it is interesting that the Torah scroll and its ritual reading in the synagogue share some characteristics with the veneration of divine images or other symbols of the presence of God. The thesis Friedhelm Hartenstein and Hanna Liss discussed was that the interplay between visible objects and mental images of the divine is a common element of religious practice in general: without 'material anchors' there are no religious symbols at all. If this is true, the explicit formulation of the biblical image ban by the exilic authors seems to presuppose a growing insight into a basic condition of humanity: the need and desire for images. The authors of the biblical texts were well aware of this need and of the dangers of human attention often being fixated only on the object itself and thereby possibly getting lost in immanence (cf. Exodus 32). How did the Bible and later Jewish traditions solve the unavoidable tension between the necessity of images and the confusion caused by treating them as idols? And how can exegetical insights contribute to Jewish studies in this respect? Do the categories of visual science (*Bildwissenschaft*) help to clarify the specific status of the Torah scroll in Jewish worship as a 'non-idolatric' cultic artefact? And finally: what are the possible implications for the question of Jewish scepticism?

[DE19] 10 April, 2018
José María Sánchez de León Serrano and Ze'ev Strauss: **Jewish Appropriations of Hegel's Philosophy of Religion**

Hegel's philosophy, in particular his philosophy of religion, played a crucial role in the way nineteenth century Jewish philosophers conceived their own religion. Thinkers like Nachman Krochmal (1785–1840), Salomon Formstecher (1808–89), and Samuel Hirsch (1815–89) developed a philosophy of Jewish religion based on Hegelian premises and articulated through Hegelian concepts. At the same time, they opposed Hegel's dismissive view of Judaism as a stage of religious consciousness that would be—along with Greek and Roman paganism—surpassed by Christianity. Thus, by presenting Judaism as the true religion of the *Absolute* (instead of Christianity), they attempted to refute Hegel's view of Judaism with Hegel's own logic. In this Dialectical Evening, the convenors discussed the assumptions, limits and strengths of Jewish appropriations of Hegel.

[DE20] 8 May, 2018
Michael Engel and Yoav Meyrav: **Elijah Del Medigo between Philosophy and Religion**

Elijah Del Medigo (c. 1460–93), a Cretan Jewish author living and working in Northern Italy, wrote about Aristotelian themes in Hebrew and Latin and is considered a 'Jewish Averroist.' Drawing on his different works, contemporary scholars have attempted to discern Del Medigo's general attitude toward the relation between philosophy and religion. In this evening, we asked whether a coherent approach to this relationship can indeed be extracted from Del Medigo's corpus, or whether he adopted a more *ad hoc* approach, adapting his view in a given context to his audience. The specific case of Del Medigo was then expanded to a general methodological discussion about scholars' tendency to search for a cohesive meta-philosophical approach within other medieval Jewish authors.

[DE21] 5 June, 2018
Timothy Franz and José María Sánchez de León Serrano: **The General Pattern of Solomon Maimon's Philosophy**

The works of Solomon Maimon (c. 1753–1800) published in his lifetime extend from 1789 to his death in 1800. Drawing largely on the perspective of his *Autobiography* (1792–93) and arguments from the *Essay on Transcendental Philosophy* (1790), scholars have written commentaries on Maimon which interpret him as an aporetic thinker, a sceptic, or a severe combination of rationalist dogmatist and empirical sceptic. Since Maimon combined his acute scepticism with ambitious and evolving theological speculations, we asked whether a broader view of his thought can be taken, also involving later works which have escaped the notice of tradition. And if this general pattern is found, what does this mean for Maimon as a *Selbstdenker* and for our philosophical and cultural traditions?

[DE22] 24 July, 2018
Stephan Schmid and Oded Schechter: **Spinoza's Scepticism about Religion? The Question of Secularism in the TTP**

Spinoza's *Theological Political Treatise* (anonymously published in 1670 as *Tractatus Theologico-Politicus* or *TTP* for short) is, next to Hobbes' *Leviathan*, often described as the founding text of modern and secular political philosophy. But in what does the secular moment of Spinoza's *TTP* consist? According to an influential line of commentators—comprising such famous scholars as Strauss and Nadler—Spinoza's secularism is identified in his questioning of the authority and truth of the Bible. For among the main claims defended in Spinoza's *TTP* are those that the Bible is but a historical document and no 'Letter God has sent men from heaven' (12.1), that prophecy is but a form of imagination, that miracles are just unusual as opposed to super-natural events, and that the goal of Scripture consists in instilling obedience, and not in conveying some super-natural truth. In this Dialectical Evening, Stephan Schmid and Oded Schechter wanted to present this secularist or sceptical reading of Spinoza's *TTP* and explore the tenability of the opposing view. According to this opposing view, far from discarding religion and considering it a useful means to control the superstitious masses, Spinoza takes revelation to be an integral element of the modern state, which leaves room for free political agency.

[DE23] 7 August, 2018
Bernard Cooperman: **Cultural Pluralism Seen from the Ghetto or: Is Tolerance Possible in a Religious Society?**

Bernard Cooperman presented a series of texts by a range of Jewish writers dating from the second half of the sixteenth and first half of the seventeenth centuries. These texts, written originally in Hebrew, Italian, and Latin, seem to express quite radical positions about the relation between Christianity and Judaism and the possibilities of Jews living within Christian society. The first three authors, all of whom lived in Venice at least for a while, include a Portuguese-trained New Christian physician (Elijah Montalto) who became famous as a Jewish polemicist, a Jewish physician (David de' Pomis) trained at the University of Perugia who lost his right to practice medicine on Christians, and a rabbi (Simone Luzzatto) who is well known as a defender of the Jewish presence in his city. All three men, not irrelevantly, authored significant works aimed at a non-Jewish audience, works devoted to medical science, lexicography, and philosophical scepticism respectively. All three represent the type of (Jewish) intellectual whose career and writings elucidate the transitional position of those who enter into another world of discourse and claim status within it without abandoning their claims to independent status. Finally, Cooperman used their arguments to offer a contextualisation of Spinoza's *Theological-Political Tractate* that may help to understand why the Dutch author presented the relation between religion and the state as he did.

Reading Evenings

The Reading Evening is an informal meeting every four weeks (in fortnightly rotation with the Dialectical Evening). Fellows and researchers read and discuss primary texts that are specifically relevant to their respective projects. Each meeting, one fellow or research team member selects and presents a text of particular importance for her research. In reading together, the group benefits from the expertise of the individual researcher.

[RE16] 8 August, 2016
Máté Veres: **Scepticism about Theology in Sextus Empiricus**

Given the prevalence of religious diversity in the Graeco-Roman world and the dominance of theological tenets in the philosophy of the time, it is hardly surprising that reflections concerning the rationality of religious belief came to the fore in the Hellenistic age. Importantly, both religious and anti-religious dogmatism proved to be a prime target for sceptical examination, as evidenced by Sextus Empiricus, a Pyrrhonian sceptic and our primary source for the early encounter between scepticism and dogmatic theology. The Reading Evening was focussed on some arguments concerning theology as they are presented by Sextus in his *Outlines of Pyrrhonism*, Book III, and parts of his *Against the Physicists*, Book I.

[RE17] 5 September, 2017
Ehud Krinis: **Judah Halevi's Use of Sceptical Arguments**

Articles 11–25 in Book I of Judah Halevi's *Kuzari* form the opening section of the dialogue between the Khazar king and the Jewish sage (the ḥaver). It is in this section that Halevi presents his definition of Judaism vis-à-vis the dogmatic-rationalistic definition of religion. In this section, we can detect Halevi's most elaborated use of some sceptical arguments. The Reading Evening was devoted to the examination of Halevi's use of sceptical arguments in I, 11–25 as part of his elucidation of the uniqueness of the Jewish religion.

[RE18] 24 October, 2017
Thomas Meyer: **The Quest for Certainty in Saadiah's Philosophy**

Abraham Joshua Heschel's article "The Quest for Certainty in Saadiah's Philosophy" is an important contribution to Jewish scepticism on at least three levels: as a close reading of Saadiah's concept of 'certainty', as part of Heschel's own theology (for example 'God in Search of Man'), and as an example of the use of medieval thinkers and their concepts during the Second World War. The aim of the Reading Evening was to understand how one and three are mixed and what that means for our interpretation of Jewish scepticism (keywords: historicism, systematical vs. historical reading, persecution and the art of writing, etc.).

[RE19] 19 December, 2017
Friedhelm Hartenstein: **Is the Book of Job a Work of Sceptical Literature?**

This Reading Evening raised the question whether the biblical book of Job could be characterised as a work of sceptical literature. Hartenstein considers the dissertation of Katherine J. Dell (supervised by John Barton, University of Oxford, 1988) as the only monograph which is explicitly dealing with the question in considerable length—taking into account aspects of content as well as of form. Dell follows a more open definition of scepticism with regard to Greek sceptics (cf. pp. 168–171). The discussion was based on chapter 4 of this thesis as well as on various chapters of the book of Job (ch. 1–7; 19; 38 and 42).

[RE20] 16 January, 2018
Andreas Brämer: **Abraham Geiger—A Reluctant Pioneer of Systematic Theology?**

Andreas Brämer's research at the Maimonides Centre was dedicated to Rabbi Abraham Geiger (1810–74), both an intellectual spearhead of liberal Judaism and an iconic figure of critical Jewish scholarship in Germany during the era of *Verbürgerlichung*. Considering the fact that Geiger, rabbi first in Wiesbaden, then in Breslau, Frankfurt and Berlin, was so eager to define 'jüdische Wissenschaft' as a Jewish theology, it may seem appropriate to enquire after Geiger's contributions to a systematic description of the Jewish belief system. The Reading Evening was based on a number of passages from Geiger's private correspondence that have been published in German as well as in English translation in order to comprehend his rather reluctant stance when it comes to the presentation of doctrines of faith.

[RE21] 20 February, 2018
Zev Harvey: **Ḥasdai Crescas' Scepticism about Proofs of God**

Medieval philosophers, like Avicenna, Maimonides, or Thomas Aquinas, composed famous 'proofs of God.' God, they held, is found not only in Holy Scripture, but also in the physical or metaphysical demonstrations of philosophers. The Catalan Rabbi Ḥasdai Crescas (c. 1340–1410 or 1411), in his Hebrew philosophical book *The Light of the Lord* (*Or Adonai*), was profoundly sceptical about such proofs. One may prove a first cause of our world, he allowed, but there may be *many* worlds, perhaps an *infinite* number of them, and each world could have its own first cause, that is, each could have its own God. Reason, he concluded, has no way of freeing itself from doubt. Only prophecy, he argued, truly proves the existence of One God. The aim of this Reading Evening was to understand the motives, spirit, and scope of Crescas' scepticism.

[RE22] 6 March, 2018
David Ruderman: **Defending the Integrity of Rabbinic Judaism in Nineteenth-Century Europe: The Creative Response of Isaac Baer Levinsohn to the Missionary Assaults of his Day**

Alexander McCaul (1799–1863) was one of the most prominent figures in *The London Society* for promoting Christianity amongst Jews during the first half of the nineteenth century. In 1837, he published a formidable attack against the Talmud entitled *The Old Paths,* engendering considerable consternation and alarm among Jews when the work appeared in Hebrew translation two years later. His work evoked a series of long responses from Jewish intellectuals attempting to defend traditional Judaism from his stinging criticisms, especially several written by Eastern-European *maśkilim* (proponents of the Jewish enlightenment) who had previously condemned the rabbis and their restrictive Talmudic laws in calling for radical religious and educational reform. The irony of these same critics of Rabbinic Judaism feeling obliged to defend their hallowed traditions is at the heart of Ruderman's study of McCaul's critique and the Jewish response.

David Ruderman examined in the Reading Evening the response of Isaac Baer Levinsohn (Ribal, 1788–1860), the most important figure in this group, and his bold attempt to articulate the relevance of Jewish civilisation for Christians and Jews alike. Armed with vast erudition in Rabbinic sources, knowledge of ancient and modern history, and broad exposure to contemporary scholarship, Ribal offered not merely a thorough answer to McCaul but a thoughtful and nuanced articulation of how Judaism might retain its authentic character while reforming itself in the light of the new exigencies and challenges of the modern era.

[RE23] 24 April, 2018
Diego Lucci: **The Limits of Human Understanding in John Locke's Philosophy: Political Scepticism, Moral Scepticism, and Ontological Scepticism**

John Locke (1632–1704) is widely known as the founder of modern empiricism and the father of liberalism. However, not many people are aware of the sceptical aspects of Locke's philosophical, political, moral, and religious thought. The sceptical dimension of Locke's thought manifests itself in different ways in his reflections on religious toleration, the foundations of morality, and the scope of human knowledge. Locke's rejection of the imposition of 'true religion' in *A Letter concerning Toleration* (1689) mainly relies on a sceptical argument—the argument from error. Moreover, Locke's moralist soteriology in *The Reasonableness of Christianity* (1695) largely resulted from his attempt to overcome his own moral scepticism. Furthermore, in *An Essay concerning Human Understanding* (1690), Locke denied that we could get behind ideas to things themselves, in that he defined substance as an unknown substratum or support of qualities—thus discarding the metaphysical concepts that underlie the trinitarian dogma and other Christian beliefs, as Edward Stillingfleet and other contemporary critics noted. Nevertheless, Locke did not call into question the existence of true religion, the demonstrability of morality, or the actuality of substances. What he doubted was the human capacity to actually comprehend and communicate religious truth, to find solid foundations for morality, and to know any substance. Briefly, Locke's sceptical attitude originated in his recognition of the limits of human understanding.

[RE24] 22 May, 2018
Lukas Lang: **Common Sense and Scepticism**

There is a tradition in philosophy, which began with Berkeley and Reid and continues up until today, that opposes scepticism with common sense. A common-sense-based attack is especially threatening because it allegedly rests on no assumptions or because it proceeds from a pretheoretical point. Other attacks on scepticism do rest on assumptions, and this weakens their position in the sense that the sceptic can (try to) resist them. However, Lukas Lang wanted to argue that a common-sense-based attack requires an obvious contradiction between common sense and scepticism. If they are not obviously contradictory, then the contradiction must be shown, presumably by argument, and so a common-sense-based attack would lose its chief advantage of ruling out scepticism *prior to* philosophical discussion. The problem is most obvious when we turn towards Moore's list of common sense truths ('There exists at present a living human body,' and so on) and Berkeley's assent to them. In Berkeley's theory, all common sense propositions are rendered true. But then there is no contradiction, not even disagreement, for the attacker to use a common sense proposition against Berkeley. With this situation in mind, Lukas Lang surveyed both sides of the debate: on the one hand, the common sense conception of Moore and Berkeley; on the other hand, the conception of contemporary Mooreans such as David Lewis and Jonathan Schaffer. Additionally, he took a look at two attempts to reach a contradiction between common sense and scepticism, namely via a theory of meaning or via Reid's theory of perception. Both, he argued, either fail because they are too weak or because they can claim no support from common sense and so gamble away the attack's main advantage.

[RE25] 19 June, 2018
Guido Bartolucci: **Jewish Scepticism in Christian Eyes**

In 1704, the Lutheran scholar Jakob Friedrich Reimmann (1668–1743) anonymously published a treatise on Solomon as a sceptic philosopher. He maintained that all the Jewish Patriarchs could be interpreted as sceptic philosophers, and in order to demonstrate his statement, he examined the figure of Solomon. The work is divided into two parts: in the first part, Reimmann shows the links between Solomon's philosophy and sceptic philosophy. In the second part, he defends his statements from the accusation of one philosopher and theologian, Joachim Lange, by maintaining that scepticism is the only true philosophy because it is based on the idea that 'man knows nothing.' Reimmann maintains that after Adam's fall the human mind could no longer attain true knowledge of the world: only God could give men *vera sapientia*, true wisdom. By quoting passages from different books of the Old and the New Testament, Reimmann used the classical fideistic instruments of scepticism in order to demonstrate the weakness of the human mind. He argues that Solomon was the best example of the Jewish philosophical tradition, and he also adds that because the Jewish king lived centuries before Pyrrho, he could therefore be seen as the real founder of scepticism. The relationship between scepticism and the Jewish tradition, according to Reimmann, was to strengthen the main characteristic of that kind of Greek philosophy, that is, its acknowledgement of human ignorance and doubt. Reimmann, however, uses the fideistic garb in order to legitimise the sceptical strategy towards dogmatism and traditional knowledge. During the Reading Evening, the first part of the work (translated into English for the first time) was read and Reimmann's interpretation of scepticism was discussed.

[RE26] 3 July, 2018
Jürgen Sarnowsky: **Miracles and Saints in Doubt**

During the later Middle Ages, the number of pilgrim places increased, as did the number of saints and relics. People were looking for support in their daily lives or collected indulgences for the salvation of their souls and to further their afterlives. Even if many people believed in what they were told by the clerics in these places of veneration, others, inside as well as outside the ecclesiastical sphere, doubted. This collection of sources for the Reading Evening offers examples from three cases: the 'Holy Blood' of Wilsnack, the canonisation process of Dorothea von Montau at Marienwerder in Prussia (1404), and the pilgrim's report of Arnold von Harff (1496–98). While the events in Wilsnack were doubted from the beginning and became the subject of a theological debate, the hearing of the witnesses for the canonisation process at Marienwerder offers several examples for popular doubts in saints and miracles. Finally, the Rhenish nobleman Arnold von Harff is included as a critical pilgrim who had his own thoughts about the veneration of relics.

Occasional Events

Workshops

Workshops are small conferences devoted to a specific topic or aspect of scepticism, bringing together different experts to present on the topic in question. In most cases, we design our workshops to include ample time for discussion in order to foster an exchange of ideas and help presenters improve their own research. The workshops are organised by MCAS fellows or team members. This allows them to present their distinctive field of study to other members of MCAS working in other disciplines or focussing on other topics. This encounter between different perspectives inspires very often new cooperations such as future interdisciplinary reading groups and workshops.

7–8 November, 2017
Scepticism and Religion in Al-Ghazali, Maimonides, and Hume
Convenors: Stephan Schmid, Universität Hamburg/Germany, Josef Stern, University of Chicago/USA, and Máté Veres, Université de Genève/Switzerland

In David Hume's *Dialogues concerning Natural Religion*, Cleanthes challenges Demea: 'Or how do you mystics, who maintain the absolute incomprehensibility of the Deity, differ from sceptics or atheists, who assert, that the first cause of All is unknown and unintelligible?' By the eighteenth century, we find questions of religion and scepticism tightly intertwined but this dialectic goes back to the ancient sceptics' critique of the gods and, when the three revealed monotheistic faiths encounter philosophy in the Middle Ages, it comes to embrace a rich variety of classical epistemological and metaphysical questions reconfigured in light of the medieval philosophical/theological context. Not only do thinkers grapple with issues of how knowledge can be acquired—by direct intuition, human reasoning, and/or divine revelation—but also with the classical question of the very possibility of knowledge, at least in the realms of metaphysics and theology. And if knowledge cannot be possessed, how should one act: by denying the claims as Academic sceptics are said to have argued, by embracing them despite, or because of, their lack of rational justification as fideists recommend, or by simply suspending judgment to free oneself from the conflict between religion and philosophy as Pyrrhonists would have reacted? In this workshop, the participants proposed to explore parallels and discrepancies between three of the greatest philosophers in the three faiths to have canvassed this rich and inadequately studied territory between religion and scepticism leading to an even wider range of questions from atomism and causation to knowledge and the self: Abū Ḥāmid Muḥammad ibn Muḥammad Al-Ghazali (ca. 1058–1111), Moses Maimonides (ca. 1135–1204), and David Hume (1711–76). Although no claims of influence among these three thinkers are made, there are striking and sometimes uncanny moments of convergence and divergence in their arguments and strategies, whose mutual investigation can serve to illuminate the thought of each.

Programme

Stephan Schmid, Universität Hamburg/Germany
'Welcome and Introductory Remarks'

Máté Veres, Université de Genève/Switzerland
'"Philosophy's happy escape?" Ancient Scepticism and the Project of Hume's Natural History of Religion'

Andreas Lammer, Ludwig-Maximilians-Universität München/Germany
'Al-Ghazali's Critical Theology'

Blake Dutton, Loyola University Chicago/USA
'Al-Ghazali and Hume on Causal Connection and Scepticism'

Josef Stern, University of Chicago/USA
'Maimonides' Guide and Hume's Dialogues: A Tale of Two Sceptics'

Mark Steiner, Hebrew University of Jerusalem/Israel
'David Hume: the First and Last "Kalamist"'

Ramona Winter, Humboldt-Universität zu Berlin/Germany
'Fictional Beliefs about the Self in Hume's Treatise. In what Sense are Fictional Beliefs Defective?'

Paul Russell, University of British Columbia/Canada and Göteborgs Universitet/Sweden
'Hume's Scepticism and the Problem of Atheism'

14–16 November, 2017
Buddhism and Scepticism: Historical, Philosophical, and Comparative Perspectives
Convenor: Oren Hanner, Universität Hamburg/Germany, in cooperation with the Numata Center for Buddhist Studies, Universität Hamburg/Germany

From their earliest stages, Buddhist traditions have displayed a sceptical attitude towards various types of accepted knowledge. Buddhist thinkers, beginning from the historical Buddha, questioned metaphysical assumptions, the realistic view of the world, and the reliability of our sources of knowledge, and expressed doubt about common social norms and religious views. In this way, philosophical scepticism played a pivotal role in the way Buddhist thought evolved. It served both as a method for arriving at a reliable and liberating understanding of reality and, as some argue, as an aspect of spiritual practice. The workshop on Buddhism and Scepticism investigated the place of scepticism in the development of classical Buddhist thought from historical and philosophical perspectives. From a historical standpoint, the conference explored the development of sceptical strategies in Buddhism and their relation to non-Buddhist systems of thought in Europe and Asia. From a philosophical point of view, it explored the ways in which sceptical arguments are used in Buddhist philosophical works, and how they resemble, and differ from, sceptical methods in other, non-Buddhist philosophies.

Programme

Oren Hanner, Universität Hamburg/Germany
'Welcome Addresses and Greetings'

Mark Siderits, Seoul National University/South Korea
'Keynote: Some Sceptical Doubts about "Buddhist Scepticism"'

Ethan Mills, University of Tennessee at Chattanooga/USA
'Nāgārjuna's Scepticism about Philosophy'

Georgios T. Halkias, University of Hong Kong/China
'The Soteriology of Scepticism: Historical and Philosophical Readings on Pyrrhonism and Buddhism'

Adrian Kuzminski, Independent Scholar
'The Evident and the Non-Evident: Buddhism through the Lens of Pyrrhonism'

Eli Franco, Universität Leipzig/Germany
'Why Madhyamaka Philosophy Is Not Sceptical'

Amber Carpenter, Yale-NUS College/Singapore
'Ethics of Atomism and Scepticism'

Dong Xiuyuan, Shandong University/China
'The Epistemological Foundation of the Debate between the Samaniyya and the Early Mutakallimūn'

Serena Saccone, Österreichische Akademie der Wissenschaften/Austria
'Abandoning the Doubt through Doubting: cintāmayī prajñā in the *Vajracchedikāṭīkā by Kamalaśīla'

Vincent Eltschinger, École pratique des hautes études, Paris/France
'Between Faith and Scepticism: Probabilism as a Philosophical Approach to Scripture in Dharmakīrti's Thought'

Gordon F. Davis, Carleton University, Ottawa/Canada
'Buddhist Variations on Axiological Scepticism and Ethical Pluralism'

James Mark Shields, Bucknell University, Lewisburg/USA
'Sceptical Buddhism as Provenance and Project'

11–12 Dezember, 2017
Visuelle Skepsis. Wie Bilder zweifeln
(in German)
Convenor: Margit Kern, MCAS und Department of Art History, Universität Hamburg

Bilder als Erkenntnismedien spielen heute eine größere Rolle denn je. Die Bilderflut, unter anderem in den Neuen Medien, lässt sie allerdings auch problematisch werden. Vor diesem Hintergrund erhält die Frage größere Bedeutung, wie Bilder ihren eigenen Status als Erkenntnismedien problematisieren—zum einen ausstellen und zum anderen in Zweifel ziehen—können. Bisher wurde die Auseinandersetzung mit Positionen des Skeptizismus in der Kunstgeschichte geführt, indem man philosophische Strömungen einer bestimmten Zeit auf die Ikonographie von Gemälden bezog. Die wenigen Publikationen, die sich mit Skepsis beschäftigen, fragen vor allem danach, wie philosophische Texte ihren Niederschlag in Gemälden oder Druckgraphiken fanden. Die Tagung wählte hier einen anderen Zugang. Es wurden explizit die Diskurse untersucht, die nicht darauf zurückgehen, dass Texte des Skeptizismus in Bilder übersetzt wurden. Stattdessen wurde gefragt, wie Bilder aufgrund der ihnen eigenen medialen Struktur zum Ort von performativen Prozessen werden, die mit den dialogischen Strategien des Skeptizismus vergleichbar sind. Eine Hauptthese des Workshops lautete, dass hier Widersprüche und Negationen auftreten müssen, die den Charakter einer medialen Selbstbefragung haben.

Programm

Margit Kern, Universität Hamburg
‚Visuelle Skepsis—Eine Einführung'

Jürgen Müller, Technische Universität Dresden
‚Alle Kreter lügen. Überlegungen zu Pieter Bruegels "Misanthrop"'

Janne Lenhart, Universität Hamburg
‚Zweifel am niederländischen Trompe-l'oeil: Cornelis Gijsbrechts' Rückseite eines Gemäldes'

Nicola Suthor, Yale University/USA
‚Scheinhafter Realismus und die Spaltung des Bildes: Zu Caravaggios "Kreuzigung Petri" und "Paulussturz" in der Cappella Cerasi'

Karlheinz Lüdeking, Universität der Künste Berlin
‚Caravaggios skeptischer Thomas (eine doppelte Gewebeprobe)'

Meinrad von Engelberg, Technische Universität Darmstadt
‚Die Kunst des "als ob": Skepsis als ästhetische Prämisse im 18. Jahrhundert'

Werner Busch, Freie Universität Berlin
‚Goyas "Caprichos". Der Zweifel an der Wirksamkeit aufklärerischer Moral'

Gerd Blum, Kunstakademie Münster/Universität Wien
‚Isosthenie und skeptischer Selbstwiderspruch: Manets "Déjeuner sur l'herbe"'

Kristin Drechsler, Leuphana Universität Lüneburg
‚Morandis Zweifel'

Monika Wagner, Universität Hamburg
‚Hinter Glas. Visuelle Dialoge mit einem transparenten Medium'

Wolfgang Kemp, Universität Hamburg/Leuphana Universität Lüneburg
‚Skepsis von Grund auf: Kurze Einblicke in werkgenetische Prozesse'

Adi Louria-Hayon, Tel Aviv University/Israel
'The Dialectics of Failed Perception in Bruce Nauman's Art'

Beate Pittnauer, HBK Braunschweig
‚Framing the real? Excluding the inventive? Über fotografische Gewissheiten und mediale Selbstzweifel'

Margit im Schlaa, Berlin
‚Blanks'

Sophia Kunze, Universität Hamburg
‚Momente visueller Skepsis im Video Game'

Postersektion

Anne-Kathrin Hinz, Friedrich-Schiller-Universität Jena
‚"Spur Andreas B." – Zweifel an der Darstellbarkeit von Geschichte?'

Constanze Fritzsch, Staatliche Kunstsammlungen Dresden
‚"Das Bild als Vorbild" A.R. Pencks Zweifel an der Sprache'

Lukas R.A. Wilde, Eberhard Karls Universität Tübingen
‚"Methodischer Zweifel" an Comic- und Manga-Bildern? Bildobjekte, referential meaning und der dritte Zeichenraum'

27 – 28 March, 2018
A Touch of Doubt: On Haptic Scepticism
Convenor: Rachel Aumiller, Universität Hamburg/Germany

Touch can serve as a 'reality check' that awakens an individual from her slumber. We pinch ourselves to confirm we are not dreaming. We slap a comrade across the cheek to bring him to his senses. In everyday speech, the sceptic is often presented as a 'Doubting Thomas' with the compulsion to touch what others accept on faith alone. Philosophical scepticism, however, casts doubt on the certainty of touch: Perhaps I am dreaming—dreaming even of the sensation of pinching myself awake. Is touch the guarantee of what is real? Or is the real precisely that which slips through the epistemologist's grasp?

Programme

Rachel Aumiller, Universität Hamburg/Germany
'Introduction: Framing the Sceptic as the Compulsive Toucher'

Noli me tangere

Mirt Komel, Univerza v Ljubljani/Slovenia
'Touch Me (Not) and the Question of Sense Certainty'

Libera Pisano, Universität Hamburg/Germany
'The Profaning Touch that Challenges Authority'

Religious Belief and the Imperative to Touch

Bill Rebiger, Universität Hamburg/Germany
'A Magic Touch: The Imperative to Touch in Jewish Magic from the Hebrew Bible to the Middle Ages'

Robert Pfaller, Kunstuniversität Linz/Austria
'When to Touch—And What to Doubt'

Haptic Cinema

Rachel Aumiller, Ana Jovanović, Bara Kolenc, Mirt Komel, Goran Vranešević
A Screening and discussion of a film project on touch and language

Questioning the Paradox of Touch

Ana Jovanović, Univerza v Ljubljani/Slovenia
'Touched in the Head: The s(k)epsis of Reason'

Goran Vranešević, Univerza v Ljubljani/Slovenia
'An Atom of Touch'

Touching the Other | Touching Oneself

Bara Kolenc, Univerza v Ljubljani/Slovenia
'The (Un)Touchable Touch of Pyramus and Thisbe: Doubt and Desire'

Jacob Levi, Johns Hopkins University/USA
'"Es wird Leib, es empfindet": Hands and Auto-Affection in Husserl's Ideen II'

Blind-Touch

José María Sánchez de León Serrano, Universität Hamburg/Germany
'Diderot's Letter on the Blind: Metaphysical Sobriety and the Priority of Touch'

Adi Louria-Hayon, Tel Aviv University/Israel
'The Weak Relations of Touch and Sight through the Passage of Lapsed Time'

Closing Discussion
'Emerging Concepts of Haptic Scepticism'

4 June, 2018
Early Modern (Anti-)Scepticism
Convenor: Stephan Schmid and Lukas Lang, MCAS, Universität Hamburg/Germany

The rise of scepticism in the early modern period led to new and innovative theories on both the sceptical and the anti-sceptical sides of the debate. This workshop aimed to investigate the sceptical and anti-sceptical elements in the philosophies of David Hume, Thomas Reid, and Baruch Spinoza. In particular, the questions, which were addressed, are first, in what respect these philosophers embraced scepticism or made use of sceptical strategies, and second, how, and by which means and at what cost, they resisted sceptical arguments.

Programme

Ramona Winter, Humboldt-Universität zu Berlin/Germany
'Are Fictional Persons a Problem for Hume?'

Lukas Lang, Universität Hamburg/Germany
'The Status of First Principles for Reid'

James Van Cleve, University of Southern California, Los Angeles/USA
'Two Ways to Skin a Sceptic: Reid's Realism and Kant's Idealism'

José María Sánchez de León Serrano, Universität Hamburg/Germany
'Spinoza on Adequacy and Common Notions'

Lecture Series 'Feminism and Scepticism'

The Maimonides Centre established a lecture series which focusses on feminist approaches to and perspectives on scepticism. The Centre invites researchers to give a public lecture on this topic, and—following this lecture—to meet with the female researchers in order to share their experiences and career paths in their academic systems. The female fellows expressed the wish to learn more about academic career advancement opportunities in different countries.

7 December, 2017
Judith R. Baskin, University of Oregon, Eugene/USA
Rabbinic Forensics: Distinguishing Egg White from Semen in bGittin 57a

This lecture began with a discussion of a brief passage within a passage in Babylonian Talmud, Gittin 57a that demonstrates how rabbinic knowledge of a forensic technique for distinguishing egg white from semen protected a woman from her husband's fabricated accusation of adultery. Judith Baskin then went on to discuss how this investigative procedure is cited in medieval and early modern Jewish exegeses of the story of Joseph and Potiphar's wife (Genesis 39), where the same forensic test is used to absolve a man who was falsely accused of rape by a woman. Interestingly, this scientific test is also cited in a medieval Muslim source. Additionally, the lecture looked at the values these narratives attach to female passivity and agency, and establishes, as well, how the anecdote about the husband who was found guilty of falsely accusing his wife in the talmudic passage is also part of a late ancient polemic against Christianity.

30 January, 2018
Tsippi Kauffman, Bar-Ilan University, Ramat Gan/Israel
Hasidism and Gender: Shades of Scepticism

Did the hasidic movement's revolution of the Jewish world include women? The lecture examined the case of Temer'l Sonenberg-Bergson, a patron of Polish ṣaddiqim. Using feminist criticism of religion studies, Tsippi Kauffman demonstrated the implications of the patriarchal approach to setting the boundaries of religious phenomena —in this instance, the question of whether this extraordinary woman may properly be called a ḥasida. A review of several hasidic stories showed how Temer'l expressed her Hasidism and how she was viewed within hasidic circles as a sort of hermaphrodite, with scepticism towards both her femininity and her religiosity.

Maimonides Lectures on Scepticism

The Maimonides lectures were established to invite international researchers to give a talk within the field of scepticism. The lectures are recorded and published on the webpage of the Centre in order to make them available to a larger audience.

21 February, 2018
Moshe Halbertal, Hebrew University of Jerusalem/Israel
Facing Uncertainty: Maimonides' Concept of Law

Uncertainty is an essential feature of the human condition; it is simultaneously a source of deep anxiety and of thrill. The present state of the world, its past, and what it holds for us in the future are frequently unknown to us. This lecture examined the moral and legal implications of uncertainty, exploring the subject through Maimonides' legal work as it faces the challenges of uncertainty in Jewish law. Jewish law takes a keen interest in this feature of the human condition, and it has vast and intense discussions which address the following question: 'what are the norms that have to be applied in conditions in which we do not know the facts of the matter?' The talmudic tradition also addresses situations in which we might have a full grasp of the facts of the matter, but deep uncertainty about the proper norms that have to be applied to these facts. In such cases, our uncertainty is not factual but normative, and while affirming our normative uncertainty, the Talmud attempts to formulate rules that will be applied in conditions of uncertainty about the rules. What we can learn from these attempts to regulate conditions of uncertainty is how Maimonides understood its moral and legal significance and how his attempts to regulate these conditions reflected his conception of Jewish law.

7 May, 2018
Christoph Schulte, Universität Potsdam/Germany
Metaphysical Scepticism concerning the Philosophy of History: Mendelssohn's Arguments against the Progress of Humankind

In his seminal work *Jerusalem* (1783), Moses Mendelssohn explicitly refuses his close friend Lessing's ideas of a successive education of humankind and a general progress in the development of human rationality and morality in world history. This scepticism towards the upcoming modern philosophy of history and the idea of an infinite progressive evolution of humankind from the beginnings of world history is based on the principles of Mendelssohn's metaphysics, his anthropology, and his philosophy of natural law. This lecture discussed Mendelssohn's arguments and their philosophical relevance in some philosophers of the twentieth century.

29 May, 2018
Glenn Dynner, Sarah Lawrence College, Yonkers/USA
'I began to have doubts:' Defection from Orthodoxy and the Traditionalist Jewish Response in Twentieth-Century Poland

The early twentieth century was a period of accelerated acculturation among Polish Jews. As many young people discovered rationalist literature and joined modern political movements, rabbinic and hasidic leaders evinced panic over youth defections and the 'emptying-out' of their study halls. However, secularising Jewish youths in the Second Polish Republic encountered formidable barriers to integration, including restrictions on university admissions and frequent physical assaults on campuses. Many found themselves in a state of cultural limbo. At the same time, hasidic and rabbinic leaders revitalised their institutions by appropriating secularist educational, political, and institutional modes—a defensive acculturation strategy that inadvertently transformed Polish Jewish traditionalism itself. This lecture examined both Polish Jewish youth 'defections' and the innovative traditionalist responses to this perceived crisis.

12 – 15 March, 2018

International Conference: Abulafia and the Early Maimonideans: Trends, Approaches, and Sceptical Strategies

Convenor: Racheli Haliva, Universität Hamburg/Germany

The conference focussed on the different trends and sceptical attitudes Maimonideanism took in the thirteenth and fourteenth centuries by examining various approaches to major religious topics such as the nature of the Torah, the commandments, the Hebrew language, the people of Israel, and the land of Israel. This comparative approach points to distinctive philosophical trends—as represented by ibn Tibbon, Shem Tov ibn Falquera, Joseph ibn Caspi, Levi ben Abraham, Isaac Albalag, Moshe Narboni, Zerahyah Hen, and Hillel of Verona—focussing on major Jewish religious topics. Among these trends, the place of Abraham Abulafia and the early writings of R. Joseph Gikatilla, who wrote some forms of commentaries on Maimonides' *Guide of the Perplexed* stands out. The questions to be asked were whether it is possible to draw a map of radical versus conservative Maimonideanism and whether the two kabbalists are as radical as the philosophers when dealing with the same topics.

Programme

Life in Naples

David Abulafia, University of Cambridge/UK
'Naples as Mediterranean Crossroads'

Moshe Idel, Hebrew University of Jerusalem/Israel
'Abulafia's Commentaries on the Guide of the Perplexed'

Gitit Holzman, Levinsky College Tel Aviv/Israel
'Commentaries on the Guide of the Perplexed II'

Yossi Schwartz, Tel Aviv University/Israel
'Abulafia and Hillel of Verona on the Guide of the Perplexed'

Arje Krawczyk, Jewish Historical Institute, Warsaw/Poland
'Inner Speech (endophasia) in the Thought of Maimonides and Abulafia'

Torah, Tablets of Stone, and Mount Sinai's Revelation

Steven Harvey, Bar-Ilan University, Ramat Gan/Israel
'The Law of Moses in Maimonides, Abulafia, and Maimonideans'

Daniel Davies and Racheli Haliva, Universität Hamburg/Germany
'Tablets of Stone—between Maimonides and Abulafia'

Adam Afterman, Tel Aviv University/Israel
'Kabbalistic Reading of Maimonides' Concept of Revelation'

Fabrizio Lelli, Università del Salento/Italy
'Translations and Commentaries of Abulafia'

Between Prophecy and Philosophy

Haim Kreisel, Ben-Gurion University of the Negev, Beer-Sheva/Israel
'Maimonides and Abulafia on Prophecy'

Elke Morlok, Goethe-Universität Frankfurt/Germany
'The Status of the Text and the Use of Language in Maimonides and Abulafia'

Ofer Elior, Ben-Gurion University of the Negev, Beer-Sheva and Hebrew University of Jerusalem/Israel
'The Account of the Chariot in Maimonides, Abulafia, and Provençal Thinkers'

The Land of Israel and the Hebrew Language

Josef Stern, University of Chicago/USA
'The Role of Language in Maimonides and Abulafia's Thought'

Hanna Kasher, Bar-Ilan University, Ramat Gan/Israel
'Maimonides, Abulafia, and Joseph ibn Kaspi on the Hebrew Language'

Zev Harvey, Hebrew University of Jerusalem/Israel
'Maimonides, Abulafia, and Spinoza'

José María Sánchez de León Serrano, Universität Hamburg/Germany
'Response'

Lecture Series 'Reason and Revelation in Jewish Tradition'

Organised by the Institute for Jewish Philosophy and Religion, in cooperation with MCAS
Convenor: Lilian Türk, Institute for Jewish Philosophy and Religion, Universität Hamburg/Germany

The lectures introduced Jewish thought to the interested public and exposed the relationship between reason and revelation in specific Jewish writings. They revolved around the following questions: under which circumstances can we speak of reason within the framework of Judaism? Can we erroneously read reason into the sources of heavenly revelation? How can the presupposition of reason/ratio be justified by Jewish thinkers and deduced from traditional Jewish sources? Does reason concur with faith, or are they exclusive epistemological spheres?

Programme

16 March, 2018
Giuseppe Veltri, Universität Hamburg/Germany
Glaube und Vernunft im Judentum: Eine philosophisch-skeptische Einführung

25 March, 2018
Meir Buzaglo, Hebrew University of Jerusalem/Israel
The One: Towards a Talmudic Approach

5 May, 2018
Bill Rebiger, Universität Hamburg/Germany
Gershom Scholems Erforschung der Kabbala und die Frage nach Vernunft und Offenbarung im Judentum

7 May, 2018 [Maimonides Lecture]
Christoph Schulte, Universität Potsdam/Germany
Metaphysical Scepticism concerning the Philosophy of History: Mendelssohn's Arguments against the Progress of Humankind

14 May, 2018
Ze'ev Strauss, Universität Hamburg/Germany
Wenn die Offenbarung selbst die hypostasierte Vernunft Gottes ist: Der Offenbarungsbegriff des Philon von Alexandria

28 May, 2018
Elchanan Reiner, Tel Aviv University/Israel
The 'Ten Questions' of Eliezer of Eilenburg—Scepticism, Heresy or Exegesis? An Alternative Reading

4 June, 2018
Daniel Davies, Universität Hamburg/Germany
The Jacobs Affair: Revelation and Schismatic Jewish Theology

6 June, 2018
Lilian Türk, Universität Hamburg/Germany
Offenbarungsverständnis und Vernunftkritik im jüdischen religiösen Sozialismus

11 June, 2018
Aryeh Botwinick, Temple University, Philadelphia/USA
Negative Theology in the Context of Rabbi Akiva as a Rabbinic Precursor and Infinity as the Point of (Non-)Contact

13 June, 2018
Yair Lorberbaum, Bar-Ilan University, Ramat Gan/Israel
The Rise of Halakhic Religiosity, of Mystery, and Transcendence in the Jewish Tradition

18 June, 2018
Michael Engel, Universität Hamburg/Germany
Apologetic Tendencies vs. Apologetic Works: Evaluating the Historiography of Medieval Jewish Thought

25 June, 2018
Rachel Aumiller, Universität Hamburg/Germany
The Comic Slapstick of Resistance and Revelation: Walter Benjamin and WWII Political Satire

27 June, 2018
Libera Pisano, Universität Hamburg/Germany
The 'Speaking Language' of Revelation beyond Reason: Franz Rosenzweig's Grammatical Thought

2 July, 2018
Daniel Boyarin, University of California, Berkeley/USA
Kommentar innerhalb der Grenzen der bloßen Vernunft: The Philosophical Grounds of Pilpul

9 July, 2018
Michela Torbidoni, Universität Hamburg/Germany
Challenging Religious Authorities: The Scientific Commitment of the Jews in Seventeenth Century Venice

29 July–3 August, 2018
Second Summer School

Sceptical Strategies, Methods, and Approaches in the Middle Ages: Jewish, Christian, and Islamic Traditions

The second Summer School was focussing on major sceptic concepts, strategies and key terms in medieval Hebrew, Arabic, and Latin literature. Participants and instructors focussed on sceptical and anti-sceptical enquiry of concepts of truth and knowledge as well as sceptical methods of doubting and arguing. The Summer School offered a unique platform to discuss the tension between philosophy and faith, and between reason and revelation within medieval discourses. Participants were engaged with primary Hebrew, Latin, and Arabic texts. The aim was to provide participants with the tools to examine scepticism and anti-scepticism within Jewish, Christian, and Islamic contexts in relation to attaining true knowledge.

Course leaders were Racheli Haliva and Giuseppe Veltri. They were supported by an international team of experts in scepticism from the fields of medieval philosophy and religious studies: Elena Baltuta, Guido Bartolucci, Daniel Davies, Heidrun Eichner, Yehuda Halper, Elon Harvey, Steven Harvey, Gitit Holtzman, Henrik Lagerlund, Giovanni Licata, Ariel Malachi, Yoav Meyrav, and Ronny Vollandt.

The Summer School was attended by 15 participants from Argentina, Austria, China, Germany, Israel, Morocco, the United Kingdom, and the United States.

MCAS Participation in External Conferences (Selection)

6–10 August, 2017
17th World Congress of Jewish Studies in Jerusalem/Israel

Panel: Scepticism and Anti-Scepticism in Medieval Jewish Philosophy and Thought

Giuseppe Veltri
Saadiah's Anti-Scepticism among Sceptical Movements in the Middle Ages

In his introduction and first section of the *Emunot ve-De'ot*, Saadiah makes a genuine attempt and devotes great efforts to rebutting and refuting sceptical movements that were active in his time. He argues that mistakes and changes of opinion are part of the quest for the truth. These mistakes and changes of opinion are not to be taken, according to Saadiah, as a proof that nothing can be known. The fact that Saadiah devotes in his work long discussions to deal with sceptical problems should not be underestimated. Indeed, it is not a purely introductory question but rather a historical testimony of an extent phenomenon of sceptical theories in his time. The lecture focussed mainly on the presence of sceptical movements before and during Saadiah's time as reflected in his work(s). Moreover, the analysis of Saadiah's anti-scepticism was addressed through the lenses of modern studies on medieval scepticism.

Ariel Malachi
'Our eyes saw, not a stranger's:' Sceptical Aspects in Epistemological Conceptions of Halevi, Ibn Daud and Maimonides, through the Question of the Certainty of Tradition

What is scepticism, and what is the definition according to which one can be characterised as sceptic, is a fascinating question. However, be our answer to this fundamental enquiry wide or narrow, inclusive or exclusive, casting doubt is clearly at its basis. According to the logical Islamic–Aristotelian tradition, the distinction between an argument whose conclusion is certain and an argument whose conclusion is uncertain, depends on the distinction between the value of a demonstrative argument and the value of a dialectical or rhetorical arguments. In this context, it is noteworthy to analyse in which manner Islamic and Jewish thinkers faced the question of the certainty of tradition. In the talk, the following arguments were addressed:

    1. With regard to this question, one can distinguish Al-Farabi's position from that of Ibn Sina's; while Al-Farabi doubts tradition, and states that the epistemological status of prepositions which derives from tradition is uncertain, Ibn Sina, on the other hand, argues that in case of consecutive tradition, the consecutiveness might unravel the doubt we attribute to these prepositions, and one may accept them as certain.

    2. The analysis of relevant texts reveals that this distinction found its way to the Jewish thought in the following surprising way: Halevi, much like Maimonides, supports Al-Farabi's more doubtful attitude, while Ibn Daud emphasises the less sceptical approach of Ibn Sina.

Racheli Haliva
The Esoteric Scepticism of the Rational Jewish Thinker: Isaac Polqar on the Talmud and the Commandments

The tension between revelation and reason, between tradition and intellectual investigation, has occupied thinkers of all religions. These thinkers, who sought to reconcile faith and philosophical enquiry, were obligated to their religious traditions on the one hand, and to philosophical principles on the other. Naturally, the traditionalists were sceptical towards the rationalists, for, according to their view, the philosophers shake the foundations of faith. At the same time, the philosophers were sceptical towards the traditionalists, arguing that some aspects of tradition contradict philosophical principles and therefore must be re-interpreted.

Isaac Polqar, the Jewish philosopher from the fourteenth century, was intrigued by the relationship between philosophy and Judaism. Despite his attempt to exoterically argue that there is no contradiction between philosophical principles and the principles of Judaism, he esoterically challenges the authority of basic religious foundations such as the Mosaic Law.

In this lecture, it was shown how Polqar's sceptical approach towards some traditional views strengthens his philosophical/natural point of view, as a result of which philosophy is placed in a superior position than tradition, or more precisely, aspects of tradition.

Bill Rebiger
Sceptical Strategies Used by Simone Luzzatto and Leon Modena in their Examination of Kabbalah

The Venetian rabbis Simone Luzzatto (1583–1663) and Leon Modena (1571–1648) adopted a critical approach towards Kabbalah; and yet their criticism was manifested in different ways. While Leon Modena devoted an entire book written in Hebrew, his *Ari Nohem* ('Roaring Lion'), to a comprehensive and sharp attack on Kabbalah, Simone Luzzatto included merely a few pages in his *Discorso circa il stato degli Hebrei et in particular dimoranti nell'inclita città di Venetia* ('Discourse Concerning the Condition of the Jews, and in particular those living in the Fair City of Venice') where he presented in Italian apparently only several basic concepts and historical data of Kabbalah. In the lecture, various sceptical strategies inherent in their examination of Kabbalah were compared and discussed. Thus, the lecturer presented the complex relationship between the purpose of the writing, the choice of language, the addressed audience, the modes of publication, and sceptical strategies.

5–8 March, 2018

Annual Conference 2018, European Academy of Religion (EURARE) in Bologna/Italy

Panel: Jewish Philosophy: A Controversial Issue between Judaism and Christianity (Seventeenth and Eighteenth Centuries)
Guido Bartolucci, Libera Pisano, and Michela Torbidoni

The meaning of Jewish philosophy has been, is, and continues to be a controversial issue within the broad field of Jewish studies. It would be paradoxical to attempt to draw the boundaries of this category, since it is at the same time a conjunction and a disjunction of two different perspectives. In fact, the concept of Jewish philosophy on the one hand addresses the secular tendencies of Jewish thinking and its critical approach to religion, and on the other hand necessarily involves the results of the dialogue between Jewish and Christian traditions. In this regard, the panel aims to explore the blurred boundaries of such a significant subject by presenting the point of view of some Christian and Jewish authors, such as Johann Franz Budde, Simone Luzzatto, and Moses Mendelssohn, and how they have developed a philosophical interpretation of Judaism from this.

15–19 July, 2018

11th EAJS Congress in Krakow/Poland

Panel: Jewish Scepticism

Giuseppe Veltri
Jewish Scepticism? Origins and Development of a Definition

It is perhaps no surprise that the period in which the main concept of a 'Jewish philosophy' was developed, i.e. early modernity, is also the origin of the idea of a 'Jewish' scepticism. In the lecture, Veltri dealt with the many elements which created a Jewish sceptical tradition in the early modern period parallel to the discussion of a *philosophia perennis* that was developed in Christianity in an attempt to dogmatise the Jewish philosophical tradition by assuming a genealogy of wisdom as well as mystical or kabbalistic speculation to back it. The curious element which will be analysed is that discussion of the sceptical 'nature' (or, to use a sceptical category, 'attitude') of Judaism originated contemporaneously in two different areas, in northern Italy, particularly in Venice, and in Germany.

Guido Bartolucci
Simone Luzzatto's Political Thought: Between Scepticism and Reason of State

Simone Luzzatto's political thought has been interpreted by several scholars as being linked to the tradition of the Reason of State, to which the Venetian rabbi makes constant reference in his work, particularly in the *Discorso*. Upon analysing Luzzatto's works in depth, however, it is possible to recognise other fragments of a political reflection that cannot be traced back to the tradition of Reason of State and which in some cases is contrary to it. By comparing the different political positions expressed by Luzzatto in his works, a new political thought emerges, transformed by using the sceptical tradition. In fact, in both the *Discorso* and the *Socrates*, Luzzatto recognises the impossibility of formulating a 'universal' political theory, and identifies the sceptical concept of the 'probable' as the only guide that man has for living in a social community.

The paper aimed to compare Luzzatto's different positions and to recognise the sources of his most radical interpretation, the politics of the probable, which may be useful in order to understand the influence of scepticism in Jewish and Christian political thought in seventeenth-century Europe more generally.

Michela Torbidoni
Challenging the Authority of Antiquity: The Influence of Francis Bacon on Simone Luzzatto's Sceptical Thought

The aim of the paper is to explore the purposes underlying the sceptical enquiry led by Rabbi Simone Luzzatto in his works. Through his sceptical arguments, Luzzatto develops a criticism of human knowledge specially aimed to deconstruct the authority of ancient dogmatic wisdom. In this respect, Torbidoni argued that Luzzatto's project was deeply influenced by the reading of Francis Bacon's philosophy, well-known for having promoted a reformation of human learning by challenging the relationship between antiquity and modernity and thus the method whereby knowledge is apprehended and passed on. The statement, which is based on relevant indirect quotations of Bacon's works raised throughout Luzzatto's writings, intends to disclose the crucial role played by this source in understanding the arguments and goals of Luzzatto's scepticism. Bacon's philosophy fulfils a double task in this regard: on the one hand, it provides a significant speculative pattern to be taken into account by reading some of the main issues raised by Luzzatto, like those of time, dogma, free critical investigation, sincere truth, and temporary suspension of judgement. On the other hand, this source narrows the field of research upon the still-unknown intellectual interlocutors of Luzzatto. As no other Jewish reader of Bacon's writings is known so far, this source builds a bridge between Luzzatto and those Venetian Christian intellectuals who were closer to the Protestant world and highly critical of both the Roman Church and the Scholastic tradition, such as Paolo Sarpi and his circle.

Libera Pisano
***Sprachkrise* as Sceptical Philosophy of Language**

The so-called *Sprachkrise* is a complex phenomenon of language critique diffused in the philosophical and literary debate among poets and intellectuals before World War I. The specific trait of the theoretical constellation that was characterised by the collapse of language as an epistemological, logical, and ontological tool was to consider linguistic boundaries. In this contribution, Pisano investigated this phenomenon for two reasons: firstly, the *Sprachkrise* helps us to better understand how the critique of language became the focus of philosophical thought at the beginning of the last century long before the linguistic turn; secondly, this phenomenon particularly acquired special attention among German-Jewish thinkers. In fact, since all these authors have a double cultural background in common, or better, a double belonging both to Jewish tradition and to German philosophy, their sceptical attitudes or critical distance towards language also have their premises in autobiographical factors. Thanks to the mediation of Fritz Mauthner, whose work was the *trait d'union* between literature and critical thought, the phenomenon of *Sprachskepsis* spread throughout the milieu of German-Jewish philosophy; in fact, it involves the whole generation of thinkers whose elective affinities were analysed by Löwy in *Redemption and Utopia*, i.e. Landauer, Benjamin, Buber, Scholem, Bloch, and others, who linked together language, messianism, libertarian utopias, and romanticism.

Bill Rebiger
Sceptical Elements in a Dogmatic Stance: Isaac Polqar against the Kabbalah

Despite the generally accepted opinion that the Jewish Averroists were—at least ultimately—dogmatics or anti-sceptics, certain sceptical elements and strategies can notwithstanding be detected in their works. Rebiger presented a case study devoted to the Jewish Averroistic philosopher and polemicist Isaac Polqar (second half of the thirteenth century—ca. 1330) and his attack on kabbalists included in his main work *'Ezer ha-Dat* ('In Support of the Religion'). According to Polqar, the kabbalists are dangerous because they claim to have knowledge that does not accept the philosophical methods and logical rules of Aristotle. In contrast, the kabbalists' supposed knowledge is supplied by an esoteric tradition reaching back to the time of the prophets, as they claim. Therefore, following the epistemological criteria defined by Maimonides, Kabbalah cannot be accepted as a certain source of knowledge. Accordingly, Polqar tried to undermine the authority and legitimation of the kabbalists' claims about a traditional knowledge by using various sceptical elements in his argumentation.

Israel Netanel Rubin
Omnipotence, Scepticism, and Logic: What Is Remaining When Everything Is Possible?

God is almighty, as every child knows, at least since the time when monotheism conquered the cultural world. However, can God really do everything? Is He able to create a square with a diagonal which has the same length as its side? Can God create another God like Himself? Can God commit suicide? Among the family of such quaint heretical paradoxes, the most famous is that about God's ability to create a stone that He is unable to lift. So, the principal question is whether God's omnipotence, which originally meant His superiority over physical laws, also extends to the world of logic and mathematics. But it becomes clear that this question leads in fact to the basic question about the rationality of religion and even the issue of whether a rational religion is possible at all. One of the solutions to the problem, adopted both by philosophers like Descartes and by Jewish kabbalists and mystics in recent generations, indeed prefers the totality of divine omnipotence over any other consideration. This position leads to what the American philosopher Alvin Plantinga called 'universal possibilitism,' since even the most basic laws of logic are declared to be contingent and determined by the arbitrary will of God alone. The result of this is that everything is possible, that anything can be, and that there is no situation, sentence, or object whose existence, or non-existence, can be absolutely determined. Here, then, is the touching point between the problem of divine omnipotence and the sceptical worldview. Each of them begins at a different point of origin, but eventually they find themselves draining together into the impasse of philosophical nihilism that comes from unlimited possibilitism.

José María Sánchez de León Serrano
Spinoza on the Cartesian Circle

The so-called 'Cartesian circle' designates a predicament in Descartes' attempt to prove God's existence and eliminate sceptical doubt. The predicament can be described as follows. Descartes argues that we cannot be certain of anything—even of the most evident truths, such as mathematical truths—as long as we do not know if God exists. However, God's existence is not self-evident and requires a demonstration. Yet such a demonstration appears to be impossible, for a demonstration must be based on certain premises and we have just assumed that nothing is certain. In this paper, Sánchez de León focussed on Spinoza's approach to this predicament. Although Spinoza was strongly influenced by Descartes, it is usually assumed that the just described problem plays no role in his philosophy, due to Spinoza's full-fledged rationalism. The lecturer argued, on the contrary, that the Cartesian circle resurfaces in Spinoza's philosophy *precisely because* of its rationalistic character. Moreover, Sánchez de León showed how Spinoza circumvents the difficulty through a proof of God's existence that is simultaneously cosmological and ontological.

Ze'ev Strauss
On the Boundary between Dogmatic Platonism and Academic Scepticism: Philo of Alexandria's Sceptical Judaism

It is by no means a new revelation within the scholarly work done on Philo of Alexandria thus far that his multi-layered body of thought has recourse to various elements of the rich philosophical tradition of academic scepticism. The leading Philo scholar David T. Runia draws our attention to this fact when he alludes to the 'mixture of scepticism and dogmatism' present in Philo's Jewish philosophy (1986, 129). This view might come as a surprise to some, since Philo can be perceived as a dogmatist in the truest sense of the word: on the one hand a dogmatic Platonist, and on the other hand and *a fortiori* a dogmatic Jewish thinker who strictly adheres to the tenets of Mosaic faith. In his paper, Strauss endeavoured to show that Philo cannot be easily cast aside as merely a dogmatic exegete of scripture who occasionally makes only eclectic references to Greek philosophy. Rather, he should be considered a serious metaphysician, who quarrels with sceptical notions in order to delineate his own speculative understanding of Jewish philosophy. Strauss argued that Philo held the stance that without the revealed truth of Judaism, we are forced to resort to a radical sceptical position, where we are left to battle for our mere opinions without ever being able to attain basic metaphysical knowledge of reality. He also aimed to concretely demonstrate a point touched on by Carlos Lévy (2010, 94), namely how Philo sophisticatedly utilises sceptical patterns of thought for the formulation of his apophatic theology.

Yoav Meyrav
Report on the International Conference on Abraham Abulafia and the Early Maimonideans: Trends, Approaches, and Sceptical Strategies (March 12–15, 2018)

The purpose of the conference organised by Racheli Haliva was to celebrate and discuss Moshe Idel's new book, *Abraham Abulafia's Esotericism: On Secrets and Doubts.* The book will be published by De Gruyter (Berlin) during 2018–19 in the MCAS's publication series *Studies and Texts in Scepticism* (STIS).

The conference focussed on the different trends and sceptical attitudes Maimonideanism took in the thirteenth and fourteenth centuries by examining various approaches to major religious topics such as the nature of the Torah, the commandments, the Hebrew language, the people of Israel, and the land of Israel. This comparative approach points to distinctive philosophical trends—as represented by Samuel ibn Tibbon, Shem-Tov ibn Falaquera, Joseph ibn Kaspi, Levi ben Abraham, Isaac Albalag, Moshe Narboni, Zeraḥyah Ḥen, and Hillel of Verona—focussing on major Jewish religious topics. Among these trends, the place of Abraham Abulafia and the early writings of Joseph Gikatilla, both of whom wrote commentaries on Maimonides' *Guide of the Perplexed*, stands out. The questions asked here concern the possibility of drawing a map of radical versus conservative Maimonideanism and to discern whether or not the two kabbalists are as radical as the philosophers in treating the same subject matter.

The conference was comprised of Kabbalah and Jewish philosophy scholars, including internationally renowned and established experts alongside new voices of a younger generation. All of the participants had received advance copies of Idel's book and had explored its various themes and intersections with their own respective research focusses. The conference combined formal lectures with a workshop format, and a considerable amount of time was allocated to free discussion. The report here will provide a chronological talk-by-talk overview and conclude with a short summary of a number of recurring themes that came up during the discussions, which can perhaps provide occasion for subsequent scholarship.

The conference opened with David Abulafia (University of Cambridge/UK), whose presentation "Naples and Mediterranean Crossroads" outlined the complicated history of the kingdoms of Sicily and Naples, mainly in the thirteenth century, and provided historical context for the intellectual undertakings explored in the conference. The presentation focussed on the reigns of Frederic II and his successor Charles I of Anjou, their politics and attitude to scholarship and non-Christian groups, and the condition of the Jewish community under both monarchs' rules. By the time Abraham Abulafia arrived at Capua in 1279, Charles had already stabilised his regime and had made attempts to convert the Jews, who until that period had been an integral part of society, enjoying the court's protection. A short time afterwards, a period of political and military turmoil begun, persisting for over 200 years, bringing with it rich apocalyptic literature.

Moshe Idel (Hebrew University of Jerusalem/Israel) outlined the conceptual framework of the subsequent presentations, describing "Abulafia's Commentaries on the *Guide of the Perplexed*" in terms of structure, circumstances of composition, reception, and influence. Abulafia wrote three commentaries on Maimonides' *Guide of the Perplexed* within a span of nine years (significantly more than any other scholar): *Sefer Ge'ulah* ('Book of Redemption,' 1273; probably written in Spain), *Ḥayyei ha-Nefesh* ('Life of the Soul,' 1278/9; written in Byzantium), and *Sitrei Torah* ('Secrets of the Torah,' 1280; written in Capua). Of these, *Sitrei Torah* was the most read and the most influential. In fact, it survives in more manuscripts than all other thirteenth-century commentaries on the *Guide*—by any author—and was also translated into Latin.

According to Idel, Abulafia was a passionate teacher of the *Guide*, which he taught in Barcelona, Castile, Byzantium, Capua, and Sicily. The three different commentaries arise from the fact that Abulafia's writings at the time addressed different audiences in different places. Idel claimed that Abulafia's teachings about the *Guide* and his exposing its secrets would have been one of the reasons he was forced to move from place to place. The commentaries were written for specific students, to whom Abulafia assigned numbers, complaining they were bad or poor students. His complaint was founded on his observation that whenever he progressed to a more advanced stage in understanding the *Guide* those students abandoned him.

Idel noted that when exploring Abulafia's works on the *Guide* it is important to keep in mind that he wrote them as a kabbalist rather than a philosopher. Indeed, Idel argued that, to a certain degree, Abulafia took the *Guide* to be the *source* of his Kabbalah. In so doing, he attempted to uncover the secrets of the *Guide*, which he deemed contained a kabbalistic nature. Abulafia, for instance, is one of the few commentators who implemented gematria when reading the *Guide*, facilitating it in an ecstatic context. Moreover, the work is understood not only as a guide to *knowing* secrets, but also as a guide to an *experience*: this particular experience being a Maimonidean prophetic experience.

In discussing the lasting influence of Abulafia's commentaries, Idel tentatively suggested considering the possibility that later commentaries on the *Guide* were written as a form of reaction to Abulafia. Whether or not this is the case, the wide distribution of manuscripts, especially of *Sitrei Torah*, is an extremely significant indicator of the dissemination and impact of Abulafia's commentary. Idel presented a long list of authors (Jewish as well as Christian) who have directly quoted or alluded to Abulafia's commentaries with or without proper attribution.

Idel argued that Abulafia's Kabbalah is intertwined with Maimonidean influence, which Abulafia never marginalised, even long after writing the commentaries. This influence is also felt in the negative reaction with which other kabbalists received

Abulafia's commentaries after Abulafia was compelled to leave Spain. Abulafia's influence is tied in with his unique blend of Kabbalah and philosophy. His Kabbalah is idiosyncratic, but not to any extremes that would prevent his work from attracting audiences in significant circles. This form of 'Maimonidean Kabbalah' has interesting connections to Abulafia's fierce critique of rabbinic Jewry, his conception of Judaism as a universal entity, and his opening of the Jewish experience to non-Jews.

Idel ended his talk by musing about the transformation in the reception of Abulafia in Jewish orthodox literature; from being completely outcast to appearing frequently on the shelves of the bookshops of Jerusalem's ultra-orthodox neighbourhood *Me'ah She'arim*.

Gitit Holtzman (Levinsky College, Tel Aviv/Israel) discussed "Esoteric Philosophy, Prophecy, and Mysticism: R. Moshe Narboni's commentary on the *Guide of the Perplexed* as Revealed in the Commentary on al-Ghazali's *Intentions of the Philosophers*." Holtzman argues that Moshe Narboni's distinction between the exoteric and esoteric levels in Maimonides' *Guide* is reflected by his distribution of information among his different commentaries on philosophical works. Most importantly, she stressed Narboni's refusal to reveal the secrets of the *Guide* in his commentary on the work, referring his reader to his commentaries on al-Ghazali's *Intentions of the Philosophers*, Averroes' *Letter about the Possibility of Conjunction with the Agent Intellect*, and Ibn Tufail's *Ḥayy ibn Yaqẓān*. In other words, to understand Narboni's views about the esoteric level of the *Guide*, one should study texts *other* than Narboni's commentary on the *Guide*.

Holtzman demonstrated this by analysing key passages of Narboni's commentary on Al-Ghazali's *Intentions of the Philosophers*, exploring the possibility that Narboni used what he took to be Maimonides' esoteric doctrine to explain al-Ghazali's text. Here Narboni claims, for instance, that al-Ghazali lived in an era in which the teaching of philosophy was forbidden and his apparent 'rejection' of philosophy is merely a ploy to communicate philosophical knowledge. In this context, Narboni borrows an idea he finds in Maimonides on the sages' necessity to disperse the knowledge that emanates from them. Another esoteric element is introduced regarding al-Ghazali's classifying fields of knowledge and their susceptibility to error, to which metaphysics is most prone. By way of explanation, Narboni indicates Maimonides' identical sentiment in the *Guide*. Other examples are given in the context of the need to accommodate positions to a different time and place. In conclusion, Narboni appears to think that Maimonides based all of the secrets of the *Guide* on the imaginative faculty.

The final example dealt with Idel's contention that, in a certain passage, Narboni is quoting Abulafia. Holtzman provided an alternative explanation, claiming them both to be drawing on Maimonides. Here she suggested Narboni is subtly criticising Maimonides for placing too much emphasis on the imaginative faculty.

In his presentation "Some Thoughts Regarding the 1270–1290 'Windows of Opportunities': Abulafia, Zeraḥyah, and Hillel on the *Guide of the Perplexed*," Yossi Schwartz (Tel Aviv University/Israel) proposed widening the intellectual and geographical scope of Idel's notion of the 20-year 'window of opportunities'—a period of exceptional fertility in kabbalistic literature. The 'window of opportunities,' Schwartz argued, is wider than Castile and encompasses not only Kabbalah but Maimonideanism as well. Schwartz's presentation here pointed out the complex relation between Abulafia, Zeraḥyah ben Sha'alti'el Ḥen, and Hillel of Verona, the latter two having been active in Italy during the relevant time frame, a period in which Abulafia also spent much time there.

Aside from offering revisions to some accepted views on the chronology of events concerning Hillel and Abulafia, Schwartz argues that Abulafia, Hillel, and Zeraḥyah not only present three versions of Maimonideanism, but also three versions of Jewish Averroism. Unlike Abulafia, Hillel and Zeraḥyah were late bloomers and were only acknowledged for their work at a much later stage. There are interesting parallels in Zeraḥyah and Hillel's projects regarding the texts they translated (or for which they commissioned translations) that seem to indicate they were engaged in some sort of competition. This might have been a reflection of a professional dispute between physicians.

Aryeh Krawczyk (Jewish Historical Institute, Warsaw/Poland) discussed the notion of "Inner Speech (Endophasia) in the Thought of Maimonides and Abulafia." Introducing a multidisciplinary approach, Krawczyk employed neuro-cognitive theories of endophasia to shed interesting light on Maimonides' and Abulafia's respective approaches to the possibility of conjunction with the agent intellect. Krawczyk argued that inner speech plays an important role for both to achieve this effect.

After acknowledging the methodological challenges associated with research of this nature and the necessary caution it requires, Krawczyk addressed the distinction between ordinary and acute cases of endophasia. In neuropsychology, ordinary endophasia indicates a normal phenomenon such as talking to oneself, whereas acute cases indicate instances of hallucinations whereby the individual experiences voices speaking to them from outside. Krawczyk suggested that although one can find ordinary endophasia in Maimonides regarding the intellect and noetics by reference to sound and hearing in different chapters of the *Guide of the Perplexed*, Abulafia's writings contain several techniques and rituals that seem to be aiming at *prompting* acute cases of endophasia and heautoscopy (vision of oneself from the outside). To this end, Krawczyk analysed several examples from Abulafia's works like *Sefer ha-Ḥesheq* ('The Book of Desire') and *Sefer ha-Ot* ('Book of the Letter').

Steven Harvey (Bar-Ilan University, Ramat Gan/Israel) discussed "The Law of Moses in Maimonides, Abulafia, and Maimonideans." Prior to addressing the main issue, Harvey expressed reservation concerning the scholarly tendency of shifting away from the idea of esotericism in the medieval period. He argued that the denial of the historical phenomenon of the persecution of philosophers is factually incorrect and provided several counterexamples from the Islamic world. These examples are better suited to Plato's open reference to the danger of philosophy, as its opinions are in such contradistinction to those of the multitude, that philosophers are compelled to conceal them. Plato's position set the tone for much subsequent philosophical literature that took heed of his warning.

Having reinforced esotericism within the philosophical tradition, Harvey suggested treating Abulafia as a missing link in the history of Maimonideanism and set out to express this through his silent absorption of Maimonides' conception of divine law in the *Guide*. The immediate context is Maimonides' distinction between divine and conventional law, of which only the former interests Maimonides. The criterion for the divinity of a law is its reference to the welfare of the body and to belief. Only with the existence of the two can a law be divine. Another criterion is that the lawgiver should be a prophet and denounce bodily pleasures. By putting forth these criteria, Maimonides followed in the footsteps of al-Farabi, as did Falaquera and Isaac Albalag, who nevertheless appropriate al-Farabi's views to neutralise his subordination of religious practice to philosophical truth.

An implicit difficulty in Maimonides' view is that it is hard to see how his understanding of divine law (according to the aforementioned criteria) harmonises with the idea of the singularity of Mosaic Law. Harvey showed that Averroes (who also follows al-Farabi's notion of divine law) is open to the possibility of a better religion emerging, which would also better represent the philosophical ideal. This, in fact, is what we find in Abulafia. Abulafia never addresses Maimonides' conception of the uniqueness of Mosaic Law but talks explicitly about a *new Torah*. According to Harvey, Abulafia thinks that Mosaic Law can be superseded, for a new prophet (he himself) has arrived.

Daniel Davies and Racheli Haliva (Universität Hamburg/Germany) explored the idea of "Tablets of Stone—Between Maimonides and Abulafia." The basic problem with which Davies and Haliva grappled was the ontological status of the tablets of stone. Although Maimonides insists that the tablets are 'natural' rather than 'artificial', it is unclear whether this means that 'natural' contains the 'miraculous' or denies both the 'artificial' and the 'miraculous'. Maimonides compares this issue to the notion of 'divine speech', which complicates matters further, as it is difficult to understand how the distinction between nature, miracle, and artifice applies to God's speech and will, or more broadly, to the issue of causality as applied to God.

In Abulafia this problem is translated into a multi-levelled understanding of the tablets and their significance. In *Sefer ha-Melammed* ('Book of the Teacher') Abulafia distinguishes—within the context of Mount Sinai—between tablets, letters, and writing in the general sense. In *Or ha-Śekhel* ('The Light of the Intellect') three levels of understanding are identified: either exoteric, or esoteric, or both (in which the exoteric is false). In reference to what is written on the tablets, in *Shomer Miṣwah* ('Keeper of the Commandment') Abulafia tells us that the tablets have two sides—front and back—corresponding to God's front (face) and back (actions).

Regarding speech and writing Abulafia distinguishes three kinds of sounds, which emerge from different parts of the mouth, and three kinds of speech, corresponding to physical writing, the spoken word, and the mental conception. It appears that Abulafia distinguishes divine speech from human speech on the basis that divine speech is creative. The presenters asked whether Abulafia's elaborations and distinctions could be understood as an interpretation of Maimonides' account of the tablets and the writing.

Adam Afterman (Tel Aviv University/Israel) discussed "Kabbalistic Reading of Maimonides' Concept of Revelation." In his presentation, Afterman talked about mystical and noetic union in the Kabbalah and the Aristotelian tradition, with reference to the Neo-Aristotelian background of the Kabbalah, eschatological union in Maimonides, Abulafia, and other kabbalists. Afterman showed how Maimonides was used by various kabbalists to present different versions of eschatological union.

The Aristotelian background of Abulafia and other kabbalists in the thirteenth century is relevant, particularly concerning the possibility of conjunction with the agent intellect, and even the First Cause. The basic formula is the equation between knowledge and union, a point that has become increasingly important for several kabbalists who sought an ontological bridge between man and god. In this tradition, there is an important Neoplatonic presence, which adds the notion of communion to the notion of union, as the former involves the receipt of emanation (*shefaʿ*) from the agent intellect through the imaginative faculty. Maimonides links this to prophecy. The idea of a union with God, with no mediation from imagination or emanation, is a more radical one.

Within this framework, Afterman argued that Maimonides is relatively moderate. He does not permit a union with the active intellect unless it is at the instant of death or after death. It is appropriate to medieval metaphysics to be free of the body to arrive at the realm of unity. This is the union of intellect-intellection-intelligible, liberation from plurality and individuality into something simple, unified, and eternal.

Abulafia, in turn, uses this metaphysics to explain acute and immediate transformation from man to angel, or son of God. He proposes many techniques, sometimes alongside the agent intellect. Abulafia deviates from Maimonides and permits this in this life. However, Afterman claimed that Abulafia sides with Maimonides by stating that this is rare and difficult to arrive at. Nevertheless, this is a radical reading of Maimonides, and it is enabled by Abulafia's contemporary philosophical climate.

After Abulafia, other, different forms of Kabbalah emerge. Naḥmanides, for example, describes a process of purification of the body, the soul, and the intellect. In other words, a gradual integration into the Godhead. This differs from Abulafia, whose model is either/or. But for this different picture, Naḥmanides also uses Maimonides. Naḥmanides refers to Maimonides' discussion of posthumous unification when describing his own idea of an eschatological level in which man achieves unity with the Godhead at the end of the integration process. But Naḥmanides takes this to the next level, stating that there are rare individuals who can fully integrate with the Godhead while still embodied, with no need to go through all of the steps. This recurs in various kabbalists, e.g., Isaac of Acre, in his book *Oṣar Ḥayyim* ('Treasure of Life'). When one reaches this stage, it is presented as being in accordance with the Maimonidean eschatological union.

Fabrizio Lelli (Università del Salento, Lecce/Italy) talked about "Translations and Commentaries of Abulafia," particularly into Latin during the fifteenth century. Starting from the discussion of humanist interests in Kabbalah, Lelli retraced Pico della Mirandola's connections with Jewish scholars by reference to Pico's search for Hebrew sources that can fit into his Christian fields of interest. He believes that Pico's views on universalisation and the idea of unity with the agent intellect may be based, in part, upon Abulafia via some kind of mediation.

Some of Abulafia's works were translated (or perhaps appropriated) into Latin at Pico's request by Mithridates, a Sicilian convert from Judaism. In Sicily there was a continuous tradition of Kabbalah stemming from Abulafia's students. It is possible that Mithridates' father—with whom Mithridates studied before his conversion—was part of this tradition. Mithridates' translations featured many adaptations that enabled an understanding of Abulafia in a Christian manner. Mithridates also adds several notes to prove that Maimonides was a kabbalist, which had a major impact on Pico. Lelli suggested the possibility that subsequent Jewish interest in Abulafia is an effect of the Christian interest in him and perhaps even an attempt to correct Mithridates and recheck Abulafia.

Haim Kreisel's (Ben-Gurion University of the Negev, Beer-Sheva/Israel) "Maimonides and Abulafia on Prophecy" was premised on the assumption that Maimonides would not recognise himself as the person whose positions Abulafia presents. According to Kreisel, it is strange to think of Abulafia's commentaries on the *Guide* as actual commentaries, as they are so different from what Maimonides writes. Although the order of 'secrets' in Abulafia's commentaries is in accordance with the *Guide*, their discussion has little or nothing to do with the *Guide* itself. Instead, there is some kind of link to the content of the secrets with occasional reference to Maimonides' text, which Kreisel labelled 'impressionistic'. In this respect Kreisel shared the frustration of Abulafia's students, who were also unlikely to see the connection between Abulafia's commentary and Maimonides' text. Kreisel suggested viewing Abulafia as drawing inspiration from Maimonides but focussing on the secrets themselves, particularly in letter combinations. Nevertheless, some influence is apparent, for instance, in the theory of prophecy.

Kreisel characterised Maimonides' theory of prophecy as understanding prophecy as a 'natural' phenomenon; there are certain preliminary conditions and preparations, which when met, render prophecy inevitable or nearly inevitable. This appears to be a radical departure from rabbinic literature and may have inspired Abulafia's view on preparing oneself for prophecy. Accordingly, the definition of prophecy is not the reception of a specific divine message or a specific revelation, but emanation—the question about the actual content of prophecy remains open. Kreisel noticed a slight shift between Maimonides' legal writings, in which prophecy is described as an intellectual phenomenon, and the *Guide*, in which the imaginative aspect is emphasised and there is no reference (in that context) to the Aristotelian vocabulary of the acquired intellect and the idea of conjunction. Instead, the intellect becomes acquired in the perfection of the intellect and the culmination occurs when prophecy is over, as prophecy is concerned with the body. Prophecy, as a message, is completely natural as an extension of the overflow. According to Kreisel, Abulafia seems to have adopted a Maimonidean model—at least its theoretical framework—which Abulafia modified according to his needs.

Elke Morlok (Goethe-Universität Frankfurt am Main/Germany) discussed "Gikatilla on Language and the Status of the Text—On the Transition between Abulafian Concepts and the Theosophic-Theurgic Matrix." Morlok focussed on the difference of approach between the kabbalist Joseph Gikatilla, who was Abulafia's student, and Abulafia himself. According to Morlok, after Gikatilla left Abulafia he turned to theosophic/theurgic Kabbalah, which is incompatible with Abulafia's noetic-linguistic approach. Gikatilla wrote *Ginnat Egoz* ('Garden of the Nut'), one of his most important early works, at the age of 26, while he was still Abulafia's student. After being exposed to new currents, he moved from an Aristotelian–Pythagorean approach to the Neoplatonic camp. Gikatilla also moved from Abulafia's idea of universalisation and interiorisation to a more traditional-liturgical and less abstract narrative focussing on the priority of the Jewish tradition. Hence, according to this sociological and epistemic criterion, only Jews, who keep the Halakha, can access truth on the basis of a complex mystical exegesis, into which one has to be initiated by a kabbalistic teacher. This differs from Abulafia's approach, which also propagates initiation into highly manipulative linguistic techniques, but simultaneously tends to expand the Kabbalah to encompass a universal application.

In the early works of Gikatilla, the fact that the Tetragrammaton is comprised of those consonants which can usually serve as vowels prescribes a special place for Hebrew vocalisation symbols (*niqqud*). For Gikatilla, the mystic operates within the sphere of the vowels, and becomes the middle point for the relation between the divine and human spheres. He arrives at the centre of the cosmos through language.

Morlok also referred to Gikatilla's notes on Maimonides' *Guide* in his *Haśśagot* ('Critiques'), an early work Gikatilla wrote while still very much under the influence of Abulafia. In the *Haśśagot*, Gikatilla interprets the 'Account of the Chariot' (*maʿaśeh merkavah*) as the secret of the causal chain of everything and their existence from one another, from the first emanation to the middle of earth (which is not found in Abulafia). The idea of order has a performative aspect of language and ontology—the human organ becomes the seat for the divine. In this respect, the ritualistic aspect is emphasised, as there is correspondence between the human and divine being, which is also dependent upon the ethics of human behavior, explaining the centrality of the commandments, as exemplified later in his *Shaʿarei Orah* ('Gates of Light').

Ofer Elior's (Ben-Gurion University of the Negev, Beer-Sheva/Israel and Hebrew University of Jerusalem/Israel) presentation focussed on "The Account of the Chariot in Maimonides, Abulafia, and Provençal Thinkers." Elior discussed various interpretations of the 'Account of the Chariot' as a mirror through which he would then explore the thinkers' approach to scientific enquiry, particularly at junctures where tension arises between science and religion. The presentation did not focus on the entire account, but only on Ezekiel 1:24–25 ('When they [i.e. the creatures] moved, I could hear the sound of their wings like the sound of mighty waters, like the sound of Shadday, a tumult like the din of an army. When they stood still, they would let their wings droop. From above the expanse over their heads came a sound. When they stood still, they would let their wings droop.').

In Maimonides' exploration of this passage in the *Guide*, he refers to the Pythagorean theory of celestial sound as an interpretation for the sounds that the animals make. He notes that Aristotle disagrees with the Pythagoreans, but his criticism is not of this theory but of the *basis* of their explanations: a cosmological picture in which the stars are self-moving and the spheres are fixed. Elior claimed the question here to be whether or not Maimonides agrees with Aristotle; if he does, this means that Maimonides admits that a prophet was wrong.

According to Elior, many scholars addressed this issue, but no one referred to Abulafia's take on the matter. Before turning to Abulafia, Elior discussed several Provençal thinkers and presented a wide array of engagements with this problem, ranging from ascribing to Maimonides a rejection of Aristotle, to acknowledging that Ezekiel had in fact erred but dissociating this from his prophecy. Moving to Abulafia, Elior found difficulty in understanding his position but believed that he basically accepted the interpretation according to which Ezekiel was in fact wrong. Elior indicated several points where Abulafia refers to the interpretation of the *Cherubim*. In *Sitrei Torah*, for example, there is a passage where Abulafia—gematria aside—seems to be directly drawing from Maimonides' interpretation. However, Abulafia does not seem to address the problem resulting from Maimonides' understanding. Elior wonders whether Abulafia thinks that the problem of tension between science and faith is marginal. Gikatilla, for instance, directly addressed the contradiction between Aristotle and Ezekiel, and stressed the importance of explaining the contradiction and its genesis.

Josef Stern (University of Chicago/USA) spoke about "The Role of Language in Maimonides and Abulafia's Thought." Unlike many medieval philosophers and theologians, Maimonides denies the divinity of language and the literal attribution of speech to God. Instead, he follows al-Farabi in distinguishing between things, utterances (or 'outer speech'), and traces in the soul (or 'inner speech'). For Maimonides, the relationship between logic and the intellect is analogous to the relationship between grammar and language. The traces in the soul comprise a complete system of interrelated concepts—a language with structure and syntax—a composite entity. On the background of the distinction between internal and external speech, Maimonides severely criticises external speech, limiting its function to communicating concepts to another person (this is why the spheres only have inner speech). The mental representations are the primary language, which functions independently of external speech, although access is only attained through external speech.

For Maimonides, languages in the sense of external speech (and only in that sense) are conventional rather than natural. The conventionality is expressed by the accidental relationship between the word and the mental representation it reflects; conversely, the relationship between the mental representation and the external object is natural and universal (the same thought points to the same object). External speech is inferior to internal speech, just as the conventional is inferior to the natural. But despite this, Maimonides maintains that both inner and outer speech have syntax, composition, and structures. This is conditioned upon the imagination, the faculty of representation, which cannot perceive anything immaterial, hence it is still not good enough to represent immaterial simple beings; syntax is the matter that prevents the intellect from apprehending the subject matter of metaphysics, hence, from being perfected.

This is the point of friction with Abulafia, who sympathises with Maimonides' insight, but draws different conclusions. Abulafia takes the 22 consonants to be the matter (i.e., the 'linguistic potentiality') of the words. There is a natural process that creates, from this matter, the combinations of consonants whose vast number is capable of constructing any language. At the same time, there is an ontological process of emanation of things. The consonants in language are parallel to physical elements. For Abulafia, words are nothing but combinations of sounds, so that all languages are equal and generated in the same manner. What elevates Hebrew is that it offers the best phonetic articulation of the 22 consonants (the matter)—not that it is divine. As such, Hebrew becomes the representative of universal sound. The mission of the sage, then, is not to think the form of the words, but their matter—in precise opposition to Maimonides.

At the end of his talk, Stern addressed Maimonides' and Abulafia's parables of the pearl, even though (as Idel observes) we have no explicit evidence that Abulafia based his parable on Maimonides'. Stern, however, argued that there is indirect evidence in that the tri-partite structure of Abulafia's parables (as analysed by Idel) parallels the tri-partite semantic levels of the Maimonidean parable, a structure not found elsewhere. However, for Maimonides this semantic structure reflects the expressive function of a parable, not political esotericism, for which Idel argues, in the case of Abulafia. Further research will be necessary to delineate the exact contours of influence between the master and his disciple.

Hanna Kasher (Bar-Ilan University, Ramat Gan/Israel) discussed "Maimonides, Abulafia, and Joseph ibn Kaspi on The Hebrew Language." Maimonides and ibn Kaspi offer two opposing views on the status of Hebrew and the reason for its holiness, whereas Abulafia's view is difficult to discern.

Kasher showed that human language, for Maimonides, is conventional rather than natural. Accordingly, Hebrew is the holy language for circumstantial reasons, namely because it is part of a perfect climate area. According to this climatology, the pronunciation of its words is balanced, a feature of similar languages, such as Greek, Hebrew, Persian, and Aramaic. As regards the script, Maimonides seems to contrast it with Arabic, whose script is connected and contains many identical letters. There was probably a need to respond to the Arabs, who claimed Hebrew vocabulary to be lacking. Maimonides responds that the limited vocabulary in Hebrew is an advantage, as all of the inferior things (reproductive organs, for instance) do not have their own words, but are only alluded to. This is the mark of a divine language.

Kasher noted that neither ibn Kaspi nor Abulafia refer to Maimonides' attitude toward Hebrew. Ibn Kaspi addresses the issue of the Hebrew language in his *Commentary on the Torah* in which he advances that Arabic and Hebrew words are derived from reality, unlike Latin, whose words are random. Arguing with a Latin scholar on the Latin translation of the Bible, ibn Kaspi says that all of the Hebrew words have an informative meaning. The authors of this language understood this and made sure that each root has one meaning. Hence, the creators of language were philosophers, and Hebrew cannot be translated into other languages. Translation entails a 'unification of tongues,' whereas God wanted a 'division of tongues.'

Abulafia, who was active before ibn Kaspi, openly advocated the unification of languages, saying that there are many names to one being. Kasher wondered whether Kaspi's account can be taken as including a critique of Abulafia. She further noted Abulafia conceives language as natural and is also interested in bi-lingual education of children. The idea of a 'holy language' as that which is developed on a desert island—a commonplace idea since Herodotus—is for Abulafia nothing but a noble lie.

In his talk "Maimonides, Abulafia, and Spinoza," Zev Harvey (Hebrew University of Jerusalem/Israel) addressed three points of striking similarity between Abulafia and Spinoza, which, in his opinion, would be difficult to explain without recourse to some historical connections.

The first point is the identification of God and nature, well known from Spinoza's formula *Deus sive Natura* ('God or nature'). According to Harvey, Abulafia was the first to note that the gematria of God (*elohim*—אלהים) and nature (*ha-ṭeva'*—הטבע) is the same, namely 86. This identification is frequent in Abulafia's corpus, appearing ten times in his known works. This gematria was widely quoted in Jewish and Christian literature, some of which was familiar to Spinoza. The idea that God is nature suits Maimonides' thought as well. Abulafia returns frequently to this theme in the context of the tablets of the law. This is also frequent in other kabbalists and in Hebrew philosophical literature. According to Idel, Spinoza disentangled the linguistic/gematric mode and focussed on the content.

The second point takes on the issue of the intellectual love of God. According to Harvey, Abulafia was the first to coin the term *ahavah elohit śikhlit*, of which he maintained that *amor Dei intellectualis* is a good translation. The passage in which Abulafia coins the term is quoted in Narboni and in Abraham Shalom with no reference to Abulafia as its original author. The Maimonidean connection is established through the term *or ha-śekhel* ('the light of the intellect') which appears in the *Guide*.

The third and final point is the reestablishment of the Jewish state as a natural occurrence. In the *Theologico-Political Treatise*, Spinoza claims that laws are meant to be observed in a certain place and are irrelevant to other places. Hence, Jewish law belongs to the Jewish state, so it will become relevant again only if the Jews return to their homeland. Harvey noted that Shlomo Pines had detected the similarity between this idea and Joseph ibn Kaspi's contention that the possibility of the Jews returning to their homeland is not irrational. Spinoza explains that the return to the land of Israel is natural rather than miraculous. This idea, too, goes back to Abulafia.

In his *Response*, José María Sánchez de León Serrano (Universität Hamburg/Germany) focussed on the attempt to find precedents for Spinoza's identification between God and nature, arguing that thinking about sources for Spinoza changes the way we perceive him as an innovator. However, Sánchez de León attempted to stress the fundamental differences underlying the equivalence in formula. Alluding to studies that attempt to bridge the conceptual gap between Spinoza and his predecessors in this respect, Sánchez de León noted several areas in which the differences seem to outweigh the similarities; such as the availability of the concept of God to the human intellect, the philosophical status of language, and the radical transformation of the concept of nature.

Throughout the various discussions in the conference, a few recurring themes came up, which can perhaps prompt further scholarship on Abulafia within a Maimonidean context:

(1) The ambiguity of Abulafia's theoretical framework: Idel has shown that for Abulafia the use of contemporary philosophical jargon is instrumental rather than theoretical, namely to facilitate a certain experience in terms with which his audience could relate. Nevertheless, the question whether and how a coherent metaphysical backdrop can indeed be extracted from Abulafia—even if it has an *ad hoc* status—seems to warrant further study.

(2) In various cases it seems as if a key difference between Maimonides and Abulafia is that although Maimonides' *Guide*, in many cases, tries to *address* various philosophical topics (e.g. the structure of the cosmos, the phenomenon of prophecy, and the relation/tension between scripture and scientific truth), Abulafia is interested in *facilitating change* (e.g. elevating nature, becoming a prophet, altering the Bible). This distinction between static and dynamic undertakings raises interesting questions when exploring the manner in which Abulafia appropriates themes from Maimonides.

(3) The identification between God and nature in Abulafia and Maimonides can mean different things and can be employed (among other things) to assert transcendence as well as reinforce immanence. Furthermore, understood within the context of creativeness, the status of the artifice and the miraculous, derivatively, require additional clarification. The different options can be explored more fully, also concerning subsequent developments in the Kabbalah.

(4) The status of gematria has raised some questions, especially assuming that letters are the building blocks of the cosmos. The gematric equivalence of different expressions, Abulafia argues, is not accidental or random but seems to point to some logical connection between them. Hence, if gematria is not only a tool for mystical experience but also an expression of the architecture of the world, it should be explained within a metaphysical framework. Moreover, and perhaps significantly, within the context of language, the question of the relationship between 'The Holy Language' and Hebrew emerges at various junctures here.

Silke Schaeper
Report on the Library of Jewish Scepticism

One Person Library

The Library of Jewish Scepticism is a one person library (OPL), a special collection managed by a single librarian. The librarian is responsible for all tasks involved in setting up, developing, coordinating, and constantly evaluating this highly specialised academic research collection. Since research at the Maimonides Centre for Advanced Studies is broad in historical and linguistic scope, the library purchases books from a great variety of sources, nationally and internationally. The librarian undertakes detailed bibliographic research in Israel, negotiates with bookdealers and publishers about prices and conditions for access to e-resources, and catalogues library materials to the latest international standard (RDA), including materials in non-Roman script (Hebrew, Judaeo-Arabic, Arabic, Cyrillic). The librarian liaises with all research projects at the Institute for Jewish Philosophy and Religion and engages in in-depth bibliographic research. The librarian is responsible for the IT infrastructure of the library (hardware, software, backups) and for selecting and ordering books and e-resources for current and planned research projects. She places orders with bookdealers, negotiates rebates, pays bills, keeps inventory records, and oversees the work of student library assistants. She also processes international shipping and customs duties.

Student Assistants

Student assistants contribute to the daily running of the library. Ms Nora Gutdeutsch, a student of Protestant theology with knowledge of Hebrew and bookkeeping, worked for us successfully. Now we are supported by Ms Vanessa Zerwas, a student of sign language.

Subject Information Service in Jewish Studies

The 'Fachinformationsdienst Jüdische Studien' (FID Jewish Studies) provides national access to electronic resources in Jewish Studies. In July 2018, the FID issued a beta version of its new web portal in Jewish Studies: www.jewishstudies.de

A considerable programming effort was undertaken in order to make older transliterated cataloguing records from one of Germany's leading Hebraica collections accessible in original script (University Library Frankfurt am Main). Another innovative IT project is under way: enriching the metadata of Frankfurt's digitised Hebraica collections with 'entities', i.e. links to other web-based information (author's biographies, geographic information, and similar).

The librarian continues to manage access permissions to the subject information service for staff and fellows of the Centre.

FID subscriptions at our Centre in the academic year 2017/2018:

    Staff   14
    Fellows, Post Docs   4

Periodicals

We subscribe to the *Jüdische Allgemeine*, a German weekly. We were interested in subscribing to the Israeli newspaper *Haaretz*, which has online editions in Hebrew and in English. After lengthy and difficult negotiations, directly and through a bookdealer, we decided not to buy an institutional access licence.

Faculty Library Committee

The librarian has made purchasing suggestions for 4 campus-licences for electronic dictionaries and encyclopaedias in the field of Hebrew and Jewish Studies to the library committee of the Faculty of Humanities in April 2018. The suggestions were not followed up due to other priorities.

Association of Judaica Collections

The 'Arbeitsgemeinschaft Jüdische Sammlungen' was founded in 1976, in Cologne. Its annual meetings are a valuable forum providing an exchange of information for professionals working in public and private collections, academic and public institutions, libraries, and archives in German-speaking countries (Germany, Switzerland and Austria).

In September 2016, the librarian introduced the library of the Centre at the annual meeting in Berlin. In September 2017, the librarian attended the annual meeting in Würzburg. In September 2018, the librarian plans to give a progress report at the annual meeting in Bamberg.

Collaboration

The library cooperates nationally and internationally with other special collections in the field in order to obtain or exchange books and theses. It collaborates successfully with the State and University Library of Hamburg and Faculty libraries and special collections in Hamburg for the planning of e-resource provision. We have enhanced the local version of the national web portal DBIS ('Datenbankinformationssystem') by contributing 10 new records for e-resources in Jewish Studies.

It has been agreed that the Universität Hamburg's Philosophy Faculty Library will receive the collections of the Library of Jewish Scepticism once the research project of the MCAS has come to an end. From the beginning of the MCAS project, the librarian is therefore in close contact with the team of the Philosophy Faculty Library, ensuring professional sustainability.

Book Donations

We wish to thank for donations of books received from Giuseppe Veltri (Universität Hamburg), Moshe Goncharok (St. Petersburg), Hannelore Wilke (Universität Hamburg), Reuven Kiperwasser (Berlin), Michael Studemund-Halévy (Hamburg), Friedhelm Hartenstein (München), the National Library of Russia (St. Petersburg), Asher Salah (Jerusalem), Bill Rebiger (Universität Hamburg), and Ehud Krinis (Beer Sheva).

Interlibrary Loan and Document Delivery

From the founding of the Centre in October 2015, the library has promptly met more than 300 specialist interlibrary loan and document delivery requests, of which 85 were made in the 2017/2018 academic year.

Statistics July 2017 to June 2018

Institute for Jewish Philosophy and Religion

Bibliographic units (editions)	190
Of which: Donation (editions)	20
Of which: E-Book—campus licence	7
Of which: E-Book—CD-ROM	1
Periodical holdings reported to ZDB	34
Volumes on shelf (print)	287

Maimonides Centre for Advanced Studies

Bibliographic units (editions)	229
Of which: Donation (editions)	5
Of which: E-Book—campus licence	29
Of which: E-Book—PDF	2
Of which: Repro—PDF on CD-ROM	9
Of which: E-Resource—encyclopaedia	3
Of which: E-Resource—dictionary	1
Periodical subscription—print	2
Periodical subscription – online	1
Volumes on shelf (print)	219

Statistics October 2014 to July 2018

MCAS cataloguing records	606
IJPR cataloguing records	866

By language(s)

English	694
Hebrew	278
German	218
Italian	60
French	36
Spanish	22
Arabic	21
Latin	9
Yiddish	8
Judaeo-Arabic	3

Library Webpages

In the Centre's first year, when library IT and catalogues were not yet up and running, the librarian published an occasional newsletter entitled 'Library News,' in order to keep staff and fellows informed about progress in library provision. This is no longer necessary. Information about local and international catalogues and other resources is now found on the webpages of the library.

www.ingramcontent.com/pod-product-compliance
Lightning Source LLC
Chambersburg PA
CBHW060418300426
44111CB00018B/2892